SUPERVISION
TODAY'S SCHOO

SUPERVISION
for
TODAY'S
SCHOOLS

SECOND EDITION

Peter F. Oliva

GEORGIA SOUTHERN COLLEGE

Longman
New York & London

Again to grandson Gregory, *who now at age 11*
no longer feels the necessity
for supervising the production of this manuscript.

Supervision for Today's Schools, 2nd Edition

Longman Inc., 1560 Broadway, New York, N.Y. 10036
Associated companies, branches, and representatives
throughout the world.

Copyright © 1976, 1984 by Longman Inc.

Developmental Editor: Lane Akers
Editorial and Design Supervisor: Ferne Y. Kawahara

Library of Congress Cataloging in Publication Data
Oliva, Peter F.
  Supervision for today's schools.
  Bibliography: p.
  Includes index.
  1. School supervision. I. Title.
LB2805.058 1983   371.2   83–5417
ISBN 0-582-28420-1

Manufactured in the United States of America
Printing: 9 8 7 6 5 4 3 2 1   Year: 92 91 90 89 88 87 86 85 84

Contents

Preface to the
Second Edition

This book is an overview of the field of instructional supervision. It is designed as a text for basic graduate courses such as Introduction to Supervision, Supervision of Teaching, and Supervision in Education. Like the first edition it is directed also to the practitioner in supervision.

Every chapter of the first edition has been carefully scrutinized and revised. Greatly expanded is the second chapter on issues in supervision. Completely new to this edition is the chapter on clinical techniques in supervision.

This text introduces the reader to the three domains of supervision: instructional development, curriculum development, and staff development. Training programs for supervisors normally follow the overview course with one or more specialized courses in each of the three domains.

Philosophically and functionally, this text is geared as much toward competency-based programs as toward the more traditional programs of professional preparation. At the beginning of each chapter I have set forth desired objectives. Objectives are of two types: cognitive, specifying intellectual tasks, and affective, designed to bring out the reader's personal positions and attitudes. Appendix A is a list of competencies which the preservice and in-service supervisor should be able to demonstrate after completing study of the text. Appendix B consists of examples of supervisory positions.

At the end of each chapter you will find a generous number of activities for further study. These activities have two purposes: (1) to clarify the content of the chapter and (2) to extend study beyond the chapter.

Notes follow each chapter. Asterisks are used to footnote within the text instead of at the end of the chapter in those relatively few cases where the information footnoted is an elaboration or clarification of the narrative. When additional information had an immediacy to it, I felt it desirable to asterisk it and place it contiguous to the narrative.

I have consciously tried to provide examples of all the major points discussed in the text. In so doing I have made a special effort to provide illustrations from actual school systems whenever possible.

To indicate the directions of study to be taken in this book, I have in mind the following goals for supervisors:

1. To develop a concept of supervision compatible with the needs of students, teachers, the community, society at large, and their own personalities.
2. To become aware of what to look for in each of the topics discussed in the book.
3. To find suggestions for measures that can be taken to improve areas of supervision discussed in the text.
4. To become sensitive to the instructional needs of teachers.
5. To be confronted with recent developments, thought, and research within the domains of supervision discussed in the text.
6. To gain ideas for training programs for teachers.
7. To feel the need for becoming proficient in areas discussed in the text and to take what measures are needed to improve their own competence in each of the areas.
8. To become aware of some of the trends and issues in the field of supervision.
9. To become familiar with the work of some of the specialists in the field.

I want to thank all the professors, students, and practitioners who have used the first edition of this text. Special thanks go to all those who kindly wrote me expressing their satisfaction with the first edition.

I would like to extend special thanks to Mr. Lane Akers, Director, College and Professional Book Division, Longman Inc., for making this second edition possible.

Acknowledgments

Excerpts from Ben M. Harris, *Supervisory Behavior in Education*, 2nd ed., Englewood Cliffs, N.J.: Prentice-Hall, 1975, pp. 2–3, 10–12. Reprinted with permission of Prentice-Hall, Inc.

Excerpts from William H. Lucio and John D. McNeil, *Supervision: A Synthesis of Thought and Action*, 3rd ed., New York: McGraw-Hill, 1979, pp. 3, 26–27, 155. Reprinted with permission of McGraw-Hill Book Company.

Excerpts from Ralph L. Mosher and David E. Purpel, *Supervision: The Reluctant Profession*, Boston: Houghton Mifflin, 1972, pp. 3, 81, 83, 84, 92–95, 97–98, 110–111. Copyright © 1972 by Houghton Mifflin Company. Used by permission.

Excerpts from Ross L. Neagley and N. Dean Evans, *Handbook for Effective Supervision of Instruction*, 3rd ed., Englewood Cliffs, N.J.: Prentice-Hall, 1980, pp. 4, 20, 137–138. Reprinted with permission of Prentice-Hall, Inc.

Excerpts from John T. Lovell and Kimball Wiles, *Supervision for Better Schools*, 5th Edition, © 1983, pp. 4, 46, 64, 89, 114, 143, 183, 287–290. Reprinted by permission of Prentice-Hall, Inc., Englewood Cliffs, New Jersey.

From *Supervisors and Teachers: A Private Cold War*, 2nd ed., by Arthur J. Blumberg Berkeley, Calif.: McCutchan, 1980, pp. 5–6, 88–89. McCutchan Publishing Corporation © 1980. PERMISSION GRANTED BY THE PUBLISHER.

Excerpts from William H. Burton, *Supervision and the Improvement of Teaching*, New York: D. Appleton-Century, 1922, pp. 9–10. Reprinted with permission of Prentice-Hall, Inc.

From *The Supervisor*, by Robert C. McKean and H. H. Mills, New York: Center for Applied Research in Education, 1964, pp. 42–44. © 1964 by Center for Applied Research in Education. Published by Center for Applied Research in Education, West Nyack, New York.

Excerpts from A. W. Sturges, *The Roles and Responsibilities of Instructional Supervisors*, Alexandria, Va.: ASCD Working Group on the Roles and Responsibilities of Supervisors, Association for Supervision and Curriculum Development, October 1, 1978, pp. 72–73. Reprinted with permission of the Association for Supervision and Curriculum Development. Copyright © 1978 by the Association for Supervision and Curriculum Development. All rights reserved.

Excerpts from Adolph Unruh and Harold E. Turner, *Supervision for Change and Innovation*, Boston: Houghton Mifflin, 1970, p. 8 Copyright © 1970 by Houghton Mifflin Company. Used by permission.

Excerpts from Harold Spears, *Improving the Supervision of Instruction*, Englewood Cliffs, N.J.: Prentice-Hall, 1953, p. 27. Reprinted with permission of Prentice-Hall, Inc.

Excerpts from Lloyd W. Dull, *Supervision: School Leadership Handbook*, Columbus, Ohio: Charles E. Merrill, 1980, pp. 7, 110, 111. Reprinted with permission of Charles E. Merrill Publishing Company.

Excerpts from Jon Wiles and Joseph Bondi, *Supervision: A Guide to Practice*, Columbus, Ohio, Charles E. Merrill, 1980, pp. 20, 21, 161. Reprinted with permission of Charles E. Merrill Publishing Company.

Excerpts from Thomas J. Sergiovanni and Robert J. Starratt, *Supervision: Human Perspectives*, 2nd ed., New York: McGraw-Hill, 1979, pp. 5–6, 15, 290–291. Reprinted with permission of McGraw-Hill Book Company.

Excerpts from Morris Cogan, *Clinical Supervision*, Boston: Houghton Mifflin, 1973, pp. 9, 10–13, 16–17. Copyright © 1973 by Houghton Mifflin Company. Used by permission.

Excerpts from Arthur J. Lewis and Alice Miel, *Supervision for Improved Instruction: New Challenges, New Responses*, Belmont, Calif.: Wadsworth, 1972, p. 47. Reprinted with permission of Wadsworth Publishing Company.

Excerpts from Robert H. Davis, Lawrence T. Alexander, and Stephen L. Yelon, *Learning System Design: An Approach to the Improvement of Instruction*, New York: McGraw-Hill, 1974, p. 41. Reprinted with permission of McGraw-Hill Book Company.

Excerpts from *Taxonomy of Educational Objectives: Handbook I: Cognitive Domain* by Benjamin S. Bloom et al. Copyright © 1956 by Longman Inc. Reprinted by permission of Longman Inc., New York.

Excerpts from *Taxonomy of Educational Objectives: Handbook II: Affective Domain* by David R. Krathwohl.et al. Copyright © 1964 by Longman Inc. Reprinted by permission of Longman Inc., New York.

Excerpts from Jack L. Davidson and Freda M. Holley, "Your Students May Be Spending Only Half the School Day Receiving Instruction," *American School Board Journal* 166, no. 3 (March 1979): 40–41. Reprinted, with permission, from The American School Board Journal, March. Copyright 1979, the National School Boards Association. All rights reserved.

Excerpts from Barak V. Rosenshine, "Content, Time and Direct Instruction," from Research on Teaching, Penelope L. Peterson and Herbert J. Wahlberg, eds., p. 52, McCutchan Publishing Corporation © 1979. PERMISSION GRANTED BY THE PUBLISHER.

Excerpts from Agatha Christie, *The Mystery of the Blue Train*, New York: Dodd, Mead, 1928, p. 1. Reprinted with permission of Dodd, Mead and Hughes Massie Ltd.

Excerpts from Rachel Carson, *Silent Spring*, Boston: Houghton Mifflin, 1962, pp. 1–2. Copyright © 1962 by Houghton Mifflin Company. Used by permission.

Excerpts from Benjamin S. Bloom, J. Thomas Hastings, and George F. Madaus, *Handbook on Formative and Summative Evaluation of Student Learning*, New York: McGraw-Hill, 1971, pp. 43, 46, 53, 54. Reprinted with permission of McGraw-Hill Book Company.

Excerpts from Harvey F. Clarizio, *Toward Positive Classroom Discipline*, 3rd ed., New York: John Wiley, 1980, pp. 1, 4, 8, 11, 12. Reprinted with permission of John Wiley & Sons.

Excerpts from William Glasser, *Schools Without Failure*, New York: Harper & Row, 1969, pp. 13–14, 26, 29–30, 37, 52–53. Copyright © 1969 by William Glasser, Inc. Reprinted by permission of Harper & Row, Publishers, Inc.

Excerpts from Don E. Hamachek, *Encounters with the Self*, 2nd ed., New York: Holt, Rinehart and Winston, 1978, p. 33. Reprinted with permission of Holt, Rinehart and Winston, Inc.

Excerpts from Arthur W. Combs, "A Perceptual View of the Adequate Personality," in *Perceiving, Behaving, Becoming*, 1962 Yearbook, Alexandria, Va.: Association for Supervision and Curriculum Development, 1962, pp. 51, 53. Reprinted with permission of the Association for Supervision and Curriculum Development. Copyright © 1962 by the Association for Supervision and Curriculum Development. All rights reserved.

Excerpts from Earl C. Kelley, "The Fully Functioning Self," in *Perceiving, Behaving, Becoming*, 1962 Yearbook, Alexandria, Va., Association for Supervision and Curriculum Development, 1962, p. 222. Reprinted with permission of the Association for Supervision and Curriculum Development. Copyright © 1962 by the Association for Supervision and Curriculum Development. All rights reserved.

Excerpts from Allison Davis, "Socialization and Adolescent Personality," *Adolescence*, 43d Yearbook, Part I, Chicago: National Society for the Study of Education, 1944, p. 210. Reprinted with permission of National Society for the Study of Education.

Excerpts from B. Othanel Smith, Saul B. Cohen, and Arthur Pearl, *Teachers for the Real World*, Washington, D.C.: The American Association of Colleges for Teacher Education, 1969, 51–52, 55, 63. Reprinted with permission of The American Association of Colleges for Teacher Education.

Excerpts from Charles E. Silberman, *Crisis in the Classroom: The Remaking of American Education*, New York: Random House, 1970, p. 10. © 1970 by Random House, Inc. Reprinted with permission.

Excerpts from Peter F. Oliva, "High School Discipline in American Society," *The NASSP*

Bulletin 40, no. 216 (January 1956): 7–8, 14. Reprinted with permission of National Association of Secondary School Principals Bulletin.

Excerpts from Puran J. Rajpal, "What Behavior Problems Do Teachers Regard as Serious?" *Phi Delta Kappan* 53, no. 9 (May 1972): 591–592. Reprinted with permission of Phi Delta Kappa.

Excerpts from Barbara Bree Fischer and Louis Fischer, "Styles in Teaching and Learning," *Educational Leadership* 36, no. 4 (January 1979): 246–250, 251. Reprinted with permission of the Association for Supervision and Curriculum Development. Copyright © 1979 by the Association for Supervision and Curriculum Development. All rights reserved.

Excerpts from Johanna Kasin Lemlech, *Classroom Management*, New York: Harper & Row, 1979, pp. 8–26. Copyright © 1979 by Johanna Kasin Lemlech. Reprinted by permission of Harper & Row, Publishers, Inc.

Excerpts from Jacob S. Kounin, *Discipline and Group Management in Classrooms*, New York: Holt, Rinehart and Winston, 1970, p. 127. Reprinted with permission of Holt, Rinehart and Winston, Inc.

Excerpts from Laurel N. Tanner, *Classroom Discipline for Effective Teaching and Learning*, New York: Holt, Rinehart and Winston, 1978, pp. 14–16. Reprinted with permission of Holt, Rinehart and Winston, Inc.

Excerpts from J. Michael Palardy and James E. Mudrey, "Discipline: Four Approaches." Reprinted with permission of Macmillan Publishing Company from *Teaching Today: Tasks and Challenges*, J. Michael Palardy, ed., New York: Macmillan, 1975, pp. 315, 318–319, 323, 324. Copyright © 1975 by J. Michael Palardy.

From *Teaching I: Classroom Management* by Wesley C. Becker, Siegfried Engelmann, and Don R. Thomas. © 1975, Science Research Associates, Inc. Reprinted by permission of the publisher.

Reprinted with permission of Macmillan Publishing Company from *Curriculum Development: Theory into Practice* by Daniel Tanner and Laurel N. Tanner, New York: Macmillan, 1975, pp. 620, 631–632, 2nd ed., 1980, p. 103. Copyright © 1975, 1980 by Macmillan Publishing Company.

Excerpts from National Study of School Evaluation, *Elementary School Evaluative Criteria*, 1981, p. 39, and *Middle School/Junior High School Evaluative Criteria*, rev. ed., 1979, p. 39, Falls Church, Va.: National Study of School Evaluation. Reprinted with permission of National Study of Evaluation.

Carbondale High School, *A Philosophy of Education*, reprinted with permission of Carbondale Community High School District 165, Carbondale, Illinois.

Excerpts from Educational Policies Commission, *Education for All American Youth*, Washington, D.C.: National Education Association, 1944, p. 216. Reprinted with permission of NEA Publishing, National Education Association.

Excerpts from Robert M. Gagné, "Curriculum Research and the Promotion of Learning," *AERA Monograph Series on Evaluation, no. 1, Perspectives of Curriculum Evaluation*, Rand McNally, 1967, pp. 21–23. Reprinted with permission of the American Educational Research Association.

Excerpts from Michael Scriven, "The Methodology of Evaluation," *AERA Monograph Series on Evaluation, no. 1, Perspectives of Curriculum Evaluation*, Rand McNally, 1967, pp. 53–57. Reprinted with permission of the American Educational Research Association.

Excerpts from Fenwick W. English and Roger A. Kaufman, *Needs Assessment: A Focus for Curriculum Development*, Alexandria, Va.: Association for Supervision and Curriculum Development, 1975, pp. 3–4. Reprinted with permission of the Association for Supervision and Curriculum Development. Copyright © 1975 by the Association for Supervision and Curriculum Development. All rights reserved.

Excerpts from Willard Crouthamel and Stephen M. Preston, *Needs Assessment: User's Manu-*

al; *Needs Assessment: Resource Guide; Needs Assessment: Checklist of Steps*, Atlanta, Ga.: Research and Development Utilization Project, Georgia State Department of Education, 1979. Reprinted with permission of Georgia State Department of Education.

Excerpts from Savannah-Chatham County Public Schools, *System-Wide Needs for a Comprehensive Educational Plan*, adopted by the Board of Public Instruction for the City of Savannah and the County of Chatham (Georgia), May 6, 1981. Reprinted with permission of Savannah-Chatham County Public Schools.

Excerpts from Fenwick W. English, "Curriculum Mapping," *Educational Leadership* 37, no. 7 (April 1980): 558, 559. Reprinted with permission of the Association for Supervision and Curriculum Development. Copyright © 1980 by the Association for Supervision and Curriculum Development. All rights reserved.

Excerpts from Fenwick English, "Curriculum Mapping," *The Professional Educator* 3, no. 1 (Spring 1980): 11–12. Reprinted with permission of Association of Teacher Educators.

Excerpts from E. Lawrence Dale, "What Is Staff Development?" *Educational Leadership* 40, no. 1 (October 1982): 31. Reprinted with permission of the Association for Supervision and Curriculum Development. Copyright © 1982 by the Association for Supervision and Curriculum Development. All rights reserved.

Excerpts from John T. Lovell, "Instructional Supervision: Emerging Perspectives," in A. W. Sturges, chairman, *The Role and Responsibilities of Instructional Supervisors*, Report of the ASCD Working Group on the Roles and Responsibilities of Supervisors, Alexandria, Va.: Association for Supervision and Curriculum Development, October 1, 1978, pp. 35, 43. Reprinted with permission of the Association for Supervision and Curriculum Development. Copyright © 1978 by the Association for Supervision and Curriculum Development. All rights reserved.

Excerpts from Fred H. Wood and Steven R. Thompson, "Guidelines for Better Staff Development," *Educational Leadership* 37, no. 5 (February 1980): 374, 377. Reprinted with permission of the Association for Supervision and Curriculum Development. Copyright © 1980 by the Association for Supervision and Curriculum Development. All rights reserved.

Excerpts from David W. Champagne, "Does Staff Development Do Any Good?" *Educational Leadership* 37, no. 5 (February 1980): 403. Reprinted with permission of the Association for Supervision and Curriculum Development. Copyright © 1980 by the Association for Supervision and Curriculum Development. All rights reserved.

Excerpts from John Dewey, *The Sources of a Science of Education*, New York: Liveright, 1929, p. 17. Reprinted with permission of the Center for Dewey Studies, Carbondale, Illinois.

Excerpts from Toni Sharma, "Inservicing the Teachers," *Phi Delta Kappan* 63, no. 6 (February 1982): 403. Reprinted with permission of Phi Delta Kappa and Toni Sharma.

Excerpts from Fred H. Wood, Steven R. Thompson, and Sister Frances Russell, "Designing Effective Staff Development Programs," in *Staff Development/Organization Development*, 1981 Yearbook, Alexandria, Va.: Association for Supervision and Curriculum Development, 1981, pp. 61–63. Reprinted with permission of the Association for Supervision and Curriculum Development. Copyright © 1981 by the Association for Supervision and Curriculum Development. All rights reserved.

Excerpts from Leonard C. Burrello and Tim Orbaugh, "Reducing the Discrepancy between the Known and the Unknown in In-service Education," *Phi Delta Kappan* 63, no. 6 (February 1982): 385–386. Reprinted with permission of Phi Delta Kappa and Leonard C. Burrello.

Excerpts from Jay Lutz and Garrett Foster, "Greater Involvement Urged," *Florida Schools* 37 no. 3 (February 1975): 20–21. Reprinted with permission of Florida State Department of Education.

Excerpts from *Inservice Training Needs Assessment*, Fort Myers, Fla.: Southwest Florida Teacher Education Center, 1975. Reprinted with permission of Southwest Florida Teacher Education Center.

Excerpts from *Inservice Program Survey*, Miami: Dade/Monroe Teacher Education Center, June 1982. Reprinted with permission of Dade Monroe Teacher Education Center.

Excerpts from Linda L. Jones and Andrew E. Hayes, "How Valid are Surveys of Teacher Needs?" *Educational Leadership* 37, no. 5 (February 1980): 390, 391. Reprinted with permission of the Association for Supervision and Curriculum Development. Copyright © 1980 by the Association for Supervision and Curriculum Development. All rights reserved.

Excerpts from Sol C. Johnson High School, *Staff/Department Improvement Plan: 1981–82*, Savannah, Ga.: Savannah-Chatham County Public Schools. Reprinted with permission of Savannah-Chatham County Public Schools.

Excerpts from James M. Lipham, "Leadership and Administration," *Behavioral Science and Educational Administration*, 63d Yearbook, Part II, edited by Daniel E. Griffiths, Chicago: National Society for the Study of Education, 1964, p. 122. Reprinted with permission of National Society for the Study of Education.

Reprinted with permission of Macmillan Publishing Company from *Handbook of Leadership: A Survey of Theory and Research*, by Ralph M. Stogdill, New York, Macmillan, 1974, pp. 62–63. Copyright © 1974 by The Free Press, a Division of Macmillan Publishing Company.

Excerpts from Robert J. Alfonso, Gerald R. Firth, and Richard F. Neville, *Instructional Supervision: A Behavior System*, 2nd ed., Boston: Allyn and Bacon. Copyright © 1981 by Allyn and Bacon, Inc. Reprinted with permission.

Excerpts from Wendell L. French and Cecil H. Bell, Jr., *Organization Development*, Englewood Cliffs, N.J.: Prentice-Hall, 1973, p. 15. Reprinted with permission of Prentice-Hall, Inc.

Excerpts from Richard Beckhard, *Organization Development: Strategies and Models* © 1969. Addison-Wesley, Reading, Mass., p. 9. Reprinted with permission.

Excerpts from Gilbert R. Weldy, *Time: A Resource for the School Administrator*, Reston, Va.: National Association of Secondary School Principals, 1974. Reprinted with permission of National Association of Secondary School Principals.

Excerpts from "The Man from Plains Sums It Up," *Time* 120, no. 5 (October 11, 1982): 63. Reprinted with permission of *Time* and Jimmy Carter.

Excerpts from *The Silent Language* by Edward T. Hall. Copyright © 1959 by Edward T. Hall. Reprinted by permission of Doubleday & Company, Inc.

Excerpts from Ben M. Harris and William R. Hartgraves, "Supervisor Effectiveness: A Research Resume," *Educational Leadership* 30, no. 1 (October 1972): 78. Reprinted with permission of the Association for Supervision and Curriculum Development. Copyright © 1972 by the Association for Supervision and Curriculum Development. All rights reserved.

Excerpts from Stuart Chase, *Roads to Agreement*, New York: Harper & Row, 1951, pp. 235–238. Copyright © 1951 by Stuart Chase. Reprinted by permission of Harper & Row, Publishers, Inc.

Excerpts from *Interaction Laboratory for Teacher Development*, Roy, Utah: Interaction Associates, 1971, pp. 1–3. Reprinted with permission.

Excerpts from Georgia State Department of Education, *Teacher Performance Assessment Instruments: A Handbook for Interpretation*, Atlanta, Ga.: State Department of Education, Division of Staff Development, revised 1980. Reprinted with permission of Georgia State Department of Education.

Excerpts from Dwight Allen and Kevin Ryan, *Microteaching* © 1969. Addision Wesley, Reading, Mass., p. 15. Reprinted with permission.

Excerpts from Russell N. Jensen, Darleen Videen, and Charles F. Grubbs, *Teacher Self-Appraisal Program*, 1967–68, Tucson, Ariz.: Research and Development, Tucson Public Schools, July 1968. Reprinted with permission of Research and Development, Tucson Public Schools.

Excerpts from Robert Goldhammer, Robert H. Anderson, and Robert J. Krajewski, *Clinical*

Supervision: Special Methods for the Supervision of Teachers, 2nd ed., New York: Holt, Rinehart and Winston, 1980, pp. 26–29, 32; and Robert Goldhammer, 1st ed., 1969, 54, 89. Reprinted with permission of Holt, Rinehart and Winston, Inc.

Excerpts from Barbara Nelson Pavan, "Clinical Supervision: Some Signs of Progress," *Texas Tech Journal of Education* 7, no. 3 (Fall 1980): 242, 250. Reprinted with permission of Texas Tech Press.

Excerpts from *Techniques in the Clinical Supervision of Teachers: Preservice and Inservice Applications* by Keith A. Acheson and Meredith Damien Gall. Copyright © 1980 by Longman Inc. Reprinted by permission of Longman Inc.

Excerpts from Noreen Garman, "The Clinical Approach to Supervision," in Thomas J. Sergiovanni, ed., *Supervision of Teaching*, 1982 Yearbook, Alexandria, Va.: Association for Supervision and Curriculum Development, 1982, pp. 38, 42, 52. Reprinted with permission of the Association for Supervision and Curriculum Development. Copyright © 1982 by the Association for Supervision and Curriculum Development. All rights reserved.

Excerpts from Robert J. Alfonso and Lee Goldsberry, "Colleagueship in Supervision," in Thomas J. Sergiovanni, ed., *Supervision of Teaching*, 1982 Yearbook, Alexandria, Va.: Association for Supervision and Curriculum Development, 1982, pp. 91, 94, 107. Reprinted with permission of the Association for Supervision and Curriculum Development. Copyright © 1982 by the Association for Supervision and Curriculum Development. All rights reserved.

Excerpts from George C. Kyte, *How to Supervise: A Guide to Educational Principles and Progressive Practices of Educational Supervision*, Boston: Houghton Mifflin, 1930, pp. 138, 142, 147, 149–150, 151, 156–157, 160, 171, 187–188. Copyright © 1930 by Houghton Mifflin Company. Used by permission.

Excerpts from Elliot W. Eisner, "An Artistic Approach to Supervision," in Thomas J. Sergiovanni, ed., *Supervision of Teaching*, 1982 Yearbook, Alexandria, Va.: Association for Supervision and Curriculum Development, 1982, pp. 55–57, 59, 60–61. Reprinted with permission of the Association for Supervision and Curriculum Development. Copyright © 1982 by the Association for Supervision and Curriculum Development. All rights reserved.

Excerpts from Madeline Hunter, "Six Types of Supervisory Conferences," *Educational Leadership* 27, no. 5 (February 1980): 408, 409–412. Reprinted with permission of the Association for Supervision and Curriculum Development. Copyright © 1980 by the Association for Supervision and Curriculum Development. All rights reserved.

Excerpts from Carl D. Glickman, *Developmental Supervision: Alternative Practices for Helping Teachers Improve Instruction*, Alexandria, Va.: Association for Supervision and Curriculum Development, 1981, pp. 22, 29, 34. Reprinted with permission of the Association for Supervision and Curriculum Development. Copyright © 1981 by the Association for Supervision and Curriculum Development. All rights reserved.

Excerpts from Theresa Reilkoff, "Advantages of Supportive Supervision Over Clinical Supervision of Teachers," *The NASSP Bulletin* 65, no. 448 (November 1981): 29–31. Reprinted with permission of National Association of Secondary School Principals Bulletin.

Excerpts from Arthur Shaw, "Improving Instruction through Evaluation: One Teacher's View," *Action in Teacher Education* 2, no. 1 (Winter 1979–80): 1, 4. Reprinted with permission of Association of Teacher Educators.

Excerpts from Perry A. Zirkel, "Teacher Evaluation: An Overview," *Action in Teacher Education* 2, no. 1 (Winter 1979–80): 19–20. Reprinted with permission of Association of Teacher Educators.

Excerpts from John D. McNeil, "A Scientific Approach to Supervision," in Thomas J. Sergiovanni, ed., *Supervision of Teaching*, 1982 Yearbook, Alexandria, Va.: Association for Supervision and Curriculum Development, 1982, p. 23. Reprinted with permission of the Association for Supervision and Curriculum Development. Copyright © 1982 by the Association for Supervision and Curriculum Development. All rights reserved.

PART **I**

THE ROLE OF
THE SUPERVISOR

1

What Is Supervision?

OBJECTIVES

After studying Chapter 1 you should be able to accomplish the following objectives:

1. Write a working definition of supervision.
2. Draw and explain a conceptual model of supervision.
3. Identify supervisors in a school system.
4. List common tasks of supervision.
5. Describe various roles of supervisors.
6. State what you believe to be minimal qualifications of a supervisor.
7. Show your position on supervision as a career.

A FIELD ILL-DEFINED

One of the best kept secrets outside the education profession and, to a considerable degree, even within the profession is the existence of a large shadow army of school personnel known by the collective title of supervisors. Parents and sometimes teachers profess not to know of the presence of these specialists in the school systems of the nation. Although laypersons may be aware that school systems employ a variety of personnel such as custodians, secretaries, cafeteria workers, and counselors, the concept of school personnel held by a typical layperson is a teacher in every classroom and a principal in every school. Were members of the community asked to identify a school supervisor, they would probably indicate the principal, who may or may not be the sole supervisor. Or, they might refer to the superintendent, who plays a very small part in the type of supervision we shall be concerned with in this book, namely, instructional supervision.

Yet, as the alien-watchers say about extra-territorial beings, supervisors are out there. In fact, they are all around us. We could discover to what degree they are present if we had the power to equip every supervisor for one day with a coal miner's hat and to turn on all the light beams. If we could then photograph the light trails, we would trace a pattern of motion as astounding as any sketch drawn by a computer. We'd see almost endless movement as supervisors journey from class to class, school to school, and school system to school system. Whereas teachers are usually place-bound, supervisors are in periodic motion. A distinguishing feature of true supervisors lies in the fact that they leave their offices frequently for the purpose of helping other school personnel to do their jobs better.

Motion itself can, of course, be aimless. It must be accompanied by knowledge and skills which we will discuss later in this chapter. For a moment, however, let's glimpse a few specialists in action.

The superintendent "supervised" teachers on casual strolls through the schools, believing a teacher's effectiveness could be judged by glancing through the open door or the window of the teacher's classroom. He sometimes met teachers in the halls and talked with them, which he believed to be a more effective means of supervision than visiting them in their classrooms.

The vice-president for academic affairs of the university ruled on the question of tenure for a faculty member by counting publications in refereed journals and presentations at conferences of learned societies.

The dean of the College of Education made the rounds of the corridors of the college, buttonholing unwary students to ask about one of their professors, "Can she teach?" The dean listened carefully to their spontaneous comments.

The dean of instruction of the community college sent a memorandum to all department heads requesting copies of the syllabi for all their courses.

The assistant superintendent in charge of curriculum and instruction returned from a national meeting during which open-space education was discussed and decided that all elementary schools in her school system should initiate open-space programs. She sprang the matter on them suddenly and cajoled them into trying out this "innovation."

The director of elementary education presided over a meeting of developmental reading teachers, allowing every participant to be heard and permitting each one to speak as long as he or she desired. At the end of lengthy meetings the director always summarized, neatly tying up the discussion into a package representing the consensus of the meetings.

The science supervisor favored an inquiry approach and, traveling from school to school, insisted that all science teachers in the school system use it. He watched for deviations from this approach.

The general supervisor stayed in her office at the superintendent's headquarters the entire academic year, sifting through papers, writing memos, reacting to situations, and conferring with teachers who elected to come in for a visit. She regretted not having enough time to get out into the schools.

The senior high school principal required teachers on the staff to turn in lesson plan books every two weeks with lessons outlined in them for the next two weeks.

The junior high school principal hastened through the corridors of the school and stopped in front of a classroom. The bell had just signaled the beginning of the class hour, but students had not ceased their chitchat in the first 30 seconds after the bell had finished sounding. The principal barged into the classroom shouting, "Everybody quiet. The bell has rung. Settle down now." He glared at the teacher, who stood agape at the front of the room.

The assistant principal for curriculum of a middle school wrote the school's statement of philosophy and passed out copies of it to the faculty for its information and, presumably, acceptance.

The head of the social studies department began the after-school faculty meeting with a coffee hour to help develop a sense of warmth and camaraderie among the faculty. The head of the department spent a lot of time fostering a feeling of togetherness.

The kindergarten team leader reprimanded the other members of the team in front of the children because she felt they were too lenient in their handling of the pupils.

All the school personnel mentioned above consider themselves supervisors and render, either deliberately or incidentally, a type of supervision. In discharging supervisory functions they operate within their own frames of reference and have their own ideas of the supervisor's role.

Supervision Defined

Considering the veritable army of supervisors on local and state levels of schooling throughout the country, it is surprising to find that the role of the supervisor in education is rather ill-defined. Business and industry are not troubled by this same malady. The position of commercial or industrial supervisor is highly visible and well-defined in the managerial structure of the organization. Educational supervisors may or may not be a part of the managerial structure of school systems. Whether they should be a part of management is, as we will examine later, a storm center among specialists in supervision.

Responsibilities of educational supervisors are not at all clear from locality to locality and from state to state. Indeed, supervisory roles even within localities are often poorly delineated. To compound the problem the titles of supervisors are almost as varied as their roles.

Ben M. Harris attributed the variations in roles to differing theoretical perspectives when he said:

Supervision like any complex part of an even more complex enterprise can be viewed in various ways and inevitably is. The diversity of perceptions stems not only from organizational complexity but also from lack of information and absence of perspective. To provide perspective, at least, the total school operation must be the point of departure for analyzing instructional supervision as a major function.[1]

To varying degrees many occupations outside education utilize the services of supervisors, be they office boss, telephone supervisor, floor manager, construction foreman, department-store head, or assembly-line supervisor. These individuals carry out the task of supervision in the original sense of the Latin word *supervideo*, to oversee. They demonstrate techniques, offer suggestions, give orders, evaluate employees' performance, and check on results (products).

Historical Approaches

Inspection.   Historically, school supervisors fulfilled their function by giving directions, checking on compliance with prescribed teaching techniques, and evaluating results of instruction by teachers in their charge. In an authoritarian mode early supervisors set strict requirements for their teachers to follow and visited classrooms

1872

Instruction to the Teacher

Harrison, S.D.

1. *Teachers will fill lamps, clean chimneys and trim wicks each day.*

2. *Each teacher will bring a scuttle of coal and a bucket of water for the day's use.*

3. *Make your pens carefully. You may whittle nibs for the individual tastes of children.*

4. *Men teachers may take one evening each week for courting purposes or two evenings a week if they go to church regularly.*

5. *After ten hours in school, the teacher should spend the remaining time reading the Bible and other good books.*

6. *Women teachers who marry or engage in other unseemly conduct will be dismissed.*

7. *Every teacher should lay aside from every pay a goodly sum of his earnings for his declining years so that he will not become a burden on society.*

8. *Any teacher who smokes, uses liquor in any form, frequents pool or public halls, or gets shaved in a barber shop will give good reasons to suspect his worth, intentions, integrity and honesty.*

9. *The teacher who performs his labors faithfully without fault for five years will be given an increase of 25ᶜ a week in his pay—providing the Board of Education approves.*

SOURCE: Board of Education, Harrison, South Dakota and Leo W. Anglin, Richard Goldman, and Joyce Shanahan Anglin, *Teaching: What It's All About*, New York, Harper & Row, 1982, p. 11. Reprinted by permission of Board of Education, Harrison, South Dakota.

to check on how closely the teachers complied with the stipulated requirements. The appeal to authority was very evident in the widely reproduced set of instructions to teachers of Harrison, South Dakota in 1872.

Inspection, often derided as "snoopervision," was the prevailing approach to supervision in nineteenth-century America. To some extent school supervisors, or inspectors, as they are called in other countries, continue to fulfill their tasks with an authoritarian approach. The classic illustration of this—though, of course, not entirely true—is France, where it is said that the Minister of Education can tell on any day exactly where each teacher is in any textbook anywhere in the country. Such a situation implies a highly structured form of instruction and supervision.

In America we have no instructional inspectors in the foreign sense of the word. There are no inspectors from the United States Department of Education whose duty it is to check on teachers and schools. Some states do provide or have provided a limited type of inspection of teachers prior to full certification in a subject or grade level, but this is more uncommon than common. Even today, however, some individuals behave like inspectors although their job specifications do not call for such behavior.

Scientific Management. Some supervisors subscribe to principles of scientific management, which influenced the professional behavior of both school administrators and supervisors in the first quarter of the twentieth century. William H. Lucio and John D. McNeil pointed out that during this period:

Teachers were regarded as instruments that should be closely supervised to insure that they mechanically carried out the methods of procedure determined by administrative and special supervisors.[2]

"Scientific" supervisors look for fixed principles of teaching drawn from the research which can be related to teachers. The teachers' performances then are judged on how well they follow the instructional principles in their teaching. To supervisors of this persuasion teaching is a science rather than an art and they believe that by following a prescribed set of rules teachers are bound to be successful.

Laissez-faire. To some, supervision is a laissez-faire task. Supervisors who are thus inclined agree with a goodly number of teachers that the less supervision, the better. Nondirective in their approach, they may visit the teachers' classrooms or stop by the teachers' lounge for a cup of coffee. They tend to consider a classroom visit and an appearance in the teachers' lounge as equally important; some, in fact, might rate the chat in the teachers' lounge as more important. They see their task as giving the teacher a benevolent pat on the head now and then.

Group Dynamics. To others, supervision is a continuous exercise in group dynamics. They see improvement of instruction as a continuing exercise in human relations. Viewing themselves as resource persons to the group, they spend considerable time fostering a positive group climate, using social affairs to establish a happy, cooperative frame of mind. They hope that after a period of deliberation groups will reach consensus on points under discussion. Supervision in mid-twentieth-century America was dominated by the human relations approach.

Neither an authoritarian nor a laissez-faire approach is adequate or suitable for today's schools, nor is an exclusively "scientific" or group-process approach. Supervisors are called on to work with both groups and individuals and many of the innovations in schools are products of experimentation by one or two individuals rather than by groups.

It is extremely difficult to create a sharp, clear-cut definition of supervision. Ralph L. Mosher and David E. Purpel described this difficulty as follows:

The difficulty of defining supervision in relation to education also stems, in large part, from unsolved theoretical problems about teaching. Quite simply, we lack sufficient understanding of the process of teaching. Our theories of learning are inadequate, the criteria for measuring teaching effectiveness are imprecise, and deep disagreement exists about what knowledge— that is, what curriculum—is most valuable to teach. . . . When we have achieved more understanding of *what* and *how* to teach, and with what *special effects* on students, we will be much less vague about the supervision of these processes.[3]

Looking at the way specialists in supervision have defined the term may help us in our quest for a viable definition. William H. Burton and Leo J. Brueckner, for example, gave supervision a broad interpretation, viewing supervision as a technical service requiring expertise the goal of which is improvement in the growth and development of the learner.[4]

Stressing the helping nature of supervision, Jane Franseth stated:

Today supervision is generally seen as leadership that encourages a continuous involvement of all school personnel in a cooperative attempt to achieve the most effective school program.[5]

Kimball Wiles viewed supervision as a service activity when he wrote:

Supervision consists of all the activities leading to the improvement of instruction, activities related to morale, improving human relations, in-service education, and curriculum development.[6]

Ross L. Neagley and N. Dean Evans pointed to the democratic nature of modern supervision in their definition:

Modern supervision is considered as any service for teachers that eventually results in improving instruction, learning, and the curriculum. It consists of positive, dynamic, democratic actions designed to improve instruction through the continued growth of all concerned individuals—the child, the teacher, the supervisor, the administrator, and the parent or other lay person.[7]

Contemporary definitions of supervision stress *service, cooperation,* and *democracy.* Since the word supervision by itself connotes so many different meanings, some specialists in the field have found it expedient to add modifiers. Thus, we encounter *administrative, clinical, consultative, developmental, educational, general,* and *instructional* preceding *supervision*. Each of the adjectives offers a special interpretation of the term supervision.

Whereas *educational supervision* and *general supervision* suggest responsibilities encompassing many aspects of schooling, including administration, curriculum, and instruction, *instructional supervision* (or *supervision of instruction*) narrows the focus to a more limited set of responsibilities. *Clinical, consultative,* and *developmental supervision* are subsumed under *instructional supervision*. *Administrative supervision* covers the territory of managerial responsibilities outside of the fields of curriculum and instruction.

In this book you will find the emphasis placed on instructional supervision. For that reason it will pay us to take a look at ways in which some of the experts view this term. Harris wrote as follows:

Supervision of instruction is what school personnel do with *adults* and *things* to maintain or change the school operation in ways that *directly* influence the teaching processes employed to promote pupil learning.[8]

Robert J. Alfonso, Gerald R. Firth, and Richard F. Neville defined instructional supervision in this way:

Instructional supervision is herein defined as: *Behavior officially designated by the organization that directly affects teacher behavior in such a way as to facilitate pupil learning and achieve the goals of the organization.*[9]

John T. Lovell in revising the earlier work of Kimball Wiles looked at instructional supervisory behavior in the following way:

Instructional supervisory behavior is assumed to be an additional behavior system formally provided by the organization for the purpose of interacting with the teaching behavior system in such a way as to maintain, change, and improve the design and actualization of learning opportunities for students.[10]

These last three definitions focus on (1) the behavior of supervisors, (2) in assisting teachers, and (3) for the ultimate benefit of the student. Supervision, as presented in this text, is conceived as a service to teachers, both as individuals and in groups. To put it simply, supervision is a means of offering to teachers specialized help in improving instruction. The words *service* and *help* should be underscored and they are used repeatedly in this text.

That service and help are not stressed by some supervisors is seen in the attitudes teachers often bear toward supervisors. Some teachers distrust supervisors, fearing that the supervisors will report their shortcomings to the school administrators. To some teachers the supervisor's presence in the classroom can be a traumatic experience.

Other teachers view supervisors with contempt, feeling, sometimes rightly and sometimes wrongly, that they are more capable than the supervisor or that the supervisor has nothing of value to offer them. Many teachers simply ignore supervisors, choose not to ask for their help, and avoid opportunities to work with them.

Arthur Blumberg pictured the tensions between supervisors and teachers in the following passage:

the character of relationships between teachers as a group and supervisors as a group can be described as somewhat of a cold war. Neither side trusts the other and each side is convinced of the correctness of its position. Supervisors seem to be saying, "If *they* would just listen to us, things would really get better." Teachers seem to be saying, "What *they* give us doesn't help. It would be better if they left us alone."[11]

These negative, fearful, or hostile attitudes are symptoms of the malaise brought on by uncertainties about the role, function, and efficiency of the supervision profession. Great needs exist to clarify duties and responsibilities of supervisors, to discover the most effective techniques and skills, and to identify who the supervisors are.

WHO ARE THE SUPERVISORS?

In the traditional meaning of supervision anyone who oversees the work of another is a supervisor. Hence, every administrator is ipso facto a supervisor. If we limit the concept of supervision to management of resources and personnel, we are on firm ground in labeling the administrator a supervisor. Yet, if we delimit supervision to the means of improving the curriculum and instruction, we may not conclude that every administrator is an instructional supervisor.

Logically, it would seem that any school official who assists teachers in the improvement of curriculum and instruction is a supervisor. In practice, however, some individuals in the school system are charged with the management of resources and personnel as their primary task whereas others are assigned the improvement of curriculum and instruction as their major function.

Many an argument is waged over whether the building principal, for example, is a supervisor. When we consider primary duties, we would not classify the *typical* school principal as an instructional supervisor. Although principals have responsibility for the curriculum and instruction of the school, supervision of those aspects is only one of their many tasks. It is unfortunately true that instructional supervision is often a secondary task to many school principals who commonly lament that they do not have time to devote to curriculum and instructional leadership because they are too busy with the day-to-day operation of the school.

Having eliminated the typical school principal from our list of instructional supervisors, we must hasten to add that in those small schools throughout the country which employ a principal, several teachers, and no one to assist the principal with any of his or her duties, the principals do, by necessity if not by desire, perform the function of instructional supervisor. Perhaps, we would do well if we referred to those principals by a title used more often in earlier days, supervising principals, as distinguished from instructional supervisor.

"By their fruits ye shall know them" is more pertinent in the world of supervision than "by their titles ye shall know them." Controversy swirls around the issue, which we will examine more fully in Chapter 2, as to whether supervisors should assume administrative responsibilities. We should note at this point that this issue is not ordinarily reversed, i.e., whether administrators should assume supervisory responsibilities. For both legal and practical reasons administrators already possess these responsibilities. Whether they perform these duties effectively is another matter. In their mind's eye principals perceive themselves as managers of instruction as well as directors of resources and personnel.

As we try to identify supervisors, it might be helpful to depict the degree to which administrators and supervisors take on the role of leading in instructional improvement. We can chart varying degrees of supervisory responsibility in the following manner:

Full-time Administrators	Administrators Who Supervise Part-time	Supervisors Who Administer Part-time	Full-time Supervisors

A full-time administrator (e.g., superintendent of schools; many principals, especially of large schools) is deep into budgeting, transportation, staffing, pupil personnel services, and public relations. He or she devotes little or no time to curricular and instructional supervision but delegates that duty to others. Some administrators, however, although preoccupied with managerial problems, expend some time and energy on supervisory activities. They may visit—and, in fact, in many cases they are required by law to visit—teachers in their classrooms, observe their teaching, make judgments, and offer advice. When they behave in this fashion, administrators become supervisors, if only for a portion of their time.

Some school personnel who by job description are classified as supervisors are charged with or assume on their own initiative administrative duties such as annual assessments of teacher performance. When they accept managerial tasks, they join the ranks of the administrators. Finally, those personnel who spend all their time and efforts in helping teachers directly with the improvement of instruction may be called full-time supervisors. Thus, with a nod to Izaak Walton, we have the Compleat Administrator on one side of the spectrum and the Compleat Supervisor on the other.

Types of Supervisors

The American system of education is a confusing diversity of systems which confounds people from abroad who attempt to study it. In fact, at times our system even confuses Americans themselves. This confusion extends even to the provision of special services like supervision.

In the pages of this book we talk about a person whom we call the supervisor. Unless otherwise specified, we are talking about the instructional supervisor. In agreement with many specialists but not all, I include curriculum supervision within the context of instructional supervision.

Because of the great diversity in roles and duties of supervisors, I urge the reader to keep in mind the distinction between the *supervisor* with *supervisor* emphasized and *the* supervisor with *the* emphasized. In discussing the *supervisor* we make the assumption that principles and practices of supervision may apply *generally, to most, but not to all situations nor to all persons* who wear the hat of supervisor. This book concentrates on the *supervisor*. Were we to talk about *the* supervisor, we would be conveying the erroneous notion that there is a single, accepted role which supervisors can, do, or should play. The effort to identify a single role applicable under all circumstances is akin to searching for that unrealizable will-o'-the-wisp, the best model of teaching.

Supervisors are special service personnel to be found on the staffs of administrators at the state, local district, and school building levels. In administrative parlance these service personnel are *staff* employees whereas the administrators, equipped with the mantles of status and authority, are *line* employees. Staff personnel are hired by and responsible to the line employees. Supervisors are often referred to as auxiliary personnel or, more simply, staff. Although titles and responsibilities of these auxiliary personnel differ from state to state and from school district to school district, we can

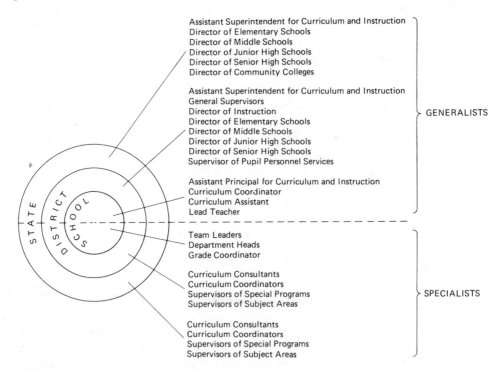

Figure 1.1 Types of Supervisors

identify the major types of supervisors. Figure 1.1 shows some of the varieties of supervisors on the different levels. Included among the types of supervisors are both part-time, i.e., administrators who spend a portion of their time in supervising, and full-time supervisors. Figure 1.1 also distinguishes generalist supervisors whose duties cut across subject matter lines and grade levels from specialist supervisors whose responsibilities fall within a subject area or grade level.

State Supervisors

The chief supervisor on the state level is the assistant superintendent for curriculum and instruction. Although this position may bear other titles, it is this person's responsibility to supervise the entire instructional and curricular program of the public schools in the state, with the help of staff members. The assistant superintendent interprets state department of education and state legislature mandates concerning education, and is directly responsible to the state superintendent of public instruction. The assistant superintendent's office frequently directs teachers in the preparation of certain curricular materials and often supervises textbook adoptions. It provides consultant service to the schools, sponsors conferences on curriculum and instruction, and acts as liaison with the federal government in the preparation of proposals for grants for federal projects. This office encourages experimentation in curriculum design and instructional techniques.

The assistant superintendent for curriculum and instruction is aided by a staff of specialists who may be designated as supervisors, directors, consultants, or coordinators. Frequently found are specialists in curriculum and instruction such as directors or supervisors of elementary education and directors or supervisors of secondary education. These staff members aid in fulfilling the assistant superintendent's tasks. They generally confine themselves, however, to providing leadership at their own levels.

Well-developed state departments of education provide a variety of specialists in particular areas or disciplines such as science, English, social studies, and reading. These supervisors operate throughout the state in their own areas of specialization assisting teachers, suggesting materials, giving advice, and demonstrating effective methods of teaching their specialties. They are generally responsible to the director of elementary education or director of middle schools, junior high schools, or senior high schools, depending on their level of responsibility. It is not uncommon, for example, to find a supervisor of elementary language arts and a supervisor of secondary language arts on the assistant superintendent's staff.

Local Supervisors

The presence and effectiveness of the supervisor is felt more keenly on the local than on the state level. The state supervisor's area is so large and responsibilities so many that he or she cannot possibly make the rounds of all the schools and teachers demanding services. Consequently, local supervisors become key people in the school system.

On the school district level supervisors are on the staff of the local school superintendent. They are referred to in the literature and in practice as central office personnel, which distinguishes them from school-based personnel employed to serve in particular schools.

On the central office staff customarily an assistant superintendent for curriculum and instruction serves the school district although sometimes he or she is replaced by a director of instruction. This key local official provides curricular and instructional leadership throughout the local district and is in charge of the entire curriculum of that district. This official aids teachers in developing materials; encourages experimentation and research; provides schools with up-to-date materials and consultants; leads the district in the continuous task of curriculum development; and meets with teachers and administrators on problems of curriculum and instruction.

Helping the assistant superintendent are personnel of various types. Often there are one or more general supervisors, responsible for supervision from kindergarten through twelfth grade. They are frequently in the schools assisting individual teachers and groups of teachers in a variety of fields. These persons are familiar with learning theory, adolescent psychology, methods of handling groups and individuals, and new ways to organize for instruction. Some of the smaller school districts limit their central office personnel to positions of this type.

Larger school systems employ supervisors or directors of elementary and secondary education. Whereas the general supervisor must be spread thin over the entire school system, these two specialists may concentrate on their individual levels.

Large school districts often provide a variety of supervisors or consultants in special fields such as reading, guidance, foreign languages, and vocational education. Some of the special-area supervisors divide their time between the elementary and secondary levels as, for example, in art, music, and physical education, while others confine their work to one level. These specialists are in a strategic position for effecting change in individual classrooms. They have expertise in a particular field and may devote their full time and energies to the development of curriculum and instruction in their specialties. They can be knowledgeable about latest content, materials, and methods of their fields of specialization.

Within the individual schools of a district can be found people who could be designated as supervisors. Often, a school will employ an assistant principal whose main duty is the supervision of curriculum and instruction. This person devotes full energies to developing the curriculum of his or her own school and helping teachers with the improvement of instruction.

Curriculum coordinators or lead teachers are sometimes found in the individual schools either as assistants to or replacing the assistant principal for curriculum and instruction. It is their task to assist teachers with curricular and instructional problems and to give leadership to the improvement of instruction and the development of the curriculum.

Key supervisors in the individual schools are the team leaders, grade coordinators, and department heads. With the new staffing patterns followed by many schools at all levels, the person who heads an instructional team plays a significant role as supervisor for that team. The department head in middle, junior high, and senior high schools fulfills for a department a supervisory function similar to that fulfilled by the team leader. Since elementary schools are ordinarily not departmentalized, the grade coordinators for all sections of a grade level and the team leaders for each section of a grade level serve as quasi department heads and carry heavy responsibilities for supervision. In the middle, junior high, and senior high schools we may find both team leaders and department heads with team leaders who are within departments responsible to the department heads.

School-based supervisors will lead in curriculum development, assist teachers in the production of instructional and curricular materials, and help teachers to improve their teaching methods. Principals have the obligation of freeing their coordinators and leaders so that they will not be bogged down with either administrative details of running their grades, teams, or departments or full-time teaching schedules which prohibit them from giving adequate time to instructional and curricular leadership.

It will be debated whether those personnel shown in Figure 1.1 who hold line or administrative positions are truly supervisors; for example, the assistant superintendents and directors on both state and district levels, who often work only minimally with teachers. The assistant superintendent for curriculum and instruction and frequently the directors on the local district level occupy line rather than staff positions. Depending upon the school district, line persons may or may not work directly with teachers. Figure 1.1, however, does classify these line officials as supervisors since they devote at least part of their time to supervisory duties. Whereas some specialists in supervision restrict their concept of a supervisor to those staff persons who work full-time directly with teachers, others include within their concept line officers who have responsibilities for curriculum and instruction. In this vein, for example, Lucio and McNeil listed the assistant superintendent and director among supervisory positions in urban school districts.[12]

Since many line administrators do engage in supervision, we should interject at this point that they should be trained in supervision as well as those who pursue full-time careers in supervision. It is an unfortunate commentary on the licensing process in many states that the requirements for the preparation of administrators and supervisors, which are often minimal, are one and the same. By taking a handful of college courses in educational administration and supervision, a person can become certified in both administration and supervision at the same time.

However delightful such an arrangement is for prospective administrators and supervisors since one preparation program opens up two job markets, differentiation in training programs for administrators and supervisors is a crying need of the profession. The training requirements of these two related careers are not identical.

TASKS OF SUPERVISION

We might gain a clearer insight into the field of supervision if we focused our attention for a few moments on what it is supervisors actually do. As long ago as 1922 William H. Burton listed the tasks which he saw as pertinent to the supervisor. These tasks, which some might label arenas, were:

1. The improvement of the teaching act (classroom visits, individual and group conferences, directed teaching, demonstration teaching, development of standards for self-improvement, etc.).

2. The improvement of teachers in service (teachers' meetings, professional readings, bibliographies and reviews, bulletins, intervisitation, self-analysis and criticism, etc.).

3. The selection and organization of subject-matter (setting up objectives, studies of subject-matter and learning activities, experimental testing of materials, constant revision of courses, the selection and evaluation of supplementary instructional materials, etc.).

4. Testing and measuring (the use of standardized and local tests for classification, diagnosis, guidance, etc.).

5. The rating of teachers (the development and use of rating cards, of check-lists, stimulation of self-rating).[13]

A. S. Barr, William H. Burton, and Leo J. Brueckner credited Burton's listing as "the first modern statement and concept" of supervision.[14] Burton's list looks surprisingly current when we examine the numerous tasks which today's supervisors actually perform.

Writing a half century later Harris enumerated 10 tasks of supervision in a rather detailed list as follows:

Task 1: Developing curriculum. Designing or redesigning that which is to be taught, by whom, when, where, and in what pattern. Developing curriculum guides, establishing standards, planning instructional units, and instituting new courses are examples of this area.

Task 2: Organizing for instruction. Making arrangements whereby pupils, staff, space, and materials are related to time and instructional objectives in coordinate and efficient ways. Grouping of students, planning class schedules, assigning spaces, allocating time for instruction, scheduling, planning events, and arranging for teaching teams are examples of the endeavors associated with this task area.

Task 3: Providing staff. Assuring the availability of instructional staff members in adequate numbers and with appropriate competencies for facilitating instruction. Recruiting, screening, selecting, assigning, and transferring staff are endeavors in this task area.

Task 4: Providing facilities. Designing or redesigning and equipping facilities for instruction. The development of space and equipment specifications is included in this task area.

Task 5: Providing materials. Selecting and obtaining appropriate materials for use in implementing curricular designs. Previewing, evaluating, designing, and otherwise finding ways to provide appropriate materials are included in this task area.

Task 6: Arranging for in-service education. Planning and implementing learning experiences that will improve the performance of the staff in instruction-related ways. This involves workshops, consultations, field trips, and training sessions, as well as formal education.

Task 7: Orienting staff members. Providing staff members with basic information necessary to carry out assigned responsibilities. This includes getting new staff members acquainted with facilities, staff, and community, but it also involves keeping the staff informed of organizational developments.

Task 8: Relating special pupil services. Arranging for careful coordination of services to children to ensure optimum support for the teaching process. This involves developing policies, assigning priorities, and defining relationships among service personnel to maximize relationships between services offered and instructional goals of the school.

Task 9: Developing public relations. Providing for a free flow of information on matters of instruction to and from the public while securing optimum levels of involvement in the promotion of better instruction.

Task 10: Evaluating instruction. Planning, instrumenting, organizing, and implementing procedures for data gathering, analysis, and interpretation, and decision making for improvement of instruction.[15]

Harris classified tasks 1, 3, and 4 as preliminary; 6 and 10 as developmental; and the other tasks as operational.[16] You will note both similarities and differences in the Burton and Harris listings. We can find supervision specialists who would be willing to accept either the Burton or the Harris compilation of supervisory tasks. On the other hand, we can find experts in the field who would reject both lists. Those who view supervision as a one-to-one, clinical relationship between the teacher and supervisor would eliminate many of the tasks from both lists. Those who view supervision as a field distinctive from administration would delegate administrative tasks like scheduling, staffing, and public relations to the administrator rather than to the instructional supervisor.

What is more revealing about the functions of supervisors are the statements of expectations as shown in the job descriptions of various school personnel. In Appendix B you will find several examples of actual job descriptions of supervisory personnel at the school, school district, and intermediate unit level. Were we to compare these examples with illustrations from other school systems, we would inevitably discover differences in the duties assigned to the various personnel even though they may bear the same titles. What is universally true throughout school systems, however, is the fact that much is expected of all supervisors.

A MODEL OF SUPERVISION

The supervisor plays a variety of roles within certain domains and the expertise demonstrated in the particular domains is derived from a number of bases or foundations. One way to explain the dimensions of supervisory behavior is in the form of a schematic model. Figure 1.2 depicts the concept of supervision followed in this text.

The model shows three large domains or territories within which supervisors work. Within the model several concentric wheels rest on a foundational bed. The four inner wheels show four primary roles of the supervisor while the outer wheel surrounds the three supervisory domains. The foundational bed undergirds the whole system and indicates the sources of the supervisor's knowledge and skills.

The conceptual design of this model conveys the notion that supervision is both dynamic and service-oriented. The dynamic nature of the model is shown by the arrows which point out that any of the wheels may turn in either direction. This conceptual model visualizes the supervisor's playing four major roles: coordinator, consultant, group leader, and evaluator in three domains: instructional development, curriculum development, and staff development.

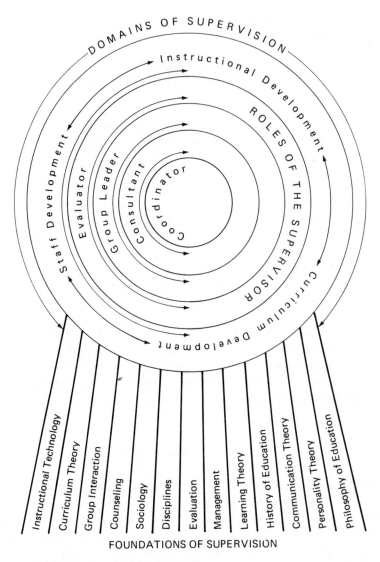

Figure 1.2 A Conceptual Model of Supervision

A model of this nature can quickly reveal the concepts held by the person who designs it. Let's play for a moment with the same basic design but follow a different set of assumptions about the role(s) of the supervisor. Some people, for example, might take issue with the three domains, cut them to one or two, or expand them beyond three. They might eliminate supervisory duties in the area of curriculum development, leaving instructional development and staff development. They might delete instructional development as well as curriculum development, allowing only staff development to remain. They might feel in so doing that instructional development, that is, improvement in the classroom, is a by-product or part of staff development. To them staff development would mean assistance to teachers in improving personal and professional qualities.

In restricting the domains to staff development alone, these people might perceive the roles of the supervisor as two in number: consultant to individual teachers and consultant to groups of teachers. Some might even go further and restrict the supervisor to one role: consultant to individual teachers, i.e., clinician.

A design of the kind herein presented is, in fact, a graphic description of supervision. In presenting a model of supervision I have taken the position that supervisors *do* and *should* work in all three domains and carry out *at least* the four roles. This model can accommodate limited and required administrative functions of supervisory personnel through the four roles already charted.

Domains of Supervision

The supervisor exercises various roles within one of three domains: instructional, curricular, and staff development. Following one or more of these major areas the supervisor assists teachers in the improvement of instruction, curriculum planning and improvement, and personal and professional growth and development. In fulfilling the various roles within these domains the supervisor must bring to bear a wide repertoire of knowledge, skills, and techniques. In Figure 1.2 two-headed arrows connect the three domains to show that all are interrelated and overlap. Staff development activities may center on personal growth, instructional development, or curriculum development. When a supervisor works, for example, as a group leader in curriculum development, he or she may at the same time work in the domain of instructional development and/or staff development. It is possible at the same time to be working in the domain of instructional development and/or staff development.

Roles of the Supervisor

It is true, as has already been mentioned, that the roles which supervisors play vary from state to state and from locality to locality. The roles are defined by the superintendents or principals to whom the supervisors are responsible and, as happens in most positions of leadership, by the supervisors themselves. Although some variation will be found in the roles supervisors may fulfill, it is more than likely that the service-oriented supervisor will perform at varying times each of the four roles shown in the model:

Coordinator. The supervisor serves as a coordinator of programs, groups, materials, and reports. It is the supervisor who acts as a link between programs and people. It is the supervisor who knows of the disparate pieces of the educational process and directs the actions of others to make the pieces blend. As a director of staff development the supervisor plans, arranges, evaluates, and often conducts in-service programs for teachers.

Consultant. The supervisor serves in a consulting capacity as a specialist in curriculum, instructional methodology, and staff development. In this capacity he or she renders service to teachers both on an individual basis and in groups. At times the supervisor may simply furnish necessary information and suggestions. At other times he or she may help teachers define, set, and pursue goals. The supervisor should be a prime source of help to teachers wishing to improve either their generic or specialized teaching skills. Though some will disagree with me, I believe the supervisor-consultant should be able to demonstrate to teachers particular techniques either inside or outside a classroom setting.

Group Leader. The supervisor as group leader works continuously to release the potential of groups seeking to improve the curriculum, instruction, or themselves. To perform this role the supervisor must be knowledgeable about group dynamics and must demonstrate leadership skills. The supervisor assists groups in consensus building, in moving toward group goals, and in perfecting the democratic process. As a group leader the supervisor seeks out, identifies, and fosters leadership talent from within the group.

Evaluator. As an evaluator the supervisor provides assistance to teachers in the evaluation of instruction and curriculum. The supervisor helps teachers to find answers to curricular and instructional problems, aids them in identifying research studies which may have a bearing on their problems, and assists them in conducting limited research projects. Additionally, the supervisor helps teachers to evaluate their classroom performance, to assess their own strengths and weaknesses, and to select means of overcoming deficiencies.

Foundations of Supervision

The supports which constitute the bed for the wheel of supervision are areas of learning from which the supervisor derives expertise. A look at the multiplicity of areas from which a knowledgeable and skilled supervisor must draw suggests that a broad training program is in order for the supervisor.

When the conceptual model of supervision with its domains, roles, and foundations is studied, we may deduce competencies that supervisors should be able to demonstrate. Supervisors should possess (1) certain personal traits and (2) certain types of knowledge and skills.

Personal Traits

The literature on supervision is remarkably silent on what personal characteristics are necessary for successful supervisory behavior. Perhaps this silence can be attributed to one or more of the following reasons.

1. Personal characteristics can be inferred from the skills supervisors should possess. Thus, if supervisors are expected to demonstrate a high degree of skill in

human or interpersonal relations, they should exhibit human and humane traits like empathy, warmth, and sincerity.

2. Educational research has been notably unsuccessful in identifying personal qualities which are common to all successful administrators and supervisors. The presence of generally valued personal traits in a leader does not guarantee success on the job nor does the absence of these traits assure failure. Since the search for universal traits has been unproductive, the experts have concentrated on the more certain requisite knowledge and skills.

3. Personal traits necessary for success in positions of leadership appear so obvious that they need no elaboration. Some specialists in the field may feel that a compendium of supervisory traits is on the order of the oath which Boy Scouts take, promising to be trustworthy, loyal, helpful, friendly, etc.

4. The search for personal traits is a somewhat dated activity in a time when researchers are attempting to identify competencies which school personnel should demonstrate. Nevertheless, in spite of these encumbrances I believe we should at least briefly consider the question of personal characteristics needed by supervisory personnel. Robert C. McKean and H. H. Mills deemed the following personal characteristics essential to fulfillment of the role of supervisor:

- ability to win respect and confidence
- empathy and sensitivity
- enthusiasm
- feeling of adequacy
- originality
- sense of humor
- sense of relative value
- sincerity
- resourcefulness[17]

The successful supervisor is one who is in constant contact with people. He or she should possess those personal traits of warmth, friendliness, patience, and a sense of humor which are essential not only to supervision but also to teaching as well. As a service-oriented agent for improvement the supervisor must be imbued with the spirit which counselors refer to as "the helping relationship," the desire to give of oneself in order to be of assistance to others. Beyond this the supervisor needs a type of persuasiveness, and infectious enthusiasm to cause teachers to want to make changes for the better.

The supervisor should be an "idea person," one who starts people thinking about new and improved ways of doing things. At the same time he or she needs to convey the attitude of valuing and seeking the ideas of others. The leader must avoid giving the impression of having all the answers to problems faced by teachers.

The supervisor who is a helper to teachers is able to effect a democratic environment in which the contributions of each participating member are valued. Above all, the supervisor needs to possess a predisposition to change and must constantly promote improvement. If the supervisor, whose chief responsibility is to bring about improvements, is satisfied with the status quo, he or she can be sure that the teachers will be too. The supervisor must be able to live with change and help teachers to adapt to changing needs of society and of children and youth. To accomplish this mission the supervisor should be able to work effectively in both one-to-one relationships and in group settings.

Knowledge and Skills

Whereas discussions of personal traits of supervisors are less frequently encountered, we can find an abundance of statements about the knowledge and skills essential to successful supervisors. There is general agreement that supervisors should have experienced:

- a sound general education program
- a thorough preservice professional education program
- a major field of study
- a solid graduate program in supervision
- three to five years of successful teaching at the elementary or secondary school level

In preservice and in-service training programs supervisors should develop a grounding in:

- learning theory and educational psychology
- philosophy of education
- history of education, especially of curriculum and instructional development
- the role of the school in society
- curriculum development
- instructional design and methodologies
- group dynamics
- conferencing and counseling
- assessment of teacher performance

Lovell and Wiles pointed to necessary knowledge and skills when they wrote that supervision is:

- releasing human potential
- leadership
- communications
- coordinating and facilitating change
- curriculum development
- facilitating human development[18]

Alfonso, Firth, and Neville drew implications for instructional supervisory behavior from organizational, leadership, communication, decision, and change theories.[19]

Take the table of contents of any textbook on supervision and you will become cognizant of the broad knowledge and special skills demanded by the profession. To identify knowledge and skills required for effective supervision we may also turn to Figure 1.2 and analyze the domains, roles, and foundations presented in the conceptual model. To perform effectively the supervisor must possess broad knowledge of both a general and professional nature and must be able to translate that knowledge into skillful practice. At appropriate points in this book you will encounter further discussion of the knowledge and skills essential to instructional supervisors.

Persons considering the job of supervisor might begin by taking a look at themselves. They should decide whether they possess the fund of knowledge and skills required by the job. Prospective supervisors should ponder whether they have a type of personality for dealing with teachers in a supervisory capacity. They should know whether they enjoy working intimately with people in a helping relationship. A beginning point in supervision is the determination by the prospective supervisor of his or her adequacy to fill the roles demanded.

SUMMARY

The roles and titles of supervisory personnel vary among the school systems of the nation. Supervision is defined in this text as a service provided to teachers for the purpose of improving instruction. It is the student who is the ultimate beneficiary of instructional improvement.

A supervisor is a trained auxiliary or staff person whose primary function is the provision of service according to a conceptual model. The model presented in this chapter portrays the supervisor as fulfilling the roles of coordinator, consultant, group leader, and evaluator within the domains of instructional, curricular, and staff development.

The supervisor should evidence personal traits which will enable him or her to work harmoniously with people and should possess sufficient knowledge and skills to perform all functions effectively. Leadership, human relations, and communications skills appear to be especially important to successful supervision.

Supervisors perform a wide variety of tasks, which may or may not include managerial or administrative duties. The focus of this book is on instructional supervision, which is an inclusive term to signify service to teachers in developing the curriculum, instruction, and themselves.

ACTIVITIES FOR FURTHER STUDY

1. Cite at least four definitions of supervision to be found in references at the end of this chapter, show their similarities and differences, state whether you agree or disagree with each definition, and give your reasons for your position.

2. Formulate your own definition of supervision.
3. Design your own conceptual model of supervision.
4. Poll a sampling of teachers and inquire (a) whether they know what supervisory help is available to them and (b) how they perceive the functions of each supervisor.
5. Identify at least two improvements in curriculum and/or instruction that have been made in a particular school system in the last three years and postulate on how these came to be.
6. State your position on the following questions:
   a. Is the principal a supervisor?
   b. Would our system of education be better if the United States Department of Education employed inspectors to check on instruction throughout the country?
   c. Would our system of education be better if state departments of education regularly sent out inspectors to check on instruction throughout their states?
   d. How much teaching experience is essential for a supervisor?
7. Inquire of several teachers how often supervisors visited them in their classrooms during the past school year. Identify the supervisors by title, such as assistant principal for curriculum, supervisor of language arts, et al.
8. Interview one or more of the following supervisors and write a brief description of their chief duties:
   a. Assistant superintendent for curriculum and instruction
   b. General supervisor
   c. Team leader
   d. Grade coordinator (Grade chairperson)
   e. Lead teacher
   f. Department head
   g. Director of elementary, middle, junior, or senior high schools
9. Describe supervisory assistance available to teachers in your field from the following sources:
   a. The state Department of Education
   b. Cooperative educational service agencies (intermediate school district level)
   c. The school superintendent's office
10. Write a short paper utilizing references in the bibliography at the end of this chapter, expanding on the list of qualifications found in this chapter.
11. Write a short paper utilizing references in the bibliography at the end of this chapter, expanding on the list of functions, roles, or tasks of supervisors found in this chapter.
12. Outline a desirable university training program for supervisors and compare it with a training program with which you are familiar.
13. Tape an interview with a supervisor on the central office staff and write a summary covering the following points: (1) How does the supervisor

perceive his or her role? (2) What are major problems in supervision as he or she sees them? and (3) What training is required for the job?

14. Outline the state requirements for certification as (1) a school principal and (2) a supervisor. Write a brief summary contrasting the differences and comparing the similarities.

15. Examine the staffing pattern of a school system you know well and list as many different types of supervisors as you can discover.

16. Write an analysis of your own knowledge, skills, and personal traits as they bear on the role of the supervisor. Describe your strengths and indicate areas in which you feel you need improvement.

17. Use Appendix A: *Competencies* as a self-diagnosis instrument by rating yourself on each competency to determine the degree to which you believe you can now demonstrate the particular competency. Rate yourself by applying the scale:

     5—Completely competent
     4—High degree of competency
     3—Average degree of competency
     2—Limited degree of competency
     1—Lack of competency

NOTES

1. Ben M. Harris, *Supervisory Behavior in Education*, 2d ed., Englewood Cliffs, N.J., Prentice-Hall, 1975, 2–3.
2. William H. Lucio and John D. McNeil, *Supervision: A Synthesis of Thought and Action*, 3d ed., New York, McGraw-Hill, 1979, 3.
3. Ralph L. Mosher and David E. Purpel, *Supervision: The Reluctant Profession*, Boston, Houghton Mifflin, 1972, 3.
4. William H. Burton and Leo J. Brueckner, *Supervision: A Social Process*, 3d ed., New York, Appleton-Century-Crofts, 1955, 11.
5. Jane Franseth, *Supervision as Leadership*, Evanston, Ill., Row, Peterson, 1961, 19.
6. Kimball Wiles, *Supervision for Better Schools*, 3d ed., Englewood Cliffs, N.J., Prentice-Hall, 1967, 5.
7. Ross L. Neagley and N. Dean Evans, *Handbook for Effective Supervision of Instruction*, 3d ed., Englewood Cliffs, N.J., Prentice-Hall, 1980, 20.
8. Harris, 10–11.
9. Robert J. Alfonso, Gerald R. Firth, and Richard F. Neville, *Instructional Supervision: A Behavior System*, 2d ed., Boston, Allyn and Bacon, 1981, 43.
10. John T. Lovell and Kimball Wiles, *Supervision for Better Schools*, 5th ed., Englewood Cliffs, N.J., Prentice-Hall, 1983, 4.
11. Arthur Blumberg, *Supervisors and Teachers: A Private Cold War*, 2d ed., Berkeley, Calif., McCutchan, 1980, 5–6.
12. Lucio and McNeil, 23.
13. William H. Burton, *Supervision and the Improvement of Teaching*, New York, D. Appleton-Century, 1922, 9–10.
14. A. S. Barr, William H. Burton, and Leo J. Brueckner, *Supervision: Democratic Leadership in the Improvement of Learning*, 2d ed., New York: Appleton-Century-Crofts, 1947, 5.

15. Harris, 11–12.
16. Ibid., 13.
17. Robert C. McKean and H. H. Mills, *The Supervisor*, New York, Center for Applied Research in Education, 1964, 42–44.
18. Lovell and Wiles, 3–6, 8, 10.
19. Alfonso, Firth, and Neville, Part II.

BIBLIOGRAPHY

Alfonso, Robert J., Gerald R. Firth, and Richard F. Neville. *Instructional Supervision: A Behavior System*, 2nd ed., Boston: Allyn and Bacon, 1981.

Barr, A. S., William H. Burton, and Leo J. Brueckner. *Supervision: Democratic Leadership in the Improvement of Learning*, 2nd ed. New York: Appleton-Century, Crofts, 1947.

Blumberg, Arthur. *Supervisors and Teachers: A Private Cold War*, 2nd ed., Berkeley: McCutchan, 1980.

Burton, William H. *Supervision and the Improvement of Teaching*. New York: D. Appleton-Century, 1922.

——— and Leo J. Brueckner. *Supervision: A Social Process*, 3d ed., New York: Appleton-Century-Crofts, 1955.

Dull, Lloyd W. *Supervision: School Leadership Handbook*. Columbus, Ohio: Charles E. Merrill, 1981.

Eye, Glen G., Lanore A. Netzer, and Robert D. Krey. *Supervision of Instruction*, 2nd ed., New York: Harper & Row, 1971.

Franseth, Jane. *Supervision as Leadership*. Evanston, Ill.: Row, Peterson, 1961.

Grimsley, Edith E., and Ray E. Bruce. *Readings in Educational Supervision from Educational Leadership*. Alexandria, Va.: Association for Supervision and Curriculum Development, 1982.

Harris, Ben M. *Supervisory Behavior in Education*, 2nd ed. Englewood Cliffs, N.J.: Prentice-Hall, 1975.

Harrison, Raymond H. *Supervisory Leadership in Education*. New York: Van Nostrand Reinhold, 1968.

Kyte, George C. *How to Supervise*. Boston: Houghton Mifflin, 1930.

Leeper, Robert R., ed. *Role of Supervisor and Curriculum Director in a Climate of Change*, 1965 Yearbook. Alexandria, Va.: Association for Supervision and Curriculum Development, 1965.

——— and Fred T. Wilhelms, eds. *Supervision: Emerging Profession*. Alexandria, Va.: Association for Supervision and Curriculum Development, 1969.

Lewis, Arthur J., and Alice Miel. *Supervision for Improved Instruction: New Challenges, New Responses*. Belmont, Calif.: Wadsworth, 1972.

Lovell, John T., and Kimball Wiles. *Supervision for Better Schools*, 5th ed. Englewood Cliffs, N.J.: Prentice-Hall, 1983.

Lucio, William H., and John D. McNeil. *Supervision: A Synthesis of Thought and Action*, 3rd ed. New York: McGraw-Hill, 1979.

McKean, Robert C., and H. H. Mills. *The Supervisor*. New York: The Center for Applied Research in Education, 1964.

Marks, James R., Emery Stoops, and Joyce King-Stoops. *Handbook of Educational Supervision: A Guide for the Practitioner*, 2nd ed. Boston: Allyn and Bacon, 1978.

Mosher, Ralph L., and David E. Purpel. *Supervision: The Reluctant Profession*. Boston: Houghton Mifflin, 1972.

Neagley, Ross L., and H. Dean Evans. *Handbook for Effective Supervision of Instruction*, 3rd ed. Englewood Cliffs, N.J.: Prentice-Hall, 1980.

Pfeiffer, Isobel, and Jane Dunlap. *Supervising Teachers: A Guide to Supervising Instruction.* Phoenix: Oryx Press, 1982.

Sergiovanni, Thomas J., ed. *Supervision of Teaching*, 1982 Yearbook. Alexandria, Va.: Association for Supervision and Curriculum Development, 1982.

———— and Robert J. Starratt. *Supervision: Human Perspectives*, 2nd ed. New York: McGraw-Hill, 1979.

Unruh, Adolph, and Harold E. Turner. *Supervision for Change and Innovation.* Boston: Houghton Mifflin, 1970.

Wiles, Jon, and Joseph Bondi. *Supervision: A Guide to Practice.* Columbus, Ohio: Charles E. Merrill, 1980.

Multi-Media

Vimcet Associates, P.O. Box 24714, Los Angeles, California 90024. *Instructional Supervision: A Criterion-referenced Strategy.* Filmstrip-tape program #17.

2

Issues in Supervision

OBJECTIVES

After studying Chapter 2 you should be able to accomplish the following objectives:

1. Identify several pressing, current issues in supervision.
2. Recognize varying positions on each issue.
3. Choose and defend your position on each issue.

NUMEROUS UNRESOLVED PROBLEMS

The educational world is replete with a host of unresolved problems or issues. Whether we are talking about learning theories or the curriculum or methodology, it sometimes seems that there are no certainties to which we can subscribe. Take, for example, the issue of the specification of behavioral objectives. This procedure is roundly attacked by its opponents and strongly supported by its adherents. As is the case with many issues, a polarity has developed with vocal camps on both sides of the issue. One camp holds the writing of behavioral objectives to be a waste of time whereas extremists in the opposite camp feel that teaching can scarcely survive unless teachers design behavioral objectives.

Somewhere in between the extreme poles we find groups who champion portions of an issue and reject other aspects. For instance, some educators encourage writing behavioral objectives in the cognitive and psychomotor domains but not the affective; others insist on writing behavioral objectives in all three domains. Some claim that it is impossible to write behavioral objectives in the affective domain; others assert that affective objectives must be specified. Some advocate a formula-

28

like approach to writing objectives; others are willing to be more permissive. Some accept general goals in place of specific objectives; others accept only objectives which can be observed and measured. When we discuss helping teachers plan for instruction, we will return to the issue of behavioral objectives. We introduce it at this point solely as an illustration of one controversial issue in professional education.

The unresolved issues in education are almost as plentiful as the sands of the desert. If we were to compile a quick list of current issues in education, our list would surely include:

- open-space education
- corporal punishment
- behavior modification
- mainstreaming of handicapped children
- inquiry learning
- integration of subject matter
- minimal competencies for graduation
- state assessment of student achievement
- methods of teaching reading
- relevancy of subject matter
- placement of subject matter
- grouping learners
- the role of vocational education

The foregoing list, which is far from being a complete set of issues in education, illustrates unresolved problems with which supervisors must contend. As is the case with its companion disciplines, sociology and psychology, education is besieged with problems, since by their very nature, education, sociology, and psychology are imprecise sciences, i.e., social and behavioral sciences. These disciplines lack precision primarily because they deal with human beings, who do not lend themselves well to preciseness. Unlike machines, people are notoriously unpredictable. Whereas natural scientists may manipulate elements and equipment in the science laboratories, the social and behavioral scientists experience difficulty in manipulating people. People, especially in a literate, democratic environment, tend to reject manipulation. Of course, we can all point to exceptions to the rule, as studies of mob behavior, demagoguery, and totalitarianism readily show. People living in a democracy, as a rule, prefer to think through answers to problems themselves. As a result, we often find that there are multiple answers to specific problems. The presence of multiple answers causes consternation to many people in education who are seeking *the* definitive answers to particular problems. We cannot even be sure, for example, that 5 and 4 equal 9. If we are working with a base of 6 instead of 10, 5 and 4 equal 13. Perhaps John Dewey and his progressive followers were right after all when they averred that truth was relative.

To know whether 5 and 4 equal 9 or 13, we must know, as they say in that esoteric language called psycho-babble, "where you're coming from." If you're working with the base 6 and trying to communicate with a person who thinks in terms of base 10, and to compound the problem, who believes 10 is the only base possible, the message does not get through. Thus, for those who see supervision only as a specialist who works with individual teachers, many of the issues in the field are either nonexistent or spurious.

Since supervision, along with teaching, counseling, and administration, is one of the subsystems of the enterprise of education, we should not be surprised to find it embroiled in a number of unresolved problems. We find supervision beset with more issues than the other subsystems because the role of the supervisor is drawn so ambiguously. Teachers, counselors, and administrators usually have a clearer perspective of their behavior systems and the roles expected of them than do supervisors. We can show the relationship between these four major behavior systems in the diagram below.

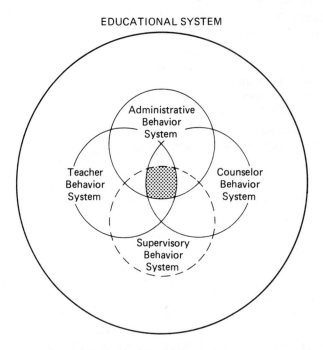

EDUCATIONAL SYSTEM

All systems interact with each other. Perhaps, as the saying goes, never the twain shall meet, but the four behavior systems decidedly meet, relate, reinforce, and sometimes lock horns. The educational commons where the four come together (shaded area on the diagram) is both bedecked with roses and strewn with nettles. The supervisory behavior system is enclosed within a broken circle to indicate that its borders are less firm than those of the other three subsystems. Whereas the uncertainty of the supervisor's role creates some problems, at the same time it has the saving grace of permitting specialists the oportunity to refine the role. In this respect supervision is more malleable than the other systems.

ASCD Working Group

The Executive Council of the Association for Supervision and Curriculum Development (ASCD) in 1975 created the Working Group on Supervisory Practices, which identified issues in supervision. The Working Group surveyed 163 public school supervisors and persons associated with colleges and universities, all of whom were members of ASCD. The public school personnel comprised 70 percent of the respondents. Those surveyed ranked the following seven statements (which I have restated as questions) as high-priority issues:[1]

Should supervisors evaluate teachers or should they evaluate instruction only?

Should supervisors help individual teachers or should they provide leadership for instructional change?

Should the teacher and the school's program be the central focus of supervision or should the emphasis be on the child and learning?

Should supervisors be proactive in initiating change or should they be reactive and respond to needs?

Should the supervisor's authority be based on expertise and interpersonal relationships or should it be on the basis of conferred status and decision-making responsibility?

Should supervisors work to develop curricula and materials or should they work to improve instruction?

Should supervisors rely on teachers to promote their own improvement or should they work cooperatively with teachers toward fulfilling goals?

At the same time the respondents viewed the following 10 issues as significant but less important:

Should supervision be carried out by generalists or by specialists?

Should supervisors be assigned instructional program responsibilities only or should they be members of the administrative staff?

Should supervisors maintain collegial relationships with principals or should they be members of the staff?

Should supervisors have assignments within a single school or should they be assigned to serve several schools?

Should the supervisor's schedule be highly structured or should it be flexible?

Should supervisors' assignments focus on program or subject tasks or on broad issues?

Should responsibility for supervision be diffused or should it be concentrated in the hands of the supervisory staff?

Is it the supervisors' task to model, advise, and suggest or is it to facilitate, interest, and collaborate?

Should supervisors represent management in collective negotiations, should they represent teachers, or should they represent neither?

Should supervision be a team approach or should it be an individual assignment?

The 17 issues uncovered by the ASCD Working Group show some of the problems which members of the profession consider important. Some persons may be inclined to say that the either/or dichotomy of these issues is unrealistic. They would conclude that supervisors must be occupied with both sides of the issue. They would take the position that you cannot, for example, evaluate instruction without evaluating teacher performance.

Yet, affirming that supervisors must fulfill responsibilities on both sides of every issue is as simplistic as rejecting out of hand one side or the other. It is true that we find supervisors devoting energies to both sides of some issues. In some few cases they expend equal energies on the dual tasks of an issue. On the other hand, some supervisors throw greater efforts into one dimension of an issue than into the other. It is safe to say that supervisors tend to lean toward one side of an issue even if only slighty past the midpoint. They may not be Leaning Towers of Pisa with pronounced inclinations but they lean far enough to show their preference.

An even larger question than where *do* supervisors spend their time is where *should* supervisors spend their energies? To answer the normative question *should* we must bring to bear not only a knowledge of prevailing practice but the philosophical assumptions we hold about supervision. We find so many conflicting views on what supervision is because the viewers start with varying sets of assumptions. This textbook, of course, is no exception. I will present certain positions for your consideration and analysis. I would be the last to say that every position, yes even bias, in this book represents *the right answer*. "Right" answers are hard to come by. What is right for one situation *may* be right generally, which we will hope. On the other hand, what is right in one situation may not be right in other situations. We need to think in terms of "situational supervision" in much the same way we think of "situational leadership." Leadership is a function of both the characteristics of the leader and of the situation in which the leader may demonstrate his or her abilities. Successful supervision is the judicious application of the supervisor's skills in a particular setting.

The practitioner, therefore, must exercise professional judgment in determining what is right in a given situation. However, the practitioner must know what the options are and, if he or she rejects a practice which has been found generally effective elsewhere, he or she should be able to explain the reasons for the rejection.

In the following pages of this chapter we will examine what seem to me to be some of the more pressing issues in supervision. These are:

1. Is supervision necessary?
2. For whom should supervision be provided?
3. Should the supervisor's authority be based on expertise and interpersonal relationships or on conferred status and decision-making responsibilities?
4. Should the supervisor be an administrator?

5. Is supervision staff development?
6. Is supervision curriculum development?
7. Should supervisors work with groups of teachers or with individual teachers?
8. Should supervision be carried out by supervisors based in the central office or in the individual schools?
9. Should the supervisor use a directive or nondirective approach?
10. Should the supervisor represent management or the teachers in collective bargaining?
11. Should school systems organize for supervision by employing generalists or by hiring specialists?

By their very nature issues are problems whose answers are not fully settled and on which specialists may disagree. In the case of each issue you will see a figure representing a scale:

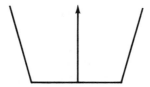

The reading shows graphically the position I have taken on each issue. The indicator moves from the midpoint with each issue to one side or the other. Unless the indicator is all the way over to one side and touching, latitude has been left for some degree of responsibility on the other side of the issue. If the indicator remains in the middle, the reading should be interpreted as giving equal weight to both sides of the issue—taking the middle ground. An *N* appears in place of the indicator to signify that I believe neither side of the issue is appropriate.

In the pages to follow the positions I have taken apply to the instructional staff supervisor, the protagonist of this book. The positions may or may not be the same for line supervisors (administrators). When there are differences of this nature, I have noted it in the narrative. It is not the purpose of this discussion to persuade supervisors and prospective supervisors to accept the positions presented in this chapter but rather to assist them in thinking through the issues and reaching their own decisions.

ISSUE 1: IS SUPERVISION NECESSARY?

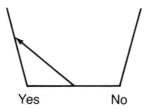

Yes   No

The question, Is supervision necessary? may seem out of place in a text on supervision. The mere fact that there are supervisors and a body of literature on supervision would seem to indicate the necessity of supervision. Yet, this fundamental question has probably not been given enough consideration. Teachers, administrators, and supervisors assume the necessity for supervision as a given. In their memory supervisors have been like the firmament; they have always existed and so presumably they will always exist.

We might phrase our question in another way. Can we do without supervisors? As the system now operates, the answer is apparently that we could not. Supervisors meet a need in our current educational structure and will undoubtedly continue to do so for a long time to come. Theoretically, however, we could dispense with the services of supervisors *if*—a very improbable *if*—all teachers were dynamic, knowledgeable, and skillful. In one sense the supervisor is like the preacher who strives to make his or her parishioners into sinless beings. When all churchgoers have reached this happy utopian state, the need for the minister will have been obviated. Since it is not likely that all humans will achieve this state of sinlessness, the task of the preacher will not be relegated to obsolescence. Since not all, perhaps few, teachers have reached a state of perfection, the need for supervision remains.

In analyzing this issue we must make certain assumptions. It is assumed that the preservice programs of teachers do not turn out finished products. The typical training program consists of general education, concentration in a teaching field, and professional education. In a time of rapid development in all fields of knowledge prospective teachers cannot begin to learn in college all that they will need to know when teaching. Nor can they gain a full mastery of techniques of instruction; study of curriculum and teaching constitutes only a beginning point. In many college programs the work in curriculum and instruction exists in a hypothetical context which students may translate into practice only in limited participation programs and in student teaching. Student teaching gives the preservice teacher merely a taste of teaching—10 to 12 weeks in a school under the direction of a supervising teacher. It is literally impossible for the teacher education institutions to assure perfection in their products. To the limited program of the teacher education institution must be added the differences among individuals themselves. Teachers develop their capacities at different rates of speed. Some are ready to move into the classroom with a sense of confidence and demonstrable ability at the end of—sometimes even before—the student teaching experience. Others will take a few years to develop their potential, while some, unfortunately, will never realize their full potential. The assumption can be made then that teachers need the help of supervisors because they have not been fully prepared by their teacher education programs and because there is a great difference in the abilities and needs of individual teachers.

Limitations on Teaching

By providing supervision, the educational system is declaring in effect that teachers are not completely free to run their own classrooms as they see fit. Limitations are imposed by school regulations, state legislative regulations, types of students, and type of communities. A supervisor is more aware of or more sensitive to these limitations and can help teachers to work within the restrictions.

Supervision skirts dangerously close to the issue of academic freedom, the teacher's right to teach as he or she sees appropriate within his or her realm of competence. The doctrine of academic freedom, however, raises many questions. Do teachers have the right to teach topics that have been explicitly forbidden by the administrators? Can teachers reject textbooks that have been adopted by a state textbook commission or by colleagues of their own grade or department? May a teacher follow a curricular program that disrupts the sequence from one grade level to another?

Academic freedom has its limitations. Realistically, it is more limited on the public school level than in institutions of higher education. For a number of reasons public schools are more susceptible to pressures from the community than are colleges and universities. What this means is that a public school teacher must live within certain limitations and must seek individuality within a context generally agreed in the school system. The supervisor helps teachers understand the context of their positions and to find their own ways of teaching within that context. A simple illustration of this is the case of the teacher who does not like a particular textbook that is used in the school. The teacher cannot simply ignore the school's investment in the textbook or arbitrarily declare that pupils must buy a different textbook. If the particular textbook is part of a sequence, that teacher cannot disrupt this sequence without destroying previous planning done by colleagues and without confusing students. The supervisor can help the teacher find ways to use the textbook, expand on the textbook, use additional text materials, and provide supplementary, original activities which go beyond it.

When the teacher and supervisor sit down to discuss the thorny issue of academic freedom, they should not ignore another dimension of academic freedom that some teachers overlook, namely, that academic freedom does not exist for the teacher alone. Not only does academic freedom provide an environment in which a teacher is free to teach—within established parameters—but it should also provide a climate in which the learner is free to learn—within the same parameters.

In providing a program of supervision the assumption is made that change is desirable, necessary, and indeed, inevitable. School programs and methods of instruction must keep pace with changing times. If all teachers were professionally dedicated enough to keep up-to-date in their fields, the need for supervision might diminish. Unfortunately, teaching has not fully reached a professional status. Consider, for example, the continuing debate in educational circles on whether teaching is a profession. Individuals choose to go into teaching for a number of reasons. Some are dedicated to teaching and over the years become dedicated teachers. Others enter into teaching because they have majored in a particular field and by adding some professional education courses can be certified to teach. They may have no great interest in teaching but reason that teacher training will equip them for the job market. Others in teaching are marking time until they can move into another profession. Some are in teaching because of the sense of power they hold over the lives of young people. It can be said, therefore, although teaching is referred to as a profession, and is so more than in past decades, it is not yet a true profession. Until such a time a considerable degree of supervision will need to be provided for teachers.

Need for the Supervisor

Observing many teachers will lead to the conclusion that without assistance some teachers will not make changes. We make the further assumption, therefore, that supervisors are able to help teachers to bring about changes. Whether this assumption is translated into fact depends upon the supervisor, the teacher, and the interaction between the two. Possibly, if existing patterns of educational organization were changed, means other than the presence of a live supervisor might—stress *might*—help teachers to effect change. Dissemination of professional literature from the central office and self-evaluation techniques, including the use of media also might enable the teacher to change faster than a supervisor is able to stimulate changes. So far the evidence seems to point to the need for supervisors. As Stanley W. Williams observed, "Unquestionably the central problem facing instructional leaders is how to help people change."[2]

It is an accepted goal that there should be some internal consistency to sequences of subject matter and that there should be articulation between grades of a school and levels of the school system. A supervisor is the one person in a school system who can help achieve these goals. The district supervisor, for example, moving from school to school knows what materials are being used in each class and what the objectives of teachers are in the various schools. The supervisor of language arts in the elementary school, for example, helps teachers coordinate their sequences, avoid duplication of content, define goals, and work cooperatively.

The district supervisor is concerned with sequences across levels, that is, with the problem of articulation. The supervisor of language arts in the elementary school works with the supervisor of language arts in the middle or secondary school to develop coordinated, sequential programs between the elementary and middle or secondary levels. The provision of coordinated sequences of subject matter between levels, elementary and middle school or junior high, middle school or junior high and senior high, senior high and college, is a problem in need of solution in many communities. Solution of the problem requires joint planning on the part of teachers at the various levels. The supervisor can act as catalyst in getting teachers at the various levels together so they can cooperatively work out sequences whose parts will bear some relationship one to the other.

At the individual school building level the principal, assistant principal, or curriculum coordinator can oversee the planning for continuous sequences among courses or grades within his or her own school with help from team leaders and department heads. At both the school building level and the district level someone needs to be assigned to work with teachers so that they are not all going off in different directions. It should be expected that the learner will go through an orderly progression of study from the elementary school through high school. This orderly progress is a well-planned, well-formulated sequence in each area of study. To achieve this sequence requires the cooperation of teachers at all school levels. The supervisor serves to bring these teachers together and to make known to them the problems of sequence and articulation.

Neagley and Evans explained the need for supervision in the following way:

Supervision, then, seems destined to be essential to deciding the nature and content of the curriculum, to selecting the school organizational patterns and learning materials to facilitate teaching, and to evaluating the entire educational process. Effective coordination of the total program, kindergarten through high school, has never been achieved in most school systems, although this is one of the most pressing needs in American public education today.

We can no longer afford the waste of human resources in overlapping courses, duplication of teaching effort, and lack of continuity from one school level to the next. A careful curriculum plan embracing the entire school experience from entry to graduation is imperative and long overdue. An effective supervisory program is needed in every school district—small, intermediate, or large—to launch or coordinate this effort.[3]

Supervision is, therefore, a necessary service to teachers for a number of reasons. That stage has not yet been reached where the services of these specialized personnel may be eliminated. The fact is, there exists a present need for more supervisors who are better trained and more highly skilled in the performance of their tasks.

ISSUE 2: FOR WHOM SHOULD SUPERVISION BE PROVIDED?

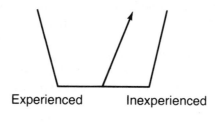

Experienced   Inexperienced

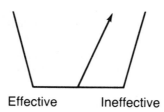

Effective   Ineffective

Should supervision be provided for new teachers only? For older as well as newer teachers? For experienced as well as inexperienced? For poor as well as able teachers? Ostensibly, supervision is made available to all teachers and supervisors make choices as to where they will spend most of their time and energies.

Naturally, most effort is devoted to those who seem to need the help most: the new, the inexperienced, and the less able teachers. Teachers who are new to the school system must be helped to become accustomed to the ways the particular system operates. The supervisor assists them to become familiar with resources of the school and community and to understand the types of students and parents found in the system. The teacher new to a school district has special needs which those who have been in the system awhile do not have. A supervisor must be tuned in to these special needs and must make a greater effort to help new teachers become familiar with the system.

The supervisor will spend more time assisting those teachers who are inexperienced. The supervisor knows that the inexperienced teacher is not a finished product. Although those who are in their first years of teaching are often uncertain of themselves, they often make up in enthusiasm what they may lack in experience. The chances are that they will be eager to receive whatever help is extended to them. They are often more approachable and more receptive to suggestions than more experienced teachers who are convinced that they know the answers from years of experience. It is little wonder that many supervisors choose to spend more of their efforts on new and inexperienced teachers.

The less able teacher requires particular help from the supervisor. The less able teacher may or may not be a new or inexperienced teacher and may or may not seek help from the supervisor. There are, of course, less competent teachers among the new and inexperienced. In many cases the supervisor can help the less effective but new or inexperienced teachers to improve their teaching. With familiarity to the school system and with a few years of teaching experience problems of some ineffective teachers will disappear.

On the other hand, we can find the less able among the experienced teachers and among those who have been in a school system for years. These teachers fall into several categories. There is, first of all, the teacher who is ineffective in the supervisor's judgment but sees himself or herself as effective. This teacher is identified by the poor progress of students, by lack of rapport with students, by a lack of knowledge of the material being taught, by lack of skill in presenting the material, and by lack of classroom control. A supervisor works with this type of person by helping the individual take an inventory of personal strengths and weaknesses. In this particular case the supervisor receives support for his or her judgment of the teacher in that the teacher is considered ineffective by the school principal and by colleagues as well. A much more difficult problem for the supervisor consists of a second category of teacher whom the supervisor considers ineffective but whom either the principal or the teacher's colleagues may consider effective. This teacher considers himself or herself to be effective, even superior. To put it simply, the teacher does a great job of teaching the wrong things in the wrong way.

In the opinion of some teachers and some principals rigid discipline is a virtue. The strict disciplinarian keeps all learners under thumb, allowing no freedom for adolescent exuberance. Some teachers and principals believe that the subject matter is king and the learner should be adjusted to the subject matter rather than vice versa. Some feel that the "old ways" of teaching are better than the "new ways," if we may so distinguish between subject-centered and learner-centered approaches to presenting content. Thus, the stern disciplinarian, the subject-centered personality, and the follower of tradition is often labeled an effective, indeed superior, teacher.

If the supervisor believes that some allowances should be made for young learners, this same 'effective' teacher would be considered ineffective. The supervisor would consider an authoritarian, regimented classroom inappropriate, a type of educational climate more suitable to a totalitarian than a democratic society.

If the supervisor believes that the learner should take precedence over subject matter and that subject matter ought to be tailored to fit the learner rather than vice versa, he or she will consider the subject-centered teacher ineffective. The supervisor works with such a teacher to bring about an understanding of the motivation of learners and to review learning theories. The supervisor will recall with the teacher some of the principles of educational psychology with which the teacher became acquainted during preservice training and will try to point out to the teacher that these psychological principles were not simply truisms for college students but have their applications in the classroom.

In working with a strictly subject-centered teacher the supervisor may well find the route to change in teacher behavior slow going, for the weight of tradition is on the side of the teacher. Tradition is a powerful block, especially when it is supported by school administrators and other teachers who resist change. Experienced teachers are often in greater need of supervision with respect to rigidity and subject-centered-ness than inexperienced teachers. Inexperienced teachers who have just recently completed their teacher preparation programs know some of the latest thinking in education and in their teaching field and are not set in fixed ways of teaching. They are still flexible and have not developed a set of particular techniques, plans, and procedures to which they are committed and repeat from year to year, nor have they as yet become tainted by the cynicism which some of the experienced teachers develop. The supervisor will have less difficulty working with inexperienced teachers who have open minds than with experienced teachers who are certain they have all the answers.

A third category of ineffective teacher is the teacher who is clearly ineffective and knows it. Supervisor, principal, and colleagues may agree that the teacher is ineffective. A willingness on the part of the teacher to improve is a first step. Yet, ineffective teachers who recognize their ineffectiveness are often defensive about their instruction and refuse to seek the help of the supervisor or other resource people. Refusing to participate in teachers' workshops or institutes for fear of revealing their own inadequacies, they develop defensive excuses for their lack of competence. Often they blame the students, claiming they are unmotivated. Or, they blame uncooperative administrators for their difficulties. They are placed in the wrong grade or in their minor teaching field, or in the wrong school, they reason. But deep within they know that they lack the preparation or other qualifications to be effective teachers. They see improvement in their instruction as an insurmountable barrier and often exhibit the same lack of motivation that they ascribe to their learners. It is one of the unfortunate concomitants of tenure regulations and lifetime certificates that it is almost impossible to correct situations like this no matter how hard a supervisor tries unless the teacher is willing to be helped.

The supervisor can work with teachers who are willing to cooperate. He or she must develop a relationship with the teacher in which the teacher will not be fearful of revealing inadequacies. The teacher must know that no retribution will result from revealing problem areas. Since retribution can be harsh—a change of grade level or school or even dismissal—no teacher will willingly make personal inadequacies known if punishment is expected to follow.

The supervisor must not act surprised at whatever low level of preparation or skill is shown. The supervison begins with the fact that, like Mount Everest, the teacher is there. It is of little avail to wring hands and lament that ineffective teachers are found in many school systems for it is unrealistic to believe that every school system in the United States could fill all its vacancies with effective teachers. The supervisor can only work with these individuals after allaying all fears that exposure of the teachers' difficulties will result in unpleasantness.

It is standard practice that supervision is provided for all teachers, not just the new, the inexperienced, and the ineffective. Supervisors can be of help to experienced and effective teachers. Those who are capable and see themselves as capable tend to welcome advice and suggestions and go out of their way to seek new ideas. These are the teachers who urge supervisors to drop in to see them and to talk to them. These teachers are completely at ease when supervisors, administrators, and their colleagues stop into their classrooms and observe them teach. Some enjoy the experience of demonstrating to others that they are effective teachers.

The supervisor can help the better teachers by offering suggestions drawn from personal experience and from visits to other classrooms. The supervisor can assist the more able teachers by making known to them new publications and materials which they have not had a chance to examine. The supervisor can be a time-saver for teachers. In some ways the supervisor may get "better mileage" from suggestions to the more able teachers than to the less able. The more able will take the suggestions seriously and try them out while the less able will be reluctant or hesitant to try out new ideas. Since they possess the self-confidence to surmount failures, the more able teachers do not fear failure of a new plan or technique. Cooperative, able teachers are a joy to the supervisor. Whereas some uncooperative or ineffective teachers keep their doors shut to the supervisor, teachers who are eagerly looking for assistance throw open their doors and welcome the supervisor.

The supervisor will have to decide where the priorities for help lie. He or she may decide to concentrate on troubleshooting. This would yield short-term results but would be unfortunate in long-term gains. If leadership is to be given in improving instruction, the supervisor must do more than troubleshoot. He or she must work with individuals and groups in developing the curriculum and improving instruction. Together they must study goals, means of reaching the goals, and ways of evaluating what they have accomplished, a process which requires considerable time. The supervisor must achieve some balance between short-term and long-term projects. There must also be balance in work load between helping teachers individually and working with them in groups. Like the teacher who has 35 students in a class, the supervisor cannot give complete attention to one individual who has a problem but has to devise ways to handle both individuals and groups.

Ideally, supervisors should provide help to all teachers, experienced and inexperienced, effective and ineffective. In practice, they will need to spend more time with the inexperienced and ineffective.

ISSUE 3: SHOULD THE SUPERVISOR'S AUTHORITY BE BASED ON EXPERTISE AND INTERPERSONAL RELATIONSHIPS OR ON CONFERRED STATUS AND DECISION-MAKING RESPONSIBILITIES?

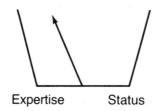

Expertise   Status

Authority is derived from various sources. Whereas we tend to think of conferred power as the only source of authority, actually many leaders derive their authority from their ability to influence other people. A role is prescribed either directly or indirectly for each position in an organization. With each role go certain expectancies. Power to varying degrees undergirds positions so that leaders may fulfill their role expectancies. Thus, role expectations are often met because of the power attached to them.

On the other hand, some leaders fulfill their roles without resorting to the use of power. Some leaders by the force of reason, persuasiveness, and personality can achieve their goals without exerting power and flaunting status. These leaders would be able to perform their duties even if the props of power and status were removed.

Other leaders, lacking the ability to reason, to demonstrate vision, or to relate to other people must fall back on bestowed power to get the tasks done. Some of these leaders spend more time preserving the authority of their office than solving the problems of the organization. Instead of emulating the wisdom of Solomon, they adhere to the dictum of Louis XIV, "*I* am the state."

Thomas Briggs and Joseph Justman counseled supervisors not to be arbitrary or authoritative, nor to rely on power of the position or of personality.[4] In considering this issue we must again distinguish between line supervisors (administrators) and staff supervisors. The line supervisors, like the assistant superintendent, the principal, and the assistant principal, possess certain powers conferred on them through law and state and local regulations, whereas the staff supervisor possesses only those powers narrowly prescribed by regulation and by the administrator. The supervisor's power is greatly circumscribed. One needs only to look at a school system's table of organization to realize that supervisors are not high in the power structure and, as a result, their jobs are not high-status positions. Let me add quickly before anyone laments this condition that I believe that the staff person who serves as instructional supervisor needs neither conferred power nor exalted status. Supervision, like teaching, has an importance of its own without the trappings of power.

Line supervisors can fall back on power and status if they must in order to effect their orders. The staff supervisor cannot command nearly as much power. That is not to say that the supervisor has no power. In fact, supervisors bask in the reflected power of the administrator and the organization. Teachers may follow a supervisor's direction *because* they perceive the supervisor to possess powers which, in reality, he or she does not possess.

We will examine the larger issue next when we address the question about whether the supervisor should *be* an administrator. At this point we wish to decide whether supervisors should seek to use what limited powers they may have, call on the administrator's power, or convey the impression of possessing derived administrative powers in fulfilling their roles.

Lucio and McNeil maintained that the authority of office and influence cannot be separated and that there are times when supervisors must use the authority of their position. They explained:

Popularly, supervisors are seen as those who justify themselves as they are able to influence fellow executives at all levels by virtue of their factual or technical mastery, consultative skill, advisory persuasiveness—in short, by their educational effectiveness. . . . We question the notion that within a line-and-staff organization school leaders are administrators and not supervisors when they exercise initiative in movements for the improvement of teaching and learning, making decisions, coordinating the work of others, and issuing directions. They are supervisors when using authority as well as supervisors when exerting influence. . . . Supervisors are sometimes delegated authority and held responsible for results. Hence, they must hold others responsible for carrying out instructions.[5]

Resorting to authority of office, however, can get in the way of helping teachers. Since falling back on power implies punishment of some kind if the teacher fails to respond to the supervisor's directions, a threatening climate is created. Like most human beings teachers perform more effectively in a threat-free environment. Adolph Unruh and Harold E. Turner corroborated this point when they observed:

Normally, the full-time supervisor operates from the central office and reports directly to the superintendent. In many such instances the line authority, either real or implied, tends to blunt the total effectiveness of the position. To the extent that teachers feel threatened in their relationship with the supervisor, good supervision becomes difficult to achieve.[6]

Burton and Brueckner took the position that the supervisor's authority is derived from the situation itself. If the supervisor needs to use personal authority, according to these experts, he or she derives it from planning done by the group.[7]

Numerous studies have shown that if teachers seek help at all—and many do not[8]—they wish the supervisor to demonstrate the type of expertise which will help them in the classroom.[9] They also expect the supervisor to be able to develop rapport with them and to work with them in a cooperative way.

As a matter of fact, it probably does not matter to teachers whether the supervisor possesses power or not if the supervisor is able to help them do their jobs better. If the supervisor is able to provide teachers with the kind of help they need, the supervisor will not find it necessary to call upon power. We should make an exception, of course, in the case of the incompetent teacher, as contrasted with the ineffective teacher. The ineffective teacher can be helped; the incompetent teacher should be removed from the classroom.

ISSUE 4: SHALL THE SUPERVISOR BE AN ADMINISTRATOR?

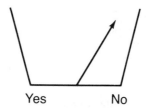

Yes   No

In Chapter 1 you have already noted the uncertainty and ambiguity which exist as to whether the supervisor should be an administrator and vice versa. It has been mentioned that administrators by the very nature of their positions have supervisory responsibilities. It has also been observed that many administrators unfortunately are not able to give primary attention to the main purpose for which schools have been established—instruction of the young. They are too busy with plant maintenance, record keeping, personnel management, scheduling, directing auxiliary services, and public relations.

Whether supervision should be an arm of administration is a controversy of long standing. We have already averred that administrators are supervisors. The question remains whether supervisors are or should be administrators. On one side of the issue are those who view supervision as a fundamental appendage of administration. On the other side are those who would divorce supervision from administration. Harold Spears stated the issue clearly, pointing out the lack of success in resolving the problem:

Ever since supervisors were added to school management, there has been a concerted attempt to draw a line of demarcation between administration and supervision, between the job of administering and that of supervising. But this campaign for strict interpretations is still far short of its goal, for those who have dared to set the stakes have reached no common agreement.[10]

Burton and Brueckner distinguished administration from supervision but saw them as inseparable, complementary functions. They perceived the function of administration as general operation of a school system whereas supervision focuses on the improvement of the learning environment.[11]

Historically, supervision has been a part of administration. Glen G. Eye and Lanore A. Netzer when they wrote in 1965 held that supervision is an extension of administration. In the first edition of their textbook entitled *Supervision of Instruc-*

tion: A Phase of Administration they defined supervision as "that phase of administration which deals primarily with the achievement of the appropriate selected
instructional expectations of educational service."[12]

Kathryn V. Feyereisen, A. John Fiorino, and Arlene T. Nowak saw supervision as the function of administration which is concerned with making improvements
in educational programs.[13]

Lloyd W. Dull coined two terms to connote individuals with varying supervisory
roles:

> The term *supervisor* refers to a staff person who is normally assigned *full-time* responsibility
> for leadership in instructional improvement. . . . The second terminology for supervision work
> is *supervisory leader* or *supervisory personnel*. . . . They include supervisors and other staff
> personnel who do supervisory tasks; for example, principals, superintendents, and departmen-
> tal heads.[14]

I prefer to classify principals and superintendents as administrators and department
heads as supervisors.

James P. Esposito, Gary E. Smith, and Harold J. Burbach have created a four-
part taxonomy of the supervisor's role which encompasses both administrative and
supervisory responsibilities. Their taxonomy is reproduced in Table 2.1.

From the mid-1950s to the present specialists in supervision have been inclining
toward reducing the administrative roles of the supervisor—some on philosophical
grounds, some on the basis of role definition, and some for the very practical reason
that supervisors have too much to do when they take on administrative duties as well
as supervisory duties.

Jon Wiles and Joseph Bondi noted a drift taking place during the 1980s back
toward supervision as administration. They warned:

> By returning to the administrative camp, instructional supervisors will further remove them-
> selves from the classroom and diminish their ability to work with teachers to improve
> instruction.[15]

The problem might be resolved if the administrator assumed more of a supervisory role and turned over to assistants some managerial aspects of running a school
system. Most administrators are unwilling to relinquish management responsibilities.
They may, therefore, concentrate on administrative and operational matters and
delegate responsibilities for curricular and instructional leadership to a subordinate.
Or, they may call in outside help, specifically staff persons who are employed to fulfill the supervisory roles they cannot fill.

The question is not so much whether administrators should assume supervisory
tasks since they already do this to one degree or another and since they already
possess responsibility for supervision. We must examine more carefully the opposite
side of the coin. The question is whether the supervisor should assume administrative
tasks and responsibilities. Should the administrator require or permit a person
charged with leadership in curriculum and instructional development to perform
administrative duties? Should teachers recognize the supervisor as one who has direct

Table 2.1   Taxonomy of the Supervisory Role

Helping Role		Administrative Role	
Factor I Indirect Service to Teachers	*Factor IV Direct Service*	*Factor II Administrator*	*Factor II Evaluator*
Plan and arrange in-service education programs and workshops	Assist in the orientation of new and beginning teachers	Coordinate instructional programs	Plan and arrange in-service education programs and workshops
Participate in in-service education programs and workshops	Assist teachers in the location, selection, and interpreatation of materials	Assist in the evaluation and appraisal of school programs	Participate in in-service education programs and workshops
Coordinate instructional programs	Visit and observe in the classroom	Routine administrative duties	Assist in the evaluation and appraisal of school programs
Assist in the orientation of new and beginning teachers	Teach demonstration lessons	Participate in the formulation of policy	Arrange intersystem visitations to observe promising practices
Assist teachers in the location, selection, and interpretation of materials	Hold individual conferences with teachers	Engage in public relations	Arrange intrasystem visitations to observe promising practices
Collect and disseminate current curriculum materials		Work with citizens' or lay groups	
Develop curriculum designs and coordinate curriculum improvement efforts		Arrange intersystem visitations to observe promising practices	
Assist in the development of curriculum guides and other publications			
Assist textbook selection committees			
Develop and prepare new instructional media			
Assist in the evaluation and appraisal of school programs			

SOURCE: James P. Esposito, Gary E. Smith, and Harold J. Burbach, "A Delineation of the Supervisory Role," *Education* 96, no. 1, Fall 1975, 66. Reprinted with permission.

line authority over them, determines promotions, passes on salary increments, decides on retention, makes decisions on expenditures for materials and equipment, and determines specifications for construction of new facilities teachers will use?

Should the supervisor think of himself or herself as an administrator? If administrative authority is not delegated to the supervisor per se, should the supervisor act as the agent of the administrator in the sense of a liaison who reports back to the administrator? Are the supervisor and administrator in cahoots, so to speak? Is the supervisor the administrator's alter ego when setting foot in the teacher's classroom?

If we conceive of supervision as service, it is difficult to see how supervisors can maintain rapport with teachers if teachers perceive them as people who control their destinies. For supervision to be successful teachers must want the services of the supervisor. They must feel that the supervisor is there to serve them and to help them become more effective teachers.

We find ourselves in a real dilemma with respect to rating teacher effectiveness, an issue discussed more fully in Chapter 13. Shall the supervisor rate the teachers and, having rated them, report to the administrator? When this happens, what does it do to the teachers' willingness to call on the supervisor for help and to reveal their inadequacies?

Supervisors are often required by their administrators to perform administrative tasks, such as rating of teachers. By their close proximity to the superintendent, frequently sharing office space in the same building, they fall heir to administrative duties which they might not have if they were housed away from the center of administrative power. The supervisor, as a subordinate, cannot refuse to accept assigned administrative duties. The fact that supervisors must accept such duties prompts the suggestion—though perhaps impractical—to house supervisors away from the administrator's headquarters.

Such a move would be understood by teachers as affirming that supervisors are really employed primarily to help them and not to assist the administrator. While such a move might not appeal to those supervisors who see themselves as administrators, it might be welcomed by those supervisors who see themselves as service-oriented people. We might hypothesize that those supervisors who maintain they have no time to visit schools and are unduly loaded with paper work see themselves as administrators rather than as supervisors. They have become involved in administrative decision-making activities assigned to them by the administrator or assumed on their own initiative.

Thomas J. Sergiovanni and Robert J. Starratt described differences between administrative and supervisory behavior as follows:

Behavior of administrators and others in school organizations which is characterized by action toward achievement of school goals but is *not* dependent upon others for success is described as administrative rather than supervisory. When administrators and supervisors work with things and ideas rather than people in pursuing school goals, they tend to be operating in an administrative way rather than in a supervisory way. . . . We need at this point to differentiate between working with and through people to achieve school goals and using people to achieve these goals. . . . Using people is consistent with classical-traditional management styles. . . .[16]

It would be unrealistic if we were to take the extreme position that the supervisor must never accept administrative tasks. Sometimes the administrator requires the supervisor to fulfill administrative duties. At other times, as in the case of teacher evaluation, for example, the supervisor is in a most advantageous position to assess teacher performance and to suggest remedial measures to the teacher when necessary.

What is needed by today's supervisors is a penchant to emphasize supervisory behavior and to deemphasize administrative behavior. We must admit that there are individuals who enjoy being near the center of power without sharing the responsibilities borne by the administrator. There are also supervisors who are closet administrators. If so, they should admit it, come out, and seek to join the ranks of the administrators. Like many teachers some supervisors are administrators-in-waiting, looking forward to the day when they might be able to trade in their staff job for a line position. Those supervisors who view instructional leadership as their career will seek to keep administrative responsibilities to a minimum.

ISSUE 5: IS SUPERVISION STAFF DEVELOPMENT?

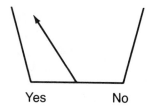

Yes   No

As conceptualized in this book staff development is one of the domains of supervision. It is not, however, as it appears in some school systems, the sole domain. The role of the supervisor as shown in the model in Chapter 1 involves instructional development on which there is little or no controversy; curriculum development, on which there is disagreement; and staff development, on which there is also argument.

In large school systems more than one person may be employed to carry out the multiple tasks of supervision. Their responsibilities may range across all three domains or individuals may devote themselves entirely to one or two domains. We find, for example, directors of staff development, directors of curriculum development, and directors of both staff and curriculum development. Interestingly enough, the assistant superintendent to whom these directors report is sometimes called the assistant superintendent for *instructional* improvement.

If supervision is a service designed to help teachers become more effective so that as a result their students will benefit, then staff development is an important domain of supervision. Leslee J. Bishop described staff development in the following terms:

Staff development focuses upon professional growth rather than upon credentialing or maintaining . . . the emphasis here is upon those attitudes, competencies, and knowledges that enhance learning, program effectiveness, and professional adequacy. These are related to the systematic efforts to improve the conditions, objectives, resources, and processes that are the responsibility of the school district.[17]

Many people equate staff development with in-service education. Dull, for example, used the terms *in-service education* and *staff development* synonymously and went on to define in-service education (hence, staff development):

In-service education can be defined as follows: *It is the sum of all activities designed for the purpose of improving, expanding, and renewing the skills, knowledge, and abilities of staff personnel.*[18]

Harris took the position that a distinction should be made between staff development and in-service education. He divided staff development into two aspects: staffing and training. The staffing aspect he viewed as the assignment of the best qualified person to a task to be done. The training aspect he separated into in-service education and advanced preparation. By in-service education he meant:

any planned program of learning opportunities afforded staff members of schools, colleges, or other educational agencies for purposes of improving the performance of the individual in already assigned positions.[19]

Advanced preparation, according to Harris, is training for a different and higher position.

Not only is staff development often equated to in-service education but it is also used sometimes interchangeably with instructional development. Sir James R. Marks, Emery Stoops, and Joyce King-Stoops explained the difference in these two concepts:

Staff development focuses on the staff. It attempts to provide the means for the total staff to meet the students' needs—the academic, personal, social, intellectual, and career objectives that are perceived as essential to the goals of students and society.

Instructional development concentrates more narrowly on the objectives concerned with curriculum and instruction. Its objectives include developing a more effective, systematic way of providing efficient, meaningful, effective instruction based on clearly specified objectives.[20]

We might say that instructional development or improvement is one hoped-for result of staff development. Although I concede that staff development is a somewhat broader term, I have no real objection to equating staff development to in-service education, if by in-service education we mean a program of organized activities of both a group and individual nature planned and carried out to promote the personal and professional growth of staff members, in this case, teachers. In Chapter 13 we will discuss the task of supervising in-service education.

Instructional development consists of those staff development activities which center directly on the improvement of instruction, e.g., perfecting testing techniques. Instructional development focuses on *instructional* design, implementation, and evaluation. Another way of viewing instructional development is to consider it a specialized domain of staff development. I do not include within the concept of instructional development those staff development activities which aim primarily at the personal growth of the teacher such as learning to demonstrate empathy, to be more cooperative in group settings, and to treat parents courteously and professionally.

Because we are examining the specialized field of supervision our discussion places emphasis on activities which are organized and planned by the supervisor. We would be remiss if we did not note that a good deal of staff development goes on which is much less structured; it is planned and engaged in by the individual teacher for that teacher's self-improvement.

As we shall see when we consider issue 6 we encounter a problem with curriculum development similar to the question of distinguishing between staff development and instructional development. Staff development activities relate to curriculum development when they consist of organized, planned activities of a group or individual nature which target on *curriculum* design, implementation, and evaluation.

In effect, staff development, instructional development, and curriculum development flow into each other. To paraphrase Gertrude Stein we might say staff development is instructional development is curriculum development is staff development . . . ad infinitum. Each set of two domains is like a pair of Siamese twins; it is very difficult and sometimes impossible to separate them. Perhaps we need not separate them if we are aware of the extent and limitations of each. Supervisors will find staff development high on their agenda.

ISSUE 6: IS SUPERVISION CURRICULUM DEVELOPMENT?

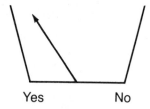

Yes   No

When supervisors help teachers either individually or in groups to make decisions about programs as opposed to methodology, they are working in the domain of curriculum development. As curriculum leaders supervisors direct teachers in the study of scope and sequence, of balance, and of articulation.[21] When they chair or serve as resource persons to curriculum councils, they engage in curriculum development. When they conduct a curricular needs assessment, involving students, teachers, administrators, and parents, they are exerting curriculum leadership. They are in the curriculum arena when they help faculties to try out innovative programs like learning centers, remedial laboratories, open education, and nongrading.

Helping teachers to make decisions about programs can be a full-time job in and of itself. The scope of curriculum development is so vast that supervisors once committed to the domain may never exit. There is constant need for review and revitalization of the curriculum in order to keep current with rapidly developing knowledge.

Those who feel that people who direct or coordinate curriculum are not really supervisors point out that these staff people spend so much time in curriculum development, running from school to school and group to group, that they never have time to get into the classrooms where the real action is. Teachers who desperately need help with the improvement of instruction go without assistance. Since some supervisors put all their eggs in the curriculum basket, those who reject curriculum development as a domain of supervision believe that students would benefit more if supervisors worked in a clinical setting on a one-to-one basis with classroom teachers.

Yet, programmatic decisions must be made daily and continually. The decisions are usually difficult and complex. They call for a knowledge of the research and intelligent deployment of human and physical resources. They require a match between the school's philosophy and its practice and they must be accompanied by an appropriate evaluation plan.

Groups must be assembled to study ramifications of curriculum problems, make recommendations, and translate plans into operation. Leadership is essential for successful completion of these tasks.

We can argue about whether it is better for school systems and for education in general to limit supervision exclusively to one domain or to provide attention to two or three domains. We have no evidence to prove conclusively that restricting supervision to one domain would result in a better product than providing assistance to teachers in three domains. By limiting help to one domain we could do a respectable job in one area while neglecting other areas. Consequently, I believe supervision must be provided in all three domains. Whether we assign full-time supervisors to each domain or whether all supervisors work in all domains is not a significant question. Supervision becomes questionable when the supervisory staff, no matter how large or how small, restricts itself to one domain, whether that domain is staff development, instructional development, or curriculum development.

The supervisory job can be done by (1) choosing priorities carefully, (2) managing time more wisely, (3) placing energies where they will be of most benefit, and (4) making better use of personnel, even if they have to be trained on the job. School systems could make far better use of assistant principals, department heads, team leaders, and grade coordinators. We are sitting on a largely untapped gold mine of supervisory talent which is eager to be released. These people could be of enormous help to administrators, curriculum directors, and other instructional supervisors.

Supervisors must set objectives, manage their time, and direct their energies so as to enhance their efficiency. Some supervisors run frantically at top speed from one problem to another without asking whether the problem is serious, without delegating authority and responsibility for resolution of some problems, and without completing one task before they leap to the next.

A review of the literature on supervision reveals many specialists who include curriculum development within the responsibilities of the supervisor. Lovell and Wiles asserted that "supervision is curriculum development . . . an important function of instructional supervisory behavior."[22] Bondi and Wiles identified eight leadership roles of modern supervisors in curriculum development as follows:

1. Coordinating curriculum planning and development.
2. Helping identify and apply curriculum theory.
3. Designing and applying curriculum research.
4. Identifying resources and support systems for curriculum development.
5. Helping develop a systematic approach to curriculum development.
6. Maintaining balance in the curriculum.

7. Determining curriculum priorities.
8. Determining curriculum needs in a pluralistic society.[23]

Feyereisen, Fiorino, and Nowak stressed curriculum change in their book *Supervision and Curriculum Renewal: A Systems Approach.*[24] Lucio and McNeil assigned a large leadership role for the supervisor. In a chapter on curriculum planning and change entitled "Strategies and Tactics for Program Improvement" they wrote:

The public relies on supervisors who possess certain professional competencies to present to the elected representative body definite recommendations for improving the curriculum for children and youth.[25]

Morris Cogan, however, narrowed the definition of supervision to clinical supervision which focuses on ways of helping teachers to improve their performance in the classroom.[26] Cogan labeled all supervisory activities that occur outside the classroom as general supervision.[27] Cogan made his attitude toward general supervision known when he said:

It is clear that general supervisors themselves have often expounded the virtues of diffuse, group-centered, nonspecific supervision. In doing so, they have effectively barred themselves from many areas of direct action with teachers out of fear of arousing resentment and distrust, only to find themselves still faced with deep, easily aroused, continuing hostility from their teachers.[28]

However desirable it might seem to throw all the supervisory forces into either staff development or instructional development I believe the supervisor must continue to function in the curriculum development domain as well as the other two domains.

ISSUE 7: SHOULD SUPERVISORS WORK WITH GROUPS OF TEACHERS OR WITH INDIVIDUAL TEACHERS?

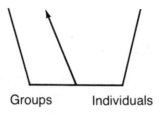

Groups   Individuals

Supervisors must decide repeatedly whether their time is best used when allocated to groups of teachers or to individual teachers who need and want their help. As much as my sentiments lean to flipping the meter to the individual side of the scale, my judgment counsels me that such a rating is not practical. If a rating for individualization of supervision implies assistance to all or even most teachers in a school system, very few school districts have either the funds or the person-power to serve every teacher or the majority of teachers on an individualized basis.

Traditionally, supervisors have worked with groups of teachers in an in-service mode with workshops, conferences, encounter sessions, and the like. The work of a number of specialists in recent years in the field of clinical supervision has resulted in bringing this issue to the forefront. The specialists in clinical supervision encourage us to move the pendulum toward the individual side of the scale.

Group supervision possesses the following merits:

1. It is less costly in the supervisor's time; it eliminates excessive travel from classroom to classroom.
2. It is a more efficient use of resources. For example, if we are offering training in the classroom use of computers, it would be foolhardy to provide this instruction to teachers on an individual basis.
3. In a time when there is a great deal of concern with the phenomenon of burn-out, we can reduce the wear and tear on supervisors when they do not have to repeat learning experiences for teachers individually. For some strange reason the literature in referring to administrators talks about stress rather than burn-out. It is the teachers who burn out. Like the pillars of strength they are, administrators presumably can learn to manage their stress and avoid burn-out. We cannot be sure where the supervisor comes in the stress/burn-out syndrome. Are they like administrators who suffer only stress or like teachers who suffer only burn-out? Do they suffer from both or from neither? Or, have their psychological problems simply been ignored since they hold lesser status than administrators and are outnumbered by the teachers?
4. Some activities necessitate group decisions, as in the case of curriculum proposals.
5. Some activities require the efforts of more than one person, as in the conduct of a curriculum needs assessment for a school system.
6. Some activities cannot achieve their objectives if they are to be attempted on an individual basis, as training in group dynamics.

Individualized supervision has the following advantages:

1. It meets the special needs of the individual teacher; it is, therefore, tailor-made supervision.
2. It demonstrates the supervisor's personalized interest in the teacher.
3. If it meets the teacher's need, it overcomes some of the hostility teachers feel toward unproductive group sessions.
4. If conducted properly, it permits teachers to reveal inadequacies without fear of exposure.
5. It allows personal relationships to build between the supervisor and teacher which are not possible in a group setting.

Unless we are talking about a one-room school with a handful of teachers—a vanishing phenomenon—adequate individualized supervision for all teachers is remote. As a result, we must make some compromises. Supervisors can continue to spend more than half of their time working with and through groups. They can provide individualized help to (1) those teachers who call for it; though we may lament it, it is perhaps fortuitous that not all teachers seek help for if they did the demand would exceed the supply of helpers; (2) those teachers for whom administrative assessments reveal deficiencies; and (3) inexperienced teachers who need help initially. Whereas good, effective, experienced teachers would welcome individual help which would contribute to their professional development, time in most school systems does not permit supervisors to render a great deal of that aid.

To fulfill the need for individual help to every teacher we would require a greater army of supervisors than we now have. In a time of tight money when staff personnel are among the first to be axed, it would be unrealistic to expect boards of education to expand the cadre of supervisors. Given the typical makeup of our democratically elected boards of education, we cannot look forward to a posture of largesse in expending public moneys. Boards are notoriously tightfisted with the dollar, aware as they are that an increase in the property tax—the source of local support for the schools—could bounce them out of the office which for various reasons they may covet.

Supervisors must plan for a judicious mixture of both group and individual activities. They can often plan training which combines both features; for example, group instruction in using higher-order questions followed by observation and advisement in the classrooms of those teachers who participated in the group training session.

School administrators show partiality to group-oriented supervision on a cost-effectiveness basis. They want, as they say in the vernacular, more bang for the buck. In working with groups supervisors can reach more people with more training in a shorter period of time.

I would laud school systems which exhibit effective, completely or predominantly individualized programs of supervision. These school systems would be rarities which should receive national recognition as models for emulation. Until such a time, however, when the horn of plenty—which is promised by many candidates for public office—reappears as it did in the 1950s, supervisors will devote a somewhat larger percentage of their time to working with groups. The balance of their time will be devoted to helping teachers on an individual basis. An effective program of supervision consists of a combination of both group and individualized activities.

ISSUE 8: SHOULD SUPERVISION BE CARRIED OUT BY SUPERVISORS BASED IN THE CENTRAL OFFICE OR IN THE INDIVIDUAL SCHOOL?

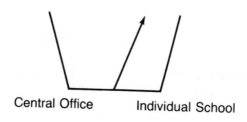

Central Office   Individual School

In practice today supervisory services to the local schools are furnished by supervisors who are headquartered at one of four locations: (1) the state level, (2) an intermediate level between the state and local school, (3) the school district (central office) level, and (4) the individual school level.

State Level

Education, as we know, is one of the powers reserved to the states by the Tenth Amendment to the U.S. Constitution. In principle, the state has the authority to manage and supervise all public schools within its boundaries. For practical and political reasons, with the notable exception of Hawaii, states choose not to oversee the daily operations of their school systems. Though some may disagree, state education officials by and large restrict their roles to activities which they can handle with a degree of efficiency.

State Departments of Education

Instructional supervision from the state level is extremely limited. Leaders from the state Department of Education may direct research studies, supervise state assessments of student achievement, and help define statewide educational goals. They may assemble groups to work on statewide curricular and instructional problems, e.g., identifying minimal competencies for high school graduation or specifying important generic teaching competencies. They may get together groups to write curriculum guides which unify the scope and sequence of disciplines and which can be (though are not necessarily required to be) used throughout the state. Some state departments of education offer limited consultative help to local school systems. We can visualize, however, the modicum of help a state supervisor of mathematics education, for example, could give to any one local school system in the state.

State supervision is often of an administrative rather than an instructional nature, as in checking compliance with state-mandated programs. Instead of being broad based, if it is provided at all, state supervision concentrates on the state legislature's or state Department of Education's concerns of the moment, as, for example, early childhood education, reading, mathematics, or exceptionalities. The state of Georgia, as a case in point, furnishes the services of a few (presently, eight) highly specialized employees of the state Department of Education known as regional consultants, who are distributed throughout the state and who offer supervisory help to teachers in their assigned territories. A single consultant may serve a geographical area comprising as many as 20 county and city school systems. It is the function of these consultants to provide assistance exclusively to the K–4 level, grades which the state has selected to receive special attention.

Learning Resource Systems

The various states have created through federal funding agencies known as learning resource systems. In Florida, learning resource centers (FLRS) are referred to popularly as "Flurz"; in Georgia they are known simply by their initials GLRS. The learning resource systems are part of a nationwide network of special education resource centers.

Each state network is a teacher support system for people who work with exceptional children. The state of Georgia, as an illustration, maintains 16 centers within its network. These centers provide the following services to special educators:

1. Maintenance of instructional materials which may be borrowed on a short-term basis for diagnosis, teacher training, and children's use
2. In-service training of teachers
3. Sponsorship of innovative projects
4. Dissemination of information
5. Diagnosis and referral

These centers come under the jurisdiction of the state Department of Education.

Practically speaking, the state level is too far removed from the scene to be of significant help to teachers and schools directly and consistently. To many people, the state capital, where most state agencies are housed, is at the far side of the globe, even though modern, albeit expensive, transportation links exist between the capital and local communities. We must look to lower levels for more adequate supervisory services.

Intermediate Level

When we come to the intermediate level of school organization and administration we become entangled in a veritable maze. No example of the organizational structure of American education shows so vividly the effects of decentralization as the permutations and commutations of the intermediate level.

Most of us are aware that responsibility for education in America rests with the states. The prevailing pattern of school administration within a state places school systems under the direction of a state commissioner or superintendent who is, as a general rule, responsible to some type of state board of education. We also are even more aware that local school districts exist which are administered by a superintendent elected by the people or appointed by a local school board, which itself may be either appointed (by a grand jury, for example) or, more often, elected by the people. Local school superintendents are responsible to the local school board. However, both local school administrators and the boards of education serve as agents of the state.

County Superintendents

Thirteen states administer schools (K–12) through the county-unit system. In those states the school territory is congruent with the political entity called a county. County-unit school systems are governed by a county school board and administered by a county school superintendent. The models for the county-unit system vary state by state. Florida, for example, is divided into 67 counties in each of which we find a county superintendent and board who exercise jurisdiction over all public schools in the county. Dade County, the largest county in Florida, with over 20 incorporated communities within its borders, including populous Miami, with some 250 schools and over 10,000 teachers, gets along with but one school board and one superintendent of schools. Holmes County in the rural panhandle of Florida likewise has one board and one superintendent of schools to govern its eight schools. Each county is a single school district. School systems of this type are local school districts, not intermediate units.

The pattern in Georgia, another county-unit state, is slightly different. In Georgia we find 187 school districts of which 159 are county units and 28 city districts. The city districts operate independently from the county units.

Outside the county-unit states the patterns of school organization vary widely. Hawaii forms a single school district. In Illinois we can count close to 1,100 school districts (out of some 16,000 nationally). In an Illinois community we may find an elementary school district and a secondary school district, each with its own board, administrators, faculties, and facilities.

We must explore the position of county superintendent to understand the intermediate unit. County superintendents come in three varieties, which are somewhat difficult to describe. First, we have the *county* county superintendent. These are the superintendents of schools in the 13 states which manifest the county-unit system. They are elected by the people or hired and fired by the local school board. They are responsible to the local board of education. We have little difficulty understanding this species of county superintendent. He or she heads a local school district whose boundaries are coterminous with the county's.

Second, we have the *state* county superintendent. The state of New Jersey has complicated the picture of the intermediate unit by appointing county superintendents who are members of the state Department of Education and who are paid by the state.[29] These superintendents take the state's business to the provinces. They are a rare species.

Third, we have the *intermediate* county superintendent, once a plentiful but now a dying species. The *intermediate* county superintendency has a long history. This official functions somewhere between the state level and the local school level. In cases where these administrators' territories expanded beyond the confines of a county, they were often called intermediate district superintendents. I'll not burden you with a lengthy discussion of the fact that units smaller than the counties called townships formed intermediate units prior to the establishment of the county superintendency.

Roald F. Campbell, Luvern L. Cunningham, Raphael O. Nystrand, and Michael D. Usdan credited 35 states with intermediate units.[30] Campbell et al. reported that Michigan has strengthened the intermediate units, currently operating 58 intermediate districts which serve all local school districts of the state.[31] Stephen J. Knezevich observed that Idaho and Kansas dissolved all county superintendencies and Indiana, Hawaii, and Nevada never established any.[32] He pointed out that intermediate units are known by the following names:

intermediate school district (in Michigan); county school district (in California, Illinois, and Pennsylvania); cooperative educational services agency (in Wisconsin); multicounty educational service unit (in Nebraska); board of cooperative educational services (in New York); and regional education service center (in Texas).[33]

Campbell et al. described the evolution of the intermediate unit in New York State from deputy superintendency appointed by a county board of supervisors, to town superintendency, to elected county superintendent, to supervisory district superintendent, to district superintendent hired by a district board of school directors, to district superintendent selected by a board of cooperative educational services.

What is important for our purposes is to remember that the *intermediate* county superintendent has fewer powers than the *county* county superintendent or the *state* county superintendent. The intermediate units are by-products of a rural society. Although the functions of the intermediate unit are undergoing study and change in the states which have them, the typical intermediate unit does not manage schools or programs; it does not hire and fire teachers; it does not mandate curricula, provide transportation to students, or handle disciplinary problems. Its traditional mission is to furnish the local districts with services which they cannot afford or choose not to perform themselves. Among these services are centralized purchasing of supplies, pupil testing services, school health services, reporting services, research, and, what interests us most, curriculum development, in-service education, and instructional supervision. It is possible that as the intermediate units continue to evolve they may depart from their traditional role and take on some limited operational responsibilities in addition to their traditional service functions.

Cooperative Educational Service Agencies

A metamorphosis has taken place with the intermediate unit. The intermediate county unit has evolved in some states into cooperative educational service agencies which encompass wide service areas. The Board of Cooperative Educational Services (BOCES) in the state of New York provides through its 46 centers service to most of the local school districts of the state. In Georgia 16 Cooperative Educational Service Agencies (CESAs) serve 170 school systems.

The cooperative educational service agencies are funded by the state or through a combination of state and local moneys. In New York the BOCES unit is administered by a district superintendent who serves as executive officer of the district board of cooperative educational service. At the same time the BOCES superintendent reports to the state commissioner of education. In Georgia the head of each CESA is a director responsible to a board of control which consists of all the superintendents of the participating school districts.

Emery Stoops, Max Rafferty, and Russell E. Johnson suggested that local school districts could look to the intermediate units for the following services:

1. Direct supervision of classroom teachers. (This diminishes as school districts grow larger.)
2. Coordination of area programs among districts.

3. In-service education of certificated and classified personnel.
4. Preparation of communication and publication aids.
5. Adoption and preparation of courses of study.
6. Provision of audio-visual, library, educational TV, and other materials or programs.
7. Consultant help with pupil personnel services.
8. Operation of federal programs, such as Title III (ESEA), and assistance to districts that apply for federal programs under the several titles of ESEA.
9. Cooperation with business and industry to improve vocational education.
10. Scoring, interpreting, and summarizing standardized testing.
11. Furnishing leadership toward innovations such as flexible scheduling, programmed instruction, team teaching, Head Start and preschool education, collective bargaining or professional negotiation, continuing education in business and industry, citizenship, and skills in human relations.
12. Coordination and cooperation with problem departments, law enforcement agencies, legislative committees, character-building organizations, and community support groups.[34]

A considerable amount of instructional supervision is provided by the intermediate level. What has been said about supervision from the state and intermediate levels is prologue to consideration of the heart of issue 8, which revolves around the question of whether local school districts should make use of central office supervisors or assign supervisors full-time to the individual schools.

We could introduce a related issue at this point which time and space do not permit me to discuss, i.e., should supervision be provided by the intermediate unit or by the local school districts? Is service from the intermediate unit the only way small school systems can conduct supervisory programs? Is it only the larger and wealthier local school districts which can establish their own staff, curriculum, and instructional development programs?

Local School Districts

Let's look at the table of organization of an urban school district, that of Savannah-Chatham County, Georgia in Figure 2.1. You will note that the assistant superintendent for instructional development supervises a large number of coordinators in a variety of disciplines and specialties. These coordinators assume leadership for program development in their assigned fields. As such, they represent a typical staffing pattern for a large school system.

The effective central office supervisor must be an itinerant staff member, which means that he or she cannot spend a great deal of time with any one teacher or in any one school. He or she will more likely concentrate on working with groups than with individual teachers.

Neagley and Evans outlined duties of the K–12 central office subject-area coordinator in the following list:

1. Visits classrooms and works with teachers from K–12 on instructional and curricular matters peculiar to the discipline or subject area.

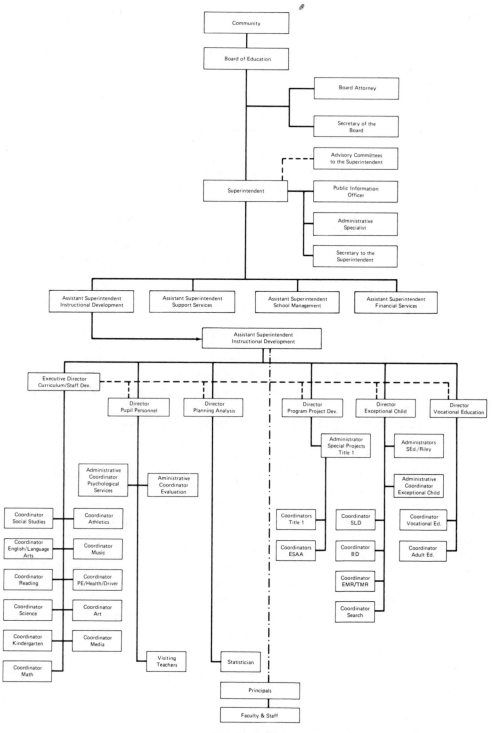

Figure 2.1 Table of Organization, Savannah-Chatham County, Georgia Public Schools

2. Includes teachers in decision making and change.
3. Works with the principals and coordinators of elementary and secondary education in a staff relationship and shares particular knowledge and competence as needed.
4. Reports to the assistant superintendent and informs this person of the developing curriculum and new trends and research in the area of specialization.
5. Chairs the district curriculum committees in the discipline or subject area.
6. Makes recommendations to the appropriate officials of instructional and curricular materials and resources.
7. Works closely with the appropriate curriculum consultants in the intermediate unit office or the regional curriculum center, and keeps abreast of the latest research and trends in the field.
8. Conducts parent and community meetings for the lay public and interprets the latest methods and content in the subject area.
9. Prepares written materials for the lay public on topics related to the discipline.
10. Participates actively in the sessions of the curriculum council, especially when the coordinator's area of concern is on the agenda.
11. Meets and works with the other subject-area coordinators, under the leadership of the assistant superintendent in charge of instruction, in order that a balanced curriculum may be developed.[35]

Instructional and curricular supervision at the individual building level throughout the country is generally very limited. Most supervisory service within school systems comes from the central office. What little supervision that can be identified as an individual school activity is carried out by the principal or assistant principal, occasionally with the help of lead teachers, team leaders, grade coordinators, and department heads.

The lead teacher is a newer position roughly equivalent to a school-based curriculum coordinator. Few are the schools, however, which employ lead teachers or curriculum coordinators as members of the individual school's staff.

Team leaders, grade coordinators, and department heads are allocated so little released time for supervisory duties as to make their roles in supervision meaningless. As has been noted earlier in this chapter, these leaders represent a reservoir of talent which should be developed and put to use in a supervisory capacity.

Arthur J. Lewis and Alice Miel proposed a solution to the central office/individual school issue by separating responsibilities for curriculum leadership and instructional leadership. Central office supervisors would carry heavy responsibility for curriculum development while the staff of the individual school would concentrate on instructional development. They explained:

The separation of curriculum and instruction lends itself well to this view of a useful sharing of responsibility and authority between central office and semiautonomous individual schools. Certain kinds of curricular decisions may be made at the school system level in the interests of a broad range of young people. The decisions may be refined and implemented or greatly modified at the building level where those to be educated can be known quite well.

Initiative for curriculum change can be exercised by anyone at any level and provision for coordination makes it more likely that innovative ideas will be shared. Responsibility for instruction clearly belongs in the individual school.[36]

Lovell observed that if we separated curriculum leadership from instructional leadership, we might designate the two categories of personnel as "curriculum supervisors" and "instructional supervisors."[37] While the notion of separating curriculum from instruction may be appealing and can be done for purposes of analysis, I find it extremely difficult to do in practice.

Writing for the ASCD Working Group on the roles and responsibilities of supervisors Sturges recommended that school systems recognize two types of instructional supervisors: the *consultative* instructional supervisor and the *administrative* instructional supervisor. He described their functions as follows:

The *consultative* instructional supervisor is primarily concerned with the improvement of instruction and works closely with teachers. Teachers prefer this type of supervisor be assigned to a specific building . . . The *administrative* instructional supervisor is also concerned with the improvement of instruction, but more from a controlling and coordinating level. More often housed at a central office, duties will include administrative functions such as requesting and administering Federal grants, acquisition of materials, quality control of the learning environment, and the overall coordination of the instructional program. Responsibilities of the administrative instructional supervisor are often assigned to a principal or department head at the building level, or directors/assistant superintendents/coordinators at the district level.[38]

In recent years administrators have extolled the virtues of school-based management, which means that the superintendent has delegated limited powers to the principal to manage his or her own budget and to run his or her own shop. With school-based management comes the growing conviction that we also need more school-based supervision.

School-based supervisors are on duty in the school building full time. They can devote all their energies to assisting teachers. They can respond to teachers when they are needed and can serve as the schools' designated leaders in curriculum and instruction.

While we cannot conceivably nor should we duplicate the kinds of supervision the central office can provide, we do need to find additional ways for individual schools to create their own supervisory programs in conjunction with central office assistance. If this were done, schools could provide more of the clinical type of supervision recommended by experts like Cogan. What is needed is a well-planned team approach which carefully divides supervisory responsibilities between central office and individual school staff, with a somewhat heavier share of the responsibility falling on the supervisors of the individual school. Both central office and individual school personnel would work in all three domains of supervision.

In passing, we should observe that the department head of the secondary school is in a precarious position. The department head is often perceived as a member of the administrative team. In systems bound by teachers' union contracts, however, the department head, i.e., a teacher, may be designated as a member of the bargaining unit and, as such, is prohibited from conducting or participating in formal evaluations of teacher performance, a function which is reserved to the administrator. In spite of contractual limitations department heads can still be available to assist teachers at the teachers' request and can work with them on an informal basis. Such an approach might be even more productive in the long run.

ISSUE 9: SHOULD THE SUPERVISOR USE A DIRECTIVE OR NONDIRECTIVE APPROACH?

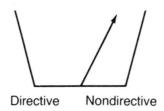

Directive   Nondirective

This issue raises the question of whether the supervisor should adopt a direct approach or an indirect approach in working with teachers. Is it the supervisor's mission to tell teachers how to go about their tasks or does the supervisor attempt to effect change by persuasion and example?

Some supervisors see their role as a highly directive one and prescribe content, materials, and techniques for teachers to follow. Others prefer to help teachers to come to their own decisions about content and methodology.

An indirect approach in supervision is similar to the nondirective approach followed by guidance personnel and psychologists. The nondirective counselor refrains from claiming to know the answers. Such a counselor does not sit down, listen to a client, and write a prescription, but rather allows the client to express his or her own concerns and ideas. Often the teacher merely wants the reassurance the supervisor is in a position to give. The teacher wants help in thinking through problems and wishes to try out solutions on another person whose judgment can be trusted.

An effective supervisor is ready with suggestions for a teacher to consider, knowing that until the teacher has accepted the suggestions and has, in effect, incorporated them into his or her behavior, the suggestions fall on barren land.

Of course, teachers expect the supervisor to be of help to them and to have *some* answers. But they do not expect always to receive the "right" or "approved" or "only" answers, and want the freedom to feel that their solution to an instructional problem is as good as or better than the supervisor's solution.

Teachers can argue with the nondirective supervisor who serves as a sounding board, but not with the directive supervisor, the one who tells them what and how they must teach. We are raising a basic question in human relations: are persons motivated to change, cooperate, and work effectively by telling or demanding or ordering? In the case of supervision, moreover, can we tell or demand or order highly trained professionals?

Directive Administrators and Supervisors

Even the administrator who possesses the sanction of society and the law for telling or demanding or ordering finds that in dealing with people a cooperative approach is far more effective in most cases than the hard-nosed approach.

The hard-nosed administrator says, "You must do this because I say so." He or she falls back on status and legal authority for enforcing compliance. Individuals commonly react to the hard-nosed or highly directive approach in one of a number of ways. They may comply with the administrator's wishes because they happen to be in accord with them and choose to ignore the manner in which they are made known. If they take issue with the directive manner of an administrator, they may, and probably will, still comply, though in a sullen, resentful way. They will do just enough to meet the minimal requirements of the administrator's edict. They will be cooperative on the surface and uncooperative deep down inside.

Still another type of individual may simply throw up his hands and withdraw in body or spirit from teaching. The creative teacher who feels compelled to accept the administrator's or supervisor's prescribed methods down to the last detail may despair and give up teaching entirely. Others silently ignore edicts, remain in teaching, and resign themselves to the fact that their reluctant behavior will result in penalizing them in assignments, recognition, salary, and promotions.

Bolder individuals will speak out, resist prescriptions of the administrator and actively rebel. If they happen not to be on tenure, the administrator may deny it to them. If they are already on tenure, continuing animosity may exist between the hard-nosed administrator and rebellious teachers.

Of course, administrators should have the authority to be directive when they need such authority. If a teacher contemplates an activity which might be dangerous to the bodies and minds of youngsters, the administrator has not only the right but the duty to be directive and to say "No." Teachers recognize this authority as necessary to the administrator's job. It is more often the manner of the administrator than the actual requests which antagonize teachers. The same is true of the directive supervisor whose manner may rub a teacher the wrong way and destroy rapport even when the validity of specific suggestions is not disputed.

Those supervisors who behave in a highly directive fashion are more likely to perceive supervision as a function of administration than those who behave in a nondirective fashion. Directive supervisors tend to see themselves as line administrators rather than as staff service personnel.

If a supervisor is not an administrator, then, in effect, he or she does not have the implied sanction of status and legal position to be prescriptive. Prescriptive behavior may turn out to be particularly ineffective, if teachers realize that the supervisor has no administrative authority and cannot compel them to behave in ways he or she has decided are the best ways. To effect change the prescriptive supervisor must then appeal to the administrator to apply considerable administrative authority to making recalcitrant teachers see things the supervisor's way. If the supervisor frequently appeals to the authority of the administrator to effect change, he or she then becomes aligned in the teachers' minds with the administrator and is no longer perceived as a service-oriented person whom they can count on, confide in, and trust. The supervisor has destroyed the very fabric which should have been maintained—rapport with the persons to be served and assisted.

"Have you ever thought of ...?" "Why don't you try ...?" "What would you think of ...?" are much better ways to phrase suggestions to a teacher than "Do it this way," "Never mind your way," and "It is required."

It is a simple psychological principle that individuals will go out of their way to comply with a directive they feel they have helped formulate, about which they made a choice. Whether they had a choice or not is not nearly as significant as whether they feel they had a choice. They need to feel also that it is not just the beliefs of one individual which necessitate compliance with requirements in curriculum and instruction, but that compliance is necessary for the best interest of all concerned— the students, the community, and colleagues.

Blumberg contrasted the direct and indirect approaches as follows:

A supervisor using predominantly *direct* behavior might well be assuming that:

- The control of a situation is based on the authority of one's position in an organizational hierarchy.
- People in higher organizational positions have more expertise.
- People in lower organizational positions can best be evaluated by those who are higher.
- The most important external rewards of a job come to a person primarily from a person who holds a higher position.
- Empathic listening to the teacher is not a necessary dimension of helping.
- People learn best by being told what to do by someone in a higher organizational position.
- Work is rational; there is little place in supervision for discussion of feelings or interpersonal relationships.
- Collaborative problem solving between supervisor and teacher is not a critical concern in supervision.
- Teaching as a skill can generally be separated into the right and wrong ways of doing things.

The assumptions about people that appear to accompany a supervisor's heavily loading *indirect* behavior are that:

- Control of the situation depends on the demands of the problem. The problem determines the direction that events take.
- Expertise is a function of knowledge and experience, not necessarily of organizational position.
- The product of a teacher's work is the best evaluative tool to use in measuring his performance.
- The important rewards of teaching are intrinsic to the job, but they need to be supplemented by external rewards.
- People learn best by being confronted with a situation and, with help, finding their own solution.
- It is important for teachers to feel that they have been listened to and understood.
- Work is both rational and emotional; that discussion of feelings and interpersonal relations may be as important as discussion about the job.
- Collaborative problem solving between supervisor and teacher is an important concern of supervision.
- Teaching is a complex process and what works well for one person may not for another, so that most of what goes on in a classroom needs to be viewed experimentally.[39]

Let us take as an illustration of the two different approaches the case of the teacher mentioned earlier in this chapter who wants to change textbooks. The elementary school at which he is employed is using a particular publisher's arithmetic books. The teacher hears of a set of books which he believes are better for his fourth grade. He feels that the content is more clearly explained than in the ones he is using. Let us suppose that he even has access to a set of the books, perhaps supplied to him for experimental use by the publisher and decides that he will use the new books.

A directive supervisor would flatly tell him, "No, you cannot use these books. We require the other books." A nondirective supervisor would explain why the first books had been chosen, how the decision to use these books was one made by teachers of the school, how his rapid shifting to another set of materials might destroy a particular sequence, affecting not only the students but the teacher's colleagues at higher levels. Such a supervisor would help the teacher to see the consequences of his action and suggest alternative procedures to the teacher, such as taking a set of the new materials to a representative group of teachers who might be concerned. The new materials could be evaluated and even adopted at a later date if the teachers agreed that the new materials were actually better and if they could be obtained by the school.

The supervisor would acquaint the teacher with the problem of structuring a discipline and would point out that there are threads that run through a discipline, that a sequence is formed starting with the simplest elements and moving into the more complex, and that the orderly progression of a sequence is taken into consideration in the choice of materials. Introduction of materials into the middle of a sequence may result in duplication of material or omission of significant learnings. A break in the coordinated sequence may also confuse the learners as they move from one level to another.

The supervisor helps the teacher understand the necessity for considering other factors before introducing a completely new set of materials. The question might be raised as to what happens if the teacher persists in his wish to use the new materials. Since the issue is a serious one, it may then be referred to the person who is responsible for decision making, the principal or superintendent. The principal may talk with the teacher, other teachers affected by the teacher's action, and the supervisor. He or she will examine the materials the teacher wishes to use, compare them with what is then being used, and may actually decide that the new materials do no harm to the sequence and authorize their use. The principal may authorize them on a permanent or temporary, experimental basis, or may deny the teacher the request to substitute the new materials.

Through the actions of both the supervisor and administrator, the teacher has been permitted to state his case, and his opinions have been listened to and evaluated. Whether he is granted the right to use the new materials, he can at least feel that he has been treated as an intelligent, professional, and valued person. This is the basic distinction between the directive and nondirective approaches.

ISSUE 10: SHOULD THE SUPERVISOR REPRESENT MANAGEMENT OR THE TEACHERS IN COLLECTIVE BARGAINING?

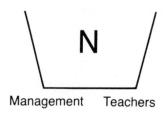

Management   Teachers

In recent years powerful teachers' organizations have appeared on the educational scene. Through strong teachers' unions and other educational associations, teachers are making demands and packing enough muscle to force acquiescence to their demands. Though demands most often concern administrative matters such as salary, hiring and dismissing, amount of free time, and supervision of extra-class activities, they also concern matters of curriculum and instruction. As teachers gain experience and success in the use of strong professional associations, the chances are that they will scrutinize the curriculum and make increasing demands in that area.

School administrators have been feeling the pressures from militant teachers' organizations for a number of years now. They know that teachers are no longer going to sit back placidly like the gentle schoolmarms of yesteryear and accept a pittance for their work. The collective power of teachers has been felt in the legislative halls of a number of states. Strikes and absences from the classroom are recognized phenomena of the day. Even the threat of legal reprisal has not served to quell teachers who are angered by unacceptable working conditions.

School systems in many localities have been forced to recognize bargaining agents among the teachers. In many school systems local chapters of the National Education Association or the American Federation of Teachers have been selected by the teachers themselves to represent their interests before the administration and school board. The aims and procedures of these two powerful associations have been steadily converging and might even someday result in a merger at local, state, and national levels.

Whether the two professional organizations merge or not, teachers at all levels may be expected to exercise their authority through potent associations. This is one of the realities with which administrators must now contend. During a teacher strike or prolonged holiday or work stoppage the administrators are on a hot spot. If they side with the school board, the teachers view them as the enemy. If they side with the teachers in their desire to better their own and the school's lot, they may turn their school boards against them. It is one of the unfortunate paradoxes of education today that administrators and teachers are so far apart that they consider each other antagonists.

Looking back on the development of schools, we see that the administrator was once the "headmaster" or "principal teacher," a master teacher who happened to be assigned certain administrative and supervisory tasks. How far we have departed from the principal teacher concept is seen in the polarity of administrators and teachers in conflicts brought to a head by strong teachers' associations.

As sure as the sun rises and sets, collective bargaining for public employees is to be here for a while. Those small communities which now watch complacently, expecting the tide of teacher militancy elsewhere to ebb, will discover that the teachers' organizations have made an end run, bypassed the localities, and taken their campaign to the state level. They may obtain on a statewide basis what they could not obtain district by district, much to the chagrin of school administrators who attempt to stem the tide.

Already more than 30 states have enacted collective bargaining laws to permit public employees to enter into negotiations with management. An adversary relationship has been codified by the force of law; representatives of management (i.e., administrators) must sit down on one side of the table with representatives of the teachers (i.e., members of the teachers' organization or union) on the other side of the table. If public employees in every state were granted the right to strike, there would be no holding back the march of collective bargaining.*

Only enlightened school administration can turn the tide. Given the vastness of the American educational enterprise, we should not be surprised to find in some status positions administrators whose behavior evokes problems.

A fact of life today is that administrators must cooperate with strong, often militant, teachers' organizations. They must meet with representatives, seriously consider demands, work toward achieving goals on which all agree, and try to find ways to resolve problems about which there is disagreement. Unless administrators recognize that their roles have changed dramatically from strict line officials, their positions may very well be made untenable in a school system perpetually in crisis. In former days the decision to admit teachers to participation in the decision-making process was left to administrators. Teachers' associations have wrenched much authority from administrators. To be successful today administrators must, of necessity, share decision making with teachers. The wise administrator extends decision making beyond the teachers to other constituents of education, the students, and the community. He or she tries to keep ahead of crises by working with groups which will be affected by administrative decisions.

Which brings us to the question of whether supervisors should become involved in collective bargaining. My reply is an unequivocal no. They should represent neither the administration nor teachers. Supervisors bridge the gap between administration and teaching. If they choose (or are asked) to represent management, teachers will no longer respond to them as ally and helper. If they choose (or are asked) to represent teachers, they will with certainty face confrontation with the administrator. It serves no useful purpose for a supervisor to sit at the bargaining table on either side or to become entangled in the process in any way. This is not a "copout" but rather is prudent. No good can be gained by supervisors' participation in negotiations. Involvement can undermine or destroy the very fabric of their position and render them useless. An irate administrator can cut the supervisor's position out of the

---

* Teachers in a few states have a limited right to strike.

budget; hostile teachers can make the job untenable. In either situation the supervisor and the cause of supervision lose.

Collective bargaining is bringing about changes in education. Wiles and Bondi commented that early collective bargaining centered on salary and working conditions. They predicted:

By the mid-1970s, however, professional groups were bargaining for input or control in areas that historically were administrative domain. . . . It is probable that collective bargaining will deal with issues of a curricular and instructional nature as soon as major extrinsic issues have been addressed by professional groups.[40]

Supervisors should be aware of the changing roles of teachers and administrators. They should not find their role unduly limited by strong teachers' associations unless they consider their own role as administrative and unless they feel they must take a directive approach to supervision. If they are highly directive, they will view teachers' demands for changes in curriculum and instruction as an intrusion on their authority.

If they see themselves as special service people they should be able to maintain rapport with teachers and should be able to continue working with them. They may, in fact, find that some or all of the demands of militant teachers' organizations are justified and reasonable. In one respect the teachers' organizations may come to the assistance of supervisors who are in the uncomfortable role of evaluating teachers' performance by insisting on peer participation in the evaluation of teachers. Strong teachers' associations may be able to effect changes which supervisors are not in a position to bring about.

ISSUE 11: SHOULD SCHOOL SYSTEMS ORGANIZE FOR SUPERVISION BY EMPLOYING GENERALISTS OR BY HIRING SPECIALISTS?

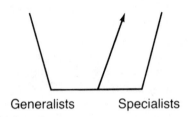

Generalists   Specialists

The chief school administrator—the superintendent—must make some difficult decisions on what qualifications to look for in hiring supervisors and how to utilize personnel. He or she must decide how many supervisors and what kind will be needed and develop a plan for organizing supervision in the district.

The administrator takes into consideration a number of factors in making these decisions including the size and financial resources of the district. He or she is aware not only of the number of teachers in the system but also their particular strengths and needs as well as their attitudes toward supervision.

The superintendent will have his or her own views regarding organizational patterns for supervision but must also take into consideration the philosophy of the board of education and attitudes of the public. Since the employment of specialized personnel will have to be justified to the public, the administrator will have to offer strong reasons for adopting supervisory programs, particularly if they entail a sizable staff. The patterns of organization which are adopted will have to conform to limitations imposed by the school district and to resources available.

Granted the freedom to adopt whatever pattern of organization seems wisest, the superintendent must decide on the kinds of personnel desired: director of instruction, consultants, coordinators, and so forth. But perhaps more basic than the kinds and titles of supervisory personnel is a question which has been debated inside and outside curriculum circles for many years. Should the superintendent employ generalists or specialists to perform the supervisory functions?

Generalist Supervisors

The generalist may be described as a supervisor who has responsibilities for supervising teachers in a number of grades or in a variety of subjects. Possessing expertise and experience in at least one teaching field, the generalist may and usually does supervise in areas in which he or she does not have special training or has had no training at all. The generalist is an expert at teaching and knows what constitutes good general methods. He or she can recognize, for example, a good classroom environment, knows when a teacher is presenting a lesson well, and can judge effectiveness of planning.

The generalist understands learning theory, is conversant with principles of evaluation and measurement, understands the use of audio-visual materials, has a good background in resources and materials, and knows where to locate additional sources.

The generalist has a broad view of curriculum and can compare what teachers in various grades, classes, subjects, and schools do. He or she can assist the teacher with problems of discipline and may be able to help the teacher develop techniques of counseling. The able generalist has a good overall knowledge of curriculum and instruction. By helping teachers of different grades and subjects to work together this leader can serve as a unifying force.

Personnel who are generalists possess titles such as assistant superintendent of curriculum and instruction, director of instruction, director of elementary education, director of middle schools, director of secondary education, and general supervisor.

Specialist Supervisors

The specialist supervisor has depth of preparation and experience in a particular level or subject. He or she not only knows the level or subject thoroughly but also knows modern techniques and latest trends in teaching.

The specialist possesses some of the same knowledge and skills as the generalist. He or she understands learning theory and can help a teacher with discipline, classroom climate, and guidance. The specialist's forte lies in the ability to relate principles and techniques to a particular grade level or field.

The specialist can help a teacher apply techniques of evaluation to a particular subject. He or she can discuss the use of audio-visual materials with the teacher in relation to a specific grade or field. Planning is considered with the teacher in relation to a specific field rather than to principles of planning in the abstract.

The specialist knows sources of specific materials of use to the teacher. He or she can detect when teachers are making mistakes in teaching particular topics and can help them to correct the errors. The specialist has a more limited view of curriculum and instruction than the generalist since the specialist works within one area whereas the generalist works across areas.

Special supervisors bear such titles as supervisor of language arts, supervisor of science. coordinator of foreign languages in the elementary school, and consultant in social studies.

If you will look for a moment at the Table of Organization of the Savannah-Chatham County Public Schools shown earlier in this chapter (Figure 2.1), you will note a large number of specialists (coordinators) who are responsible to several generalists (the assistant superintendent, instructional development and directors).

At the school building level a schematic representation of a school in a typical school district as in Figure 2.2 might show the principal administering a supervisory staff composed of one or two generalists while the team leaders, grade coordinators, or department heads perform the roles of specialist supervisors.

Should teachers be supervised by generalists or specialists? Which type of supervision is the most effective? This is one of the more difficult issues to resolve. Both types of supervision are found throughout the country. While some school systems provide the services of both generalists and specialists, others must limit their choice to one or the other.

Since they normally have limited financial resources, small school systems tend to employ generalists who can work in a number of areas and across grade levels. Thus, the general supervisor is a common position in those small school districts that can afford the services of a supervisor. If their resources permit, small school systems may employ one or two specialists to help the generalist, particularly in those fields which require a fairly high degree of technical skill such as reading, guidance, vocational education, science, and mathematics.

In a large school system with its greater financial resources, however, the choice may be open to the superintendent and the chief school officer must decide whether to provide supervisory help through general supervisors or special supervisors or both.

Opinions differ as to which type of supervisor is most helpful to the teacher. McKean and Mills appeared to lean toward the use of the generalist:

Today's recognition of the values of correlation and integration of different subjects seems to point up an advantage of general supervision. . . . Special supervision, while it presents the real advantage of expert assistance, may result in increasing compartmentalization of subjects.

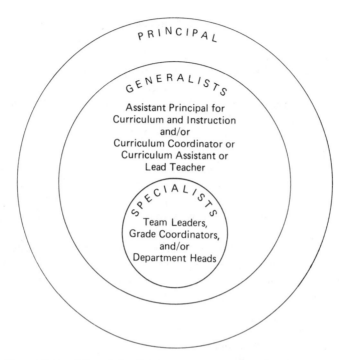

Figure 2.2 Generalist and Specialist Supervisors in an Individual School

At the elementary school level teachers sometimes report the unhappy experience of being caught in the middle of conflicting pressures from helpful special supervisors. Each special supervisor attempts to promote the teaching of his specialty, often without recognizing that his great interest and concern is only one of the subjects with which the elementary teacher must deal.

Generally, the weight of evidence would seem to favor general supervision over special supervision.[41]

There are without doubt roles for both the generalist and specialist in school supervision. A school system that can afford the services of a full staff of both generalists and specialists is a fortunate system. The generalists provide broad, unifying supervision while the specialists can provide narrow, in-depth supervision.

The critical problem arises when a choice has to be made, when a school system must elect one type or the other. The superintendent's philosophy and the wishes of teachers will loom large in answering this problem. Although I would not minimize the contributions generalists can make to a system, I lean toward wider use of specialists in supervision. At the elementary level, since most, although not all, of elementary classrooms are self-contained, the superintendent may wish to begin a supervisory program by using generalists. Generalists can work very effectively at the elementary school level. They have a breadth which corresponds to the breadth of training provided elementary school teachers.

Need for Specialists

Elementary teachers, however, are increasingly in need of help from specialists. Mathematics, science, and reading programs have posed problems both for teachers and general supervisors who are not trained in the latest techniques of these programs. Teaching foreign languages in elementary school and programs of bilingual education have created the need for specialized supervision in these areas. General supervisors often lack the depth of training to help teachers write objectives, select appropriate methods, and evaluate results in the specialized fields. They may work effectively in the phases of the program which are more generic in nature, such as language arts, social studies, or humanities. Probably they feel more at home supervising in fields for which they have had preparation and experience. Given this condition they may minimize or omit assistance to teachers in some critical areas of the school's program.

As school systems move into the creation of middle schools, nongrading, team teaching, differentiated staffing, and departmentalization, the need for special supervisors becomes increasingly clear. Whereas an elementary school might get along satisfactorily with the use of generalists, I believe that it is imperative today to provide specialists in supervision at the secondary level. Content and methodology have changed—and continue changing—so rapidly that no generalist can possibly keep up with the changes in all fields.

What school systems really need are specialists who are, in effect, generalists, or conversely, generalists who are, in effect, specialists. It is possible to prepare these types of workers. A specialist who is well trained should have had at least the usual preparation in principles of teaching. He or she will ordinarily have had work in the foundations of education and should be able to identify a suitable learning environment as readily as a generalist. The specialist should know the necessity for the teachers' maintaining rapport with their students. From prior training and experience he or she should know principles of discipline, evaluation, and counseling.

Special supervisors who are professional will not push their own vested interest any more than any enthusiastic teacher. An administrator always has the power to maintain controls which would prohibit vested interests from being stressed out of proportion.

Some generalists are both generalist and specialist. They have responsibilities in a number of areas and have depth in one or two areas. They can provide the coordinating function of generalists while at the same time providing skillful supervision in one or two fields. It would be a mistake to conclude that all specialists are so narrow that they cannot provide more general types of supervision or that all generalists were so shallow that they could not provide any supervision in depth.

Generalists such as the director of instruction may assume more responsibilities for coordinating the work of the specialists. They may devote their energies to working with groups composed of representatives of different fields. Specialists may work with individual teachers and groups of teachers in the same field.

Little if any solid research exists on the relative merits of using general or special supervisors. Barring experimental evidence as to which type of supervision is better for which teachers and in what kinds of situations, administrators might well poll their teachers to see what type of supervision they would respond to best. The question might be posed: If there were both a generalist and a specialist in your secondary field or a specific field of the elementary school program available, which one would you call on first for help? The teachers would be directed to assume that both kinds of specialists are competent and easy to work with.

Some Parallels

The issue of generalist versus specialist is encountered in other situations within and outside the profession of education. Universities continue to wrestle with this problem in providing faculty supervision of student teachers. Some teacher training institutions have set up their programs in such a way that generalists supervise student teachers at both the elementary and secondary school levels.

It is easier to employ generalists than specialists and it is easier for a university to administer a student teaching program in which supervision is conducted by generalists. Generalists are easier to schedule and can be used more flexibly. Specialists are harder to come by and assignment in their cases is more difficult. Administrative considerations in operating the student teaching program play a more prominent role than efficacy in supervision.

Outside the field of education, medicine has long since resolved this question in favor of specialists over general practitioners. The situation is such that it is sometimes difficult for a patient to know which type of specialist should be consulted. The specialist has all but supplanted the general practitioner. Although we may lament it, the "GP" is rapidly disappearing from the American scene. With the mighty strides made in medicine it has become extremely difficult for the general practitioner to keep up to date in all subfields of a specialization.

How then shall we organize for supervision? Shall we provide wide-sweeping supervision or supervision in depth? These questions must be decided when a school system is organizing for supervision.

SUMMARY

We have explored 11 issues in supervision. First, supervision is seen as a continuing and necessary service to teachers. Second, the supervisor can provide help to all teachers whether they are experienced or inexperienced, effective or ineffective; more time should be allocated to the inexperienced and the ineffective. Third, the supervisor's authority should be derived from expertise and interpersonal relationships. Fourth, the supervisor is likely to maintain a higher degree of rapport with teachers and render more effective service if not perceived as an administrator and if the supervisor does not perceive himself or herself in that role. Fifth and sixth, staff development and curriculum development are legitimate domains of supervision.

Seventh, supervisors should work with both individuals and groups of teachers, with a somewhat greater allocation of time to working with groups. Eighth, supervision is best carried out by a judicious combination of central office and individual school supervisors with greater weight given to the supervisory program of the individual school. Ninth, supervisors should, as a rule, manifest a nondirective approach in working with teachers. Tenth, the supervisor should not represent either the administration or the teachers in collective bargaining and should avoid involvement in the process. Eleventh, supervision requires the services of both generalists and specialists, with a slightly greater preponderance of specialists.

ACTIVITIES FOR FURTHER STUDY

1. For each of the 11 issues discussed in this chapter draw a scale similar to the one shown with each issue, and on each scale draw an arrow which shows your position.
2. Interview several practicing supervisors and determine with which types of teachers they spend most of their time: new, inexperienced, experienced, effective, or ineffective.
3. Poll a group of teachers at the school level in which you are most interested and ask them whether they prefer help from generalists or specialists.
4. Poll a group of teachers to see whether they believe that supervisors in their school system are directive or nondirective and ask them which approach they prefer.
5. Find out what Ben M. Harris (*Supervisory Behavior in Education*, 2nd ed.) means by *tractive* and *dynamic* supervision.
6. Find out what Carl D. Glickman (*Development Supervision: Alternative Practices for Helping Teachers Improve Instruction*) means by developmental, directive, collaborative, and nondirective supervision.
7. Study the objectives of local chapters of the National Education Association and the American Federation of Teachers. How many of these objectives concern curriculum and instruction? How would the actions of these organizations affect the status and duties of supervisors?
8. Describe characteristics of ineffective teachers and state how you would work as a supervisor with ineffective teachers.
9. Conduct a limited research study in a local school system to confirm or deny the hypothesis that experienced teachers are more effective teachers than inexperienced teachers.
10. Write a brief paper on one of the following questions:
    a. Is the supervisor of elementary education a specialist or generalist? Is there an area of specialization called elementary education?
    b. Is the supervisor of secondary education a specialist or generalist? Is there an area of specialization called secondary education?
11. Talk with a sampling of school principals and find out what percent of their time is devoted to supervision of instruction. Find out if they would prefer to spend more or less time on this task.

12. Interview one of the top administrators of the school system you know best and tape his or her comments and views on the role of supervisors on the staff. Inquire about, among other things, how the administrator rates supervisors.

13. Participate in small-group discussions in class on each of the 11 issues which are examined in this chapter. Try to reach consensus on each issue first in the small group and then with the class as a whole.

14. Prepare position statements on each of the 17 issues identified by the ASCD's Working Group on Supervisory Practices which has not been examined in this chapter.

15. Analyze the staffing pattern of a school system you know well and make a critique of its strengths and weaknesses.

16. Find out if your state has intermediate units and report on their organizational structure and the services they provide to local schools.

17. Cite one or more issues other than those discussed in this chapter and show your position on each.

NOTES

1. ASCD Working Group on Supervisory Practices, "Issues in Supervisor Roles: What Do Practitioners Say?" *Educational Leadership* 34, no. 3 (December 1976): 217–220.
2. Stanley W. Williams, *New Dimensions in Supervision*, Scranton, Pa., Intext Educational Publishers, 1972, 22.
3. Ross L. Neagley and N. Dean Evans, *Handbook for Effective Supervision of Instruction*, 3rd ed., Englewood Cliffs, N.J., Prentice-Hall, 1980, 4.
4. Thomas Briggs and Joseph Justman, *Improving Instruction through Supervision*, rev. ed., New York, Macmillan, 1952, 127.
5. William H. Lucio and John D. McNeil, *Supervision in Thought and Action*, 3rd ed., New York, McGraw-Hill, 1979, 26–27.
6. Adolph Unruh and Harold E. Turner, *Supervision for Change and Innovation*, Boston, Houghton Mifflin, 1970, 8.
7. William H. Burton and Leo J. Brueckner, *Supervision: A Social Process*, 3rd ed., New York, Appleton-Century-Crofts, 1955, 85.
8. Arthur Blumberg, *Supervisors and Teachers: A Private Cold War*, 2nd ed., Berkeley, Calif., McCutchan, 1980, 19–20.
9. A. W. Sturges, *The Roles and Responsibilities of Instructional Supervisors*, Alexandria, Va., ASCD Working Group on the Roles and Responsibilities of Supervisors, Association for Supervision and Curriculum Development, October 1, 1978.
10. Harold Spears, *Improving the Supervision of Instruction*, Englewood Cliffs, N.J., Prentice-Hall, 1953, 27.
11. Burton and Brueckner, 85.
12. Glen G. Eye and Lanore A. Netzer, *Supervision of Instruction: A Phase of Administration*, New York, Harper & Row, 1965, 12. The second edition (1971) with added coauthor Robert D. Krey dropped the subtitle *A Phase of Administration* and modified the definition of supervision.
13. Kathryn V. Feyereisen, A. John Fiorino, and Arlene T. Nowak, *Supervision and Curriculum Renewal: A Systems Approach*, New York, Meredith, 1970, 15.
14. Lloyd W. Dull, *Supervision: School Leadership Handbook*, Columbus, Ohio, Charles E. Merrill, 1981, 7.
15. Jon Wiles and Joseph Bondi, *Supervision: A Guide to Practice*, Columbus, Ohio, Charles E. Merrill, 1980, 21.

16. Thomas J. Sergiovanni and Robert J. Starratt, *Supervision: Human Perspectives*, 2nd ed., New York, McGraw-Hill, 1979, 15.
17. Leslee J. Bishop, *Staff Development and Instructional Improvement: Plans and Procedures*, Boston, Allyn and Bacon, 1976, 1.
18. Dull, 110.
19. Ben M. Harris, *Improving Staff Performance through In-service Education*, Boston, Allyn and Bacon, 1980, 21. See also Ben M. Harris, E. Wailand Bessent, and Kenneth E. McIntyre, *In-service Education: A Guide to Better Practice*, Englewood Cliffs, N.J., Prentice-Hall, 1969.
20. James R. Marks, Emery Stoops, and Joyce King-Stoops, *Handbook of Educational Supervision: A Guide for the Practitioner*, 2nd ed., Boston, Allyn and Bacon, 1978, 163–164.
21. See Peter F. Oliva, *Developing the Curriculum*, Boston, Little, Brown, 1982.
22. John T. Lovell and Kimball Wiles, *Supervision for Better Schools*, 5th ed., Englewood Cliffs, N.J., Prentice-Hall, 1983, 143.
23. Wiles and Bondi, 161.
24. Feyereisen, Fiorino, and Nowak.
25. Lucio and McNeil, 155.
26. Morris Cogan, *Clinical Supervision*, Boston, Houghton Mifflin, 1973, 9.
27. Ibid.
28. Ibid., 16–17.
29. See Roald F. Campbell, Luvern L, Cunningham, Raphael O. Nystrand, and Michael D. Usdan, *The Organization and Control of American Schools*, 4th ed., Columbus, Ohio, Charles E. Merrill, 1980, 129.
30. Ibid., 116.
31. Ibid., 117.
32. Stephen J. Knezevich, *Administration of Public Education*, 3rd ed., New York, Harper & Row, 1975, 234.
33. Ibid.
34. Emery Stoops, Max Rafferty, and Russell E. Johnson, *Handbook of Educational Administration*, Boston, Allyn and Bacon, 1975, 72–73. See also Ralph B. Kimbrough and Michael Y. Nunnery, *Educational Administration: An Introduction*, 2nd ed., New York, Macmillan, 1983, 174–183.
35. Neagley and Evans, 107. Adapted from Ross L. Neagley and N. Dean Evans, *Handbook for Effective Curriculum Development*, Englewood Cliffs, N.J., Prentice-Hall, 1967, 137–138.
36. Arthur J. Lewis and Alice Miel, *Supervision for Improved Instruction: New Challenges, New Responses*, Belmont, Calif., Wadsworth, 1972, 47.
37. Lovell, in Sturges, ASCD Working Group on the Role and Responsibilities of Supervisors, 32.
38. Sturges, 72–73.
39. Blumberg, 88–89.
40. Wiles and Bondi, 20.
41. Robert C. McKean and H. H. Mills, *The Supervisor*, New York, Center for Applied Research in Education, 1964, 22–23.

BIBLIOGRAPHY

Association for Supervision and Curriculum Development. "Instructional Supervision: Trends and Issues." *Educational Leadership* 34 (May 1977): 563–618.
ASCD Working Group on Supervisory Practices. "Issues in Supervisor Roles: What Do Practitioners Say?" *Educational Leadership* 34 (December 1976): 217–220.
Bishop, Leslee J. *Staff Development and Instructional Improvement: Plans and Procedures.* Boston: Allyn and Bacon, 1976.

Blumberg, Arthur. *Supervisors and Teachers: A Private Cold War*, 2nd ed. Berkeley, Calif.: McCutchan, 1980.

Briggs, Thomas, and Joseph Justman. *Improving Instruction through Supervision*, rev. ed. New York: Macmillan, 1962.

Burton, William H., and Leo J. Brueckner. *Supervision: A Social Process*, 3rd ed. New York: Appleton-Century-Crofts, 1955.

Caswell, Hollis L. "The Generalist—His Unique Contribution." *Educational Leadership* 24 (December 1966): 213–215.

Cogan, Morris. *Clinical Supervision*. Boston: Houghton Mifflin, 1973.

"Collective Bargaining." *Phi Delta Kappan* 63 (December 1981): 231–256.

Douglass, Harl R., Rudyard K. Bent, and Charles W. Boardman. *Democratic Supervision in Secondary Schools*, 2nd ed. Boston: Houghton Mifflin, 1961.

Dull, Lloyd W. *Supervision: School Leadership Handbook*. Columbus, Ohio: Charles E. Merrill, 1981.

Esposito, James P., Gary E. Smith, and Harold J. Burbach. "A Delineation of the Supervisory Role." *Education* 96 (Fall 1975): 63–67.

Eye, Glen G., Lanore A. Netzer, and Robert D. Krey. *Supervision of Instruction*, 2nd ed. New York: Harper & Row, 1971. Eye and Netzer, 1st ed., 1965.

Feyereisen, Kathryn V., A. John Fiorino, and Arlene T. Nowak. *Supervision and Curriculum Renewal: A Systems Approach*. New York: Meredith, 1970.

Glickman, Carl D. *Development Supervision: Alternative Practices for Helping Teachers Improve Instruction*. Alexandria, Va.: Association for Supervision and Curriculum Development, 1981.

Gwynn, J. Minor. *Theory and Practice of Supervision*. New York: Dodd, Mead, 1961.

Harris, Ben M. *Improving Staff Performance through In-service Education*. Boston: Allyn and Bacon, 1980.

———. *Supervisory Behavior in Education*, 2nd ed. Englewood Cliffs, N.J.: Prentice-Hall, 1975.

Harrison, Raymond H. *Supervisory Leadership in Education*. New York: American Book, 1968.

Leeper, Robert R., and Fred T. Wilhelms, eds. *Supervision: Emerging Profession*. Alexandria, Va.: Association for Supervision and Curriculum Development, 1969.

Lewis, Arthur J., and Alice Miel. *Supervision for Improved Instruction: New Challenges, New Responses*. Belmont, Calif.: Wadsworth, 1972.

Lovell, John T., and Kimball Wiles. *Supervision for Better Schools*, 5th ed. Englewood Cliffs, N.J.: Prentice-Hall, 1983.

Lucio, William H. *The Supervisor: New Demands, New Dimensions*. Alexandria, Va.: Association for Supervision and Curriculum Development, 1969.

——— and John D. McNeil. *Supervision in Thought and Action*, 3rd ed. New York: McGraw-Hill, 1979.

McKean, Robert C., and H. H. Mills. *The Supervisor*. New York: The Center for Applied Research in Education, 1964.

Marks, James R., Emery Stoops, and Joyce King-Stoops. *Handbook of Educational Supervision: A Guide for the Practitioner*, 2nd ed. Boston: Allyn and Bacon, 1978.

Mosher, Ralph L., and David E. Purpel. *Supervision: The Reluctant Profession*. Boston: Houghton Mifflin, 1972.

Neagley, Ross L., and N. Dean Evans. *Handbook for Effective Supervision of Instruction*, 3rd ed. Englewood Cliffs, N.J.: Prentice-Hall, 1980.

Raths, James, and Robert R. Leeper, eds. *The Supervisor: Agent for Change in Teaching*. Alexandria, Va.: Association for Supervision and Curriculum Development, 1966.

Sergiovanni, Thomas J., ed. *Supervision of Teaching*, 1982 Yearbook. Alexandria, Va.: Association for Supervision and Curriculum Development, 1982.

——— and Robert, J. Starratt. *Supervision: Human Perspective*, 2nd ed. New York: McGraw-Hill, 1979.

Spears, Harold. *Improving the Supervision of Instruction*. Englewood Cliffs, N.J.: Prentice-Hall, 1953.

Stoops, Emery, Max Rafferty, and Russell E. Johnson. *Handbook of Educational Administration.* Boston: Allyn and Bacon, 1975.

Sturges, A. W., chairman. *The Roles and Responsibilities of Instructional Supervisors.* Alexandria, Va.: ASCD Working Group on the Roles and Responsibilities of Supervisiors, Association for Supervision and Curriculum Development, 1978.

Subcommittee on National Security and International Operations. *Specialists and Generalists, A Selection of Readings.* Washington, D.C.: U.S. Government Printing Office, 1968.

Unruh, Adolph, and Harold E. Turner. *Supervision for Change and Innovation.* Boston: Houghton Mifflin, 1970.

Wiles, Jon, and Joseph Bondi. *Supervision: A Guide to Practice.* Columbus, Ohio: Charles E. Merrill, 1980.

Williams, Stanley W. *New Dimensions in Supervision.* Scranton, Pa.: Intext, 1972.

Wilson, L. Craig, T. Madison Byar, Arthur S. Shapiro, and Shirley H. Schell. *Sociology of Supervision: An Approach to Comprehensive Planning in Education.* Boston: Allyn and Bacon, 1969.

PART **II**

LEADERSHIP IN
THE IMPROVEMENT
OF INSTRUCTION

3

Helping Teachers to Plan for Instruction

OBJECTIVES

After studying Chapter 3 you should be able to accomplish the following objectives:

1. Describe your own model of instruction.
2. Demonstrate skill in following a systems approach to instructional design.
3. Demonstrate skill in following a model of instruction.
4. Demonstrate skill in writing instructional goals and objectives.
5. Demonstrate skill in applying taxonomies of instructional objectives.
6. Demonstrate skill in describing and analyzing learning tasks.
7. Demonstrate skill in organizing instructional plans.
8. Show acceptance of the necessity for adequate advance planning.

MODELS OF INSTRUCTION

Years ago a postcard arrived at my university address. The card came from an elementary school teacher who requested that a plan for the year's work be sent to her for use with her first graders. It apparently had not occurred to her in spite of whatever preservice training she had had that planning for instruction was her responsibility. She sought a ready-made, complete year's plan—to be given to her—with no knowledge of her school, her community, her pupils, and her own objectives.

With varying degrees of success every teacher education institution provides instruction in planning, primarily in its preservice training program. Students are taught basic techniques of planning and usually are given some opportunity for demonstrating their plans and putting them into practice.

However, the teacher education institution can simply offer an introduction to instruction, providing a foundation and limited practice in demonstrating teaching skills. These skills become refined as a teacher gains experience on the job. It is a central thesis of this book that all teachers, no matter how long they have taught, can develop new skills and improve old skills. As more becomes known about the instructional process with every passing year, newer and better ways of providing instruction are continuously being developed. It is the supervisor's function to assist teachers in becoming familiar with newer approaches to instruction and in developing and improving instructional skills.

The alert supervisor becomes aware of the extent of planning and the degree of proficiency in this skill shown by teachers who are to be supervised. It is not uncommon, for example, to find teachers with no written plans for instruction. Given the complexities of education today it would surely appear that some sort of written plan is in order and should be expected for each lesson a teacher presents.

Supervisors might begin to examine the problem of planning as they try to ascertain what kinds of plans are being made by teachers. As they spot deficiencies in planning, they may work with individuals or groups in devising better ways to go about this fundamental task.

The supervisor may encounter resistance to planning in a variety of forms. There are teachers who fully believe that they need not write anything down because they have sufficient mastery of the content of the program. They overlook the value of a written plan as a communication device for the learner to know what to expect from subsequent instruction.

Some teachers view their role in the Socratic tradition, hoping that young people will flock around them for unorganized bits of wisdom. Other teachers will readily admit that they realize the value of planning but rationalize that they do not have sufficient time to write plans. The supervisor needs to show that planning is a much more complicated and important phase of instruction than many teachers believe. There are many variables which conscientious teachers will have to consider as they begin to plan. Each group of pupils has varying abilities, needs, and interests. There is a seemingly inexhaustible pool of content from which to draw. Certain parameters such as the schedule and budgetary limitations must be considered, as well as expectations of other teachers, the public, school administrators, and even the state legislature. Faced with many methods or strategies for presenting a given lesson the teacher must make choices, knowing that some of these strategies are likely to be more effective than others for certain purposes, with certain groups, with certain individuals, in certain settings, and for the teacher's particular personality. Consequently, when the teacher jots down in a small plan book a reference to a particular chapter or exercise or topic and views that as an adequate lesson plan, he or she is ignoring many of the significant variables. It is possible for all teachers at all levels to improve planning skills and it is the supervisor's task to help them to improve these skills.

Simplified Model

Planning is the first stage of a continuum which is followed by the *implementation* or *presentation* stage and then goes into the *evaluation* stage. Some specialists in instruction would diagram the phases of the continuum as follows:

Planning → Presentation → Evaluation

They would refer to the diagram as a simplified model of instruction, which is a pattern providing teachers with a guide for following certain aspects of teacher behavior. The model indicates simply that the teacher begins the instructional process with initial planning, proceeds through the strategies of presentation of instruction, and moves finally to evaluating what the plan set out to achieve.

CLASSROOM PLANNING: A SIX-POINT PROGRAM

In practice, teachers become involved in planning on a school, district, state, regional, and national level—even on rare occasions on an international level. In this text stress is placed on planning that relates to curriculum and instruction at the classroom, school, and district levels and on the role of the supervisor in fostering curricular and instructional planning at those levels. This chapter considers techniques for the improvement of instruction in the individual teacher's classroom. Chapter 7 discusses faculty involvement in curriculum development on the various levels.

An effective classroom presentation requires a great deal of thought and preparation on the part of the teacher. To assist teachers with the task of planning the supervisor may embark on a six-point program. The supervisor can help teachers plan by providing training in the development of the following competencies:

1. skill in following a systems approach to instructional design
2. skill in following a model of instruction
3. skill in writing instructional goals and objectives
4. skill in applying taxonomies of instructional objectives
5. skill in describing and analyzing learning tasks
6. skill in organizing instructional plans

The supervisor should begin by surveying the degree to which these skills are possessed by the various teachers. Some teachers may possess a high degree of expertise in all these competencies. If that is the case, the supervisor, after verifying the fact that the teachers demonstrate these skills, encourages them to continue their good work and turns his or her attention to those teachers who need assistance in perfecting one or more of these skills. The supervisor may utilize the skilled teachers as models to emulate and may call on them to serve as resource persons to those teachers who need assistance. Since these skills involve concepts which are relatively new on the educational scene, such as a systems approach, instructional design, and the specification and classification of behavioral objectives, it is probable that the majority of teachers could profit from training in their development.

Following a Systems Approach to Instructional Design

No teacher today can long remain unaware of the existence of a concept called systems. Phrases like systems approach, systems view, and systems analysis have seeped into the educational language. The concept of systems and systems approach has been borrowed from the fields of industry and the military. The designs of weapons and industrial processes have followed principles of systems analysis. A new generation of educators has borrowed the principles of systems analysis and translated them into educational practice.

To explain in a somewhat oversimplified fashion, a systems approach seeks the answers to four questions: What is it that you wish to achieve? What resources do you have and need to achieve your objectives? How will you go about achieving your objectives? How well have you accomplished your objectives?

Whenever a teacher creates a course outline or lesson plan, he or she is engaging in instructional design. That design can be made more efficient and more effective by following a systems approach. The systems approach replaces a haphazard form of planning by requiring a careful examination of all the parts of a plan and how the parts relate to each other.

Though the systems approach to instruction is drawn from the complex worlds of industry and military science, its basic principles are rather simple. For our purposes a system is a planned, integrated, complete design for the use of materials, media, and personnel (input) in order to accomplish certain predetermined purposes (output). Each of the component parts of a system interrelates with the others, providing continuous feedback for modification of the system. A systems approach to instruction is the process of creating a systematic learning design in which all the component parts are specified, assembled, and interrelated.

Although the language of a systems approach is foreign to the realm of education, there need be nothing esoteric about it. A course is an instructional system. On a smaller scale a unit is an instructional system. On an even smaller scale a daily plan is an instructional system. When we hear an instructional specialist (a teacher or programmer) say, "The teacher should design a learning system," we may interpret this to mean, "The teacher should write a program (or course or unit or plan)—following principles of systematic design."

At this point let us take a quick overview of the systems approach to instruction by setting forth 10 steps in the process. Let us suppose for purposes of illustration that we wish to design a year's program in a particular subject or for a particular grade level. We might equally illustrate the process with a sequence of a particular curriculum extending over several years, for example, the language arts curriculum, or with a portion of a program extending over a few weeks or in abbreviated form a plan for a day or a class period. The steps which follow will give us a global look at the process. We will single out steps 1, 3, 4, and 6 for more extended treatment in this chapter. Because of their complexity we will devote greater attention to steps 7 and 8 separately in Chapter 4, and steps 5 and 9 in Chapter 5. The process of systems planning entails the following steps.

1. *Establishing a design for the system.* The teacher chooses a pattern or model of instruction to be followed. As we will see below, a number of models in current use provide a form or scheme for the teacher to follow and serve to indicate a logical sequence in planning.

2. *Taking stock of the present system.* The teacher reviews the present program, analyzes what has been covered in the past, and reexamines the current goals and objectives of the program. He or she examines the procedures for presenting the content, the varied resources which have been available, and the existing limitations. Decisions must be made whether the program fits into the total scheme of the curriculum and whether it meets the needs of the learners for whom the program is intended. Before redesigning an old program or designing a new program the teacher must consider the past and the present in order to plan for future instruction.

3. *Specifying the goals of instruction.* The teacher decides on the general purposes of the program. The goals provide a sense of direction for subsequent instruction and help the teacher to define the specific objectives.

4. *Specifying the objectives of instruction.* One of the most important phases of systems design is the specification of objectives, the specific outcomes of instruction. The objectives state what it is the learner is expected to learn, to accomplish, to do. They serve as the source of the evaluation process.

5. *Designing an evaluation plan.* The instructor must determine whether the presentations have been successful, must know whether students have mastered the content and whether they have reached the objectives set out at the beginning. The teacher may choose from a variety of evaluation techniques to find out how well students have achieved.

6. *Describing and analyzing the learning tasks.* If the learning tasks are complex ones, the teacher must break the tasks down and describe the sequence in which instruction is to be presented. He or she must know what skills the learners must bring to the tasks in order successfully to achieve the objectives and must analyze the tasks and decide whether they are appropriate for the particular group of learners who will be confronted with the material. The teacher must call on his or her knowledge of learning theory and decide what types or conditions of learning are involved in the pursuit of the tasks.

7. *Designing instructional procedures.* The teacher makes decisions about the strategies of instruction to be employed, choosing those instructional procedures which appear to have the best chance for success given the nature of the program, any constraints which have been imposed, and the nature of the learners. Techniques of instruction must be compatible with the teacher's own abilities and personality.

8. *Implementing the instructional procedures.* At this stage the design moves from thinking and planning to the actual process of instruction. The instructor meets with the learners and leads them in study of the content, then enters into a process of interaction—the learners interacting with the teacher and with each other and both the learners and the teacher interacting with the content.

9. *Implementing the evaluation plan.* Both during implementation of the instructional procedures and at the end of implementation the teacher puts the evaluation plan into operation and seeks to obtain continuous feedback as to whether the students are, indeed, learning the material and mastering the tasks. It is necessary to know whether students are successful not only for traditional purposes of evaluation but also for the purpose of modifying the instructional process.

10. *Redesigning the system.* The teacher utilizes feedback from evaluation in making revisions in the system, modifying the program and making changes. If the objectives are inappropriate for any reason, the objectives must be redesigned. If the data show that instructional procedures have been ineffective, different procedures must be tried. The systems approach permits, in fact mandates, that continuous redesign take place.

If we were to contrast older approaches to planning with the systems approach, we could note the following differences.

Systems Approach	*Older Approach*
Focus on learner's objectives, what the learner does	Focus on the teacher's objectives, what the teacher does
Objectives apparent before instruction begins	Objectives not apparent or apparent during instruction or after instruction
Continuous feedback	No feedback or feedback at the end of instruction
Continuous redesign	Redesign after instruction and for the next group of learners
Evaluation of all objectives	Evaluation of selected objectives
Achievement of the learner related to mastery of the objectives	Achievement of the learner related to achievement of other learners

The supervisor may wish to design an in-service training program which takes teachers through the 10 steps of the systems approach to instruction.

Following a Model of Instruction

Instructional designers follow a logical sequence of steps which they refer to as a model of instruction. A model is a pattern which provides a logical progression from one step to the next. Earlier in this chapter we became acquainted with a simplified model of instruction consisting of three components: planning, presentation, and evaluation. Models are normally shown in the literature on instruction as charts or schematic representations using a series of boxes, lines, and arrows. The simplified model of instruction above can be diagrammed as follows:

A model serves as a guide to the teacher for instructional design. It reveals both the essential elements of the instructional process and the sequence in which these elements are put into practice. Figure 3.1, a simplified model of instruction, however, is not an adequate guide. It is not detailed enough. It omits one or more essential elements and it does not show the important characteristic of feedback.

Figure 3.1 Simplified Model

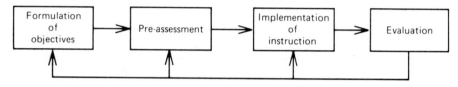

Figure 3.2 Four-part Model

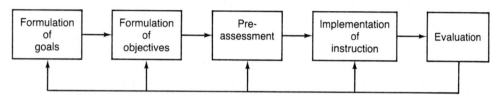

Figure 3.3 Five-part Model

Figure 3.1 can be expanded into a four-part model which is slightly more explicit in form and substance.

Robert J. Kibler et al. discussed a four-part model which they referred to as the General Model of Instruction.[1] W. James Popham and Eva L. Baker described a four-part model which they call a "Goal-Referenced Instructional Model."[2] We might convert the four-part model shown in Figure 3.2 by adding one block at the beginning labeled Formulation of Goals, as in Figure 3.3, thus creating a five-part model.

The Five-Part Model of Instruction calls for the formulation or specification of the goals and objectives of instruction. It incorporates an assessment of the learners' skills prior to initiating study of the subject matter. Evaluation of student achievement follows implementation or presentation of instruction. Feedback lines cycle back from Evaluation to the preceding stages. This model has the virtues of simplicity and adaptability to all subject areas.

The models found in the literature show many similarities in essential elements. They differ mainly in their detail and in the choice of components they emphasize. Some vary the sequence of components slightly while others are a bit more sophisticated. Some attempt to sketch every instructional act in the model itself. Bela H. Banathy singled out six parts of a design of an instructional system, that is, a model of instruction, shown in Figure 3.4.

Like the Five-Part Model of Instruction, Banathy's model starts off with a formulation of the objectives of instruction. Banathy then recommends as the next step the development of a terminal evaluation instrument—a test—based on the

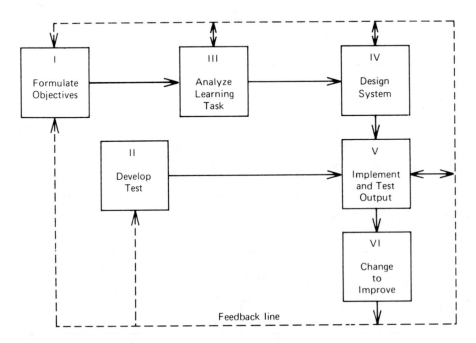

Figure 3.4   Banathy Model

SOURCE: Bela H. Banathy, *Instructional Systems*, Belmont, Calif., Fearon Publishers, 1981, p. 28. Reprinted with permission of Fearon Publishers.

objectives. The third step is a description of the content to be studied and an assessment of skills and knowledge the learners bring to the study of the content. The Five-Part Model of Instruction does not incorporate description of the learning task as an integral part of the model but does feature preassessment as an important feature. Banathy's fourth step calls for an analysis of what has to be done during the course of study, who will do each of the tasks, and in what time-frame tasks will be done. The fifth step involves both presentation of the content using selected instructional procedures and evaluation of the learners' achievement. The last step provides for redesign of the system.

Somewhat different from either the Banathy model or the Five-Part Model of Instruction is the instructional model (Figure 3.5) for the preparation of elementary school teachers developed at the Florida State University as a result of a grant from the United States Office of Education.

We may note again similarities of models as well as differences. The Florida State University model called attention at the beginning to the analysis of goals and the specification of instructional objectives. What is shown as pre-assessment in the Five-Part Model of Instruction appears as an analysis of learner status in the Florida State University model. Unlike the Banathy model, the Florida State University model does not depict the development of the terminal evaluation instrument immediately after formulation of the objectives. The differences in models are not so great as to recommend one model over the other. The important responsibility of the

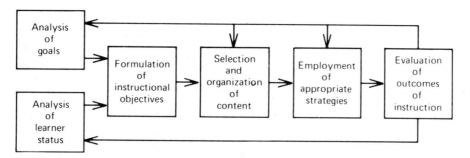

Figure 3.5 The Florida State University Model

SOURCE: G. Wesley Sowards, *A Model for the Preparation of Elementary School Teachers: Final Report.* Tallahassee, Fla., Florida State University, 1968.

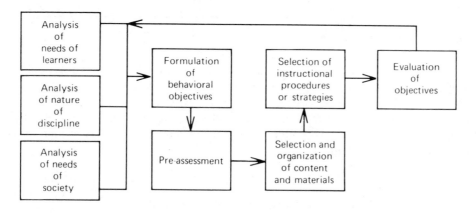

Figure 3.6 Oliva Model

SOURCE: Peter F. Oliva, *The Secondary School Today*, 2nd ed., New York, Harper & Row, 1972, p. 292.

teacher is to select a model compatible with his or her style of teaching or to create a model and follow that model in the design of instruction.

The teacher could combine components of various models and come up with a model such as shown in Figure 3.6.

We could even recast the steps in the process of systems planning which we discussed earlier in this chapter in the form of a model of instruction. Such a model could be charted as in Figure 3.7.

The feedback lines at the top and bottom of the model show that as a result of evaluation the component parts of the system may be redesigned.

It does not matter greatly which of the models of instruction a teacher follows, but for purposes of perfecting the skill of following a model it is preferable that the teacher select a model carefully and stick with it for a period of time. In this way an easy familiarity with the model can be developed which simplifies the planning process.

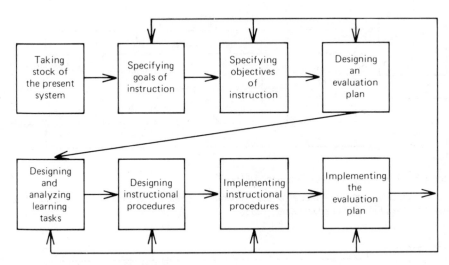

Figure 3.7 Alternative Systems Model

If supervisors are going to help teachers work with models of instruction, it is incumbent upon them to try out various models for themselves and see how they work in the actual process of instructional design. After analyzing models of instruction supervisors must help teachers become acquainted with various models, assist them in selecting models compatible to their own needs, and encourage them to try their own hands at creating a model.

Writing Instructional Goals and Objectives

The educational literature is peppered with the words "aims," "purposes," "goals," and "objectives." We hear and read about "the aims of education," "the purposes of American education," "goals of education for the twentieth century," and "objectives of secondary education." The terms are used interchangeably and loosely. It should be observed that in spite of the fact that the dictionary equates objective with goal, in instructional planning goal and objective are not necessarily the same and in my opinion should not be used interchangeably. For purposes of instructional design it is best to avoid using the words "aims" and "purposes." These terms should be relegated to philosophical discussions of education on a broad scale.

When some persons speak of goals, they mean the broad aims or purposes of education, which we might also refer to as educational goals. In this chapter we are not concerned with broad educational goals but rather with more limited instructional goals. Whereas educational goals may apply to the whole process of education and schooling, instructional goals apply only to particular content. We make a sharp distinction between goals and objectives as they apply to instruction and instructional design. Both relate to the instructional process and both are concerned with specific content.

Instructional goals may be thought of as general statements of hoped for learning on the part of the student. Goal statements contain such language as, "The student should become familiar with ...," "The student should become aware of ...," "The student should gain an understanding of ...," and "The student should develop an appreciation for...." These expressions cannot be evaluated with any degree of precision. In fact, these expressions may contain statements of outcomes which are not even observable, such as, "to develop an appreciation for. . . ." A teacher may or may not be able to discover whether a student has indeed developed an appreciation for the particular subject matter.

Goals provide the teacher with a general sense of direction. They are rough indicators of where instruction is taking the student. As such they are written in terms of the student and not the teacher. The teacher's goals may or may not be the same as the learners' goals. It must be remembered that the whole thrust of instructional design is on output, that is, achievement of the learner. For this reason statements of goals of instruction are put into the form of expectations on the part of the learner.

Let us illustrate some goal statements from a variety of disciplines:

The student should develop an appreciation for the music of Mozart by listening to recordings performed by the London Philharmonic Orchestra.*

As a result of study of Darwin's *Origin of Species* the student should better understand the basic principles of Darwin's theory of evolution.

The student should understand the role of a citizen in a democratic society.

The student should be able to evaluate critically the novels of James A. Michener.

When encountering persons of an ethnic group different from his or her own the student should have empathy for them.

The student should become acquainted with a variety of linguistic pattern drills.

The learner should understand the system of checks and balances written into the U.S. Constitution.

The pupil should learn the nines multiplication table.

The child should enjoy reading Dr. Seuss's books.

The student should develop an understanding of his or her role as a member of a family.

The learner should recognize the hazards of cigarette smoking.

The student should develop the ability to solve mathematical problems.

The student should comprehend the necessity for conservation of energy.

The pupil should learn to take responsibility as a member of a committee.

The pupil should understand why it is necessary to wash his or her hands before eating.

The student should know the differences between goals and objectives.

---

* Some teachers prefer *will* instead of *should*, as in "The student will develop an appreciation, etc." This text uses *should* in goal statements and *will* in objectives.

The verbs used in the above statements—understand, know, learn, appreciate, and recognize, for example—are nonbehavioral. That is, they do not tell exactly what it is the learner must demonstrate or do to show the teacher that the learner has accomplished what the teacher expected to be accomplished. Goals serve the useful purpose of giving direction to instruction, but their breadth, their lack of specific learner behavior, and their vagueness do not permit evaluation of the learner's mastery of content. The writing of instructional goals, however, is an important exercise, for it aids the teacher in deriving instructional objectives.

After pointing out the general direction of instruction by specifying the goals, the teacher turns to the task of deciding upon instructional objectives—the specific outcomes of learning.

Instructional objectives, alternately known as behavioral or performance objectives, state clearly expected behavior on the part of the learner. Instructional objectives differ from the goals in that they are written in terms of student performance which can usually be observed and measured. I employ the word "usually" advisedly, for when we enter the unexplored world of the affective domain it is not always possible to observe or measure expected student behavior.

Most instructional planners recommend that instructional objectives possess three characteristics:

1. *The expected behavior on the part of the learner*. The teacher must answer the question, "What will the student actually do to show that he or she has learned the material?" The teacher decides upon the expected behavior by examining the goals, by describing and analyzing the learning task, and by considering the world outside this class where the expected behavior may be applied. Following discussion of writing objectives the process of describing and analyzing learning tasks will be examined. At this point it may be said that a description and analysis of a learning task may cause a teacher to revise the behavioral objectives already specified.

The teacher should give some thought to the applicability of the behavior in situations outside the classroom both in the present and in the future. We are really talking about the problem of transfer of training. We must ask ourselves in what way the expected behavior may be of value to the learner either in other school situations or outside the school.

Whether the objectives are in the cognitive domain, the area of knowledge; the affective domain, the area of feeling; or the psychomotor domain, the area of perceptual-motor skills, the teacher should consider their usefulness beyond the walls of the classroom. Many objectives, particularly those of a cognitive nature, are useful at next higher levels of education. They are useful in the next grade, in an advanced sequence, or in a higher institution of learning. As such they are preparatory to additional and continuing education. Other objectives are useful in the learner's day-to-day life in the school, in the home, and in the community. Others are useful in part-time jobs while the learner is in school or in a full-time career after finishing school. It is relatively easy to see the transferability of instruction in auto mechanics, for example. Provided the instruction in auto mechanics has been adequate the learner can leave school, accept a job as an auto mechanic, and apply the skills learned in school. It is more difficult to explain the transferability—or relevancy—of study of Pizarro's conquest of Peru or of Giuseppe Verdi's opera *Rigoletto*.

Whenever possible, verbs used in statements of instructional objectives should reflect some overt behavior on the part of the learner. The words chosen should be action verbs such as *list, define, interpret, draw, analyze, compare, construct, organize, write, explain, produce, decide, classify, synthesize, type, summarize,* and *report.* While writing the objectives, the teacher should be thinking of ways to determine whether or not the learners achieve the objectives. The teacher's evaluation plan should begin to take shape in the mind while selecting objectives.

The supervisor can aid individual teachers and groups of teachers in writing goals and objectives by collecting and sharing with the teachers examples of nonbehavioral goals and behavioral objectives and asking teachers to distinguish between goals and objectives. The supervisor should demonstrate ways in which nonbehavioral goals can be translated into behavioral objectives by means of action words.[3]

2. *Conditions under which the learning takes place.* A complete behavioral objective stipulates the situational elements in which the learner works to fulfill the objective. The teacher specifies the tools the learner will use or the setting in which the learning experience goes on. For example, a mathematics teacher might decide upon the following behavioral objective: Given a pencil, ruler, paper, and compass the student will construct an isosceles triangle in five minutes. The pencil, ruler, paper, and compass, the tools with which the learner performs the task, are the conditions necessary for accomplishing this particular task. A business education teacher might wish the learners to be able to type 45 words per minute on an IBM electric typewriter with a maximum of two errors. The IBM electric typewriter is the condition written into this objective. Or, a science teacher may write the following objective: "In the science laboratory using paper, matches, a small ashtray, and a glass tumbler the student will demonstrate the fact that oxygen is necessary for combustion to take place."

Some of the experts on construction of performance objectives seem to show a preference for expressing conditions by starting with the word *Given.* Thus, you find such statements as, "Given a set of problems . . .," "Given a list of authors . . .," "Given a paper and pencil test. . . ." Although the use of the word Given followed by the conditions is one satisfactory way of stating conditions, it is by no means the only way. The exclusive use of Given tends to make the construction of behavioral objectives border on writing formulas rather than creative ideas. As a matter of fact, when the conditions are obvious, it is not necessary even to state them. For example, it is not necessary for the teacher to state, "Given a paper and pencil test. . . ." When the teacher prepares the test and distributes it, it becomes obvious that that is the condition imposed. Behavioral statements should include the conditions when the conditions are not readily apparent. The supervisor should avoid the pedantic or dogmatic position of insisting that all behavioral objectives contain written statements of conditions. Belaboring the obvious turns off teachers and discourages them from writing behavioral objectives.

3. *Level of mastery.* A behavioral objective should show or imply a level or degree of mastery of the behavior sought. The teacher should ask what quality of performance is expected of the learner. The teacher needs to specify the standard of performance unless that standard is an obvious one. Standards of performance may be expressed in the form of time to complete a task, number of correct responses,

number of errors permitted, or percentage of correct demonstrations of the behavior. For example, the earlier illustration, "Given a pencil, ruler, paper, and compass the student will construct an isosceles triangle in five minutes," contains a time standard—in five minutes. The illustration from the business education curriculum, "The student will type 45 words per minute on an IBM electric typewriter with a maximum of two errors," requires a two-part standard—45 words per minute with a maximum of two errors. The following example calls for a degree of mastery in terms of number of correct responses and percentage: "On this test of 25 items the student will achieve a score of at least 20 (80 percent)." The teacher could make the objective more demanding by adding a time element, as, "On this test of 25 items the student will achieve a score of at least 20 (80 percent) in 10 minutes."

When the standard is implied or obvious there is no necessity for writing it into the objective. Take the following example from the field of Spanish: "The student will be able to write with correct spelling the names of the months of the year." The statement includes two levels of mastery, one specified (correct spelling) and one implied (all twelve months). No standard need be written into the objective: "Define the word 'ethnic.' " The student's answer is either right or wrong. It would be superfluous or artificial to tack on "with 100 percent accuracy." Unless a teacher indicates differently, 100 percent mastery is expected, as in the illustration: "Given a series of measures in miles, the student will convert them to kilometers." The teacher is requiring the correct conversion of all items in the series.

Some objectives are so complex that it is a difficult or forced procedure for teachers to stipulate levels of mastery. It would take a rather lengthy description to write a standard for the objective: "Draw a graph showing the growth of population of California for the last decade." To spell out a standard for this objective the teacher would have to say something about the accuracy of figures used, the learner's skills in graphing, even the learner's artistic ability. There comes a point of diminishing return in terms of the time it would take a teacher to refine an objective to the point of including all standards. We must rely on the teacher's judgment for determining whether this objective has been achieved. A similar problem exists in a typical social studies learning task: "The student will present to the class his or her views on welfare payments to the poor." This objective involves personal views, informational content, and skills of oral presentation.

There are times when it is not possible to write a level of mastery. This is particularly true of objectives in the affective domain. It is of more than passing interest to note that much of the literature on behavioral objectives stresses the importance of affective learning and then proceeds to illustrate behavioral objectives in the cognitive and psychomotor domains. The implication is often left that writing affective objectives is analogous to writing objectives of a cognitive or psychomotor nature. Both conditions under which behavior is demonstrated and level of mastery can evade the teacher in the affective domain. What level of mastery might be required from the objective, "Respond to an appeal from fellow students by helping to collect food and clothing for needy families of the community"? This could be a very important learning. The appeal might be seen as the condition, but how much help and what kinds of help should be expected? It might be said simply that any degree of help would fulfill this objective. A teacher of environmental studies might desire that students "express disapproval of actions that pollute the air and water supplies." Under what conditions should this disapproval take place? What degree of disapproval is required?

Writing affective objectives is much more difficult than writing cognitive and psychomotor objectives. The expected behavior of the learner cannot always be observed when we are dealing with the affect. We cannot always be sure of the learner's feelings and attitudes. It cannot always be known under what conditions or to what degree he or she may show the desired behavior. The expected behavior, if it takes place at all, often takes place outside the classroom and outside the school. Sometimes the expected behavior does not occur until a long time after the learning experiences which sought to produce the behavior. This should not dissuade teachers, however, from writing affective objectives but make them realize that they need not strain to write conditions and levels which they can neither control nor predict with accuracy.

Most of the instructional specialists who have written on the subject of behavioral objectives have recommended three components in an objective: (1) the expected or terminal behavior, (2) the conditions under which the behavior takes place, and (3) the level of mastery which the learner is expected to demonstrate. Robert H. Davis, Lawrence T. Alexander, and Stephen L. Yelon suggested a fourth component.[4] They distinguished between performance standards, that is, level of mastery, and performance stability. They believed that a stability standard or criterion should be included to indicate the number of times the learner must perform the behavior at or above the performance standard. They provided two examples of objectives which contain both a performance standard and performance stability: "The student will run the 100-yard dash in 15 seconds, three out of five times." The expected behavior is "run the 100-yard dash." The performance standard is one of time—"in 15 seconds." The stability criterion is "three out of five times." The conditions under which the behavior is to be performed, incidentally, have been left out of the statement. It is assumed that the student will have a place to run and will probably have to be dressed properly for the activity. The second example reads: "The student will prepare and present three persuasive speeches (eight to ten minutes) on topics of his own choosing, using the Dewey Problem-Solving Format. He must change the attitude of at least 25 percent of the audience in two of the speeches." The expected behavior is the preparation and presentation of three persuasive speeches. The conditions specified are "eight to ten minutes," "topics of his own choosing," and "using the Dewey Problem-Solving Format." The performance standard is a change of attitude on the part of at least 25 percent of the audience. The performance stability criterion is two successful speeches out of three. Whether the expected behavior is one which can be achieved and how a change of attitude will be measured are problems separate from our immediate concern about the components of a behavioral objective. A supervisor may wish to acquaint teachers with the distinction between a performance standard and performance stability and suggest that a stability criterion be written into an objective when it seems plausible to do so.

Planning for instruction begins with the writing of instructional objectives. Since objectives are detailed and numerous in many cases, setting them down on paper is essential to avoid overlooking important ones and omitting significant learnings. Writing objectives is essentially a creative and thought-provoking activity. Different teachers will decide on different objectives. Each teacher brings to bear on this task all he or she knows about the learner, the subject, instruction, and society. The writing of instructional objectives is no simple task. It is an extremely important job, however, since all subsequent steps of the instructional process hinge upon the objectives which have been specified.

To help teachers with the planning process, the supervisor might institute an in-service program on the writing and use of instructional objectives. He or she might consider dividing this program into two distinct phases: (1) writing objectives following criteria described in this text or in other sources and (2) using objectives already developed elsewhere.

Some practice in writing objectives would be desirable to help teachers perfect the skill. It is probable that teachers have had some exposure (perhaps in some cases overexposure) to writing instructional objectives in their preservice training. If teachers are already familiar with the technique, they may apply the technique and develop objectives for their particular courses and grade levels. The objectives which they develop may be retained to build a local bank of objectives from which teachers may later draw. As a group activity the process of writing objectives can be beneficial when teachers examine, exchange, and present critiques of objectives written by their peers.

Since teachers and organizations in various parts of the country have been involved in developing instructional objectives in a variety of disciplines in recent years, the supervisor should acquaint the teachers with sources of objectives which have already been written.[5] The teachers would examine objectives in their fields of interest to see whether or not they meet the criteria for instructional objectives and to decide whether or not specific objectives would be useful in their own programs. This activity would be essentially a process of selection of objectives from a pool or pools of objectives which have already been prepared. We continue consideration of the skill of writing performance objectives in the following section of this chapter where we discuss taxonomies of instructional objectives.

Applying Taxonomies of Instructional Objectives

Earlier in this chapter we used the terms *cognitive domain*, *affective domain*, and *psychomotor domain*. Each domain implies a large area of related learnings. The cognitive domain encompasses learnings of a factual and intellectual nature; cognitive tasks are mental exercises leading to knowledge. The affective domain takes in learnings of an emotional nature; affective tasks produce feelings and attitudes toward things and people. The psychomotor domain comprises learnings which may require some cognition but are primarily skills which demand movement of parts of the body. Since psychomotor learnings involve both mental and bodily activity, they are often called perceptual-motor skills.

A task description and analysis, discussed later in this chapter, will reveal whether the learning tasks are primarily those of the cognitive, affective, or psycho-motor domain. The content of a given course may include learnings from all three domains. The supervisor should encourage teachers to write objectives in all three domains whenever all three are applicable. Since cognitive and psychomotor objectives are the most apparent, affective objectives are often overlooked by teachers. Of course, not all content will lead to outcomes in all three domains. On the other hand, much of the content studied in school is of such a nature that learnings in at least two and often all three of the domains should be sought.

It soon becomes evident to an experienced teacher that not all learnings of a given domain are of equal merit. Some learnings are more complex than others. Some are more important than others in terms of their significance to the learner and their permanency. Some learnings are clearly of a lower level of competence than other learnings.

The three domains have been subjected to study for the purpose of answering the questions: What categories of learnings may be classified in each domain? What is the order of importance of each category? In 1956 Benjamin S. Bloom et al. published a classification system—a taxonomy—of educational, i.e., instructional, objectives in the cognitive domain.[6] Krathwohl and others produced a system in 1964 for classifying objectives in the affective domain.[7] A taxonomy of objectives in the psychomotor domain by Elizabeth Jane Simpson appeared in 1972.[8] These taxonomies have been widely cited and implemented.

In the discussion which follows I have described each domain and given three examples of instructional objectives in each major category of each domain. The first example in each category of all three domains is drawn from the same learning unit so that we can trace objectives on one theme through all levels of all three domains. In order to follow a topic through all three domains I have had to choose a unit from a discipline in which psychomotor learnings are sought as well as cognitive and affec-tive. I have, therefore, turned to a unit at the secondary school level on impression-ist painters.

The second examples illustrate a theme through all levels of two domains: the cognitive and affective. For this series of illustrations I have selected the topic of federal income tax applicable to a course in consumer education at the junior or senior high school level. Psychomotor learnings are of little importance in studying federal income tax. This same theme, therefore, cannot be carried through the psychomotor taxonomy. A unit on tumbling in physical education at the elementary, junior, or senior high school level furnishes the second examples of psychomotor objectives.

The third examples are taken from many disciplines of the elementary and secondary school; there is no relationship among the third examples across domains or at any levels within a domain. The third examples are a miscellaneous collection of objectives which serve as additional illustrations.

The Bloom Taxonomy

The Bloom taxonomy of the cognitive domain set forth six general categories.[9] From the lowest level to the highest these categories are:

1. Knowledge
2. Comprehension
3. Application
4. Analysis
5. Synthesis
6. Evaluation

The taxonomy further subdivides each of the above categories into subcategories according to levels of importance but it will serve our purposes to confine discussion to the six major categories. The taxonomy says, in effect, those instructional objectives which are designed to seek only the acquisition of knowledge are at the lowest level of both complexity and importance. It is no secret to anyone who has ever gone to school that most of the learnings sought are in the cognitive domain and that most of those learnings hover around the low end of the taxonomy. All a supervisor needs to do to verify this point is to examine several tests given by teachers and he or she will see how frequently learners are asked to recall specific factual information as opposed to interpreting, applying, analyzing, synthesizing, and evaluating data. A supervisor needs to help teachers to write higher-level objectives. Let's illustrate what behavioral objectives look like at each level of the Bloom system of classification.

1. Knowledge
   a. The student will name four impressionist painters.
   b. The student will give the number of the short form used for filing his or her federal income tax statement.
   c. On an outline map of the United States showing the Great Lakes the student will print the name of each lake in its proper location.
2. Comprehension
   a. The student will explain what is meant by *impressionism*, citing the chief characteristics of this school of painting.
   b. The student will tell the difference between an *exemption* and a *deduction* as applied to the federal income tax.
   c. Given a graph showing the increase in population of the state of Arizona for the last 30 years, the student will interpret to his or her classmates the facts shown by the graph.
3. Application
   a. From a series of reprints of classical and modern paintings and applying characteristics studied in class the student will select those which are the works of impressionist painters.
   b. Given a set of data, the student will correctly calculate the tax due the federal government using the appropriate tax table.
   c. The student will correctly solve 8 out of 10 problems in long division.
4. Analysis
   a. The student will examine reprints of one painting of an impressionist painter and one painting of a nonimpressionist painter and contrast the differences in the styles of the two painters.

     b. Given a completed 1040 tax form the student will determine whether there are any errors in filling out the form and whether the tax due has been calculated correctly.

     c. The student will watch several commercials on television and decide whether they meet the standard of "truth in advertising."

5. Synthesis

     a. The student will write a biography of an impressionist painter.

     b. The student will fill out a 1040A tax form using data furnished by the teacher.

     c. The student will produce a documented research paper on the effects of drugs on the human body.

6. Evaluation

     a. The student will examine a reprint of a painting by a lesser-known impressionist and evaluate it as to the quality of the work, applying characteristics studied in this unit.

     b. From background data about a fictitious taxpayer and a completed income tax return the student will evaluate the deductions taken by the taxpayer and decide whether he or she was entitled to all the deductions claimed. The student will give reasons for all decisions.

     c. The student will read a short story by O. Henry and evaluate it in respect to (1) mood, (2) vocabulary burden, and (3) impact on the reader.

Although I have used the style, "The student will . . .," in each of the preceding examples, teachers may prefer an abbreviated style which is equally acceptable. "The student will" can simply be omitted, leaving, for example, "Name four impressionist painters;" "Given a graph showing the increase in population of the state of Arizona for the last 30 years, interpret to your classmates the facts shown by the graph."

It would be possible for a teacher or group of teachers to develop their own classification system. They might create, for example, a simplified system consisting of two levels: low-order objectives and high-order objectives.[10] However, since the Bloom taxonomy has been with us for many years and has been widely followed with considerable success, it provides a ready-made guide which teachers might well choose to follow. In either case the object is to raise the level of behavioral objectives to a higher order than is commonly found in many classrooms.

We should point out that in all of the three taxonomies discussed in this chapter objectives may overlap levels of each domain. Each level within a domain builds on the preceding level, adding a degree of complexity with each ascending step in the hierarchy. It is difficult, sometimes impossible, and not always necessary for a given objective to fit precisely and clearly within one level. The important understanding which we should hold is that the thrust of the objectives should be upward in each hierarchy.

The Krathwohl Taxonomy

Krathwohl and his colleagues enumerated five levels in their classification of objectives in the affective domain.[11] These categories are:

1. Receiving
2. Responding
3. Valuing
4. Organization
5. Characterization by value or value complex

Like the Bloom taxonomy, the Krathwohl classification breaks each major category down into subcategories in a hierarchy from low to high level. As we have done in the discussion of the Bloom taxonomy we will illustrate by referring only to the major categories and rely on the reader to consult the taxonomies for the detailed subdivisions of each category. Following are examples of objectives for each of the five categories.

1. Receiving
   a. The student will demonstrate in conversation an awareness of impressionistic art which he or she encounters in daily life.
   b. The student will evidence an awareness of the need for paying one's federal income tax and the consequences of not filing when required to do so.
   c. The student will show an awareness of the fact that the American Indian has suffered at the hands of the white settlers of America.
2. Responding
   a. The student will choose and read a book on impressionism.
   b. The student will observe the deadline for filing his or her tax return.
   c. The student will volunteer to serve on a committee for a class project.
3. Valuing
   a. The student will express an appreciation for the contributions of the impressionists to our aesthetic life.
   b. The student will support the income tax system by pointing out worthwhile government expenditures financed by tax revenues.
   c. The student will defend physical fitness exercises.
4. Organization
   a. The student will decide whether he or she likes impressionist painting and what the characteristics are which cause him or her to like it or dislike it.
   b. The student will analyze the reasons why some persons cheat on their income tax returns and decide whether he or she approves or disapproves of this behavior.
   c. The student will account for his or her reasons for subscribing to a particular moral value.
5. Characterization by value or value complex
   a. The student will express a positive predisposition toward the fine arts as an enrichment of our lives.
   b. The student will consistently demonstrate honesty in paying his or her income tax.
   c. The student will develop the habit of collecting facts before making a decision.

The preceding illustrations show some of the inherent problems of affective objectives. Some of the objectives are both unobservable in school and unmeasurable. We cannot know for sure whether the student in affective category 2b. above, for example, will indeed file an income tax return. The student can tell the teacher that he or she is aware of the laws requiring the filing of income tax returns, and can express agreement with the need for a federal income tax and measures to enforce the laws. We have no way of knowing, however, whether the student has complied with the law. We do know, of course, that there is often a discrepancy between what people profess to do and what they actually do.

Few people would argue the importance of learnings such as those illustrated in the five categories of the affective domain. Affective objectives can point the way toward hoped for ends. The fact that students may achieve the affective objectives, if not immediately perhaps in the future, makes these types of objectives worth writing. A caution is raised at this point to which we will return in the discussion of the evaluation of instruction in Chapter 5. Unless an affective objective is structured in such a way that it can be both observed and measured, it cannot be evaluated and scored in the same way as cognitive and psychomotor learnings.

The Simpson Taxonomy

More recent is the Simpson classification of instructional objectives in the psychomotor domain. Simpson recommended a classification system consisting of seven categories.[12] Her major categories from lowest to highest are:

1. Perception
2. Set
3. Guided response
4. Mechanism
5. Complex overt response
6. Adaptation
7. Origination

Anita J. Harrow, who also created a taxonomy of the psychomotor domain, suggested that Simpson's category of perception may be considered as interpreting; set as preparing; guided response as learning; mechanism as habituating; complex overt response as performing; adaptation as modifying; and origination as creating.[13] The following examples serve to illustrate the Simpson scheme for classifying psychomotor objectives.

1. Perception
   a. The student will perceive the visual impact (blurred effect, dots) of impressionist painting.
   b. The student will recognize the mat as appropriate equipment for demonstrating skill in tumbling.
   c. The student will identify the sound of the piano.

2. Set
   a. The student will demonstrate how to hold a paintbrush.
   b. The student will demonstrate the correct stance from which to begin tumbling.
   c. The student will demonstrate the proper way to hold the clarinet.
3. Guided response
   a. The student will imitate the teacher's demonstration of mixing water colors.
   b. The student will imitate the teacher's demonstration of tumbling.
   c. Following directions on the box the student will mix a batch of batter for pancakes.
4. Mechanism
   a. The student will mix water colors to prepare the shades he or she will use in copying a reprint of a classical landscape or seascape.
   b. The student will perfect proper form by practicing several tumbles each of which the teacher will critique.
   c. The student will sand manually the top of a small wooden table.
5. Complex overt response
   a. The student will copy a reprint of a classical landscape or seascape.
   b. The student will do a triple tumble, demonstrating proper form at the beginning, while tumbling, and in regaining standing position.
   c. The student will transcribe dictation which has been recorded on a dictating machine.
6. Adaptation
   a. The student will paint a second copy of the same reprint of a classical landscape or seascape converting it to impressionist style.
   b. The student will introduce a variation on the tumbling exercise taught by the teacher.
   c. The student will convert a popular ballad or classical theme to disco beat (using any musical instrument).
7. Origination
   a. The student will do an original painting in water color or in oils in impressionist style.
   b. The student will create a new exercise using the mat without additional props.
   c. The student will create and build a model house of original design and of unusual building materials.

Each succeeding category from perception to organization demands a higher degree of skill from the simplest to a complex set of skills. Some of the psychomotor objectives—mainly in the category of perception—are mastered during preschool years. Psychomotor skills share with cognitive learnings the fact that it is somewhat easier to write conditions and levels of mastery into these kinds of objectives than into affective objectives. Some of the examples above specify conditions; others merely imply them. Many of the examples but not all of them imply a level of mastery—right or wrong, correct or incorrect.

It becomes clear on examination of all three taxonomies that they are not discrete and mutually exclusive. Learnings often cut across all domains. All perceptual-motor skills contain elements of cognition and often of the affect. Affective objectives require mastery of cognitive and often psychomotor learnings. The cognitive domain may reach into the affective and many times the psychomotor. The whole area of language learning, for example, may bounce back and forth among the three domains. When the student completes a sentence correctly whether written or oral, he or she may be at the same time in all domains. Knowledge of the correct grammatical form and sentence structure places the student in the cognitive domain. Pleasure at giving the right response and being rewarded for it by the teacher's approval leads the student into the affective domain, while the physical action of writing or moving vocal chords, tongue, and lips puts the student in psychomotor territory.

The teacher should, therefore, classify instructional objectives under the domain which seems to be the primary nature of the task. A workshop on the classification of instructional objectives and the application of a system of classification to instructional planning could be a valuable in-service program for a supervisor to organize.

Describing and Analyzing Learning Tasks

Task Description

A task description and analysis of each instructional objective (i.e., the task) are helpful to the teacher in refining planning. Some instructors combine the concepts of task description and task analysis and think in terms simply of task analysis; others distinguish between them. Davis, Alexander, and Yelon clearly separated description of a task from analysis.[14] A task description is a determination of the steps or sequence in which a learning task is studied. A task analysis, according to Davis et al., is the identification of characteristics of the learner, the types of learning involved, and the conditions or constraints imposed. This distinction between description and analysis is a useful one.

Certain tasks must be taught in a step-by-step procedure. It is desirable for the teacher to describe that procedure before attempting to present the content. The concept of task description is more useful in some content areas than in others, being particularly helpful in developing competencies in the psychomotor domain. Complex perceptual-motor skills must often be taught in a particular sequence of steps. For example, there are generally accepted sequences for teaching the following:

- baking a cake
- refinishing a table top
- parallel parking
- cleaning a rifle
- repairing an automobile generator
- drawing a blood specimen
- making a papier-mâché figure

- laying vinyl tiles
- filling out an airline ticket and reserving space for a customer
- developing film
- cutting a piece of lumber with an electric hand-saw

These tasks involve both mental and manual skills. To accomplish the tasks correctly the learner must follow a particular or fixed sequence of steps. Let us describe the task of parallel parking by listing the steps which must be followed. Let's assume that we have the car in motion and spot a parking space which requires us to demonstrate this skill. The driver's handbook furnished by a state's Department of Motor Vehicles will furnish an excellent illustration of a description of the task of parallel parking. The required steps are as follows and woe be to the applicant for a driver's license who does not follow them exactly:

1. Stop even with car ahead and about two feet away from it.
2. Turn wheels sharply right and back slowly toward the car behind.
3. As your front door passes the back bumper of car ahead, quickly straighten the wheels and continue to back straight.
4. When clear of car ahead turn wheels sharp left and back slowly to car behind.
5. Turn wheels sharp right and pull toward center of parking space.
6. Put gear in park position.
7. Set parking brake.
8. Shut off motor.
9. Remove key from switch.

We hypothesized a car in motion for a specific reason—to show a single sequence of steps. Let us suppose for a moment that the car is parked in the driveway and that we wish to give Junior—who has a learner's permit—a real test before he goes for the driver's license examination by having him drive downtown and parallel park. Junior would have to demonstrate several series of steps. In a fixed order he would have to:

1. Start the car.
2. Back out of the driveway.
3. Drive straight ahead.
4. (Possibly) Pass a car.
5. Make right and left turns.
6. Respond to signal lights and road signs.
7. Parallel park.

Each of these skills requires its own particular sequence of steps. A driver-training instructor would need to describe each sequence.

Task descriptions are less common, less necessary, and less readily apparent in the cognitive and affective domains. The task description is obvious when a student is called upon to "list the names of the five leading oil-producing nations of the world." There is no sequence involved in a simple cognitive task of this type. An element of sequence might be provided by asking the students to list the nations in the order of number of barrels of oil they produce annually but that is not a sequence of steps to be followed in mastering the objective.

In the affective area of learning it is almost impossible to describe a fixed sequence of steps. What would be the sequence of steps for the affective objective that seeks to have a student "demonstrate empathy for an ethnic group different from his or her own by writing an essay which supports the ethnic group's desire for improved conditions of living"? Students will approach this task in a variety of ways.

Some of the more complex cognitive tasks may lend themselves to task description if there is a generally accepted sequence which most experts follow. Solving types of mathematical problems is an illustration of a complex cognitive task which can be described. For example, suppose that we wish to teach pupils to multiply one factor (the multiplicand) by another factor (the multiplier) of three digits. We might ask the student to demonstrate ability to perform this task by requiring him or her to multiply $2{,}326 \times 247$.

$$
\begin{array}{r}
2326 \\
\times\ \ 247 \\
\hline
16282 \\
9304\ \ \\
4652\ \ \ \ \\
\hline
574522
\end{array}
$$

Though the operation can be done rather mechanically, the learner should be taught that a particular sequence of steps is being followed. The steps are:

Step 1: multiply 2326 by 7	$2326 \times\ \ \ 7 = \ \ 16282$
Step 2: multiply 2326 by 40	$2326 \times\ \ 40 = \ \ 93040$
Step 3: multiply 2326 by 200	$2326 \times 200 = 465200$
Step 4: add 16282, 93040, and 465200	574522

There is likely to be agreement among mathematicians that these four steps are the proper ones in teaching this learning task. If there is no agreed upon correct sequence for performing a learning task, the teacher can still make his or her own task description which would show the learner the sequence to follow.

A foreign language specialist in a teacher education institution, for example, might wish students in a methodology class to teach some principles of grammar by means of a selected number of oral pattern drills. Although there is no particular sequence to this task, and variations in sequence might occur from instructor to instructor, the specialist would undoubtedly want the students to begin the study of this task with the simpler kinds of drills and proceed to the more complex.

The instructor might phrase the performance objective: "In the methodology class before peers the student will demonstrate during one class period four different types of pattern drills for teaching points of grammar." For students to reach this stage the instructor must teach them the various types of pattern drills and break the task down into four steps:

Step 1: Work on simple analogy drills.
Step 2: Work on item-substitution mutation drills.
Step 3: Work on fixed-increment drills.
Step 4: Work on paired-sentence drills.

The instructor next recasts the steps of the description into behaviorally stated subobjectives, which are often referred to as enabling objectives or, simply, enablers. They are the subcompetencies which must be mastered before the major objective, the competency, itself is attempted. In behavioral terms the enabling objectives may be stated:

1. The student will construct and present orally in class a simple analogy drill.
2. The student will construct and present orally in class an item-substitution mutation drill.
3. The student will construct and present orally in class a fixed-increment drill.
4. The student will construct and present orally in class a paired-sentence drill.

By highlighting the steps in a learning task a description of the task makes it easier to identify the subobjectives that must first be achieved by the learners. The description also helps to refine the major learning task itself.

Though a teacher may often write task descriptions even if the experts in the discipline are in disagreement on the order in which learning should be presented, it is not always possible or desirable for the teacher to attempt a task description for every kind of learning task. It is questionable whether there can be or should be a fixed progression of steps in such activities as suggesting ways to solve the nation's energy problems, writing a poem, designing the floor plan of a house, doing an original painting in water colors, or composing a song. These learnings appear to be of a creative nature, cutting across the cognitive, affective, and psychomotor domains. To try to establish a fixed order for which learnings of this type are undertaken could result in squelching the very creativity they are designed to foster.

Task Analysis

Task analysis follows task description. After the steps of the task have been determined, the teacher examines the nature of the task, seeking answers to such questions as: What is the background of the learners who will encounter the task? Do they have the necessary prerequisite skills for beginning study of the topic? What skills do learners really need to be successful in mastering the content? In this regard the supervisor should help teachers develop the ability to assess prerequisite (entry) skills, a topic considered in Chapter 5, on the evaluation of instruction.

The teacher's analysis proceeds by identifying the kind of learning involved in the task so the best choice of teaching procedures for presenting the content can be made. Some preservice or in-service training in learning theories and their application in the classroom is essential for this task. Learning theory would be a very appropriate topic for an in-service program arranged by a supervisor. To help the supervisor recognize types of learning Robert M. Gagné's categories might be used as a guide.[15] Gagné has classified what he referred to as conditions of learning from simplest to most complex types. Gagné's classification includes eight types of learning. In very brief summary form these types are:

1. *Signal learning.* This is classical conditioning—the formation of conditioned responses to planned or unplanned stimuli. Experiments of the Russian scientist Ivan Pavlov to train a dog to salivate at the ringing of a bell are the classic illustrations of this type of learning. Fear of thunder is a conditioned response. Somewhere in the past the individual heard a sudden clap of thunder which was followed by a fright reaction—perhaps a scream—of another person which provoked a fear reaction. Although teachers need to be aware of both positive and negative kinds of conditioning which may be going on in school, signal learning has little place in planned school instruction.

2. *Stimulus-response learning.* This type of learning is also known as operant conditioning and appears to be particularly relevant to the development of motor learning of animals and young children. Gagné illustrated this type of learning with examples of a person teaching a dog to shake hands and someone teaching a child to say "mama." He pointed out that reinforcement of the desired response is an important feature. Gagné observed that it is difficult to find pure examples of this type of learning in humans. What appears to be stimulus-response learning in humans is more likely to be chaining (type 3) or verbal association (type 4).

3. *Chaining.* Gagné limited chaining to motor learning and described it as connecting a series of stimulus-response links. To perform a complex motor skill successfully the learner must complete the individual stimulus-response links—or subskills—in a particular order. Applying a tourniquet to stop bleeding furnishes a good illustration of chaining. To stop the bleeding, each of the stimulus-response links must be followed in order:

STIMULUS	RESPONSE
Sight of person bleeding	Desire to stop the bleeding
Pad and strip of cloth or piece of cloth alone if no pad available	Place pad over artery which is bleeding, put cloth over pad and around limb between wound and body, tie cloth over pad
Stick	Slip stick under the cloth next to the limb and turn stick, tightening cloth until bleeding stops
Bleeding stopped	Note time tourniquet applied and take person to doctor

4. *Verbal association.* This type of learning is similar to chaining but differs in that it applies to verbal learning. Verbal association involves the connecting of a series of verbal links—a verbal chain. The naming of objects and the memorization of

passages are examples of verbal association. A two-link verbal chain can be shown in teaching youngsters the name of the geometric figure *rectangle*.

STIMULUS	RESPONSE
Picture of a rectangle or an actual rectangular object	Observation of the picture or object
Teacher says the word *rectangle*	Pupils repeat the word *rectangle*

The test of the pupils' learning would be to see if they recognize rectangles when they are next presented to them.

A three-part verbal chain can be illustrated in teaching both a noun and its definite article in Spanish:

STIMULUS	RESPONSE
Picture of a church	Pupils observe picture
Teacher says *iglesia*	Pupils repeat *iglesia*
Teacher says *la iglesia*	Pupils repeat *la iglesia*

If the pupils have mastered the noun and the article, they will be able to repeat *la iglesia* when the teacher next shows them a picture of a church.

5. *Discrimination learning.* Human beings master a large number of motor and verbal chains many of which, though distinct, are at the same time similar. Learners discriminate, for example, when they learn to distinguish the different skills required in driving a car with automatic transmission, a car with standard stick transmission, a car with "four on the floor," and a trailer-truck. Pupils who have learned separate verbal chains for *rectangle*, *square*, and *triangle* must learn to discriminate among these figures. Pupils who have been taught that *iglesia* means *church* and *la iglesia* means *the church* must distinguish churches from other buildings, must recognize churches as a class even though each church may be architecturally different, and must repeatedly use *la* with the noun and not *el*, which they have seen in other verbal chains. They must further recognize that *la* when used as an article means *the* and not something else. In spite of the fact that they have been exposed to hundreds of other verbal chains for other words they must always remember that the word *iglesia* means *church*.

6. *Concept learning.* We get into a higher order of learning when we seek to teach learners concepts. Concepts are abstractions—some more abstract than others—which require the medium of language for their learning. The property of a rectangle—its rectangularness—is a concept. The color blue and the number three are concepts. An office building is a concept which differs from the concept, school building. First, last, and always are concepts, as are north and south, up and down, large and small, left and right. Concepts may refer to concrete objects such as a football, to properties of objects such as the color red, and to ideas such as democracy. Brotherhood, excellence, and honesty are concepts. Students must have the necessary mastery of language to be able to understand concepts. The beauty of language is that it permits us to talk about concepts and to communicate these abstractions to others. We do not need the football to talk about it. We do not have to be in the presence of an office building to discuss it. We cannot even see the concept of honesty

but we know what traits an honest person exhibits and can communicate those traits to others. Much of the instruction in school involves teaching concepts.

7. *Rule learning.* A rule is a chain of concepts. The learner puts together the relationship between concepts and formulates a rule or principle. We are constantly teaching rules in school. The science instructor teaches learners that litmus paper turns red when dipped into an acid. Three concepts are involved in this rule: litmus paper, acid, and red. The relationship between the litmus paper and the acid is the action of turning red. We teach the principle that yellow plus blue makes green. We teach that $a^2 + b^2 = c^2$. Pupils learn that *la* in Spanish is used with feminine words and *el* with masculine. Students learn that life insurance is a way of protecting one's family. We teach that some drugs have a harmful effect on the health of the individual. Rule learning brings out the relationships and applications of the concepts which are linked together to form the rule.

8. *Problem solving.* This is the highest-order and most complex type of learning. The problem-solving process is the development of the ability to think. The learner puts to use all the rules learned which have a bearing on a particular problem in order to seek a solution to that problem, and in the process generates new rules and new knowledge. Problem solving is the process of reasoning. In other contexts problem solving is equated with the scientific method. Each attempt at problem solving reveals new ideas and adds to the store of knowledge which may in turn be applied to the solution of subsequent problems. The various disciplines teem with illustrations of both successful and unsuccessful attempts to solve problems such as the discovery of cures for smallpox, undulant fever, and polio; the search for ways to convert garbage into energy, more effective means of providing for the nation's housing needs, combating crime, growing disease-resistant grain, and piecing together the origin of the human species.

We have reviewed these eight types of learning in order to help teachers recognize the different types of learning evident in their learning tasks. A supervisor should study a classification system of types of learning such as Gagné's in order to help teachers make task analyses.[16]

A task analysis should include in addition to a review of the learners' characteristics and identification of type of learning an appraisal of any special conditions or constraints under which the learning tasks will be experienced. The teacher should ask: Do the tasks require special equipment or other resources? Can the tasks be performed in the space provided? Are there time constraints? Are there limitations imposed by the school, the community, or the state? If we may go back to our example of parallel parking and place it as a topic in a driver education course, we might analyze this task in the following manner:

1. *Nature of the learners.* The learners must be of age to obtain a learner's permit to drive. They must possess sufficient physical coordination skills to handle an automobile. They must know the rules of the road and recognize road signs.
2. *Type of learning.* This task is primarily chaining, the development of a series of perceptual-motor skills.

3. *Special conditions and constraints.* The students must have obtained their learners' permits. Assuming a class of 25 students the teacher can allot only one half-hour of actual practice in parallel parking to each student. The school must possess a driver education automobile which is fully insured and equipped with dual controls.

By understanding the nature of the task the teacher is more likely to realize the goal of instruction—mastery of the content by the learners. Task description and analysis aid the teacher in designing enabling objectives and in perfecting the main objective itself. The supervisor can serve as a consultant to teachers who wish to develop the skills of task description and analysis.

Organizing Instructional Plans

At some point the teacher must assemble the various products of planning, must put it all together in some form of comprehensive plan. We are concerned in the remaining pages of this chapter with types of plans which will be put to immediate use in the classroom, and defer discussion of broader plans such as curriculum guides to Chapter 7.

To begin to organize his or her plans the teacher looks at the content: knowledge, skills, and affective outcomes as a whole and the time available for presenting that content to the students. A year, a half year, a quinmester of nine weeks, or possibly six weeks may be available for dealing with the particular subject matter. The next step is to break that content into its principal topics. It is conceivable that a teacher would need the entire time to treat one topic. It is most likely, however, if the period of time is a long one, several topics can be covered. The teacher should estimate the amount of time necessary for most—and hopefully all—of the students to master the material.

Unit Plans. After identifying the topics and the time available for each topic, the teacher proceeds to create a type of plan known as a unit, learning unit, or teaching unit, sometimes referred to as a module. A unit or module is a segment of an instructional program. If mastery of one unit is dependent upon mastery of previous units, the units must be put into sequence. The unit could follow a number of formats. Drawing on the earlier discussion of models of instruction we can devise a functional format such as the one below:

1. *Goals.* At the beginning of each unit the teacher should state the nonbehavioral instructional goals.
2. *Objectives.* Following the goals should come the instructional objectives. The objectives and subobjectives should be stated behaviorally, classified, and grouped by domain.
3. *Preassessment.* The teacher should indicate what procedures are to be used to answer the question: Do the students already possess the knowledge and

skills which the teacher plans to develop in the unit? This information is needed so that the teacher may alter the content or choose different content if the pupils demonstrate they have already sufficiently mastered the content to be studied. The teacher must also specify the entry skills, if any, needed in order to successfully begin study of the unit and the means by which possession of the prerequisite skills would be determined.

4. *Instructional procedures.* In this part of the unit the teacher should detail the learning strategies to be used to present the material and the human and material resources needed. The following chapter of this text, on presentation of instruction, is designed to help the supervisor work with teachers in the selection of instructional procedures.

5. *Resources.* The teacher should list the physical and human resources which will be used in the unit.

6. *Evaluation.* The final section of the unit is devoted to evaluation techniques. The teacher chooses those techniques most appropriate to the content and the learners and writes whatever tests are to be used to measure student achievement. Chapter 5 will explore some ways to help teachers evaluate instruction.

The unit outline suggested here is general enough to be adaptable to a broad range of the curriculum: elementary and middle school content; segments of a high school discipline; mini-courses (for example, Purchasing Life Insurance); interdisciplinary topics (for example, Homes of the Colonial Period); and even phases of the extra-class program of the middle, junior high, and senior high schools.

Although the six points covered in the suggested unit format may apply in planning in most fields and at most levels of learning, there will be variations in the substance, extent, and complexity of plans from teacher to teacher and from program to program. While a unit plan in the social studies, for example, would be quite different from a unit plan in skill areas such as typing, gymnastics, or instruction in playing the clarinet, and in creative areas such as art, writing, and other crafts, teachers in all areas need to spell out goals, objectives, preassessment techniques, instructional procedures, resources, and evaluation techniques on more than a day-to-day basis. A unit plan requires the teacher to look at instruction on a longer-range basis than the next day's work. The supervisor should help teachers to find a planning format which is compatible with their own disciplines or grade levels.

If the unit is primarily for the teacher's use and is not to be put into the hands of the pupils, the teacher has the choice of incorporating tests under the appropriate section—preassessment or evaluation—or placing them in appendices or keeping them separate from the unit itself.

Some instructors who teach mature learners, particularly at the college level, like to give an entire unit to the students. In that case tests cannot be made a part of the unit. It is not essential that the students have a copy of the entire unit but instead may receive an abbreviated version which outlines goals, objectives, entry skills needed, and resources to be used. It is of paramount importance, however, that the teacher communicate to the students the goals and objectives of the units.

Lesson Plans.   The unit serves as a basis for day-to-day planning. It is from the unit that the teacher derives daily lesson plans. The word *daily* should be stressed. If study of a particular unit in a high school course is to last six weeks, a course which meets five days per week would require 30 lesson plans. The elementary school teacher in a self-contained classroom will find it necessary not only to outline the work of an entire day but also to develop mini-lesson plans for each subject area or topics studied during the day.

A lesson plan need not be lengthy. The supervisor must remember that planning is a continuing activity of teachers and the demands on teachers' time are many. Each lesson plan should include at least the following elements:

1. *Objectives of the particular lesson plan.* It is recognized that not all objectives can be accomplished in one day's time. Some will carry over to the next day or for several days. Some daily plans, in practice, will require more than one day's presentation. What the teacher must do is review the plan at the conclusion of the day and make whatever revisions are needed for the next day. That teachers must make a plan for every class every day does not mean that each plan must be totally new—it may legitimately be a revised plan based on the accomplishments of the preceding day.

2. *Instructional procedures and resources.* The teacher will select from the unit plan those procedures pertinent to the particular day's activities and will utilize those resources applicable for that day.

3. *Evaluation.* The teacher should employ some evaluation techniques no matter how simple to reveal whether or not the day's lesson has "gone over."

We have omitted from the lesson plan the goals, which normally apply to the entire unit, and preassessment, which is conducted at the beginning of the unit and relates to the whole unit.

The formats of a unit and lesson plan can be seen in the following abbreviated unit and lesson plan on *The Use of the Dictionary* for an upper middle school or lower junior high school class.

ILLUSTRATIVE UNIT PLAN: THE USE OF THE DICTIONARY

Goals

The child should become familiar with the kinds of help which can be found in a dictionary.

The child should gain an appreciation of the dictionary as a useful tool in language learning.

Objectives

Cognitive and Psychomotor

Using a dictionary supplied in class the child will look up words given orally by the teacher and will write the correct spelling of those words.

Using a dictionary supplied in class the child will look up words given in written form by the teacher or encountered in books or magazines and will write definitions of the words.

Using a dictionary supplied in class the child will look up words given in written form by the teacher or encountered in books or magazines and will pronounce them correctly.

Using a dictionary supplied in class the child will look up words given in written form by the teacher or encountered in books or magazines and will find synonyms for those words.

Using a dictionary supplied in class the child will look up words given in written form by the teacher and will tell the language origin of those words.

Given words in written form which the child cannot find in the dictionary supplied in class the child will go to the library and look up the definition and pronunciation and will verify the spelling in *Webster's Unabridged Dictionary*.

Given three different dictionaries the child will state the differences in systems for noting division of words into syllables, differences in marking pronunciation, and differences in preferred definitions.

Affective

When asked by his/her parents to look up the spelling, meaning, pronunciation or origin of words not familiar to them, the child will find pleasure in carrying out this task.

On encountering a new word while reading the child will find satisfaction in being able to find out what the word means.

Preassessment

A pretest (not included in this illustrative unit) will be administered which requires the children to look up the spelling, meaning, pronunciation, and origin of selected words. A mastery level of 90 percent accuracy will indicate that a child already possesses the competencies to be learned in the unit.

The child will be able to read most of the materials of the fifth grade, will be able to write the letters of the alphabet in sequence, and will be able to alphabetize a word to four letters (as, *dict*ionary).

Instructional Procedures

The children will take a spelling test of words dictated by the teacher and will look up in the dictionary words they misspell.

The children will read passages from a book, identify words whose meanings they do not know, and look up in the dictionary the definitions of those words.

The children will be taken on a tour of the school library by the librarian, who will show them the various kinds of dictionaries the library has, discuss the value of dictionaries, and show them how to use *Webster's Unabridged Dictionary*.

The children will listen to a presentation by the teacher on how to read the pronunciation of words in the dictionary. The teacher will utilize transparencies on the overhead projector for explanations and will distribute a dittoed sheet which shows words broken into syllables and marked for sounds and stress.

The child will look up the same word in three dictionaries supplied in class and compare differences in noting syllables, in indicating pronunciation, and in preferred definitions.

Resources

Dictionaries such as *Webster's New World Dictionary*, *Webster's New Collegiate Dictionary*, paperback dictionaries, *Webster's Unabridged Dictionary*, overhead projector and transparencies, librarian.

Time allotted for the unit: 45 minutes per day for five days.

Evaluation

The children will attempt to achieve a 90 percent mastery level on a performance test (not included in this illustrative unit) which requires them to look up words in the dictionary and give their correct spelling, definition, pronunciation, and origin. Students who score less than 90 percent will need individualized help in mastering the content of the unit.

ILLUSTRATIVE LESSON PLAN

Objectives

The children will write 20 words dictated by the teacher, look up the correct spelling of the words in a dictionary supplied in class, and verify their spelling of the words.

Instructional Procedures and Resources

*Set Induction:** The teacher will ask pupils whether they have ever used the dictionary, whether they have ever wanted to know how to spell words correctly, whether *recieve* or *receive* is the correct spelling of the word, and why it is important to know the correct spelling of words. (5 min.)

The children will write words dictated by the teacher. (10 min.)

The children will use a dictionary supplied in class to verify the spelling of each word and to correct words misspelled. (20 min.)

*Closure:** (last 2 min.) The teacher will summarize the pupils' success in finding and correcting words they had misspelled and will stress the usefulness of the dictionary for helping them with spelling unfamiliar words.

Resources: dictionaries; dittoed sheet with correct spellings.

* See Chapter 4 for discussion of these terms.

Evaluation

The children will double-check the correct spelling of the words from a dittoed sheet distributed by the teacher giving spellings which they should have found in the dictionary and will report to the teacher how many words they had written correctly after looking them up. (8 min.)

The foregoing outlines of two types of instructional plans—the unit plan and the lesson plan—offer means of organizing products of the planning process into a logical and intelligible form. A great deal of thought and creativity go into constructing instructional plans. Plans may and should differ from teacher to teacher even when topics are the same; no two teachers approach the task of planning in the same way, a fact which makes the planning process such a highly creative endeavor. The supervisor may aid teachers in developing unit and lesson plans by showing them models of well-constructed plans. In so doing he or she should make it clear to them that plans are not written to please the administrator or supervisor but to enable the teachers to carry out instruction more effectively.

SUMMARY

Instructional planning is seen as the first step in a continuum whose subsequent steps are presentation and evaluation of instruction. Plans must be continuously revised as feedback from the output—learner achievement—shows modifications that should be made.

It is recommended that the supervisor implement a six-point program to help teachers develop and improve skills in following a systems approach to instructional design, using a model of instruction as a guide to planning, writing nonbehavioral goals and behavioral objectives, describing and analyzing tasks, applying taxonomies of instructional objectives, and organizing instructional plans. Two types of instructional plans are recommended: the lesson plan, which shows the planning for one day, and the unit plan, which shows the planning for longer periods of time and from which the lesson plans are derived. Planning requires a good deal of thought and time but it is an essential process with the ultimate aim of enhancing student learning.

ACTIVITIES FOR FURTHER STUDY

1. Define the following terms:
   systems approach   instructional (behavioral) objective
   feedback   taxonomy of instructional objectives
   instructional design   cognitive domain
   model of instruction   affective domain
   instructional goal   psychomotor domain
2. Diagram a model of instruction and explain its parts.
3. Select a learning task, describe and analyze it.

4. Apply the taxonomies of the three domains of learning by writing one behavioral objective for each of the major categories of each domain.
5. Construct one unit plan and one lesson plan.
6. Locate one model of instruction which is different from any model in the text and compare it to the Five-Part Model of Instruction described in this chapter.
7. Describe the differences between task description and task analysis.
8. Write one instructional goal for a particular topic which you might teach in school and three instructional objectives derived from the instructional goal.
9. Describe the following types of learning and give one illustration of each:
   chaining   rule learning
   concept learning   problem solving
10. List two behavioral terms (verbs) which might be used in stating cognitive objectives in each of the six categories of the Bloom taxonomy.
11. List two behavioral terms (verbs) which might be used in stating affective objectives in each of the five categories of the Krathwohl taxonomy.
12. List two behavioral terms (verbs) which might be used in stating psychomotor objectives in each of the seven categories of the Simpson taxonomy.
13. Compare Harrow's taxonomy of the psychomotor domain with the Simpson taxonomy as to (a) categories and (b) use.
14. Compare the taxonomy of the psychomotor domain found in Kibler et al., *Behavioral Objectives and Instruction*, Chapter III, with the Simpson taxonomy as to (a) categories and (b) use.
15. State three components of complete behavioral objectives.
16. Distinguish a performance standard from a stability standard in writing an instructional objective.
17. Describe ways in which a supervisor can decide whether teachers are doing adequate planning.
18. Observe two teachers in their classrooms and try to determine from their presentations whether there is evidence of planning. If you believe there is such evidence, attempt to judge the quality of planning that went into the presentation.
19. Talk with the teachers in activity 18 above and report to the class on planning procedures they use. Determine whether the teachers follow planning procedures discussed in this chapter or other techniques.
20. Classify the following instructional objectives as to domain and category within the domain. For answers see below. The student will:
   a. Evaluate and compare the nutritive value of six breakfast cereals.
   b. Demonstrate how to hold a tennis racket and ball in order to serve.
   c. Listen to a native speaker of a foreign language which he or she is studying and summarize what the speaker has said.
   d. Respond to a call for a contribution to a leading charity.
   e. Assemble a kite following instructions on the wrapper.

    f. Using a 12″ ruler, measure and record in inches and fractions of inches the lengths of several straight lines on a handout distributed by the teacher.

    g. Regularly demonstrate sensitivity in his or her relationships with other people.

    h. Write a biography of a famous political or military leader on either side in World War II.

    i. Practice cutting chunks of raw cabbage into pieces for cole slaw.

    j. Name the president and vice-president of the United States.

    k. Express admiration for the fine work which has been put into a hand-made afghan.

    l. Identify marijuana by its smell.

    m. Demonstrate an awareness that vandalism is hurting the school's image.

    n. Create an original fruit punch.

    o. Decide whether a proposed solution to a community problem is likely to work.

    p. Change a tire (leaving it on the rim) by substituting the spare for the front left tire.

    q. Decide whether saving money "for a rainy day" is worthwhile or not.

    r. Using a dresser which has been painted a solid color, refinish it in antique white.

Answers to activity 20:

a. cognitive-evaluation	j. cognitive-knowledge
b. psychomotor-set	k. affective-valuing
c. cognitive-comprehension	l. psychomotor-perception
d. affective-responding	m. affective-receiving
e. psychomotor-guided response	n. psychomotor-origination
f. cognitive-application	o. cognitive-analysis
g. affective-characterization by value or value complex	p. psychomotor-complex overt response
h. cognitive-synthesis	q. affective-organization
i. psychomotor-mechanism	r. psychomotor-adaptation

21. For each of the following behaviors identify the type of learning using Gagné's classification of types. For answers see below.

    a. Define *charity*.

    b. Baby repeating "Da-Da" on hearing his/her father say "Da-Da."

    c. Choosing the right computer for the needs of the office.

    d. Fear of high places.

    e. Learning that smoking may be hazardous to your health.

    f. Child sees an elephant in a zoo. An adult points to the animal and says "elephant." When seeing an elephant again, the child says "elephant."

    g. Pitching a baseball.

    h. Distinguishing oak from other woods.

Answers to activity 21
  a. concept learning
  b. stimulus-response learning
  c. problem solving
  d. signal learning
  e. rule learning
  f. verbal association
  g. chaining
  h. discrimination learning

NOTES

1. Robert J. Kibler, Donald J. Cegala, David T. Miles, and Larry L. Barker, *Objectives for Instruction and Evaluation*, Boston, Allyn and Bacon, 1974, 20–27.
2. W. James Popham and Eva L. Baker, *Systematic Instruction*, Englewood Cliffs, N.J., Prentice-Hall, 1970, 11–18.
3. For additional help in writing instructional objectives consult: Benjamin S. Bloom, J. Thomas Hastings, and George F. Madaus, *Handbook on Formative and Summative Evaluation of Student Learning*, New York, McGraw-Hill, 1971; Norman E. Gronlund, *Stating Objectives for Classroom Instruction*, 2d ed., New York, Macmillan, 1978; Robert F. Mager, *Preparing Instructional Objectives*, 2d ed., Belmont, Calif., Fearon, 1975; Newton S. Metfessel, William B. Michaels, and Donald A. Kirsner, "Instrumentation of Bloom's and Krathwohl's Taxonomies for the Writing of Educational Objectives," *Psychology in the Schools* 6, no. 3 (July 1969): 227–231; W. James Popham and Eva L. Baker, *Establishing Instructional Goals*, Englewood Cliffs, N.J., Prentice-Hall, 1970.
4. Robert H. Davis, Lawrence T. Alexander, and Stephen L. Yelon, *Learning System Design: An Approach to the Improvement of Instruction*, New York, McGraw-Hill, 1974, 41.
5. See *Catalog*, Instructional Objectives Exchange, P.O. Box 24095, Los Angeles, Calif. 90024; *Florida Catalogs of Objectives*, Panhandle Area Educational Cooperative, Chipley, Fla.; and assessment programs of various states.
6. Benjamin S. Bloom, ed., *Taxonomy of Educational Objectives: The Classification of Educational Goals: Handbook I: Cognitive Domain*, New York, Longman, 1956.
7. David R. Krathwohl, Benjamin S. Bloom, and Bertram B. Masia, *Taxonomy of Educational Objectives: The Classification of Educational Goals: Handbook II: Affective Domain*, New York, Longman, 1964.
8. Elizabeth Jane Simpson, "The Classification of Educational Objectives in the Psychomotor Domain," *The Psychomotor Domain*, Vol. 3, Washington, D.C., Gryphon House, 1972, 43–56. See also Anita J. Harrow, *A Taxonomy of the Psychomotor Domain: A Guide for Developing Behavioral Objectives*, New York, Longman, 1972.
9. Bloom, p. 18.
10. See VIMCET filmstrip–audio tape program, *Selecting Appropriate Educational Objectives*. (See multi-media in the bibliography.)
11. Krathwohl, Bloom, and Masia, p. 35.
12. Simpson.
13. Harrow, 27.
14. Davis, Alexander, and Yelon, chs. 5 and 7.
15. Robert M. Gagné, *The Conditions of Learning*, 2d ed., New York, Holt, Rinehart, and Winston, 1970.
16. For a useful discussion of three types of learning (humanistic, cognitive, and behavioral) see Carl D. Glickman, *Developmental Supervision: Alternative Practices for Helping Teachers Improve Instruction*, Alexandria, Va., Association for Supervision and Curriculum Development, 1981, 3–5.

BIBLIOGRAPHY

Armstrong, Robert J., Terry O. Cornell, Robert F. Kraner, and E. Wayne Roberson. *The Development and Evaluation of Behavioral Objectives*. Worthington, Ohio: Charles A. Jones, 1970.

Baird, Hugh W., Dwayne Belt, Lyal Holder, and Clark Webb. *A Behavioral Approach to Teaching*. Dubuque: William C. Brown, 1972.

Baker, Eva L., and W. James Popham. *Expanding Dimensions of Instructional Objectives*. Englewood Cliffs, N.J.: Prentice-Hall, 1973.

Banathy, Bela H. *Instructional Systems*. Belmont, Calif.: Fearon, 1968.

Becker, Wesley C., Siegfried Engelmann, and Don R. Thomas. *Teaching 2: Cognitive Learning and Instruction*. Chicago: Science Research Associates, 1975.

Bloom, Benjamin S., ed. *Taxonomy of Educational Objectives: The Classification of Educational Goals: Handbook I: Cognitive Domain*. New York: Longman, 1956.

———, J. Thomas Hastings, and George F. Madaus. *Handbook on Formative and Summative Evaluation of Student Learning*. New York: McGraw-Hill, 1971.

Briggs, Leslie J. *Handbook of Procedures for the Design of Instruction*. Washington, D.C.: American Institutes for Research, 1970.

Davies, Ivor K. *Objectives in Curriculum Design*. London: McGraw-Hill, 1976.

Davis, Robert H., Lawrence T. Alexander, and Stephen L. Yelon. *Learning System Design: An Approach to the Improvement of Instruction*. New York: McGraw-Hill, 1974.

De Cecco, John P., and William R. Crawford. *The Psychology of Learning and Instruction*, 2nd ed. Englewood Cliffs, N.J.: Prentice-Hall, 1974.

Dick, Walter, and Lou Carey. *The Systematic Design of Instruction*. Glenview, Ill.: Scott, Foresman, 1978.

Dillman, Caroline Matheny, and Harold F. Rahmlow. *Writing Instructional Objectives*. Belmont, Calif.: Fearon, 1972.

Education Commission of the States. *Directory of Measurable Objectives Sources*. Denver: Education Commission of the States.

Florida Department of Education. *Florida Catalogs of Objectives*. Chipley: Panhandle Area Educational Cooperative.

Gagné, Robert M. *The Conditions of Learning*, 2nd ed. New York: Holt, Rinehart and Winston, 1970.

———and Leslie J. Briggs. *Principles of Instructional Design*. New York: Holt, Rinehart and Winston, 1974.

Glickman, Carl D. *Developmental Supervision: Alternative Practices for Helping Teachers Improve Instruction*. Alexandria, Va.: Association for Supervision and Curriculum Development, 1981.

Gronlund, Norman E. *Stating Objectives for Classroom Instruction*, 2nd ed. New York: Macmillan, 1978.

Hannah, Larry S., and John U. Michaelis. *A Comprehensive Framework for Instructional Objectives: A Guide to Systematic Planning and Evaluation*. Reading, Mass.: Addison-Wesley, 1977.

Harrow, Anita J. *A Taxonomy of the Psychomotor Domain: A Guide for Developing Behavioral Objectives*. New York: Longman, 1972.

Henson, Kenneth T. *Secondary Teaching Methods*. Lexington, Mass.: D. C. Heath, 1981.

Hunter, Madeline, and Douglas Russell. "How Can I Plan More Effective Lessons?" *Instructor* 87, no. 2 (September 1977): 74–75f.

Instructional Objectives Exchange. *Catalog*. Los Angeles: Instructional Objectives Exchange.

Kibler, Robert J., Larry L. Barker, and David T. Miles. *Behavioral Objectives and Instruction*. Boston: Allyn and Bacon, 1970.

———, Donald J. Cegala, David T. Miles, and Larry L. Barker. *Objectives for Instruction and Evaluation*. Boston: Allyn and Bacon, 1974.

Krathwohl, David R., Benjamin S. Bloom, and Bertram B. Masia. *Taxonomy of Educational Objectives: The Classification of Educational Goals: Handbook II: Affective Domain*. New York: Longman, 1964.

Lee, Blaine Nelson, and M. David Merrill. *Writing Complete Affective Objectives: A Short Course*. Belmont, Calif.: Wadsworth, 1972.

McNeil, John D. "Deriving Objectives." In *Designing Curriculum: Self Instructional Modules*. Boston: Little, Brown, 1976.

Mager, Robert F. *Developing Attitude Toward Learning*. Belmont, Calif.: Fearon, 1968.

———. *Preparing Instructional Objectives*, 2nd ed. Belmont, Calif.: Fearon, 1975.

Metfessel, Newton S., William B. Michaels, and Donald A. Kirsner. "Instrumentation of Bloom's and Krathwohl's Taxonomies for the Writing of Educational Objectives." *Psychology in the Schools* 6, no. 3 (July 1969): 227–231.

Morine-Dershimer, Greta. "Instructional Planning." In *Classroom Teaching Skills: A Handbook*, James M. Cooper, ed. Lexington, Mass.: D. C. Heath, 1977.

Oliva, Peter F. *The Secondary School Today*, 2nd ed. New York: Harper & Row, 1972.

Popham, W. James. "Practical Ways of Improving the Curriculum Via Measurable Objectives." *The Bulletin of the National Association of Secondary School Principals* 55, no. 355 (May 1971): 76–90.

——— and Eva L. Baker. *Establishing Instructional Goals*. Englewood Cliffs, N.J.: Prentice-Hall, 1970.

———. *Systematic Instruction*. Englewood Cliffs, N.J.: Prentice-Hall, 1970.

Program Development Center of Northern California. *A Programmed Course in the Writing of Performance Objectives*. Bloomington, Ind.: Commission on Educational Planning, Phi Delta Kappa, 1972.

Simpson, Elizabeth Jane. "The Classification of Educational Objectives in the Psychomotor Domain." *The Psychomotor Domain* 3 (1972).

Tenbrink, Terry. "Writing Instructional Objectives." In *Classroom Teaching Skills: A Handbook*, James M. Cooper, ed. Lexington, Mass.: D. C. Heath, 1977.

Tyler, Ralph W. *Basic Principles of Curriculum and Instruction*. Chicago: University of Chicago Press, 1949.

Westinghouse Learning Press. *Behavioral Objectives: A Guide to Individualizing*. Sunnyvale, Calif.: Westinghouse Learning Press, 1977. 4 volumes.

———. *Learning Objectives for Individualized Instruction*. Sunnyvale, Calif.: Westinghouse Learning Press, 1977. 4 volumes.

Multi-Media

Davis, Robert H., Lawrence T. Alexander, and Stephen L. Yelon. *Learning System Design: An Approach to the Improvement of Instruction*. New York: McGraw-Hill Book Company, 1974. 342 pp. Twelve filmstrip/audio tape presentations, student workbook, and instructor's manual to accompany this text available from Instructional Media Center, Michigan State University, East Lansing, Michigan.

General Programmed Teaching. *Designing Effective Instruction*. Workshop consisting of fifteen units with twelve filmstrips in color, fifteen cassette tapes, workbooks, monitor's manual, and scriptbook. General Programmed Teaching, Post Office Box 402, Palo Alto, California.

Insgroup, Inc. *Objectives for Instructional Programs*. Filmstrip, audio cassette, coordinator's guide, viewer response forms, response manual, reference pamphlet, and wall chart. In-service training materials on various types of objectives. Insgroup, Inc. (Instructional Systems Group), One City Boulevard West, Suite 935, Orange, California 92668.

Vimcet Associates. *Validated Instructional Materials for the Continuing Education of Teachers*. Thirty filmstrip/audio tape programs on a variety of topics. Most pertinent to this chapter are:

#1 *Educational Objectives*
#2 *Systematic Instructional Decision-Making*
#3 *Selecting Appropriate Educational Objectives*
#9 *Defining Content for Objectives*
#10 *Identifying Affective Objectives*
#11 *Analyzing Learning Outcomes*
#13 *Teaching Units and Lesson Plans*
#28 *Humanizing Educational Objectives*

The Vimcet materials are coordinated with the book *Systematic Instruction* by W. James Popham and Eva L. Baker. Vimcet Associates, Post Office Box 24714, Los Angeles, California 90024.

4

Helping Teachers to Present Instruction

OBJECTIVES

After studying Chapter 4 you should be able to accomplish the following objectives:

1. Select resources applying appropriate criteria.
2. Select teaching strategies applying appropriate criteria.
3. Demonstrate set induction.
4. Demonstrate appropriate lecturing techniques.
5. Demonstrate skill in conducting a class discussion
6. Demonstrate nonverbal cues.
7. Demonstrate oral questioning techniques.
8. Provide for variation of stimuli.
9. Provide for variation of learning activities.
10. Demonstrate closure.
11. Apply a checklist for observing lesson presentations.
12. Express a desire to master skills of presentation so that in your capacity as a supervisor you can help teachers become more effective at lesson presentation.

STEPS IN IMPLEMENTATION

An old saw prescribes the steps for presenting a lesson. It directs the teacher to:

1. Tell them what you're going to tell them.

2. Tell them.
3. Tell them what you told them.

Like old wives' tales, old saws sometimes have a ring of truth about them. Today we couch our ideas in more technical language but this old prescription is not completely off target. We talk now of *set induction* instead of the pedestrian "tell them what you're going to tell them," of *explaining* instead of the pointed "tell them," and of *closure* instead of the mundane "tell them what you told them."

To initiate our discussion of helping teachers present instruction let us use the Five-Part Model of Instruction discussed in Chapter 3 as our referent point. You will recall that the fourth block of the model is implementation of instruction. In the ensuing discussion implementation of instruction is seen as including the selection of resources and the selection and implementation of teaching strategies.

The selection of resources and the decisions on strategies are parts of the planning phase, while implementation of the resources and strategies is the actual presentation phase. The task of selecting resources and strategies prior to presentation reinforces a concept discussed in the previous chapter, namely, that the instructional process is a continuum. There are no sharp divisions between planning and presentation, between planning and evaluation, and between presentation and evaluation. Each component of a model of instruction glides into the other and doubles back on the other.

SELECTION OF RESOURCES

The great disparities in school financing are nowhere more readily visible in a school system than they are in the case of instructional resources. The resources at the teacher's command vary considerably from community to community, from state to state, even from school to school within a community. Some schools have only the barest essentials while others have a superabundance of materials and equipment, some of which lie dormant in media storage rooms. A few fortunate schools are blessed with an instructional material center which produces audio-visual aids in support of instruction throughout the school.

A major task of the teacher is to identify whatever resources are available for instructional purposes. A central task of the supervisor is to assist the teacher in locating, obtaining, and creating instructional aids. There are very few teachers who would not like additional resources and who do not feel that they would be more effective teachers if these resources were available to them. The task of selecting resources is twofold. First, teachers must make effective use of the resources which they do have and second, teachers must uncover resources which are available but untapped.

Even the most poorly financed classrooms possess as a general rule some limited instructional resources. Normally most classrooms contain a blackboard, bulletin board, textbooks, dictionary, and often maps and a globe. In some classrooms these time-honored aids could be put to more effective use.

One of the first jobs of teachers new to a school system is to find out what instructional materials and equipment are available in that school system, not only in the school itself but also from the central office. A supervisor can speed up this initial orientation process by advising new teachers what is available and providing in written form lists of available resources, their location, and the means of obtaining them.

Teachers must develop the habit of thinking beyond the confines of the school for aids in carrying out instruction. Some communities are rich in educational resources. To varying degrees all communities can provide significant educational experiences for young people. We must get away from the old notion that the only educational experiences which are important are those which take place within the walls of the school and develop the corollary notion that the community is the school's campus. A supervisor can do much to break down the traditional barriers between the school and the community by suggesting sources of aid and by encouraging teachers to make full utilization of resources which are available. One helpful technique for promoting the use of community resources is an organized tour of the community for teachers who are new to the system. This would give teachers an early chance to see the neighborhoods from which their students come and to pinpoint places which might be of future help to them in instruction.

Teachers must think in terms of human as well as physical resources of the community. They should identify individuals and groups inside and outside the school system who might help them present particular topics. People with unique and pertinent experiences should be invited into the classroom or have classes taken to them so they may share their experiences with students. The movement of alternative schools in recent years is based on the premise that worthwhile learning experiences can be provided at settings away from the school and by resource persons other than certificated teachers. Thus, we find alternative schools calling on the voluntary services of artists, tradesmen, bankers, salespeople, writers, farmers, and scientists for supplementing studies. These kinds of resources are available to the traditional school as well as to alternative schools. Retired specialists in the community can be of service when their fields are under study. They are often eager to help and are delighted when they are asked to speak to young people. Teachers customarily identify libraries, museums, and art galleries as sources of educational experiences for students, but except for the field of vocational education teachers often overlook experiences which can be derived from stores, banks, garages, hospitals, prisons, insurance agencies, or travel agencies.

The supervisor might recommend that teachers who are engaged in the process of selecting resources apply a check-list such as the one below for purposes of evaluating resources and making choices.

CHECKLIST FOR USE IN SELECTING RESOURCES

	YES	NO
1. The resources relate directly to the objectives.	____	____
2. The resources are in keeping with the abilities of the learners.	____	____

	YES	NO
3. The resources are in keeping with the age level of the learners.	____	____
4. The resources will be of interest to the learners.	____	____
5. The resources are varied enough to make provision for individual differences.	____	____
6. The resources are accurate and up-to-date.	____	____
7. The resources are without bias or if with bias, the bias is clearly stated and the resources are balanced to reveal different biases.	____	____
8. The resources are easily accessible to the learners.	____	____
9. The resources are without cost to the learners.	____	____

It is clear that the resources must relate to the predetermined objectives, for the resources are the vehicles which carry the learners to their destination. There would undoubtedly be agreement that resources should be selected which meet the learners' abilities, age level, and interests. If at all possible, the resources chosen should be stimulating and motivating.

The teacher, while searching for resources with the class as a whole in mind, should also seek resources which might appeal to individuals within the group. Some materials should be relatively easy, others more difficult. Some should be concrete, others more abstract. Whatever resources are brought to the learners' attention—whether in the form of media or in the form of resource persons—should be accurate and incorporate the most recent data available.

Some teachers may take issue with the use of biased materials. Yet, many of the problems facing mankind are controversial ones with no clear-cut, factual solutions. Men and women of good will and ill will differ on the resolution of controversial issues. It is impossible to study opposing views on controversial subjects without examining biased points of view. Whenever an individual takes a side in a controversial issue, he or she is presenting a bias. When dealing with controversial content the teacher may offset the bias of one side by presenting the biases of other sides.

The checklist suggests that resources be readily accessible and without cost to the learners. In the public schools where learners are immature and a captive population, it is the teacher's responsibility to see that instructional resources which have been chosen are at the command of the learner. The teacher must also assure that the materials to be used will be either without cost or of insignificant cost to the learners and their parents. The public school is not like a college or university where a professor may order mature students who choose to be there to purchase books and other instructional materials and to pay a variety of laboratory fees.

The checklist offers the teacher some guidelines for the selection of resources. The alert teacher is constantly on the lookout for new instructional materials, particularly those which are free or inexpensive. It is a duty of the supervisor to supply teachers continuously with references to new resources which have come to his/her attention and which appear worthwhile. Further, teachers can be encouraged to evaluate resources they might use by applying a set of criteria such as suggested in the preceding checklist.

SELECTION OF STRATEGIES

When teachers consider the problem of selecting strategies for presenting content to students, they might well paraphrase the poet: 'How shall I teach thee? Let me count the ways. . . ." Many strategic avenues are open to them. Like the streets of any city some avenues are more traveled than others, some thoroughfares receive little traffic, and some are unknown except to those in the neighborhood.

Pedagogy has borrowed the word strategy from the armed services. We can envision the military brass mapping out a campaign and planning their tactics. Some teachers might well point out that there is another analogy in the use of the word strategy—it applies to the field of battle. We prefer not to conceptualize the classroom as a battlefield with the teacher and students on opposing sides but rather as a team effort with the teacher as the leader and both teacher and students working together for a common cause.

The terms *procedures* or *strategies* appear within some of the models of instruction which we saw earlier. Whichever term is used we are talking about methodology—the means of providing opportunities for students to encounter content. We find not only these terms in the pedagogical literature but we also meet the terms *tactics, methods, techniques*, and *modes of instruction*.

Some specialists in instruction see differences in the concepts mentioned in the preceding paragraph. We could, if we wished, make some subtle distinctions in these concepts. For example, we could identify the use of nonprint media as a strategy while the use of a specific medium—a film—could be labeled a technique. But we shall not make these fine distinctions in our discussion. We use the aforementioned terms when they apply to teaching or instruction as synonymous and interchangeable.

We do need to distinguish, however, between a teaching strategy and a learning strategy. In this text we are concerned with teaching or instructional strategies—those methods which teachers select and use to present subject matter. We are further concerned with the ability of the supervisor to help teachers select and use appropriate strategies.

Learning strategies are personalized ways by which a learner internalizes content, that is, learns the subject. Some learners will outline subject matter so they can grasp the points in logical sequence. Some memorize words or sentences as keys to learnings. Can any school child forget "Able was I ere I saw Elba," which has the dubious virtue of not only reminding the learner of Napoleon's first place of confinement but also being a completely reversible sentence? Some pupils put together both real and nonsensical words which have meaning only to them to help them recall facts. Some pupils like to read a passage in its entirety quickly, then go back and study segments in depth. Some students subject themselves to silent question-and-answer sessions on content they have under study. These are all learning strategies, not teaching strategies. When we use the word strategy by itself in this text, we mean teaching or instructional strategy and we equate it with procedure, method, technique, mode, or tactic.

The reader is reminded that the process of selection of strategies is still a part of the planning process. Not until the teacher walks into the classroom and initiates a lesson does he or she move out of the sphere of planning and into the area of implementation or presentation.

A teaching strategy may be defined as a procedure or set of procedures for utilizing resources and for deploying the central figures in the instructional process— the teacher and the learners. With this definition in mind we might list some of the many strategies a supervisor might suggest teachers consider as possible procedures:

lecturing	oral reports
discussion	written reports
textbook exercises	drill
recitation	use of audio media
grouping by ability, achievement, or interest	use of video media
questioning	laboratory
discovery	programmed instruction
role playing	field trips
tutoring	tests
problem solving	homework
	independent study

This list is far from complete, but it indicates that there is a variety of strategies which teachers may use in presenting content. Variations are possible in a number of the strategies listed above. For example, the teacher might lecture to large groups or small groups. Discussion might be conducted in small groups or even smaller seminars. Textbook exercises might be written or oral. Grouping students for learning may be implemented according to varying criteria; subgroupings are possible within larger groups; given a team of teachers, groupings may be arranged around team teaching or differentiated staffing patterns. Without delineating all the combinations of strategies possible, it is evident that the range of procedures open to teachers is broader than they sometimes realize.

The difficult task is to select that strategy or those strategies which would be most productive for the learners. By way of illustration, suppose an elementary school teacher wishes the pupils during science study to become familiar with the concept of the Nitrogen Cycle, the process whereby nitrogen undergoes change, nitrites and nitrates are formed for nourishment of green plants, and nitrogen returns to its original state, a process vital to the maintenance of life on this earth. Let us do as Don Quixote advises his fellow prisoners in the opening scene of *Man of La Mancha*: come enter into (the teacher's) imagination. How can this content be placed before the learners in such a way that they will readily master the principles involved? A number of alternatives run through the teacher's mind:

1. Prepare a lecture and use only written notes.
2. Prepare a lecture and use an overhead projector to sketch the Nitrogen Cycle for the students.
3. Prepare a lecture and use charts which have been prepared by the teacher or former students or an instructional materials center.
4. Show a film on the Nitrogen Cycle.

5. Ask students to open their textbooks to the section on the Nitrogen Cycle and have students read aloud the passages in the text describing the cycle. The teacher could follow each reading with oral questions to see if pupils understand the concept.

6. An alternative to 5 is to have the students open their books and the teacher read to them—a still far too common procedure in many classrooms.

7. Introduce the content by raising questions such as, What is nitrogen? Is there more nitrogen in the air than oxygen? Animals, bacteria, and green plants play a part in the Nitrogen Cycle—what are their roles? The teacher may ask students to look up the Nitrogen Cycle in the textbook and/or reference books either as class work or homework. Pupils report their findings to class.

8. Lecture and ask pupils to follow up the lecture with drawings of the Nitrogen Cycle.

9. Use a programmed text to teach the content.

10. Ask a committee to study the Nitrogen Cycle and prepare a report to be given to the class.

11. Bring in a small bag of fertilizer; for example, 6-6-6 100 percent organic. The class could discuss the difference in meaning between organic and inorganic. The teacher can show them the label on the bag which describes the contents and explain to them that 6-6-6 means 6 percent nitrate, 6 percent phosphate, and 6 percent potash. The teacher explains the necessity for growing plants to have these chemicals, singles out the nitrate, and relates it to the Nitrogen Cycle, which the class will then study.

12. Lead the class up to study of the Nitrogen Cycle over a period of time during which the class experiments with growing plants in the classroom. Several plants are given proper water and chemicals; other plants are given proper water and inadequate chemicals; some plants are given proper water and no chemicals. Students will observe the necessity for plants to get sufficient food.

13. Take the class on a field trip to a farmer's pasture which is complete with cows, manure, green plants, and decaying plants. The teacher can point out the Nitrogen Cycle at work.

How can the teacher know which of the alternative strategies would be most effective? It is apparent that more than one road leads to Rome. Contrary to the classic expression, however, not all roads lead to Rome, or certainly some roads are more circuitous than others.

The teacher can choose one strategy at random and try it out. If it doesn't work, another strategy is tried and then another until one that will work is found. To some extent all teachers follow a trial-and-error procedure. Intuitively, they select a strategy that seems on the surface as if it would be effective. These teachers would verify the notion that experience is the best teacher. Over the years after considerable trial and error they have learned which strategies have been most effective under which conditions.

But what guidance can the supervisor give the new teacher in order to avoid the lengthy process of trial and error? Or what help can the supervisor give the experienced teacher who wants to test intuition against some criteria? How can a teacher judge in advance whether a given strategy will work? Although one can never be absolutely sure that a given procedure will work until it is put to the test in the classroom, chances for success will be greatly enhanced if the supervisor will help the teacher develop some simple guidelines such as the following.

1. *The strategy must be right for the learners.* The teacher must consider the age level of the students and the interests of that age level, remaining cognizant of the learners' achievement levels. If we refer to our illustration of the elementary school teacher's presenting the Nitrogen Cycle to elementary school pupils, a formal lecture by the teacher using written notes could be a disaster. Short minutes after the lecture has begun the teacher may well be confronted with a classroom full of wiggling, twisting, disinterested urchins. If the teacher has a room full of poor readers, requiring them to go to reference works and encyclopedias to dig out information may be an unrewarding approach.

2. *The strategy must be right for the teacher.* Each teacher is a unique personality. Some function well in certain situations and not so well in others. Some teachers, for example, are master lecturers. Others work more effectively in small groups. Teachers who adopt a counseling point of view toward education and life are more effective in one-to-one situations than teachers who are more remote and detached.

Some teachers have a knack of dramatizing content while other teachers are more matter of fact. Some teachers are extroverted while others are introverted. Some have more background and skill in a particular subject field than others. Teachers need to be aware of their strengths and limitations. We will examine in chapter 11 ways in which a supervisor may help teachers to evaluate themselves. We would make the observation here that whatever strategy teachers select must be compatible with their skills, knowledge, values, and personality.

3. *The strategy must be right for the subject matter.* This guideline is such an obvious one that it seems impossible that it could be violated. Yet, how often do teachers teach *about* the content of a subject rather than teach the subject? How often do teachers accept pupils' verbalization of rules, for example, without probing to see if the pupils understand the rules? How often do teachers accept memorization of content for mastery of content? How often do teachers structure tests in such a way that students can cram for the tests, regurgitate the content on the tests, then immediately proceed to let the content float off into oblivion?

How many supervisors and other visitors have walked into modern language classrooms, for example, and wondered whether the teacher was teaching a foreign language or English? When English is consistently substituted for the foreign language in the modern language classroom, the strategy does injustice to the subject matter.

Teachers violate this guideline when they select and use out-dated resources. The teacher must exercise care in the selection of printed and other resources which may present as fact that which is no longer true. Media libraries are understandably reluctant to retire old films which were an expensive investment to begin with. The job falls on the teacher to be discriminating about materials placed before the learners.

An injustice is done to the subject matter when the teacher either intentionally or unintentionally directs learners to one-sided treatments of the content. For example, if the teacher selects a research paper as a strategy for studying the racial problem in America, students should be directed to books and articles written by both black and white authors. If we are studying poverty in Latin America and looking at pictures of slum areas of some Latin American cities, we should at the same time study problems of the poor in urban and rural areas in our own country. Teaching controversial topics calls for careful selection of resources and strategies to bring out all dimensions of the topics.

Because their resources are often limited—sometimes to a single textbook— teachers frequently but unintentionally present a distorted picture of content. It is only in recent years that social studies teachers have begun to dispel some of the myths that have surrounded great personalities of history. We have begun to see famous men and women from the past as real, once living, breathing human beings, not as larger than life supermen and superwomen. How many of us still believe that Washington chopped down the cherry tree and threw his half-dollar across the Potomac? How many schoolchildren were ever made aware that the nation's first president was rather tight-fisted with a nickel, had slaves working at his splendid home at Mount Vernon, and was, perhaps, a bit pompous? How many children believe that when Abraham Lincoln wasn't splitting rails, he was wandering around in top hat and tails? How many children learned that Abraham Lincoln had an earthy sense of humor and enjoyed a salty joke? The teacher must select strategies which bring out the essence and preserve the integrity of the subject matter.

4. *The strategy must be right for the time available.* How much practice, follow-up, review, independent study, and research will be conducted on a topic will depend upon the relative importance of the topic and the time allotted for its study. Some procedures take more time and move more slowly. Study in depth will require more time than a superficial survey. The achievement of the learners of an active mastery of the content will require more time than the goal of passive acquaintance with the subject matter. Time frames have already been established in every school system in terms of the number of hours in the school day and the number of days in the school year and marking periods.

Time on task and direct instruction. Whatever the strategies selected, the teacher must make the best use of the time available. Recent studies have confirmed what many educators have long observed, that there is a great deal of lost time in a typical classroom.[1] John I. Goodlad related that research funded by the Kettering Foundation and conducted over a period of eight years in some 38 schools, primarily at the elementary school level, revealed a considerable amount of time wasted in such activities as recess and cleaning up. As a result, students are deprived of an adequate amount of instructional time for some of the disciplines.[2] Jack L. Davidson and Freda M. Holley, summarizing a study in the Austin, Texas public schools, reported:

The most dramatic finding produced by the study, however, was that all students spend *more than one-fifth* of each school day involved in noninstructional "management" activities:

listening to announcements; taking out and putting away supplies; bathroom trips; discipline; or simply waiting for teacher instruction. When this time—along with lunch, recess, and other such activities—was subtracted from the school day, only about three hours and forty-five minutes of that six and one-half hour school day were left to spend in actual instruction.[3]

Not only must time be used for instructional rather than noninstructional purposes but it should also be noted that achievement gain of learners is associated with what is called *"direct instruction,"* i.e., techniques such as advance planning by the teacher, using questions with a factual basis, and focusing on subject matter. Barak V. Rosenshine noted:

the frequency of nonacademic activities such as arts and crafts, reading stories to a group, or questioning students about personal experience usually are negatively related to achievement gains.[4]

Supervisors in classroom visits should observe the amount of time teachers keep the learners on task and should help teachers to analyze where they went off task, how to remain on task, and how to focus on content.

Self-pacing. Teachers must consider whether they can or should permit an element of self-pacing to enter the picture. The concept of self-pacing allows learners to take varying amounts of time to complete a particular learning task. Some students may take a shorter period of time than average, others may take a longer period of time. Time, then, becomes a variable. The traditional approach to instruction is to hold time constant and vary content. All learners work within the same time framework. Some learners master the learning task while others never achieve the objective. When a teacher introduces the notion of self-pacing, content is held constant and time is variable.

Self-pacing is a feature of most competency-based approaches to instruction. Certain objectives (competencies or learning tasks) are stipulated for the learner to master. This approach recognizes the fact that some individuals take more time to master specific content than other learners. The important aim is the attainment of the objectives by all learners even if it takes some learners longer than others.

A companion concept of self-pacing is criterion-referenced measurement, which is discussed in Chapter 5. In a competency-based approach to instruction a learner earns credit and receives a grade when the objectives have been mastered. When the criterion, the minimal level of competency, is met, the learner receives full credit. In a more traditional approach the teacher follows a norm-referenced system of measurement and compares students to each other rather than to the criterion. The teacher considers the degree to which various learners have accomplished the task. Whether individual learners have had sufficient time or not to complete a learning task is not considered an important factor under a norm-referenced system. We will return to these distinctions later on.

Ideally, if a teacher subscribes to the concept of self-pacing, learners should be able to take all the time they need to accomplish a task. One consequence of such a procedure would be completely individualized learning. Under these conditions the teacher's role would be a much different one for this would mean working in different ways with different learners.

There is always a gap between the ideal and the practical. An instructional staff must live within certain institutional parameters. Unlimited time is simply not available to any teacher or class. A published school calendar shows the dates when the school year and terms within the year begin and end. Classes change, teachers change, and content changes at the beginning of new instructional periods. Therefore, if teachers wish to introduce self-pacing, certainly a defensible practice, they will have to institute a modified self-pacing plan that allows some variation in time within the larger time parameters which have been set by the school. Instead of unlimited time to complete a task, a learner may have more than the average amount of time up to a fixed limit established by the teacher. A teacher might give the learner several opportunities to achieve an objective, permitting the learner to attempt a task more than one time, a process which some educators refer to as "recycling." The teacher may permit the learner to recycle only a reasonable number of times, say, two or three, after which the press of time forces the teacher to move on. A modified self-pacing plan will permit more learners to achieve objectives than is the case when time is held constant. Some learners will still fail to attain the objectives even if permitted several attempts unless through remedial work and tutoring they can achieve the objectives.

5. *The strategy must be right for the resources available.* A decision to use a number of reference books to explore a topic is contingent upon the availability of those reference books. The finest film in the world is useless without access to a projector to show it. Duplicated practice work sheets are possible only if the school has the supplies and duplicating equipment.

Earlier in this chapter we cautioned that resources must be accessible and without cost to the learners. A teacher cannot assume that resources outside the school are always available to students. A home economics teacher cannot, for example, assume that all homes are equipped with sewing machines. The language arts teacher cannot assume that all homes are fortunate enough to have magazines and books. The social studies teacher cannot assume that reference books and encyclopedias are available in homes of the students. Since most of the teaching force are products of the middle class, they sometimes forget that children from many homes, particularly those of the lower socioeconomic levels, do not have the cultural and educational resources children of upper socioeconomic levels might be accustomed to.

Nor can the teacher assume that if resources are not available in the home students can locate them somewhere in the community. Even if the desired resources are available many students will be prevented from reaching them through lack of transportation, a part-time job after school, and duties at home. Lack of resources will reduce the range of strategies open to the teacher.

6. *The strategy must be right for the facilities.* A strategy which calls for laboratory experiences in a particular discipline implies appropriate materials, equipment, and space. Learning centers, clinics, and remedial areas make demands similar to laboratories.

To put into practice, for example, a plan which advocates large-group instruction, small-group instruction, and independent study, space problems must be resolved. Varying-sized meeting rooms are needed. Library facilities are required. Sliding partitions may have to be installed. Faculty may have to be deployed differently. Existing facilities must be considered when a strategy is being selected.

7. *The strategy must be right for the objectives.* Perhaps the most important guideline of all is that there must be a direct fit between the strategy chosen and the objectives which the strategy is designed to achieve. If a teacher has specified objectives at higher levels of the taxonomies, he or she must choose strategies for reaching the higher levels. A strategy to achieve the cognitive level of evaluation will differ from a strategy to achieve the level of knowledge. A strategy to achieve the affective level of valuing will be different from techniques for reaching the level of responding. A procedure which would bring about attainment of the psychomotor level of adaptation would differ from a procedure to reach the level of set. The relationship between the objectives and strategies is direct and intimate. Alone, the objectives are nothing but ideas from the teacher's mind. The strategy is the vehicle for carrying the objectives from the teacher's mind to the learner's mind and body. Some years ago I was asked to talk to a group of teenagers on what seemed to me a rather silly topic, "Ideas with Legs." This metaphor, however, appears an apt one for the relationship between objectives and strategies. The objectives are the ideas and the strategies are the legs.

By engaging in periodic analyses and discussion of these seven guidelines with teachers the supervisor may assist them to develop the skill of selecting appropriate strategies and to avoid the uneconomical process of trial and error.

LESSON PRESENTATION

The goals are written, the objectives are stated, the tasks are analyzed and described, resources and strategies are selected, entry skills of learners are assessed, the unit plan is developed, the first lesson plan is created, and the planning process phases out. The implementation process is about to begin: the teacher starts the first lesson of the unit by initiating study of the unit's topic.

When the teacher steps into the classroom, the hours of prior planning stand him or her in good stead. They provide a sense of confidence that all systems are "go." Can any experienced teacher ever forget the first time he or she soloed in front of a group of students? Can the butterflies in the stomach be compared to the actor's stage fright? Did the teacher wonder how the audience would react? How would the lesson go over?

We might even say the teacher conducts a silent dress rehearsal the night before each lesson, running through the unit and reviewing how the lesson plan fits into the unit plan. Each part of the lesson plan must be checked to fix clearly in mind the details of each of the components. The teacher makes an inventory of the materials and equipment needed and tries to anticipate problems likely to be encountered.

In practice, of course, teachers do not carry out a full-scale review of each lesson prior to presentation the following day. They do not have time for exhaustive checks, but in a cursory or abbreviated fashion they do make a quick check. It is likely that they will spend somewhat more time readying the lesson plan for the introductory class of each unit and less time as the unit moves along lesson by lesson.

Each day's lesson provides feedback for review and modification of the next day's lesson plan. The competent instructional supervisor who has helped the teacher plan for instruction must now help the teacher to translate the plans into action.

The discerning supervisor who visits a class in session should be able to tell with little difficulty whether or not the teacher has done any planning for instruction. The clues are there for any perceptive visitor to see:

> Are there any visible written plans to which the teacher refers?
> Does the teacher exhibit confidence?
> Does the teacher appear to know where learners are going?
> Has the teacher communicated the objectives to the learners?
> Is there a flow to the day's activities?
> Does the class experience blocks of time during which nothing constructive seems to be taking place?
> Are the learners kept busy at constructive tasks?
> Does the teacher rely on constructive learning tasks for managing the class or on threats and reprimands?
> Are the needed materials and equipment on hand and ready for use?
> Does the teacher appear to be improvising, moving from one tangent to another, prolonging activities beyond their productive time?
> Does the teacher repeat content after it is apparent that all the learners have mastered it?

The experienced supervisor can attest that adequate planning does make a difference in both teacher behavior and student behavior during the course of a lesson presentation. Let us examine more closely the elements of a well-conducted lesson presentation. The theatrical model will serve our purpose well. For a lesson presentation to be effective the teacher attends separately to the beginning, the middle, and the end of the lesson. For each of these three parts the teacher uses different strategies, Several of the most frequently used strategies will be examined in our analysis of lesson presentation.

Beginning the Lesson

The skilled teacher realizes that the problem of starting a lesson is a little like the problem faced by a storyteller in the initial paragraphs of a story. The storyteller knows that the reader's interest must be stimulated at the very beginning. The master storyteller knows how to grab the reader's attention in the first few sentences. The first two verses of *Genesis* make us want to read on:

In the beginning God created the heaven and the earth. And the earth was without form, and void; and darkness was upon the face of the deep. And the Spirit of God moved upon the face of the waters.

Who can resist reading Agatha Christie's *The Mystery of the Blue Train*, which starts:

It was close on midnight when a man crossed the Place de la Concorde. In spite of the handsome fur coat which garbed his meager form, there was something essentially weak and paltry about him.
A little man with a face like a rat.[5]

We want to hear Rachel Carson's message about the dangers of pollution from chemicals when she commands our attention in the first three paragraphs of *Silent Spring*:

There was once a town in the heart of America where all life seemed to live in harmony with its surroundings. The town lay in the midst of a checkerboard of prosperous farms, with fields of grain and hillsides of orchards. . . . Along the roads, laurel, viburnum and alder, great ferns and wildflowers delighted the traveler's eye. . . . Then a strange blight crept over the area and everything began to change. Some evil spell had settled on the community: mysterious maladies swept the flocks of chickens; the cattle and sheep sickened and died. Everywhere was a shadow of death.[6]

Each author attempts at the very beginning of the story to arouse the reader's interest and establish a particular frame of mind or "set." The author seeks to influence the reader to respond to the message in such a way that the reader will want to learn more. An aura of mystery and suspense lures the reader on, sometimes to the point where he or she cannot put the book down until the last page is finished. How many people have read a fascinating book until the wee hours of the morning! Some enduring books and movies have had such an impact on readers and viewers that they have read or seen them again and again.

On a smaller scale we see the phenomenon of set in our daily lives as we attempt to influence others' predispositions about people, places, or things. Two girls are talking, for example, and one tells the other, "I met the coolest guy last night. I want you to meet him." The drama critic writes in a review, "The new musical which opened last night was a smash hit." Our neighbors invite us into their home to see slides of their recent trip to Switzerland and wax ecstatic with words such as, "If you ever go to Switzerland, you mustn't miss Lucerne." I was once walking on the street in a Latin American republic and a young man from a disadvantaged neighborhood came alongside and started to rave, "This country is ugly. Everything about it is ugly." The endless television commercials exhort us to rush out to buy the sweetest smelling soap, the longest lasting deodorant, and the softest toilet tissue. Daily we try to put others into a certain frame of mind or are recipients of others' attempts to motivate us to take certain actions.

A teacher shares a similar need to stimulate learners to put themselves in a frame of mind receptive to pursuing the content of the lesson. The teacher wants to pique the learners' interest and cause them to want to go on for more. The teacher wants to make the forthcoming content interesting to learners as well as to give learners some notion of the relationship of the ensuing content to previous content and some idea of its relevance to them and their lives. When planning, the teacher should design some means of eliciting student interest at the start of the lesson.

The techniques a teacher uses to put the learners in a receptive frame of mind are referred to by some specialists on instruction as set induction.[7] Set induction is a pedagogical term used to label various techniques employed by teachers to gain students' attention, stimulate their interest, and make them receptive to further instruction.

We have all sat in classes where the teacher's opening ploy has been deadening. What kind of reactions may we expect from the following classic openings?

"Open your books to page 113."
Calling the roll, consuming five minutes of valuable class time.
"O.K., who's scheduled to give a report today?"
Handing out corrected exam papers, the teacher comments, "This was a terrible set of examinations."
"Class, today we're going to study about volcanoes." The teacher then plunges into the lesson plan.
"Take out your workbooks and work the problems on page 30."

What kind of mind set may be expected from the learners? Will they react with a "Ho-hum, just another day"? Will the class that did poorly on the examinations react positively when they are told how bad their papers were? Will calling the roll bring them to attention and the expectation of learning something interesting? Is the teacher's statement that the class is going to study about volcanoes sufficient to motivate the learners to proceed with the topic?

Teachers need to inject an element of the dramatic or semidramatic into an introduction. They should ask themselves questions like, "What technique—or stunt, if you wish—will be likely to attract the students' interest?" "What do I know about my students that I can capitalize on to make them want to learn this material?"

Techniques of set induction can be most personal. Some teachers can carry off some techniques better than others. Some teachers have almost an innate flare for the dramatic. Others find a modicum of just plain hammyness a useful tool in dealing with children and adolescents. No supervisor should expect that every lesson of every day will be a polished gem and that teachers will succeed in making youngsters become wildly excited and eager for each day's study. But supervisors have a right to expect that teachers will make more than a token gesture at putting the learners into the proper frame of mind for studying the material. There are several guidelines which any teacher may follow in an effort to establish set. Even if the teacher is not able to put all learners into a receptive state of mind, at the very least they can be pointed in the right direction.

Let us assume first that we wish to establish an appropriate set for studying a topic new to the class. After we examine several suggested ways of arousing interest in the new topic, we will consider ways of inducing set with continuing topics. Each lesson, whether it is the first or part of a series, should incorporate a planned introduction. What techniques can we borrow from the repertoire of experienced, skilled teachers to motivate learners to pursue the topic of a unit we have planned for them?

The teacher can bring in an article from a current magazine or recent edition of the daily newspaper pertinent to the topic and read it to the class. If the article is a controversial one, so much the better. Using a story reported in the press immediately shows that the topic has currency and relevance to the students' daily lives. A report on the discovery of asbestos filings in the drinking water of a city on one of the Great Lakes would stimulate interest in study of the Great Lakes much more effectively than the teacher's announcement, "Today we're going to study the Great Lakes." Such an article could introduce not only a unit on geography of the Great Lakes region but also a unit on water or other pollution. A chart from a magazine article showing stock market cycles could be used to introduce either a unit on the stock market or a unit on graphing. The timelier the article, the better. The fact that some students may already have read the article serves to underscore that what they will study has importance to them. This technique can bring the past and the future as well as the present to the students' attention. A news account of the damage being done to the Colosseum by modern day traffic in Rome could be used to introduce a variety of units, including the significance of the Colosseum itself and ancient Rome's contributions to the present. A unit on space could begin with the dramatic news report of the Venus probes which revealed the facts that Venus' atmosphere is mainly carbon dioxide, and its surface temperature 900° Fahrenheit.

The teacher can introduce a lesson with realia—physical objects—or barring tangible materials, pictures, which may provoke a reaction. Geographical units can be initiated with samples of arts and crafts from various countries. A jade necklace, an onyx chess set, a hand-tooled leather purse, and a straw hat can arouse a curiosity about the places from which they originated and the people who created them. Samples of foreign currency can be used to start a unit on international money and banking. Three-dimensional geometric figures which may be taken apart and reassembled have proved helpful in beginning mathematical units.

If it is impractical or not feasible to carry physical objects to the classroom, photographs, slides, or filmstrips can be used effectively to induce set. Pictures of breadfruit, papaya, and passion fruit, edibles not customarily seen in most parts of the United States, can replace the fruits themselves at the start of a unit on products of the tropics. The photograph of the raising of the American flag on Iwo Jima symbolizes the war in the Pacific, 1941–1945. Pictures of the Berlin Wall can be used to commence a unit on divided Germany, the cold war, or human values.

Audio impressions can be as effective as visual impressions. Recordings of the voices of John F. Kennedy, Franklin D. Roosevelt, Martin Luther King, and other men and women of history help learners think of these personalities of the past as real people rather than myths. A particular atmosphere can be created in class by the judicious selection of recorded music or poetry or drama. The teacher's aim is to provide just enough stimulation to cause students to want to get into the study of the topic.

A simple means of creating student curiosity is the technique teachers use when they write an unfamiliar word or expression on the board and let students ponder it.

The word *cloning* written across the blackboard can bring about a discussion of both philosophical and biological dimensions when students debate whether it is possible or desirable for human beings to be able to reproduce themselves asexually. Significant words of low familiarity will serve as brain teasers. The teacher might scrawl "deoxyribonucleic acid" on the board and ask the learners to define it. Some bright student may know or guess it to be DNA, the main complex compound found in chromosomes. From there the teacher can move into a unit on heredity and genetics. The words *habeas corpus* can instigate a unit on fundamental freedoms. It is unlikely that history students will at first recognize the names Vladimir Ilyich Ulyanov or Iosif Vissarionovich Dzhugashvili, but world history would have been far different without Lenin and Stalin, names by which they were better known. Unfamiliar though significant words and names may be found in all subject fields. The device of writing such words on the board to bring forth questions and discussion offers a simple but effective way of introducing a lesson.

The teacher may stage an action which may even startle the learners. To introduce a unit on psychology he or she may spend the first few minutes of class berating them, calling them "dumb," telling them they are the worst class ever and predicting no good for all of them. Then with a smile, the teacher lets them in on the secret that it was just playacting to illustrate a point and proceeds to ask them how it felt to be on the receiving end of such a harangue. An endless variety of role-playing situations can be concocted with the aid of other teachers, parents, and students. For example, an angry parent (whose role is played by an adult friend of the teacher) barges into the classroom and accuses the teacher of using obscene, Communist, irreligious, and unpatriotic textbooks. The parent storms out of the room to the bewilderment of the learners. At this point the teacher breaks the shock effect and starts them on a study of censorship, freedom of the press, or church-state relationships. As another illustration, a class in journalism or criminal justice might have its powers of observation tested when (by prearrangement) two boys who resemble each other rush into the classroom. One angrily accuses the other of "ratting" on him and threatens to "beat him up." The teacher shoos them out of the room and then asks the class to relate what they saw and heard. These contrived situations can make the topic to be studied dramatic.

Needless to say, the teacher cannot fruitfully employ dramatic means of introducing every lesson. After a unit or module has been started, more routine methods of beginning a lesson will be in order. Yet, each lesson should have some planned introduction even if it is only an explanation of the transition to the particular lesson from the previous day's lesson. Some of the more routine introductory procedures would include:

1. *An explanation of the reasons for studying the content.* The teacher will tell the students why the content is important to them and how it can have meaning in their daily lives. Some content is easily justified on the basis that it meets both immediate and long-range needs of students. Other content is more difficult to justify but still important, and, sad to say, some content is not justifiable at all and would be better removed from the curriculum.

2. *A review of yesterday's lesson.* A quick review can be conducted in a number

of ways. The teacher can summarize what took place the day before and how it relates to today's lesson. A student can be asked to summarize what was learned in class yesterday. The teacher can pose some questions based on the previous day's work and see how well the students comprehended the material. Sometimes only a very few minutes of review will be necessary. Other times the entire work of the preceding day must be repeated to assure mastery of the content.

3. *An analysis of results of a test taken the preceding day.* If the preceding day's work included a test or examination and the papers have been scored, the teacher should give them back immediately and go over them. The test should be used as a learning device and a review. The teacher should show students where they made their mistakes and how to correct them.

The supervisor should help the teacher devise effective procedures for initiating lessons and provide the teacher with feedback on how the introductory procedures appear to go over with the students. The supervisor should make the teacher aware of the fact that half the battle is won if students are interested, have developed a receptive frame of reference, understand the value of the content to be studied, comprehend the relationship of the present day's lesson to the previous day's and to future lessons, and are oriented to the direction their study will take.

The Middle of the Lesson

When the teacher feels that the class is in the proper frame of mind, it is time to move into the heart of the lesson. The word *feels* is stressed here not only in connection with lesson presentation but also in relationship to the entire teaching process. Though the teaching act strives to be as scientific as possible, much of teaching still remains an art. A great deal of teaching is intuitive. We cannot say, for example, that set induction should occupy the first five minutes of each class. The teacher has to develop almost a sixth sense to judge when the learners are ready. With experience the teacher can detect the nuances and know when to start, change pace, recapitulate, and end. Teachers must learn when to switch from one technique to another, which techniques most frequently achieve the best results, and which procedures are adaptable to which types of students.

Ordinarily, many strategies are available to present any given lesson and many combinations of those strategies are possible. As any experienced supervisor can attest, not all teachers are equally skilled in implementing all stategies. One of the big advantages of some team-teaching plans is that they capitalize on the strengths of teachers. Those who are skilled at lecturing to large groups, for example, may put those skills to use when team teaching and differentiated staffing patterns are employed. When the individual teacher is alone in the self-contained classroom, however, he or she must develop at least a passable level of performance in the most frequently called upon strategies.

Efforts have been made by teacher educators in recent years to identify the component skills of the teaching process. Dwight Allen and Kevin Ryan have identified 14 general teaching skills.[8] In this chapter we will concern ourselves with five.

The first of these general (or generic) skills has already been introduced: opening the lesson or set induction. The chapter will terminate with a discussion of the skill of closing the lesson, or closure. To help the teachers with the presentation of the central part of a lesson the supervisor may examine with them three major skills which are discussed below: (1) lecturing, (2) conducting a discussion, and (3) providing for variation. A sixth skill (or set of skills) evaluation, will be discussed in Chapter 5.

Lecturing

Included in the concept of lecturing are telling, explaining, describing, demonstrating, and teacher talk generally. Chapter 11 shows that these skills are grossly overworked. It is a fact of school life that teachers by and large talk far too much. Yet, lecturing is a time-honored technique not soon to be shunned by instructors. It *can* be an efficient means of getting across large quantities of information to a large group of students in a short period of time. It can also be an extremely inefficient mode of instruction and one unsuited to many learners. The strategy of lecturing can be improved if the teacher will follow a few guidelines, among which are the following:

1. *The learners should be mature enough to accept the mode of lecturing.* As a general rule, the younger the child, the less receptive he or she is to the technique of lecturing. Young children do not have the powers of concentration possessed by older youth. Lecturing requires a self-discipline not yet developed by young children who must be active rather than passive. Youngsters cannot sit still for long while the teacher drones on. Consequently, straight lecturing, that is, sustained talk, is the stock-in-trade of the college professor. Whether college professors should indulge in relentless lecturing is another story, but the fact that college students are older, more disciplined, more motivated, and not a captive audience makes the strategy of lecturing at least a passable one at the college level.

2. *The learners should have developed adequate listening skills.* The development of listening skills is a function of both maturity and training. In recent years the language arts have incorporated instruction in the skills of listening. It is generally agreed that listening skills can be learned and improved. One only needs to attend some committee meetings to realize that maturity alone is no guarantee that listening skills have been perfected. Through faulty instructional procedures teachers sometimes encourage the development of poor rather than good listening skills. The teacher must know whether the learners have sufficient skill in listening before choosing lecturing.

3. *The teacher must use language the learners understand.* The teacher must neither talk over their heads nor down to them. Either case will lose listeners. The teacher must be careful of the vocabulary burden, making sure that all students understand the words in the lectures. If puzzlement is detected after using an unfamiliar word, the teacher should stop and define the word. Teachers need to exert some caution in the use of children's slang and street language. Some teachers feel that to communicate they must use the current slangy expressions. Thus, they pepper their lectures with expressions like "ripoff" instead of "fraud," "split" instead of "leave," and "beautiful" or "fantastic" for "good" or "correct." A little argot goes

a long way. Children and youth do not expect teachers to use their language; they expect teachers to play their roles as adults. Youngsters often resent or are amused by adults' attempts to mimic them. Judicious use of selected words may help the teacher get the message across but overworking the youngsters' jargon may cause the teacher to lose the audience.

4. *Every lecture should be planned.* The teacher should have prepared a written outline that sets forth the key points to be made, key questions to be raised, and illustrations to amplify key points. Like a good lesson plan a lecture should have an introduction, a middle, and an ending. Amusing illustrations will help carry the lecture across. A summarization of the main points of the lecture is essential.

5. *Talk alone is not sufficient.* A lecture should be supplemented whenever possible with actions (demonstration) and visual aids. Slides, charts, pictures, and transparencies help create interest. Even the use of the blackboard for a "chalk talk" is superior to talk by itself.

6. *Provision should be made for feedback and follow-up.* Time should be allotted for questions from the class. The teacher should conduct some sort of evaluation to make sure that learners have mentally digested the points made in the lecture. The technique of following up a lecture to a large group in small discussion groups has much to recommend it.

The supervisor should counsel teachers who have a penchant for lecturing to help them decide whether lecturing is indeed the most effective way to teach and, if so, what measures can be taken by the teachers to achieve the maximum advantage from use of this strategy.

Conducting a Discussion

Discussion and lecturing are often confused. Many teachers claim to be conducting a discussion when, indeed, they are lecturing to students. Discussion implies an interaction between the teacher and learners. I have used the term *discussion* somewhat loosely in referring to the narration in this text. I do so with the assumption that the instructor who adopts this text will use the narration in developing discussions with the students. An effective discussion involves not only certain individual mental and oral skills but also skills in group participation, for discussion is a group activity, not a lecture nor a dialogue. Three subcomponents of the generic skill of discussion, (1) student participation, (2) nonverbal cues, and (3) questioning should be brought to the attention of teachers by the supervisor.

Student Participation.   The teacher must provide continuous and frequent opportunity for students to express themselves. Discussion time should give students a chance to develop skills of listening, thinking, speaking, and participating as members of a group. Maximum student participation should be sought. It is often difficult for teachers to restrain themselves and give students a chance to express their thoughts, but this is a must. In conducting a discussion the teacher is not only concerned with illuminating the material under study but also with perfecting the discussion skills themselves. So much of the world's social and business activities is transacted through discussion that these skills cannot be slighted in any course or grade.

Teachers should attempt to provide opportunities for all learners to participate and not be content with participation by only a few students. They should not let individuals dominate a discussion but should seek to develop a kind of atmosphere where students feel free to state their opinions and to raise questions. Students should be encouraged to volunteer responses and to contribute illustrations and anecdotes from their own experiences. The teacher needs to make the students feel that class participation is an important part of the day's lesson. Students will participate more frequently when they are reassured that their opinions count for something and when they do not fear ridicule or disapproval by the teacher or their classmates.

One of the teacher's tasks in conducting a discussion is to keep it on track and under control. Students must learn to take turns talking and listen while others are speaking. The teacher generally serves as moderator but can often turn over this function to students so they can gain additional skills. The teacher should help the students evaluate the significance of their own responses and questions by urging them to support their positions with facts and logical argument.

When the supervisor sits in on a discussion lesson, he or she should observe which students are actively participating and which ones are sitting back, which ones the teacher calls on repeatedly and which ones are never called on. The supervisor should observe whether the discussion stays on its course, whether participants listen to and understand each other, and whether they accept each other's ideas. If problems are detected in these areas, the supervisor should confer with the teacher about ways the discussions can be improved.

Nonverbal cues.   Messages are often conveyed through means other than the spoken or printed word. A look, a nod, a frown, or just silence may transmit meaning to the listener. A discussion can be started, stopped, moved along, or turned in another direction by the judicious use of teacher gestures or movement. A nod and a smile from the teacher can reinforce a student's contribution. A frown at a student who is not paying attention can bring him or her back into participation. A period of complete silence can often quiet a group and cause it to return to the subject at hand. The old technique of tapping on the backboard with a piece of chalk can call for increased attention to the topic under consideration.

The teacher is conveying a message to students when moving around the room and directing discussion from varying vantage points. The message may be, "I want to see everybody participating," or it may be, "The noisy clique in the corner must pay attention to the discussion," or it may be, "I am just as interested in the participants in the back row as in the front row." The teacher's movement acts as a stimulus for the learners to continue participating.

When the teacher adopts a puzzled expression, the student who is responding knows that the response is not clear. Teachers who are adept at charades can often draw out responses from students. Audio-lingual foreign language teachers, for example, have developed a whole range of nonverbal signals for specific types of student responses.

Using silence and nonverbal cues is a little like directing an orchestra. The teacher can point to the students who are to respond, can appear to follow a student's comment with an accepting "uh, huh," can show bewilderment with an audible "hmmmmm," and can show amusement with a broad smile and rolling eyes. The analogy of teaching to dramatics comes forth again as we employ movement, gesture, and silence to convey certain meanings. Some of these are habitual traits with some individuals while others may learn to develop the cues by watching other teachers and by studying their own performance. A supervisor should help teachers analyze their use of silence and nonverbal cues by watching them in action and providing them with feedback on their performances.

Questioning.   What is often called lecturing or discussion in reality turns out to be an oral question-and-answer session. The teacher poses questions and the students are expected to furnish the right answers. Of all classroom strategies questioning may well be the most overworked and the most often abused.

Contrary to common practice questioning sessions should be planned. It is apparent to the supervisor when a teacher is firing questions at students from the "top of the head." The questioning session should have specific purpose and an internal consistency which can be achieved only through advance planning. In any question-and-answer session the teacher should write key questions into the lesson plan to avoid forgetting essential points.

Questioning is a skill which can be developed by following the few rules below.

1. *Since questioning is essentially a verbal, cognitive type of activity, the teacher should strive to raise the questions to the highest possible level of the cognitive domain.* Reference is made to the six levels of the Bloom taxonomy: knowledge, comprehension, application, analysis, synthesis, and evaluation.[9] Whenever possible teachers should pose questions at the higher end of the classification spectrum. Too often they settle for simple recall or yes/no types of responses from learners. Such responses neither encourage thought nor give students practice in formulating their ideas and opinions.

Though the teacher may seek to raise the level of the questions to those of a higher order, certainly we would not eliminate the lower levels completely. There are times when lower level questions are perfectly legitimate, particularly in conducting drill sessions on materials of a repetitive nature. The important consideration, however, is that the teacher's questioning not remain at the lower levels of the taxonomy but consciously and deliberately move toward the higher levels. Questions at the lower level may sharpen the memory process but they do little to develop the more important abilities—to think and to express one's thoughts. Let's illustrate briefly questions at the six levels in the teaching field of English.

> *Knowledge*: Name three novels of Charles Dickens.
> *Comprehension*: Give me a résumé in your own words of the first chapter of *David Copperfield*.
> *Application*: Is there any moral lesson in any of the novels of Dickens you have read that would apply to our society today?

Analysis: What is there about *A Christmas Carol* that has made it a favorite story for more than 100 years?

Synthesis: What human values run through all three novels: *David Copperfield*, *Oliver Twist*, and *Great Expectations*?

Evaluation: In your judgment which is the better novel: *David Copperfield* or *Great Expectations*? Why?

It is not always possible, depending on the content, to structure higher order questions. Nor is it always possible to run the full gamut of questioning from lowest level to highest. The teacher's goal, however, is to raise the level of questioning to the highest order possible wherever possible.

2. *Questions should be phrased clearly and in language the learner will understand*. The importance of using language geared to the level of the learner has already been stressed in the previous discussion of the strategy of lecturing. The same principle holds true with any oral activity which transpires in the classroom. Not only should questions be clear but they should also be in the teacher's own words, not those of the text materials. Questioning should be considered supplementary to text materials, an approach to content different from that used by authors of the text materials. By the same token, students should be expected to respond in their own words instead of repeating the language of the text materials.

3. *Since the teacher is concerned with the development of listening skills as well as speaking and comprehending skills, he or she should not develop the habit of repeating the questions and the answers given by students*. The teacher should speak loudly and clearly enough so all students can hear. Repetition encourages students to allow their attention to wander and wait for the second go-around. Only if it is apparent that students have not understood the question should it be repeated or, preferably, rephrased. Students should be taught to develop the habit of listening the first time and to make their own responses clear and audible so their classmates can understand them.

4. *A questioning session should consume only a portion of a lesson*. Long, extended question-and-answer periods can cause the teacher to lose the audience and defeat the purposes for which the questioning was intended. One help in livening up questioning sessions is to cast them in the form of games. For example, by creating teams to field questions, the teacher can introduce a pleasant competitive spirt. This technique, however, is adaptable only for the lower level questions and is too awkward for more complex and probing questions.

5. *The affective learning which takes place along with the cognitive should be kept in mind by the teacher*. Student responses should be positively reinforced by the teacher with words or gestures of approval when the responses are satisfactory. When the responses are not correct, the student's attempt at responding should be encouraged even though the content of the response itself may have to be corrected. The teacher is responsible for maintaining a classroom climate that permits students to respond, encourages all to participate, and develops a spirit of acceptance for each other's ideas.

Supervisors should encourage teachers to examine their questioning technique to see if it meets guidelines such as those cited above.

Providing for Variation

In the fields of literature, drama, and television a fast-moving story commands reader or viewer attention. A television producer who wants to hold an audience through the commercials knows how important it is to present the actors in varying situations, provide action in the story, change scenery, and use appropriate audio and visual effects. The teacher can borrow some of the film and television producer's tricks for, like the producer, the teacher must attempt to prevent boredom and disinterest from setting in.

Unlike the producer the teacher is up against the inexorable laws of human growth and development. Youngsters tend to be restless and in need of movement and change. Their attention span is much shorter than adults', and the younger the child, the shorter the span of attention. Since not all young people are intrinsically motivated to encounter the material the teacher is presenting, the teacher must devise extrinsic means of attempting to arouse interest in the topic of study.

Variation is a key word in the task of stimulating student interest. The teacher must vary the content, the pace of learning, the activities of the lesson, even his or her own style of teaching. The supervisor may observe in the teacher's performance three components of the generic teaching skill which we call variation. These components are (1) variation of the stimuli, (2) variation of learning activities for the group, and (3) variation of learning activities for the individual.

Variation of the Stimuli. Every second of every class hour countless stimuli effect certain responses in the learners and in the teacher. The human beings in the classroom, the lighting, the color of the paint on the walls and ceiling, the furniture and equipment in the room, the loudspeaker and clock, and the activity which takes place outside the doors and windows all have a bearing on the learning or lack of learning in the classroom. By far the most significant stimuli are the teacher and the learners, each of whom interacts with the other and provokes certain responses in the other.

The stereotype teacher who sits or stands motionless, makes no gestures, is unaware of the impact of nonverbal cues, and leads the class through a single, long, unchanging learning activity is violating a premise of good teaching namely, frequent altering of the stimuli. This means, of course, that a teacher must be able to detect stimuli which affect learning in the classroom and must be able to read the impact of these stimuli. When spotting the telltale signs of boredom, the teacher needs to shift gears rather quickly in the hope that the change will refuel the learners and bring them back to life.

The staff of the Stanford Teacher Education Program has developed a training program to help teachers perfect the skill of stimulus variation. The Stanford program trains teachers in the behaviors of movement, gestures, focusing, interactional styles, pausing, and shifting sensory channels.

An earlier section of this chapter on conducting a discussion considered the effectiveness of teacher movement, the use of gestures to transmit meaning, and the use of silence (pausing) to secure the attention of the students. Allen and Ryan suggested that teachers master the skills of focusing, interactional styles, and shifting sensory channels as well as the skills of movement, gestures, and pausing.[10] By focusing, these authors meant directing learner attention to particular objects or concepts. Typically, focusing is done with a statement such as "Keep this point in mind," or "Let's look at the table on page 25." The teacher zeros in on an item and gives it special emphasis.

The term interaction has been used elsewhere in this text and it has been postulated that learning is an interactive process. Allen and Ryan supported this view by cautioning against teacher monologs and recommending training in varying inter-actional styles.[11] The monologist may hold an honored place in the entertainment world but that style is decidedly out of place in the classroom, where learner achievement is the goal. Teachers should not only interact with the learners but should change the style of interaction frequently. Teachers customarily interact with groups but may also interact with individuals within a group and may direct interaction between students. All three of these interactive styles are superior to the monolog.

Shifting sensory channels as set forth by Allen and Ryan is a simple skill which is often overlooked. The most common sensory channel in teaching is the path from the teacher's mouth to the student's ears—spoken communication. Allen and Ryan recommended switching stimuli from oral to visual and back again. There may even be times when the senses of smell and touch may become the primary modes of communication.

The teacher's objective is to maintain, hold, or recapture, if necessary, the learners' attention. Manipulating and varying the stimuli can more readily gain and keep student interest.

Variation of Group Learning Activities.   If we identify all the learning activities which take place in class as stimuli, then this second point in our discussion of providing for variation is identical to the first point: stimuli must be varied; therefore, learning activities, which are stimuli, must be varied. By employing the stimulus variation of focusing, I wish to distinguish between the specific stimuli mentioned above and more general learning activities or strategies. The supervisor should suggest to teachers that they build into their lesson plans a variety of activities for each lesson. As a general rule, a single, prolonged activity—be it lecture, panel discussion, or film—will not hold a group's attention and interest as well as a variety of activities. Key activities should be written into the teacher's lesson plans along with the estimated amount of time the class should devote to each activity. The object of variation of group activities is learner motivation.

Variation of Individual Learning Activities.   Not only must activities be varied for the group as a whole but special activities are necessary for individuals who comprise that group. With this skill we enter the difficult realm of individualizing instruction. The individualization of instruction is a noble teaching goal and it has been described, analyzed, and advocated in countless books and articles. It is often made to seem like a simple task to which easy formulas can be applied. In reality, individualization of instruction is extremely difficult. The ultimate would be an individualized curriculum, individual programming, and tutorial instruction using either human or machine tutors. However, education is a mass venture quite unlike the one-to-one relationship of doctor to patient or lawyer to client. We must handle individuals within groups and as members of a larger group, the student body. Given the mass nature of education we can partially adapt instruction to individual differences as we attempt to move toward the ideal of individualization of instruction.

In the last analysis learning is an individual activity. No one can learn for another; one human being can help another learn but what goes on in the mind of the individual is an intensely personal affair. The teacher, who is the principal helper during the formal education process, will put into practice whatever skillful means he or she can employ to help differentiate instruction and make it more personal to the learner. The supervisor may point out that instruction is individualized when the teacher:

1. *Subgroups students within the class.* The teacher may create special interest groups, ability groups, or remedial groups. By subgrouping learners the teacher reduces the range of abilities or interests and makes instruction more individualized albeit not completely individualized. Students may be grouped and regrouped for specific tasks and for special purposes. The teacher can more effectively help individuals within smaller subgroups to realize their own personal goals. Subgrouping is simpler and possibly more successful in schools where teachers are assisted by aides or where teachers are members of a teaching team.

2. *Allows choices.* The teacher should make a habit of extending the opportunities for selection to students whenever possible during the school year. Students can be given a choice, for example, of subgroups to which they wish to belong. They can be offered choices of learning activities which have equal value, approaches they would like to take to the study of a topic, and resources they would prefer to use.

3. *Provides for independent study.* Those students who are mature and interested enough to pursue a topic of study independently should be given the chance to do so. The teacher may allot a portion of the student's time to independent study under supervision.

4. *Differentiates questions to individuals on the basis of their particular interests and abilities.* When conducting an oral question-and-answer session, the teacher can vary the complexity of questions according to the abilities of the intended responder.

5. *Provides differentiated assignments.* Minimal assignments may be set for slower students and more difficult assignments for faster students. The teacher may distinguish among a series of tasks those which are most difficult and assign them to the brighter students. Some extrinsic device may need to be used to motivate the faster learners to do the more difficult tasks but the practice of bonus tasks or honors assignments sometimes helps.

6. *Utilizes resources of varying levels of difficulty.* It is advisable to provide learning resources beyond a single adopted textbook. There should be supplementary text materials available for varying levels of readers. There should be materials which

present the topic being studied in different ways so that if the treatment in the text-book is not clear students may approach the topic in another way.

7. *Makes use of learning resources outside the classroom.* The teacher will want to call on the services of the reading clinic, if there is one, and learning resource centers, where students may study more or less on their own. Worthwhile community resources should be utilized.

The fact that the goal of complete individualization of instruction may never be reached should not dissuade the teacher from using those techniques that are available for providing for individual differences. The supervisor should strongly reinforce the efforts of teachers who try to achieve the goal of individualization of instruction.

Closing the Lesson

It has been observed that not only should each lesson have a beginning, a middle, and an end but also a *planned* beginning, middle, and end. The closing of the class lesson should be controlled by the teacher, not by the ringing of the bell or the passing of groups or classes.

Toward the end of the day's lesson, teachers customarily make the assignment for the next day. In analyzing a lesson presentation with a teacher, the supervisor should not neglect the skill of assignment making. The classic distortions of assignment making are the hurried directives from the teacher, "Read the next chapter," "Study pages 115–135," and "Work the next 10 problems in your book." Such assignments are common and far too simplistic for the most effective learning. The supervisor might encourage teachers to take a sampling of the assignments they have given their class the last few days and see how the assignments stack up against the following guidelines.

1. *The assignment should be clear to all students.* This means that the teacher must take enough time during the lesson to make the job understood. The directions must be in language the learners understand. Time should be allotted for questions about the assignment from the students.

2. *The assignments should be on work the class has already covered or the teacher is sure the learners are able to do.* If the assignment involves new principles the teacher has not yet explained to the students, it is best that they not be directed to go ahead without adequate instruction. If students attempt work ahead of instruction, they may do the work incorrectly and develop wrong learnings which are then difficult to correct.

3. *Difficulties students may experience in the assignment should be anticipated and suggestions given by the teacher on how to overcome them.* The teacher may review the points of difficulty and direct the students to resources which will prove helpful.

4. *Assignments should be differentiated for varying interests and abilities.* The element of choice can often enter at this point. Though more difficult to plan than a single, blanket assignment for all, multiple assignments have the advantage of appeal to a wider number of learners.

5. *The assignments should be reasonable in terms of the amount of out-of-class work expected.* Secondary school teachers in particular must be aware of the amount of homework they are piling on students.

6. *Assignments should not only be reasonable in length, they should be necessary.* "Busy work"—assignments for assignments' sake—should be avoided. Busy work only serves to discourage rather than promote interest. If there is no real need for an assignment, none should be made.

7. *Resources for accomplishing the assignment must be available.* The teacher cannot assume the availability of resources in the home. Consequently, he or she must know what resources are called for and direct students to their location.

8. *It is helpful if assignments are given through more than one sensory channel.* Instead of relying exclusively on an oral direction the teacher can supply instruction in written form as well. An oral explanation based on written instructions makes the task to be done that much clearer, for the student not only hears but sees the assignment and, as a result, is better able to carry out the instructions.

Before the class ends the teacher will want to know whether the objectives of the day's lesson have been achieved. Success with the lesson may have been evident all through the day's activities. However, before the group leaves for the day the teacher should evaluate achievement of the objectives no matter how limited they may be. This may be accomplished by posing a few summary questions to see if the students have understood the work of the day and by encouraging questions from the group. It can be misleading, however, if the group has no questions. The customary teacher's remark, "Any questions?" does not always bear fruit. Students may not have understood enough of the lesson to ask intelligent questions. They may not know what they don't know and therefore cannot raise questions. Further, they may be tired or disinterested, and ready to leave class, not to prolong the lesson.

The teacher must allow at least a few minutes before the end of the class for a wrap-up or closure. For a few moments the students will reexamine what they have achieved that day and attempt to fix the more important learnings in their minds. The teacher may effect closure by reviewing the main points of the day's lesson or by asking one of the students to summarize the main points. It is advisable to review with them what they have learned—or at least what was expected to be learned. The teacher not only looks back over the day's work but shows the learners the connections with previous lessons and with future lessons, particularly with tomorrow's lesson. The supervisor should look for lesson closure when visiting teachers and observing them in action.

A CHECKLIST

Based on principles discussed in the preceding pages, the check-list below is supplied to help the supervisor evaluate lesson presentations. The more items the supervisor can check "Yes" when observing a teacher teaching, the better that lesson presentation may be said to be. "No" responses serve as indicators of points calling for dialog between the supervisor and the teacher.

A CHECKLIST ON LESSON PRESENTATION

On the basis of classroom observation the supervisor will check "Yes" for those items observed in the lesson presentation and "No" for those items not observed.

	YES	NO
SELECTION OF RESOURCES		
related to objectives	____	____
in keeping with abilities of learners	____	____
in keeping with age of learners	____	____
of interest to learners	____	____
varied for individual differences	____	____
accurate and up-to-date	____	____
without bias or balanced as to biases	____	____
easily accessible to learners	____	____
without cost to learners	____	____
SELECTION OF STRATEGIES		
right for learners	____	____
right for teacher	____	____
right for subject matter	____	____
right for time available	____	____
right for resources available	____	____
right for facilities	____	____
right for objectives	____	____
CONDUCT OF THE LESSON		
General		
written plans present	____	____
teacher exhibits confidence	____	____
teacher appears to know where class is going	____	____
communicates objectives to learners	____	____
flow to the day's activities	____	____
avoids periods of inactivity, waste time	____	____
learners busy at constructive tasks	____	____
materials and equipment on hand	____	____
avoids unnecessary repetition of content	____	____
Beginning of lesson		
establishes set		
Middle of lesson	____	____
lecturing	____	____
learners mature enough		
learners developing listening skills	____	____
learners understand language	____	____
evidence of advance planning	____	____
supplemented with aids	____	____
provision for feedback and follow-up	____	____

	YES	NO
student participation		
continuous opportunity to express selves		
use of silence and nonverbal cues		
effective questioning		
higher order questions		
learners understand language		
avoids repeating questions and answers		
consumes only portion of lesson		
teacher aware of affective learning		
provision for variation		
varies stimuli		
varies activities for the group		
varies activities for individuals		
End of lesson		
provides for evaluation		
assignment making		
assignment clear		
on work covered or students able to do		
anticipates difficult points		
differentiates for varying interests and abilities		
reasonable length		
necessary		
resources available		
uses more than one sensory channel		
achieves closure		

SUMMARY

Lesson presentation involves a complex variety of component skills. The supervisor can be a help to teachers as they translate their unit and lesson plans into action. The supervisor looks to see if the teacher has chosen suitable resources and selected appropriate strategies. In this chapter we have provided guidelines for selection of both resources and strategies. The supervisor helps teachers in developing generic skills of instruction which include effective ways of beginning, carrying through, and closing a lesson.

The supervisor should encourage teachers to increase student participation and incorporate a variety of stimuli and activities in both their planning and actual presentation. To help the supervisor work with teachers on lesson presentation we have examined the specific skills of set induction, lecturing, discussion, the use of silence and nonverbal cues, questioning technique, stimulus variation, providing activities for both groups and individuals, making assignments, and closure. Supervisors should help teachers discover whether they are using time most productively for instructional purposes.

It is in the presentation stage that the carefully laid plans come to fruition—or unfortunately, fail. Lesson presentation is the phase of instruction the public knows as teaching, since they tend to be unaware of or ignore the hours of planning, grading papers, and other miscellaneous duties required of today's teacher. It is the presentation phase which is the most rewarding to the teacher and which keeps most teachers in the classroom. It is during this stage that ideas leap from mind to mind, skills are mastered by those who lacked them before instruction, and knowledge is stored in the brain—primarily because of the efforts of the teacher.

ACTIVITIES FOR FURTHER STUDY

1. Define:
   teaching strategy   stimulus variation
   set induction   closure
2. Summarize common errors made by teachers in presenting a lesson and describe ways in which you, as a supervisor, could help teachers to overcome the errors.
3. Prepare a lecture/demonstration such as you would give to an in-service group of teachers on one of the following topics: selection of strategies, set induction, lecturing, conducting a discussion, questioning, stimulus variation, or closure.
4. Summarize two or three recent articles in professional journals on ways to individualize instruction and critique the articles as to (1) applicability elsewhere, (2) soundness of approach, and (3) cost.
5. Observe a teacher who is presenting a lesson and apply the check-list included at the end of this chapter. As a result of the observation, decide how effective you believe the presentation was in respect to each of the items on the check-list.
6. Write a 50-minute lesson plan that incorporates skills studied in this chapter.
7. Select a topic, choose three strategies for presenting that topic to a particular group of learners, and decide which one of the three strategies would be most effective as an initial strategy.
8. Examine the text materials used at one grade level or in one subject and apply the criteria for resources cited in this chapter.
9. Choose a topic and demonstrate set induction.
10. Describe or outline ways of evaluating the development of listening skills by the students.
11. Prepare and demonstrate effective lecturing following the guidelines presented in this chapter.
12. Prepare and demonstrate a discussion lesson using at least four nonverbal cues.
13. Select a topic that could be taught to a particular group of learners and write two questions (which you would present to a class orally) at each level of the Bloom taxonomy of cognitive objectives.

14. Prepare and conduct a short question-and-answer session and point out how frequently you used higher-order questions.
15. Observe a teacher conducting a questioning session and evaluate the effectiveness of the questioning, applying guidelines presented in this chapter.
16. Write a lesson plan and indicate where you are incorporating variation of learning activities for the group.
17. Observe a teacher presenting a lesson and decide whether the teacher varied the stimuli and in what ways.
18. Demonstrate closure.
19. Collect at least five assignments given by teachers and decide whether or not each assignment meets the guidelines as presented in this chapter.

NOTES

1. See David C. Berliner et al., *Phase III of the Beginning Teacher Evaluation Study*, San Francisco, Calif., Far West Laboratory for Educational Research and Development, 1976; J. E. Brophy and C. M. Evertson, *Process-Product Correlation in the Texas Teacher Effectiveness Study*, Austin, Tex., University of Texas, 1974; Diana Hiatt, "Time Allocation in the Classroom: Is Instruction Being Shortchanged?" *Phi Delta Kappan* 61, no. 4 (December 1979): 289–290; John D. McNeil, "A Scientific Approach to Supervision," in *Supervision of Teaching*, 1982 Yearbook, Thomas J. Sergiovanni, ed., Alexandria, Va., Association for Supervision and Curriculum Development, 1982; Donald M. Medley, "The Effectiveness of Teachers," in *Research in Teaching: Concepts, Findings, and Implications*, Penelope L. Peterson and Herbert J. Wahlberg, eds., Berkeley, Calif., McCutchan, 1979, 11–27. See also notes 2, 3, and 4 below.
2. See the following series of articles: John I. Goodlad, Kenneth A. Sirotnik, and Bette C. Overman, "An Overview of 'A Study of Schooling,'" *Phi Delta Kappan* 61, no. 3 (November 1979): 174–178; M. Frances Klein, Kenneth A. Tye, and Joyce E. Wright, "A Study of Schooling: Curriculum," *Phi Delta Kappan* 61, no. 4 (December 1979): 244–248; Barbara J. Benham, Phil Giesen, and Jeannie Oakes, "A Study of Schooling: Students' Experiences in Schools," *Phi Delta Kappan* 61, no. 5 (January 1980): 337–340; Mary M. Bentzen, Richard C. Williams, and Paul Heckman, "A Study of Schooling: Adult Experiences in Schools," *Phi Delta Kappan* 61, no. 6 (February 1980): 394–397; John I. Goodlad, "A Study of Schooling: Some Findings and Hypotheses," *Phi Delta Kappan* 64, no. 7 (March 1983): 465–470; "A Study of Schooling," *Educational Leadership* 40, no. 7(April 1983), 4–37. See also John I. Goodlad, *A Place Called School: Promise for the Future*, New York, McGraw-Hill, 1983.
3. Jack L. Davidson and Freda M. Holley, "Your Students May Be Spending Only Half the School Day Receiving Instruction," *American School Board Journal* 166, no. 3 (March 1979): 40–41.
4. Barak V. Rosenshine, "Content, Time, and Direct Instruction," in *Research on Teaching*: *Concepts, Findings, and Implications*, Penelope L. Peterson and Herbert J. Wahlberg, eds., Berkeley, Calif., McCutchan, 1979, 52. See also Barak V. Rosenshine, "Academic Engaged Time, Content Covered, and Direct Instruction," *Journal of Education* 160, no. 3 (August 1978): 38–66.
5. Agatha Christie, *The Mystery of the Blue Train*, New York, Dodd, Mead, 1928, 1.
6. Rachel Carson, *Silent Spring*, Boston, Houghton Mifflin, 1962, 1–2.
7. See H. E. Aubertine, *An Experiment in the Set Induction Process and Its Application*, doctoral dissertation, Stanford University, 1964; Committee on Establishing Set, Metcalf Laboratory School, Illinois State University, *Set Induction Materials*, mimeographed, n.d.;

and Dwight Allen and Kevin Ryan, *Microteaching*, Lexington, Mass., Addison-Wesley, 1969, 18–19.
8. Allen and Ryan, 15.
9. See Chapter 3 of this text.
10. Allen and Ryan, 15–18.
11. Ibid., 17.

BIBLIOGRAPHY

Allen, Dwight, and Kevin Ryan. *Microteaching*. Reading, Mass.: Addison-Wesley, 1969.
Berenson, David H., Sally R. Berenson, and Robert B. Carkhuff. *The Skills of Teaching: Lesson Planning Skills*. Amherst, Mass.: Human Resource Development Press, 1978.
———. *The Skills of Teaching: Content Development Skills*. Amherst, Mass.: Human Resource Development Press, 1978.
Berenson, Sally R., David H. Berenson, and Robert R. Carkhuff. *The Skills of Teaching: Teaching Delivery Skills*. Amherst, Mass.: Human Resource Development Press, 1979.
Borg, Walter R., et al., *The Minicourse: A Microteaching Approach to Teacher Education*. Beverly Hills, Calif.: Macmillan Educational Services, 1970.
Brown, George. *Microteaching: A Programme of Teaching Skills*. London: Methuen, 1975.
Carkhuff, Robert R., David H. Berenson, and Richard M. Pierce. *The Skills of Teaching: Interpersonal Skills*. Amherst, Mass.: Human Resource Development Press, 1977.
Goodlad, John I. *A Place Called School: Promise for the Future*. New York: McGraw-Hill, 1983.
Henson, Kenneth T. *Secondary Teaching Methods*. Lexington, Mass.: D. C. Heath, 1981.
Hutchins, C. L., Barbara Dunning, Marilyn Madsen, and Sylvia Rainey. *Minicourses Work*. San Francisco: Far West Laboratory for Educational Research and Development, n.d.
Intermediate Science Curriculum Study. *Individualizing Teacher Preparation*: *Individualization*. Morristown, N.J.: Silver Burdett, 1972.
———. *Individualizing Teacher Preparation: Questioning*. Morristown, N.J.: Silver Burdett, 1972.
Martorella, Peter H. "Teaching Concepts." In *Classroom Teaching Skills*: *A Handbook*, James M. Cooper, ed. Lexington, Mass.: D. C. Heath, 1977.
Mid-Continent Regional Educational Laboratory. *Cooperative Urban Teacher Education Program Manual*. Kansas City, Mo.: n.d.
Miltz, Robert. *How to Explain: A Manual for Teaching*. Palo Alto, Calif.: Stanford Center for Research and Development in Teaching, 1972.
Nichols, Ralph G. *Listening and Speaking: A Guide to Effective Oral Communication*. New York: McGraw-Hill, 1972.
Peter, Laurence J. *Competencies for Teaching*, vols. I, II, and III. Englewood Cliffs, N.J.: Prentice-Hall, 1975.
Peterson, Penelope L., and Herbert J. Wahlberg, eds. *Research on Teaching: Concepts, Findings, and Implications*. Berkeley, Calif.: McCutchan, 1979.
Popham, W. James, and Eva L. Baker. *Planning an Instructional Sequence*. Englewood Cliffs, N.J.: Prentice-Hall, 1970.
———. *Systematic Instruction*. Englewood Cliffs, N.J.: Prentice-Hall, 1970.
Postman, Neil. *Teaching as a Conserving Activity*. New York: Delacorte, 1979.
——— and Charles Weingartner. *Teaching as a Subversive Activity*. New York: Delacorte, 1969.
Sadker, Myra, and David Sadker. "Questioning Skills." In *Classroom Teaching Skills: A Hand book*, James M. Cooper, ed. Lexington, Mass.: D. C. Heath, 1977.
Shostak, Robert. "Lesson Presentation Skills." In *Classroom Teaching Skills: A Handbook*, James M. Cooper, ed. Lexington, Mass.: D. C. Heath, 1977.

Smith, B. Othanel, et al. *Teachers for the Real World*. Washington, D.C.: American Association of Colleges for Teacher Education, 1969.

Sokolove, Sandra, Myra Sadker, and David Sadker. "Interpersonal Communication Skills." In *Classroom Teaching Skills: A Handbook*, James M. Cooper, ed. Lexington, Mass.: D. C. Heath, 1977.

Multi-Media

Mincourses of the Far West Laboratory for Educational Research and Development. Minicourses utilize microteaching and consist of filmed ot taped instructional materials, handbooks, evaluation forms, and daily course schedules. The following minicourses are available from Macmillan Company, Front and Brown Streets, Riverside, New Jersey 08075.

> *Effective Questioning—Elementary* (Grades 1–6)
> *Developing Children's Oral Language* (Grades K-6)
> *Individualizing Instruction in Mathematics* (Grades 1–6)
> *Organizing Independent Learning: Primary Level* (Grades K-3)
> *Higher Cognitive Questioning* (Grades 4 and up)

Instructional systems of the Northwest Regional Educational Laboratory, 400 Lindsay Building, 710 S.W. Second Avenue, Portland, Oregon 97204:

> *Facilitating Inquiry in the Classroom*. Participant materials, four audiotapes, and leader's guide. Forty to forty-five hours of instruction on teaching strategies which encourage student inquiry.
> *Development of Higher Level Thinking Abilities*. Participant materials and instructor's manual. Forty-two hours of instruction on teaching strategies which increase abilities of students to solve problems.

Westinghouse Learning Corporation, 100 Park Avenue, New York, N.Y 10017:

> *Designs for Individualization*. Fifteen performance objectives with learning activities; criterion-referenced tests; teacher's handbooks; administrator's handbook; three sound color films; and two audio tapes. A preservice and in-service teacher-training program on competency-based, student-centered education.

Audiotape

John I. Goodlad, Kenneth A. Tye, and M. Frances Klein. *About a Study of Schooling*. Association for Supervision and Curriculum Development, 225 North Washington Street, Alexandria, Virgina 22314, 1979. 90 min.

Videotape

Teacher and School Effectiveness. Discussion of characteristics of effective teachers and schools. Barak V. Rosenshine discusses the importance of academic focus, selection of activities, grouping of students, demonstration-practice-feedback, and mastery. Ronald Edmonds discusses five characteristics: principal's leadership style, instructional emphasis, climate, expectation, and assessment of pupil progress. Peter Mortimore reinforces these characteristics. Association for Supervision and Curriculum Development, 225 N. Washington Street, Alexandria, Virginia 22314, 1981. 21 minutes.

5

Helping Teachers to Evaluate Instruction

OBJECTIVES

After studying Chapter 5 you should be able to accomplish the following objectives:

1. Explain the differences between evaluation, measurement, and testing.
2. Contrast norm-referenced and criterion-referenced measurement.
3. Define formative and summative evaluation and explain when to use each.
4. Describe purposes and techniques of preassessment.
5. Write and identify well-constructed essay test items and explain the purposes for which they should be used.
6. Write and identify well-constructed objective test items and explain the purposes for which they should be used.
7. Develop and lead faculties to adopt and apply guidelines for a sound marking system.
8. Develop and lead faculties to adopt and apply guidelines for a sound reporting system.
9. Formulate your philosophical position about evaluating student achievement.

EVALUATION: AN ESSENTIAL PHASE

From the day of birth until the day of death human beings are subjected to continuous evaluation by fellow human beings. In fact, a person's deeds may continue to be evaluated long after he or she is gone from the scene. The infant is told by parents

156

with appropriate gestures and tone of voice, "That was very naughty." The teenage girl views her boy friend as a combination of Hercules and Apollo. The housewife lets her husband know of her displeasure with her appraisal, "You never help me around the house." The boss produces a feeling of elation in an employee by saying, "That was brilliant work. I'm going to give you a raise." The teacher is happy when the supervisor gives praise for a job well done with, "That was a great class you had today." And the student, who is at the low end of the educational totem pole, knows that no day will go by without some kind of evaluation and hopes today will be the day to hear, "You answered every question correctly on the test."

The evaluation of instruction requires a complex set of skills on the part of the teacher. It is an essential phase of the instructional process but a phase which can lead to inaccuracies and even abuse if not performed skillfully. It is the purpose of this chapter to examine some fundamental concepts of evaluation and to suggest evaluation techniques which the supervisor should encourage.

PREASSESSMENT

Recall the little boxes which represent the Five-Part Model of Instruction as shown in Chapter 3. The third box has the label "preassessment" and the fifth box "evaluation." The model shows the feedback lines from evaluation to each of the other blocks: formulation of goals, formulation of objectives, preassessment, and implementation of instruction.

Terms other than preassessment and evaluation might be used, such as pre-evaluation and evaluation, or pretesting and posttesting. Whatever the terms used, both the third and fifth blocks of the Five-Part Model of Instruction are evaluation components. They are similar in that the teacher may use some of the same techniques to conduct a preassessment as in conducting the Evaluation. They are different in respect to both timing and purpose.

As the name implies, preassessment takes place before instruction. The purpose of preassessing is twofold. First, the teacher wants to find out whether the students have already mastered the skills and knowledge planned for presentation. The teacher does not wish to perpetuate the archmistake of elementary schools and force students to study Indians at every grade level. Students may well have mastered the content to be studied in other grades, at other times, and even outside the school. There is no sense beating a dead horse, an evil which unfortunately takes place when no preassessment is made.

Second, the teacher wants to know if the students possess the requisite skills and knowledge to begin study of the material. The literature on instruction talks of entry skills or entry behavior. The lack of student entry skills is often apparent in programs which are part of a sequence. Students enter into higher levels of the sequence (for example, fourth-grade language arts, sixth-grade arithmetic, second-year algebra, third-year French) without sufficient level of mastery of the preceding skills and knowledge. The teacher must determine whether students are ready to begin the new study.

What should preassessment say to the teacher when the results are uncovered? In the first place, if students do *not* know the content of the material to be studied, the teacher should be satisfied and permit them to encounter the material. If the students already have sufficiently mastered the content, the teacher should omit study of that material and move on to the next material in the curriculum. Second, if students are discovered to possess the requisite entry skills, the teacher can confidently introduce them to the content to be studied. If they do not possess the necessary entry behaviors, remediation must be provided before encounter with the new material can begin. In previous days students who had not mastered the content which had arbitrarily been placed at a particular grade level were "put back"—it might be said "drummed out." This alternative is no longer a realistic one, is not sound educationally, and is not supported by public opinion. "Putting students back" is an old form of tailoring the learner to the curriculum rather than tailoring the curriculum to the learner.

The supervisor should encourage teachers to conduct a preassessment at the beginning of each unit. Preassessments can be conducted through the use of evaluation techniques such as teacher-made tests, standardized tests, student essays, or less formal means such as oral questioning. The supervisor should encourage teachers to go beyond the traditional forms of preassessment: prerequisite courses, grades in other courses, and other teachers' comments about the performance of students in their classes. The information from these sources may prove helpful but there are no substitutes for teachers' conducting their own preassessment of learners' entry skills.

A favorite and commendable technique of teachers who conduct preassessments is the pretest, posttest. The terminal evaluation (posttest) is created at the beginning of the unit. Another version of the posttest is given to students as the pretest. Students take the pretest at the beginning of instruction and the posttest at the end of instruction. The teacher compares the results of the pretest and posttest to see how much gain has been made during the period of instruction. If students have shown gain on the posttest, the teacher cannot always be sure that the gain has resulted from classroom instruction alone. The students may have picked up some of the skills and knowledge elsewhere, but unless the teacher is attempting to determine whether the treatment has alone made the difference, where they obtained the skills and knowledge is not paramount. The important fact is that they have performed at a satisfactory level of mastery on the posttest whereas they had performed less well on the pretest.

A pretest on the content to be studied may not reveal with certainty which entry behavior students lack. Consequently, further probing or testing may be necessary to pinpoint which entry behaviors must be learned before instruction begins on the new material.

In the suggested outline of a unit in Chapter 3 it was recommended that the teacher incorporate into the plan a statement of the entry skills necessary to begin study of the unit. This exercise forces the teacher to identify those skills and knowledge which the learners must have if they are to be successful with the ensuing content.

CONTINUING ASSESSMENT

A group of teachers, asked why they assess or evaluate, would offer a variety of answers. Some teachers would say they evaluate so they may inform students of their progress in the subject. Others would say they evaluate to provide a basis for assigning marks. Still others, that they evaluate so that they may send report cards home to parents and advise them of their children's work.

If asked what it is that they evaluate, they would likely again give multiple answers. Some teachers would say they evaluate the student's performance in class. Others would venture that they evaluate students in relation to each other in the class. Fewer teachers state that they evaluate the instruction, the instructional procedures, or the instructor.

The process of evaluation may be viewed as assessing achievement of the objectives of instruction by each of the learners who make up a class. There should be a direct line from the objectives originally set forth at the beginning of a unit or course to the evaluation techniques before, during, and at the end of instruction. Evaluation seeks to find out whether students have mastered the objectives. The results of evaluation are also used to make necessary modifications in the instructional design. Whether the students achieve or not says something to the teacher about the effectiveness of the design itself and the effectiveness of the instructional procedures. When students fail to achieve the objectives of instruction, several hypotheses for this failure may be explored. It could well be that the students have failed through lack of effort, lack of study, or lack of motivation. But it also may be true that:

- The objectives were not related to the task.
- The objectives were not clear.
- The objectives were not behaviorally stated and therefore not subject to accurate evaluation.
- Preassessment was poorly conducted.
- Remediation was not provided before proceeding with the content.
- Resources were inappropriate or unavailable.
- Strategies were not appropriately selected.
- Content did not relate directly to the objectives.
- Continuing assessment was neglected.
- Terminal evaluation did not relate directly to the objectives.
- The teacher was ineffective in managing the group and presenting the content.

Evaluation should be thought of as an integral part of instruction, not an activity separate from instruction. For this reason evaluation should always be present and continuing. In some manner, no matter how brief or informal, evaluation should take place every day with every lesson. The teacher wants to know not only how well students will perform at the end of a unit or course but also how well they have mastered each day's work. The supervisor can help teachers to master a variety of formal and informal evaluation techniques which they can call on as the need arises.

Evaluation at the end of the lesson or day may be nothing more than some oral questions posed to the students by the teacher. It may be but silent observation of the way students tackle the work of the day. The alert teacher can tell by student actions and questions whether they seem to have understood and whether they are able to do the work. Calling for a summary of the day's lesson by a student can serve as an evaluation technique. Periodic progress checks during the course of the unit should be conducted to find out whether the learners are staying up with the teacher and what needs to be reviewed and perfected.

When evaluation is mentioned in a school setting, testing—largely of the paper-and-pencil variety—immediately leaps to mind. This reaction may be only natural since schools have traditionally administered paper-and-pencil tests, schooling is to a great extent cognitive in nature and assessment is most easily served by paper-and-pencil tests, and teachers and the public are test conscious. Since teachers devote a good deal of time to the construction and administration of paper-and-pencil tests, some time will be devoted in this chapter to principles of testing which the supervisor may wish to incorporate into an in-service training program. The supervisor must not overlook, however, evaluation techniques other than testing such as:

oral questioning	actual performance of skills
observation of students at work	self-evaluation
oral and written reports	anecdotal reports
evaluation of group work	autobiographies
surveys and questionnaires	projective techniques
attitude inventories	evaluation of class participation
evaluation conferences	summaries and résumés

NORM-REFERENCED AND CRITERION-REFERENCED MEASUREMENT

Before proceeding further some common agreement is necessary on the language of evaluation. As most teacher trainees are aware, many colleges and universities offer courses in tests and measurement or in measurement and evaluation. Unless the words in each pair of titles are redundant—a distinct possibility given the professorial penchant for embellishment—we must assume that each word in each pair signifies something different from the other word in each pair.

Although all three terms are related, testing is different from measurement and measurement is different from evaluation or assessment. In this text the global concept is evaluation and is synonymous with assessment. Evaluation or assessment as it relates to instruction means the process of making judgments about specific aspects of a learner's behavior; it consists of a set of skills by which an instructor determines whether or not the learner has mastered the objectives established.

Measurement is a phase of evaluation during which the instructor quantifies instances of the learner's behavior; the quantitative data provide the teacher with a basis for assigning marks—at least in the cognitive and psychomotor domains. A test is an instrument for measuring, for ascertaining the presence of expected behaviors and discovering the degree of mastery of those behaviors. Testing is the process of administering the test instrument.

The distinctions among evaluation, measurement, and testing are more than semantic ones and the supervisor will do well to explore these differences with teachers. The behavior of a learner can be evaluated without measuring but behavior cannot be measured without testing. In Chapter 3 it was noted that it is not always possible to observe and to measure the achievement of objectives in the affective domain. It is possible to measure mastery of cognitive objectives—at least learner achievement of these objectives can be sampled and the presence of psychomotor skills can be measured; but in dealing with attitudes, feelings, interests, and emotions—the affect—it may or may not be possible to observe the attainment of these objectives. Less possible is measuring or quantifying the degree of mastery of affective outcomes. How enthusiastic must an attitude of enthusiasm be? How much willingness must be shown to be passing?

Attempts to measure and quantify the attainment of affective objectives exist in the form of personality tests and interest tests. More accurately, these instruments are personality inventories and interest inventories. Standardized inventories of personality and interest provide behavior norms for the groups which took the inventories. But these norms or standards should not be thought of as accurate measurements of individual behavior in the same way as reading skills can be measured and physical fitness demonstrated. With affective instruments we encounter difficulty in attempting to label answers "right" or "wrong." The affective behaviors of an individual might be compared with socially stated norms and those which do not agree with socially stated norms might be labeled "wrong" and those which do agree with them as "right." Failure to live up to middle-class norms might be called wrong, neurosis wrong, interest in illegal activities wrong, and racism wrong. The point is that these outcomes cannot be measured with any degree of certainty. There is no certainty that the socially stated norms are really the norms practiced by many—possibly even the majority—of the population, as Alfred Kinsey and later sex researchers discovered.

What is possible in the domain of the affect is to specify as best the instructor can objectives which hopefully can be observed in the classroom. Some of these objectives will not be visible during the time the learner spends with the teacher but may blossom in later years. Attitudes and feelings can be surveyed with various types of inventories asking for agreement or disagreement or for gradations of agreement and disagreement. Instructors may even measure the achievement of affective outcomes if they are willing to accept a binary measure as a satisfactory indicator of presence or absence of the outcome. For those outcomes which are observable, they may evaluate their presence or absence with a yes, the outcome is present, or no, the outcome is not present. They cannot use this crude measurement, however, to form a basis for marking students on the affect in the same manner as they mark on the achievement of cognitive and psychomotor skills.

This discussion of evaluation of the affect is preliminary to observing that most of the measurement which takes place during schooling is assessment of achievement in the cognitive and psychomotor domains. Though we will return to the problems of evaluating and reporting the attainment of affective objectives, the major part of this chapter is devoted to the measurement of cognitive and psychomotor behaviors and to those aftermaths of measurement—marking and reporting pupil progress and achievement.

Norm-referenced Measurement

In practice, schools utilize two different approaches to measurement: norm-referenced measurement and criterion-referenced measurement. Norm-referenced measurement is the historic approach to measurement in the schools and is still predominant. Both approaches to measurement weigh the student's achievement against some standard or norm. When following a norm-referenced approach, the instructor compares a learner's achievement against the norm of some group which was subjected to the same measuring instrument. That group may be and most frequently is the learner's own class. The teacher may, first of all, create a test, administer it, and score it, making judgments about individual performance relative to the performance of all members of the group. The teacher determines the mid-score or "average" around which the majority of scores cluster. Some students will achieve above that average and some below. The average group has, in effect, set the standard against which each individual's performance is compared. The average group may or may not have achieved the objectives specified at the beginning of instruction and the teacher has the option to set the average on any given test as high or low as the group's performance seems to indicate. What the scores on a test may mean in terms of mastery of the objectives is not always clear.

If teachers administer the same test or equivalent forms of a test to successive groups of learners, they may over the years build up a set of standards or norms which show the performance of these previous groups. Teachers may then choose, as a second option, to measure an individual's achievement against these standards, called local norms. As a third alternative, teachers may choose to administer a standardized test if there is such a test available for their particular need. In this case, teachers compare the performance of their students on the test against the norms of the group or groups to which the test maker administered the test. These groups may be and commonly are groups far distant from the local scene and they may or may not be representative of the teacher's own current group of students. The standards achieved by these groups are reported as norms in the test manuals which accompany the test, and it is against these standards that the students' performance is compared.

If teachers choose to use a standardized instrument—the limitations of which are discussed later in this chapter—they have the same alternative as in the case of their own teacher-made tests. As a fourth procedure, teachers may accumulate local norms on the standardized test and compare performance of learners in their current classes against the performance of previous learners on that same standardized test or equivalent form. Thus, teachers who follow a norm-referenced approach to measurement have four options as bases for comparison of student achievement:

1. The performance of all other individuals in the class on the basis of a teacher-made test.
2. The performance of previous groups in past years to whom the teacher has administered the same teacher-made test or equivalent form thereof.
3. The performance of previous groups in the same subject in the same school on the same standardized test or equivalent form thereof.
4. The performance of groups to whom the standardized-test maker has administered the test.

The key qualifiers of a norm-referenced system of measurement are *comparative*, *relative*, and *competitive*. Norm-referenced measuring seeks to compare learners with each other; its standards are relative rather than absolute; it recognizes degrees of mastery; and it encourages competition among learners. Our schools by and large employ and champion the norm-referenced approach to measurement. The competitive approach to measurement is espoused by the majority of the teaching profession, by the public at large, and, perhaps, though this is less certain, by the majority of students. The letter-grade system, A-F, discussed later, is an integral part of the norm-referenced system. The C grade represents a mystical (perhaps mythical) average. A and B reflect above average performance, and D and F below average.

The roots of the norm-referenced system lie in the statistical concept of the normal curve, which assumes that certain attributes such as intelligence are distributed among the population as a whole and the possession of these attributes can be depicted in the form of a bell-shaped curve. When a test of intelligence, for example, is administered to a large, random sample of the population, a mean score (the sum of all scores divided by the number of scores) may be determined. This mean score coincides with the median score (middle score) and the majority of those who took the test cluster around this mean/median score. Thus, it may be said somewhat loosely and unscientifically a quotient of 100 determined as a result of dividing the mental age of a student shown on a test of intelligence by the chronological age of the student and multiplying by 100 represents average intelligence.

Of the four options which serve as bases for comparison of student achievement the prevailing option is the first one—comparison of an individual's achievement against the performance of all other individuals in the class on the basis of a teacher-made test. Since the performance of a particular group sets the standard, that standard may vary from section to section of the same subject and it may vary from year to year. The standard for a group which as a whole performed poorly may be lower than the standard for a group that performed well on the test. This is what is meant in saying the standards under a norm-referenced approach to measurement are relative.

The norm-referenced system serves the purpose of showing how well students perform in relation to their peers and of providing data for assigning competitive marks. Since the nature of norm-referenced measurement is comparative and competitive, the norm-referenced approach must be used in situations in which screening individuals and selection are required.

Criterion-referenced Measurement

Under a criterion-referenced system of measurement an individual student's performance is compared not against the achievement of other learners but against the attainment of the objectives of instruction themselves. Following this approach the teacher determines whether each student has mastered the objectives specified in the planning stage of instruction. The student either masters the objectives or does not. Once the student has mastered those objectives he or she is considered to have passed that content and proceeds to the next objectives. If the student has not shown mastery of the objectives, he or she takes more time for study and practice and then again attempts to demonstrate mastery.

The application of criterion-referenced measurement is seen most readily, perhaps, in the psychomotor domain. An elementary school pupil can demonstrate skill in tying shoes, writing letters of the alphabet, and using a crayon. The secondary school student can show the ability to construct an angle of 60° using a pencil, paper, ruler, and protractor; type 40 words a minute accurately on an electric typewriter; remove, clean, properly gap an auto's spark plugs, and replace them; and chin on a horizontal bar 10 times without stopping.

The application of criterion-referenced measurement in the cognitive domain is a little less apparent. On any test of cognitive outcomes the teacher must set some level of mastery. For example, an objective in fifth-grade social studies might read, "Given a paper-and-pencil test on this unit the pupil will achieve 80 percent mastery (or will answer correctly 8 out of the 10 questions)." The 80 percent level of mastery is an arbitrary one set by the teacher after due reflection and consideration of what the group is likely to do. It may be based on the teacher's experience with previous classes. It is often overlooked in the literature of evaluation that levels of mastery on criterion-referenced tests are to a large extent determined by norm-referenced means. A level of mastery set on the basis of the teacher's experience with other groups at other times brings norm-referenced principles into play. Mastery in the cognitive domain, therefore, is somewhat different from mastery in the psychomotor domain. Mastery in the psychomotor domain represents the presence or absence of the particular skill. Mastery in the cognitive domain is revealed by a score of 80 percent or any other arbitrary level—even 100 percent represents but an approximation of mastery of the total content, for any cognitive test is but a sampling of the whole content. The learner achieves a level of 80 percent on the test items which the teacher has chosen to put on the test.

As already noted, caution must accompany the use of the term measurement in respect to affective objectives. I believe that the attainment of affective outcomes may and should be evaluated but these outcomes should not be subjected to statistical treatment nor scoring nor marking with the traditional symbols of a grading system. The problem of reporting attainment of affective outcomes is dealt with in the section of this chapter on marking and reporting.

The choice between a norm-referenced approach to measurement and a criterion-referenced approach has always been a possible decision for teachers. Yet, criterion-referenced measurement has only become an attractive alternative to norm-referenced measurement in recent years. The behavioral objectives movement which has blossomed since the late sixties has given impetus to criterion-referenced measurement. Underlying concepts of this movement are a competency-based approach to instruction, self-pacing, and learning for mastery.

In discussing learning for mastery of a subject Benjamin S. Bloom, J. Thomas Hastings, and George F. Madaus clearly pictured the conflicting philosophical positions on measurement:

Each teacher begins a new term or course with the expectation that about a third of his students will adequately learn what he has to teach. He expects about a third to fail or to just "get by." Finally, he expects another third to learn a good deal of what he has to teach, but not enough to be regarded as "good students." This set of expectations, supported by school policies and practices in grading, is transmitted to the students through the grading procedures and through the methods and materials of instruction. This system creates a self-fulfilling prophecy. . . .

This set of expectations, which fixes the academic goals of teachers and students, is the most wasteful and destructive aspect of the present educational system. . . .

Most students (perhaps more than 90 percent) can master what we have to teach them, and it is the task of instruction to find the means which will enable them to master the subject under consideration. A basic task is to determine what we mean by "mastery of the subject" and to search for the methods and materials which will enable the largest proportion of our students to attain such mastery.[1]

If teachers are teaching for mastery and students are learning for mastery, a measurement system must test for mastery, which implies a criterion-referenced approach whereby student achievement is compared to some standard of mastery of the content set by the teacher and not by group norms.

Evaluation begins with the statement of the objectives of instruction. Sometimes the objectives, which are stated in the form of learning tasks, are the test items themselves. Let's take the following examples:

- Define the words *cognitive*, *affective*, and *psychomotor*.
- Sightread a musical passage.
- Balance a series of chemical equations.
- Compare the weekly cost of food for a family of four in different parts of the country and account for variations.
- Produce a documented research paper on the causes and effects of inflation.
- After studying several conflicting proposals for solving the country's energy problem, choose the proposal which seems to be the best solution to the problem, and state your reasons for your choice.

These cognitive illustrations are drawn from the lowest to the highest levels. Each objective is, in effect, a test itself, although the complexity of each objective as a test is increasingly more involved as we go from the lowest order of knowledge to the highest order of evaluation.

In the psychomotor domain the following objectives may also serve as test items:

- Recognize a broken water pump in the automobile by the noise it causes.
- Demonstrate the proper way of holding the clarinet.
- Imitate the instructor's karate movement.
- Plant tomato seeds in a suitable container.
- Correctly operate a data-processing machine.
- Use traditional hula dance movements to express a story.
- Design and create a ceramic jar.

These psychomotor objectives are actually performance tests rather than verbal tests. The teacher can evaluate these kinds of performance by observing the learner in the act of demonstrating the perceptual-motor skills.

In the case of both the cognitive and the psychomotor illustrations given here, mastery of the objective can be measured. An acceptable level of mastery can be established by the teacher for each of the objectives. It is not possible to establish a level of mastery of affective objectives, however, such as:

- Develop a sensitivity to the problems of the elderly.
- Enjoy reading historical novels.
- Express a positive school spirit.
- Judge persons of different ethnic groups as individuals rather than as groups.
- Develop the habit of collecting facts before making a decision.

Although some objectives in the cognitive domain may serve as tests of performance themselves, this is not always the case. The illustration, "Given a paper-and-pencil test on this unit the pupil will answer correctly 8 out of 10 questions," is not a test in itself. The teacher must carry this objective one step further and write the actual test items. The teacher may also have to refine the criteria for measuring accomplishment of some objectives. For example, the objective which calls for students to produce a research paper requires a statement of the bases on which the paper will be graded, if the teacher intends to require more of the student than simply handing in a paper regardless of quality. The teacher may choose as criteria a minimum length, correct English usage, proper footnoting, and proper form for bibliography.

Many teachers—perhaps a majority—tend to write cognitive tests at the end of instruction. They wait to see what they have covered and then sample the content of the material covered. Experts in evaluation and instruction recommend the opposite—that teachers write cognitive tests at the beginning of instruction or early in the course. Some recommend that the terminal evaluation for a unit or course be written right after the objectives are written. The teacher would have two tasks then right after writing the objectives: preparing the preassessment instrument and preparing a preliminary terminal assessment instrument. Michael Scriven recommended the construction of a pool of test items in the early phase of instruction. He said:

Even though the project is only at the stage of finishing the first unit of a projected ten-unit curriculum, it is entirely appropriate to be formulating questions of the kind that it is proposed to include in the final examination on the final unit or, for that matter, in a follow-up quiz a year later.[2]

By designing the test items before instruction starts or in the early phase of instruction the teacher can more readily achieve consistency between the objectives and the test items. When the teacher waits until instruction is finished, some of the objectives specified at the beginning may be overlooked. It is not that the teacher must be compelled to accomplish every objective originally sought. The teacher may, anytime feedback is received, modify, add, or eliminate objectives. But there should be consistency between all remaining objectives and items on any final examination. The teacher and supervisor should not read into this discussion that a final examination on an entire course or a year's work is a must. The teacher may choose to administer a final examination covering only the final unit, but if the choice is made to administer a final examination covering the whole course, the pool of test items should be initiated at the very beginning of the course. In a like manner if the teacher administers a final test on a unit of a program, construction of the test items should begin when the unit is introduced.

By starting the evaluation process at the beginning stage of instruction the teacher can more readily conduct what Scriven called a "consistency analysis."[3] Scriven urged that there be consistency among the goals (i.e., objectives) of a course, the content of the course, and the pool of test items.

The supervisor should help teachers clarify the distinctions between norm-referenced measurement and criterion-referenced measurement and should point out the appropriate uses of each approach. The supervisor needs to help teachers define the meaning of "mastery" and identify ways of assessing mastery.

FORMATIVE AND SUMMATIVE EVALUATION

The literature on evaluation and research is rich with technical terms, some of which will become familiar in this text, others being left to the specialists in measurement and evaluation. The focus of this text is on the needs of classroom teachers and the supervisor who works with the teachers in carrying out evaluation for the improvement of instruction.

Two terms, *formative evaluation* and *summative evaluation*, have gained great currency in recent years and are concepts with which the supervisor should help teachers develop familiarity. Stripping the terms down to their essentials, formative evaluation comprises those assessment procedures the teacher uses during the course of instruction, and summative evaluation those evaluation techniques which the teacher uses at the end of instruction. In the cognitive domain, formative evaluation may be equated with progress tests and summative evaluation with final tests. The reaction of many teachers to these terms may be, "I've been doing that for years." What the teachers may not having been doing is refining the formative and summative processes in order to achieve maximum effectiveness.

An evaluation process is effective when the teacher can determine whether the learner has achieved mastery of the subject. The evaluation is less likely to show learners' mastery of the subject when the teacher:

- Does not prespecify the instructional objectives.
- Does not relate test items directly to the objectives.
- Waits until the end of instruction to create the test items.
- Fails to capitalize on the results of formative evaluation and modify instruction.
- Writes tests which poorly sample the content and which contain poorly written test items.

Bloom, Hastings, and Madaus encouraged teachers to "break a course or subject into smaller units of learning" and to administer at the end of each unit "brief diagnostic progress tests," which they referred to as formative evaluation.[4] Though many teachers follow this practice, they often stop at this point and simply use the results of these progress tests to form part of the student's grade at the end of a marking period. Bloom, Hastings, and Madaus recommended frequent progress tests and saw the use of these as helping to "ensure that each set of learning tasks has been thoroughly mastered before subsequent tasks are started."[5] They described the purposes of these frequent tests:

For the student who has thoroughly mastered the unit, the formative tests should reinforce the learning and assure him that his present mode of learning and approach to study are adequate.

For the student who lacks mastery of the unit, the formative test should reveal the particular points of difficulty—that is, the specific questions he answered incorrectly and the ideas, skills, and processes he still needs to work on.[6]

Bloom, Hastings, and Madaus stressed the importance of using the formative tests for the purposes of diagnosis of learning difficulties and for prescribing what the student needs to do to overcome these difficulties. These authors take a position with which many teachers may not agree when they state,

We are of the opinion that formative tests should not be assigned grades or quality points. The tests are marked to show *mastery* and *nonmastery*. The nonmastery evaluation is accompanied by a detailed diagnosis and prescription of what has still to be done before mastery is complete. It is likely that the use of grades on repeated progress tests prepares students for the acceptance of less than mastery.[7]

They admit that there is limited evidence on this point and certainly teachers who do use progress tests for the dual purpose of diagnosing and grading would not be remiss.

It should not be forgotten that the purpose of both formative and summative evaluation is to furnish feedback for redesigning the instructional model. Formative evaluation provides feedback for ongoing revision of objectives and instructional procedures while summative evaluation provides feedback for later revision. Summative evaluation in the form of a final examination serves not only to provide a score which will be used in grading the learner's achievement but also to indicate changes which should be made in instruction with subsequent groups. Bloom, Hastings, and Madaus saw summative evaluation as less threatening to students if they have undergone frequent progress tests. They said, "The student who consistently demonstrates mastery on the recurring tests should be able to reduce his anxiety about his course achievement."[8]

TESTING

While tests may be described by the teacher as opportunities for students to demonstrate mastery of the content, to students they are usually distasteful hurdles, something to be tolerated as a part of this enterprise called education. Most students take testing in stride. Some small percentage of students even welcome tests as an opportunity to show what they know and as challenges to be met, while others regard each test as a traumatic experience. Certainly most students learn the power of tests in the early years of schooling and come to know full well the implications of performance on tests. These are the instruments which determine marks, scholastic status, promotions, entrance into higher levels of education, and employment. The impact of tests can be readily observed in any class when the teacher remarks, "This is going to be on the test." Every ear in the classroom perks up and tunes in to the teacher's comments.

The supervisor might on some appropriate occasion with a group of teachers raise the question, "Why do we test?" After the initial teacher reaction that this is an absurd question, the supervisor might start to get answers such as:

- To find out what students know.
- To discover who are the best students in the class.
- To discover who are the poorest students in the class.
- To accumulate data for figuring marks.
- To gather data to share with parents about their children's work.

After some discussion it develops that teachers test:

- To provide incentive for study.
- To serve as a punitive device for controlling unruly classes.
- To help students develop practice in the skill of taking tests.

It may take some probing before the supervisor draws out responses like:

- To see if the learners have attained the objectives.
- To diagnose learning difficulties.
- To appraise the effectiveness of instruction.
- To judge the effectiveness of the teacher.

The last response raises the spectre of a concept in education today which is not too popular with teachers, namely, accountability. Historically, when students fail to achieve in school, the fault has always been assigned to the students themselves. It is said that they do not study, they are lazy, they are unmotivated, they don't have the proper background, any number of both legitimate reasons and rationalizations for learners' lack of achievement. Teachers have been in the past accountable for their teaching performance to their superintendent, principal, and school board, and in a rather indirect and vague way to parents and the public at large.

Today the public has grasped the notion that learners' achievement is in direct relationship to the effectiveness of teachers as instructors and that some judgment should be made of the teachers' effectiveness. This has been an appealing concept to the taxpayers who must foot the bill for public education and who in the past have had no reckoning of the effectiveness of their investment. Accountability implies that teachers are instrumental in the success or failure of students, and when students fail, teachers are as much or more responsible than the learners. Teachers' groups have resisted the accountability movement because they claim with some justification that they are unable to control all the variables which affect learners' achievements. There are forces outside the school and sometimes years of educational neglect which are beyond the capacities of even the best instructors to overcome.

However, the concept of accountability cannot be completely eliminated. Most supervisors can attest that there are poor, sloppy, and unmotivated teachers as well as poor, sloppy, unmotivated students. It is a fact of educational life that both effective and ineffective teachers are employed in the schools. The supervisor's primary task is to help ineffective teachers become effective teachers.

One product of the accountability movement has been to make teachers more conscious of their responsibilities in respect to learners' achievement and to refrain from shrugging off learners' failure as completely the fault of the learner. Consequently, they strive harder in order that their students will score well on both standardized achievement tests and on their own teacher-made tests. The norm-referenced approach to measurement in one way obstructs accountability, for by varying standards of performance some learners will always do poorly in relation to other learners. The concepts of criterion-referenced measurement and learning for mastery of content are compatible with accountability. If the objectives of instruction are clear and realistic, if content and methodology directly relate to achieving the objectives, and if tests are designed to measure learners' attainment of the objectives, fewer students will wind up doing poor work. Bloom, Hastings, and Madaus reiterated the generalization that most students can master what we have to teach them when they said:

Thus, we are expressing the view that, given sufficient time and appropriate types of help, 95 percent of students . . . can learn a subject with a high degree of mastery. To say it another way, we are convinced that the grade of A as an index of mastery of a subject can, under appropriate conditions, be achieved by up to 95 percent of the students in a class.[9]

Standardized Tests

A fairly wide variety of standardized tests and inventories is available for use of school personnel. We can find standardized instruments to measure intelligence and achievement and to inventory interest, aptitude, attitude, and personality. Each of the tests comes with its manual of norms reporting the performance of the groups on which the tests were standardized.

The classroom teacher will have occasion to make use of some or all of these types of tests for general background information about the learner. If the teacher administers a standardized test, it is most likely that it will be a test of achievement in a discipline. Other types of tests and inventories such as intelligence, interest, and the like are often administered by specialized school personnel and the results are made available to teachers to help them plan instruction.

Standardized tests will be dealt with only briefly in this text for I believe them to be inappropriate instruments for measuring instructional objectives in particular classrooms and for serving as a basis for marks or promotion. Standardized tests of achievement do serve a very valid purpose, however, in permitting comparison of the local group's achievement with the achievement of the norm groups. It is helpful to the teacher to find out how well the students have done in comparison to groups elsewhere and the data do provide some guidance to the teacher in terms of what content should be included in the scope of the program. Admittedly, it is good public relations to run an article in the local press to show the public that local students compare favorably with students elsewhere. The public is pleased when its students "measure up" to national norms and displeased when they do not. Though some schools attempt to squelch negative findings that local students achieve below national norms, in the long run it is best to report the situation as it is.

As far as classroom teachers are concerned in the matter of standardized tests, they should know how to (1) select an appropriate standardized achievement test, (2) administer and score the test, and (3) interpret results of standardized tests. The supervisor should aid teachers in developing these skills and can direct them to catalogs of test publishers and to such standard references as *The Mental Measurements Yearbook*,[10] which contains reviews of various kinds of standardized tests and provides information on the reliability and validity of the tests as well as the adequacy of the norms reported and costs of the tests. Manuals which accompany the tests describe procedures for administering and scoring the tests and for interpreting the results. Chapter 8 discusses some of the common statistical concepts the supervisor will wish teachers to be familiar with in order that they may interpret test results.

Teacher-made Tests

Each time a teacher feels it is appropriate to give a test he or she is confronted with a number of decisions. The teacher must decide whether to give a paper-and-pencil test or require the students to demonstrate actual physical performance of an objective; whether to administer a written test or an oral test; whether to administer the test to the group all at once or to students individually. If the decision is for written tests, the teacher must decide whether to give an objective test, an essay test, or combination thereof. If a test is defined as a student's try at demonstrating achievement of specific objectives, oral and written reports or written papers may be substituted for objective and essay type examinations. The choices the teacher will make depend upon the objectives students are to achieve and the nature of the content.

The tests must be an accurate reflection of what the teacher set out to achieve with the learners and what has been covered in the course. Oral tests are clearly called for in assessing a student's ability to speak in courses in speech and dramatics and in foreign languages. Both aural (hearing and auditory discrimination) and oral skills must be assessed in phases of instruction in music and foreign languages.

Both the actual demonstration of skills and tangible products of instruction must be evaluated in phases of the fine arts, business education, industrial arts, and vocational and technical education. No written report or paper-and-pencil examination can substitute for actual performance when the teacher wishes to know if a student can create an attractive piece of pottery, take shorthand at a certain speed with a minimum number of errors, put paneling on the walls of a room, or weld two pieces of metal.

When tests of actual performance are to be used, teachers must make known to the students in advance what the criteria are which constitute a level of mastery of the particular skills. The time it takes to complete a job and the number of errors that will be permitted may be appropriate criteria. Qualitative judgments of a finished product are also necessary. A piece of pottery, for example, may be judged on such characteristics as originality, symmetry, size, finish, and color. The evaluation of tangible end-products and psychomotor skills is more difficult than the scoring of paper-and-pencil objective tests. In some ways it is analogous to scoring essay tests. The task of evaluating both actual performance and essay tests is made easier and more reliable if teachers specify in advance the criteria which they as experts will apply and communicate these criteria to the learners.

In all fields of study there are times when tests of actual performance may be more appropriate than paper-and-pencil tests and when oral examinations may be more pertinent than written examinations. Generally speaking, the type of test the typical classroom teacher will use most frequently is the paper-and-pencil, group test. Given the exigencies of mass education and the cognitive nature of most of what goes on in schools, the paper-and-pencil, group variety of test is the most economical and practical solution to testing cognitive achievement. Individual tests, though highly desirable, are impractical except for certain diagnostic and remedial purposes. Individual conferences covering the content could conceivably be substituted for examinations but, however laudatory, they are too time-consuming to be practical. Lengthy written reports place too much of a demand on teacher time to represent a routine solution to the problem of assessing achievement. Nor is there sufficient time for either individual or group oral reports from all members of a class on all the content of a program. Consequently, teachers must resort to administering group, written tests as indicators of performance in the cognitive domain.

Essay Tests

Two major types of paper-and-pencil tests are in wide use in the schools—the essay test and the objective test, which might also be called the subjective test and the objective test. However, essay tests are not completely subjective nor are objective tests completely objective: subjectivity comes into play in the construction of both types of tests. In scoring these two types of tests, objective tests reduce the element of judgment on the part of the scorer and for that reason may be labeled objective.

If the supervisor provokes a discussion on the use of essay and objective tests, teachers will disclose attitudes from antipathy to essay tests to almost exclusive use of this type of test, and from complete rejection of objective tests to their exclusive use. What discussions of this nature sometimes omit is the recognition that the two types of tests serve different purposes. Although both types are designed to measure students' mastery of content, they do not fulfill the same functions.

An essay test may measure a limited amount of content but in addition may evaluate a student's ability to write coherently, to organize thoughts, to describe situations, to make comparisons, to use English properly, to make applications of content, to demonstrate writing style, to summarize content, to cite research, and to elaborate reasons for positions taken. Essay tests may sample a limited portion of the content while objective tests sample a much wider range of content. Whereas an essay test may consist of but one or a few test items, an objective test may consist of many items. Some balance needs to be struck between essay testing and objective testing. Consistent use of objective tests from elementary school through secondary school can leave the learner deficient in sustained writing, a deficiency lamented by many college professors who receive the products of the high schools. Consistent essay testing would, on the other hand, leave instructors uncertain of the learners' breadth of mastery of content.

Essay tests are more difficult to construct than many teachers believe and they are certainly difficult to score. It is unfortunately true that in the press for time some teachers have a tendency to dash off both essay and objective test items. Such a practice is much more harmful in the case of essay tests than in the case of objective tests, for an objective test allows learners many opportunities to reveal knowledge of the subject while essay tests limit the number of items and therefore the learners' chances of demonstrating achievement.

Essay test items should communicate to learners exactly what they have to do and what degree of mastery is considered an acceptable performance. A common and unsatisfactory essay test item is seen in the example, "Discuss détente between the United States and the Soviet Union." The supervisor might ask a group of teachers what is wrong with such an item. Those teachers who have had training in measurement and evaluation may quickly respond that the question is not specific enough. It does not indicate to the students what they must do to give a complete answer and to achieve maximum credit for the question. Unfortunately, far too many essay test items are of this caliber. Even training in measurement and evaluation has not served as a preventive for teachers' writing inadequate essay items. Thus, there is mileage in a supervisor's calling for analysis of test questions if only to serve as a reminder to teachers that it is possible to improve test items.

An interesting exercise which a supervisor may conduct with a group of teachers is to administer an essay item such as the previous example on détente to the teachers and then ask teachers to score each other's answers. This is often an illuminating activity to many teachers, for if their experiences run parallel to those of other groups the scores they have assigned to each other's answers will range from failing to outstanding, from F to A, and probably all grades in between. If the teachers are short of time or if the supervisor feels that answering a test item themselves will inject too much personal involvement in the exercise (for example, if individuals did not have sufficient command of the content called for), the supervisor may duplicate the response made by a student to an essay item and ask teachers to grade that response. I have on occasion used an editorial written by a school principal for the school paper for this purpose and without any identification as to position the unnamed principal has consistently been graded from failing to superior.

This little exercise shows the unreliability of many essay tests. A test should yield the same score or close to the same score regardless of who scores it or when it is scored. A group of teachers should be expected to come up with the same or close to the same scores on a test item, particularly if they are all experts in the field being tested. The unreliability of essay test items can also be demonstrated when the same scorer grades the items at different times. A particular mood at a particular time can affect the grade a learner receives. Almost everyone who has ever taken essay tests has suffered at some time from this abuse of this type of test. If an essay item is subject to such variation in its scoring, we cannot say at all that that item measures mastery of content. It measures only those aspects of content and learner behavior the teacher or teachers subjectively determine it to measure at the time they are scoring the item.

The example given could be sharpened and thereby made a more reliable item by expanding it and specifying what the teacher desires for a full answer. An improvement in the item can be made as follows:

Discuss détente between the United States and the Soviet Union. In your answer state two advantages and two disadvantages for each of the superpowers. State what has been reported in the sources you have read to be the position of each of the following regarding détente: (1) The President of the United States, (2) The Soviet Premier, (3) The U.S. Congress, and (4) The People's Republic of China. Finally, state your own position on détente and the reasons for your position.

This revised version will help increase the reliability of scoring of the item. However, it will still not eliminate the problem, for some teachers will still score other behaviors in addition to the content called for. Some will grade spelling, grammar, style of writing, length of response, even handwriting. The teacher's prerogative to grade these additional behaviors is not in dispute but the fact that the behaviors are being graded must be communicated to the learner as well as the relative weights to be assigned to each behavior.

A task of the teacher preliminary to any scoring is the construction of a key which outlines the points the learners should touch on in their answers. The construction of a key is a step many teachers short-circuit and the absence of a key contributes to the unreliability of the grading. Without a key against which to compare a student's response the teacher is liable to forget significant points which he or she is supposed to be looking for and can also be unduly swayed and sidetracked by students who write well or at length but who fail to include significant points of content. The supervisor could ask the teachers once again to score an answer to an essay question and this time supply a key to each member of the group to see if the use of a key decreases the range of scores on the test item.

A student's chances of demonstrating mastery of content are improved when the teacher increases the number of test items on any given essay test. As a general rule, it is an unwise procedure to give an essay test consisting of only one test item. The more test items there are on a given test, the wider is the sampling of the content. While a student may "bomb out" on a particular test item of which he or she has an inadequate command or neglected to study, additional test items provide an opportunity to demonstrate at least some degree of mastery. The single-item test induces unnecessary anxiety in the learner anticipating whether or not he or she will be lucky enough to be able to respond to the item the teacher selects to put on the test.

More test items will require shorter answers, which is not necessarily a bad feature. If a teacher wishes to test for sustained writing, an occasional or term paper which students do outside of class may serve this purpose much better than an essay test. Let us illustrate a few variations of essay test items, following the classification in Bloom's taxonomy of the cognitive domain. Essay test items may be constructed for each of the six major categories of the taxonomy as the following illustrations show:

1. *Knowledge*: State the steps by which a federal bill becomes a law.
2. *Comprehension*: Explain in 50 words or less what message John Donne was conveying when he wrote, "Never send to know for whom the bell tolls, it tolls for thee."
3. *Application*: Briefly describe what is meant by the economic law of supply and demand and give three examples of the operation of this law in the American marketplace in the last five years.
4. *Analysis*: Contrast the characteristics of a developed nation and an underdeveloped nation by citing four ways in which a developed nation differs from an underdeveloped nation. Following your statement of differences tell whether you would classify each of the following as an underdeveloped nation or a developed nation: (1) The United States, (2) El Salvador, (3) Thailand, (4) Israel, (5) Great Britain, (6) Algeria. Select one additional nation of your own choice which meets the characteristics of an underdeveloped nation and describe efforts which that nation is making to become a developed nation.
5. *Synthesis*: If you were the chief of police of this community, describe what actions you would recommend to reduce the number of automobile accidents in the community. In your answer show that you are familiar with principal causes of accidents and data on fatalities, injuries, and property damage from automobile accidents in the community.
6. *Evaluation*: A legislator of our state, which has no state income tax, proposed that an income tax of 2.5 percent on taxable income above $10,000 be levied. Evaluate this proposal as to (1) the need for such a tax, (2) pos-

sible uses to which the tax might be put, (3) effects of the tax on various socioeconomic classes of the state, and (4) likelihood of its acceptance by the people. Compare the benefits and disadvantages of the proposed income tax with the benefits and disadvantages of increasing the state sales tax from 4 to 5 percent.

The supervisor should encourage teachers to write full and clear essay test items and to avoid the common, inadequate "Discuss. . . ." Generally some elaboration is necessary beyond the simple command to "discuss." Essay test items can be given a particular twist by substituting other words for discuss, including *describe*, *compare*, *contrast*, *outline*, *analyze*, *apply*, *summarize*, *evaluate*, *state the reasons*, and *show the relationships*.

One final suggestion might be offered to teachers on scoring essay tests. When a test consists of more than one essay item, many teachers prefer to rate each item for all the papers before going on to the next item. In that way they avoid skipping around from item to item and are able to keep in mind the specific points they are looking for in each response. Essay tests have a definite place in the instructional process. They must be carefully constructed and used for the purposes they serve best.

Objective Tests

While essay tests sample limited content in depth, objective tests can sample breadth but not depth of content. The length of answers to essay test items sometimes deludes the teacher into thinking that breadth of content is being tested. If a teacher wishes to test for sheer knowledge of a subject field, the supervisor should recommend an objective test as a far better instrument for this purpose than the essay test. The objective test can cover much more ground and can sample a field of study in a much shorter time than can the essay test.

A test is said to be objective if it eliminates the need for judgment on the part of the scorer. Any person—or a machine for that matter—should be able to take the key to an objective test and arrive at the same score as any other person. Consequently, the reliability of objective tests is much higher than the reliability of essay tests. Subjectivity does enter into objective testing, however, in two ways. At the beginning the teacher must make subjective decisions on which items to include on a test. He or she must refer to the objectives and then analyze the content. Since each test at best represents a sampling of content, the teacher will incorporate only certain items of content in a test, deciding which are the more important items. Subjectivity can also enter into the process of scoring objective tests. There are times, for example, when a student will give a correct response to an item which is different from the response expected by the teacher. The wording or construction of a test item sometimes leaves the item open for judgment by the student and fails to elicit the response indicated by the teacher.

In their own way good objective test items are as difficult to write as are good essay test items. It is difficult but not at all impossible to write objective test items which measure cognitive behavior above the lowest levels of the Bloom taxonomy. A fruitful exercise for the supervisor to carry out with a group of teachers is to ask them to bring in for analysis and discussion an assortment of objective test items which have appeared on tests of theirs. The supervisor must assure the teachers that the discussion and analysis will be carried on in a friendly, positive manner so that teachers will not feel threatened by the exercise. Through this exercise the teachers will ordinarily come to realize that many of the best items confine themselves to low-level cognitive, many items are worded ambiguously, some do not relate to the unit or course objectives, and some call for obvious answers.

A collection of teachers' objective test items will usually consist of at least five major types of items: (1) recall, (2) multiple choice, (3) alternative response, (4) matching, and (5) rearrangement. The text will describe and illustrate each of these types of items and then applications of objective testing to the Bloom taxonomy of the cognitive domain will be made.

Recall Items.   A recall item offers no choice of responses for the test taker and requires a direct answer that must be retrieved from the learner's memory. In its varied forms it is probably the most common type of objective item used, one of the easiest to construct, and the one which is subject to original answers if the teacher has not carefully structured the item. It is found in the form of direct questions, commands, and statements to be filled in, which we also call completion items. The student's life is filled with both oral and written recall items in the form of direct questions which require short answers such as the following:

> Where did the Mayan Indians live?
> Who succeeded President Kennedy as President of the United States?
> How much are 12 and 9?
> What colors are found at the extremes of the color spectrum?
> When did Columbus first reach the New World?

To be an objective item the questions must yield single or separate short answers. The direct question, "Why did we fight in Vietnam?" would lead to an essay answer and would not be appropriate as an objective item.

Recall items may be structured as commands, for example:

> Name the present United States Secretary of State.
> Give the nickname of New York State.
> List three sources of protein in the diet.
> Translate the word *agricola*.
> Mention four contributions of ancient Rome.

Each of these commands can be responded to in brief form. No elaboration is necessary or wanted. The student must draw on his or her own fund of information to supply the correct answers.

Recall items may also be written in the form of statements to be completed, as:

The result obtained when we divide 12 by $\frac{1}{2}$ is _____.
The chemical formula for table salt is _____.
_____ is the name of the capital of France.
The Gift of the Magi was written by _____.
The 50th state admitted to the United States is _____.

Questions, commands, and completion are three styles of recall items. It will be noted that all the illustrations call for low-level cognition—specific factual data. It will also be noted that recall items reduce the chronic problem of objective items—guessing by the student. Naturally, the student can guess at the whole answer but does not have alternative responses presented which may suggest answers. An active command of the knowledge is necessary for the answer to be a right one.

Subjectivity can enter into the scoring of recall items when the items call for more than one response. For example, one of our illustrations above asks students to mention four contributions of ancient Rome. Let us suppose the teacher expected the responses *laws*, *roads*, *aqueducts*, and *military weapons*. A student might respond, *military tactics*, *language*, and *literature* as well as a number of other possible acceptable answers. In each case the teacher must judge whether the unexpected answer is correct and if it is, give the student credit for it. If a teacher gets responses to an item which are different from the responses expected, the fault lies with the test item and not with the students. For this reason the teacher must exercise care in writing items in such a way that students will respond in the way desired.

Students' answers can sometimes contain surprises for the teacher, if the teacher's test items are poorly constructed. The following example is an ambiguous item: "George Washington was born in _____." The teacher might be looking for the answer 1732, but might receive the answer Virginia, an equally creditable response. Would it help, assuming that a date is the expected answer, to construct the item: "George Washington was born on _____"? Probably not, for the student could answer Pope's Creek Farm or February 22 or February 22, 1732. A real sharpie might answer February 11 or February 11, 1732, which was the actual date according to the calendar in use at that time. To avoid ambiguity, completion items sometimes must be cued, as, "George Washington was born in _____ (year)," or written more fully, as, "George Washington was born in the year _____." The recall item must be directed to the specific response or responses which the teacher desires the students to make. A student who gives a correct answer regardless of where that answer has been learned should be given full credit for the answer.

The teacher will not, of course, give credit for frivolous answers, as, *pest* instead of *German roach* or *German cockroach* in completing the item, "The common name for *Blattella germanica* is _____."

The supervisor should help teachers detect ambiguity in test items and suggest ways to avoid this problem. He or she should point out to them that the function of the test item is to find out whether the students know that particular item of content. Teachers sometimes inadvertently provide clues to the correct responses by varying the length of the blanks in completion items and by using "a" or "an" unwisely. If a student is debating, for example, whether to respond "Nile" or "Amazon" to the statement, "The longest river in the world is the _____," the short blank would sway him or her to writing the correct response and would be especially noticeable if subsequent completion items had blanks of varying lengths. All blanks on a completion test should be of uniform length to prevent guessing. In a similar vein the correct answer might be suggested by the article *a* or *an* in an item such as, "A house made of blocks of ice and inhabited by Eskimos is called an _____." If the student is conscious of language, he or she knows the correct answer must start with a vowel. An improved version of this item would be "Houses built of blocks of ice and inhabited by Eskimos are called _____." A single blank should always be used rather than a number of blanks equal to the number of words in the correct response. Would not the student be most likely to respond *Saudi Arabia* to the item, "_____ _____ is the nation in the Middle East which produces the most barrels of oil annually"?

Some measurement specialists recommend that the blank come at the end of the item. While that format is desirable and perhaps most common, there may be times when the teacher wishes to vary that procedure.

Though even objective tests should strive to measure higher levels of cognition, it is necessary many times to test for lower-level cognition; recall items perform that function admirably.

Multiple Choice.   A multiple-choice test item provides students with a statement or question and a number of responses from which the student selects one or more responses according to the directions with the items. This type of item is favored by most teachers and professional test makers for its versatility and for its ability to sample content in a limited time. Though the multiple-choice item is subject to guessing to a much greater degree than is a recall item, compared to other types of objective items discussed later in this section, the multiple-choice test item reduces the student's ability to guess the correct response. When there are four responses, for example, from which a student must select one, the chances of guessing are one in four; with five responses, one chance in five; etc.

Multiple-choice items can be used in any cognitive field and may range from very simple to very complex in nature. They may be used to test for low-level cognition and for higher levels, as we shall illustrate later in this section. They come in a number of varieties, such as "Select the right answer," "Select the incorrect answer," and "Select the best answer." They may call for one response or many responses and they may require considerable thought as anyone who has wrestled with responses such as "all of the above," "none of the above," "a, c, and d but not b," can attest. Let's examine a few of these items from a number of subject fields:

$$12 + 4 = 3 + \square$$
a. 12
b. 13
c. 14
d. 15

Las gafas are
a. Gloves
b. Groves
c. Glasses
d. Gallons

Day: Night = _____: Black
a. Blue
b. White
c. Green
d. Red

Mark Twain is author of all the novels except
a. *Huckleberry Finn*
b. *Tom Sawyer*
c. *Pudd'nhead Wilson*
d. *Henry Esmond*

If $x = 2$ and $y = 4$, $2x + 2y =$
a. 6
b. 12
c. 4
d. 10

The opera *Madame Butterfly* takes place in
a. Italy
b. China
c. France
d. Japan
e. Spain

The formula for water is
a. H_2SO_4
b. H_2O
c. H_2O_2
d. HCl

The proper response a driver should make when his or her auto begins to skid
on ice is
a. jam on the brakes and slide through
b. throw the shift into neutral and coast
c. hold the wheel tight and keep steady
d. turn the wheel in the direction of skid
e. turn the wheel in the opposite direction
f. step hard on the accelerator

A person with *savoir-faire* is
a. reticent

b. knowledgeable
c. impressionable
d. contagious

It is more than likely that as the supervisor and teachers examine sample test items they will find some common errors of construction. Analysis of these errors will suggest some guidelines which the supervisor may suggest to teachers to help them write multiple choice items, as the following:

1. *As a rule of thumb, it is a good idea to provide at least four responses for each item.* The more responses there are, the fewer the opportunities for guessing. There comes, of course, a point of diminishing return in terms of time for pupils to read items and respond to them and in terms of actual space required to duplicate the items. A general practice is the use of four or five responses.

2. *The answers to a multiple-choice test consisting of many items should not follow a consistent pattern which the student can guess.* Although it expedites scoring if the answers are a, b, c, d, a, b, c, d, for example, many students can decipher the pattern and respond accordingly. The teacher wants to know if the students have mastered the content not whether they are good at breaking codes.

3. *Responses should be the same or almost the same length and consistent in form.* For example, let's take the Mark Twain item above. Suppose it read as follows:

Mark Twain is author of all the novels except
a. *Huckleberry Finn*
b. *Innocents Abroad*
c. *Pudd'nhead Wilson*
d. *Call of the Wild*

Which response would you have made if you did not know the title of the novel Twain did not write? Chances are you would select *Call of the Wild*, which is different in form—four words instead of two, as in all the others. The tendency of the test taker is to select a response which is different in length or form from the other responses. If the different form is the correct response, the student may guess it and be rewarded for the guess. Dostoevsky sticks out like a sore thumb in the following item:

Crime and Punishment was written by
a. Capote
b. Dostoevsky
c. Lewis
d. Doyle

The student who did not know would likely guess Dostoevsky and would be right. On the other hand, the teacher may play the game with the student a bit and make one of the incorrect responses different, as in the following example:

All were famous generals of ancient times except:
a. Caesar

   b. Hannibal
   c. Cicero
   d. Scipio Africanus

If the student chooses Scipio Africanus because it is different in form from the others, the choice would be an incorrect one, since Cicero is the correct answer. The purpose of writing an item like this is not to trick a student deliberately—there is no trick, as these were all personnages of history and Scipio Africanus was, indeed, a general. The teacher wants to reward knowledge and not the ability to guess.

   4. *It is generally accepted practice not to put the correct response first in the sequence.* Along with choosing an item that is different, a student who attempts to guess will often choose the first item if none of the responses are known. The same principle operates here as on a voter's ballot. It is conceded that the person whose name appears first on the ballot has a built-in advantage over the other candidates.

   The supervisor should encourage teachers to build up a pool of test items so they can mix them on subsequent testing. They should strive to create items with increasing complexity and those which test more than low-level cognition. Teachers who work within the same field of study can help each other critique test items and can even share items where applicable.

Alternative Response.   Alternative-response items provide the test takers, as the name implies, two choices from which they must select one. The most common form of this type is the true-false item, a much overworked kind of objective item. A major advantage of alternative-response items is their ability to sample an extensive amount of content in a short space and short time. Their major disadvantage lies in the fact that students have a 50–50 chance of guessing correctly. Typical of a multitude of true-false items are the following to which students would respond by circling the T for true or the F for false:

   T   F   Thomas Jefferson was the third president of the United States.
   T   F $6 \times 9 = 54$
   T   F   The seasons of the northern hemisphere are the reverse of the seasons in the southern hemisphere.
   T   F   Leap year comes every other year.

   True and false items can be made more difficult and therefore less objective if the student is required to state the reason for any false answer. Asking a student to state why an answer is false is a perfectly acceptable testing procedure but the teacher will soon realize that this slows down the scoring process and often leads to the necessity for making judgments about the stated reason.

   Alternative-response items may appear in forms other than true and false. Language concepts, for example, can be tested in the following ways:

   (Its, It's) time to go.

The student may circle or underline the correct response or strike out the incorrect response. The teacher may simplify scoring by placing blanks after each item in a column and asking students to write the correct responses on the blanks.

The language arts teacher might ask students to tell whether the italicized words are prepositions:

	YES	NO
After he left, I found the note.	____	____
I saw *her* come in.	____	____
The man spoke *to* his dog.	____	____
I couldn't hear, *for* he had turned his head.	____	____

The pupil would check "Yes" if the underlined word is a preposition and "No" if it is not.

One of the vowel sounds of the English language is tested in the following example of an alternative-response item:

Are the sounds of *a* in each of the following words the same as in the word *cat*?

	SAME	DIFFERENT
Hat	____	____
Hate	____	____
Jar	____	____
Had	____	____
Hall	____	____

Alternative-response items hover around the low levels of cognitive learning. This is particularly the case with true-false items. Our language arts illustrations at least move us up to the level of application. True-false items seem especially easy to create and, as a result, the teacher stumbles into pitfalls—or it should be said the learner stumbles into pitfalls dug by the teacher.

A supervisor might collect or write and share examples of true-false items such as the following and ask teachers what the problem is in their construction.

T F It is always cold in Alaska.
T F It is never legal in the United States to make a right turn on a red light.
T F It is sometimes permissible in the United States to make a right turn on a red light.
T F Every country of South America has Spanish as its official language.
T F No country of South America has two official languages.

Discussion will bring out that all these statements have qualifiers which make it easy for a learner to guess the answer. This same deficiency can be found in the construction of other types of objective test items. Words like *always*, *never*, *sometimes*, *every*, *all*, and *no* should be avoided and the question structured so as not to use these terms. If the question cannot be restructured, it should not be placed on a test. The student already has a 50–50 chance of guessing and the teacher does not want to give away the items.

Another common error can be found in the following examples:

T   F   Tourism is the most important business of Florida.
T   F   Watergate is the worst political scandal in U.S. history.
T   F   It is warm in Hawaii all year round.

Each of the above items calls for some judgment on the part of the test taker. Qualifiers like *important* or *most important* should be avoided unless they are clearly spelled out: most important in what way? Dollars generated? Number of persons employed? Number of people affected? Possibly, historians will judge Watergate to be the worst political scandal but we did have Teapot Dome and Watergate has not yet been subjected to the test of history. By whose criteria is Watergate the worst or not the worst scandal? The third example, "It is warm in Hawaii all year round," may be designed to test knowledge of Hawaii's tropical climate but *warm* is a relative term. Warm to whom? How many degrees is warm? If anyone has been in Hawaii when the thermometer occasionally hits 60° in February, he or she might wish for a touch of heat in the house.

Alternative-response items, like all objective items, must be clear. The double negative does not lend clarity to an item, as "T F It is not uncommon to find snow in Yellowstone National Park in the summer." The teacher should avoid involved, obtuse, and convoluted statements. They should be direct, clear, and precise and yield only one correct answer.

Because of the problem of guessing, alternative-response tests should not be used consistently or exclusively. When they are used, it is advisable to construct a test with a fairly good number of items. One additional guideline should be mentioned: By no means should the teacher copy statements verbatim from the textbook for tests. Students who are familiar with the text may remember the passages from the book and receive unwarranted help from this familiarity.

Matching and Rearrangement Items.   Matching and rearrangement items are two varieties of objective items which provide a little stimulation and challenge on the order of puzzles and make for good variation. Both are somewhat difficult to construct and both require more time to score than is the case with any of the three other types of items, with the possible exception of recall items. The matching test item seeks to find out if students can recognize and pair up a specific stimulus with a specific response. A single theme runs through the pairs of stimuli and responses as in the case of writers and their novels below:

1. Swift   _____   *The Vicar of Wakefield*
2. Scott   _____   *Gulliver's Travels*
3. Carroll   _____   *The Forsyte Saga*

4. Goldsmith   _____   *Ivanhoe*
5. Galsworthy   _____   *Alice in Wonderland*
                    _____   *Little Women*

In the above matching item students write the numbers they find to the left of the authors' names in the appropriate blank to the left of the titles. To reduce guessing by the process of elimination the teacher should provide at least one more response than there are stimuli, otherwise if a student knows all the responses except one, the last response would be a "freebie."

A math item is shown in the following example which requires students to solve each problem before pairing them:

	_____ $2 \div \frac{1}{2}$
1. 54	_____ $21 \div \frac{1}{7}$
2. 9	_____ $24 \div \frac{2}{3}$
3. 4	_____ $12 \div \frac{3}{4}$
4. 32	_____ $18 \div \frac{1}{3}$
5. 16	_____ $8 \div \frac{1}{4}$
	_____ $6 \div \frac{2}{3}$

In constructing matching items the teacher should take care that members of the pair are not opposite each other and that the correct answers do not form a pattern, as 1, 2, 3, 4, 5 in succession.

Rearrangement items test for knowledge of a particular sequence. If order is an important feature to the teacher, the rearrangement item fulfills this task. The teacher provides a statement or command and a set of responses out of sequence. The student must put the items into their proper sequence by writing 1 beside the first item in the sequence, 2, next, etc. as in the two examples below:

Rank the states below from 1 to 7 according to their 1980 U.S. Census population figures:

( ) Ohio   ( ) Pennsylvania
( ) Michigan   ( ) California
( ) New York   ( ) Texas
         ( ) Illinois

In listing a book which has a single author in a bibliography there is a standard order in which items are written. Mark from 1 to 6 the order in which the items should appear.

( ) city of publisher
( ) number of pages
( ) name of author
( ) name of publisher
( ) title of work
( ) date of publication

Recall, multiple-choice, alternative-response, matching, and rearrangement questions all have their place on objective tests. They each have their distinct advantages and disadvantages. Students should be exposed to all types of items if for no other reason than for stimulus variation, which serves to heighten a student's interest.

The question may be raised as to whether objective test items can measure achievement in the highest levels of cognitive learning. Let's take a look at some illustrations of objective test items for each of the major categories of the Bloom taxonomy.

Knowledge

A synonym for lethargic is
a. cool
b. taut
c. slow
d. long

Of the planets listed below the one which is closest to our sun is
a. Pluto
b. Jupiter
c. Venus
d. Saturn
e. Mars

Comprehension

The question, "Do you mean American time or Latin time?" implies
a. North Americans have the custom of arriving late for appointments.
b. Latin Americans have the custom of arriving late for appointments.
c. North America lies in time zones different from South America.
d. Time zones in South America are the reverse of North America.

The moral of Daphne Du Maurier's short story, *The Birds*, is
a. People can triumph over anything.
b. Nature can get out of balance.
c. Birds are vital to humankind's existence.
d. Birds are rapidly becoming extinct.
e. People should help their feathered friends.

Application

If a man loads 50 kegs of nails on a truck in 1 hour, to find out how many cases he could load in 8 hours you would
a. subtract 8 from 50
b. divide 50 by 8
c. add 8 to 50
d. multiply 50 by 8

Which of the following Spanish nouns follow the regular rule for identifying feminine nouns? Underline all the nouns which follow this rule.

a. casa
b. mano
c. cosa
d. mesa
e. pelo
f. pozo

Analysis

The following sentence contains two errors:
My friend Jimmy Lane don't know how to read.
The errors are:
a. absence of commas
b. use of the apostrophe
c. agreement of the verb
d. spelling of *friend*

The snake in the picture shown you by the teacher has all the characteristics
of a
a. king snake
b. chicken snake
c. coral snake
d. milk snake

Synthesis

Add the fifth step in the sequence of steps for multiplication on the pocket
calculator which we used in class:
a. Punch "clear" button
b. Punch the number to be multiplied
c. Punch the × (multiplication) button
d. Punch the number of the multiplier
e. _____
f. Read the product in the window

A boy went into a store with 25 cents. He wanted to buy lollipops which cost
3 cents each and bubble gum which costs 2 cents each. He decided to buy six lollipops
and spend the remainder for as many pieces of bubble gum as he could buy. To find
out how much change he would receive you would need to follow certain steps. Mark
from 1 to 5 the steps you would take to solve this problem in the order in which you
would take them.
( ) Multiply 3 × 2
( ) Subtract 18 from 25
( ) Multiply 6 × 3
( ) Subtract 6 from 7
( ) Divide 7 by 2

Evaluation

Of the four test items below select the one which meets the characteristics of a well-constructed T-F item as described in this text:

a. T F It is not uncommon to find mountain streams which are polluted.
b. T F Milk is the best beverage.
c. T F It never snows in Florida.
d. T F Washington, D.C. is the capital of the United States.

The students will preview three films made for children. On the basis of criteria studied in class, the students will assign each film a rating of 1, 2, 3, or 4 stars (four is the highest rating). The rating for the first film is:

a. one star
b. two stars
c. three stars
d. four stars

Although it is common and acceptable practice for both teacher-made and standardized tests to consist of a single type of objective test item, as multiple choice, I recommend as a general rule that teacher-made tests include a variety of objective test items.

EVALUATING AFFECTIVE OBJECTIVES

Earlier in this chapter it was observed that cognitive objectives may be measured by essay and objective tests and psychomotor skills by tests of actual performance. Standards of mastery may be set and observed for learnings in these two domains. Judgmental kinds of decisions must be made in the case of cognitive essay tests and in the case of assessment of performance of psychomotor skills. In both these cases the standards against which the cognitive and psychomotor performance will be weighted should be established beforehand, written down, and communicated to the test takers.

It is difficult or impossible to observe mastery of many affective objectives and for that reason it is preferable to think of assessment of affective objectives as evaluation rather than measurement. Though we may administer instruments to assess attainment of affective objectives and even subject the results to statistical treatment, the assessment of affective objectives should be used for purposes other than marking and reporting in the traditional sense of marking and reporting.

The affective domain, which comprises feelings, emotions, and attitudes, may be assessed in a variety of ways. Among these techniques are the following.

1. *Observation.* Observation is the most common technique for evaluating performance in any domain. The experienced teacher develops skills in observing the performance of individuals and groups both in and outside class. Affective behavior is shown through comments students make in class, by their behavior in school and out, by the enthusiasm they show, and by questions they raise. The teacher may elicit certain kinds of behavior by placing students in particular situations, by asking them to role-play, and by posing controversial issues.

2. *Essays.* Students may be asked to write compositions which will reveal their feelings and positions on issues. The teacher may suggest personalized topics such as "My Favorite Subject in School," "The Worst Experience of My Life," and "What It Means to Be Cooperative," The teacher might also suggest topics which are more cognitive in nature but still designed to bring out attitudes of the learner, as "The Role of Welfare in Our Society," "Equal Rights for Women," and "Opportunities for Service in the Community."

3. *Opinionnaires.* Attitudes of students may be surveyed with alternative response items such as:

Circle the letter A if you agree with the statement and D if you disagree.
A   D   Handguns should be outlawed.

Some teachers and professional inventories provide for a continuum of responses from strongly agree to strongly disagree, as

Circle SA if you strongly agree, A if you agree, U if you are undecided, D if you disagree, and SD if you strongly disagree with the statement.
SA   A   U   D   SD   The personal use of marijuana should be a criminal offense.

Attitude inventories may yield scores but these scores should be considered simply compilations of responses to give a picture of the positions taken by individuals and the group but not considered correct and incorrect responses.

To construct items and exercises for evaluating affective objectives the teacher goes back to the objectives in the same way as for assessing objectives of the cognitive and psychomotor domains and tries to design assessment items which come as close as possible to finding out whether the learner has met the affective objectives.

The supervisor should engage the teachers in discussion of ways to evaluate affective objectives and should raise questions with them such as: "Which affective objectives should we seek?" "In what ways can accomplishment of these objectives be observed?" "Which affective objectives should be stressed over others?" "What shall we do with the results of evaluation of affective objectives?" "Are there any affective objectives which we should insist on or do all affective objectives pertain only to the individual? For example, if a student believes that dishonesty is the only way to get along in life, should this attitude be of any concern to the teacher?"

Whatever tests are used should be considered an instructional strategy. In order to make most effective use of tests as instructional techniques the teacher should score them and convey the results to the learners as rapidly as possible.

OTHER EVALUATION TECHNIQUES

The major portion of this chapter has been devoted to a discussion of testing. Yet, evaluation through means other than testing occupies a far greater portion of a teacher's time than testing.

EVALUATION OF CLASS PARTICIPATION					
Student:_____					
CHARACTERISTIC	A Excellent	B Good	C Fair	D Poor	F Failing
Attentiveness and interest shown					
Frequency of participation					
Merit (quality) of answers and questions raised					
Extent of volunteering					
Contributions of significant anecdotes, illustrations, and facts to assist in topics under discussion					
Composite Letter Grade_____					

Figure 5.1   Evaluation of Class Participation

SOURCE: Peter F. Oliva, *The Secondary School Today*, 2nd ed., New York, Harper & Row, 1972, p. 528.

Observation of Class Participation

While tests are not and should not be given every day, observation of pupil achievement, usually the most common evaluation technique, occurs daily. Most observation is informal and unstructured. Teachers gain impressions about the work of pupils in their classes. By carefully examining how pupils go about their work, the depth of their understanding of the content, and the quality of their questions and responses, the teacher can make judgments about their achievement.

The teacher is concerned not only with the pupils' achievement but also with their participation—how they interact with each other and with him or her. The teacher looks for attentiveness and interest shown, frequency with which pupils participate, and whether certain pupils are unresponsive. If active class participation by all class members is a goal, the teacher can devise a systematic way of observing and evaluating class participation. The rating instrument shown in Figure 5.1 is one means of providing feedback to the pupils on their class participation as judged by the teacher.

Oral Reports

Oral reports by individuals, committees, panels, and the like provide the teacher with another way to assess student performance. The teacher should provide pupils who are to present oral reports with some criteria against which they will be rated. Common standards include clarity of presentation, correct language usage, supporting

INDIVIDUAL ORAL REPORT

Student: _____

CHARACTERISTIC	Low 1	2	3	4	High 5
Was there evidence of preparation on the speaker's part?					
Was the speaker's presentation clear to the listeners?					
Was his or her voice audible?					
Was his or her voice free of monotony?					
Was his or her language usage correct?					

Figure 5.2 Individual Oral Report

SOURCE: Peter F. Oliva, *The Secondary School Today*, 2nd ed., New York, Harper & Row, 1972, p. 533.

GROUP ORAL REPORT

Group: _____

_____

CHARACTERISTIC	Low 1	2	3	4	High 5
Was there evidence of preparation in respect to content?					
Was there evidence of preparation in respect to organization and presentation of the report?					
Did all the students in the reporting group have the opportunity to participate in the report?					
Did all the students speak audibly?					
Did all the students use language correctly?					

Figure 5.3 Group Oral Report

SOURCE: Peter F. Oliva, *The Secondary School Today*, 2nd ed., New York, Harper & Row, 1972, p. 534.

data, enunciation, and evidence of preparation. Both individual and group reports can be rated using instruments such as shown in Figures 5.2 and 5.3.

Whenever evaluation instruments are used the assumption is made that the teacher will make the results known to the pupils so that they may make improvements in future presentations.

Written Assignments

As common as oral reports are written assignments of varying types from a set of problems to be worked or questions to be answered to brief compositions to research papers. In each case the teacher should provide the learners in advance with a set of standards by which the work will be judged. For routine written homework that standard may simply be completion of the assignment, for it is impossible for teachers to grade all written assignments. On the other hand, the teacher must take the time to grade major written assignments and report the results to the learners.

Creative Assignments

Creative assignments such as scrapbooks and art work give evidence of certain types of learning. Many of the areas of the curriculum offer opportunities for pupils to create some tangible products which demonstrate various skills and knowledge. Whether or not each of the creative assignments is to be graded, pupils must know in advance on what criteria they will be judged.

Group Work

When pupils' work on assignments in groups efforts should be made by the teacher and the members of the group to evaluate their work as a group. Evidence should be obtained as to how effectively each member of the group carried out his or her responsibilities. From time to time it is possible and desirable for the class to participate in evaluating the work of individuals and groups in the class. This technique requires care on the part of the teacher to lay certain ground rules for students' criticism of the performance of other students. When students are asked to evaluate the work of their peers, they must be taught to critique work of their classmates in a positive, constructive vein. An instrument which permits pupils to evaluate their own work as a member of a committee or group can be constructed as shown in Figure 5.4.

This particular instrument utilizes the letter grading system. Should the teacher not wish to couple the evaluation with the letter grades, a numerical scale or categories such as excellent, very good, good, fair, and poor could be used.

Self-evaluation and Joint Evaluation

A total evaluation plan should include opportunities for pupils to develop the skill of evaluating their own performance. It can be helpful for pupils to share their own perceptions of their work with the teacher. Not that the pupils' self-evaluations would substitute for the teacher's evaluation of their work nor ultimately determine a mark but the self-appraisals would serve to provide the teacher with a type of information often otherwise missed and with clues for assisting individual students. Pupils—particularly those at the secondary school level—might be asked to rate themselves on such criteria as their performance on tests, quality and regularity of homework,

```
┌─────────────────────────────────────────────────────────────────┐
│                                                                   │
│              EVALUATION FORM FOR COMMITTEE MEMBER                 │
│                                                                   │
│                                                                   │
│       Please rate yourself on each of the following phases of your committee's │
│       work by encircling the appropriate letter.                  │
│                                                                   │
│                                                                   │
│       PLANNING   (Extent of your participation in planning sessions) │
│                                                                   │
│                           A  B  C  D  F                           │
│                                                                   │
│       PREPARATION  (Library research, search for materials, committee │
│                      work outside of planning and class sessions) │
│                                                                   │
│                           A  B  C  D  F                           │
│                                                                   │
│       TEACHING   (Performance during class periods devoted to your topic) │
│                                                                   │
│                           A  B  C  D  F                           │
│                                                                   │
│                                                                   │
│                                                                   │
│                     Composite grade: _____        │
│                                        Write A, B, C, D, or F      │
│                                                                   │
│       NAME:_____                       │
│                                                                   │
└─────────────────────────────────────────────────────────────────┘
```

Figure 5.4 Evaluation Form for Committee Member

SOURCE: Peter F. Oliva, *The Secondary School Today*, 2nd ed., New York, Harper & Row, 1972, p. 537.

participation in class discussions, participation as a member of a small group, effort expended, cooperation with teacher and fellow pupils, ability to listen, and conduct in class. It is of interest to discover how realistic students' perceptions are of their own work and how far apart are their appraisals and the teacher's appraisal of their work.

A self-appraisal instrument can be designed which reflects the various criteria which the teacher deems important. It can be made into a joint evaluation process which would necessitate appraisal conferences with each pupil at the end of each marking period. Such an instrument is shown in Figure 5.5.

While testing may occupy a prominent place in the instructional program, the teacher should not rely exclusively on testing as a means of evaluation. As has been shown, some of the outcomes of education may not be assessed by ordinary testing. The teacher's evaluation skills should include more than expertness in the construction and administration of essay and objective tests and should include a variety of techniques other than testing. When the supervisor discovers the need for teachers' development of evaluation skills, some in-service training is in order.

MARKING STUDENT ACHIEVEMENT

At the end of each marking period every teacher engages in a pseudo-science known in the "trade" as marking. Marking or grading as it is also called—a concept which

---

JOINT EVALUATION

Student: _____

Teacher: _____

Place an A, B, C, D, or F in each blank.

	Student's Appraisal	Teacher's Appraisal	Weight
Achievement (tests)	_____	_____	2/6
Written assignments (homework, class work, research papers, term reports, book reports)	_____	_____	1/6
Reports to class (preparation, delivery)	_____	_____	1/6
Assigned readings (completed, understood)	_____	_____	1/6
Participation in class discussions (value of contributions, frequency, attentiveness)	_____	_____	1/6
Composite grade	_____	_____	

Figure 5.5 Joint Evaluation

SOURCE: Peter F. Oliva, *The Secondary School Today*, 2nd ed., New York, Harper & Row, 1972, p. 537.

conjures up visions of a steamroller leveling a road—has all the appearance of a science. Teachers administer tests, collect data, subject the data to statistical treatment, and finally come up with a symbol, the letter grade. They place that grade on some sort of reporting form and share it with the student, the parents, and others who may be interested. The school divides its year into a number of marking periods and teachers repeat the grading process at the end of each marking period and wrap up student achievement in one symbol which represents performance for the year. The most common system of grades, particularly at the secondary school level, is a five-letter system: A, D, C, D, F. We know that the student who receives an A will be a much happier person than the student who receives an F. If a student or his parents ask a teacher what a given symbol means—say a B—some teachers will give answers akin to the line from Alice in *Through the Looking Glass*, "It means just what I choose it to mean."

Let us assume for a moment the role of the mathematics department head in a school which has no consistent policy on marking and leaves marking decisions entirely in the hands of each individual teacher. This department head is concerned about the marking practices among the teachers of the department for at the end of the current marking period he has made the rounds of the teachers' classrooms and has discovered a variety of practices. For example:

- A teacher adding up all numerical scores compiled by each student during the marking period, dividing by the number of scores, determining the mean or average score, then converting the scores to letter grades based on an arbitrary scale:
  A = 95–100; B = 85–94; C = 75–84; D = 65–74; F = scores below 65.
- A teacher fitting grades to a modified normal curve with a few As, a few Fs, a larger number of Ds, and the majority of grades Bs and Cs.
- A teacher who gave only As and Bs.
- A teacher who gave Fs to two-thirds of the class.
- A teacher who gave every student an A.
- A teacher who based grades exclusively on written tests.

The inconsistencies in marking practices among teachers in this same department leads the department head to open a discussion with the teachers during one of their joint planning periods. The department head asks the teachers to consider two questions: What are the purposes of marking? On what guidelines can we as a group agree?

A group of elementary school teachers would be in agreement with this group of high school teachers if the high school group saw the purposes of a marking system as:

- Reporting to pupils how well they have done during the marking period and at the end of the year.
- Reporting to parents of the pupils how well their children have done in the subject.
- A means of deciding on promotions to the next grade level.
- A way of motivating students.
- A means of deciding which students' names will be placed on the honor roll.

A group of high school teachers like our math group will also state the purposes of marking as:

- Reporting to employers and colleges. (This purpose is often paramount with high school teachers.)
- Deciding on graduation and awards at graduation.

Marking is a serious business with both teachers and students. Learners are conditioned from the day they set foot in the school that marks—regardless of the symbols used, be they pass-fail, satisfactory-unsatisfactory, 0 to 100 percent, or A–F—are important. Both teachers and parents have pushed students to bring home as high grades as possible. It is not uncommon to find parents who pay their children for each A they bring home. And it is far too common that marks produce conflict between parents and their children, particularly when parents lack patience and understanding of their children's difficulties. It is apparent that teachers, students, and parents alike see tangible and intangible rewards stemming from high grades.

For this reason marks do serve as motivators for many children and conversely they serve as sources of frustration and despair for those pupils who do not or cannot achieve at least passing standards.

The responsibility for marking is a real form of power which teachers exert over the learners. Conscientious teachers spend many anguished moments during their teaching careers over the grades assigned to students. They recognize the pressure marks put on students and seek by every means possible to make those grades a fair and just approximation of student achievement. No matter how scientific the process of marking may appear marks are at best approximations of achievement. Every mark given by a teacher calls for a judgment, which is sometimes based on very limited evidence. It is also unfortunate that, given the premium on marks, the symbols themselves have become for many students more important than the achievement which the marks are supposed to represent.

All marking systems have certain innate problems, some of which are seeds for controversy among teachers and between teachers and the public. It would be a most rewarding in-service activity if the supervisor could lead the teachers to consensus on certain practices they will follow in implementing the marking system of their school. There need to be resolution and common agreement on such issues as:

Shall grades be based on mastery of content (criterion-referenced) or on comparative achievement of learners (norm-referenced)?

How much evidence do you need for determining a grade?

What factors should be considered in arriving at a grade in subject matter achievement?

Should grading practices in homogeneous classes differ from grading practices in heterogeneous classes?

How should achievement in the affective domain be evaluated and reported?

What do letter grades mean?

What score constitutes passing a test? a marking period? a course? a grade level?

Should a student's ability be considered in assigning a mark?

Should a student's effort be considered in assigning a mark?

Is it justifiable for some teachers to be "easy markers" and others "hard markers?"

A heated argument can be started among teachers on any of the foregoing questions. It should be recognized that teachers base their practices not only on empirical data but also on philosophical premises which they hold concerning the learner, the learning process, and society. By sharing their beliefs teachers may come to modify their views and reach some common understandings. The supervisor should strive to obtain consensus among teachers on a few basic principles of marking, specifically:

1. *Marks should reflect as nearly as possible mastery of content.* As Bloom, Hastings, and Madaus pointed out, most learners in school can learn most of the content if they are properly placed in school to begin with and if instruction is skillfully implemented.[11]

2. *A multitude of evidence is necessary for determining a grade.* Success at any level or in any program should not rest on a single examination or a couple of tests. A variety of evaluation techniques should be employed and repeated opportunities should be provided for the learners to demonstrate achievement.

3. *The meaning of each letter symbol should be defined in behavioral terms and those meanings communicated to students and parents.* Whatever factors teachers consider in basing their grades should be made known and no factors which are not communicated should be considered. A frequent and often subliminal abuse of this principle is found in situations where teachers consider a student's deportment in class and penalize him or her for misbehaving by reducing his or her mark in subject matter achievement.

4. *In schools which have set up a competency-based education program the faculty must decide what letter grade represents satisfactory attainment of minimal competencies at each grade level and in each course.* Whether students are grouped heterogeneously or homogeneously for learning, the minimal grade for satisfactory achievement of the prescribed minimal competencies should be, in my estimation, equivalent to a B. We are really dealing here with two conflicting systems when competency-based education is superimposed on an A-F letter grade system. Competency-based education is really binary in nature. You master the competencies or you don't. Thus, we are dealing with a situation which begets satisfactory-unsatisfactory, pass-fail, or A-B. Since many students, teachers, and parents regard a C grade, supposedly average, as unsatisfactory work, C will not suffice as the grade for achievement of the minimal competencies. If B is the grade for acceptable performance on minimal competencies, there is still latitude for brighter or more industrious or more motivated students to excel, perform at a higher level, and attain A grades.

5. *Symbols for marking and reporting conduct, attitudes, personal habits, and other affective outcomes should be different from the symbols for reporting achievement in the cognitive and psychomotor domains.* I make no brief for any particular set of symbols. In practice, secondary schools have tended to stick with the A-F system for marking cognitive and psychomotor achievement, while elementary schools have tended to use two- or three-point systems such as satisfactory(S)–unsatisfactory(U), or S–U and N (needs improvement). If affective objectives are evaluated and reported—and I believe some of them should be—other letters or numbers should be used for this purpose. A three-point scale such as 1, 2, 3 or H(high), M(moderate), L(low) is a feasible alternative.

6. *Whatever measures teachers can take to reduce or remove the threatening nature of marks should be taken.* They can reduce the stress placed on tests and marks and report cards and help learners to adjust to them more easily. Teachers sometimes contribute to students' low marks by the manner in which they emphasize tests. A little positive set induction when administering a test can reduce students' anxiety and help them develop a sense of confidence.

Marking practices can serve the purposes for which they were intended if a careful set of guidelines is developed and put into practice. Improper marking practices can serve as a continuing source of conflict between students and teachers and between parents and teachers. Supervisors need to assist faculties in developing sound marking systems.

REPORTING STUDENT ACHIEVEMENT

Sooner or later the inevitable happens. The student receives his or her piece of paper with the symbols to take home to announce how well or how poorly he or she has done in school for that particular marking period. In theory the report card is meant to communicate to parents the progress and achievement made by the learners. In practice a report card by itself tells parents very little. It tells nothing about the process by which the teacher decided on the grade. If a student brings home low grades, the report card does not reveal why the student's grades are low or what the student must do to bring the grades up.

Over the years, schools have experimented with a variety of forms of report cards and varying procedures for handling them. Some schools mail cards directly to the home instead of sending them home with the pupils. Some secondary schools use single cards for reporting all subjects while other schools use individual report forms for each subject. Some reporting forms consist of but a single card while others are made up of multiple copies. Some are handwritten by the teacher and some are machine processed. Some provide space for teacher's comments while others add space for parents' comments. Some cards must be returned to the school while other report forms are kept at home. If report cards have any common characteristic, it is the inadequacy of information supplied on the card and of the interpretation of the meaning of the symbols used. True, there are often words or phrases which seek to interpret the grades, such as "A means excellent work," "C is average work," etc. But these words tell little more than the letter grade itself.

Unfortunately, teachers are locked into the reporting system and it requires lengthy and concerted action on the part of a total faculty in conjunction with the community to make a change in a reporting system. There are, however, ways to make the reporting system more meaningful and informative. Three ways are suggested by which the reporting system can be improved. First, teachers might supplement the limited information on the report card by a narrative report of student progress. In the narrative the teacher can point out areas in which the student does well and areas in which the student needs improvement. The narrative form of reporting has been popular with elementary school teachers and has, in fact, supplanted other types of reporting in many elementary schools. With the large number of students taught by secondary school teachers a narrative for every student though ideal would be impractical. The secondary school teacher might reserve the narrative for students who have done something exceptionally well and for those students who are having particular difficulty. The secondary school teacher may take advantage of space on those reporting forms which provide for teacher's comments. Both elementary and secondary teachers should be willing to supplement the reporting system with parent conferences.

Second, the school might adopt the practice of sending home progress reports during the marking period instead of waiting until the end of the period to report to parents. If parents know in enough time that their children are doing poor work in school, they may be able to work with them and help them to improve. If the numbers of students preclude progress reports for each student, interim reports could be sent out only when students are experiencing difficulty and appear in danger of failing the course or grade.

Third, the teacher should as a regular practice schedule an evaluation conference, preferably with each student but certainly with students who are not succeeding in class. The conferences need not be lengthy or formal but they should provide the opportunity for the teacher to counsel students on their work, to make suggestions for improving, and to hear from students about difficulties they are experiencing.

These supplements to the report card can go a long way toward enabling both students and parents to understand what the symbols on the cards mean, where the learners are having problems, and what the students must do to achieve mastery of the content. Supervisors need to help faculties to analyze and improve their reporting systems.

SUMMARY

Evaluation is conceived as an integral part of the instructional system. The main purpose of evaluation is to find out if students have met the prespecified objectives.

The process of evaluation begins with preassessment of entry skills which students must exhibit in order to pursue the subject successfully. Formative evaluation should be conducted to check learners' progress during a unit and summative evaluation should assess terminal behaviors.

Testing is one of the tools for assessing cognitive and psychomotor objectives. The teacher customarily makes use of two types of tests: essay and objective. Care must be exercised in the construction of test items so that they accurately measure attainment of the objectives.

In addition to testing teachers may employ observation, oral and written reports, creative assignments, group evaluation, and self-evaluation. The accomplishment of affective objectives may be evaluated through techniques other than testing such as observation, surveys, inventories, essays, opinionnaires, and self-evaluation techniques.

Marks should be an accurate reflection of the objectives of instruction. Efforts should be made to define marks and make them as meaningful as possible. In the case of affective objectives symbols used should be different from those used for reporting achievement of cognitive and psychomotor objectives.

Reporting systems are designed to let students, parents, and others know how well the learner is performing in school. The reporting system can be improved through the use of narrative reports, progress reports, and evaluation conferences.

The supervisor is urged to develop a number of in-service activities to help teachers with the improvement of skills of evaluation, measurement, testing, marking, and reporting.

ACTIVITIES FOR FURTHER STUDY

1. Define:

evaluation	formative evaluation
assessment	summative evaluation
measurement	criterion-referenced measurement
testing	norm-referenced measurement

2. Select a topic for a unit in a subject you know well and specify the entry skills necessary for initiating study of that unit. Specify the means you would use to assess those skills.

3. Select a unit you have prepared in the past and describe in written form the total evaluation plan for that unit, including formal and informal evaluations, continuing and terminal evaluations.

4. Describe how you would calculate marks for a student at the end of the year and how you would determine whether a student passes the course or level.

5. *For those who are currently teaching*: Examine a unit test that you have given to a group of students and on which they have not done well. Describe in what way results of the test have a bearing on the objectives of the unit, preassesment, and instructional procedures. *For those who are not currently teaching*: Secure test data from a teacher you know and make a similar analysis.

6. Prepare an instrument or a set of criteria for evaluating a group oral report and administer it either to your own or another teacher's students where a group oral report is being given.

7. Suggest entry skills which pupils should possess to begin study of:
   a. first grade
   b. beginning typing
   c. World History
   d. eighth-grade algebra

8. Confer with at least two teachers and find out whether they are using a norm-referenced or a criterion-referenced approach to measurement and (tactfully) whether they know the distinctions between the two approaches to measurement.

9. Specify a usable set of criteria for evaluating:
   a. a four-legged wooden stool made in ninth-grade Industrial Arts
   b. a fifth-grader's oral report on the Grand Canyon
   c. a sixth-grade committee report (oral) on "History of the American Flag"
   d. the American crawl (eleventh-grade physical education)
   e. a pair of earrings made of black coral (eighth-grade arts and crafts)
   f. a senior's term paper on "The Uses of Computers"

10. State whether each of the following test items is well or poorly constructed. If you decide an item is poorly constructed, state your reason and tell how the item can be improved.

    T   F   Television is the most important source of news today.

T F Popes have always had their residence at the Vatican.
An Indian tribe which inhabited the continental United States was:
a. the Aztecs
b. the Mayans
c. the Sioux
A communist country is:
a. Peru
b. Yugoslavia
c. Mali
d. Iraq
List four products France exports for sale.
The American Revolution ended in _____.
Discuss the Federal Reserve System.

11. State the way you believe the attainment of affective objectives should be evaluated and reported.
12. Confer with at least two teachers and determine whether any attempt has been made by them to preassess entry skills for the units they are presently teaching.
13. Create an instrument for evaluating students' participation in class.
14. Attend a teacher's class for 30 minutes and, using the instrument which you have designed for activity 13, evaluate the class participation of the students.
15. Obtain a report card of a friend's or relative's child, bring it to class, and try to interpret to the class the meaning of the grades on the report card.
16. Create two essay test items and two each of the following objective test items: recall, multiple choice, alternative response, matching, and re-arrangement, which you feel are examples of well-constructed items.
17. Confer with at least two teachers and gather their reactions to the use of essay and objective tests.
18. Write a position paper on the Bloom, Hastings, and Madaus thesis that more than 90 percent of the students could learn most of what we have to teach them.
17. Find out the passing grade in the high school you attended as a student. Compare passing grades of your high school with those of other high schools and account for the differences, if any.
18. Interview at least two teachers, find out how they determined the marks they gave to their students at the end of the last marking period, and summarize your findings in a written report.
19. Obtain a teacher-made objective test (it can be your own) and classify the test items on it according to the six major categories of the Bloom taxonomy of the cognitive domain. Decide at which level most of the test items lie.
20. Create two sample multiple-choice items to measure achievement at the following levels of cognition: application, analysis, synthesis, and evaluation.
21. Obtain an essay test (it can be your own) and evaluate it on the basis of the criteria in the check-list below.

Checklist for Evaluating Essay Tests

	Yes	No
a. The questions relate to the objectives.	____	____
b. The purpose of the test items is clear.	____	____
c. The wording of the items is unambiguous.	____	____
d. There is more than one essay item.	____	____
e. The questions are focused so students know what will constitute a complete answer.	____	____
f. Students are told what factors will be evaluated in scoring.	____	____
g. Students are told weights assigned to each question.	____	____
h. A scoring key has been prepared showing key points which students must cover in order to receive full credit for each answer.	____	____
i. There is sufficient time for students to respond fully.	____	____
j. English usage is correct.	____	____

22. Obtain an objective test (it can be your own) and evaluate it on the basis of the criteria in the checklist below.

Checklist for Evaluating Objective Tests

	Yes	No

General

	Yes	No
a. The test items relate to the objectives.	____	____
b. There is a sampling of types of test items.	____	____
c. The items sample the content.	____	____
d. The items are clearly written.	____	____
e. The items avoid clues which give away the answers.	____	____
f. The items avoid the language of the text materials.	____	____
g. A key has been prepared.	____	____
h. The items can be scored objectively.	____	____
i. English usage is correct.	____	____

In addition to the general criteria the following specific criteria apply to the various types of objective test items.

Recall Items

	Yes	No
a. The items allow for only one correct answer.	____	____
b. Each item when completed will make a sentence.	____	____
c. Each item has only one blank to be filled in.	____	____
d. All blanks to be filled in are of equal length.	____	____

Multiple-Choice Items

a. There are at least four responses for each item. ____ ____
b. The test avoids a consistent pattern of response. ____ ____
c. The responses to each item are plausible. ____ ____
d. The responses to each item are of approximately the same length. ____ ____
e. Unless students are directed otherwise, the items call for but one answer. ____ ____

Alternative-Response Items

a. The items avoid qualifiers which give away the answers. ____ ____
b. The items avoid double negatives. ____ ____
c. The items avoid opinions and judgments. ____ ____
d. The test avoids a consistent pattern of response. ____ ____

Matching Items

a. For each item there is at least one more response than stimuli. ____ ____
b. Stimuli and matching responses are on different lines. ____ ____
c. Each item is complete on one page. ____ ____
d. The test avoids patterns of response. ____ ____

Rearrangement Items

a. The responses are approximately the same length, where possible. ____ ____
b. The responses for each item are scrambled so correct responses do not follow each other. ____ ____
c. The test avoids patterns of response. ____ ____

NOTES

1. Benjamin S. Bloom, J. Thomas Hastings, and George F. Madaus, *Handbook on Formative and Summative Evaluation of Student Learning*, New York, McGraw-Hill, 1971, 43.
2. Michael Scriven, "The Methodology of Evaluation," *AERA Monograph Series on Evaluation: Perspectives of Curriculum Evaluation*, no. 1, Chicago, Rand McNally, 1967, 56–57. Now available from Xerox University Microfilms, 300 North Zeeb Road, Ann Arbor, Mich. 48106.
3. Ibid., 57.
4. Bloom, Hastings, and Madaus, 53.
5. Ibid., 54.
6. Ibid.
7. Ibid.
8. Ibid.

9. Ibid., 46.
10. Oscar K. Buros, ed., *The Mental Measurements Yearbook*, Highland Park, N.Y., The Gryphon Press. Revised periodically.
11. Bloom, Hastings, and Madaus, 46.

BIBLIOGRAPHY

Becker, Wesley C., Siegfried Engelmann, and Don R. Thomas. *Teaching 3: Evaluation*. Chicago: Science Research Associates, 1975.

Beggs, Donald L., and Ernest L. Lewis. *Measurement and Evaluation in the Schools*. Boston: Houghton Mifflin, 1975.

Bloom, Benjamin S., J. Thomas Hastings, and George F. Madaus. *Handbook on Formative and Summative Evaluation of Student Learning*. New York: McGraw-Hill, 1971.

De Cecco, John P., and William R. Crawford. *Psychology of Learning and Instruction*, 2nd ed. Englewood Cliffs, N.J.: Prentice-Hall, 1968.

Dembo, Myron H. *Teaching for Learning: Applied Educational Psychology in the Classroom*. Santa Monica, Calif.: Goodyear, 1977.

Ebel, Robert L. *Essentials of Educational Measurement*. Englewood Cliffs, N.J.: Prentice-Hall, 1972.

Gay, L. R. *Educational Measurement and Evaluation: Competencies for Analysis and Application*. Columbus, Ohio: Charles E. Merrill, 1980.

Gorow, Frank F. *Better Classroom Testing*. Chicago: Science Research Associates, 1966.

Gronlund, Norman E. *Constructing Achievement Tests*, 2nd ed. Englewood Cliffs, N.J.: Prentice-Hall, 1977.

————. *Measurement and Evaluation in Teaching*, 3rd ed. New York: Macmillan, 1976.

————. *Preparing Criterion-Referenced Tests for Classroom Instruction*. New York: Macmillan, 1973.

Hedges, William D. *Evaluation in the Elementary School*. New York: Holt, Rinehart and Winston, 1969.

Henson, Kenneth T. *Secondary Teaching Methods*. Lexington, Mass.: D.C. Heath, 1981.

Intermediate Science Curriculum Study. *Evaluating and Reporting Progress*. Tallahassee: Florida State University, 1972.

————. *Individualized Teacher Preparation: Individualizing Objective Testing*. Tallahassee: Florida State University, 1972.

Lien, Arnold J. *Measurement and Evaluation of Learning*, 3rd ed. Dubuque, Iowa: William C. Brown, 1976.

Lyman, Howard B. *Test Scores and What They Mean*, 2nd ed. Englewood Cliffs, N.J.: Prentice-Hall, 1971.

Oliva, Peter F. *The Secondary School Today*, 2nd ed. New York: Harper & Row, 1972.

Payne, David A. *The Assessment of Learning: Cognitive and Affective*. Lexington, Mass.: D.C. Heath, 1974.

Popham, W. James. *Educational Evaluation*. Englewood Cliffs, N.J.: Prentice-Hall, 1975.

————. *Evaluating Instruction*. Englewood Cliffs, N.J.: Prentice-Hall, 1973.

————, ed. *Evaluation in Education: Current Applications*. Berkeley, Calif.: McCutchan, 1974.

———— and Eva L. Baker. *Systematic Instruction*. Englewood Cliffs, N.J.: Prentice-Hall, 1970.

Simon, Sidney B., and James A. Bellanca, eds. *Degrading the Grading Myths: A Primer of Alternatives to Grades and Marks*. Alexandria, Va.: Association for Supervision and Curriculum Development, 1976.

Smith, Fred M., and Sam Adams. *Educational Measurement for the Classroom Teacher*, 2nd ed. New York: Harper & Row, 1972.

Strenio, Andrew J., Jr. *The Testing Trap*. New York: Rawson, Wade, 1981.

Tenbrink, Terry. "Evaluation." In *Classroom Teaching Skills: A Handbook*, James M. Cooper, ed. Lexington, Mass.: D.C. Heath, 1977.

Tyler, Ralph W., Robert M. Gagné, and Michael Scriven. "Perspectives of Curriculum Evaluation," *AERA Monograph Series on Curriculum Evaluation*. no.1. Chicago: Rand McNally, 1967.

Films

Critical Moments in Teaching series. Sound. Color. New York: Holt, Rinehart and Winston. Available from BFA Educational Media, 468 Park Avenue South, New York, New York 10016.

Films in the series pertinent to evaluation are:
Give Me Instead a Catastrophe. 10 min.
Image in a Mirror. $8\frac{1}{2}$ min.
Report Card. 12 min.
What Do I Know About Benny? 10 min.

Multi-Media

Vimcet Associates, P.O. Box 24714, Los Angeles, California 90024. Filmstrip-tape programs. Programs on evaluation:
#4 *Establishing Performance Standards*
#7 *Evaluation*
#16 *Modern Measurement Methods*
#23 *Current Conceptions of Educational Evaluation*
#26 *Alternative Measurement Tactics for Educational Evaluation*
#30 *Writing Tests Which Measure Objectives*

6

Helping Teachers with Classroom Management

OBJECTIVES

After studying Chapter 6 you should be able to accomplish the following objectives:

1. Identify common sources of behavior problems.
2. Describe the characteristics of a fully functioning personality and its relationship to the problem of discipline.
3. Analyze your attitudes toward (a) behavior problems, (b) children, and (c) yourself.
4. Describe common teaching styles.
5. Describe common learning styles.
6. Describe several measures which can be taken to prevent disciplinary problems.
7. Describe several models of discipline.
8. Describe several approaches to discipline.
9. Contrast the strengths and weaknesses of behavior modification.
10. Contrast strengths and weaknesses of psychodynamic or diagnostic approaches to discipline.
11. List steps in behavior modification.
12. Analyze the methods of discipline you prefer.
13. Select appropriate corrective measures.
14. Explain the role of punishment.
15. Formulate your own views on discipline.

DISCIPLINE: A SERIOUS PROBLEM

A frazzled young elementary teacher holds her head at the end of a particularly rough day with her group of superactive children. As she fumbles for an aspirin in her handbag it is obvious to the supervisor, who happened to drop in on this inauspicious occasion, that the children's behavior that day had been less than ideal. The supervisor empathizes with her and hopes that the painkiller will relieve her headache. If only the problems of classroom management would respond to a simple formula like aspirin and vanish overnight!

Even Socrates, one of the most famous teachers in history, must have been holding his head when he lamented.

Children now love luxury. They have bad manners, contempt for authority. They show disrespect for elders and love chatter in place of exercise. Children are now tyrants, not the servants of their households.[1]

Sometimes it seems that not much has changed since 400 B.C. Not even the venerable Socrates was able to concoct a formula which would serve as either a vaccine or a cure for misbehavior on the part of young people. Fantasizing, harried teachers feel that student behavior problems would disappear:

If only children were mature—but they are not.
If only children were as motivated as the teacher—but they are not.
If only children could choose whether they wanted to come to school—but they cannot.
If only children had no problems—but they do.

If only—teachers could go on and wistfully hope never to encounter a disciplinary problem, and proceed smoothly from planning to presentation to evaluation without stumbling on the pebbles and boulders of behavior problems. But the road is rocky and the stones are there. It is the teacher's task to clear the stones out of the way, go over them, go around them, or even push them out of the way if need be, and it is the supervisor's task to help the teachers in this arduous job.

The teacher's task when it comes to matters of discipline and control should not be minimized. Discipline is constantly on the minds and tongues of most teachers in the elementary and secondary schools, particularly in the case of new and inexperienced teachers. The frustration of dealing with disciplinary problems has driven many teachers out of the classroom. Some have left the profession, while others, ironically, have gravitated to administrative positions where they have responsibility for the disciplinary problems of an entire school instead of just the problems of their own classes. Some have taken on the mantle of the college professor, whose disciplinary problems are usually few and far between.

High school teachers have it roughest when it comes to discipline, for they have students during the stormy period of adolescence. There are many days when high school teachers would agree with the eminent writer who observed that adolescence is so precious that it is a shame to waste it on youth.

Discipline is a word that is easily understood by everyone but difficult to define. Perhaps, the difficulty of defining the word stems from the fact that like a Portuguese man-of-war it has so many and such long tentacles. If we go back far enough—say 2,000 years—the little Roman *discipulus* was a pupil, a learner, who was subjected to *disciplina*—instruction, training, or education. Hence the use of the term discipline to mean an organized body of knowledge, a subject field. The Disciples of Christ were those who had been instructed in the teachings of Christ.

Though the word discipline still refers to organized fields of specialization, discipline in its "training" sense has come to signify order, management, conduct, deportment, and even punishment. People talk about the discipline of the school and the discipline of the class. We say the teacher maintains good discipline and disciplines the pupils. This text defines discipline as a state of order in the class or school environment which permits learning to proceed smoothly and productively.

Behavior is another of those words which can be understood only in context. Previous chapters discussed learning behaviors meaning, in that context, outcomes or objectives of learning in any of the three domains of learning. To speak of behavior in the context of discipline (as opposed to *a* discipline) is to equate it with conduct or deportment just as misbehavior means misconduct. The student who has learned to take responsibility for his or her own actions in socially acceptable ways is said to possess self-discipline, a major goal not only of discipline but of the entire process of education in our society. Those who behave in socially unacceptable ways are said to have—or, in personified form, to be—behavior problems or disciplinary problems.

A teacher not only teaches classes, but manages them, or more properly, manages the learning environment in such a way that learning can go on. The skills the teacher employs for this purpose are called classroom management. Included within the scope of this definition are classroom routines, prevention of misbehavior, and correction of behavior problems.

Both teachers and school administrators are in agreement that discipline is the most serious problem faced by teachers, particularly inexperienced teachers. Harvey F. Clarizio put the problem in perspective as follows:

Classroom management has always been one of the foremost problems for teachers. Indeed, the adequate control of a class is a prerequisite to achieving instructional objectives and to safeguarding the psychological and physical well-being of students.[2]

Since 1969 George H. Gallup has conducted for Phi Delta Kappa, the national society in education, an annual survey of the public's attitudes toward public schools. Lack of discipline has consistently appeared at or near the top—usually in first place—of the public's list of problems in the public schools. The public has repeatedly ranked lack of discipline ahead of such other thorny issues as lack of proper financial support, use of drugs, poor curriculum/poor standards, difficulty in getting good teachers, teachers' lack of interest, and integration/busing.[3]

The students, in their role as potential misbehavers and recipients of disciplinary measures, are intimately concerned with the problem of discipline. Students expect teachers to foster a classroom environment where, whether productive learning goes on or not, at least their security and self-esteem are protected.

Students realize that they are a part of the American school culture. As such, they expect to encounter misbehavior on the part of their peers and they anticipate that they themselves may indulge in some infractions of the rules, if only to maintain their status in the culture. As a result, they expect responses from the teacher to misconduct. Earlier Gallup surveys showed that the majority of students felt the discipline of their school was about right. Only a small percentage believed the discipline was too strict and a significant percentage considered the discipline not strict enough.[4] What students expect is not absence of response to their misbehavior but attitudes of concern and fairness for them as people.[5]

With all the stress placed by the constituents of the school on discipline the supervisor's work is cut out. Classroom management may well be the single most difficult task of public school teaching. If there is any one aspect of teaching with which beginning teachers especially need help from a supervisor, discipline fits that description.

The principal, the assistant principal for administration, or the dean of students may well ponder the question of discipline in their school as they sit in their offices and receive a steady flow of "discipline problems" from the various classrooms of the school. They note that there are great variations among what teachers consider serious behavior problems—those sent to the administrators' offices. They observe that some of the teachers on the faculty have either a greater skill in handling disciplinary problems than other teachers or else a greater tolerance for enduring them, for some teachers never send misbehaving pupils to an administrator's office while other teachers repeatedly send children out of their classrooms because of misconduct. They realize with a touch of amusement that the teachers who send their misbehaving children to them expect them to handle the problems where they have failed; they expect them to take some drastic action on each case whether the culprit has simply sassed the teacher or pulled a knife.

These administrators cannot help but notice as they stroll through the corridors of the school great differences in teaching styles among the faculty. They conjecture that there must be some relationship between teaching style and the presence or absence of behavior problems in the classroom. And yet, no single variable can be found to be a sure predictor of skill in discipline except perhaps for the fact that the beginning teacher seems to have more difficulty with discipline than the experienced teacher. Even the variable of experience, however, is not an accurate predictor of a teacher's success or failure in handling disciplinary problems. It cannot be said with certainty that an inexperienced teacher is always less skillful in maintaining discipline than an experienced teacher; it can be seen that that is not always the case. It cannot be stated that an older teacher is better at maintaining discipline than a younger teacher, for it is apparent that that is not always true. It cannot be stipulated that male teachers are more skillful at discipline than female teachers; quite the reverse is often true. Sometimes it seems as if some mysterious body chemistry of a teacher is the secret of discipline. Among teachers in the same school, working with the same students, some teachers experience few or no disciplinary problems while others experience constant problems. Administrators may finally conclude that those teachers who are having difficulties in respect to discipline lack certain understandings about behavior—both the student's behavior and their own—and certain skills in classroom management.

What kind of program, then, can a supervisor institute to help teachers develop and improve both their understandings of behavior and skills of classroom management? The program should include at least three components:

Teachers should be engaged in discussions of causes of behavior problems and helped to develop basic understandings about discipline.

Teachers should be helped to develop skills for preventing disciplinary problems.

Teachers should be helped to choose suitable corrective measures.

CAUSES OF BEHAVIOR PROBLEMS

The disciplinary problems of the schools today range from the trivial to the terrifying and from the casual to the criminal. Since the days of the Latin Grammar School, teachers in America have had to contend with children who scrapped with each other, carved their initials on school furniture, scribbled on the walls, failed to pay attention, were impertinent, and disrupted learning in a variety of ingenious ways. Some of the troublemakers in school have gone on to become prominent and productive citizens. Only in recent times have teachers had to cope with students who bring handguns to school, use drugs, and threaten both teachers and other students with bodily harm. A pessimist might conclude that young people and society have gone to hell, hedonism is in the saddle, religion has failed, and we have entered an era of darkness.

Such a pessimistic outlook makes the mistake of generalizing that a large percentage of children and youth in all schools are serious troublemakers. True, some schools do have more than their share of serious offenders. But these schools are not the norm of our educational operation. The extent of this enterprise we call public education can be seem in some recent statistics. Our children are schooled in some 67,000 elementary public school attendance centers and some 25,000 secondary public schools.[6] It takes more than 2 million teachers employed by some 16,000 school districts to instruct these young people: over 1,200,000 teachers are engaged in the education of some 25,000,000 elementary school children and more than the 800,000 teachers serve to educate over 17,500,000 secondary school boys and girls.[7]

Great variations in disciplinary climate exist among these more than 90,000 schools some of which are located in rural and small-town America, some in urban settings including the inner city, and some in suburbia. Some of these schools are characterized by relatively few behavior problems and only a very small percentage of serious problems while other schools experience many behavior problems, a sizable percentage of which are serious. The serious problems such as racial conflicts, sex offenses, the use of drugs, and violence tend to be highlighted and featured in the news media. Although the serious problems are numerous—more numerous than we would wish them to be—the truth of the matter is that most children and youth are law-abiding, fortunately for our society. Although the headlines of the daily press feature rising crime rates throughout the nation, the majority of our population still subscribes to the rule of law. When corrective measures are discussed later in this chapter it will be observed that in those schools where serious problems are frequent strict measures must be taken to cope with them. What plagues most teachers, however, is the continuing, repeated, frustrating behavior of students who impede not only their own learning but the learning of others.

Well-disciplined schools share two characteristics: (1) the absence of disciplinary problems and (2) a total program which promotes the teaching of self-discipline. Both these characteristics are goals which schools should strive to achieve even though both are difficult to realize. Self-discipline means the individual's ability to exercise self-control and to take responsibility for his or her own conduct. When self-discipline is present in a school, behavior problems disappear.

The absence of disciplinary problems per se is, however, no guarantee that self-discipline is present. Behavior problems can be held in check—at least temporarily—by strict regimentation. Stern disciplinary measures on the part of the faculty can repress behavior problems but at the same time they prevent the development of self-discipline on the part of the students.

Since discipline is such a pervasive problem and teachers are eager for answers to their problems, supervisors sometimes initiate the study of discipline with a case approach. Teachers share anecdotes of misbehavior with their colleagues and jointly try to recommend the best strategies for dealing with each case. Though this procedure is a useful and practical approach to the study of discipline, the case approach is more effective after the teachers have developed some understandings of the causes of behavior problems. When they can form some hypotheses as to why a child has behaved in a certain way, they can more intelligently recommend solutions to the problem. Understanding causes of behavior problems may serve to indicate additional information teachers must gather before they can attempt to resolve a problem. The supervisor should help teachers to clarify the reasons why children become disciplinary problems.

Some years ago in researching the subject of discipline I classified causes of behavior problems under six broad categories: causes originating with the child, causes originating with the child's group, causes originating with the teacher, causes originating with the school, causes originating with the home and community, and causes originating in the larger social order.[8] Analysis and discussion of each of these categories can contribute to the teachers' understanding of pupil behavior. The six categories of this classification scheme are in reality sources or roots of disciplinary problems. An early conclusion which teachers will reach is the understanding that behavior may be manifested in class but its origins may lie somewhere else. Teachers will come to realize on study of sources of misbehavior that problems in the classroom may very well be symptoms of trouble rather than the trouble itself. Teachers are usually already aware that there are causes of behavior problems over which they have little or no control. For that reason our discussion of prevention and correction of behavior problems later in this chapter will emphasize those measures which are within the powers of the teachers. As a prelude to an examination of what the teacher may do about disciplinary problems let's consider why pupils exhibit behavior problems.

Causes Originating with the Child

Personal Problems

Children experience a variety of physical, mental, social, and emotional problems which can create disciplinary difficulties in the classroom. A typical class includes youngsters with physical handicaps, slower intellectual capacities, and social and psychological problems. Defects in hearing and vision are common handicaps which sometimes go undetected for years. When a youngster cannot see well or hear well, he or she can easily become a disciplinary problem for the teacher. Malnutrition is a more common problem than we sometimes realize. Not only is malnutrition a problem among children of parents who cannot afford to provide their children with a nutritious diet but it is also a problem in middle- and upper-class families who can afford nutritious diets but for one reason or another do not follow sound principles of nutrition. If there is some truth to the saying, "You are what you eat," then a good many classroom behavior problems can be traced to faulty diets. The general health of the child, the presence or absence of fatigue, endocrine deficiencies, and past diseases may all be factors in the child's performance and behavior in class.

Of all the physical factors which contribute to disciplinary problems the most common and most obvious is the child's stage of growth and development. The handling of concepts, the ability to solve problems, the ability to sit still, the ability to listen, the ability to pay attention, the ability to take turns in speaking, and the ability to get along with others are all functions of growth and development. Biological determiners join with sociocultural determiners to make growing up in twentieth-century America a protracted experience for children and adolescents. Biologically, youngsters develop in a fixed pattern—they learn to walk before they learn to talk, they learn to talk before they learn to read, they learn simple numbers concepts before they can solve equations. Ultimately, they learn to take responsibility for their own behavior. Culturally, the American public keeps its children in school for longer periods of time than many other societies. One reason is that the American public accepts the dictum that education opens doors for its youth. Don't every American mother and father secretly wish they could point with pride to their offspring and say, "Our child, the doctor"? Don't repeated public opinion polls show doctors, lawyers, and engineers at the top of lists of preferred occupations—all calling for prolonged education? (Teaching, which once ranked among the most preferred of occupations, has moved down somewhat but in spite of all its problems still enjoys a wide popularity as evidenced by numbers of young people aspiring to be teachers.)

The American public keeps its youngsters in school longer and therefore in a less than mature status in order to reduce competition of young people with adults for jobs. Raising the age for compulsory school attendance over the years has been a direct function of the efforts of the public to safeguard jobs for the adult bread-winners of the family. Though growth and development are significant factors in discipline at all levels, many teachers seem to feel that the middle school and junior high years are the most difficult. Caught as they are between puberty and adolescence preadolescents often exhibit simultaneously problems of childhood and adolescence.

An analysis of the mental abilities of children in any heterogeneous class will show a range from very slow to gifted. Any of these levels—slow, average, or fast—can become behavior problems given an inappropriate learning environment. When slow learners are frustrated by their inability to cope with their studies, when average learners find nothing stimulating about their studies, and when bright students find their studies no challenge, they can create disciplinary problems for the teacher.

Self-concept

All human beings have common socio-psychological needs. All need love, security, recognition, approval, and success and the lack of awareness, the frustration, even the squelching of these needs breeds countless behavior problems. William Glasser, exponent of Reality Therapy, identified love and self-worth as the most important needs of all humans. Said Glasser:

Love and self-worth are so interwined that they may properly be related through the use of the term *identity*. Thus we may say that the single basic need that people have is the require-ment for an identity: the belief that we are someone in distinction to others, and that the someone is important and worthwhile. Then *love and self-worth may be considered the two pathways* that mankind has discovered lead to a successful identity.[9]

Perceptual psychologists have called educators' attention to the necessity for recognizing the importance of the self-concept. Every human being has the need to become, as Carl R. Rogers termed it, "a fully functioning personality,"[10] or, as A. H. Maslow called it, "a self-actualizing"[11] person or, as Arthur W. Combs labeled it, "a truly adequate person."[12]

Don E. Hamachek described how the self-concept is formed:

How we view ourselves is determined partially by how we perceive ourselves as really being, partially through how we view ourselves as ideally wanting to be, and partially through the expectations we perceive that others have for us.[13]

Combs identified four characteristics which seemed to him to underlie the behavior of truly adequate persons. "These characteristics are: (a) a positive view of the self, (b) identification with others, (c) openness to experience and acceptance, and (d) a rich and available perceptual field."[14] Of the self-concept Combs wrote:

The self concept, we know, is learned. People *learn* who they are and what they are from the ways in which they have been treated by those who surround them in the process of their growing up. . . . People develop feelings that they are liked, wanted, acceptable and able from *having been* liked, wanted, accepted and from *having been* successful. One learns that he is these things, not from being told so, but only through the experience of *being treated as though he were so*. Here is the key to what must be done to produce more adequate people. To produce a positive self, it is necessary to provide experiences that teach individuals they are positive people.[15]

Maslow placed self-actualization at the top of a hierarchy of basic needs. Self-actualizing persons hold a positive view of the self. Many children, however, in their association with "significant others" have learned self-doubt, low esteem, and fearfulness. "The self is built almost entirely, if not entirely," said Earl C. Kelley, "in relationship to others.... Unfortunately, many people in the world today suffer from inadequate concepts of self. . . . An inadequate concept of self, so common in our culture, is crippling to the individual."[17]

In contrasting behaviors commonly observed in students Hamachek noted that students with high, positive self-concepts get along well with others, are friendly, and show self-confidence. Students with low, negative self-concepts generally worry, exhibit shyness, and can be overassertive.[18]

Self-fulfilling Prophecy

Many students who hold inadequate self-concepts have become victims of what is known as the *self-fulfilling prophecy*. Friends, relatives, or teachers or possibly all have led them to believe that they are inadequate and, as a result, they have come to believe in their own inadequacies. They may have been told that they cannot read, they cannot do math, they cannot draw, they cannot excel in sports; they cannot, you name it. If told enough times, they agree they are inadequate. This belief leads to failure, which deepens their conviction that they cannot achieve, which leads to more failure.

On the other hand, if they are told that they are adequate and that they can do the tasks asked of them, they are more often successful. With success comes the belief that they are adequate, which leads to continued success. Somehow negative attitudes toward the self need to be replaced by positive ones. Teachers are in a vital position to help young people gain a sense of adequacy, which is fundamental to living and learning.

Supervisors should help teachers to realize that when a child takes a seat the first day of class, he or she has brought along certain physical, mental, social, and emotional attributes which during the course of the year may lead to disciplinary problems.

Causes Originating with the Child's Group

Children act not only as individuals but also as members of groups. Most notably, all children are members of their classes and react with one another in their classes. To varying degrees the behavior of one individual in a class shapes the behavior of other individuals in that class. The learning environment of which the teacher is the chief manipulator can contribute to behavior problems in the group.

Children are not only members of their classes but they participate as members of other groups both inside and outside school. Unless they are "loners," they will have a small circle of intimate friends with whom they constantly associate. Subgroups develop within classes and can become powerful shapers of student behavior. Some young people are more gregarious than others and are members of many groups: school clubs, church organizations, community groups, and street gangs. For many, youth groups outside school permit them to achieve a sense of identity they cannot find in school.

The groups to which a child belongs exercise a potent influence on his or her behavior. This influence can be positive or negative depending on whether the aims of the group are social or antisocial. Peer-group pressures, particularly among adolescents, force youngsters often into patterns of behavior which may be against their own best inner judgments. Long ago Allison Davis observed:

The example of the adolescent's play group and of his own kin, however, is the crucial determinant of his behavior. Even where the efforts of the parent to instill middle-class mores in the child are more than half-hearted, the power of the street culture in which the child and adolescent are trained overwhelms the parent verbal instruction. The rewards of gang prestige, freedom of movement, and property gain all seem to be on the side of the street culture.[19]

We cannot blame youth alone for responding to group pressures. The hand-shaking, back-slapping, gregarious, conforming Organization Man is still an ideal of our society. Those who are critical of social customs and practices are not always appreciated. American society has placed a great emphasis on outer-direction as evidenced by our preoccupation with encounter groups and other forms of sensitivity training, by personality "testing" which places a high value on conformity, and by the joining syndrome which the Frenchman Alexis de Tocqueville observed about Americans in the nineteenth century.

Neither conformity to a particular group's pressures nor nonconformity should be considered an end in itself. Conformity to the rule of law and to conventions subscribed to by society as a whole is a must—whether in the classroom or out. Conformity of thought, of ideas, and of opinions is not a goal to be sought—whether in the classroom or out.

Teachers need to be aware that there are groups outside the class group vying for the interests of members of the class. They need to be aware also that the aims and activities of those outside groups are often more appealing to the members of their classes than is membership in the class group. They are literally in competition with other forces which demand the time, interest, and loyalty of members of their class. The textbook answer to this problem is the creation of a learning environment so appealing that children will choose academic pursuits over other interests. Whether this can be achieved is highly problematical. Even the experienced supervisor may be hard pressed to advise the teacher how to make learning more attractive to young people than avocational, recreational, and other out-of-class activities. The supervisor feels as if he or she were the grasshopper who envied the household roach for his good fortune at being able to live inside where he could find food and be sheltered from bad weather. The grasshopper asked the roach, "How can I share your good fortune?" The roach answered, "That's easy. Just turn yourself into a roach." The grasshopper, perplexed, inquired, "But how can I do that?" The roach replied, "Well, I've given you the principle. Now you work out the details."

What the supervisor can advise the teacher is to create as favorable and positive a classroom climate for learning as possible. Some of the dimensions of this positive climate are examined further on in this chapter. The supervisor can advise the teacher, at the risk of being accused of tautology, to try to develop groups of nonconforming conformists or, vice versa, conforming nonconformists by providing a climate where there is freedom to learn. But freedom, the supervisor hastens to add, is accompanied by restraint on the part of all members who make up the groups. Without restraint, preferably self-restraint, there can be no freedom for anyone.

Causes Originating with the Teacher

It will take a complete change of thought before the point has been reached where the majority of teachers are willing to admit that teachers themselves can be causes of pupil behavior problems. It takes an open, introspective personality to look within oneself and recognize that the teacher can be a source of student problems. Such introspection flies in the face of tradition, for it has been the custom since schools were first established to place the blame for misbehavior with the offender himself. It is the pupil, after all, who is not behaving properly. We may on occasion look beyond the child and lament, as the refrain goes, "Poor helpless child, he's not to blame, his father's folks are just the same." From time to time we might listen instead to Cassius' words, "The fault, dear Brutus, is not in our stars, but in ourselves." Chapter 11 develops the theme of teacher behavior and suggests ways in which a supervisor can help teachers to evaluate themselves.

A common source of disciplinary problems can be found in the methods of instruction employed by the teacher. Objectives which are inappropriate to the learners (or lack specified objectives) or poorly conceptualized, haphazard planning, ineffective presentations, unsuitable materials, inadequate evaluation, and lack of provision for feedback—dealt with at length in previous chapters—create and magnify pupil behavior problems. While many behavior problems are caused by poor methodology, this aspect of teaching fortunately can be improved with training. It is far easier and less threatening for a teacher to admit that methods of instruction are causing disciplinary problems than it is to admit that something about his or her personality provokes problems. The supervisor who is a specialist in the teacher's field or grade level should continuously work with teachers in helping them to improve their methods of instruction. Fortunately too, improvement in methodology can be observed and measured by both the teacher and the supervisor. Improvement—translate this *success*—spurs the teacher on to continued improvement and helps develop rapport between the teacher and supervisor.

Unfortunately, not all teacher-caused faults lie in the methods of instruction. The attitudes which teachers reveal about students, learning, the school, the community, morality, democracy, and life in general can create a climate which either produces or reduces behavior problems, depending on whether these attitudes are negative or positive. Teachers who care about their students and show it will have fewer disciplinary problems than teachers who dislike their students, their school, and their job.

Beyond a genuine interest and affection for the level of learners they are teaching, teachers should possess certain common personal characteristics without which successful school teaching is impossible. Both a sense of humor and a sense of confidence are essential attributes of a teacher. Some people seem to be born with both these characteristics, though we know they have developed them over the years through contacts with other people. If they are lacking in an individual, they are both exceedingly difficult to develop. Of the two traits a sense of confidence may be developed more easily than a sense of humor. Good planning, for example, can give a teacher a sense of confidence. When a teacher knows how to go about the instructional process, fears of floundering disappear. The teacher can develop confidence by managing instruction in such a way that students achieve their objectives. A supervisor can help a teacher develop a sense of confidence by pointing out ways to plan for instruction and present lessons effectively and by building the teacher's sense of confidence with frequent and positive reinforcement. It is dubious whether the supervisor can help a teacher develop a sense of humor if the teacher has none. The lack of a sense of humor may be symptomatic of personal problems which will only respond to the kind of therapy a supervisor neither can nor should attempt to provide. Perhaps, just perhaps, if the supervisor displays a sense of humor and cajoles the teacher a little, a latent seed of humor may blossom forth.

Much has been written in recent years about students' rights to dress and groom themselves as they see fit. Certainly teachers should have similar rights to select their wardrobes and wear their hair in a manner pleasing to them. Yet, some bounds of propriety are essential. Though most beginning teachers are scarcely out of their teens themselves, they are still adults and must comport themselves as adults. Further, young people want to look to them as adults, not as their peers. The teacher's choice of dress and language should be such as to command the respect of young people. Teachers who attempt to imitate the life style of children in the mistaken notion that this is the way to show their interest in them run the risk of becoming ridiculous in their eyes. Whether they want the role or not, teachers are a parent substitute and as such have a certain culturally determined role they must play. To forsake this role is to invite disciplinary problems.

One attribute which must be mentioned is the teacher's voice. Confidence is communicated to youngsters through what the teacher says and how it is said as well as through what the teacher does and how it is done. Teachers with a speech impediment have a tough row to hoe, for at times children can be intolerant to the point of cruelty. The teacher's voice must be strong enough to be heard—the first time he or she speaks—if children are to be taught listening skills. A grating or shrill voice fails to command either attention or respect. What the teacher should seek to develop is a calm, well-modulated, resonant voice and well-articulated, grammatically correct speech patterns. The supervisor might recommend that teachers who have problems in speaking and voice projection take some training in speech and if necessary undergo speech therapy.

The supervisor must ask teachers to look at themselves as possible sources of some of the behavior problems they encounter in their classrooms.

Later this chapter we will return to the role of the teacher in preventing and correcting disciplinary problems.

Causes Originating with the School

A number of conditions beyond the boundaries of the classroom combine in the school to create disciplinary problems. A study of the school's curriculum from the academic program to the extra-class program to the pupil personnel services will show that the curriculum contributes to and causes many pupil behavior problems. When the curriculum is "out of joint," to use Shakespeare's expression, disciplinary problems can spring up like toadstools.

The curriculum can be out of joint in several ways. Though we have given a lot of lip service to individualized instruction, especially in the past few years, education remains a mass operation with most instruction aimed at a hypothetical average child. The curriculum often misses the large numbers of students who fall below or above the average. Couple the curriculum—the program itself—with methods of instruction which fail to meet the needs of the slow and fast ends of the spectrum and we create a breeding ground for behavior problems. When students cannot cope with the program, they find other ways to distract themselves, much to the teacher's consternation.

The word *relevance* has been so abused and distorted that I almost hesitate to use it. Nevertheless, a goodly portion of the curricula of many schools is irrelevant. For some people relevance has come to mean catering to the immediate needs of students. Preferably, a relevant curriculum is one that will help students not only in the present but also in the future. Relevant subject matter helps pupils to make decisions—to think—and to carry out life activities. B. Othanel Smith, Saul B. Cohen, and Arthur Pearl indicated relevant subject matter as helping the learner to:

choose and follow a vocation,
exercise the tasks of citizenship,
engage in personal relationships,
take part in culture-carrying activities.[20]

Glasser defined relevance as "the blending of one's own world with the new world of the school" and saw relevance working in two directions: the school curriculum must be relevant to the child's life and the child's life must be relevant to the curriculum. He said:

Thus we have both parts of relevance:
  1. Too much taught in school is not relevant to the world of the children. When it is
     relevant, the relevance is too often not taught, thus its value is missed when it does
     exist.

2. The children do not consider that what they learn in their world is relevant to the school.[21]

Glasser attacked the chronic disease of schools since time immemorial—the stress on memorization as opposed to thinking. He observed:

Children discover that in school they must use their brains mostly for committing facts to memory rather than expressing their interests or ideas or solving problems . . . beginning in the first grade . . . thinking is less valuable than memorizing for success. . . . Memorizing is bad enough. . . . Worse is that most of what they are asked to memorize is irrelevant to their world; where it is relevant, the relevance is taught either poorly or not at all.[22]

School climate impinges on pupil behavior in much the same way as the climate in the individual classroom affects pupil conduct. The perceptive visitor to a school can sense the morale of students. A visitor can tell whether students feel a pride in their school and a sense of identity with it and can judge whether there exists that intangible something called "school spirit." The care of the building and grounds by its inhabitants sometimes speaks louder than words. The school should be a place where students enjoy not only learning but living. Charles E. Silberman made some harsh judgments about the schools when he said:

It is not possible to spend any prolonged period visiting public school classrooms without being appalled by the mutilation everywhere—mutilation of spontaneity, of joy in learning, of pleasure in creating, of sense of self. . . . Because adults take the schools so much for granted, they fail to appreciate what grim, joyless places most American schools are, how oppressive and petty are the rules by which they are governed, how intellectually sterile and esthetically barren the atmosphere, what an appalling lack of civility obtains on the part of teachers and principals, what contempt they unconsciously display for children as children.[23]

Glasser feels that instead of stressing success schools emphasize failure. He hit hard the failure orientation of the schools. He pointed out that the child enters school in a successful and optimistic frame of mind. He observed, "Very few children come to school failures, none come labeled failures; *it is the school and the school alone which pins the label of failure on children....* The shattering of this optimistic outlook is the most serious problem of the elementary schools."[24]

The school climate of nine secondary schools was studied by Carl Nordstrom, Edgar Z. Friedenberg, and Hilary A. Gold.[25] They found extensive presence of a negative attitude which they called *ressentiment*. Their study of attitudes of teachers and students in these schools showed ressentiment deriving from the presses or limitations on students' behavior and from the premium schools place on conformity.

Not all schools, of course, are the joyless places these authors describe but enough of them are to cause administrators and faculty to look at the type of climate they are fostering. If a school is experiencing a large number of behavior problems, its climate may very well be at fault and in need of revitalizing. The development of a healthy school climate is everybody's business in the school not just the responsibility of an administrator or small groups of teachers. The supervisor should engage teachers in a study of the school and classroom learning climate and in identification of problem areas which need correcting.

Causes Originating with the Home and Community

The child's family, neighborhood, and community play a profound part in shaping behavior. During preschool years and on through school to adulthood, attitudes learned from closest associates affect the child's behavior. Parental love for their children is one of the most powerful determiners of behavior. Children who are rejected by their parents are much more likely to become behavior problems than children whose parents love them.

The parents' attitude toward education influences children for good or for ill. Children who receive reassuring support from their parents are more likely to succeed in school and less likely to be behavior problems than children whose parents do not care whether they succeed or not. Parents err when they provide no reassurance or exert too much pressure on their children to succeed in school. Either extreme can contribute to behavior problems. Oversolicitous parents who insist their children bring home nothing but As can induce feelings of guilt and anxiety which can erupt in disciplinary problems in the school.

Disharmony in the home can produce pupil misconduct in school. A child's relationships with brothers and sisters and parental preferences for one child over the other can create difficulties. It is far too common for parents to hold up one child in the family as a model of behavior. Each child wants to create a personal identity and be valued for himself or herself. Teachers too often compound the problems by telling a child that an older brother or sister whom they may also have had in a class was a better student.

The neighborhood and immediate community in which a child lives make their impression on his or her behavior. The ghetto child finds problems of living greatly different from the problems experienced by children from well-to-do residential areas. All children bring their problems to school. The teacher who is aware of the fact that some of a child's problems may be arising as a result of home environment can use this knowledge to advantage. For many children from unfavorable homes the school is, can be, or should be a warmer, more comfortable setting than their home or neighborhood.

The teacher will realize that there is little or nothing he or she can do to change a child's home environment. The teacher can refrain from exacerbating a child's problems and from creating a classroom environment that in itself causes behavior problems.

Causes Originating in the Larger Social Order

It is difficult to pin down the effects of conditions on the social scene which contribute to disciplinary problems. Some students cheat, for example, because they hear and read about cases of cheating by adults and conclude that that is the accepted way of making one's way in the world. Unethical and illegal conduct on the part of prominent persons is featured in the press. The young person may have a tendency as a result to conclude that the crime is not in the conduct itself but in getting caught.

Studies of class in America have shown that mores differ from one socioeconomic class to another. Classes differ in moral and spiritual values, permissiveness, patterns of aggression, sexual habits, and even language. Our schools are middle-class institutions staffed largely by middle-class teachers. But the children in these schools are not all from middle-class environments. Children from lower socioeconomic backgrounds have been taught behavior patterns which are quite different from those taught children of middle-class backgrounds and they must manifest these behavior patterns to survive in their environment. Change to middle-class values of cleanliness, industriousness, refined language, etc.—what we might call "gentlemanly behavior"—however laudable, cannot be effected overnight. Behavior patterns are difficult and often impossible to change, as every teacher knows.

The effects of violence in everyday life on individual behavior are difficult to gauge. Violence seems to be a way of life on the contemporary American scene. Young people are bombarded with reports and stories of violence daily in the press, on television, and in films. More and more parental groups, psychologists, and government officials are becoming concerned with the large doses of violence being served to children in books, television shows, and movies. In the past the public has had more of a preoccupation with sex in the arts. There is a growing concern that preoccupation with either sex or violence can be destructive to the individual and can result in behavior that can be destructive to society.

The chances of an individual teacher's making much of an impact on behavior problems which stem from the social scene are small. Teachers can and must restrain students who exhibit antisocial behavior, but fundamental changes in society are not within their power. On the other hand, suppose for a moment that every teacher, every administrator, and every supervisor in every school system of the country were aware of the impact of the larger social order on the behavior of pupils. Could not a program be designed from kindergarten on up which would help resolve some of these social problems and even result in changes in society? Would not relevance of content take on new meaning?

PREVENTING BEHAVIOR PROBLEMS

The prevention of behavior problems should be foremost in the minds of teachers. When measures to prevent disciplinary problems are successful, the teacher has little worry about corrective measures. From an examination of causes of behavior problems can the supervisor derive ways of helping teachers to prevent problems from arising? The supervisor can help and encourage teachers to do the following.

1. Analyze Their Own Attitudes

a. Attitudes toward Behavior Problems. In 1928 E. K. Wickman conducted a study asking 511 elementary school teachers in Minnesota, New Jersey, New York, and

Ohio and 30 mental hygienists (clinicians) in Cleveland, Newark, and Philadelphia to rate 50 behavior problems as to their relative seriousness.[26] Table 6.1 shows the comparison of the ratings of the two groups.

In reviewing the Wickman study in 1952 I wrote:

Wickman summarizes the ratings in that teachers regard immoralities, dishonesties, transgressions as most serious; violations of orderliness in the classroom and application to school work as next most serious; extravagant, aggressive personality and behavior traits as less serious; and withdrawing, recessive personality and behavior traits as least serious. Mental hygienists, on the other hand, view withdrawing, recessive personality and behavior traits as most serious; dishonesties, cruelties, temper tantrums, and truancy as next most serious; immoralities, violations of school work requirements, and extravagant behavior traits as less serious; and transgressions against authority and violations of orderliness in the class as least serious.[27]

Table 6.1   Behavior Problems Rated by Teachers and Mental Hygienists as to Seriousness of the Problems

Ratings as to Seriousness by Teachers		Ratings as to Seriousness by Mental Hygienists
1	Heterosexual activity	25
2	Stealing	13
3	Masturbation	41
4	Obscene notes, talk	28
5	Untruthfulness	23
6	Truancy	22
7	Impertinence, defiance	37
8	Cruelty, bullying	6
9	Cheating	24
10	Destroying school materials	45
11	Disobedience	42
12	Unreliableness	21
13	Temper tantrums	17
14	Lack of interest in work	26
15	Profanity	47
16	Impudence, rudeness	32
17	Laziness	36
18	Smoking	49
19	Enuresis	27
20	Nervousness	19
21	Disorderliness in class	46
22	Unhappy, depressed	3
23	Easily discouraged	7
24	Selfishness	16
25	Carelessness in work	38
26	Inattention	34
27	Quarrelsomeness	31
28	Suggestible	8
29	Resentfulness	4
30	Tardiness	43
31	Physical coward	15
32	Stubbornness	20
33	Domineering	11

Table 6.1 (*continued*)

Ratings as to Seriousness by Teachers		Ratings as to Seriousness by Mental Hygienists
34	Slovenly in appearance	35
35	Sullenness	12'
36	Fearfulness	5
37	Suspiciousness	2
38	Thoughtlessness	39
39	Attracting attention	30
40	Unsocialness	1
41	Dreaminess	18
42	Imaginative lying	33
43	Interrupting	48
44	Inquisitiveness	44
45	Overcritical of others	9
46	Tattling	29
47	Whispering	50
48	Sensitiveness	10
49	Restlessness	40
50	Shyness	14

SOURCE: E. K. Wickman, *Children's Behavior and Teachers' Attitudes*, New York, The Commonwealth Fund, pp. 124, 125, 127, 1928, as reported by Peter F. Oliva in "High School Discipline in American Society," *The National Association of Secondary School Principals Bulletin*, 40, no. 216, January 1956, 15. Reprinted with permission of The Commonwealth Fund.

Over the years I have often hoped that someone would find the time and interest to replicate the Wickman study. In 1972 Puran J. Rajpal did just that, surveying 100 teachers in grades three through six and 20 school psychologists assigned to elementary schools in New York State.[28] Table 6.2 presents the ratings made by both teachers and mental hygienists in the Wickman study and teachers and school psychologists in the Rajpal study.

In the interval of 44 years we can see some pronounced changes. Rajpal commented:

The 1928 groups and the contemporary groups disagree strongly about four behaviors in particular: heterosexual activity (boys and girls working and playing together), masturbation, unhappy (depressed) behavior and unsocial (withdrawn) behavior.

The shifts in rankings of the first two were from 1 in 1928 to 32.5 today and from 3 in 1928 to 45 today. One explanation of this extreme discrepancy is the fact that classroom groups today represent a much different sample of the total population than they did in 1928. At that time many more children were retained in a class because of failure in one or two subjects, hence much older children could be in the same classroom with younger children. The age-grade promotion system means that practically all sixth-grade children are now 12 years old. Besides this, of course, folkways and mores have shifted significantly. . . .

The rankings of "unhappy" and "unsocial" behaviors are up from 22.5 to 2 and from 40.5 to 9 in seriousness respectively. In both cases there seems to be greater awareness by classroom teachers in the current study of the feelings of children and their significance in the life of the child.[29]

Table 6.2 Rank Order of 50 Behavior Problems, Based on Ratings Made by Four Groups: Rankings of Teachers and School Psychologists in This Study in Comparison with Rankings of Wickman's Teachers and Mental Hygienists in 1928

Behavior Items	Wickman Teachers	Teachers in This Study	Wickman Mental Hygienists	School Psychologists in This Study
Tardiness	30	38	43	39.5
Truancy	6	5	23	17.5
Destroying school materials	10	3	45	4
Untruthfulness (lying)	5	4	23	10.5
Imaginative lying	42	28	33	34
Cheating	9	6	23	8.5
Stealing	2	1	13.5	4
Profanity	15	34.5	47	44.5
Smoking	18	34.5	49	46.5
Obscene notes, pictures, talk	4	23	28.5	34
Masturbation	3	45	41	46.5
Heterosexual activity	1	32.5	26	36
Disorderliness	20.5	46	46	44.5
Whispering and note writing	46.5	50	50	50
Interrupting (talkativeness)	43.5	48	48	49
Restlessness (overactivity)	49	47	41	42.5
Inattention	26	20	34	20
Lack of interest in work	14	14	25	8.5
Carelessness in work	24.5	24	37.5	24
Laziness	16.5	18	35.5	16
Unreliableness (irresponsible)	12	8	21	10.5
Disobedience	11	17	41	20
Impertinence (defiance)	7	21.5	37.5	28.5
Cruelty and bullying	8	7	6	4
Quarrelsomeness	27	21.5	31	25.5
Tattling	46.5	42	28.5	39.5
Stubbornness (contrariness)	32.5	43	20	39.5
Sullenness (sulkiness)	35	27	12	22
Temper tantrums	13	13	17	14.5
Impudence, impoliteness, rudeness	16.5	19	32	28.5
Selfishness (unsportsmanship)	24.5	15	16	12
Domineering, overbearing	32.5	26	11	25.5
Shyness (bashfulness)	50	39	13.5	34
Sensitiveness	48	29.5	10	23
Unsocial, withdrawing	40.5	9	1	1
Overcritical of others	45	29.5	9	27
Thoughtlessness (forgetting)	38	32.5	39	32
Inquisitiveness, meddlesomeness	43.5	44	44	39.5
Silliness (smartness)	39	49	30	48
Unhappy, depressed	22.5	2	3	2
Resentful	29	12	4	7
Nervousness	20.5	16	18.5	14.5
Fearfulness	36	11	5	6
Enuresis	19	36.5	27	20
Dreaminess	40.5	41	18.5	37

Table 6.2 (*continued*)

Behavior Items	Wickman Teachers	Teachers in This Study	Wickman Mental Hygienists	School Psychologists in This Study
Slovenly in appearance	34	36.5	35.5	42.5
Suspiciousness	37	25	2	17.5
Physical coward	31	40	15	30.5
Easily discouraged	22.5	10	7	13
Suggestibility	28	31	8	30.5

SOURCE: Puran J. Rajpal, "What Behavior Problems Do Teachers Regard as Serious?" *Phi Delta Kappan* 53, no. 9, May 1972, 591. Reprinted with permission of Phi Delta Kappa.

One interesting finding of the Rajpal study was the escalation in ratings of the item "destroying school materials." Mental hygienists in 1928 had ranked this behavior as 45; school psychologists in 1972 ranked it number 4. Teachers in 1928 rated the same behavior tenth whereas teachers in 1972 jumped the behavior to third place in seriousness.

It is encouraging to note that there is closer agreement between teachers and school psychologists in 1972 than there was between teachers and mental hygienists in 1928. Teachers in the more recent study more or less concurred with teachers in the older study in respect to stealing, lying, smoking, profanity, and obscene notes and talk; disorderliness and impertinence do not bother teachers as much these days. Both groups of teachers agreed that inattention, lack of interest in work, carelessness, laziness, and impudence were relatively serious. The 1928 sample of teachers rated two potentially very serious behaviors—shyness and sensitiveness—at the bottom of their list. Although the 1972 group moved the ratings of these two behaviors up, we should raise the question whether we might not have expected, with all the recent emphasis on the development of the self-concept, that these behaviors would have been ranked even higher.

Neither group of teachers put a potentially damaging behavior—suspiciousness—in its top 10. And neither group, but especially the teachers in the 1972 study, seemed overly concerned with physical cowardice.

b. Attitudes toward Children. Teachers need to know what attitudes they hold about young people. They need to assess what expectations they hold for each learner. The research of R. Rosenthal and L. Jacobson,[30] W. Burleigh Seaver,[31] and J. Michael Palardy[32] provided evidence that teachers' expectations do make a difference in the achievement of the learners.[33] An astute supervisor can detect that some teachers subconsciously interact more often and more positively with some students than with others. Teachers tend to favor girls, brighter students, those from higher socioeconomic levels, those seated near the front of the classroom, those at their favored hand (right or left), in short, those who are nearest at hand, who please the teacher, and who give fewer problems of an academic or disciplinary nature.

c. Attitudes toward Themselves.   Teachers need to develop a feeling of their own adequacy as both teachers and people. Since teachers are in charge of groups of young people, it is most important that they be fully functioning personalities. Teachers can have a powerful influence on the development of the learner's self-concept. They need to exhibit qualities of cheerfulness, fairness, and sensitivity. Not only do they need to be self-actualizing people, they need also to be effective teachers, skillful at explaining and communicating.[34] Combs concluded that good teachers feel adequate, wanted, and worthy.[35]

The supervisor should invite freewheeling discussions of teacher attitudes toward types of learners, ethnic groups, the purposes of education, satisfactions from teaching as a career, and the relative seriousness of behavior problems. Discussion is likely to bring out that teachers generally view those problems that disrupt their classes such as impertinence and impudence as more serious than deep-seated personality problems such as shyness and suspiciousness.

The supervisor, in observing classes, should look for evidence of negative attitudes held by teachers and should offer personal counseling, referral to outside counseling, or various types of training in interpersonal skills to help teachers develop more positive attitudes.

2. Analyze Their Teaching Styles and Students' Learning Styles

The supervisor should ask the teachers to look within themselves and try to decide whether their teaching styles provoke disciplinary problems. Are they autocratic martinets who repress every form of childish exuberance? Do they practice laissez-faire and let the students do as they please? Are they conscientious about planning or do they adopt a what-do-you-want-to-learn-today-kids approach to instruction? Do they project a counseling, facilitating approach to instruction as opposed to an authoritarian, dispenser-of-information approach? Do they exude confidence or do they let youngsters intimidate them?

Barbara Bree Fischer and Louis Fischer identified six teaching styles as follows:

- *The task-oriented.* These teachers prescribe the materials to be learned and demand specific performance on the part of the students . . .
- *The cooperative planner.* These teachers plan the means and ends of instruction with student cooperation . . .
- *The child centered.* This teacher provides a structure for students to pursue whatever they want to do or whatever interests them . . .
- *The subject centered.* These teachers focus on organized content to the near exclusion of the learner . . .
- *The learning centered.* These teachers have equal concern for the students and for the curricular objectives, the materials to be learned . . .
- *The emotionally exciting and its counterpart.* These teachers show their own intensive emotional involvement in teaching. They enter the teaching-learning process with zeal and usually produce a classroom atmosphere of excitement and high emotion. Their counterparts conduct classrooms subdued in emotional tone, where rational processes

predominate, and the learning is dispassionate though just as significant and mean-ingful as in the classrooms of the emotionally more involved teachers.[36]

Teachers should attempt to identify the individual students' learning styles. It is quite possible that a clash between the instructor's teaching style and a student's learning style can result in disciplinary problems. Fischer and Fischer listed 10 learning styles:

- *The incremental learner.* These students proceed in a step-by-step fashion, system-atically adding bits and pieces together to gain larger understandings . . .
- *The intuitive learner.* The learning style of these students does not follow traditional logic, chronology, or a step-by-step sequence. There are leaps in various directions, sudden insights, and meaningful and accurate generalizations derived from an unsys-tematic gathering of information and experience . . .
- *The sensory specialist.* This student relies primarily on one sense for the meaningful formation of ideas . . .
- *The sensory generalist.* These students use all or many of the senses in gathering information and gaining insights . . .
- *The emotionally involved.* There are students who function best in a classroom in which the atmosphere carries a high emotional charge . . . through the teacher's use of poetry, drama, lively descriptions, and the teacher's own obvious enjoyment and involvement in the substance of learning [or] . . . in which the teacher and students carry on active, open discussions where disagreements are common.
- *The emotionally neutral.* Some students function best in a classroom where the emotional tone is low-keyed and relatively neutral.
- *Explicity structured.* These students learn best when the teacher makes explicit a clear, unambiguous structure for learning. Limits and goals are carefully stated, guiding the intellectual tasks to be achieved as well as the behaviors that will be acceptable and unacceptable in the classroom.
- *Open-ended structure.* . . . The overall structure of the classroom is sufficiently visible, yet there is place for divergence, for exploration of relevant yet not explicitly preplanned phenomena.
- *The damaged learner.* While this category is too broad, too inclusive to be identified as a learning style, it is sufficiently important and commonplace to merit discussion. These are students who are physically normal but damaged in self-concept, social competency, aesthetic sensitivity, or intellect in such a way that they develop negative learning styles.
- *The eclectic learner.* Students who can shift learning styles and function profitably may find one or another style more beneficial, but can adapt to and benefit from others.[37]

Whenever possible, the teacher should use a teaching style which is compatible with the learner's style.

3. Analyze the Classroom Environment

Is there rapport between teacher and students and among the students themselves? Teachers will want to identify both the academic and social leaders in the class and those students who seem to be left out of classroom transactions. They will need to ask themselves whether they are encouraging a success orientation on the part of the students as opposed to a failure orientation. They will want to develop an approach that is permissive enough to allow for pupil freedom but restrictive enough so that learning can take place. They should ask themselves whether their classrooms are the "grim, joyless" places Silberman talked about.

In a healthy classroom climate the teacher avoids using learning as a threat or as punishment. The object of instruction is to make learning as enjoyable an experience as possible, a pursuit that young people will want to continue all their lives. It is not unknown for teachers to penalize a rambunctious class by piling on homework, by administering tests to quiet a noisy class, by threatening students with examinations or low grades if they do not behave properly, and by making individuals perform meaningless academic tasks as a form of punishment. The pupil who has to write "Constantinople fell in 1453" 500 times may forever remember the date of the Turkish conquest of the Byzantine Empire but he or she will probably also develop a hatred for history, for the teacher, for the school, and for learning itself. With such experiences as these it is small wonder that many youngsters cannot wait to get out of school so they can cease formal education and pursue learning which has meaning to them.

4. Analyze the Curriculum Continuously

Every teacher must examine the question of relevance and determine whether the curriculum can pass the test of relevance. Teachers must decide whether the particular curriculum meets the needs of the specific groups of which they have charge. Materials of instruction must be appropriate to the learners. Content that is either too difficult or too simple can cause behavior problems. The supervisor has the responsibility of helping teachers with planning and implementing and evaluating the curriculum, which we will discuss in Chapter 7.

5. Analyze the Methods of Instruction Employed

Teachers must be able to organize the content, sequence it properly, present it lucidly, and evaluate its mastery fairly. They must decide whether they have set realistic objectives. They must apply the principle of feedback and check their instructional design to make sure they are employing appropriate strategies and engaging learners in appropriate content. They should analyze pupils' successes and failures to see whether modifications in instruction are necessary.

Johanna Kasin Lemlech suggested 18 patterns of teacher behavior which provide a useful checklist of techniques relating to good classroom management. These behaviors are:

> accepting students' statements, feelings, attitudes
> attending to students' needs, interests, problems

anticipating probable effects
awareness of developmental levels and student interests
consistency and equity
clarity
fostering cooperative behavior
democratic behavior
encouragement and praise to motivate growth
dwelling on positive behavior vs. calling attention to negative behavior
firmness
flexibility, adjusting to students' needs
individualizing and personalizing instruction to adjust to students' needs
mobility, teacher and students
monitoring progress
participation and involvement
timing
warmth and enthusiasm[38]

Teachers should stress thinking over memorization. This procedure is both a curricular problem and an instructional problem. Teachers will need to decide when memorization is essential and when problem-solving techniques should be employed. This text has urged in previous chapters that teachers aim for higher levels of cognition and move away from pupils' regurgitation and recapitulation of sheer and often isolated facts. The noted educational philosopher John Dewey long ago recommended the adoption of the scientific method—or problem solving—as the principal route to learning. Dewey's recommendation still stands as a laudable goal.

Much more research is needed on the use of repetition as an instructional technique. Teachers at all levels repeat material ad infinitum, so desirous are they of reinforcing learning. What we need to determine is how many times we can or should repeat subject matter before we meet with negative results (ad nauseam, as they say). Jacob S. Kounin called attention to the phenomenon of satiation, that is, the students' tiring of subject matter because of too much repetition. Kounin advised teachers who want to avoid pupils' satiation to assure them a feeling of progress. Said Kounin:

A feeling of progress is the most essential variable influencing the rate of satiation. Satiation does not occur, or occurs very slowly, when there is a feeling of progress since the essential condition for producing satiation is repetitiousness: doing the same thing over and over without getting anywhere. When there is a feeling of progress there is no feeling of repetition and no consequent satiation.[39]

The class should be kept moving with meaningful tasks, not with "busy work," that is, repetitive, unnecessary, and often inconsequential activities designed to fill time. Students are justified in balking at busy work. The teacher must examine each activity required of students to make sure the work has meaning and purpose.

Successful classroom management goes hand in hand with the elements of instructional design: thorough planning, effective presentation, and careful evaluation. Teachers must give attention to the factor of motivation and plan for a variety of activities. Daily lesson plans should always provide for more than enough meaningful activities so the teacher is never placed in a situation where time hangs heavy and, as a result, students become behavior problems. One back-up technique which teachers can use to fill an unplanned void is an invitation to the class to discuss problems it is experiencing during the study of the unit or lesson.

Problems of classroom management are eased when teachers carry out classroom routines with skill and dispatch. Disorder can occur, for example, if materials and equipment are not ready for immediate use. Behavior problems frequently arise during dissemination of materials, setting up of equipment, rearrangement of furniture, collecting materials, and taking attendance.

6. Gather as Much Input as Possible about Individual Learners

Information about a child's background at home and in school can help the teacher to understand some of the reasons for the child's behavior. Teachers must exert super caution, however, in evaluating and using information about a child's past history. Teachers are working with children in the present and must deal with problems in the present, not the past. Although a child's past history is important, teachers must find ways of helping children in the here and now.

Judgments of a negative nature about a child's work and behavior in previous classes may prove harmful if a teacher does not realize that children may change in the course of a year's time. Comments that can be found in children's cumulative records, for example, must often be discounted because they no longer apply or because they may represent only the opinion of one teacher. It is possible too that a personality conflict between a teacher and child has resulted in negative comments being placed in a child's record.

With the more recent legal moves which open students' records to students and their parents, teachers must be extremely careful and judicious about the remarks they place in pupils' cumulative files. A hasty, negative comment about a child has on too many occasions dogged that child through school and on into college and adulthood. I can recall reading an anecdote about a high school freshman—perhaps a harmless report and certainly trivial in the grand scheme of things—preserved presumably for posterity in the student's file: "Puts ink on tongue, sticks it out, and makes other pupils laugh." I cannot resist commenting that this childish behavior will surely eradicate itself. These observations about the dangers of using past data are not meant to imply that we should not study the past history of a child but rather that we should be wary about the data and how we use the information.

7. Analyze the Disciplinary Methods Used

We can find considerable differences in the models of discipline and approaches to discipline followed by teachers. We can also find considerable argument as to which models and approaches are the most appropriate and effective. Laurel N. Tanner described five models of discipline.[40] Two of these, *training* and *behavior modification*, she labeled as established. The other three, *psychodynamic, group dynamics,* and *personal-social growth*, she called emergent.

With the training model, children learn habits through repetition of the desired behaviors. Through drill pupils learn habitual responses such as the proper way of arranging their chairs, sharpening pencils, and going to the rest rooms. Though training is, of course, necessary, little reflection, thought, or self-direction is possible with this model.

Behavior modification, to which we will return in a moment, is a procedure for bringing about or extinguishing specific behaviors through the use of appropriate reinforcement. It is possible to shape and control behavior through this technique.

Proponents of the psychodynamic model encourage teachers to try to understand the underlying emotional causes of behavior problems. With roots in child-centered philosophy and psychoanalysis the psychodynamic model poses problems for teachers' use. Many teachers, lacking the necessary training, are not able to uncover causes of learners' problems. Further, once they have discovered the reasons for a child's misbehavior, they have difficulty deciding how to use the information they have obtained to change the child's behavior.

The group dynamics model calls for the effective management of the class as a group. The teacher literally orchestrates the group. Explained Tanner:

The group dynamics model is an action model. Knowledge about the power and authority of teachers and how individuals behave in groups is translated into strategies for preventing and dealing with discipline problems. . . . Of all the models of discipline, the group dynamics model is most concerned with classroom management. While this is a decided advantage, it can also be a drawback. For discipline is more than "managing" others. The goal of discipline is *self*-management or *self*-direction.[41]

The personal-social growth model encourages the development of self-discipline by providing pupils with opportunities to decide for themselves what constitutes appropriate behavior. The behavior chosen by the learner conforms to the goals established. Tanner said:

A central idea in the personal-social growth model is that means and goals are related. How one behaves (the means for reaching a goal) is determined by the goal. Unfortunately, in many classrooms goals remain mysterious and obscure. . . . It is tempting to misbehave when there is no objective except to finish. On the other hand, when pupils understand the value of a task, they are more likely to want to master it. Behavior then becomes *what* one does when one is learning (or trying to learn).[42]

Tanner felt the group dynamics model and the personal-social growth model to be particularly helpful, pointing out that "the group dynamics and personal-social growth models view discipline as a part of instruction rather than as something outside of instruction."[43]

Behavior Modification

Behavior modification is a technique for coping with common classroom problems. It is based on the premise that both appropriate and inappropriate behavior are learned. It is the teacher's task to reinforce appropriate behaviors by the use of rewards and to eliminate inappropriate behaviors by withholding rewards and/or using punishment. Wilford A. Weber spoke of the assumptions underlying behavior modification:

The behavior modification approach is built on two assumptions: (1) There are four basic processes that account for learning at all age levels and under all conditions; and (2) Learning is controlled largely, if not entirely, by events in the environment. Thus, the major task of the teacher is to master and apply four basic principles of learning that behaviorists have identified as controlling all human behavior. They are: positive reinforcement [introduction of a reward], punishment, extinction [removing a reward], and negative reinforcement [removing punishment].[44]

Clarizio outlined steps for modifying behavior, which he called the four phases of positive classroom discipline:

a. Choosing the behavior [that needs to be changed].
b. Doing the A, B, Cs—attention is focused on the A, B, Cs—the antecedents of behavior (A), the behavior itself (B), and the consequences attached to the behavior (C).
c. Selecting strategies . . . (1) behavior formation techniques: positive reinforcement and social modeling, to restrict, reduce, or eliminate undesirable behaviors and to strengthen existent adaptive responses, to acquire new adaptive ones, and to extend desirable behaviors to other settings; (2) behavior elimination techniques: extinction, punishment, and desensitization, to weaken undesirable behaviors.
d. Keeping track of the results.[45]

Clarizio made a strong case for the system he recommended in the following passage:

Because mental health or psychoeducational specialists (psychologists, psychiatrists, social workers, and counselors) have not fully understood the teacher's role, they have offered to teachers few specific and concrete practical suggestions pertaining to the management of the child's daily behavior. . . . Admonitions to be accepting, nonthreatening, and understanding of the child's needs have not helped teachers to cope with troublesome behavior. In giving advice to educators, mental health professionals seem to forget about the following aspects of the teacher's role, which make it difficult for a teacher to heed their advice:

1. The teacher is a group worker and, therefore, cannot usually work with just one child.
2. The teacher's primary goal is not to increase the child's personal insights but to achieve certain academic objectives.
3. The teacher must reflect cultural values and, hence, cannot be permissively accepting.

4. The teacher deals primarily with conscious or preconscious processes and materials.
5. Finally, the teacher must focus on the reality of problems as they exist in the present situation.[46]

Concerning behavior modification Weber concluded:

(1) Rewarding appropriate student behavior and withholding the rewarding of inappropriate behavior are very effective in achieving better classroom behavior; (2) Punishing inappropriate student behavior may eliminate that behavior but may have serious negative side effects; and (3) Rewarding appropriate behavior is probably the key to effective classroom management.[47]

J. Michael Palardy and James E. Mudrey defined four approaches to discipline: "the permissive, the authoritarian, the behavioristic, and the diagnostic."[48] They rejected the permissive and authoritarian approaches, found the behavioristic (behavior modification) wanting, and supported the diagnostic approach. Of the behavioristic approach they wrote:

Does behavior modification work? We think it does, but not to the degree or with the frequency behaviorists predict. For the approach, in our opinion, has several serious flaws. The most significant is that only the symptoms of behavior problems are dealt with, not their causes.

Stated bluntly, but not unjustly, proponents of behavior modification argue that teachers are wasting time in trying to discover and treat underlying causes of behavior. From the point of view of advocates of behavior modification, teachers can be effective if they deal only with the behavior itself . . . . As long as the cause of the child's problem is undiagnosed and untreated, he is hurting and sooner or later symptoms of that hurt will emerge.[49]

Palardy and Mudrey saw the diagnostic approach as "the most comprehensive and legitimate approach to discipline."[50] About this approach they said:

Contrary to behavior modification, this approach assumes that there can be lasting effects on certain behavior problems only after their causes are ferreted out and treated. . . . There is no quick, easy, or fail-proof formula for diagnosing the causes of pupils' behavior problems. But there is one absolutely essential step: to learn as much as possible about the pupils. . . .

Most critics of this approach argue that the whole effort of diagnosis is a waste of time and energy because nothing can be done anyway . . . we disagree with this argument. First, because it assumes that the causes of behavior problems are never school related or school induced. Like it or not, many are.

Second, even if the diagnosis shows that the causes are not school related or school induced, much can still be done. Pupils' ego needs can be met in school, their self-respect enhanced, their enjoyment of life increased. In school, pupils can be given love and can learn to give it in return. Schools can provide food and clothing. They can make medical, dental, and psychological referrals. They can contact community action programs, welfare departments, civic organizations, churches, and even law-enforcement agencies. Schools can provide for adult education, sex education, and early education. We disagree that diagnosis is a waste of time because nothing can be done![51]

I do not see behavior modification/diagnosis as an either/or situation. The effective teacher seeks to control the class and shape behavior by whatever legitimate techniques he or she is adept at using, which would include behavior modification. While controlling and shaping behavior, however, the teacher will want to gather as much information about the student as possible, uncover possible causes of misbehavior, and do whatever is within his or her means to treat the causes.

8. Set and Enforce Minimum Expectations of Behavior

Rules of conduct should be made known at the beginning of the year. A key factor in setting of rules of conduct is pupil participation in drawing up the rules. With each succeeding year of schooling and the accompanying increase in the learner's maturity, a greater degree of participation in determining the rules of behavior should be extended to the students. Boys and girls are much more likely to conform to standards which they have helped set than to standards which are imposed on them.

I agree with Glasser that "children should have a voice in determining both the curriculum and the rules of their school. Democracy is best learned by living it."[52] Glasser recommended, wisely I believe, that once students have participated in formulating the rules, when they break the rules, the teacher should ask them to make a value judgment about their behavior, to select a better course of behavior, and to make a commitment to change.[53]

Pupils must be given time to practice unfamiliar behaviors. The teacher should be willing to spend sufficient time to help pupils develop routines and to get accustomed to classroom organization and procedures. The supervisor should advise teachers not to hasten into the content areas until they have the procedural learnings under control. This principle is particularly significant in dealing with youngsters who come from communities where standards of behavior are greatly different from the standards expected by the school.

The supervisor should assist teachers in diagnosing the learning environments which they maintain to see if they are doing everything within their power to prevent disciplinary problems. The old expression, trite as it is, "An ounce of prevention is worth a pound of cure," has special relevance to the problem of discipline.

CORRECTING BEHAVIOR PROBLEMS

No matter how much the teacher may understand about causes of behavior problems, no matter how healthy and wholesome the learning climate of a class or school may be, no matter how hard the teacher may try to prevent disciplinary problems, behavior problems will still arise. Teachers should enter public school teaching expecting a certain amount of youthful misbehavior and they must develop rather quickly skills for coping with behavior problems. Some teachers are past masters of discipline from the first day they set foot in the classroom. Others develop disciplinary skills as they gain experience and confidence at controlling the behavior of young people. Others are in need of help and support. Sooner or later the question will come from a teacher, often in desperation, "What shall I do?" That teacher may turn to a colleague for advice or, if he or she has sufficient rapport with the principal or supervisor, may turn to one of them. At that time the principal or supervisor must supply some kind of guidance if a state of rapport is to continue between them. The supervisor cannot come up with some hackneyed platitude like "Children will be children," "Just remember that all behavior is caused," and "Show them love." These platitudes are fine in perspective, in their place, and at the right time. When a teacher has an immediate behavior problem, more than a slogan is called for. On the other hand, the supervisor cannot sit like an MD and write out a prescription of action a teacher should take to cure the malady. How often has the experienced principal or supervisor heard a litany of offenses both minor and major and wished for some medicine which would effect a quick cure? How often has he or she wished to feed into that electronic marvel, the computer, a description of a behavior problem and obtain an instant printout of the course of action which should be taken?

When a behavior problem arises in the classroom, the teacher must make some response. In fact, the students expect the teacher to make some response and often test the teacher to see what he or she will do. Let us assume a situation: a black male pupil and a white male pupil in an eighth-grade English class suddenly leap out of their seats, call each other names, and start pummeling each other. Their teacher reacts almost instinctively, hastens to the boys, forcefully separates them, firmly orders them to take their seats, and sets the class back to work. The immediate situation has been effectively handled. But the teacher meditates as to what corrective measure or punishment, if any, should be applied to these boys so neither they nor others will repeat the behavior. The teacher decides to talk with the principal. The teacher relates the incident to the principal and asks the principal what should be done as a follow-up to the incident.

The principal might say, "Send them to detention," or might suggest, "Send them to me and I'll suspend them for three days"—but neither would be commendable. He or she might rather begin by commending the teacher for keeping cool, restoring order, and preventing what could have become an inflammatory situation. And the principal could add that had more help been needed to restore order the teacher should not have hesitated to call for immediate assistance. The principal should lead up to the question of correction or punishment by asking the teacher to think through the incident again before deciding on the matter of correction or punishment. Now that the heat of the moment has dissipated the incident should be analyzed. The principal may raise questions with the teacher such as:

> Who were the boys?
> Was this the first time anything like this has taken place in the class?
> Was this the first time these two boys have behaved in this way?
> Has either of the boys displayed antisocial behavior before?
> Was there any provocation on the part of either boy?
> Were any other students actively involved in the incident?
> Do you believe this was a racial incident or simply a case of two junior high boys having a go at it?

What was going on in class at the time of the incident?
Did the teacher do anything that could have contributed to the incident?
Was anyone hurt?
Was there any damage to property?
How serious should we consider this incident?

A calm discussion of these questions might terminate with the decision to apply the same corrective measure* the teacher or principal might have selected prior to any discussion. On the other hand, consideration of questions like those above might lead the principal and teachers to choose other forms of correction.

Early in the school year when the faculty is still fresh and the pupils have not yet created a plethora of disciplinary problems, it would be beneficial for the principal or assistant principal, department head, or other supervisor to assemble his or her group of teachers and have them develop a set of guidelines for implementing corrective measures. If teachers know what guidelines have faculty and administrative support at the time a behavior problem transpires, they can more readily and more intelligently decide what action they should take as a response to the behavior problem. The supervisor might lead them to agree that:

1. *The corrective measure applied should fit the offense.* Showing off should be treated differently from defiance. Skipping school merits lesser punishment than pushing drugs. Stealing $20 is more serious than stealing 20 cents.

2. *The corrective measure applied should fit the offender.* The democratic practice would seem on the surface to treat all offenders equally. But not even the courts treat all offenders in the same way and judges do not seem to feel that they are being undemocratic when they impose differing sentences for different offenders who have committed the same crime. Mitigating circumstances are taken into consideration when imposing punishment, for example, in the case of a first offense. The goal of correction is a change in behavior—rehabilitation. For this goal to be realized the corrective measure must be chosen with both the offense and the offender in mind.

3. *Minor, routine types of childish behavior should be met with the simplest of techniques*: a glare, a stare, silence, pointing a finger at the culprit, standing beside a noisy pupil, a terse order "Let's be quiet" or "Knock it off," tapping the blackboard with chalk, suddenly increasing the volume of the voice, changing pupils' seats, any of a host of little personalized techniques which teachers have developed to maintain order and to keep the class on the track. There are teachers who never have to go beyond these simple techniques of control, but are able to maintain a productive learning environment without resorting to sterner means.

The common, garden-variety misbehavior which stems from excess childish energies should be treated with a minimum of fuss. The teacher should not make a big issue of petty misbehaviors. We find teachers who insist on continuous, complete, and absolute attention and quiet—a next to impossible goal for children and

---

* This text uses the term *corrective measure* as an inclusive term which encompasses punishment. Punishment in this context is one form of correction. Suspension of a pupil, for example, is a punitive corrective measure. An individual conference with a pupil is a corrective measure of a remedial, nonpunitive nature.

adolescents—and stamp hard on every infraction of their (the teachers') rules. From some of the classrooms of these teachers youngsters stream to the principal's office for punitive action. These teachers weaken their own image in the eyes of the children, the administrator, and the children's parents, and may place themselves in a precarious position. When they encounter a serious problem and look for help, the administrator may conclude that they are once again "crying wolf" when there is no wolf in sight.

4. *Nonpunitive, remedial measures should be taken before resorting to punishment.* Teachers should be more concerned with helping a child to change behavior than with retribution for misconduct. If they can reason with a child and obtain results in that way, they should do so. A beginning approach in cases of pupil misbehavior is an individual conference with the child during which the teacher tries to get the child to evaluate his or her behavior, to see how the particular conduct has been detrimental to himself or herself and to others, and to choose a better way of behaving. The conference provides the teacher with an opportunity for learning more about the child and the reasons for the misbehavior. The conference is a chance for the teacher to show a child who is a behavior problem that some adult cares enough to want to be of help. These conferences should be entered into in a counseling frame of mind and should not be considered occasions for laying down the law and reprimanding the perpetrator.

The conference should be conducted in private, where teacher and pupil can talk freely. Individual conferences will not always be successful in producing a change in behavior. Some pupils will respond to this kind of approach, others will not. If an individual conference with the pupil is not successful in changing a pupil's behavior after a reasonable time, the teacher may then wish to confer with the child's parents or guardians. If the teacher chooses to go this route, the parent-teacher conference must be managed very carefully. Parents may be anxious to come to school to talk about their children's academic progress but they are not so eager to visit the teacher to talk about their children's behavior problems.

A polite invitation rather than a summons should be extended to the parents in the form of a letter or phone call from the teacher. The conference should be set up as a chance for the parents and teacher to communicate and share their knowledge about the child. The goal of the conference is to find ways in which the parents and teacher can cooperate to help the child improve his or her behavior. At all costs the teacher must avoid an antagonistic view toward the parents, for this will generate their ill-will and result in the loss of their cooperation.

The teacher must also know what the parents' attitudes are toward discipline, since some parents may treat the child more harshly than the school. A united wall of parent-teacher hostility toward a child may worsen behavior rather than improve it.

The teacher should call upon the services of specialists and agencies both within the school and outside for help in working with behavior problems. Referrals to the guidance counselor, school psychologist, or school nurse are often first steps in the remediation process. Community agencies stand ready in most communities to provide certain kinds of help to school children, from needed eyeglasses to a Big Brother or Sister.

When seeking remedial help for children with problems, the teacher, it is to be hoped, will not overlook the nonaggressive, docile, timid, fearful, despondent children in the classroom. These children may not complicate the teacher's life the way aggressive children do, but in their own way they have behavior problems and many times theirs are more serious and more prolonged than the problems of overt, disruptive children.

5. *Punishment is in order if the teacher deems that there is no other way to correct an individual's behavior.* Wesley C. Becker, Siegfried Engelmann, and Don R. Thomas made a case for the use of punishment when they commented:

Probably no area of behavioral psychology has generated more emotion, confusion, and misunderstanding than the topic of punishment. Some people believe that any use of punishment under any circumstances is immoral. . . . Teachers have been told that they should not use punishment because it doesn't work and that it produces only temporary suppression of behavior, not real change. . . . Punishment is an effective method of changing behavior.[54]

Punishment and the threat of punishment serve as deterrents to repetition of misconduct by the same offender or other offenders. It is utopian to hold that punishment will never be necessary in school. No matter how hard we strive to maintain an attractive learning environment, no matter how well disciplined the school, no matter how great an effort is made to counsel students, and no matter what preventive measures are taken, behavior problems will still arise and some of these will be serious enough to merit punishment. Becker, Engelmann, and Thomas specified two circumstances when punishment may be required:

The first is when behavior is so *frequent* that there is little or no incompatible behavior to reinforce. . . . The second circumstance where punishment may be required is when the problem behavior is so *intense* that someone might get hurt, including the child himself.[55]

When punishment must be administered, it should be done in a firm and calm manner. For this reason the teacher should wait until the heat of the moment dies down before applying punitive techniques. However, punishment should be certain. The pupil who chooses to misbehave should know that misbehavior will result in some kind of punishment. If punishment is fair and reasonable, the public will support the teacher and administrator. The supervisor should help teachers to identify and use punitive measures which can be considered fair and reasonable and to reject those measures which are unfair and unreasonable.

It is not difficult to find illustrations of punitive measures which do not meet the standards of fairness, reasonableness, or soundness. Preservice and in-service education should build concepts about discipline and punishment so that teachers will employ disciplinary procedures which are both psychologically and pedagogically sound. Apparently, preservice training does not succeed in building an adequate foundation for this purpose and in-service training under the leadership of a competent supervisor must continue the task.

The position this text takes on punishment consists of the following elements: (1) every behavior problem which seems to be serious enough for punitive action should be thoroughly analyzed before any action is taken; (2) the punishment should be adjusted to both the offense and the offender; (3) the punishment should be fair, reasonable, and sound; (4) the punishment should be within the law; and (5) when punishment is clearly warranted, it is the teacher's and/or principal's responsibility to administer it. The teacher's or administrator's power derives from three sources: school personnel represent the power of the adult (mature) world over the child's (immature) world; since the school is an agency of the state, school personnel are servants of the state and are charged with the responsibility of educating the young; teachers and administrators are parent substitutes during the time children are in school and as such possess some of the same prerogatives of discipline as parents possess. Both cultural and legal factors permit school personnel to administer punishment.

Returning to the teacher's question to the principal, "What shall I do?" what helpful guidance can be provided? First, the answer falls into two parts: What *do* teachers do? and What *should* teachers do? The answers to these two questions are not always the same. Teachers can be found, sometimes in collaboration with the principal, who employ the following disciplinary measures, some of which are only mildly punitive, others, rather severe: They threaten a class or an individual, scold a class or individual, force misbehavers to apologize to them or to their classmates, ridicule children, force children to repeat their offenses until they are weary, spank children (mostly boys), banish children from the classroom, send children to the principal's office, suspend children from school for varying periods of time, take away privileges, make children pay fines, give children demerits, subject children to personal indignities, humiliate children in front of their peers, turn children over to security guards or police, expel children from school permanently, transfer children to special schools, keep an individual or class in after school, isolate misbehavers from the rest of the class, make children pay for items they have damaged, punish the whole class for an offense committed by an unidentified individual, use learning as punishment, and reduce the grades of children who misbehave. This by no means exhausts the list of punitive procedures found in the schools, for we teachers can be as ingenious at inventing punitive measures as young people are at demonstrating novel forms of misbehavior.

The question of whether any or all of the foregoing punitive measures are either justifiable or effective in changing behavior can provoke a debate among teachers. The supervisor should encourage teachers to discuss each punitive measure and try to reach some consensus on subordinate questions such as, What is the purpose of the measure? Is the meaure more damaging than helpful to the individual? Is the measure more damaging than helpful to the group? What is the long-range effect of the measure? Will the measure serve as a deterrent? Has the measure proved effective in the past? What are the legal restrictions on the measure?

Though some teachers and administrators may disagree, I believe that a reasonable case can be made for the following punitive measures:

- taking away school privileges
- requiring a student to restore, repair, or pay for damage done

- detaining a student after school
- sending a student to the principal's office
- isolating a student within the class
- suspending a student from school or class for a period of time
- referring a student to security guards or police
- expelling a student permanently from school
- transferring a student to a special school

The following types of punishment appear to me to be unreasonable:

- subjecting youngsters to personal indignities
- threatening
- humiliating
- charging fines for misbehaving
- using academic work as punishment
- lowering a child's academic mark for misconduct

In a class by itself is corporal punishment. Though I personally reject corporal punishment as unsound and ineffective, a case for spanking can be made, it is acceptable to a large segment of the public, and it is legally permitted in some communities. In 1977 the U.S. Supreme Court upheld the right of schools to administer corporal punishment.[56]
Let us take a brief look at each of the nine punitive measures listed above for which a reasonable case may be made, and then consider the thorny problem of corporal punishment.

Taking Away School Privileges.   The loss of privileges is a natural consequence of misbehavior, a form of punishment to which many children are accustomed at home. A child or group that creates a disruption at a school play, for example, may have the privilege of attending school assemblies taken away for a period of time. A group or child who causes a turmoil at a school dance or athletic event may be denied attendance at future events for a period of time. The child who has been granted the privilege of doing independent study and who abuses that privilege may be reassigned to more closely supervised study. Children who have been appointed by the faculty or elected by their peers to positions of leadership or responsibility and who become behavior problems may be removed from these positions. Generally speaking, the loss of privileges should be a temporary punishment. Privileges should be restored when the teacher is assured that the misconduct which provoked the loss will not recur.

Requiring a Student to Restore, Repair, or Pay for Damage Done.   When a pupil takes property which belongs to someone else, he or she has the obligation of bringing that property back or reimbursing the individual or individuals from whom the property was taken. When a pupil damages or destroys another person's property, he or she has the obligation of repairing, restoring, or paying for that property, or suffering other consequences of a more serious nature. Extensive destruction of school rooms and building by vandals is a major crime and must be dealt with in other ways.

Allowing for a student's age, physical condition, financial means, and the legal restrictions, the teacher or principal should seek to have the student rectify or at least help to rectify damage caused through misbehavior. If caught writing graffiti on the walls, for example, the student should be required to use some elbow grease and remove those graffiti. If discovered defacing a desk or table, the offender should be required to restore it as well as possible. If the offense is breaking a window, charges should be assessed for its replacement.

Since the acts of restoring and repairing materials may require the expenditure of work or money or both, there are times when the pupil's parents may need to be consulted and to give their consent. This punishment is practical only if a pupil has the necessary strength, skill, and knowledge to repair damage or the financial resources to pay for damage. It is sometimes possible for those who do not have the funds to pay for damage done to work off their debt at jobs in the school or by earning money in part-time jobs after school.

This form of punishment has a direct bearing on the type of misconduct shown by a student and is a common measure used by and accepted by society.

Detaining a Student after School.   Detaining pupils after school has been an historic form of punishment in the schools. It is a relatively harmless type of punishment and not always an effective one in terms of changing pupils' behavior. The teacher is always faced with the problem of what kind of activity the pupil should be engaged in while being detained. Commonly, students work on their studies during the period of detention, which raises the problem of academic requirements being used as a form of punishment and the subsequent antagonism to studies for this reason.

Punishment should follow misbehavior as soon as possible but it is not always possible for the teacher to detain a pupil the same day misconduct was demonstrated. Transportation home, part-time jobs, after-school lessons, and after-school student activities make immediate detention a problem. The teacher may create conflicts with parents and with other teachers who are making demands on the pupils' after-school time in attempting to enforce detention on the same day. Detention may have to be scheduled at a later date after the student has had a chance to readjust his schedule. Unfortunately, the delay diminishes the effectiveness of the punishment.

Some schools send all pupils who are given after-school detention to a central detention room which teachers take turns supervising. Since detention is not a severe type of punishment, teachers tend to use it for a wide variety of relatively minor offenses. As a rule, the teacher who "sentences" a pupil to detention should supervise that student. This might provide an opportunity for some helpful dialogue between the teacher and the offender and, if the student works on studies pertinent to that teacher's class, the teacher might give the student some aid. It is obvious that the requirement that the teacher supervise his or her own behavior problems means that the teacher is detained as well as the pupil, a procedure that may hold as little appeal for the teacher as for the pupil. This requirement, however, would result in reducing the number of pupils who are kept after school and the use of detention for trivial offenses.

Unless it can be established that every child in a class has misbehaved, the detention of an entire class after school is neither wise nor fair. Mass punishment can result in rebellion, particularly of older children who have not misbehaved and who feel they are being unfairly treated. Punishment of an entire group for the offense of one or several members of a group, whether these offenders can be identified or not, is an abuse of the teacher's power. If rebellion and defiance result from an attempt to implement punishment, the teacher's status can be seriously eroded to the point where misbehavior will increase and learning will cease.

Sending a Student to the Office.   When a child disrupts a group, it is perfectly within reason to remove the child at least temporarily from that group. The welfare of the group must take precedence over the welfare of an individual. Unfortunately, some teachers abuse this form of punishment and use it for minor offenses. Consistent use of this corrective measure weakens its effectiveness. For some students a reprieve from class may be more attractive that suffering through to the end of the hour or day.

When a teacher judges it essential that a child be removed from class, the child must be sent where supervision can be provided. The most logical place for that is the administrator's office. Administrators are inclined to support a teacher who on rare occasions sends an offender to their offices. They tend to view the teacher who sends many pupils to their offices as a poor disciplinarian. The supervisor should help teachers to clarify their views as to what measures they expect administrators to take with behavior problems that have arisen in their classes. Teachers must also realize that the administrator must have the full circumstances of the case before any corrective action can be taken.

Some teachers paint themselves into a corner when they banish a student from class with the command not to return. While teachers may be permitted to suspend a student temporarily from class by sending him or her to the principal's office or to a special center for behavior problems within the school, they do not have the power to suspend or expel pupils from school. That power rests in the school board and is administered through the principal and superintendent. An order to a pupil not to return is unenforceable unless the administrator agrees with the teacher that the misconduct is severe enough to merit suspension or expulsion. The teacher loses "face" when the pupil is permitted to trot back to class because the teacher's order has been an empty threat.

Isolating a Student within the Class.   Separating a misbehaving youngster from the other members of the class is a simple and justifiable procedure. The action demonstrates to the offender that the child's behavior is interfering with the work of the group and as such cannot be tolerated. I do not recommend standing the child in the corner or making the misbehaver sit on a stool with a dunce cap, common techniques of yesterday, but the individual can be physically separated to a remote seat in the room where disruptive activity will not be possible. When the offender appears to be ready to take part again in the group's activities, permission to rejoin the class should be granted.

Suspending a Student from School or Class for a Period of Time.   Suspension, the temporary denial of the privilege of attendance at school, is a corrective measure in widespread use in the schools. It is a controversial measure, one of the more severe forms of punishment, and one which is limited by legal constraints. Suspension is a means which schools should not use lightly. Those educators who reject suspension as a form of punishment point out that it does little good to turn offenders out on the streets where they are denied learning and where they may get into more serious trouble. They argue that working parents are not able to supervise their children during working hours and the children are left to their own devices.

On the other hand, when an administrator decides an offense is serious enough to merit suspension of the offender, he or she has in mind the welfare of the group of which the student is a part and the welfare of the school generally. The administrator must resort to some measure to protect the other students from a serious offender. Suspension should be used only after remedial and less severe forms of punishment have been attempted without success.

A principal can typically suspend a student on his or her own initiative for periods of one to 10 days. With the approval of the school board the principal may be permitted to suspend a student for a longer period of time. The longer pupils are suspended, the farther they fall behind in their school work and the more difficult it is for them to catch up when they return. Some provision for making up the work is necessary when they come back or else they are liable to continue as behavior problems.

Some school systems have been experimenting with alternatives to suspending students from school. Some secondary schools have established centers for special instruction which are, in effect, a form of in-house suspension. These centers within each school are rooms to which offenders are sent for the prescribed number of days during which they would ordinarily have been denied attendance at school. The centers are provided with a teacher as director and the services of aides and part-time counselors. The director is expected to supervise an academic tutoring program and to conduct group counseling sessions.

Before children are assigned to the centers their parents are contacted and advised of the action. The offenders are assigned to the centers only after other means of handling their behavior have been tried and failed. While in the center, students may be released earlier than their assigned number of days if their behavior improves and they may be held longer if they continue to misbehave. By utilizing this in-school technique the schools are able to decrease the number of students who would ordinarily be suspended. A great advantage of this program lies in the fact that students are not free to roam the streets but are kept in school under supervision and are engaged in some form of learning.

The United States Supreme Court has underscored the position that suspension of students should not be imposed arbitrarily. In two close (5–4) decisions the Court has held that students must be granted an informal hearing by the principal before they can be suspended and that school boards are liable for damages if they violate a student's constitutional right by administering suspension without a hearing.[57]

Referring a Student to Security Guards or Police. Though some educators may deplore the presence of security personnel in the schools, the security guard has become an established member of the staff of America's large urban schools. That security guards are necessary additions to the urban school staff can be seen in the rather shocking increase in school crime since the middle 1960s.[58] Offenses include assaults on teachers and other students, use of alcohol and drugs, vandalism, and robberies. Estimates of the cost of school crime range from $200 million to $500 million per year. Among the causes for school crime, according to a study conducted by the Policy Institute of the Syracuse University Research Corporation in 1970, were: the climate of violence, students' interpretation of their civil rights, permissiveness, racism, inadequate facilities, and politicization of students by the media, the community, and teachers.[59]

Recommendations for curbing the problems of crime and violence in the schools have been made by various groups and range from establishing security departments in the schools to setting up special classes and schools for problem children to modifying teacher training to include more training in human relations and in working with emotionally disturbed children. The goal to be achieved is a school climate free from violence.

While a faculty works to create a climate in which the seeds of violence will not grow, the administrator must preserve the order and safety of all school personnel and must protect the school plant and facilities. When the necessity arises, both the teacher and the principal should be free to call in the services of either the school's security guard or the local police, and offenders should be turned over to appropriate authorities for hearings and further correction.

Expelling a Student Permanently from School. Expulsion is an extreme measure, an ultimate action of school authorities, and bound by legal restrictions. It is used for the purpose of removing incorrigibles who menace the welfare of the group. While suspension is a temporary denial of school attendance, expulsion is a permanent denial. Expulsion implies that the school has given up on the offender and that no further correction is possible under the school's jurisdiction. The power to expel rests in the school board. Parents must be involved, hearings must be held, and complete justification must be made for expulsion to be sanctioned.

Transferring a Student to a Special School. When it has been decided that a child can no longer function in a regular school situation and must be removed from the school, the next question that must be raised is whether the pupil might make progress in another type of school. If a child is below the age of compulsory attendance and is to be removed from a school, other schooling must be arranged. Those above the age of compulsory attendance should have the option of attendance at a school which might be able to aid them. Chicago, New York City, and Miami have operated types of social adjustment and alternative schools. These schools have been established to accommodate and educate children who evidence behavior problems. Many of these schools are better equipped and staffed in order to handle a difficult teaching assignment. Special instructional programs, tutoring, and counseling are techniques used in working with children who have behavior problems. In some cases if a child makes sufficient progress in a special school, transfer back to a regular school is possible.

Corporal Punishment

The debate over corporal punishment has raged ever since children were herded into institutions called schools and schoolmasters first whipped out the hickory stick. Spanking is usually a last-ditch, desperate effort before suspension of a child, expulsion, or transferral. Whether it is effective is highly questionable. The supervisor should urge teachers to study the efficacy of corporal punishment, if it is permitted in their school system. They should seek answers to questions such as: How many children received corporal punishment during a school year? What were the ages of the children? What was the sex of the children? How severely were they spanked? Who administered the spankings? How many were spanked more than once during the year? For what offenses were they spanked? Do students view spanking as effective in changing their behavior? Do students actually fear corporal punishment? Do some students gain status in their peers' eyes as a result of being spanked? Is corporal punishment more effective in changing behavior than sending pupils to special rooms or suspending them?

The teachers must also familiarize themselves with the laws circumscribing corporal punishment. They must find out first of all whether corporal punishment is legal in the community and state. They must learn the conditions under which spanking is permitted. For example, corporal punishment is generally administered in private and with an adult witness present. Parents usually have to be informed of the punishment. When corporal punishment is permissible, children can be spanked only on the posterior. The teachers will certainly want to check to see if any lawsuits have arisen over cases of corporal punishment, what the circumstances were, and what the courts' decisions were. If more children of minority families and lower socioeconomic classes are spanked, teachers must be aware they skirt the possibility of being accused of discrimination. It is surprising since corporal punishment is applied almost exclusively to boys that school officials have not been charged more frequently with discrimination based on sex.

I believe that teachers should handle their own behavior problems if it is at all possible for them to do so and this applies equally to corporal punishment. They must ascertain whether they are permitted to administer corporal punishment themselves or whether in their school system only an administrator may administer the punishment. Where teachers are allowed to inflict corporal punishment it is obvious that they must have the physical strength to do so. Incongruous situations sometimes develop when a teacher attempts to spank a boy who is physically stronger than the teacher. Female teachers may have a problem paddling a strapping football player.

Corporal punishment is effective only if the pupil has a fear or distaste for the punishment. Some students are quite willing to take a few swats of the paddle in place of other forms of punishment for which they may have a greater antipathy.

Since corporal punishment is a severe measure, if it is used at all it should be reserved for serious offenses. Because it is the intent of this punishment to inflict pain on the offender, it should never be administered when the teacher or administrator is angry and likely to inflict more serious pain or even injury. Like all forms of punishment it should be administered in a dispassionate manner.

The supervisor should engage teachers in the clarification of their positions on the use of the various punitive measures. Further, the growing issue of concern for students' rights and due process for the student is today a must for faculty examination.

In recent years school systems, responding to the students' rights movement, have developed written codes of student conduct. It is the position of this text that rules of conduct and possible remedial, corrective, and punitive measures which may be taken as a consequence of misconduct should be made known to students, parents, and staff, and should apply throughout the school system.[60]

The supervisor should work with administrators, faculties, and students (as their maturity permits) to examine the school's disciplinary climate, analyze disciplinary measures, and develop codes of conduct.

SUMMARY

Classroom management is one of the more difficult aspects of public school teaching. It is an aspect which causes many teachers great concern and one with which teachers frequently need help. Preservice training programs barely scratch the surface of this complex phase of teaching and, therefore, in-service training is essential to help teachers develop classroom management skills and understandings about discipline.

Parents, students, and teachers are in agreement that lack of discipline is a serious problem of the schools and they expect the schools to take some action to prevent, reduce, or eliminate disciplinary problems. This chapter discusses six sources of disciplinary problems: the child, the child's group, the teacher, the school, the home and community, and the larger social order.

A number of models and approaches to discipline are in use in the schools. One of these models, behavior modification, is seen as a useful technique in shaping and reshaping surface behavior. Since behavior modification treats the symptoms of misbehavior rather than underlying causes, teachers are encouraged to gather information about individual pupils, try to discover causes of behavior problems, and attempt to eliminate the causes.

Schools themselves can contribute to pupils' behavior problems. A faculty should seek to order the class and school environment in such a way that disciplinary problems will be minimized. When behavior problems do arise, remedial, nonpunitive measures should be tried to correct those problems before punitive measures are taken.

The following corrective measures are suggested as reasonable: taking away school privileges; requiring a student to restore, repair, or pay for damage done; detaining a student after school; sending a student to the principal's office; isolating a student within the class; suspending a student from school or class for a period of time; referring a student to security guards or police; expelling a student permanently from school; transferring a student to a special school.

Corporal punishment is a corrective measure acceptable to some educators and rejected by others. A school system must decide, laws permitting, whether to use corporal punishment. Within that context the faculties of individual schools of a district need to decide whether they wish to resort to corporal punishment.

The supervisor may profitably invite faculty study of four facets of the problem of discipline: causes of behavior problems, models and approaches to discipline, preventive measures, and corrective measures. The supervisor should keep before the teachers the understanding that the object of all discipline is the development of self-discipline on the part of the learner.

ACTIVITIES FOR FURTHER STUDY

1. Write a paper suggesting ways by which learners may be taught self-discipline.
2. Describe principal causes of student misbehavior.
3. Create an instrument for evaluating disciplinary climate and practices in the classroom.
4. Write a research paper on a number of court decisions (state and federal) on corporal punishment, suspension, and expulsion.
5. Visit four teachers in their classrooms, analyze the group climate in those classrooms, make a brief summary of each situation, and suggest ways in which you feel the group climate might be improved in the classrooms.
6. Talk with three teachers, compile statements of their beliefs on what they feel are the most serious behavior problems in their school and what they feel can be done about them. Drawing on these talks, summarize some teacher attitudes which a supervisor may be expected to contend with and suggest ways you would go about dealing with these attitudes.
7. Visit one or more schools and report on ressentiment practices you discovered. Report how a supervisor might go about helping teachers to correct the practices. (For reference on ressentiment consult Nordstrom, Friedenberg, and Gold listed in the bibliography.)
8. Make an audio tape recording of an interview with a group of students on their feelings and about their school. Write a report showing how a supervisor would go about using student input such as this for making changes.
9. Write a paper expounding your position on students' rights.
10. Discover and report three examples (on three different grade levels) of self-discipline being taught.

11. Make a classification of what you consider reasonable and unreasonable forms of punishment.
12. Write a paper revealing your position on corporal punishment.
13. Identify and report on schools which maintain special classes for children with behavior problems and special schools in the community for this purpose.
14. Specify steps you would recommend to a teacher who is experiencing the following behavior problems: (a) truancy, (b) excessive tardiness, (c) aggressive behavior in the classroom, (d) withdrawing behavior in the classroom.
15. Conduct a limited survey of parental attitudes on discipline.
16. Develop your own classification of causes of behavior problems.
17. Prepare a report on the relationship between pupil behavior and one of the following: (a) the teacher's attitudes on discipline, (b) instructional design, (c) grading practices, (d) peer-group relationships, (e) parental attitudes toward education, and (f) the curriculum.
18. Interview a sample of students and security guards (in schools which have security personnel) and report on the relationship between students and guards.
19. Obtain copies of the school board's policy manual and state school code and prepare a report on disciplinary measures permitted.
20. Gather and report data on assaults on teachers and students in schools of your community for the last two years.
21. Gather data on the cost of school crime in your community for the last two years.
22. Observe several experienced teachers and several inexperienced teachers and formulate a judgment as to whether or not experienced teachers have fewer disciplinary problems than inexperienced teachers.
23. Sit in the assistant principal's (or principal's) office for a day and observe and keep a log of types of disciplinary problems sent to the assistant principal (or principal).
24. Analyze a school's records of behavior problems for one school year and tabulate the number of problems by age, intelligence test scores, sex, ethnic origin, social class, and status of the home.
25. Role-play with a peer a parent-teacher conference on a case in which the son has been caught smoking marijuana in the boys' rest room.
26. Write a paper showing whether you agree or disagree with Charles E. Silberman's assertion that schools are "grim, joyless places" and state your reasons for agreeing or disagreeing. If you agree with Silberman, recommend ways to make schools more joyful places.
27. Role-play with a peer a conference between a teacher and a sixth-grade girl who has stolen a dollar from one of her classmates.
28. Write a review of Arthur W. Combs' book, *The Professional Education of Teachers*.
29. Report on the five models of discipline discussed by Laurel N. Tanner.
30. Prepare a position paper on behavior modification.

31. If your school system has a written student code of conduct, obtain a copy and critique it. If your school system does not have a written code of conduct, sketch an outline of topics which should be covered in it. (This can be a group project.)
32. Find out what Jacob S. Kounin meant by "withitness" and "overlapping."
33. Review *Teaching Students through Their Individual Learning Styles: A Practical Approach* by Rita S. Dunn and Kenneth J. Dunn and draw implications for discipline.
34. Prepare a talk which you as a supervisor would give to a group of teachers on prevention of disciplinary problems.

NOTES

1. *The Education Digest* 19, no. 5 (January 1954): 20.
2. Harvey F. Clarizio, *Toward Positive Classroom Discipline*, 3d ed., New York, Wiley, 1980, 1.
3. See annual surveys of the public's attitudes toward the public schools conducted by George H. Gallup, published each fall in the *Phi Delta Kappan*. The latest survey at the time of publication of this text is George H. Gallup, "The 15th Annual Gallup Poll of the Public's Attitudes toward the Public Schools," *Phi Delta Kappan* 65, no. 1 (September 1983): 33–47.
4. Stanley Elam, ed., *The Gallup Polls of Attitudes toward Education 1969–1973*, Bloomington, Ind., Phi Delta Kappa (1973): 57, 66–67.
5. See Kenneth T. Henson, *Secondary Teaching: A Personal Approach*, Itasca, Ill., F. E. Peacock, 1974, 3–4.
6. Stephen J. Knezevich, *Administration of Public Education*, 3d ed., New York, Harper & Row, 1975, 219.
7. See *The World Almanac and Book of Facts*, 1980, 183.
8. Peter F. Oliva, "High School Discipline in American Society," *The National Association of Secondary School Principals Bulletin* 40, no. 216 (January 1956): 1–103.
9. William Glasser, *Schools Without Failure*, New York, Harper & Row, 1969, 13–14.
10. Carl R. Rogers, "Toward Becoming a Fully Functioning Person," in *Perceiving, Behaving, Becoming*, 1962 Yearbook, Alexandria, Va., Association for Supervision and Curriculum Development, 1962, 21–33.
11. A. H. Maslow, "Some Basic Propositions of a Growth and Self-Actualization Psychology," in *Perceiving, Behaving, Becoming*, 1962 Yearbook, Alexandria, Va., Association for Supervision and Curriculum Development, 1962, 34–49.
12. Arthur W. Combs, "A Perceptual View of the Adequate Personality," in Arthur W. Combs, ed., *Perceiving, Behaving, Becoming*, 1962 Yearbook, Alexandria, Va., Association for Supervision and Curriculum Development, 1962, 50–64.
13. Don E. Hamachek, *Encounters with the Self*, 2d ed., New York, Holt, Rinehart and Winston, 1978, 33.
14. Combs, 51.
15. Ibid., 53.
16. A. H. Maslow, *Motivation and Personality*, 2d ed., New York, Harper & Row, 1970, 35–58.
17. Earl C. Kelley, "The Fully Functioning Self," in *Perceiving, Behaving, Becoming*, 1962 Yearbook, Alexandria, Va., Association for Supervision and Curriculum Development, 1962, 9–20.
18. Hamachek, 222.

19. Allison Davis, "Socialization and Adolescent Personality," *Adolescence*, 43d Yearbook, Part I, Chicago, National Society for the Study of Education, 1944, 210.
20. B. Othanel Smith, Saul B. Cohen and Arthur Pearl, *Teachers for the Real World*, Washington, D.C., The American Association of Colleges for Teacher Education, 1969, 130.
21. Glasser, 52–53.
22. Ibid., 29–30.
23. Charles E. Silberman, *Crisis in the Classroom*, New York, Random House, 1970, 10.
24. Glasser, 26.
25. Carl Nordstrom, Edgar Z. Friedenberg, and Hilary A. Gold, *Society's Children: A Study of Ressentiment in the Secondary School*, New York, Random House, 1967.
26. E. K. Wickman, *Children's Behavior and Teachers' Attitudes*, New York, The Commonwealth Fund, 1928.
27. Peter F. Oliva, "High School Discipline in American Society." Doctoral dissertation, Teachers College, Columbia University, 1952. Published in *The National Association of Secondary School Principals Bulletin* 40, no. 216 (January 1956): 14.
28. Puran J. Rajpal, "What Behavior Problems Do Teachers Regard as Serious?" *Phi Delta Kappan* 53, no. 9 (May 1972): 591–592.
29. Ibid., 592.
30. See R. Rosenthal and L. Jacobson, *Pygmalion in the Classroom*, New York, Holt, Rinehart and Winston, 1968.
31. See W. Burleigh Seaver, "Effects of Naturally Induced Teacher Expectancies," *Journal of Personality and Social Psychology* 28, no. 3 (December 1973): 333–342.
32. See J. Michael Palardy, "What Teachers Believe, What Children Achieve," *Elementary School Journal* 69, no. 7 (April 1969): 370–374.
33. See Hamachek, 225–231.
34. See Arthur T. Jersild and Frances B. Holmes, "Characteristics of Teachers Who Are Liked Best and Disliked Most," *Journal of Experimental Education* 9, no. 2 (December 1940): 139–151. See also Paul Witty, "An Analysis of the Personality Traits of the Effective Teacher," *Journal of Educational Research* 40, no. 9 (May 1947): 662–672.
35. Arthur W. Combs, *The Professional Education of Teachers: A Perceptual View of Teacher Preparation*, Boston, Allyn and Bacon, 1965, 71.
36. Barbara Bree Fischer and Louis Fischer, "Styles in Teaching and Learning," *Educational Leadership* 36, no. 4 (January 1979): 251.
37. Ibid., 246–250.
38. Johanna Kasin Lemlech, *Classroom Management*, New York, Harper & Row, 1979, 8–26.
39. Jacob S. Kounin, *Discipline and Group Management in Classrooms*, New York, Holt, Rinehart and Winston, 1970, 127.
40. Laurel N. Tanner, *Classroom Discipline for Effective Teaching and Learning*, New York, Holt, Rinehart and Winston, 1978, 5–18.
41. Ibid., 14.
42. Ibid., 15–16.
43. Ibid., 16.
44. Wilford A. Weber, "Classroom Management," in *Classroom Teaching Skills: A Handbook*, James M. Cooper, ed., Lexington, Mass., D.C. Heath, 1977, 312.
45. Clarizio, 8–16.
46. Ibid., 4.
47. Weber, 316.
48. J. Michael Palardy and James E. Mudrey, "Discipline: Four Approaches," in *Teaching Today: Tasks and Challenges*, J. Michael Palardy, ed., New York, Macmillan, 1975, 315–324.
49. Ibid., 318–319.
50. Ibid., 319.
51. Ibid., 319, 323, 324.
52. Glasser, 37.

53. Ibid., 22–23.
54. Wesley C. Becker, Siegfried Engelmann, and Don R. Thomas, *Teaching 1: Classroom Management*, Chicago, Science Research Associates, 1975, 255–261.
55. Ibid., 260.
56. *Ingraham v. Wright*, 430 US 651 (1977).
57. *Goss v. Lopez*, 419 US 565 (1975); *Wood v. Strickland*, 420 US 308 (1975).
58. See *Safe School Study Report to Congress*, Washington, D.C., National Institute of Education, 1978. See also *The School Law Newsletter* 5, no. 3 (1974): 1.
59. Stephen K. Bailey, *Disruption in Urban Public Secondary Schools*, Reston, Va., National Association of Secondary School Principals, 1970.
60. For a plan in which rules may vary from class to class see Roland S. Barth, "Discipline: If You Do That Again—", *Phi Delta Kappan* 61, no. 6 (February 1980): 398–400.

BIBLIOGRAPHY

"Assaults on Teachers." *Today's Education* 61 (February 1972): 30–32ff.
Bailey, Stephen K. *Disruption in Urban Public Secondary Schools.* Reston, Va.: National Association of Secondary School Principals, 1970.
Becker, Wesley C., Siegfried Engelmann, and Don R. Thomas. *Teaching I: Classroom Management.* Chicago: Science Research Associates, 1975.
Clarizio, Harvey F. *Toward Positive Classroom Discipline*, 3rd ed. New York: Wiley, 1980.
Combs, Arthur W., ed. *Perceiving, Behaving, Becoming*, 1962 Yearbook. Alexandria, Va.: Association for Supervision and Curriculum Development, 1962.
———. *The Professional Education of Teachers: A Perceptual View of Teacher Preparation.* Boston: Allyn and Bacon, 1965.
——— and Donald Snygg. *Individual Behavior: A Perceptual Approach to Behavior*, rev. ed. New York: Harper & Row, 1959.
Conant, James B. *Slums and Suburbs.* New York: McGraw-Hill, 1961.
Dembo, Myron H. *Teaching for Learning: Applying Educational Psychology in the Classroom.* Santa Monica, Calif.: Goodyear, 1977.
Duke, Daniel L., ed. *Helping Teachers Manage Classrooms.* Alexandria, Va.: Association for Supervision and Curriculum Development, 1982.
Dunn, Rita S., and Kenneth J. Dunn. "Learning Styles/Teaching Styles: Should They . . . Can They . . . Be Matched?" *Educational Leadership* 36 (January 1979): 238–244.
———. *Teaching Students through Their Individual Learning Styles: A Practical Approach.* Reston, Va.: Reston, 1978.
Elam, Stanley, ed. *The Gallup Polls of Attitudes toward Education 1969–1973.* Bloomington, Ind.: Phi Delta Kappa, 1973.
Epstein, Charlotte. *Classroom Management and Teaching: Persistent Problems and Rational Solutions.* Reston, Va.: Reston, 1979.
Fischer, Barbara Bree, and Louis Fischer. "Styles in Teaching and Learning." *Educational Leadership* 36, no. 4 (January 1979): 245–254.
Friedenberg, Edgar Z. *The Vanishing Adolescent.* New York: Dell, 1959. (paperback)
Furtwengler, Willis J. *Improving School Discipline: An Administrator's Guide.* Rockleigh, N.J.: Allyn and Bacon, 1982.
Gallup, George H. "The 15th Annual Gallup Poll of the Public's Attitudes toward the Public Schools." *Phi Delta Kappan* 65, no. 1 (September 1983): 33–47.
Glasser, William. *Schools Without Failure.* New York: Harper & Row, 1969.
Hamachek, Don E. *Encounters with the Self*, 2nd ed. New York: Holt, Rinehart and Winston, 1978.
Harris, Thomas A. *I'm OK-You're OK.* New York: Avon, 1969. (paperback)
Henson, Kenneth T. *Secondary Teaching Methods.* Lexington, Mass.: D.C. Heath, 1981.

Herndon, James. *How to Survive in Your Native Land*. New York: Bantam, 1971. (paperback).
————. *The Way It Spozed to Be*. New York: Simon and Shuster, 1968.
Johnson, Lois V., and Mary A. Bany. *Classroom Management Theory and Skill Training*. New
    York: Macmillan, 1970.
Jones, Vernon F., and Luise S. Jones. *Responsible Classroom Discipline: Creating Positive
    Learning Environments and Solving Problems*. Rockleigh, N.J.: Allyn and Bacon, 1981.
Kaufman, Bel. *Up the Down Staircase*. New York: Avon, 1964. (paperback).
Kindsvatter, Richard, and Mary Ann Levine. "The Myths of Discipline." *Phi Delta Kappan*
    61 (June 1980): 690–693.
Kounin, Jacob S. *Discipline and Group Management in Classrooms*. New York: Holt, Rinehart
    and Winston, 1970.
Kozol, Jonathan. *Death at an Early Age*. Boston: Houghton Mifflin, 1967.
La Grand, Louis E. *Discipline in the Secondary School*. West Nyack, N.Y.: Parker, 1969.
Larson, Knute G., and Levin R. Karpas. *Effective Secondary School Discipline*. Englewood
    Cliffs, N.J.: Prentice-Hall, 1963.
Lemlech, Johanna Kasin. *Classroom Management*. New York: Harper & Row, 1979.
Lindsey, Bryan L., and James W. Cunningham. "Behavior Modification: Some Doubts and
    Dangers." In *Discipline and Learning: An Inquiry into Student-Teacher Relationships*.
    Washington, D.C.: National Education Association, 1975.
McCarthy, Martha M. "How Can I Best Manage My Classroom? *Instructor* 87 (September
    1977): 72–73.
Madsen, Charles H., Jr., and Clifford K. Madsen. *Teaching/Discipline*, 2nd ed. Rockleigh,
    N.J.: Allyn and Bacon, 1974.
Maslow, A. H. *Motivation and Personality*, 2nd ed. New York: Harper & Row. 1970.
National Education Association. *Discipline and Learning: An Inquiry into Student-Teacher
    Relationships*. Washington, D.C.: National Education Association, 1975.
————. *Discipline in the Classroom*, rev. ed. Washington, D.C.: National Education Associ-
    ation, 1974.
Nordstrom, Carl, Edgar Z. Fridenberg, and Hilary A. Gold. *Society's Children: A Study of
    Ressentiment in the Secondary School*. New York: Random House, 1967.
Oliva, Peter F. "High School Discipline in American Society." *The Bulletin of the National
    Association of Secondary School Principals* 40, no. 16 (January 1956): 1–103.
————. *The Secondary School Today*, 2nd ed. New York: Harper & Row, 1972.
Palardy, J. Michael. *Teaching Today: Tasks and Challenges*. New York: Macmillan, 1975.
Rajpal, Puran J. "What Behavior Problems Do Teachers Regard as Serious?" *Phi Delta
    Kappan* 53 no. 9 (May 1972): 591–592.
Silberman, Charles E. *Crisis in the Classroom*. New York: Random House, 1970.
Silvernail, David L. *Developing Positive Student Self-Concept*. Washington, D.C.: National
    Education Association, 1981.
Smith, B. Othanel, Saul B. Cohen, and Arthur Pearl. *Teachers for the Real World*. Wash-
    ington, D.C.: The American Association of Colleges for Teacher Education, 1969.
Stone, James C., and Donald P. DeNevi, eds. *Teaching Multi-Cultural Populations: Five
    Heritages*. New York: D. Van Nostrand, 1971.
Tanner, Laurel N. *Classroom Discipline for Effective Teaching and Learning*. New York: Holt,
    Rinehart and Winston, 1978.
Weber, Wilford A. "Classroom Management." In *Classroom Teaching Skills: A Handbook*,
    James M. Cooper, ed. Lexington, Mass.: D.C. Heath, 1977.
Webster, Staten W. *Discipline in Classroom: Basic Principles and Problems*. Scranton, Pa.:
    Chandler, 1968.
Wickman, E. K. *Children's Behavior and Teachers' Attitudes*. New York: The Commonwealth
    Fund, 1928.
Wolfgang, Charles H., and Carl D. Glickman. *Solving Discipline Problems: Strategies for Class-
    room Teachers*. Rockleigh, N.J.: Allyn and Bacon, 1980.

Films

Classroom Management. 19 min. Sound. Color. New York: Holt, Rinehart and Winston. Supplements Kounin, *Discipline and Group Management in Classrooms*.

Critical Moments in Teaching series. Sound films. Color. New York: Holt, Rinehart and Winston. Available from BFA Educational Media, 468 Park Avenue South, New York, New York 10016. Films in the series pertinent to classroom management are:
   A Child Who Cheats. 10 min.
   The Day the Insects Took Over. 10 min.
   The First and Fundamental R. 12 min.
   Less Far than the Arrow. 8 min.
   The Poetry in Paul. 9½ min.
   Tense: Imperfect. 12 min.
   Walls. 10½ min.

Maintaining Classroom Discipline. 14 min. Sound. Black and white. New York: McGraw-Hill. Old but useful film which contrasts authoritarian and democratic methods of control.

Multi-Media

Classroom Management Modules. Four 16 mm sound films with student guides and evaluation materials. Available from Dr. Walter R. Borg, Protocol Materials Project, Department of Psychology, Utah State University, Logan, Utah 84322. On the following four topics:
   Group Alerting
   Learner Accountability
   Transitions
   Withitness

Discipline in the Classroom. Filmstrip-tape program # 15. Available from Vimcet Associates, P.O. Box 24714, Los Angeles, California 90024.

Teacher Education Resources, P.O. Box 206, Gainesville, Florida 32602:
   Fear in the School. Two filmstrips, two cassettes, leader's guide, and script books.
   Improving School Discipline: Secrets of Successful Teachers. Two filmstrips, two cassettes, and leader's guide.
   Positive Discipline. Two filmstrips, two cassettes, and leader's guide.

Videotape

Effective Classroom Management for the Elementary School. The tape demonstrates effective techniques of classroom management in the elementary school. Based on the research of Carolyn Evertson. Association for Supervision and Curriculum Development, 225 N. Washington Street, Alexandria, Virginia 22314, 1980. 30 minutes.

PART **III**

LEADERSHIP IN CURRICULUM DEVELOPMENT

7

Helping Teachers with Curriculum Development

OBJECTIVES

After studying Chapter 7 you should be able to accomplish the following objectives:

1. Draw a diagram of your preferred model for curriculum development.
2. Draft a statement of philosophy and aims suitable for submission to a faculty committee for its consideration and revision.
3. Distinguish between aims, curriculum goals, and curriculum objectives.
4. Write curriculum goals and curriculum objectives.
5. Describe and apply the Tyler Rationale.
6. Distinguish between a comprehensive approach to curriculum development and a problem-centered approach.
7. Construct an outline for a curriculum guide.
8. Construct an outline for a course of study.
9. Construct an outline for a resource unit.
10. Explain what is meant by scope of the curriculum and how scope is determined.
11. Explain what is meant by sequence of the curriculum and how sequence is determined.
12. Explain what is meant by balance in the curriculum and how balance is achieved.
13. Distinguish between curriculum goals and objectives and instructional goals and objectives.
14. Describe how to organize a school and/or school system for curriculum development.

A MODEL FOR CURRICULUM DEVELOPMENT

In the first chapter of this book we saw the responsibilities of the supervisor as falling in three domains: instructional development, curriculum development, and staff development. Chapters 7 and 8 explore the responsibilities of the supervisor in assisting teachers with the elusive undertaking called curriculum development.* The term *elusive* is used because no concept in pedagogy is slipperier and harder to "get a handle on" than curriculum development. Part of the difficulty is a semantic one. The word *curriculum* has different meanings to different people. To some people the curriculum consists of all the experiences undergone by children wherever they may be: in school, at home, or on the street. To others the curriculum is a set of subjects which children "take."

To compound the semantic problem further some educators call a written curriculum plan a curriculum. When they write curriculum guides, they say they are "writing a curriculum." Part of the elusiveness of curriculum development is a substantive one. While we can read and design curriculum plans and guides, what we see are in reality manifestations of the curriculum, not the curriculum itself. The curriculum itself is a concept—a planned concept—and observing a curriculum in action, as opposed to examining a curriculum plan which is to be put into action, reveals not curriculum but instruction.

Instruction—whether in the classroom or in extra-class activity, whether in the guidance office or the library—is the means of putting the curriculum into action. Further, attempting to observe a curriculum reveals only parts of the whole—those parts within a particular classroom or department or subject or level—not the grand design. This concept called curriculum goes beyond immediate space and time, which makes it all the more difficult for supervisors and teachers to work with.

The curriculum is also difficult to work with because it usually involves more than one teacher. A successful curriculum requires an interdependent, working relationship among all school personnel and cooperative planning for that relationship.

The word *development* tacked onto curriculum compounds the pedagogical problem. What is curriculum development? How do you develop a curriculum? Who develops a curriculum? What does a curriculum look like after it is developed? When is a curriculum fully developed? Is there such a thing as an underdeveloped curriculum? Although these questions are pertinent ones, they are not easy to answer if we wish to go beyond superficiality. The literature's answers to these problems may offer semantic difficulties which stand as barriers to clear communication. Specialists in the field of curriculum talk and write about *curriculum development*, *curriculum planning*, *curriculum improvement*, *curriculum construction*, *curriculum reform*, *curriculum change*, and *curriculum evaluation*. All the terms are, of course, interrelated but not necessarily synonymous.

Before developing the theme of curriculum development and the respective roles of the supervisor and teachers in the task of curriculum development, let us define the terms curriculum and curriculum development to provide a frame of

---

* For a full treatment of curriculum development see Peter F. Oliva, *Developing the Curriculum*, Boston: Little, Brown, 1982.

reference for subsequent discussion. By curriculum is meant those experiences of a child which come under the supervision of the school. Included in the concept of curriculum as described in this textbook are (1) all in-school experiences, including classroom learning experiences, student activities, use of the library, use of learning resource centers, assemblies, use of the cafeteria, and social functions, and (2) out-of-school learning experiences directed by the school, including homework, field trips, and use of community resources.

Here is a definition of curriculum development from the *Dictionary of Education*:

Curriculum Development: a task of supervision directed toward designing or redesigning the guidelines for instruction; includes development of specifications indicating what is to be taught, by whom, when, where, and in what sequence or pattern.[1]

This definition might be modified in one very important respect: Curriculum development is not the task of supervision alone. It is a joint endeavor of all school personnel but primarily a cooperative activity of supervisors and teachers. Curriculum development is used in this text interchangeably with curriculum planning and curriculum improvement. To make a slight distinction between curriculum development and curriculum improvement, development might be conceptualized as planning at the initial stages; then, once a curricular plan is instituted, continuous development is curriculum improvement. However, in the literature curriculum development and curriculum improvement are used synonymously and they will be so used in this book.

You will note in the foregoing definition of curriculum development that the manner in which portions of the curriculum will be taught is not included. The question of "how" takes us into curriculum's companion field—instruction. Curriculum and instruction cannot really be separated in practice. Your text gives separate attention to curriculum and instruction but this can be done for purposes of analysis only. Without a curriculum there can be no instruction; without instruction a curriculum is lifeless. The intimate relationship between curriculum and instruction underscores the necessity of the supervisor's working in both the instructional and curriculum development domains. I am in agreement with Daniel Tanner and Laurel N. Tanner when they said:

There is no domain in education that more aptly demonstrates the futility of trying to separate curriculum from instruction than supervision. The act of shooting cannot be separated from the target. So instruction cannot be separated from curriculum. Yet, as noted earlier . . . there has been a trend among curriculum theorists to conceptualize curriculum and instruction as separate entities.[2]

Neither curriculum nor instruction is subordinate to the other. Both are equally important and the supervisor has the responsibility of helping teachers with the improvement of both.

Curriculum development involves an almost continuous process of decision making. Teachers are engaged in this process when they attempt to answer questions such as:

When do we introduce fractions?

Shall we introduce an open-space plan in the elementary school?

What kind of open-space education should we adopt?

Is vocational agriculture needed in this community?

Should geometry precede intermediate algebra?

Should we offer French or should we offer Spanish?

Where should we begin study of foreign languages?

How much time should we devote to study of the American Revolution?

How many years of science should we require for graduation from our high school?

What experiences essential to young people are omitted from our curriculum?

Should our curriculum be subject-centered or child-centered?

Are we providing experiences for development of self-discipline on the part of the learner?

Shall we add sex education to the curriculum?

Are there enough carry-over sports in the physical education program?

For what jobs in the community should our vocational program prepare young people?

Should boys take a course in homemaking?

Do the elementary school pupils need the services of a guidance counselor?

Do we have a balance between general education and specialized education in the curriculum?

Should junior high pupils take typing?

Do the elementary school pupils need the service of a guidance counselor?

Are we identifying the health needs of our pupils?

Should we separate exceptional children and put them into special classes?

Should we adopt a continuous progress or nongraded plan?

Should we establish a core program in the secondary school?

What kinds of musical experiences are appropriate for elementary school children?

Are we providing opportunities for creative expression by pupils?

The foregoing questions are illustrative of the hundreds of kinds of questions which must be answered by a school system if its curriculum is not to remain dormant. Some of the questions must be asked repeatedly, for curriculum development is a continuous, nonending process. The answer to a curriculum question at one time may not suffice at another time. Circumstances change and the curriculum must change to reflect the new circumstances.

Most of the illustrative questions involve decision making by groups of teachers, sometimes the total faculty of a school, and often the faculties of all schools in a particular school system. Many of the questions are interdisciplinary in nature and call for input from many grades and fields of study.

The kinds of questions raised above require prolonged study before decisions can be reached. While instructional methods can be altered on short notice, curriculum changes take time—to examine, to make decisions, to implement, and to evaluate. Consequently, curriculum development is futuristically oriented. Improvements desired for next year or the year after should be studied this year. Some of the curricular problems schools have encountered stem from the fact that faculties have rushed into curriculum change before adequately studying all the ramifications of the change.

Curriculum development is normally a group undertaking. Not that the individual teacher does not become involved in curriculum improvement within his or her own grade level or subject. The individual teacher must make many curricular decisions. He or she must decide what limitations will be placed on the content chosen and in what order to present units. He or she must make sure that the content not only articulates with previous study and future study by the pupils but is relevant.

When curricular decisions lap across discipline lines, as they often do, a group of teachers under the leadership of a supervisor must conduct a study of the curricular problems and make recommendations to the faculty and administration for changes they deem desirable. Teachers group and regroup depending upon the nature of the curriculum problem under study. The problem of choosing a reading program for the elementary school will certainly involve all elementary school teachers in a particular school and will probably involve all elementary school teachers in the entire school system. The formation of a group that represents all teachers concerned with a problem is usually the means by which curriculum development is initiated.

Depending upon the nature of the problem and the extent of its effect, curriculum development may be carried on by a building supervisor, by a central office supervisor with the faculty or segments of the faculty of a particular school, or by a central office supervisor with the faculties of all schools of a particular level or levels throughout a school district. If a problem is localized in one particular school, curriculum development may be confined to that school. On the other hand, if a problem and its solution will affect teachers and pupils in more than one school, curriculum development must proceed on a districtwide rather than on a schoolwide basis. In practice, both schoolwide and districtwide curriculum development are frequently and continuously engaged in by teachers and supervisors.

The questions of what language arts experiences should be taught in a secondary school language arts program, for example, and the sequence in which the experiences should be programmed are appropriately the domain of the language arts faculty of that school and other schools in the district. Decisions on these matters may be made in consulation with the appropriate supervisor or supervisors such as the team leader, grade coordinator, department head, assistant principal for curriculum, supervisor of language arts, director of instruction, assistant superintendent for curriculum and instruction, and appropriate administrators. A decision on whether to require an additional year of language arts for graduation from high school is appropriately the domain of the total secondary school faculty of a school system, since any addition to or deletion of a course from a curriculum has an effect on all teachers.

The supervisor has several responsibilities in the process of curriculum development. As one approach, he or she may initiate a broad study of the curriculum by enlisting teachers in the preparation or revision of the school's philosophy. The supervisor may stimulate teachers to identify curriculum problems of concern to them or may even suggest problems which might be of interest to them. He or she helps set up the groups and subgroups needed for study of a problem. It is the supervisor's responsibility to provide time, facilities, and resources which teachers must have to perform their task of curriculum development. Unless these ingredients are made available to teachers, curriculum development is doomed to failure. The lack of these resources is a major reason why the curriculum of many schools remains static. Teachers must be granted school time to work on curriculum revision. They should not be expected to tackle the strategic problems of curriculum improvement on their own time and uncompensated. In fact, with the growing power of teachers' organizations collective bargaining is placing limitations on after-school hours which may be demanded of a teacher.

Curriculum development will cost a school system a certain amount in released time for teachers and provision of substitutes for them as needed, and in the purchase of materials which are essential for adequate study. School administrators must make a value judgment as to whether a school system can afford not to continuously revitalize its curriculum and as a result deliver an outmoded, irrelevant curriculum to its learners.

THE SUPERVISOR IN CURRICULUM DEVELOPMENT

Some supervisors mistakenly concentrate most or all of their curriculum development energies to the exclusion of leadership in the other two domains: instructional and staff development. They emphasize locating and disseminating curriculum materials, writing curriculum guides, and the like. A supervisor has been facetiously described as a person who repeatedly loads up the car with curriculum materials that he or she carries around to teachers in the schools even though teachers don't use the materials anyway.

Some supervisors feel more comfortable in the curriculum domain where much of the work takes place outside the classroom. By concentrating on programs they feel they can effect changes more readily than by working with individual teachers in improving their methods of instruction. As if journeying in the fourth dimension some supervisors enter the domain of curriculum development and rarely exit. Unless a supervisory staff is large enough to differentiate leadership responsibilities in each of the three domains, a perpetual sojourn in the territory of curriculum development is as inappropriate as a detour past the domain, as if it were the Slough of Despair out of *A Pilgrim's Progress*.

It is often said that the supervisor acts as a catalyst or change agent. In the job of curriculum development it is the supervisor who helps teachers to identify curricular problems and helps facilitate the study and search for solutions to these problems. He or she exerts leadership in stimulating teachers to take a look at the curriculum and come up with recommendations for improvements. It is the leader who sparks a dissatisfaction with the status quo and causes teachers to want to make revisions.

The supervisor is a curriculum worker, a participant in a cooperative process of which he or she is but one member—a respected member, one hopes. The supervisor's authority and claim to respect should result not only from status but from the level of credibility which can be induced in fellow workers. The supervisor is not *the* developer and should not behave in such a manner. Just as it takes two to tango it takes two or more to develop a curriculum.

In order to achieve credibility the supervisor must have specialized skills. He or she must be grounded in curriculum theory, know what solutions have been tried in the past and how they have fared, and be cognizant of current developments in curriculum, nationally and internationally. The elementary school supervisor, for example, who is unaware of developments in British schools[3] and the math supervisor who is not familiar with the International Study of Achievement in Mathematics[4] are lacking valuable input which they should be able to share with teachers who are studying related problems.

The supervisor must possess research skills, know how to help teachers develop curriculum proposals, be able to analyze research, be able to spot biases in research, and know how to interpret findings to teachers. The supervisor's role calls for a knowledge of learning theory and a sensitivity to problems of society. Among necessary skills of the supervisor is the ability to manage work groups and to facilitate their endeavors.

LEADERSHIP FOR CURRICULUM DEVELOPMENT

Where does a supervisor begin to grab hold of this task of curriculum development? Two approaches may be followed, both of which are effective and viable. The first, *the comprehensive approach*, permits a total view of the curriculum. The second, *the problem-centered approach*, is confined to study of specific curricular problems identified by teachers. Each approach has its own purposes. The comprehensive approach requires a global look at the curriculum and uncovers heretofore unidentified problems while the problem-centered approach is a response to problems already identified by faculty members. A supervisor will take both approaches, often concurrently, conducting a problem-centered study while a comprehensive study is going on. The supervisor should plan for and initiate a comprehensive study while at the same time responding to the need for study of particular problems.

The Comprehensive Approach

The comprehensive approach to curriculum development may be conceptualized in the form of the simplified model in Figure 7.1.*

---

* For discussion of models for curriculum development see Peter F. Oliva, *Developing the Curriculum*, Boston: Little, Brown, 1982, Ch. 5.

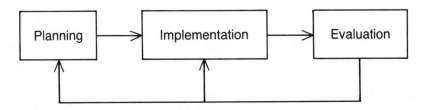

Figure 7.1   A Simplified Model for Curriculum Development

You will note that this model with its three components is the same as the simplest model of instruction discussed in Chapter 3, except that the feedback lines have been added and the word *implementation* is used instead of *presentation*. Whereas the simplified model of instruction advises us to plan, implement, and evaluate *instruction*, the simplified model of curriculum improvement guides us to plan, implement, and evaluate *curriculum*. In both cases we are following the same process but in each case we are working with a different entity.

We could readily follow the simplified model for curriculum development but the expanded model in Figure 7.2 gives us greater insights into the process.

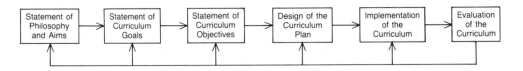

Figure 7.2   Expanded Model for Curriculum Development*

* This model is a slight revision of the model for curriculum development presented in the first edition of this book in that *aims* have been added to the first component. For a more detailed, expanded model which integrates an instructional model with a curriculum model, see Peter F. Oliva in *Developing the Curriculum*, Boston: Little, Brown, 1982, p. 169.

Both the models of instruction found in Chapter 3 and the two models of curriculum development discussed in this chapter follow a systems approach. Using the expanded, six-part model for curriculum development we begin by specifying where we are going and what we wish to achieve (philosophy and aims, goals, and objectives); we design a curriculum plan (plan design); we put a plan into operation to attempt to achieve the objectives (implementation); we evaluate the success of the plan (evaluation); and we provide feedback so we can revise the components of the model (feedback line). The process is cyclical and unending.

Faculties embarking on curriculum development ordinarily work on one of three levels: class, grade, or subject level; schoolwide level; and school-systemwide level. When the supervisor engages teachers in a comprehensive approach to the total curriculum, study groups are formed which are representative of the entire school or of the entire school system. The supervisor must take responsibility for setting up the machinery for the curriculum study and help identify the groupings of teachers which will be necessary for pursuing the study. Study committees must be established which are representative of the total faculty or faculties concerned, but at each stage of curriculum study the total faculty or faculties must be informed, approve committee reports, and consent to proposals for curriculum change before they are put into operation.

The comprehensive look at the total curriculum requires formation of groups of teachers across grade levels and across disciplines. The initial formation of these groups is exceedingly important, for they should be representative of the broad spectrum of interests of teachers. What the supervisor is after is commitment on the part of teachers and to achieve that commitment teachers must feel that they are adequately represented on groups working in their name.

The model for curriculum development implies a fixed sequence of tasks. A study of the curriculum begins with writing a statement of the philosophy and aims espoused by the school or school system, which is followed by stating curricular goals, and finally by specifying curricular objectives. Each of the statements—philosophy and aims, goals, and objectives—which may be drawn up by a representative committee or committees, should be taken to the total faculty for its endorsement.

Following approval of the objectives, curriculum proposals are developed and submitted to the faculty; those which are approved by the faculty are then implemented. In the last stage of the model evaluation plans are designed, approved by the faculty, and carried out.

One committee which represents the faculty may provide the leadership for all phases of the study, or two or three committees may divide the responsibilities. Since there is a logical flow from philosophy and aims to goals to objectives, it seems desirable to establish a Committee on Philosophy, Aims, Goals, and Objectives, which would be the task force for the first three components of the model. In addition to teachers who would constitute the majority, representatives of the nonprofessional staff, the community, and the student body (given appropriate maturity level) should serve on this committee so views of constituencies other than teachers can be made known. When the Committee on Philosophy, Aims, Goals, and Objectives finishes its task, the same or other groups will draft specific curricular plans and will design and conduct the evaluation of those plans.

The first five components of the model for curriculum development—philosophy and aims, curriculum goals, curriculum objectives, design of the plan, and implementation—are considered in this chapter. Evaluation of the curriculum is examined in the next chapter. To establish a frame of reference for our discussion in this chapter we will look at the preparation of statements of philosophy and aims, curriculum goals, and curriculum objectives which are schoolwide or school-systemwide and not specific to a particular grade or discipline.

Statements of philosophy and aims should evolve as sets of beliefs and purposes which are espoused by the entire school faculty regardless of discipline or grade level. Sets of schoolwide or school-systemwide curricular goals and objectives should be adopted by the faculty before writing curricular goals and objectives for a particular discipline or grade level. Committees within the discipline or grade level should be established at a later time for writing curricular goals and objectives which are in keeping with the broader goals and objectives agreed on by the total faculty. Leadership in the development of the curriculum of the particular teaching fields is a function of the specialist supervisor, while leadership in the development of overall curriculum rests with the generalist supervisor.

Writing a School's Philosophy and Aims

Statement of Philosophy.   Writing a school philosophy is primarily an affective exercise. Teachers who develop a statement of philosophy must verbalize their beliefs and express their feelings about education. Whether teachers realize it or not the way they behave in the classroom is a direct reflection of beliefs they hold about the learner, about education, and about society. If they believe that learning should be a pleasant experience, they behave differently from the way they do when they believe that learning must be a distasteful experience—like taking medicine—for it to do the learner any good. They also order their curriculum and methodology accordingly. If they believe in the worth of each individual, they construct a curriculum and employ methods which aim to foster individual development. When they write a philosophy, they are forced to look within themselves and to clarify, perhaps for the first time, what they truly believe about education.

Frankly speaking, the exercise of writing a statement of philosophical beliefs is not one that is terribly popular with teachers. One reason for this is cultural. The United States is not known as a nation of philosophers but as a country of pragmatists; thus, our people express a penchant for action, not thought; for practice, not theory. It is this penchant which causes students in teacher education institutions to express impatience with courses which they label "theory." The most popular courses in teacher education are the "nuts and bolts" courses and the practice courses such as student teaching. It is this deprecation of theory which has caused many students in teacher education to rank so-called foundations of education courses at the low end of the totem pole. The illustrious former president of Harvard University James B. Conant, a scientist, joined the critics of foundational courses in his study of the education of teachers.[5] Teacher educators have long been considered impractical idealists, too immersed in theory, and too remote from the firing line ("those who can, do; those who can't, teach; those who can't teach, teach teachers"). The professional educator has his or her work cut out to convince the teacher trainee that foundations such as philosophy of education indeed have a place in both preservice and in-service education. The professional educator must do what he or she advocates the teacher do with students—demonstrate that a field such as philosophy is relevant. Two ways may be attempted to achieve the goal of demonstrating relevance of philosophy. First, the the preservice trainees or the in-service teachers should at some point approach philosophy from their own personal perspectives and clarify what they believe. Second, the preservice trainees and the in-service teachers should analyze the ways in which their philosophies are applied in the classroom and the ways in which the teaching practices they use devolve from their philosophical beliefs.

Teachers often balk at writing statements of philosophy not only because they are impatient for practical solutions to problems as opposed to theoretical statements but also because writing a philosophy is an introspective exercise. The pragmatic, even materialistic outlook on life precludes time for searching minds and hearts. Nor is it just a question of the time it takes for thinking through one's beliefs. People would much rather expose their actions than their thoughts.

Teachers express impatience with writing philosophical statements because they realize that philosophical beliefs cannot be labeled right or wrong in the same way factual statements can. They know that teachers will hold differing views as to the rightness or wrongness of a philosophical statement and that such differences will produce a time-consuming hassle, which they would just as soon avoid. Yet, the hassling is the most significant part of the exercise of writing a philosophy. Discussion and argument on profound ideas help individuals to shape their own beliefs. The individual's beliefs are placed in the crucible of public opinion, a test which some teachers would prefer to bypass.

Teachers sometimes object to writing a statement of philosophy because they feel the end result will be a set of clichés devoid of meaning and impossible to translate into practice. When they enter upon the task of writing a philosophy with this attitude, the outcome is a self-fulfilled prophecy—a philosophical statement which is empty and dead.

Most commonly teachers are confronted with the necessity for producing a statement of philosophy in connection with regional accreditation of their school, a process discussed in the next chapter. Since accreditation acts as a pressure on teachers to develop a philosophical statement, there is the danger that the task can become an academic exercise for the accreditation process and not for its own intrinsic value. The supervisor should not wait until some pressure such as an accreditation process pushes a group of teachers to setting down in writing their philosophical beliefs. Nor should a supervisor or principal ever make writing a philosophy more academic and more empty by rushing into the void and writing the philosophy himself or herself. Though teachers may resist writing a philosophy, they literally deride a school philosophy which has been written by a supervisor or administrator, and rightfully reject it as an expression of a faculty philosophy.

The resistance of teachers to the task of writing a philosophy should not be magnified since the resistance is usually a gentle one. Teachers can and do intellectualize the need for some sort of philosophical statement. The job of the supervisor is to get teachers to internalize the task, to see a real need for the exercise, and to give them hope that the effort to produce the statement will be rewarded by visible results in practice.

Not that all schools are lacking in a statement of philosophy and that these statements must always be developed from scratch. Where a statement of philosophy exists, the task of the Committee on Philosophy, Aims, Goals, and Objectives is to review the previous statement, reaffirm it, modify it, or toss it out and begin anew, as they deem most appropriate.

Assume for purposes of illustration that a committee is charged with the task of drafting a statement of philosophy for a school which has never engaged in this exercise before. What should be included in such a statement? Several ideas immediately come to mind. The statement of philosophy should include the group's beliefs about:

- the purposes of education
- the nature of learning
- the nature of the learner
- the nature of society

The National Study of School Evaluation recommended 12 items which elementary school faculties should consider for possible inclusion in a statement of philosophy.[6] The items serve as guiding principles for faculties drafting a philosophical statement.

1. Relevance of the statement of philosophy to the larger purposes of the American democratic commitment.
2. Attention to intellectual, democratic, moral, and social values basic to satisfying the needs of the individual and his culture.
3. Recognition of individual differences.
4. The special characteristics and unique needs of elementary school pupils.
5. Concern for the nature of knowledge and for the nature of the learning process as they apply to learners and their total development.
6. Consistency of philosophy with actual practice.
7. Identification of the roles and relationships expected of the community, the pupil, the teacher, and the administration in the educational process of the school.
8. The role of the elementary school program of the school district and the importance of articulation with the other elements of the overall educational program.
9. The responsibility for making a determination as to a desirable balance among activities designed to develop the cognitive, affective, and psychomotor domains.
10. The relationship of the school to all other educational learning centers.
11. The responsibility of the school toward social and economic change.
12. The accountability of the school to the community it serves.

After the statement is drafted, it must be ratified by the total school faculty and it becomes the statement of principles from which the goals and objectives of the school are derived and a set of principles against which practice must be tested. Below is an illustration of a statement of philosophy developed by the faculty of the Carbondale, Illinois Community High School.[7]

CARBONDALE COMMUNITY HIGH SCHOOL
DISTRICT 165, CARBONDALE, ILLINOIS

A Philosophy of Education

We believe it is the responsibility of School District 165 to provide:

An educational program which will aid the children of this community to grow physically, intellectually, morally, and emotionally, that they may live happily as children and that they may become adult citizens of a democracy, realizing the most complete life possible within the limits of their individual needs, interests, and abilities. Complete citizenship embodies the dignity of the individual and his responsibility to the group, both of which can be nurtured best through democratic living in a democratic situation.

As a basis for building this educational program:

We believe education is a growth process by which people learn to think and act more effectively.

We believe in the individual's worth and dignity as a person.

We believe the individual's welfare is dependent upon the welfare of others and all must have an understanding of the mutual rights and problems of all people.

We believe that a respect for and an understanding of the policies of democratic government must be held by all.

We believe that the privileges of the democratic way of life enjoyed by the individual imply a responsibility to help maintain this democracy.

We believe that complete citizenship can be realized only through the development of a personality, characterized by intellectual, emotional, and social maturity.

We believe that we must provide ways and means for the individual to discover and develop his ability and personality, in the classroom and in extra-curricular activities.

We believe that in our democratic society, an opportunity for the development and mastery of fundamental attitudes, habits and skills must be offered to all the people according to their abilities.

We believe each person should acquire an understanding of and a respect for the traditions, customs and heritages of this country which have contributed to its development and which will affect its future progress.

We believe the home, the church, the community and the school must cooperate to assist young people in developing spiritually and morally.

We believe in providing for a wise use of leisure time that there may be increased pleasure in living, as well as increased efficiency.

The inevitable question is raised concerning statements of philosophy: What if the philosophical beliefs of a school faculty are divergent, as is often the case? What if there are some teachers who subcribe to essentialistic doctrines and believe that subject matter should take precedence over the learner while others adhere to the pragmatic tenet which places the needs of the learner before subject matter? What if some teachers endorse the role of the school as a passive transmitter of knowledge and cultural heritage while other teachers champion the role of the school as a leader in reconstructing society? Differences in philosophical beliefs go to the heart of the exercise of writing a statement of philosophy and cause teachers to reveal "where they are coming from."

The differences in beliefs among teachers can make the task of writing a philosophy an exciting one. The process of resolving differences of philosophy is the same as with any issue where viewpoints collide: the search for consensus. The supervisor should strive to help a group of teachers reach consensus. Since human beings differ and will continue to differ, 100 percent consensus may be an impossible goal, but the supervisor should try to bring about as wide a consensus as possible. Only those items on which there is consensus of at least a majority of the faculty should be incorporated in the finished statement. Those items on which consensus is lacking should be the subjects for continuing study and discussion and may come up for consideration when the statement of philosophy is reviewed in the future. Once consensus is achieved, however, and a statement of philosophy is accepted by the faculty as a whole, each teacher is bound by that philosophy and should behave in accordance with it. There is nothing unusual in expecting teachers to act in accordance with a group-adopted philosophical statement; that is the essence of the democratic process. While every person is assured of input in the formative stages, once adopted the statement is binding on all the participants. Neither a nation nor a school can function if every individual is at complete liberty to go his or her own way and to reject consensus which has been democratically achieved.

Statement of Aims.   A statement of aims can be considered an extension of the statement of philosophy. Faculties often produce documents entitled *Philosophy and Aims.* The philosophy itself is cast into statements of belief. An accompanying statement of aims, derived from the philosophy, is a set of broad purposes of education. Curriculum goals and objectives refine the aims. The aims themselves are value laden and, therefore, reveal philosophical positions.

Aims are often inseparable from the philosophy, nor is it necessary to separate them. The Carbondale High School example wrapped up aims in the first paragraph, where the faculty said:

We believe it is the responsibility of School District 165 to provide: An educational program which will aid the children of this community to grow physically, intellectually, morally, and emotionally, that they may live happily as children and that they may become adult citizens of a democracy . . . through democratic living in a democratic situation.

Examples of philosophical statements in this same illustration are:

We believe education is a growth process by which people learn to think and act more effectively.
We believe in the individual's worth and dignity as a person.

Typically, school philosophies begin with a statement of beliefs and then draw the aims of education from those beliefs. Instead of or in addition to writing its own aims, a faculty may wish to borrow well-known statements of aims such as the Seven Cardinal Principles, for example. The Commission on the Reorganization of Secondary Education proposed the following principles, i.e., aims for secondary education: "health, command of the fundamental processes, worthy home membership, vocation, citizenship, worthy use of leisure, ethical character."[8]

Aims are meant to be universal. In stating educational aims faculties are saying that they believe schools in general should foster these purposes, that the broad aims they subscribe to for their schools and their communities are desirable for schools and communities throughout the country. Curriculum goals and objectives turn the general aims of education into school-specific purposes.

Writing Curricular Goals

After the faculty has established the philosophical premises and aims to which it claims allegiance, it should turn its attention to a statement of curriculum goals. The same confusion exists between goals and objectives which pertain to the curriculum as exists between goals and objectives in respect to instruction. The direction of curriculum development is sharpened if goals are distinguished from objectives.

Both goals and objectives should be stated in terms of expectations of the learner, rather than expectations of the school. Curriculum goals are expectations of the learners as they encounter the curriculum and are stated in more general, nonbehavioral terms. Curriculum objectives are expectations of the learners as they encounter the curriculum and are stated in more limited, measurable, and behavioral terms.

The problem of distinguishing goals from objectives is seen in the following examples:

The *Elementary School Evaluative Criteria* contains a section on Guiding Principles for a Statement of Objectives.[9] These criteria ask for a report on philosophy, objectives, and commitments. Some people would call these objectives goals, or even aims.

The *Middle School/Junior High School Evaluative Criteria* requires completion of a section on philosophy and goals.[10] They offer several guiding principles for a statement of goals. Of philosophy, goals, and objectives they stated:

The statement of philosophy expresses ideals and beliefs. Goals are more precise delineations of those ideals and beliefs. Objectives are carefully specified statements of intended learner outcomes which contribute to the attainment of program goals and give direction to the school program.[11]

It is the goals which accompany the statement of philosophy for these criteria. Objectives are stated in the section on learning areas.

The *Evaluative Criteria* (for secondary schools) leaves out references to goals and asks for a statement of philosophy and objectives.[12] Objectives give specificity to the statement of philosophy for these criteria.

The Educational Policies Commission, a body of the National Education Association, years ago developed a classic statement spelling out what it considered to be the needs of youth in secondary schools.[13] This statement of needs, which are, in reality, aims for secondary education, is widely known as the "Ten Imperative Needs of Youth" and consists of the following declarations:

1. All youth need to develop salable skills.
2. All youth need to development and maintain good health, physical fitness, and mental health.
3. All youth need to understand the rights and duties of the citizen of a democratic society.
4. All youth need to understand the significance of the family.
5. All youth need to know how to purchase and use goods and services intelligently.

6. All youth need to understand the methods of science.

7. All youth need opportunities to develop their capacities to appreciate beauty in literature, art, music, and nature.

8. All youth need to be able to use their leisure time well.

9. All youth need to develop respect for other people, to grow in their insight into ethical values and principles, to be able to live and work cooperatively with others, and to grow in the moral and spiritual values of life.

10. All youth need to grow in their ability to think rationally, to express their thoughts clearly, and to read and listen with understanding.

If a secondary school faculty substituted *our* for *all*, it would have a statement of curricular goals, not that it is recommended that a statement of philosophy, aims, goals, or objectives be taken bodily from some source external to the school's faculty. The process of developing these statements is as important as—and may even be more important than—the products themselves.

The statement of the curricular goals is the first step in applying the school's statement of philosophy and aims. The Dade County (Florida) Public Schools have developed a statement of goals which they refer to as "Goals for Student Development." This statement is reproduced as an illustration of a school-systemwide effort to spell out the curricular goals of that system.[14] This statement of goals furnishes an excellent illustration of the way in which a local school system takes a statement of goals developed by the state and modifies that statement to fit its own needs.[15]

Goals for Student Development

Goal Area I:

Communication and Learning Skills. Students shall acquire, to the extent of their individual physical, mental, and emotional capacities, a mastery of the basic skills required in obtaining and expressing ideas through the effective use of words, numerals and other symbols.

a) Students shall achieve a working knowledge of reading, writing, speaking and arithmetic during the elementary school years, accompanied by gradual progress into the broader fields of mathematics, natural science, language arts and the humanities.

b) Students shall develop and use skills in the logical processes of search, analysis, evaluation and problem-solving, in critical thinking, and in the use of symbolism.

c) Students shall develop competence and motivation for continuing self-evaluation, self-instruction and adaptation to a changing environment.

d) Students shall have the opportunity during the elementary school years to develop and use the skills of speaking and understanding a foreign language in order to communicate effectively in the language for future personal or vocational achievements.

Goal Area II:

Citizenship Education. Students shall acquire and continually improve the habits and attitudes necessary for responsible citizenship.

a) Students shall acquire knowledge of various political systems with emphasis on democratic institutions, the heritage of the United States, the contributions of our diverse cultural backgrounds, and the responsibilities and privileges of citizenship.

b) Students shall develop the skills required for participation in the political processes of our country and for influencing decisions made by political organizations.
c) Students shall develop the competence and desire to become informed and critical participants in the electoral process of this country.
d) Students shall acquire those attributes necessary for functioning, on a daily basis, as good citizens in their own school and community settings.

Goal Area III:

Career and Occupational Education. Students shall acquire a knowledge and understanding of the opportunities open to them for preparing for a productive life, and shall develop those skills and abilities which will enable them to take full advantage of those opportunities— including a positive attitude toward work and respect for the dignity of all honorable occupations.
a) Students shall acquire knowledge of and develop an understanding of the fundamental structure and processes of America's economic system, together with an understanding of the opportunities and requirements for individual participation and success in this changing system.
b) Students shall develop occupational competencies, consistent with their interests, aptitudes and abilities, which are necessary for entry and advancement in the economic system; they shall develop those academic competencies necessary for the acquisition of technical or professional skills through post-high school training.
c) Students shall develop competence in the application of economic knowledge to practical economic functions: such as, planning and budgeting for the investment of personal income, calculating tax obligations, financing major purchases, and obtaining desirable employment.
d) Students shall develop an awareness of the relevance of the curriculum to the world of work and our social existence.

Goal Area IV:

Mental and Physical Health. Students shall acquire good health habits and an understanding of the conditions necessary for the maintenance of physical, emotional, and social well-being.
a) Students shall develop an understanding of the requirements of personal hygiene, adequate nutrition and leisure time activities essential to the maintenance of physical health, and a knowledge of the dangers to mental and physical health from addiction and other aversive practices.
b) Students shall develop skills in sports and other forms of recreation which will provide for life-long enjoyment of participation according to their own preferences and abilities.
c) Students shall develop competence in recognizing and preventing environmental health problems.
d) Students shall acquire a knowledge of basic psychological and sociological factors affecting human behavior and mental health, and shall develop competence for adjusting to changes in personal status and social patterns.

Goal Area V:

Home and Family Relationships. Students shall develop an appreciation of the family as a social institution.

a) Students shall develop an understanding of their roles and the roles of others as members of a family, together with a knowledge of the requirements for successful participation in family living.
b) Students shall develop an understanding of the role of the family as a basic unit in the society.
c) Students shall develop an awareness of the diversity of family patterns and the value of the contributions of the individuals to family and community living.

Goal Area VI:

Aesthetic and Cultural Appreciations. Students shall develop understanding and appreciation of human achievement in the natural sciences, the humanities and the arts.
a) Students shall acquire a knowledge of and an appreciation for major arts, music, literary and drama forms, and their place in the cultural heritage.
b) Students shall acquire a knowledge of the natural, physical and social sciences and their relationships to human and social development.
c) Students shall develop skills for creative use of leisure time and shall develop an interest in becoming active in one or more areas of creative endeavor.
d) Students shall develop discrimination skills in the critical evaluation of cultural offerings and opportunities.

Goal Area VII:

Human Relations. Students shall develop a concern for moral, ethical and spiritual values and for the application of such values to life situations.
a) Students shall acquire the greatest possible understanding and appreciation of themselves as well as of persons belonging to social, cultural and ethnic groups different from their own, and of the worthiness of all persons as members of society.
b) Students shall develop those skills and attitudes necessary for positive interpersonal and group relationships and shall recognize the importance of and need for ethical and moral standards of behavior.
c) Students shall recognize the value of that level of group discipline and self-discipline that promotes a sense of worth of the individual while contributing to the collective benefit of all involved.

Writing Curricular Objectives

Up to this point the first two phases of the curriculum development process have been completed—the faculty has threshed out its statement of philosophy and has adopted a statement of curricular goals. The supervisor then takes them into the task of specifying curricular objectives. Statements of curricular objectives must ultimately be drafted and accepted on two levels: first, schoolwide (or school-systemwide), cutting across disciplines and grade levels, and second, within a particular discipline or grade level. The Committee on Philosophy, Aims, Goals, and Objectives may be charged with the task of developing the set of schoolwide objectives, while special committees from the disciplines or grade levels may undertake the job of specifying curricular objectives peculiar to their special fields.

The progression from the statement of philosophy and aims to the statement of goals and finally to the statement of objectives is increasingly more specific. As was observed in writing the statements of goals, the statements of objectives should focus on what the learner does as opposed to what the school does. Well-defined curricular objectives meet the same standards as well-defined instructional objectives. They state what learners are expected to achieve, under what conditions they must demonstrate the behavior, and what level of performance they must attain. A distinction may be made between these criteria as they apply to instructional objectives and as they apply to curricular objectives. The latter is concerned with the achievement of groups of students; the former is concerned with the achievement of individual students in a class or subject.

As a general rule, it seems best when writing both goals and objectives in whatever area—instruction, curriculum, administration, supervision, or other area—to focus on the person or persons who must perform the desired behavior. This is particularly important in the case of objectives. The subsequent process of evaluation is simplified when the evaluator knows who does what under what conditions and to what degree of mastery. If the objectives do not show these elements, the evaluator needs first to revise the objectives so that these elements are clearly shown.

Some faculties write their curricular goals and objectives in terms of what the school—and by inference the school's program or curriculum—will do rather than what the learners will do. Let's contrast the two ways of writing statements of goals and objectives by hypothesizing a junior-senior high school, grades 7–12, composed predominantly of a white, English-speaking student body, whose faculty believes the students should have some exposure to another language and culture. The faculty might write a curricular goal statement—typical of many which can be found—which emphasizes the school's role: The school should promote an understanding of another culture through the medium of foreign language study. Contrast that statement with the following statement, which starts off by mentioning the learners: Students should gain an understanding of another culture through the medium of foreign language study. Admittedly, there is not a great deal of difference between these two goal statements, and the differences are not crucial in goal statements, for in practice we do not measure achievement of goals; we measure achievement of objectives.

Let us assume this same faculty attempts to write an objective for achieving the aforementioned goal. It might come up with: The school will extend the study of Spanish downward from the high school to include grades 7, 8, and 9, making a seven-year sequence. This statement omits mention of the learners, does specify the action (extend the study . . . sequence), does not mention conditions under which the action will take place, and offers no level of performance which would be helpful in subsequent evaluation.

The supervisor might suggest a revised version of the objective such as: In keeping with a three-year developmental plan, by the end of next year every student in the ninth grade will have the opportunity to elect Spanish and one-third of the ninth graders will have enrolled in Spanish; by the end of the second year every student in the eighth grade will have the opportunity to elect Spanish and one-fourth of the eighth graders will have enrolled in the study of Spanish; by the end of the third year every student in the seventh grade will have completed a one-semester exploratory course in Spanish.

Does this latter illustration of a curriculum objective meet the criteria for a well-defined objective? It can be concluded that it does. First, it focuses on the student. Second, it specifies the action; the students will have the opportunity and will enroll (enrolling actually being the action). Third, it spells out the conditions under which the action takes place; in keeping with a three-year development plan, by the end of the next year, by the end of the second year, by the end of the third year, and a one-semester exploratory course. Finally, it establishes a level of performance: every student in the ninth grade, one-third of the ninth graders; every student in the eighth grade, one-fourth of the eighth graders; and every student in the seventh grade. These levels of performance illustrate the distinction made earlier between level of performance in the case of curricular objectives and level of performance in respect to instructional objectives. The level of performance in the case of a curricular objective is measured in reference to the achievement of groups of learners, while the level of performance in the case of an instructional objective is measured for each individual.

The School Service Center of Florida Atlantic University has developed a statement of curricular objectives in connection with a needs assessment of a middle school.[16]

Curriculum

At the beginning of the school year, at least 90% of the students will complete a reading inventory.

After completing the reading inventory, each student determined to be deficient in reading skill will take reading instruction at least two days a week, at least 30 minutes each day.

During the regular school year, at least 90% of the students will take at least three exploratory courses.

When school is in session, at least 90% of the students will identify which objective to begin after completing a given objective.

During the regular school year, at least 80% of the students in years 7 and 8 will work with content material based on abstractions (abstractions as opposed to concrete) to complete at least 60% of their instructional objectives.

During the regular school year, at least 80% of the students in year 6 will work with content material that is based on concrete material (concrete as opposed to abstract) to complete at least 50% of their instructional objectives.

During the school year, at least 75% of the students will do independent research to complete at least 1% of their instructional tasks. Independent research is to be characterized by each of the following:

1. a problem
2. independence of student to study and solve problem
3. resources available for student to study
4. final product

During the school year, at least 90% of the students will work independently (individually, at their own rate) to complete at least 40% of their instructional objectives.

For each nine week period while school is in session, at least 90% of the students will spend at least 30 hours in a human relations course where students can both learn about and practice both human relations skills and group dynamics.

During the regular school sessions, at least 90% of the students will take two 12-week daily living courses which include learning experiences in each of the following areas:

buying insurance	applying for social security number
public service agencies	checking and banking accounts
using the newspaper	income tax preparation
installment loans	

It will be noted that these curricular objectives, which are referred to as performance objectives, contain the essential elements of a well-defined objective. They state what the learners will do, under what conditions, and what level of group performance is required for each curricular objective to be considered as accomplished.

Periodically, the faculty of a school should subject its curriculum to this type of comprehensive study. It gives the faculty an opportunity to look at the curriculum in toto and to avoid the common error in curriculum development, a patchwork approach of adding and dropping courses and units.

If there are specialist supervisors available in the school system which is conducting a curriculum study, these supervisors may enter into the process when the comprehensive study has been completed and initiate the development of goals and objectives pertinent to the particular specialties or grade levels. The goals and objectives of the special fields or grade levels must be compatible with the general goals and objectives of the school.

Curriculum Guides

The specialist can help teachers take a comprehensive look at an entire discipline, field, or grade level. For example, the supervisor may work with the social studies teachers of a secondary school with the object of improving the entire social studies program. Writing a curriculum guide which covers the entire sequence of a field, in this case social studies, is a common way by which teachers become involved in systematic study of a particular field or across fields.[17]

A curriculum guide is a general plan for a particular sequence of courses within a discipline, for a particular sequence of grade levels, or for interdisciplinary programs. A curriculum guide may also be written for a particular grade level or course within a discipline. The guide should include at least the following elements:

1. Introduction, which should include (1) some reference to the school's statement of philosophy and aims; (2) some reference to schoolwide curriculum goals and objectives which pertain to the field, e.g., citizenship; and (3) curriculum goals and objectives for all students in the particular field or grade levels.

2. Instructional goals.
3. Instructional objectives.
4. Learning activities.
5. Evaluation techniques.
6. Resources, both human and material.

The curriculum guide offers teachers many ideas and choices. We find guides, for example, on Language Arts K–4, Career Education in the Junior High School, and Mathematics Grades 4–6. Teachers develop a variety of curriculum materials or products. When a curriculum product is limited, as it may be, to a detailed plan for an individual course as, for example, twelfth-grade American History, it becomes a course of study (see below). When a curriculum product is limited, as it may be, to a general plan for teaching a particular topic, it becomes a resource unit (see below).

One of the advantages of curriculum projects exemplified by the creation of curriculum guides, courses of study, and resource units lies in the fact that teachers not only go through the process—a valuable outcome in and of itself—but they come out with a useful product.

The task of writing curriculum materials clearly demonstrates again the inseparability of curriculum and instruction. When we include instructional goals and objectives, activities, resources, and evaluation techniques in the materials, we are moving from programmatic concerns (curriculum) into methodology (instruction). In practice, when teachers write curriculum guides, courses of study, and resource units, they go beyond the curriculum questions of *what? when? where?* and by *whom?* and into the instructional question of *how?*

As curriculum development narrows from study of the entire curriculum of the school, to study of the curriculum of an entire sequence within the total curriculum, to study of the curriculum of a course or grade level to study of a particular topic, curriculum goals and objectives actually change into instructional goals and objectives. The emphasis shifts from levels of performance of groups of students, which would serve as an indicator of the success of the curriculum, to levels of mastery expected of individuals, which would serve as an indicator of the success of instruction.

Below are illustrations of curriculum and instructional goals and objectives. We will take one example of a goal and one example of an objective from each of four kinds of curriculum materials.

1. From a *comprehensive study* of an elementary school mathematics sequence which specified curriculum goals and objectives:
Curriculum goal: Students should complete the mathematics sequence with competencies in mathematics which will enable them to function in their daily personal transactions.
Curriculum objective: On completion of the mathematics sequence at least 90 percent of the sixth-graders will score a grade of 75 percent or better on the terminal mathematics test developed by the elementary school teachers in cooperation with the mathematics supervisor.
2. From an early childhood *curriculum guide* on health education:

Instructional goal: The student will understand the necessity for developing sanitary personal habits.

Instructional objective: The student will wash his or her hands after using the lavatory.

3. From an eighth-grade English *course of study*:

Instructional goal: The student will understand the differences between linking verbs, transitive verbs, and intransitive verbs.

Instructional objective: On completion of a learning package on types of verbs the student will be able to identify linking verbs, transitive verbs, and intransitive verbs in a literary passage supplied by the teacher with 90 percent accuracy.

4. From a *resource unit* on Common Home Repairs for a ninth-grade course in industrial arts:

Instructional goal: The student will realize how much money can be saved by doing his or her own home repairs.

Instructional objective: The student will repair a leaking kitchen faucet.

Curriculum guides are a type of product which can come out of a comprehensive curriculum study.

The Problem-centered Approach

While teachers do not always see the advantage or necessity of carrying out a complete and comprehensive review of the curriculum, they can become highly motivated to pursue study of curricular problems which they themselves have identified. One or more teachers may wish, for example, to study ways of improving the reading program of the elementary school. A group of teachers might desire to find better ways of caring for the needs of the exceptional children in the school. A number of teachers might be interested in developing a program in ethnic studies. The science teachers might express dissatisfaction with the school biology program and wish to overhaul it. A couple of teachers in English might be motivated to try out a team-teaching approach in their classes. The teachers of the primary grades might like to experiment with an open-space program in their grades. The mathematics teachers in a middle school as a result of studying the achievement of their students in mathematics might begin to raise the question of whether their mathematics program is suitable for the learners in their classes. The problems which teachers identify and the revisions of programs or innovations which they suggest may be within a particular field or grade level or may cut across fields and grade levels. In either case the problems or programs are specific pieces of the curriculum and not the total curriculum of the school nor even the total sequence of a particular field. For that reason, the study of specific problems and programs is referred to as the problem-centered approach.

Following the problem-centered approach the supervisor responds to needs identified by the teachers. This does not mean that the supervisor must act only as a responder to teachers' needs but should also serve as a galvanizer, an idea person who assists teachers in identifying curricular problems and innovative programs. In this capacity the supervisor suggests ideas to teachers and attempts to stimulate their interest by raising questions such as: "What would you think of . . .?" "Have you thought about this kind of program?" "Do you think such a plan would work in our school?" "I just came across a report of a successful program at a school in New Mexico, would you care to read about it?" The supervisor and the teachers jointly share the responsibility for uncovering problems as well as working toward their solution.

The problem-centered approach has a great deal of psychological merit, for teachers view this as an approach which will help them with problems or programs with which they are intimately involved. As an alternative to identifying a special problem or a particular program the supervisor might suggest that the teachers work with him or her on the development of a year's course of study or syllabus for a particular subject or grade or on the construction of a resource unit on a particular topic to be presented during the year.

Courses of Study.   A course of study is a curriculum document which covers only one subject or one year's work. Some people refer to a course of study as a *syllabus*. Typically, a syllabus is an outline of topics of a course whereas a course of study includes several features in addition to the topics. Minimal elements which should be included in a course of study are:

1. instructional goals
2. instructional objectives
3. entry skills necessary for successful pursuit of the subject
4. sequence of topics or units
5. suggested activities and resources
6. suggested evaluation techniques

Some courses of study include all text materials and tests in addition to the elements listed above, making the course of study highly prescriptive.

Resource Units.   The creation of a resource unit is a still narrower curriculum planning exercise in which a group of teachers prepares a curriculum document that focuses on a particular topic. For example, a group of elementary school teachers might develop a resource unit on Our National Parks. A group of secondary school teachers of history might construct a resource unit on World War I. The resource unit provides suggestions which teachers can utilize in developing unit plans for study of the topic in their own courses or grades. Minimal components of a resource unit are:

1. instructional goals
2. instructional objectives
3. suggested activities and resources
4. suggested evaluation techniques

Thus, we can trace the production of curriculum documents or products from curriculum guide, to course of study, to resource unit, to teaching/learning unit to, finally, the daily lesson plan.

The process in which a group of teachers studies its curriculum and creates curriculum materials is curriculum development, while the process by which teachers, singly or in combinations, carry out the curriculum is instruction.

The problem-centered approach should be followed in addition to but not in place of the comprehensive approach. The problem-centered approach permits the teachers to take a close look at the trees but without the comprehensive approach they may not see the forest. Both the comprehensive approach and the problem-centered approach have the same point of departure: specification of goals and objectives. It is axiomatic that teachers should define where they are leading the learners before they jump into their vehicles and take off.

Design of the Plan

Between the completion of the statement of objectives and the implementation stage, curriculum plans must be drawn up. A curriculum plan, which will ordinarily be written by a committee of teachers, should be presented in the form of a proposal to the entire faculty of which the committee is representative. When the curriculum change to be recommended is small, requiring no new resources and involving no great changes in staffing patterns or assignments, the plan may be a very simple one. When teachers decide to recommend a major innovative program which will involve new distributions of resources and staff, a detailed proposal is necessary. A good deal of study, research, and thought must go into the development of a proposed plan. A full-blown proposal consists of the following parts:

1. description of the proposed plan, including a time schedule for its implementation
2. rationale and justification for the plan or program
3. summary of the research related to the plan or program, with information on the success or failure of similar plans or programs elsewhere, if any
4. human and material resources needed, including facilities necessary
5. estimated costs of the plan or program
6. a plan for evaluating the success of the innovation

It can be seen that the development of a curriculum proposal is not a job that can be entered into lightly. It requires serious study and intelligent consideration of the many factors involved. It is all well and good, for example, for a group of teachers to propose that an elementary school institute a program of bilingual education. But what are the implications in such a proposal? What components of a bilingual education should be included? English as a second language only? Instruction for native speakers of a language other than English in their own language? What would be the justification for offering such a program? What resources would be needed?

How many new staff would be required? Where would staff be obtained? What printed materials and media would be required? Where would classes be held? What might have to be removed from the curriculum to find time for the new study proposed? What would the new program cost the school district? How will the success of the program be determined? The supervisor plays a vital role in helping teachers find answers to these questions so that a reasonable and possible proposal can be drafted.

A school or school system must establish the machinery for review and ratification of curriculum proposals, for an active faculty can generate numerous proposals and it is apparent that not all proposals can be endorsed and implemented. A common route for curriculum proposals is from a group of teachers to the principal. If the change proposed is within the jurisdiction of the school alone and the school has the resources necessary, the principal can, if he wishes, endorse the proposal and it can be implemented. If aspects of the proposal go beyond the school and particularly if they necessitate new funds and staffing, the principal will have to refer the proposal to the superintendent and the superintendent may then need to seek support from the school board. This route, however, bypasses a good many teachers who might have an interest in the proposed program or who might be affected directly or indirectly. When the reallocation of resources becomes a factor, every teacher is concerned. Consequently, some systematic procedure should be set up for faculty review, evaluation, and endorsement of curriculum proposals.

Universities typically follow a model which some public schools use and which has much to commend it. A standing curriculum committee of the university receives all curriculum proposals regardless of their source, reviews the proposals, holds hearings on the proposals, and ultimately approves or disapproves of the proposals. The curriculum committee's disapproval usually kills the proposal. If the committee approves, the proposal is placed before the entire faculty of the university for its approval or disapproval. Only after the entire faculty has given its endorsement to the proposal does it go on to the administration of the university for final approval or disapproval. The curriculum committee is elected by the faculty and its term of office is stipulated in the governance document of the institution.

The curriculum committee acts as a gatekeeper, screening out proposals, studying the implications in each proposal, and assuring a level of quality to the proposal. Each public school should have its elected curriculum committee to which all curriculum proposals emanating from its teachers should be directed. This process is slower than the route from a group of teachers directly to the administrator but it subjects proposals to a thorough and public analysis, prevents rash actions, and assures a broader basis of support from the faculty.

One of the major responsibilities of the curriculum committee and subsequently the entire faculty as it evaluates curriculum proposals is some consideration as to how the specific proposals fit into the grand scheme of the curriculum. All the bits and pieces of the curriculum should fit together and relate to each other. Reference should be made to the school's or school system's statements of philosophy, aims, goals, and objectives when action is being taken on specific proposals.

Up to this point the roles of teachers, supervisors, and administrators in the process of curriculum development have been stressed, but not to be omitted is input from students, the public, and other school personnel. While the faculty may carry the responsibility for curriculum development, efforts must be made from the stage of writing the philosophy through the endorsement of the curriculum proposal to obtain input from students, the nonprofessional staff, and the public. One way of achieving this input is through participation of these groups on school committees such as the Committee on Philosophy, Aims, Goals, and Objectives and the Curriculum Committee.

Schools have met with varying success at involving students and the public on professional committees. The maturity of the student and the availability of lay people are factors which must be weighed when school committees are established. In some cases school systems which are interested in obtaining federal grants for specific kinds of programs are required to involve lay people in planning and continuous participation, following a principle which is known as "parity." The federal government, the professional staff, and the lay persons are considered equal members of a team which initiates, develops, and administers the programs supported by federal moneys. Though the concept of parity sounds appealing, in practice it presents a number of difficulties. How the lay persons should be identified is a first question to be resolved. The continuing availability of lay people for curriculum study is a recurring problem. When the faculty is considering a professional and technical problem, lay persons may not have the expertness to make input and when this situation arises, they either defer to the professional staff or the professional staff consumes an inordinate amount of time to orient the lay people.

At any rate, input from groups other than the faculty is vitally necessary. In the following chapter the technique of needs assessment will be discussed as an alternative to or supplementary to student and public participation on school committees.

Implementation

When all the endorsements to a curriculum proposal have been obtained and the administrator has given the green light, the plan can be implemented. The proposal has indicated who would carry out the program and under what conditions. A time schedule has been established showing when the program will begin, at what points it will be evaluated, and when a decision will be made on whether or not to continue the program.

The design of the plan spells out what will be covered in the program and the curriculum organization pattern necessary for carrying out the plan. At this stage detailed instructional goals and objectives must be set forth by the teachers delivering the content and appropriate strategies and resources selected. From this point on, the success of the curriculum plan is in the hands of the instructors. The supervisor continues to assist the teachers through the implementation stage. He or she works with them to put into effect the evaluation plan which is outlined in the curriculum proposal and helps them with both formative evaluation during the course of the program and summative evaluation at the end.

CONTINUING PROBLEMS OF CURRICULUM DEVELOPMENT

As teachers involve themselves in curriculum development they will encounter three recurrent and major problems: scope, sequence, and balance. Each of the three problems must be resolved during the planning stage, requiring some very difficult decisions on the part of a faculty.

Scope of the Curriculum

The scope of the curriculum consists of the experiences or subject matter or content to which the learners are exposed. The content of every field of learning is so vast and is expanding at such a rate that it is impossible to cover any field in its entirety, although many teachers appear to strive to do so. Some hard decisions must be made as to what content should be selected for inclusion in the curriculum and what limitations will be placed on that content. The delineation of the scope of the curriculum entails a search for answers to two basic questions: Who should make the decisions as to what content should be included in the curriculum? and What content should be included?

Who Should Decide on Content?

The question, "Who should decide on content?" is simpler to answer than the question, "What content should be included in the curriculum?" The professional faculty should make the decisions on the scope of the curriculum—and on sequence and balance as well—after obtaining as much input as possible from as many sources as possible, including students and the public.

A faculty, working as a total faculty, as a portion of the faculty, or as individual teachers, must decide what experiences, what courses, and what topics will become a part of the curriculum. Whether the entire faculty, a portion of the faculty, or individual teachers make the decisions on content depends on the aspect of the curriculum under consideration. The scope of the content would appear in a curriculum proposal and in a curriculum guide. As indicated earlier in this chapter major decisions on curriculum which affect more than one teacher and which involve the allocation of resources and staff should be put through the approval process with review by the curriculum committee and by the entire faculty. Curriculum decisions involving minor changes within fields or subjects and not involving questions of resource allocation and staffing are appropriately the prerogative of the particular teachers involved and need not go through the entire review process. The supervisor should help teachers in determining whether a curricular revision should be taken to the curriculum committee and the entire faculty. It would be not necessary, for example, for a group of Algebra I teachers to submit a revised course of study in Algebra I to the curriculum committee and then to the faculty as a whole. On the other hand, if the algebra teachers wished to lengthen the study of algebra from two years to three years that decision would be the province of the curriculum committee and the faculty as a whole. It is not necessary to involve the curriculum committee or the faculty in a review of resource units which fit into the scope of a particular grade or course or field, unless a proposed unit embodies content of a controversial nature which might reflect on the entire faculty. Teachers in health or science, for example, who wish to offer a unit or course or sequenced program on sex education would be well advised to seek faculty approval since a great deal of controversy surrounds this area of study.

Broad decisions on content fall within the jurisdiction of the entire faculty of the school or, in many cases, the faculties of the school system as a whole. For example, if a group of elementary school teachers proposes that the elementary school adopt a new reading program, its proposal must be considered by all teachers. On the other hand, if a group of modern language teachers decides to shift the program from a grammar-translation method to an audio-lingual method, the modern language teachers need not clear this through the total approval process. In this latter case the total faculty has made its input through endorsement of modern language study and need not concern itself with the specifics of content (for example, which authors are read) and the methodology to be employed. A group of English teachers who draft a resource unit on Contemporary British Novelists need not take its resource unit to the curriculum committee and entire faculty but may make the decisions on content in this case itself. The individual teacher also has freedom to choose content, for example, within the resource unit. He or she may choose to have students read a novel by William Golding instead of a novel by Alec Waugh which was suggested in the resource unit, or may substitute Golding's *Lord of the Flies* for *The Spire*. In short, teachers make decisions on content, sometimes in large groups, sometimes in small groups, and sometimes individually.

Teachers are compelled to make curriculum decisions within certain restrictions. Some decisions on content have already been made for the teacher. Decisions which have been made for the teacher tend to be broader in scope than those which individual teachers or groups of teachers will make. It is apparent that some decisions are of long standing. The curriculum of a school has been fleshed out by a group of planners before that school opens its doors. The existent curriculum of a school is one limit on the individual teacher's freedom to select content. The teacher of a fifth grade, for example, whose elementary school offers a program in Spanish cannot elect to toss out the Spanish and substitute German on the personal belief that German is a more important language than Spanish. If the teacher believes strongly that German should be taught instead of Spanish, other teachers must be involved in consideration of the idea and must present a plan through the established channels for faculty approval.

The locality, through the school board, and the state, through the state Department of Education and the state legislature, place some restrictions on the teachers' freedom to choose content. The tendency is for the locality and state to mandate certain offerings. A locality may stipulate, for example, that it will exceed the state's minimum requirements in certain subject fields. Where a state might demand a minimum of three years of social studies for graduation from high schools of the state, a locality might require four years. Where a state might require 45 minutes of instruction in reading per day in the elementary school, the locality might require one hour.

The local school board, elected by the people of the district and serving as agents of the state, has the power to make these kinds of decisions for the schools which it administers.

The state Department of Education, acting on authority delegated to it by the people of the state through their elected representatives, makes curricular decisions affecting all schools of the state. It sets minimal standards which all schools must meet. It often puts forth a statement of goals of education in the state, which should be considered by local faculties in the curriculum planning process.

The state legislature occasionally makes a foray into the curriculum arena. When state legislators translate their curricular beliefs into law, their decisions are binding on the schools. Thus, found in the curriculum are legislatively mandated courses on the effects of alcohol, tobacco, and drugs on the human body; on the election process; and on Americanism versus Communism.

One other impingement on the teacher's power to select content is the textbook. The textbooks used within a school act not only as a resource but also as a limitation on the teacher's choice of content. The teacher who is new to a school will find that textbooks have already been chosen. Teachers who are already on the scene may have some input into the process of selecting textbooks. The process normally calls for faculty recommendations, but textbooks are usually purchased in quantities as a result of either local or state procedures. Frequently, certain series of textbooks are adopted which must be used at various grade levels. Consequently, the individual teacher is bound by the final choices which have been made as a consequence of group deliberations. The individual teacher may or may not be pleased by the final choices made, but must, however, live with those choices for the school life of these textbooks, which is often five years. In some states multiple adoptions of textbooks are made and the teacher may select from a number of options, a procedure which expands his or her freedom to choose content.

The textbook is less of an infringement on the teacher's freedom to choose content if supplementary materials are available. Some schools and communities are richer in this respect than others. Supplementary materials permit the teacher to go beyond the textbook for additional information and other points of view. It should be added, parenthetically, however, that in some cases where supplementary materials are available, some teachers elect not to go beyond the adopted textbook. They find that reliance on a single textbook is an easier path to follow. The search for suitable supplementary materials and their incorporation into teaching plans require more time and more decisions on the part of the teacher. The supervisor has the continuing responsibility of helping in the search for useful materials and in making them known to teachers.

These limitations on the process of selecting content—by the locality, by the state, and by the adopted textbook—are less restrictive than they appear on the surface. The locality or state may require a particular field of study and may even supply a suggested curriculum guide—usually developed by a group of teachers—but countless decisions on content remain to be made by the teacher. Within a field the teacher must choose topics and methods for presenting those topics.

What Content Should Be Included?

More difficult to answer than "Who should select the content?" is the question, "What content should be selected?" Once the curricular decision has been made that the school will offer a particular program, whether that decision has been made by the existent curriculum, by the school's faculty, by faculties of the school district, by the school board, or by the state, the teacher who is designated to present that content has a multitude of decisions to make.

Every field covers an enormous territory of facts, skills, and attitudes from which selection has to be made. It should be more obvious than it seems to be that not all knowledge is of equal worth.[18] Although we are not likely to encounter much controversy in establishing the principle that not all knowledge is of equal worth, the curricula of the schools often seem structured in such a way as to imply that all knowledge is equally valuable. The most conspicuous example of this implication is the typical high school which allocates the same amount of time for every course in the curriculum, following the concept of the Carnegie unit which goes back to the first decade of the twentieth century. In attempting to decide on the scope of the curriculum teachers must keep in mind one overriding criterion: they should include in the curriculum that knowledge, those skills, and those affective learnings which are of most worth to the individual throughout life.

The teacher is the final judge as to which cognitive, affective, and psychomotor learnings will be taught to the students. After having made the difficult decisions of which learnings will be taught, he or she must organize the content into coherent form and follow that organization by presenting the content to the students.

The teacher may choose simply to follow the selected learnings, the organization, and the methodology of the adopted textbook. He or she may take the number of chapters or topics in the textbook, divide the number of chapters or topics by the number of weeks in the school year, and thereby calculate the number of weeks on each chapter or topic. In using this mechanical approach to content selection the teacher is deferring all content decisions to the authors of the textbook.

Teachers must inject themselves into the selection process and not be passive agents. They must make the decisions as to which content is of most worth and not permit decisions over which they have jurisdiction to be made by others. Since not all knowledge is of equal value, effort must be made by the teacher to set priorities on content. The supervisor must assist teachers in developing the skills of choosing or rejecting content and establishing criteria for priority of content.

One means of making curriculum decisions, derived from the work of Ralph W. Tyler, is known as the Tyler Rationale. The rationale, described below, has proved a popular means of thinking about the curriculum and selecting content.[19]

Robert M. Gagné asserted that there is no such activity as selection of content. Gagné defined content as "descriptions of the expected capabilities of students in specified domains of human activity."[20] He used the term "unit of content," which he defined as "a capability to be acquired under a single set of learning conditions, among these being certain specified prerequisite capabilities."[21] Gagné defined curriculum:

A curriculum is a sequence of content units arranged in such a way that the learning of each unit may be accomplished as a single act, provided the capabilities described by specified prior units (in the sequence) have already been mastered by the learner. It is evident from this definition that a curriculum may be of any length, that is, it may contain any number of units. A curriculum is specified when (1) terminal objectives are stated; (2) the sequence of prerequisite capabilities is described; and (3) the initial capabilities to be possessed by the students are identified.[22]

Gagné concluded:

Once objectives have been defined, there is no step in curriculum design that can legitimately be entitled "selecting content." This is because the capabilities of the learner are directly derivable from the objectives themselves, as when from the objective "adds fractions" one derives the content statement "capability of adding fractions." One can select textbooks, motion pictures, laboratory equipment, even teachers; but one does not select content. It is derived from objectives.[23]

Agreement with Gagné that there is no step in curriculum design called selecting content forces the conclusion that much of the literature on curriculum and instruction is off target, for a great deal of discussion has taken place on the selection of content. A number of models of instruction, including two shown in Chapter 3 of this text, include a component on selecting content.

One of the difficulties in defining content may be a semantic one, depending on how narrowly or broadly we define the term and in what particular context. Banathy, for example, used the word content in two ways—to convey the idea of the sum or the components of an instructional system, including persons, places, and things; and to signify those outcomes of learning, for example, knowledge and skills, which the learner acquires as a result of instruction.[24]

This text discusses selection of content in a broad context, meaning the selection of subject matter, courses, or topics which must subsequently be broken down into instructional goals and objectives from which content within a field may be said to derive. The Tyler Rationale provides one mechanism for making decisions on content and goals and objectives of that content.

The Tyler Rationale proposes that the curriculum worker consider three sources of content: the student, society, and the subject, and two screens: philosophy of education and psychology of learning. From the three sources are derived tentative general objectives (which might be either curricular or instructional goals). The general objectives are passed through the two screens to yield precise instructional objectives.

The rationale which bears Tyler's name has been widely depicted as shown in Figure 7.3.

Content is derived from the three sources: student, society, and subject. The rationale implies that each of the three sources is important and has a bearing on the curriculum decisions being made. Content being considered for inclusion in the curriculum should be weighed against the three sources and answers should be found to the questions: Does the content meet the needs of students? Does the content

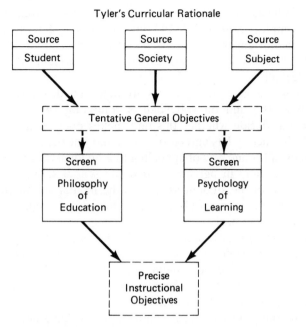

Tyler's Curricular Rationale

Figure 7.3 The Tyler Rationale

SOURCE: W. James Popham and Eva L. Baker, *Establishing Instructional Goals*, Englewood Cliffs, N.J., Prentice-Hall, 1970, p. 87. Based on Ralph W. Tyler, *Basic Principles of Curriculum and Instruction*, Chicago, University of Chicago Press, 1949. Copyright 1949 by the University of Chicago. All rights reserved. Reprinted with permission.

satisfy a societal need? Does the content fit into the internal logic of the subject matter and is it recommended by persons who are regarded as specialists in the field?

When it is determined that the content meets these tests, some tentative general objectives can be formulated. The teacher or teachers would then decide whether the content is compatible with their stated philosophy and whether the content is psychologically feasible. If the content meets these last two tests, it may be considered for inclusion in the curriculum.

Let us take as an illustration of the application of the rationale a situation in which a group of physical education teachers wish to introduce a unit on volleyball into the curriculum. First, we relate the unit on volleyball to the three sources.

Source: student. Does the unit meet needs of students? Yes, it does. Students have need for active sports. Volleyball develops a team spirit and provides an outlet for group competition. It is a sport which students themselves have requested. It is also a sport which they can carry over in adult life.

Source: society. Does the unit meet any societal need? Yes, it does. Adults have the need for wholesome recreation and volleyball is one way of satisfying this need. People of all ages can play volleyball and gain enjoyment from it.

Source: subject. Is volleyball an integral part of the field of physical education? Yes, it is. It is a sport recommended by many experts in the field of physical education as an excellent form of physical exercise and as a source of pleasure.

Since volleyball has met these three tests, we can draw up some tentative general objectives; for example, "Students should develop skills in carryover sports like volleyball," "Students not engaged in interscholastic sports should demonstrate physical fitness," "All students should learn to participate in team efforts such as those provided by volleyball."

After the tentative general objectives are determined, the teachers should ask themselves whether the unit on volleyball is compatible with their philosophical beliefs. They should decide whether this unit makes operational any philosophical statement which the faculty has agreed on. It should not be difficult to establish the position that volleyball is one way of appealing to individual differences and interests. Since faculties are usually in agreement that the school should contribute to the physical development of the student as well as the mental and intellectual development, volleyball would be compatible with the philosophy of education espoused by our hypothetical group of teachers.

The tentative general objectives must also be passed through the psychology of learning screen. The skills of volleyball are within the range of the learners at their stage of growth and development. Learners would be positively motivated to play volleyball and this activity would help them to satisfy basic psychological needs of success, approval, and movement.

The unit on volleyball has been demonstrated to have been derived from all three sources and to have successfully passed through the two screens. It is now the teacher's task to specify the precise instructional objectives; for example, "The student will demonstrate the proper way of serving," "On a paper-and-pencil test on the rules of the game of volleyball the student will achieve a score of 90 percent."

Tanner and Tanner discussed some of the problems in utilizing the Tyler Rationale, as the lack of apparent interaction among the three sources and the tendency toward mechanical application.[25] In spite of any seeming deficiencies the Tyler Rationale has provided a way of thinking about curriculum development and has withstood the test of time as a useful tool in this process.

Some systematic way of thinking is necessary in determining the scope of the curriculum. The supervisor should guide the teachers not only in the process of identification of content but in helping teachers to develop the skills of the process of thinking about the curriculum.

Sequence of the Curriculum

The scope of the curriculum tells what subject matter will be presented. The sequence of the curriculum tells in what order the subject matter will be presented. Faculties must sequence experiences, courses, series of courses (sequences of a discipline), and topics within courses. By custom pupils may not study fourth-grade mathematics until they have mastered third-grade mathematics. But what is there about the content of fourth-grade mathematics that demands completion of the content of third-grade mathematics? Some teachers never raise this kind of question. They have taken for granted grade placement of content—and placement of content within a grade level—

and have assumed that placement has been arrived at by deliberate thought, whereas placement of content has often been arbitrary. A common defense for grade placement of content is tradition—we have always done it this way. Surely, there must be more valid reasons why the content of fourth-grade mathematics follows the content of third-grade mathematics besides the fact that tradition has dictated the placement or that the number three precedes the number four in a sequence. The only defensible reason why the content of fourth-grade mathematics should follow the content of third-grade mathematics is that the content of the two levels are truly sequential— success in fourth-grade mathematics depends upon success in third-grade mathematics.

There must be some reason why teachers in the elementary school present addition first, then subtraction, follow with multiplication, and end with division. There must be a reason why algebra follows arithmetic and does not precede it. There must be a reason why calculus is delayed until the last year of the high school or until college level.

How do we account for the fact that World History precedes twelfth-grade Problems of Democracy in many high schools? Why are the civilizations of 2,000 years ago studied before those of the twentieth century? What makes the history of a state a seventh-grade subject rather than a tenth-grade subject? Why does geometry precede second-year algebra in some secondary schools? Why do students read Shakespeare's *Julius Caesar* before they read *Hamlet*?

These questions are problems of sequencing. Jerome S. Bruner caused us to think about the problem of sequencing when he hypothesized that "any subject can be taught effectively in some intellectually honest form to any child at any stage of development."[26] One inference from this hypothesis is that children are often capable of more than they have been given credit for. Must first-year algebra, for example, be reserved for eighth grade or ninth grade or can algebra be taught "in some intellectually honest form" to children as young as kindergarteners? This latter question suggests that two inquiries must be made when sequencing content. One is empirical: Can content be placed at a particular grade level or at a particular point within a grade level? The other is philosophical: Should content be placed at a particular grade level or at a particular point within a grade level? Does the fact that algebra *can* be taught to kindergarteners mean that algebra *should* be taught to kindergarteners? Over the years we have witnessed the shift of subject matter downward from college to the secondary school and from the secondary school to the elementary school. Has the shift been made after due consideration of the purposes for such a shift, or has the shift been made because of ill-defined reasons like "it seems the best thing to do"?

On what bases then may we determine the sequence of content? First, and rather obviously, simple content should precede complex content. Each step in complexity requires certain prerequisite knowledge and skills. This principle implies an analysis of the structure of the discipline, and examination of the internal logic of the subject matter. We teach the building blocks of language, the sounds, before we teach words. Mastery of the sound helps the learner in developing word-attack skills. We teach nouns before we teach pronouns—words which substitute for nouns. We teach concepts before we teach principles because we must have mastered the concepts before we can make use of them in rules.

Second, content must match the maturation level of the learners. Kindergarteners are not ready for cursive writing and this content must be delayed until children have developed enough coordination to write in cursive form. Lengthy content requiring a long span of attention must be placed appropriately for we know that the attention span of learners increases with age and acculturation. Work involving the use of hazardous tools and materials must be delayed until children are old enough to observe fundamental safety precautions.

Third, content which satisfies the immediate needs of learners usually precedes content aimed at long-term needs. The social studies curriculum of the elementary school is often organized according to this principle. Children study the world closest to them—their school, their home, their neighborhood, their community—before they look beyond to the state, then the nation, and finally the world at large. They learn to write personal letters before they learn to write essays, which meets not only the third principle—satisfaction of immediate needs of learners—but the first—simple content precedes complex—as well.

Fourth, sequences are determined often from the faculty's statements of philosophy aims, goals, and objectives. While these statements are more guides to scope, they may also provide direction for sequence. The sequence of modern language instruction today is derived from the philosophy, aims, goals, and objectives of the faculty. The goals of modern language instruction are, in order of priority: (1) understanding the language, (2) speaking the language, (3) reading the language, and (4) writing the language. Years ago reading and writing were the major goals, with little emphasis on understanding the spoken tongue and speaking it. As the goals changed, the content changed and the sequence of that content has been altered.

Fifth, chronological order serves as a guide to sequencing some content. History is normally taught in chronological order, as is the literature of certain epochs. This principle allows for a very logical sequence pattern but unfortunately it is not always the most motivating to the learner psychologically. Why, for example, couldn't the order of the history curriculum be reversed, starting with the most recent events—which would meet the criterion of immediate needs of learners—and working backward? Or, why is a more complicated pattern not possible: the study of a recent historical event coupled with the search for its antecedents in the past? What is there about nineteenth-century literature that would necessitate its study before twentieth-century literature?

Sequences must be established and sometimes these sequences will be arbitrary. When two units of content are of equal complexity and when the study of one is not dependent upon the prior study of the other, an arbitrary judgment must be made by the teacher as to which unit will come first. When each succeeding unit is progressively more complex and the series of units involves a hierarchy of knowledge and skills, some means must be found for ordering the sequence of units. Gagné recommended such a procedure, which he illustrated for a hypothetical curriculum consisting of five sequential units which require a hierarchy of skills from simpler to more complex.[27] He suggested the following steps be taken:

1. The teacher should prepare a terminal examination covering each unit of the curriculum.
2. The teacher should administer the test to a group of students who have not had instruction in any of the units to make sure that they have not learned the material elsewhere.
3. The teacher should administer the test to a group of students who have recently had the instruction. If a high percentage of students who have had the instruction pass the test, whereas a low percentage or none of the students who have not had the instruction pass the test, the teacher can deduce that the students have learned all material through the instruction and not elsewhere.
4. For each unit the teacher should analyze the results made by students who have had the instruction. If the series of five units has been properly sequenced, more students should have passed the first unit, the simplest, than the second unit, the next most difficult, on up to the fifth unit, which is the most difficult and the one which the fewest students would have passed. If the hierarchical sequence is correct, the results should correspond to the order in which the units were presented—1, 2, 3, 4, and 5. If students achieved passing scores in the order 1, 2, 4, 3, and 5, that is, more students passed the fourth unit, which is supposedly more difficult than the third unit, the units are out of sequence and should be resequenced; unit four should actually become unit three and three should become four.

In his analysis of sequencing Gagné also proposed a procedure for comparing scores made on adjacent units by pupils who passed the higher unit and pupils who passed the adjacent lower unit, a procedure which provides a further indication of proper sequencing and of the dependence of one unit upon another.

The task of sequencing content recalls the necessity of specifying and testing for entry skills. If there is a hierarchy of skills in a particular sequence and if success at each succeeding level is dependent upon success at a previous level, the teacher must preassess the presence of the necessary prerequisite skills.

When working with a group of teachers on the problem of sequencing of content, the supervisor should keep before the group the necessity of their answering the question: On what basis has the content been placed where it is?

Balance in the Curriculum

When teachers work together to outline the scope of the curriculum, they must give attention not only to what content will be included in the curriculum but also to the relationship between the various segments of the curriculum. They must strive to implement the principle of balance. The concept of balance implies that no portion of the curriculum will exert an overwhelming pressure on another portion of the curriculum.

The school's curriculum is out of balance when the school is known only for its razzle-dazzle marching band or its powerhouse of a football team. The curriculum is out of balance when children are made to study outmoded content which will be obsolete by the time they finish school. The curriculum is out of balance when it revolves completely around content of the learners' choice.

While some of the decisions on balance are internal to a particular subject or discipline, many of the decisions are interdisciplinary in nature and must be resolved by the total faculty. Vested interests play a part in making decisions on balance and it takes a larger group beyond the vested interests to assure a balanced curriculum. Among the aspects of a curriculum which require balancing are the following.

1. *There must be a balance between general education and specialized education.* Since general education is a main function of the elementary school, imbalance between general education—courses or experiences required of all students—and specialized education is more common to the secondary school. General education equips the student to cope with problems of daily living, to develop certain basic knowledge and skills, to become familiar with our culture, and to develop attitudes and competencies of good citizenship. Specialized education seeks to develop knowledge and skills within a discipline and is often preparatory to advanced study of the discipline.

When there is imbalance we find specialized education stressed over general education or vice versa. Since most teachers have a strong commitment to their own teaching fields, they naturally become strong partisans for study of their disciplines and there can be a tug-of-war for the loyalties and interests of the students. Both general education and specialized education are important and one should not eclipse the other.

2. *There must be a balance between the academic and the vocational aspects of the curriculum.* The college prep sequence of a comprehensive high school should not consume all the attention and resources of the school. In vocational schools a sizable portion of the curriculum should be allocated to general education. The movement toward career education has resulted in the inclusion of vocationally oriented experiences in the curriculum from the elementary grades through high school.

3. *There must be a balance between content aimed at the immediate and the long-range needs of learners.* Though it is advisable to begin with studies that satisfy the immediate needs of learners, a faculty is negligent if it builds its curriculum exclusively on children's immediate needs. Children are not mature enough to recognize some of the needs they will experience later in life. Teachers must help youngsters to attempt to recognize the value of certain content which is being required to satisfy future needs. On the other hand, the appeal to future needs alone is a common defense which teachers use to get pupils to pursue studies in which they have little interest. Education is both preparation for life and training in the here and now. The content of the curriculum should reflect balance between satisfaction of present and future needs.

4. *There must be a balance between the child-centered approach and the subject-centered approach to curriculum.* These two approaches have historically locked horns with the subject-centered curriculum coming out on top in most cases, with the possible exception of the heyday of progressive education in the 1930s. A rapproche-

ment has taken place since the end of World War II. The subject matter curriculum had a brief and intense revival in the late 1950s as a reaction to Russian progress in science and technology and has once again surged to the forefront with the renewed emphasis on basic skills. What is needed is an effort to balance the best features of the child-centered curriculum with the best features of the subject-centered curriculum, with the realization on the part of teachers that you cannot divorce the learner from what is being learned.

The foregoing aspects of the concept of balance require study and decisions on the part of teachers in all disciplines and at all grade levels. The principle of balance must be applied as well within disciplines and within courses. A common imbalance in the English curriculum, for example, at the secondary school level, and almost universal on the college level, is the heavy concentration on the study of literature to the detriment of the study of the language. The curriculum of a discipline is out of balance when students encounter the content through rote memorization to the exclusion of problem solving. The curriculum is out of balance when teachers consume an inordinate amount of time on special interests of their own and ignore other vital content. The supervisor should be continuously examining the curriculum for imbalance and should lead teachers in finding ways to correct the imbalance.

SUMMARY

Curriculum is conceived as all the experiences the learner undergoes under the supervision of the school. Curriculum development or improvement is a continuous process engaged in by faculties under the leadership of the supervisor.

Curriculum development begins with a statement of philosophy and aims agreed upon by consensus of the faculty. The school's statement of philosophy and aims is translated first into broad curriculum goals, then into specific curricular objectives. The curriculum goals and objectives have a direct bearing on the instructional goals and objectives in each course or grade level.

Two approaches to curriculum development are suggested: the comprehensive approach, which provides for an overall study of the curriculum, and the problem-centered approach, which focuses on problems identified by teachers and on segments of the curriculum.

A six-part model for curriculum development is presented in the text. The components of this model are: statement of philosophy and aims, statement of curriculum goals, statement of curriculum objectives, design of the plan, implementation of the curriculum, and evaluation of the curriculum. Both the comprehensive approach and the problem-centered approach have a place in curriculum study and are sometimes carried on concurrently.

Three continuing problems of curriculum development demand the attention of the supervisor and teachers: scope, sequence, and balance. Guidelines for coping with these problems are suggested.

The supervisor plays an instrumental role in promoting curriculum development. It is recommended that nonprofessional school personnel, lay persons, and students be brought into the process of curriculum development.

ACTIVITIES FOR FURTHER STUDY

1. Write a paper stating your opinions of deficiencies in curriculum leadership today and how you as a supervisor will attempt to overcome those deficiencies.
2. Outline basic philosophical beliefs you hold about education.
3. Describe responsibilities of supervisors who consider themselves "curriculum workers."
4. Select an elementary school subject at one grade level or a secondary school subject, break a year's work into units, and place the units in sequence. Justify your sequence.
5. Locate a statement of philosophy and aims of a school you know well, examine it, and report where practices in the school are in keeping with the stated philosophy and aims, and where the philosophy and aims are not being implemented.
6. Repeat exercise 5 with the school's statement of curriculum goals.
7. Repeat exercise 5 with the school's statement of curriculum objectives.
8. Find evidences of imbalance in a school's curriculum and suggest ways to correct the imbalance.
9. Give your own definition of curriculum.
10. Take a position on the premise that curriculum and instruction are interrelated but separate entities.
11. Write an illustration of a curriculum goal and two curriculum objectives derived from the goal.
12. Illustrate the difference between a curriculum goal and an instructional goal by writing an example of each.
13. Illustrate the difference between an instructional goal and an instructional objective by writing an example of each.
14. Explain the differences between a comprehensive approach to curriculum development and a problem-centered approach.
15. Locate a curriculum guide and evaluate it on the basis of criteria discussed in this chapter.
16. Locate a course of study and evaluate it on the basis of criteria discussed in this chapter.
17. Draw a chart of the Tyler Rationale and explain its components.
18. *Those who are teaching*: list several curricular problems you believe are in need of study in your school. *Those who are not teaching*: interview a teacher in a school and report problems identified by that teacher.
19. *Those who are teaching*: explain the process by which curriculum proposals are adopted in your schools. *Those who are not teaching*: explain how you believe curriculum proposals should be adopted.
20. Check on the process of curriculum development in any school of your choosing and report whether students and lay persons are involved in the process and if so, how.
21. Examine a sequence in operation in any elementary or secondary school and report on what bases the sequencing decisions were made.

22. Search the literature and report on any continuing problems of curriculum development other than scope, sequence, and balance. (Suggested reference: Peter F. Oliva, *Developing the Curriculum*, Chapter 14.)

23. Suggest curriculum elements which need balancing in addition to those described in this chapter. (Suggested reference: Peter F. Oliva, *Developing the Curriculum*, pp. 462–465.)

24. Analyze a curriculum guide or course of study in your field or grade level and explain how decisions on scope were made.

NOTES

1. Carter V. Good, ed., *Dictionary of Education*, 3rd ed., New York, McGraw-Hill, 1973, 158.

2. Daniel Tanner and Laurel N. Tanner, *Curriculum Development: Theory into Practice*, New York, Macmillan, 1975, 620.

3. See Robert J. Fisher, *Learning How to Learn: The English Primary School and American Education*, New York, Harcourt Brace Jovanovich, 1972.

4. See T. Husén, ed., *International Study of Achievement in Mathematics*, 2 vols., New York, John Wiley, 1967.

5. James B. Conant, *The Education of American Teachers*, New York, McGraw-Hill, 1963.

6. National Study of School Evaluation, *Elementary School Evaluative Criteria*, Falls Church, Va., National Study of School Evaluation, 1981, 39. See also *Middle School/Junior High School Evaluative Criteria*, rev. ed., 1979, 39, and *Evaluative Criteria*, 5th ed. (for secondary schools), 1978, 30, from the same source.

7. Carbondale Community High School District 165, Carbondale, Ill.

8. Commission on the Reorganization of Secondary Education, *Cardinal Principles of Secondary Education*, Washington. D.C., United States Office of Education, Bulletin no. 35, 1918.

9. *Elementary School Evaluative Criteria*, 40.

10. *Middle School/Junior High School Evaluative Criteria*, 37–44.

11. Ibid., 39.

12. *Evaluative Criteria*, 5th ed., 30.

13. Educational Policies Commission, *Education for All American Youth*, Washington, D.C. National Education Association, 1944, 216.

14. Dade County Public Schools, *District Comprehensive Educational Plan, Fiscal Years 1974–79*; Miami, Fla., 1974, 8–11. Reprinted with permission.

15. See State Department of Education, *Goals for Education in Florida*, Tallahassee, Fla., n.d.

16. Florida Atlantic University, *Middle School Needs Assessment Performance Objectives*, Boca Raton, Fla., Florida Atlantic University, Division of Continuing Education, School Service Center, 1972, Section 5.

17. For helpful script and transparencies on writing curriculum guides see Marilyn Winters, *Preparing Your Curriculum Guide*, Alexandria, Va., Association for Supervision and Curriculum Development, 1980.

18. See Arno Bellack, "What Knowledge Is of Most Worth?" *The High School Journal* 48, no. 5 (February 1965): 318–332. See also Herbert Spencer, "What Knowledge Is of Most Worth?" in *Education: Intellectual, Moral, and Spiritual*, New York: John B. Alden, 1885, 32. Reprinted in 1963 by Littlefield, Adams, Paterson, N. J.

19. Ralph W. Tyler, *Basic Principles of Curriculum and Instruction*, Chicago, University of Chicago Press, 1949.

20. Robert M. Gagné, "Curriculum Research and the Promotion of Learning," *AERA Monograph Series on Evaluation: Perspectives of Curriculum Evaluation*, no. 1, Chicago, Rand McNally, 1967, 21.

21. Ibid., 22.
22. Ibid., 23.
23. Ibid., 22.
24. Bela H. Banathy, *Instructional Systems*, Belmont, Calif., Fearon, 1968, 7 and 87.
25. Tanner and Tanner, 2nd ed., 1980, 83–97.
26. Jerome S. Bruner, *The Process of Education*, Cambridge, Mass., Harvard University Press, 1960, 33.
27. Gagné, 29–33.

BIBLIOGRAPHY

Association for Supervision and Curriculum Development. *Balance in the Curriculum*, 1961 Yearbook. Alexandria, Va.: Association for Supervision and Curriculum Development, 1961.
———. *Leadership for Improving Instruction*, 1960 Yearbook. Alexandria, Va.: Association for Supervision and Curriculum Development, 1960.
———. *Role of the Supervisor and Curriculum Director in a Climate of Change*, 1965 Yearbook. Alexandria, Va.: Association for Supervision and Curriculum Development, 1965.
Banathy, Bela H. *Instructional Systems*. Belmont, Calif.: Fearon, 1968.
Bruner, Jerome S. *The Process of Education*. Cambridge, Mass.: Harvard University Press, 1960. Rev. 1977.
Conant, James B. *The Education of American Teachers*. New York: McGraw-Hill, 1963.
"Curriculum Implementation." *Educational Leadership* 37 (December 1979): 204–267.
"The Curriculum Planning Process." *Educational Leadership* 38 (May 1981): 598–632.
Doll, Ronald C. *Curriculum Improvement: Decision Making and Process*, 5th ed. Boston: Allyn and Bacon, 1982.
Frymeier, Jack R., and Horace C. Hawn. *Curriculum Improvement for Better Schools*. Worthington, Ohio: Charles A. Jones, 1970.
Gagné, Robert M. "Curriculum Research and the Promotion of Learning." *AERA Monograph Series on Evaluation: Perspectives of Curriculum Evaluation*, no. 1. Chicago: Rand McNally, 1967.
Oliva, Peter F. *Developing the Curriculum*. Boston: Little, Brown, 1982.
Oliver, Albert I. *Curriculum Improvement: A Guide to Problems, Principles, and Process*, 2nd ed. New York: Harper & Row, 1977.
Popham, W. James, and Eva L. Baker. *Establishing Instructional Goals*. Englewood Cliffs, N.J.: Prentice-Hall, 1970.
Pratt, David. *Curriculum: Design and Development*. New York: Harcourt Brace Jovanovich, 1980.
Saylor, J. Galen, William M. Alexander, and Arthur J. Lewis. *Curriculum Planning for Better Teaching and Learning*, 4th ed. New York: Holt, Rinehart and Winston, 1981.
Taba, Hilda. *Curriculum Development: Theory and Practice*. New York: Harcourt Brace Jovanovich, 1962.
Tanner, Daniel, and Laurel N. Tanner. *Curriculum Development: Theory into Practice*, 2nd ed. New York: Macmillan, 1980.
Tyler, Ralph W. *Basic Principles of Curriculum and Instruction*. Chicago: University of Chicago Press, 1949.
———, Robert M. Gagné, and Michael Scriven. "Perspectives of Curriculum Evaluation." *AERA Monograph Series on Education: Perspectives of Curriculum Evaluation*. no. 1. Chicago: Rand McNally, 1967.
Wiles, Jon, and Josephi Bondi. *Curriculum Development: A Guide to Practice*. Columbus, Ohio: Charles E. Merrill, 1979.
Zais, Robert S. *Curriculum: Principles and Foundations*. New York: Harper & Row, 1976.

Multi-Media

A Curriculum Rationale. Filmstrip-tape program #8. Vimcet Associates, P.O. Box 24714, Los Angeles, California 90024.

Winters, Marilyn. *Preparing Your Curriculum Guide*. Alexandria, Va.: Association for Supervision and Curriculum Development, 1980. An illustrated script and set of transparency masters that leaders can use to explain the process of developing curriculum guides to teachers, parents, and others.

8

Helping Teachers to Evaluate the Curriculum

OBJECTIVES

After studying Chapter 8 you should be able to accomplish the following objectives:

1. Describe a model of curriculum evaluation.
2. Choose and defend your preferred model of curriculum evaluation.
3. Describe the supervisor's role in curriculum evaluation.
4. Explain the nine basic research concepts presented in this chapter.
5. Describe the four types of research presented in this chapter.
6. Explain what is meant by (1) context, (2) input, (3) process, and (4) product evaluation.
7. Outline a plan for a curriculum needs assessment.
8. Explain the nature and purposes of the *Evaluative Criteria*.
9. Explain what is meant by curriculum mapping and state its uses.
10. Cite several general references useful in researching a topic.
11. Identify the National Assessment of Educational Progress.

CURRICULUM EVALUATION: ESSENTIAL AND DIFFICULT

The distraught teacher sat across from the supervisor and began to tell her story. "Last night after our evaluation workshop I went home exhausted and flopped on the bed. I fell into a restless sleep and experienced a terrible nightmare." In his best nondirective manner the supervisor said, "Tell me about your nightmare."

The teacher, reinforced by the supervisor's interest, continued, "I dreamed that I was picked up by a tornado and set down in the middle of a conference of educational researchers. They were speaking a language which I was convinced was not of this world and for some strange reason I wanted to associate it with ancient astronauts. Their discussions were animated and from what I could gather there were differences of opinion among the conference participants. I tuned in as attentively as I could, which wasn't difficult for the voices were rather loud and I heard in rapid-fire succession.

input	context
product	t-test
CIPP	Q-sort
process	validity
CSE	reliability
norm	model
formative	inferential
summative	noninferential

"When someone yelled 'null hypothesis,' I suddenly woke up, sat bolt upright in bed, sweating." The teacher looked at the supervisor and asked plaintively, "What does this dream mean? Is there something the matter with me?"

The supervisor smiled, reassured her that there was nothing wrong, and then, departing from his nondirective manner, said, "I see four possible interpretations of your dream," hesitating to use the word hypotheses. "First, we served stale doughnuts at the evaluation workshop last night. Second, we threw too much at the group at one time. Third, you have a guilt feeling—you'd like to be doing more research but for one reason or another do not. Fourth, the researchers are not communicating to you, the teacher. Since I picked up the doughnuts myself fresh from the bakery, we can discount the first interpretation. I suspect we can attribute your nightmare a little bit to each of the other three possibilities. In fact, your nightmare brings home to me the necessity for the supervisor's clarifying the role of the teacher in evaluation and research. This is a task to which I must give priority."

This fictitious exchange between a teacher and supervisor serves to express a feeling many teachers experience when confronted with the tasks of evaluation and research. We have seen that evaluation is an integral component of models of both instruction and curriculum development. Of all components, evaluation is the one which is frequently neglected or often conducted poorly. Evaluation is such an essential phase of both instructional and curricular design that the profession cannot afford to slight it or ignore it. Chapter 5 introduced concepts of evaluation as they applied to the instructional process. This chapter will extend some of the basic evaluation concepts and apply them to the process of curriculum development. It will be primarily concerned with evaluation of the curriculum in whole or in part rather than with evaluation of instructional techniques per se. Making a rigid distinction, however, between instruction and curriculum is inadvisable, for the two are inseparable.

When we speak of curriculum evaluation, the first thing that jumps to the mind of some educators is standardized testing of student achievement in specific areas of the curriculum, as reading, math, etc. In fact, we need to evaluate much more than just the success of the learners. We need to account for the learners' success or failure. We need to know whether a program is working or not. We need to evaluate the following in addition to subject matter achievement of students in each discipline and grade:

- curriculum goals and objectives
- instructional goals and objectives
- specific programs, in both formative stage and at the end of a trial period
- student reactions to the curriculum
- parents' and other laypersons' reactions to the curriculum
- teachers' reactions to the curriculum
- the general effectiveness of the school's program
- the quality and effectiveness of curriculum materials
- the organization of the curriculum
- the process for curriculum development and its effectiveness
- projections for the future
- the evaluation program itself

Evaluation seeks to provide answers upon which decisions can be made for change and future action. Teachers employ evaluation techniques when they attempt to answer such questions as:

Is homogeneous grouping more effective than heterogeneous grouping?

Does an open-space program yield better results than the self-contained classroom?

Do students learn mathematics better by means of LAPs (Learning Activity Packets) than through more traditional methods?

Do students improve in respect to discipline if they are sent to centers for special instruction?

Does a career education program make any difference in respect to students' knowledge of the world of work?

Does geometry teach students to think?

Does Latin help improve students' English?

Is the scholastic achievement of students affected by the extra-class activity program and if so, in what way is it affected?

Does homemaking develop skills of worthy home membership?

Many of the answers given to curriculum questions such as the foregoing have been based on judgment without hard evidence. It has been assumed, for example, that the smaller a class is in size, the higher the level of student achievement will be. Or that the more years a learner is exposed to a discipline the higher will be the level of attainment in that discipline. Or that certain courses in the curriculum develop the ability to think better than other courses. All of these assumptions are based on very flimsy evidence.

Each of the curriculum questions raised suggests additional questions which must be answered. When we ask, "Is homogeneous grouping more effective than heterogeneous grouping?" we must also ask, "What do you mean by homogeneous grouping?" "What kind of homogeneous grouping are we talking about?" "What do you mean by more effective—more effective in what respects?" The ramifications of questions about a curriculum show the complexity of evaluation, which may account for one of the reasons why evaluation is omitted or handled rather poorly.

Curriculum, like the suprasystem Education of which it is a part, is a complex system comprising people, places, and things, making it extremely difficult to isolate variables. It is very difficult for a teacher to know that a particular program, a particular unit of content, or a particular treatment has made a difference in the end result. For this reason, much of the research in education terminates with conclusions such as, "There was no significant difference in two approaches," or "The results were inconclusive," or "An experimental approach achieved a result as good as the original approach." Though such conclusions may actually be significant in and of themselves, the indecisiveness of the research has created an unfortunate impatience on the part of teachers with educational research in general.

Preservice teacher education as a rule is light on training in evaluation and research, which leaves a gap that must be filled by graduate or in-service education. The supervisor must determine how wide that gap is and what particular training is called for.

One reason that teachers experience difficulties in regard to evaluation and research can be found in the esoteric language of evaluation, a method of communication which requires special training to understand. The experts in evaluation share the same problem of communicating evaluation concepts to teachers as teachers share in communicating pedagogical problems to the public. What makes the process of evaluation even more difficult are conflicting opinions of experts in the field on how evaluation and research are to be carried on.

What might prove a beneficial first step to improved communication is a summit conference of experts in evaluation to standardize the language of evaluation and research. The classroom teacher might then know whether formative evaluation is process research, whether process research is the same as process evaluation, and whether terminal evaluation is summative evaluation. Unlike the profession of writing, which requires a wide vocabulary and many synonyms, the specializations of evaluation and research demand a limited, precise vocabulary. Mathematics is sometimes called the "queen of the sciences" because its terminology is precise and its concepts clear. A hypotenuse cannot be called a diagonal or a slant-line. In deference to Gertrude Stein, a hypotenuse is a hypotenuse is a hypotenuse. It is one of the anomalies of the profession that the fields of evaluation and research, which draw heavily on mathematics and statistics, permit on occasion a looseness of language. This looseness makes it difficult for the teacher who is expected to be an applier and consumer to put sound evaluation principles into operation in the school.

One of the reasons that the evaluation component of curriculum design is slighted in school systems is the lack of qualified people to assume responsibility for leadership in this field. Some school systems are large enough and fortunate enough to be able to employ evaluators or research directors, but those categories of personnel are not common in the table of organization of most school systems. In fact, although it may seem at times that schools employ an army of supervisors, even supervisory assistance is lacking or limited in many school systems, let alone the assistance of trained evaluators.

THE SUPERVISOR'S ROLE IN EVALUATION

In the absence of fully qualified specialists in evaluation the supervisor must provide the necessary leadership in curriculum evaluation and research. Supervisors must possess or achieve a level of competence in the skills of evaluation and research at a much more sophisticated level than the level of skills possessed by most teachers. For the conduct of research the supervisor must have the teachers' cooperation and support. He or she can help teachers design proposals, collect and interpret data, and can serve as the resource person to whom teachers can turn for specialized help. A little later in this chapter we will examine ways in which the supervisor can help teachers with the task of evaluation.

As a rule, teachers serve in the evaluation process primarily as participants rather than as researchers. The terms *applier*, and *consumer*, and *interpreter* of research are often used in describing the evaluative role of the teacher. The teacher should be able to analyze completed research for any implications it has for his or her school. He or she should be able to design simple proposals under the guidance of a specialist and be able to conduct what the text will later describe as "action research." But researcher per se is not a role to be expected of the teacher. Some years ago Scriven hit the lack of competent evaluators in school systems when he said:

The very idea that every school system, or every teacher, can today be regarded as capable of meaningful evaluation of his own performance is as absurd as the view that every psychotherapist today is capable of evaluating his work with his own patients. Trivially, they can learn something very important from carefully studying their own work; indeed they can identify some good and bad features about it. But if they or someone else need to know the answers to the important questions, whether process or outcome, they need skills and resources which are conspicuous by their rarity even at the *national* level.[1]

He recommended in-service training for the staff of curriculum projects but questioned whether the task of evaluation is possible at all when he observed, "Whatever one's views about evaluation, it is easy enough to demonstrate that there are very few professionally competent evaluators in the country today."[2]

The Curriculum Director as Evaluator

Since the job of research director is not common to all school systems, the supervisor must fill the void and provide leadership in evaluation. Dominick Graziano provided some helpful insights into the way in which supervisors (in this case, curriculum directors) perceived their own roles in evaluation in their school systems.[3] Graziano surveyed 103 curriculum directors in Illinois schools, presenting to them 32 evaluative tasks. He asked the directors to respond whether each task presently was their responsibility and whether they felt it should be their responsibility.

Eighty-five percent of the respondents indicated that the following evaluative tasks were presently part of their responsibility:

To assist supervisory and administrative personnel and teachers in the adoption of materials and practices that can be evaluated in terms of specific objectives.

To encourage the adoption of innovative programs and practices.

To assist supervisory and administrative personnel and teachers in the development of materials and practices that can be evaluated in terms of specific objectives.

To aid in the interpretation of the evaluation of programs and practices.

To accumulate project or program information about similar programs in other settings.

To develop descriptive information about programs.

To explain the rationale for developmental programs.

To make judgments about programs developed, tested, or adopted in other settings.

To assess the consequences of educational programs.

To assess the relationship between what the program does and intends to do.

To prepare project or program proposals.[4]

A majority of the curriculum directors responded that five evaluative tasks were not their responsibility:

To determine the nature of the decision-making process of the institution.

To identify procedures and processes for the evaluation of the professional personnel of the institution.

To design field-testing procedures.

To implement procedures and processes for the evaluation of professional personnel of the institution.

To design procedures and processes for the evaluation of professional personnel of the institution.[5]

It is interesting to compare the curriculum directors' perceptions of which tasks should be their responsibility with their indications of tasks which are their responsibility. Although a majority accepted 22 of the 32 tasks as ones which they feel they should perform, an overwhelming majority believed the following four tasks should be theirs:

To encourage the adoption of innovative programs and practices.

To assist supervisory and administrative personnel and teachers in the adoption of materials and practices in terms of specific objectives.

To aid in the interpretation of the evaluation of programs and practices.

To assist supervisory and administrative personnel and teachers in the development of materials and practices that can be evaluated in terms of specific objectives.[6]

Conversely, a large majority identified four tasks as ones which should not be part of their assignment:

To implement procedures and processes for the evaluation of professional personnel of the institution.

To design procedures and processes for the evaluation of professional personnel of the institution.

To identify procedures and processes for the evaluation of professional personnel of the institution.

To design field-testing procedures.[7]

Seventy percent of these curriculum directors saw the need for the creation of the specific position of evaluator in their school districts. Among the duties which they felt an evaluator could better implement were:

To develop valid and reliable measurement instruments and techniques for curriculum development.

To apply valid and reliable measurement instruments and techniques to curriculum development.

To evaluate programs or practices developed, tested, or adopted in other settings.

To analyze the findings of the evaluation of programs and practices in terms of given criteria.

To assess the relationship between what the program does and intends to do.[8]

It is apparent that these curriculum directors, whom we may refer to as generalist-supervisors, do perform a sizable number of evaluative tasks. They see their role as providing leadership to teachers within a restricted set of limits. It is equally obvious that they feel the need of a specialist evaluator to help them in the conduct of evaluation and research studies. Graziano summarized the results of his study:

The results of this study strongly suggest that the curriculum director plays a major evaluative role in: (1) assisting professional personnel in the adoption of innovative programs and practices, (2) encouraging adoption of innovative programs and practices, (3) aiding in the interpretation of the evaluation of programs and practices, (4) accumulating data and developing information about various programs in other settings than his own institution, and (5) explaining the rationale for developmental programs.[9]

There is no evidence I know which would indicate a change in the perception and role of curriculum directors in respect to evaluation since Graziano completed his study in 1971. It is clear that the curriculum directors see those evaluative tasks which they accept as evaluation of programs and not of personnel, a point introduced in Chapter 2 and to be mentioned again in Chapter 11.

Given the necessity of evaluation as the route for keeping the curriculum alive and given the shortage of specialized assistance in evaluation, the supervisor must fulfill the role of leader in curriculum evaluation. In this capacity he or she should be able to help teachers in a number of ways.

Research Orientation

The supervisor should help teachers to develop an inquiring point of view—a research orientation. He or she should raise questions with teachers and encourage them to raise questions about the curriculum, such as: Does the program work? Is this program better than other programs? What effect does an innovation have on students? How can I improve a program? What do test results mean? How can I measure the success of a program? How do I know if a program is successful? What kind of data do I need to determine the effectiveness of a program? Aside from the fact that it is new, does an innovation have any other merits? What are the objectives of a program and how can I evaluate the attainment of those objectives? The supervisor should encourage teachers to try out new approaches and new programs and to find out whether they are more effective than the old approaches and programs. The supervisor should encourage teachers to develop an evaluation mentality and not to remain content with the curriculum as it is. No school has reached utopia in curriculum development nor will it ever, for the curriculum must change to reflect new needs of learners and society. Evaluation is at the heart of change. It is true that schools can and do make changes in their curriculum without evaluation through a trial and error process. Systematic evaluation points the direction of changes which need to be made and cuts down on the wasteful trials which would otherwise be experienced. The supervisor should set an example for teachers with a positive attitude toward evaluation and research and by demonstrating a disposition to seek more than empirical answers to curriculum problems.

Evaluation Related to Objectives

The supervisor should repeatedly call the teachers' attention to the feedback line between evaluation and objectives in the model of curriculum development. He or she can show teachers how evaluation is simplified when the curricular objectives contain a level of performance. For example, let us refer to an illustration of a curricular objective cited previously: "For each nine-week period while school is in session, at least 90 percent of the students will spend at least 30 hours in a human relations course where students can both learn about and practice both human relations skills and group dynamics."[10] It is a simple enough matter to determine whether the level of performance of this objective has been reached or not.

BASIC RESEARCH CONCEPTS

The supervisor should tactfully verify the teacher's understanding of basic research concepts. If the supervisor finds a teacher's understanding of the concepts to be inadequate, he or she should work out some in-service training to correct this deficiency. Though experts in measurement may disagree, most teachers can function at a minimal level of research competency through most of their professional careers with an understanding of only nine basic concepts. For advanced research concepts they may call upon the services of the supervisor or research specialist. While this text cannot begin to serve as a course in research methods, it can describe those minimal nine concepts. The supervisor may wish to review the following concepts with groups of teachers.

1. *The normal curve.* The normal or bell-shaped curve is a statistical representation of the distribution of scores made by the takers of a test designed to measure a particular trait, such as intelligence, which is presumed to be distributed "normally" throughout the human population. Built into the concept of the normal curve is the understanding that the population which took the test is a reasonably large group which has been chosen at random. With a large random sample of the population the test maker can assume that the performance of the population which took the test approximates the performance of the population in general in respect to the trait measured by the test.

Figure 8.1 is a graphic representation of a normal curve. The tallest line represents the mean. Fifty percent of the scores fall to the right of the mean and fifty percent to the left. By convention the scores to the right are greater than the mean score and the scores to the left are smaller than the mean score. In a normal distribution of scores the mean score (arithmetical average) and the median score (midscore) coincide.

The vertical lines to the right and left of the mean, which indicate standard deviations from the mean and are represented by the symbol σ, sigma, show the percentages of scores which are likely to fall within one, two, or three standard deviations from the mean. Thus, we can say that 68.26 percent of the scores will fall

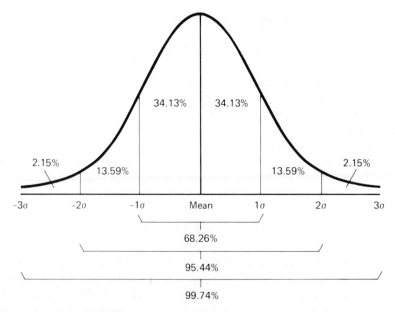

Figure 8.1 The Normal Curve

within one standard deviation on either side of the mean; 95.44 percent will fall within two standard deviations from the mean; and 99.74 percent will come within three standard deviations from the mean.

The normal curve is a useful concept in the interpretation of scores made on standardized tests which are administered to large, random samples of the population. It is not at all applicable in the manner some teachers employ it—to calculate marks made by students in their classes. It is a gross misuse of the concept of the normal curve when teachers decide that 2 percent of their students must earn As and Fs, 14 percent Bs and Ds, and 34 percent Cs. Classes are small, selected groups and they become progressively more selected as they go up the academic ladder and as students drop out of school. The supervisor should help teachers to detect abuses of the concept of the normal curve.

2. *Mean*. The mean is a measure of central tendency—that characteristic of a group of scores on a given test to group themselves somewhere between the highest and lowest scores. The mean is the arithmetical average of a group of scores: the sum of the scores divided by the number of scores. It is this concept which the layman ordinarily refers to as "average." When the householder wants to know what his or her average weekly food bill is, he or she totals the food bills for several weeks and divides that total by the number of weeks. The school principal uses the concept of the mean in calculating the average daily attendance of the school. The mean is the measure of central tendency most commonly used by statisticians.

3. *Median*. The median, which is also a measure of central tendency, is the midpoint in a set of scores. In other terminology it is known as the fiftieth percentile. Fifty percent of the scores in a given distribution fall at or below the median while 50 percent fall at or above the median. Since the median is the middle score, it is less affected by extreme scores than the mean. Of the two measures of central tendency, the mean and the median, the mean is much more widely used, for it serves as a basis for calculating other statistical concepts.

4. *Reliability*. The term reliability is equated with the term consistency, an essential characteristic of a test. A reliable test should consistently yield similar results under repeated administrations. Chapter 5 pointed out that essay tests tend to have low reliability. A test is unreliable not only when it yields different results on subsequent testings but when it yields different results on subsequent scorings of the same test—a common fault of essay tests. It was pointed out that scoring of essay tests could be made more reliable by creating a key in advance of the scoring.

No test is 100 percent reliable in the sense that identical results could be assured on repeated administrations. When teachers want to select a standardized test, they will want to know whether that test is reliable. In order to find that out, they consult the test maker's manual, which reports reliability in terms of a coefficient of correlation. The closer the coefficient of correlation, which is expressed in hundredths, comes to $+1.00$, the higher is the reliability of a test. Thus, for example, a coefficient of .90 would indicate that the test is reliable.

5. *Validity*. Besides being consistent or reliable a test should be valid, that is, it measures what it is supposed to measure. Reliability and validity are both essential characteristics of testing instruments. There is no virtue in using a test which consis-

tently measures that which it is not supposed to measure or in employing a test which inconsistently measures that which it is supposed to measure. Since no test is a perfect instrument, no test is 100 percent valid. Like the reliability coefficient the validity coefficient is reported in the test manual which accompanies a standardized test. The validity coefficient is likewise expressed in hundredths and the closer the coefficient comes to +1.00, the more valid may be considered the test. A validity coefficient of .55, for example, would be indicative of a test of moderate validity.

6. *Coefficient of correlation*. The concept of the correlation coefficient was introduced above in the definitions of the terms reliability and validity. A coefficient of correlation is a mathematical measure for showing relationships between two variables, for example, between two different types of tests, between two administrations of the same test, and between scores made on a test and some external criterion.

Coefficients are generally expressed from +1.00, which is indicative of a perfect positive correlation between two variables, to −1.00, which is indicative of a perfect negative correlation between two variables. The midpoint of this range, .00, implies that there is no relationship between the two variables. Coefficients of correlation are expressed by the mathematical symbol r.

Generally speaking, a negative coefficient of correlation can be as useful to the statistician as a positive coefficient of correlation. It is of help to know, for example, that one test correlates negatively with another test. In the cases of reliability and validity, however, an inconsistent or invalid test is of little use to a prospective test purchaser and the test maker is not likely to market tests which produce a negative coefficient of reliability or of validity.

7. *Standard deviation*. The standard deviation is a measure of variability which indicates the spread of a set of scores. Any standard textbook on research will show how the standard deviation is calculated. However, the number of classroom teachers who compute standard deviations can be counted on the fingers of one hand. The teacher will have occasion to use the standard deviation in interpreting scores made by students on a standardized test. What the teacher needs to know is that the higher the value of the standard deviation, the wider is the spread of the scores. The value of the standard deviation will be found in the test manual. We have noted that 68.26 percent or approximately two-thirds of the scores in a normal distribution are found within one standard deviation of the mean. Thus, for a test whose mean is 100 and whose standard deviation is 10, 68.26 percent of the scores may be expected to fall between 90 and 110. By the same token 95.44 percent of the scores will range from 80 to 120 and 99.74 percent will come between 70 and 130.

8. *Standard scores*. A standard score, known as the *sigma score* and designated with the symbol z, is a means of converting raw scores to figures which represent values in terms of the standard deviation. The concept of the standard score facilitates comparisons of a student's scores on different tests on which the total number of points are not the same. If raw scores are used to calculate means, a distorted picture may emerge and make it difficult to compare scores. For example, what inferences could be drawn in comparing two scores made by a student on two different tests whose means as calculated using raw scores are 50 and 46? The means are affected

by extremes and the comparison is difficult. But suppose we could start from a common mean, say 0, as we do with standard scores; we can then decide whether a student has done better on one test than on another.

Take a case of a student who has scored 60 on a test of business English and 40 on a test of business arithmetic. The mean on the test of business English is 50 and the standard deviation is 5. The mean of the business arithmetic test is 46 and the standard deviation is 6. The statistician employs a simple formula to convert the raw score to a standard score:

$$z \text{ (standard score)} = \frac{X \text{ (raw score)} - m \text{ (mean)}}{S \text{ (standard deviation)}}$$

Applying the formula to the test of business English gives $\frac{60 - 50}{5} = +2$. The business arithmetic test gives $\frac{40 - 46}{6} = -1$. In the case of the student's score of 60 on the business English test, the sigma score $+2$ indicates that the score of 60 is two standard deviations above the mean. The score of 46 on the business arithmetic test shows up as a sigma score of -1, which is one standard deviation below the mean. When comparing the standard scores on these two tests, we may conclude that the student is quite a bit better in business English than in business arithmetic. The sigma score is a procedure for weighting scores equally so that more accurate comparisons can be made than is true if raw scores are used.

9. *Norms.* Norms are scores made by the group or groups on which a test was standardized and as such these scores become standards against which individual test scores are compared. Test makers report the norms of tests in their test manuals. The norms reported are based on test scores made by a large, random sample of the population and are generally interpreted as having national significance.

Test makers report norms most frequently in terms of (1) age-norms, (2) grade-norms, and (3) percentile rank. Age-norms are expressed in years and months, for example, 10–5, which indicates a level of achievement in the trait measured by the test at an age level of 10 years, 5 months. This level of achievement must be compared with the pupil's actual chronological age. For example, a child of 8 years, 5 months chronological age who achieves a score on a standardized arithmetic test which puts the child at an age-norm of 10 years, 5 months is two whole years advanced for his or her chronological age.

The grade-norm fulfills a function similar to the age-norm but its point of reference is the year and month of school. A grade-norm of 7.8 represents the eighth month of the seventh grade. Grade-norms are written with decimals and are based on a 10-month school year. By way of illustration, a child in the fourth month of the eighth grade (8.4) who achieves a score on a standardized test which places him or her at the eighth month of the seventh grade (7.8) is reading below grade level.

The percentile rank is another means of expressing the relative position of scores made by those who take a standardized test. The middle or median score is said to be at the fiftieth percentile. Fifty percent of the scores fall at or above the fiftieth percentile and 50 percent fall at or below the fiftieth percentile. The student who achieves the middle score is considered to be equal to or surpassed by 50 percent of the student population and to have equaled and surpassed 50 percent. In layman's language the student is average in the trait measured by the test. The student who ranks at the ninety-eighth percentile has done very well on the particular trait measured by that test. That student has equaled or surpassed 98 percent of the population and is equaled or surpassed by only 2 percent.

The norm data give the interpreter of results of a standardized test some indication of how students to whom they may administer a test fare in relation to those persons who were in the sample of the population on whom the test was standardized.

A mastery of these nine concepts should enable teachers to fulfill their roles as interpreters of research at a minimal level of competency. These nine concepts can provide a beginning point for in-service training under the guidance of the supervisor.

TYPES OF RESEARCH

The supervisor should help teachers distinguish between different types of research with the view toward identifying types in which teachers may be customarily engaged and kinds which are more likely to be the responsibility of research teams. Four types of research are as follows:

1. *Basic research.* Otherwise known as fundamental or pure research, basic research is normally carried on in the laboratory or in laboratory-like situations with animals or human subjects for the purpose of testing theoretical principles of behavior and with no particular application in mind. Studies of the ways in which animals and human beings learn are basic research. It is not common for the classroom teacher to conduct basic research studies.

2. *Applied research.* Most of the research in education is applied research, the study of the applicability of instructional principles and learning theory in the classroom. Teachers are frequently involved in applied research studies under the direction of a supervisor or research specialist. Applied research follows generally accepted principles of research methodology and its purpose is to find means of improving the curriculum and the instructional process.

3. *Action research.* Many teachers are engaged in this form of research and should be encouraged to be by their supervisors. Action research consists of less controlled studies of specific applications of learning theory and methodology in a particular classroom. The teacher who tries out a new method and attempts to compare the success of that method with the success of previous methods is engaging in action research. We may think of action research as a type of applied research and as a study of the applicability of a principle or method in a specific situation. Action research is one means of fostering the research orientation of teachers. This type of research has been popular with curriculum workers but has not always been acceptable to specialists in measurement and research. The specialist in evaluation prefers to obtain results from research studies which can be generalized beyond the immediate classroom. He or she also likes to be assured that the variables in a study are

more stringently controlled than is true of much action research. As far as classroom teachers are concerned, however, their major thrust in research is likely to be either in action research or in certain types of descriptive research (below). John W. Best commented on the controversy over action research:

But whether or not it is worthy of the term *research* it does apply scientific thinking and methods to real-life problems and represents a great improvement over teachers' subjective judgments and decisions based upon folklore and their limited personal experiences.[11]

4. *Descriptive research*. Descriptive research is an accurate accounting of general or selected aspects of a given situation. This particular category of research includes a variety of types of studies in which teachers participate. What is commonly referred to as a status study, for example, a study of the extent to which schools in a state have remedial reading laboratories, is a form of descriptive research. Surveys of current practices and of opinions of groups which are conducted as a part of a needs assessment are descriptive research. A descriptive report of what goes on at a particular time in a classroom is a type of descriptive research which some evaluators call process research. Unfortunately, the term process research is used to connote formative evaluation, the testing of the prototype model and the periodic check of progress of a program, as well as a noninferential type of study of classroom activities.

Basic, applied, and action research are types of *experimental research*. Teachers frequently engage in action and descriptive research with minimal supervision and they occasionally participate in applied research with closer supervision.

TYPES OF EVALUATION

The supervisor should help teachers to distinguish between different types of evaluation and to select and use an evaluation model. For purposes of analysis, types of evaluation are distinguished from types of research. This is a somewhat arbitrary classification, since evaluation and research are so closely related. The terms which describe evaluation and research are sometimes used in the literature interchangeably. Formative evaluation, for example, may be referred to as process research but process research is not just formative evaluation. Other types of studies are subsumed under the rubric of process research. In very brief form, some of the more frequently encountered terms are described. The various terms and the models of evaluation discussed below are worthwhile topics to be explored at length in in-service programs.

Let's review first two terms which were introduced in the earlier chapter on the evaluation of instruction: formative evaluation and summative evaluation. Formative evaluation is essentially an analysis of a program at its beginning stage, the testing of a prototype program so that changes can be made before the program has gone too far. Summative evaluation is terminal evaluation, that which is conducted at the end of the program and on the basis of which the teacher or evaluator decides whether or not the program has been successful, that is, whether the objectives have been reached.

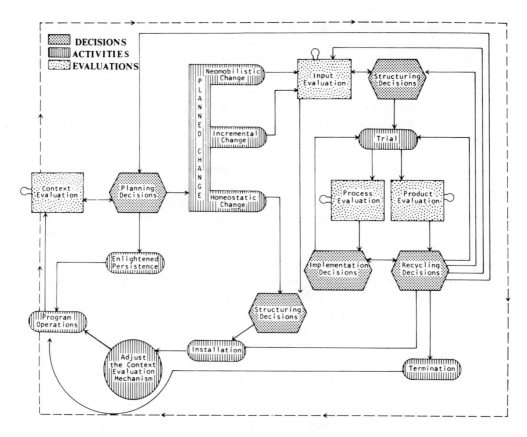

Figure 8.2   The CIPP Evaluation Model

SOURCE: Daniel L. Stufflebeam et al., *Educational Evaluation and Decision Making*, Itasca, Ill., F. E. Peacock, 1971, p. 236. Reprinted with permission of Phi Delta Kappa.

Evaluation Models

Evaluation models can serve not only to extend the teacher's understanding of evaluation concepts but also as guides for carrying out a curriculum study. The CIPP (Context, Input, Process, and Product) Evaluation Model, shown in Figure 8.2, contains four evaluation components: context evaluation, input evaluation, process evaluation, and product evaluation,[12] while the CSE (Center for the Study of Evaluation) Evaluation Model, shown in Figure 8.3, comprises five evaluation phases: needs assessment, program planning, implementation evaluation, progress evaluation, and outcome evaluation.[13] Let's briefly examine the evaluation components of each of these two evaluation models.

   1. *Context evaluation.* Context evaluation is the first component of the CIPP Evaluation Model. According to this model the evaluation process begins with an analysis of the context or environment in which a curriculum study is to be conducted.

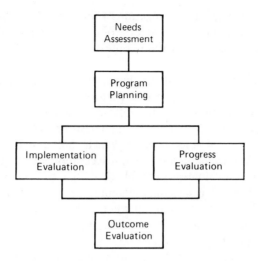

Figure 8.3 The CSE Evaluation Model

SOURCE: Center for the Study of Evaluation, *Evaluation Workshop I: An Orientation, Participant's Notebook*, Del Monte Research Park, Monterey, Calif., CTB/McGraw-Hill, 1971, p. A-2. Reprinted with permission.

It continues with a description of the conditions, both actual and hoped for, of that environment. It includes an assessment of the needs of the system and a determination of the unmet needs of the system. It includes an accounting of reasons why the unmet needs are not being met.

2. *Input evaluation*. This second phase of the CIPP Evaluation Model consists of making decisions on procedures which will be followed in pursuit of the objectives. The evaluators at this stage must choose from among alternative routes to the realization of the objectives. In making these decisions the evaluators must keep in mind the limitations of resources, including time and funds available.

3. *Process evaluation*. The third element of the CIPP Evaluation Model, process evaluation, is a monitoring of the curriculum plan as it unfolds. The evaluators look for deficiencies in the system and attempt to correct these. They maintain a continuing record of what is happening during the implementation process.

4. *Product evaluation*. The fourth and final component of the CIPP Evaluation Model bears the label product evaluation. This type of evaluation is both formative and summative in that it seeks to measure both during the curriculum study and at the end of the study whether the objectives have been reached.

Now compare the terminology of the CSE Evaluation Model:

1. *Needs assessment*. The CSE Evaluation Model begins with needs assessment as its first component. Generally, a needs assessment is the process of identifying unmet needs of a school system by comparing the achievement levels of that school system with its stated objectives. The discrepancies between achievement levels and objectives are needs which are not being met by that school system. An assessment of needs and the consequent determination of unmet needs necessitates the devel-

opment of new objectives for the realization of those needs. A little further along in this chapter we will elaborate on the process of conducting a needs assessment. Note the element of needs assessment within context evaluation of the CIPP Evaluation Model.

2. *Program planning.* The CSE Evaluation Model prescribes program planning as its second stage. It is at this stage that performance objectives are specified and a program is selected and prepared. It is also at this stage that input evaluation, as in the CIPP Model, comes into play with an analysis of various strategies for accomplishing the objectives and of the resources which can be made available.

3. *Implementation evaluation.* The third component of the CSE Evaluation Model, implementation evaluation, is a check of the various parts of the program design to see if the design has been implemented properly. This stage of evaluation is an effort to spot difficulties, to find out whether the personnel involved, the materials and equipment needs, and the facilities to be used are all in order and to learn whether the program is meeting its time and budgetary commitments. Implementation evaluation is related to process evaluation of the CIPP Model.

4. *Progress evaluation.* During the course of a program the evaluator arranges to obtain continuous feedback as to whether the program objectives are being met so that adjustments can be made in the program. Progress evaluation is the fourth element of the CSE Evaluation Model and is formative in nature.

5. *Outcome evaluation.* The fifth and final stage of the CSE Evaluation Model is outcome evaluation, which is a terminal assessment of the accomplishments of the program. It is at this stage that decisions are reached as to whether or not the objectives have been realized and whether the program should continue or not. Outcome evaluation is essentially the same as product evaluation of the CIPP Evaluation Model when conducted at the end of the program. In more general terms, outcome evaluation equals summative evaluation.

The foregoing terms are some of the most frequently encountered evaluation terms but are by no means an exhaustive listing of concepts of this complex field. The models and descriptions have been selected to give the prospective supervisor a flavor of the thinking that goes on in the field of evaluation. The supervisor should follow up these brief descriptions by turning to more detailed sources which could be helpful in working with teachers in the task of evaluating the curriculum. Ultimately, as the supervisor works with teachers in planning, implementing, and evaluating curriculum studies. Together they may select from the models described above or from other models as guides to the process of evaluation.[14]

At some point teachers and supervisors should examine the evaluation plan itself. They should ask questions such as: Are we following a model for curriculum evaluation? Do we have a comprehensive evaluation plan? Have we collected both formative and summative data? Have we used proper means of gathering data? Have we involved the right people? Do we need to use outside evaluators? Have we validated the curriculum goals and objectives?

When fulfilling the role of curriculum evaluators, supervisors and teachers would be well-advised to familiarize themselves with the standards developed by the Joint

Committee on Standards for Educational Evaluation.[15] The committee proposed 30 standards centered around four concerns: the utility, feasibility, propriety, and accuracy of an evaluation. The utility standards address questions such as the identification of the audience, the credibility of the evaluators, and the clarity and timeliness of the evaluation report. The feasibility standards include consideration of the practicality of the evaluation procedures and cost effectiveness. Propriety standards relate to such concerns as conflicts of interest, the public's right to know, and the rights of human subjects. The accuracy standards direct evaluators' attention to such items as the validity and reliability of measurement, the analysis of quantitative and qualitative information, and the objectivity of reporting. The supervisor should exercise leadership in curriculum evaluation by directing those charged with evaluation of a program in application of the thirty standards.

CONDUCTING A CURRICULUM NEEDS ASSESSMENT

The supervisor should assist a faculty in planning, conducting, and analyzing an assessment of curriculum needs. As the name implies, a curriculum needs assessment is an evaluation of programmatic needs. It is a process for deciding whether the objectives of the school are being reached and whether there are existing needs of learners which are not being met. The conducting of a needs assessment by a faculty is not only significant in terms of the data generated but it also provides an excellent vehicle for in-service training in one aspect of evaluation.

A needs assessment should be viewed not as a specific evaluation program with a fixed set of procedures which can be applied anywhere but as a general procedure which varies from school to school or school system to school system. While the general process is similar from locality to locality, the choice of instruments for collecting data, the steps followed, and the detailed procedures differ considerably.

Fenwick W. English and Roger A. Kaufman have defined needs assessment in the following manner:

Needs assessment is a process of defining the desired end (or outcome, product, or result) of a given sequence of curriculum development. . . .

Needs assessment is a process of making specific, in some intelligible manner, what schooling should be about and how it can be assessed. . . .

Needs assessment is an empirical process for defining the outcomes of education, and as such it is then a set of criteria by which curricula may be developed and compared. . . .

Needs assessment is a process for determining the validity of behavioral objectives and if standardized tests and/or criterion-referenced tests are appropriate and under what conditions.

Needs assessment is a logical problem solving tool by which a variety of means may be selected and related to each other in the development of curriculum.

Needs assessment is a tool which formally harvests the gaps between current results (or outcomes, products) and required or desired results, places these gaps in priority order, and selects those gaps (needs) of the highest priority for action, usually through the implementation of a new or existing curriculum or management process.[16]

A needs assessment has two basic purposes: (1) it seeks to determine whether stated objectives have been accomplished, and (2) it seeks to identify needs which have not been met and for which objectives have not been stated. A faculty may approach a needs assessment on a broad scale, studying academic, physical health, mental health, and social needs of learners. Or, a faculty may delimit a study to a particular set of needs which it will survey at one time.

As it has done so many times before, a faculty must go back to its statement of curriculum objectives. If it has not developed a statement of objectives, this task must be a first item of business. The objectives serve as the take-off point for a needs assessment. While a faculty will specify many curricular objectives, it may wish to assess needs in respect to those objectives which it believes to be most important or urgent. To accomplish this task the faculty will rank the curricular objectives in order of relative importance and will assess those objectives which it has placed at the top of its ranking. While it is feasible to assess a limited number of high-priority objectives, it should be understood that a faculty will ultimately survey all objectives.

Once the curriculum objectives have been specified the faculty must then plan ways by which the objectives are being or will be measured. Many data are already available in the school—in teachers' records, the principal's office, the guidance office, the school nurse's files. Additional data will need to be collected to supplement existing data. A faculty must decide on the means it will employ to collect the necessary data. Normally it will make use of standardized test data, teacher-test data, questionnaires, health records, rating scales, and check-lists.

Since the faculty is taking a broad look at the school's program, an adequate needs assessment attempts to gather data from the widest possible number of sources. Students, teachers, administrators, other school personnel, and the lay public should make input in a needs assessment.

The faculty should indicate specifically what evaluative data it will need in order to decide if each of the stated objectives is being met. Once it has gathered the evaluative data, it must then decide on the basis of those data whether the learners are reaching the objectives. For each objective that is being realized the faculty can congratulate itself. For each objective that is not being accomplished the faculty must make one of two decisions: (1) Is the objective which is not being met still valid and worth pursuing? and (2) What should be done about this situation? If the objective is deemed no longer valid, it can be dropped from the school's statement of objectives. However, if the objective is judged still worthwhile and is not being reached, some strategy for reaching it must be devised—this unattained objective is an unmet need.

But a needs assessment ought to go beyond the determination of whether the currently stated objectives are being met. The needs assessment should serve as a means of validating the goals and objectives themselves. Unstated objectives that teachers, administrators, other school personnel, students, and patrons of the school identify may also be unmet needs if enough persons believe they are. A common technique for getting at the question of unstated objectives (or, conversely, stated objectives that many people feel not to be needed) is the questionnaire or opinion survey. The opinions of students and former students (graduates and dropouts), of all school personnel, and of a representative sample of the community should be sought. In sampling lay opinion I do not hold with the technique employed by some schools—sampling only the community leaders or the power structure of the community. Nor do I recommend that sampling be confined to parents of children in the schools. Education in a community is everybody's business and not simply the domain of an elite or parents of school-age children. One of the subsets of the community easiest to ignore is the disadvantaged or poor segment; special effort should be taken to make sure faculties have gathered data from this source as well as other sources.

On questionnaires of this type the recipients are asked to identify goals and objectives of the school, problems they believe exist in the school and rank them, subject matter which they feel to be lacking, programs they would like to see incorporated into the school's program, instructional approaches they would like to see attempted, pupil services they would like to see added, ways in which they feel school funds should be expended, and qualifications which they believe teachers exhibit or should possess.

A final step in the needs assessment is the ranking of unmet needs. From this point the faculty begins to devise strategies and programs for meeting the unmet needs.

Objections have been raised to the needs assessment process. Those who object to the process maintain that it is too time consuming. They feel that teachers already know what the school needs. They claim the needs assessment focuses on lacks instead of strengths. They believe that the results from a needs assessment will repeat those of previous needs assessments.

On the other hand, the proponents of needs assessments, with whom I agree, see the process as an opportunity to involve all the constituencies of the school. The process makes teachers, students, and laypersons feel that their opinions are important. A needs assessment offers a systematic process for identifying gaps in the curriculum.

When a school system opts to conduct a needs assessment, the alert supervisor in charge might secure in advance descriptions of needs assessment processes carried out elsewhere.[17] The Research and Development Utilization Project of the Georgia Department of Education, by way of illustration, has developed a needs assessment process which local school systems of the state may choose to adopt.[18] The process consists of the following six steps, each of which is subdivided into certain tasks to be accomplished.

Checklist of Steps

This checklist describes *what to do* to conduct a system-wide needs assessment. The process recommended here consists of six basic steps. The checklist can be used in several ways. It has been designed in what experience has shown to be a logical, sequential order for use in a cookbook fashion by a project coordinator or steering committee. As with a recipe, any step or ingredient which is left out will affect the quality of the product. A second, less strict, application is to use the checklist as a directory, that is, as a source of recommendations which can be altered according to local circumstances. This checklist is also ideal as a tool for review to be sure that the planners have successfully completed each task, and to verify that any which have been left out were left out by rational choice rather than through an oversight. The sequence and detail of this six step process has been field tested over a three-year period with the help of over thirty local school systems. If this sequence is varied or the elements changed, be sure to do so only after careful consideration.

Step 1   **Initiate the needs assessment process**

This step entails gearing up for the needs assessment: selecting needs assessment committee members, orienting them and making tentative plans.

☐ **Task 1   Establish a Needs Assessment Committee**
   ☐ Select a coordinator
   ☐ Identify a resource person
   ☐ Outline required committee functions/prerogatives
   ☐ Choose a committee with cross sectional representation

☐ **Task 2   Orient the Committee to the Overall Needs Assessment Process**
   ☐ Brief committee on strategies, recommendations
   ☐ Identify current resources and constraints

☐ **Task 3   Make Tentative Plans**
   ☐ Review specific needs assessment components
   ☐ Determine desired comprehensiveness of the local plan
   ☐ Determine individual committee member responsibilities
   ☐ Set tentative timelines

Step 2   **Conduct perceived needs assessment**

School publics are surveyed to determine what they view as the *top* school needs. It is recommended that the publics surveyed include administrators, teachers, and students, and that approximately five top needs of each group be identified and then merged into one list.

☐ **Task 1   Review/Finalize the Perceived Needs Assessment Process**
   ☐ Specify target individuals or sample sizes
   ☐ Finalize instruments
   ☐ Detail administration procedures
   ☐ Define points to be made to each target group
   ☐ Finalize data analysis mechanics

☐ **Task 2   Conduct the Perceived Needs Assessments**
   ☐ Conduct school **administration** assessment
   ☐ Conduct a **teacher/school staff** assessment
   ☐ Conduct a **student** assessment

☐ **Task 3   Identify Sets of Top Needs**
   ☐ Score the instrument(s)
   ☐ Determine top needs by group
   ☐ Merge into one cross system list

Step 3   **Verify perceived needs by objective means**

The aim of Step 3 is the verification by objective means of each of the top perceived needs to determine that a major problem, limitation, or discrepancy does in fact exist. That is, do test data, structured observations, interview data, or other means (existing or new) bear out the identified needs? Thus, the list is further delineated.

☐ **Task 1　Plan for Verification**
 ☐ Orient committee on possible verification tools
 ☐ Select objective means to verify each need (existing or new)
 ☐ Plan for administration (procedures, timeline)

☐ **Task 2　Validate the Perceived Needs**
 ☐ Collect/compile existing or new data
 ☐ Analyze all data
 ☐ Compare perceived needs with analysis of objective measures
 ☐ Finalize the cross system perceived needs list

Step 4　Determine system-wide need priorities

One cross-system survey instrument is developed and administered during Step 4. A discrepancy-type instrument is suggested for surveying everyone's perception of: (1) the importance of addressing a need and (2) the degree to which this need has been met to date. From these perceptions, needs can be rank ordered, resulting in a system-wide list of priority needs.

☐ **Task 1　Organize for a System-wide Ranking of Needs**
 ☐ Review the plan for determining system-wide priorities
 ☐ Develop one cross-system survey instrument
 ☐ Determine groups to respond/sample sizes
 ☐ Determine procedures for ranking resulting needs
 ☐ Specify administrative mechanics

☐ **Task 2　Conduct the Assessment**
 ☐ Administer the instrument (distribute/collect)
 ☐ Score the instruments

☐ **Task 3　Place Cross-system Needs in Priority Order**
 ☐ Rank order the needs
 ☐ Compile priority list of cross-system needs

Step 5　Choose need to be addressed by improvement efforts

Step 5 involves deciding which of the system-wide needs is to be the focus of improvement. It is recommended that one (or possibly two if they are closely related) be identified by weighing what is most desirable to address and what resources are available. Obtaining school system approval and communicating undertakings to the educational public are also parts of the step.

☐ **Task 1　Determine Which Need Is to Be Improved**
 ☐ Estimate the resources required to tackle each need
 ☐ Select need(s) to address

☐ **Task 2　Obtain School System Approval**
 ☐ Obtain Central Administrative Approval
 ☐ Obtain School Board Approval

☐ **Task 3　Communicate Findings/Undertaking to the Public**
 ☐ Decide on points to be made to various publics/presentation modes
 ☐ Present information within the system (faculty, students)
 ☐ Communicate information to parents/community

Step 6　Conduct a causal analysis of the need to be improved

This step requires a look at factors which might have caused the identified need. Six factors are recommended for analysis in relation to the need: students, teachers, curriculum, resources, management and the community. The causal analysis study is to delimit or redefine the need with respect to possible causal influences. A master list of causes is generated and ranked, and a report published.

☐ **Task 1   Organize to Conduct the Causal Analysis**
        ☐ Review the process
        ☐ Assemble/orient representatives from the need area(s) affected
        ☐ Determine additional support required
        ☐ Set timelines, responsibilities

☐ **Task 2   Analyze the Need in Relation to Six Causal Areas**
        ☐ Decide which of the Six Causal Areas to investigate
        ☐ Describe desired conditions in each area
        ☐ Examine interrelationships across the six areas
        ☐ Select analysis tools or techniques for data collection
        ☐ Collect and analyze data

☐ **Task 3   Place Causal Factors in Priority Order**
        ☐ Generate a list of primary causal factors
        ☐ Decide which have the greatest impact on the system
        ☐ Place the causal factors in priority order
        ☐ Choose final areas to attack through an improvement effort

☐ **Task 4   Evaluate Your Needs Assessment Process Using "Needs Assessment: Checklist of Steps"**

☐ **Task 5   Develop a Report of Causal Factors**
        ☐ Submit report to Central Administration and Board for approval
        ☐ Communicate report to educational community and public

    A set of procedures like the Georgia Department of Education's is an effective evaluation process which reveals to curriculum planners where the curriculum is not meeting the needs of the learners. The process causes the planners to set priorities and develop plans for meeting student needs.

    As has been noted, procedures for a needs assessment vary from community to community depending on the desires of those charged with the task. The Savannah-Chatham County Public Schools uncovered 74 systemwide needs of an instructional, curricular, and administrative nature. Among the top curricular needs were the following:

To define procedures to assure the teaching and the assessment of the basic skills—including reading, math, science, social studies, language arts, etc.
    To improve the instruction of academically capable students based on identified strengths and weaknesses on norm-referenced reading and math tests.
    To assess the needs and interests of pupils identified as marginal achievers and/or potential dropouts and to provide programs that will meet the needs and interests of those students.[19]

The Delphi Technique

School systems can no longer afford to focus only on the here and now. Like business and industry they must anticipate future needs of the products of our schools. A promising procedure for predicting future educational needs, the Delphi Technique, has been gaining popularity in the social sciences and education.[20] When a researcher—for example, the supervisor—wishes to employ the Delphi Technique, he or she prepares a set of statements which is sent out in written form to respondents who are considered experts in the field.

The statements, which may be developed by the supervisor in collaboration with the teachers and others, consist of goals, values, and programs which might come to pass. The respondents to the instrument which contains the statements independently predict dates in the fashion of the Delphic oracle by which they believe the goals, values, or programs will come about. A number of experts in education, for example, might be polled as to the dates (years) by which they believe certain programs, such as the universal application of nongraded programs, the complete individualization of instruction, and the equalization of educational opportunities for all ethnic groups, will become reality.

The Delphi Technique involves repeated administering and refinement of the instrument and permits revisions of the answers by individual respondents, who do not collaborate or consult with each other while the technique is being carried out. The technique should not be thought of as a controlled research study or identification of specific unmet needs of a particular school. What the Delphi Technique does is to encourage futuristic thinking and the identification of the beginnings of possible trends.

The purpose of the Delphi Technique is to attempt to forecast trends by relying on informed guesses of experts. The best judgments of experts are gathered, their predictions are summarized, and the results are made known to those who may be concerned. The results of a Delphi study in education may cause school personnel to focus on modifications of aspects of education. If, indeed, for example, a number of educators believe that all children will not have mastered the basic number facts until twenty years from now (if ever), curriculum planners should stop and ponder the significance of these predictions. By finding the consensus of experts some light is shed on needs for program planning and curriculum development. If the goal is worth seeking (which respondents may indicate) and if the accomplishment of the goal will require many years, the Delphi study says, in effect, we had better get moving now on plans to reach that goal, perhaps even sooner than has been predicted.

A Delphi study can also reinforce or negate beliefs held by the supervisor and other school personnel. If the experts who respond to a study reveal that they believe that alternative schools will be commonplace within the next 10 years, they may be identifying the beginning of a trend. School systems which have already planned for and put into operation alternative schools would surmise that they are at least in keeping with a developing trend. They may even make the assumption that the trend is coming about as a response to certain needs. If, on the other hand, the experts feel that alternative schools would not become commonplace for another 25 years, school personnel would need to decide whether they have simply been negligent in promoting the accomplishment of an important goal or whether approaches other than alternative schools should take higher priority, since the experts did not see the beginning of a trend developing in respect to alternative schools.

The supervisor who wishes to try out the Delphi Technique might assemble a group of interested teachers and other school personnel and brainstorm with them some possible goals, values, and programs which could be included on an instrument to be sent out to a number of experts. When the items for the instrument have been selected, the supervisor duplicates the instrument and sends it out to the experts, for example, college professors of education, administrators, other supervisors, or state Department of Education specialists.

When the respondents return their instruments, the supervisor tabulates them and sends a revised instrument back to them along with a summary of the results, including the range of predicted dates by which they anticipate items would be realized. The respondents are encouraged to revise their predictions and to state reasons if their predictions fall at extremes of the range. The supervisor repeats the process, again furnishing a summary of the results to the respondents and reporting the reasons given by respondents for extreme answers. The supervisor may repeat the process as many times as it appears fruitful and as the respondents are willing to participate. As a general rule, after three or four times the responses tend to converge, making a consensus of the experts.

The supervisor summarizes the final results of the study and distributes the results to both respondents and others, including teachers. Following distribution of the results the supervisor would meet with groups of teachers to discuss implications of the findings and to set strategies for tackling some of the problems revealed by the study.

EVALUATIVE CRITERIA

The supervisor will find it profitable to direct the faculty in a total school evaluation periodically using a national set of standards which are called *Evaluative Criteria*.[21] A set of criteria has been developed by educators under the direction of the National Study of School Evaluation for evaluating three levels of schooling: elementary, middle school/junior high, and secondary. The secondary school standards were originally developed in 1940 and have been revised every 10 years. The middle school/ junior high and elementary school standards are newer, with the first middle school/junior high criteria appearing in 1963 and the first elementary school criteria in 1973.

These criteria stem from the efforts of the six regional accrediting associations to specify standards which the secondary schools are expected to meet in order for them to be accredited; that is, to earn the stamp of approval of the accrediting association. The purpose of the criteria is to assure fulfillment of a set of minimal standards and to provide a systematic procedure for studying and improving all phases of a school's program.

The criteria are most often used in conjunction with a school's efforts to achieve accreditation by the regional associations and are used extensively by secondary schools. Junior high schools, middle schools, and elementary schools are beginning to seek accreditation and have begun to use the respective criteria for their levels.

Whether or not the criteria are used as a part of the accreditation process they offer a valuable set of standards for use by any faculty and they set forth an effective self-study procedure which faculties might consider following.

When using the criteria the total faculty subjects its program to continuing study over a period of time, ordinarily a year. To conduct a self-study the building supervisor (the principal or someone designated by him) should provide for the following steps:

1. Appoint or elect a steering committee of the faculty to spearhead the study.
2. Assign each member of the faculty to one or more subcommittees.
3. Provide time for reports of the subcommittees to the entire faculty with subsequent discussion of each report.
4. Modify the school's program as the study moves along.
5. Arrange for the visit of a visiting committee of the regional accrediting association if the study is tied into application for accreditation. This step would be omitted if the school is not seeking accreditation.
6. Follow up and modify the school's program at the conclusion of the study. If the study has been conducted as part of the accreditation process, the visiting committee will have made recommendations for the school's consideration and these recommendations should be studied continuously in the light of possible implementation.

A look at the sections of the *Evaluative Criteria* will give a faculty an understanding of the comprehensiveness of these criteria. It will be noted that the criteria go beyond the curriculum itself and into other phases of the school's operation as well. Sections which appear in the current editions of the criteria are:

Secondary
School and Community
Philosophy and Objectives
Educational Program
   Agriculture
   Art
   Business Education
   Distributive Education
   Driver and Traffic Safety Education
   English
   Foreign Languages
   Health Education
   Home Economics
   Industrial Arts
   Mathematics
   Music
   Physical Education
   Religion

Middle School/Junior High
School and Community
Philosophy and Goals
Major Educational Priorities
Design of Curriculum
Learning Areas (same format for each
   area of the curriculum)
Individual Faculty Data
School Staff and Administration
Student Activities Program
Learning Media Services
Student Personnel Services
School Plant and Facilities

Elementary School

School and Community
Philosophy and Objectives
Design for Learning

Science
Social Studies
Special Education
Trade, Technical, and
   Industrial Education
Student Activities Program
Learning Media Services
Student Services
School Facilities
School Staff and Administration
Emerging and Unique Programs
Individual Staff Member

Areas of Learning (same format for
   each area of the curriculum)
School Staff and Administration
Individual Faculty Data
Learning Media Services
Pupil Services
School Plant
Plans and Priorities
Independent, Church-Related, and
   Other Non-Public Schools

The steering committee for a self-study will ordinarily assign teachers to two committees, a subject-area committee and a general committee. In the case of the secondary school criteria the steering committee is charged with the task of writing the summary of the self-evaluation.

Each subject-area committee follows the same format and examines the same aspects of its discipline. In the case of the secondary schools a subject-area committee would evaluate for its own area:

- organization
- nature of the offerings
- physical facilities
- direction of learning
  instructional staff
  instructional activities
  instructional materials
  methods of evaluation
- outcomes
- special characteristics
- general evaluation of instruction

Subject-area subcommittees of the junior high schools, middle schools, and elementary schools study:

- principles and premises
- nature of the program or area of learning
- evaluation
- plans for improvement
- current status scale (a rating scale which asks teachers to rate the degree of improvement they believe is necessary)

For some faculties a self-study of this kind is the first opportunity they have had to exchange views and to acquaint each other with what is happening in their fields.

The section on school and community for each of the three sets of criteria pulls together demographic data about a community and is of particular help in orienting members of the faculty who are new to a community. As noted in the previous chapter on curriculum development, these criteria require the faculty to state its philosophy, goals, and objectives as a prelude to evaluating the curriculum itself.

When schools couple the self-study with a bid for accreditation, these criteria must be applied in addition to separate sets of standards of the regional accrediting associations themselves. The regional standards add one further dimension to the process of evaluating the school's total program. Those schools which achieve accreditation are required to renew their accreditation annually, conduct an abbreviated interim evaluation of their program every five years, and conduct a full-scale self-study every 10 years. Some schools work out arrangements for obtaining the services of a consultant during a self-study and are sometimes able to reach an agreement with a university to provide a professor as the consultant and to award academic credit for participation in the study. The academic credit serves as a motivator to many teachers and is a device which the supervisor would do well to explore.

A number of years ago Vynce A. Hines and William M. Alexander conducted a study to determine the scope and extent of curriculum change in high schools as a result of self-evaluation for purposes of regional accreditation and to find out the impact of self-studies on the attitudes and practices of the teachers involved. Some of their findings were:

> Curriculum change occurs from 25 to 75 percent more often during the year of the self-study and the year immediately following in schools making the self-study than in their controls (schools not doing the self-study). Schools working on their own make 25 percent more changes; schools with consultant help make about 50 percent more curriculum changes; schools with university courses, 75 percent.
>
> Curriculum changes are most likely to be course changes, to be faculty initiated, to have a positive influence on the attainment of the school objectives, and to be judged as minor changes by the research staff. Most changes are modifications of existing courses, services, or activities. Courses, services, and activities are rarely dropped.
>
> About 50 percent of the Visiting Committee recommendations are rejected or just not implemented because of faculty and administrative disagreement, cost, lack of space and facilities, and unavailability of suitable personnel.
>
> Outstanding outcomes of the self-study and Visiting Committee recommendations, according to teachers, were increased library materials, increased audio-visual aids, and an increase in the number of teachers trying innovations. . . .
>
> Teachers felt that the most important changes influencing them were a better understanding of the school philosophy and an enhanced appreciation of the work of other departments. Negatively, about 10 percent reported worsened attitudes toward the evaluative process and smaller percents reported worsened attitudes toward pupils and toward the community. . . .
>
> To maximize the impact of school evaluations on curriculum change (a) the interval (between self-studies) should probably be not greater than five or six years; (b) schools should arrange for a field laboratory course with access to university consultants; (c) faculty and community should be involved in developing the school philosophy and studying the school and community prior to the beginning of other subcommittee work . . . (f) annual follow-up reports should be made on action taken on recommendations of the Visiting Committee.[22]

The self-study technique recommended by the *Evaluative Criteria* offers a fruitful way by which a faculty may evaluate its total program.

CURRICULUM MAPPING

Fenwick W. English has advocated a useful evaluation technique known as curriculum mapping. In essence, a curriculum map is an analysis of what a teacher has actually taught and the amount of time spent on the tasks. Explained English:

Curriculum mapping is a content analysis of the classroom curriculum as the teacher teaches it. It is an analysis of the *real* curriculum. . . .
    There are many kinds of curriculum maps (keep in mind that a map is not a lesson plan). What do the maps tell us? They tell us the level of repetition that does or does not exist, how teachers spend time on task. They help us to know what the real curriculum is in order to adjust the test and the curriculum guide.[23]

English pointed out the difference between a lesson plan and a curriculum map as follows:

The difference between curriculum mapping and a lesson plan is that a lesson plan is in the future tense and a curriculum map is in the past tense, i.e., what was taught, last week, last semester, last year, and a representation of time on task of the teacher involved.[24]

English described the characteristics of curriculum maps in the following manner:

While mapping formats may vary, most maps have at least two constants: content taught and time spent. Content may include not only conventional subject matter but anything children are expected to learn: processes, activities, or methods. The intent is to portray time devoted to each major learning task within each classroom or other functional unit. . . .
    Mapping provides the curriculum developer with a glimpse of how much time teachers spend on each major topic.[25]

Figure 8.4 is a sample classroom curriculum map of a fifth-grade social studies teacher.
    The values of curriculum mapping were summed up by English when he observed:

Curriculum mapping reveals to a staff, principal, or supervisor what is actually being taught, how long it is being taught, and the match between what is being taught and the district's testing program. Curriculum mapping invents or creates no "new" curriculum. Rather it attempts to describe the curriculum that currently exists. The curriculum developer can use the results to gradually make the written curriculum and the real curriculum more congruent with one another.[26]

```
                     Sample Classroom Curriculum Map
                        Fifth Grade Social Studies

    General Description:  U.S. history

    My fifth grade social studies program began with the early        Time*
    explorers of our nation.  These included the Portuguese
    explorers and Columbus.  We studied the conquest of Mexico          A
    and the Incas.  We examined the evolution of religious freedom
    in the U.S. by studying Lord Baltimore's development of             4
    Maryland and the Act of Toleration of 1649.  We also modeled
    for a week a mock House of Burgesses of Virginia.  We set up
    a unit on the old Southern plantation to study its economy.
```

Concepts	Skills	Attitudes	
—Realization of the impact on the New World of the Puritan Migration of 1629–40; —Understanding of the trials of Roger Williams in moving to Rhode Island	—Wrote stories —Used the proper resources to re-search the stories —Intergroup skill/making motions	—Developed respect for religious diversity —Developed aware-ness of the need for a proper forum for dialogue about sensitive issues	Time B 4
Time 1.50	Time 2.00	Time .50 Total	4

```
    General Description:  geography

    I taught the geography of the U.S. by working with four different  Time
    kinds of maps; relief, landform, political, and historical.  The     A
    students worked in committees and developed one of each for a       .50
    time period they selected.
```

Concepts	Skills	Attitudes	
—Utilized time belts —Used longitude and latitude to locate cities and places as a concept —Was able to utilize the inter-national Date Line	—Used string to measure distances on the globe —Made time esti-mates of how long it took to reach a place by various methods	—Developed an awareness of the need for inter-national agree-ment on dates/ times —Realized the need for uniformly understood map symbols	Time B .50
Time .20	Time .25	Time .05 Total	.50

```
    *Time A is the total time for the topic which should be equal to Time B,
    the total time sub–divided into three categories.  Time is expressed as the
    number of hours per week per school year.  This teacher spends about
    one half hour per week teaching social studies.
```

Figure 8.4 Sample Classroom Curriculum Map, Fifth-Grade Social Studies

SOURCE: Fenwick W. English, "Curriculum Mapping," *Educational* Leadership 37, no. 7 (April 1980): 558.

The comparison of curriculum maps of teachers of all sections of the same grade level or subject can reveal great variations in topics taught and amount of time spent on each. When school districts administer a systemwide test to students in all sections of a grade or subject, the variations in content and time can create problems for the learners. The supervisor should help teachers to examine what they have actually taught through the technique of curriculum mapping.

TEACHER PREPARATION IN RESEARCH

The supervisor will help teachers to develop curriculum proposals and to participate in research studies. The nature of the proposal and the degree of teacher participation will depend upon the magnitude of the studies. If a proposed study is to be a rigorous piece of applied research, it will ordinarily be drafted by the supervisor or research specialist and will conform to a detailed set of guidelines such as those proposed by the United States Department of Education for proposals which are submitted to it for funding. If it is a modest piece of applied research affecting a large portion of the faculty or the entire faculty of a school, a proposal may be developed along the lines suggested for plan design in the previous chapter. If a teacher or couple of teachers wish to carry out a piece of action research that will affect only their own classes, a streamlined, simplified proposal may be all that is needed, consisting of a statement of the proposal, hypotheses to be tested, and procedures to be followed, including means of evaluating.

Proposals for action research will ordinarily originate from the teachers themselves, though the supervisor may plant the seed which flowers into an action research study. Proposals for more sophisticated research may originate with teachers but more likely will originate with supervisors or research specialists. Wherever they originate, if teachers will be asked to participate, the proposals should be talked out before the first word is set down. The cooperation of the teachers must be assured and their continuous participation must be a certainty. The teachers will need to develop a sense of identity with the study. They may be called on to assist under guidance in formulating hypotheses, validating the objectives and the instruments, carrying out procedures, collecting data, analyzing data, and certainly in the decision making which takes place as a result of the data analysis.

Even with action research, teachers should seek to validate the goals and objectives of the proposed program and the instruments they will use. The instruments can be validated by subjecting them to review by other specialists in the field in which the research study falls. The goals and objectives may be validated by this same review process by experts or by reference to published findings of others who have studied the problem.

The supervisor should be as concerned with teachers' development of the skills of creating curriculum proposals as with the end product—the curriculum proposal itself. Writing curriculum proposals is one method of promoting a research orientation on the part of teachers.

EVALUATION OF MATERIALS AND STUDIES

The supervisor should assist teachers in evaluating both curriculum materials developed elsewhere and research studies conducted elsewhere which may have significance for them. It is a major responsibility of the supervisor to be on the lookout for new curriculum materials and channel them to teachers who might make use of them. The supervisor should help teachers decide whether the new materials would be useful in their situation. Together with the teachers he or she should examine the purposes of the materials, the uses to which they could be put, the limitations of the materials, and, of course, the costs.

The supervisor also has the responsibility of funneling to teachers reports of research studies which may be significant to them. It is usually much easier for the supervisor to fulfill the task of locating and disseminating curriculum materials than it is to search out and distribute reports of research. Many curriculum materials come across the supervisor's desk without any solicitation. Manufacturers and publishers of curriculum materials have a product they wish to sell and they are quick to make their products known. Supervisors encounter curriculum materials in their travels about the country and at state, regional, and national meetings. Catalogs and announcements of new materials appear in the mail regularly or can be obtained with a simple postcard.

Supervisors do not, as a rule, experience too much difficulty in bringing new curricular materials to the attention of teachers. This is one task of supervision where some supervisors overcompensate for lacks in other tasks of supervision. Where supervisors almost universally fall down is in the location and dissemination of research that is going on or has been conducted which may be of help to teachers in their school system. It is also difficult to decide whether a research study once located is important enough to be made available to teachers in the system. The sources of reports of research are conspicuous by their absence and frequently unavailable to supervisors. The identification of research studies is a research task in itself. Yet, it is an essential task and one which teachers do not have the time to fulfill.

Fortunately, there are helpful tools available to assist the supervisor in finding research studies. In some cases these tools may already be available in the school system somewhere. In other cases certain resources can be purchased by the school system for the specific purpose of helping school personnel to keep up on the research. In still other cases the supervisor may have to put in several hours at the closest public and university libraries periodically poring over research reference materials.

Where can the supervisor turn to locate research studies? The sources are many and are usually available in most college and university libraries, in some large public libraries, and sometimes in the professional libraries of school systems. A few of the more significant sources are:

1. *Education Index* (New York: H. W. Wilson Company). This is a standard reference to articles in education journals. The supervisor may locate what appears to be a pertinent article reporting a piece of research and would then need to go to the issue of the journal itself to read the article.

2. *Reader's Guide to Periodical Literature.* (New York: H. W. Wilson Company). This standard reference fulfills the same function as the *Education Index* except that this source indexes articles from journals of general interest.

3. *ERIC materials.* The most elaborate and comprehensive source of research information was established in 1964 by the former U.S. Office of Education, the system known in the profession as ERIC (Educational Resources Information Center), a system comprising some 16 clearinghouses each of which is devoted to gathering, evaluating, abstracting, and disseminating information in a particular field of specialization.

Many college libraries receive ERIC documents and some of these libraries have arranged to automatically receive all documents made available through ERIC. Though documents may be obtained in hard (paper) copy or on microfiche, the tendency for libraries today is to obtain the documents in microfiche form which is cheaper and far easier to store than hard copy.

The supervisor may wish to invest in the *Thesaurus of ERIC Descriptors* (Phoenix: Oryx Press) to help locate studies in particular fields of specialization. The *Thesaurus* provides a classification system for indexing ERIC documents and greatly simplifies the search process.

The supervisor should make use of two periodicals: *Resources in Education* (Washington, D.C.: U.S. Government Printing Office) and the *Current Index to Journals of Education* (Phoenix: Oryx Press). *Resources in Education* is a monthly abstract journal made up of résumés of studies, reports, and of indexes to these materials. The *Current Index to Journals in Education* is a monthly publication which follows the classification scheme of the *Thesaurus of ERIC Descriptors* and lists references to studies reported in education journals.

Access to ERIC materials is a must for persons who are making a search of the literature on a particular topic. ERIC clearinghouses will provide copies of biliographies which they may have developed for their particular fields of specialization.

4. *The Encyclopedia of Educational Research* (New York: Macmillan, 1969). This summarizes many educational research studies. It is revised every ten years and is sponsored by the American Educational Research Association.

5. *Research Studies in Education* (Itasca, Ill.: F. E. Peacock). This reference work is compiled under the direction of the professional education society, Phi Delta Kappa, and lists doctoral dissertations in education.

6. *Dissertation Abstracts* (Ann Arbor, Mich.: University Microfilms). This monthly publication contains abstracts of doctoral dissertations written in the United States and Canada. The user of this publication can order a copy of a dissertation on microfilm from University Microfilms. Users may also subscribe to University Microfilms' DATRIX service for locating abstracts of dissertations on particular fields of specialization.

7. Publications of the *American Educational Research Association* (Washington, D.C.). These publications contain reviews and reports of research studies on a wide variety of topics. Among the AERA publications are *American Educational Research Journal* (quarterly), *Educational Researcher* (monthly), *Monograph Series on Evalu-*

ation: Perspectives of Curriculum Evaluation (six monographs), *Review of Educational Research* (quarterly), and *Review of Research in Education* (annually).

8. *School Research Information Service and Smithsonian Science Information Exchange.* The School Research Information Service of Phi Delta Kappa (Bloomington, Ind.) and the Smithsonian Science Information Exchange (Washington, D.C.) are two information services which for a fee will run a search through the documents which they have indexed and classified. The School Research Information Service identifies documents in its own files, in ERIC, and in the *Current Index to Journals in Education.* Copies of the documents themselves can be obtained at nominal cost either in hard copy or on microfiche. The School Research Information Service has compiled bibliographies of ERIC abstracts in certain fields of specialization. The Smithsonian Science Information Exchange will furnish information on studies in progress in a number of fields of specialization.

9. *The National Assessment of Educational Progress.* Supervisors, particularly specialist-supervisors in selected fields, should keep themselves and their teachers abreast of findings of the National Assessment of Educational Progress (NAEP), funded by the National Institute of Education of the U.S. Department of Education and one of the most extensive research projects undertaken in the United States. Originally based in Denver under the aegis of the Education Commission of the States NAEP began collecting data on the achievement of four age groups throughout the country in 10 subject areas and on their attitudes toward the subjects.

The NAEP program dates from the efforts of Ralph Tyler and the Committee on Assessing the Progress of Education which under the instigation of the Carnegie Corporation in 1964 began development of a nationwide program to assess educational progress of learners. At the onset of NAEP the program came under heavy attack from professional educators who feared this assessment could lead to a national standardized curriculum, which is anathema to most educators but quite appealing to a sizable segment of the public. The educators were concerned that comparisons of schools and even individuals might be made from the data which might destroy the images of schools which showed up poorly and might cause harm to individuals. In spite of objections the NAEP moved ahead by identifying objectives in 10 subject areas: science, writing, citizenship, reading, literature, social studies, music, mathematics, career and occupational development, and art. Following specification of the objectives, criterion-referenced assessment instruments were developed.

Assessment began in 1969–1970 and the first results were reported in 1970. Over the years NAEP has conducted periodic assessments and reassessments in the various subject areas.

NAEP has been able to allay the fears of professional educators by its refusal to establish norms on the various tests or to make individual scores known. The program collects group data and reports them for the nation, by geographical region, by size of community, by type of community, by sex, by black or white ethnic group, by educational level of parents and by age groups. The target age groups are 9 year olds, 13 year olds, 17 year olds (in school and out), and young adults 26 to 35.

NAEP leaves the interpretation of the results to the local communities. The results give supervisors and teachers a useful set of data for comparative purposes and may aid in curriculum development. One of the advantages of the national assessment program is that results in certain areas may throw out clues to school districts for conducting their own local assessments. The national assessment program has also established a model which states are using in their own assessment programs.

The Education Commission of the States administered NAEP during its first fourteen years. Effective July 1, 1983 the National Institute of Education in funding a new five-year grant transferred administration of NAEP to the Educational Testing Service in Princeton, New Jersey. Supervisors seeking information on the National Assessment of Educational Progress may obtain assessment reports from the U.S. Government Printing Office. Additional reports and a newsletter which were formerly secured from the NAEP headquarters in Denver are now obtained from the Educational Testing Service, Princeton.

10. *International assessments.* Assessments of achievement in subject areas by learners in various countries are difficult to come by, but where they do exist and are available they may have at least an academic interest for supervisors and teachers and may have implications for curriculum planning. The problems of testing across cultures and making comparisons of performance are large indeed. Educational philosophies, goals, and objectives vary from country to country and affect both the curriculum and instructional methods. Student populations and socioeconomic factors as well as teacher training are variables which make comparisons tricky. Nevertheless, the supervisor who is on top of what is happening in curriculum evaluation should at least be familiar with significant studies which have been widely disseminated. One such study was mentioned in the previous chapter on curriculum development—the International Study of Achievement in Mathematics, which was conducted by the International Project for the Evaluation of Educational Achievement (IEA).[27] This landmark study, which is of special interest to mathematics supervisors, gathered data on the achievement of students in mathematics in 12 countries. Though we may have some reservations about the study, we might all wish that American pupils showed up better in the comparisons than they did.

STATE ASSESSMENT PROGRAMS

The supervisor should assume responsibility for directing teachers in state assessment programs and in evaluation of the school's program for purposes of state accreditation. States are moving into statewide assessment programs of pupil achievement in various subject areas. Some of the states are capitalizing on the model of the National Assessment of Educational Progress. Results obtained from state assessments have particular significance for communities within the state. The supervisor should discuss with teachers results of state assessments and together they should make interpretations of the data and plans for curriculum changes which seem warranted.

State departments of education are charged with the responsibility of accrediting schools within their states. Unlike accreditation by the regional accrediting association, which is voluntary, the process of accreditation by the state is mandatory for the schools. States vary in the procedures they use to decide whether individual schools will be awarded the distinction of being accredited or whether they will be placed on the list of schools which have not been accredited. As is the case with regional accreditation the purpose of state accreditation is the maintenance of minimal standards by the schools of the state.

LOCAL ASSESSMENT

The supervisor will work with teachers to plan and carry out local assessments of achievement of students in various subject areas. Whether or not the state requires participation in a state assessment program, local school districts should develop their own assessment programs. They may use input from national, state, and even international studies in developing their own assessment programs. Such programs are a part of the needs assessment referred to earlier. As well as serving to identify unmet needs, local assessment programs facilitate comparisons among schools within the school district. The selection or creation of appropriate testing instruments will be a major problem in local assessment and for help with this problem the supervisor may need to seek assistance from research specialists either inside or outside of the school system's personnel.

The supervisor will be called upon to display a wide repertoire of knowledge and skills in working with teachers on the critical task of curriculum evaluation.

SUMMARY

Evaluation is a fundamental part of the curriculum development process. It is through evaluation that teachers learn whether or not stated objectives have been reached. It is only through evaluation that intelligent curriculum decisions can be made.

The supervisor plays a major role as leader and resource person in the evaluation phase of curriculum development. Though a research director or evaluation specialist might possess a higher degree of skill in evaluation and research than the supervisor, the positions of research director and evaluator are not universally found in the school systems and the supervisor must fulfill the role of leader in evaluation.

In fulfilling this role the supervisor should seek to help teachers develop an evaluative frame of mind, an inquiring attitude, and a research orientation. The supervisor should help teachers to state curricular objectives in performance terms in order to simplify the task of evaluation.

The understanding of nine basic research concepts will help teachers in their role as consumers and appliers of research. A knowledge of these concepts will enable teachers to more effectively utilize standardized test data and to interpret research studies which have been conducted inside and outside the school system.

The supervisor should acquaint teachers with various types of evaluation and research. The purpose of acquainting teachers with kinds of studies which are conducted is to show them the range of possibilities and to indicate types of studies in which they are most likely to be involved. Generally speaking, teachers engage in descriptive research, action research, and some applied research.

The supervisor should help teachers to develop skills of conducting needs assessments in order to discover unmet needs. Thorough needs assessments obtain input from students, teachers, administrators, other school personnel, and the community. A special caution is suggested—those conducting needs assessments should be concerned that data are sought from all segments of the community and not just selected segments.

Teachers should be instructed in the use of evaluation materials developed for both state and regional accreditation. While regional accreditation is voluntary, state accreditation is required. A self-study by a faculty utilizing the *Evaluative Criteria* for its particular school level is a comprehensive way of evaluating a total school program.

The supervisor should keep teachers abreast of information on state, national, and international assessment of achievement of learners. Whether or not a school district participates in a state or national assessment program, it should under the leadership of the supervisor develop its own local assessment program. The purposes of local assessment are (1) to identify unmet needs, (2) to make comparisons of schools within a district, and (3) to make decisions about the curriculum.

The supervisor in the role of an evaluative resource person should be knowledgeable about sources of research information and should program time in such a way that he or she can review recent research and disseminate research information to the teachers being supervised.

ACTIVITIES FOR FURTHER STUDY

1. Search the literature, find, and report on a model of curriculum evaluation other than those described in this chapter.
2. Construct and analyze a curriculum map for your grade or subject for a period of one semester.
3. Find a report of a curriculum study carried on in a school outside your own district and prepare a critique of the study as to: research design, validation of the goals and objectives, validation of the instruments, procedures used, treatment of the data, conclusions, and applicability to your school district.
4. Draft a plan for an introductory in-service program on curriculum evaluation.
5. Design an instrument to assess student needs. Administer this instrument to a random sample of 20 to 25 students and summarize your findings.
6. Design an instrument to assess attitudes of the public toward the school's curriculum. Administer this instrument to a random sample of 20 to 25 laypeople and summarize your findings.
7. Choose a curriculum problem and design a plan to study that problem.
8. Define: *mean, median, reliability, validity, norm, percentile, correlation coefficient, standard score,* and *standard deviation.*

9. Choose a curriculum topic and conduct a search for information about it in ERIC.
10. Choose a curriculum topic and locate abstracts on it in *Resources in Education*.
11. Choose a curriculum topic and locate studies on it in the *Current Index to Journals in Education*.
12. Examine and write a brief report on the nature and use of the *Thesaurus of ERIC Descriptors*.
13. Examine the regional accreditation report of a school which has obtained accreditation by its regional accrediting association and decide which recommendations of the visiting committee have been implemented since the report was issued and which have not been implemented. If a recommendation has not been implemented, formulate hypotheses as to why the recommendation has not been put into practice.
14. Distinguish between hard copy, microfilm, and microfiche. Explain the advantages and disadvantages of each of these media.
15. Find out if your school system subscribes to Phi Delta Kappa's School Research Information Service. If it does, find out if the service has ever been used and cite illustrations of its use.
16. Examine and fill out a 3×5 card reporting characteristics of each of the following sources of research information:
    a. *The Encyclopedia of Educational Research*
    b. *The Review of Educational Research*
    c. *Research Studies in Education*
    d. *Dissertation Abstracts*
17. Write a position paper on "The Role of the Supervisor in Conducting Local Research."
18. Write a paper utilizing selected references accounting for objections which researchers make to action research and propose some ways to overcome these objections.
19. List at least five curricular problems in a field of specialization you know well which call for rigorous applied research studies.
20. List at least three curriculum problems or instructional problems in a field of specialization you know well which would be suitable for action research.
21. Apply one subject area section of the *Evaluative Criteria* for your particular school level in the school whose program you know best.
22. Sample and report opinions of at least five teachers as to what forces they believe have the greatest impact on curriculum change. Ask them to identify if they can any curricular change which has come about as a result of local research.
23. Write a brief account summarizing your state's accreditation process. Try to determine what beneficial results, if any, have come about in a school you know well as a result of state accreditation.
24. Find out and report whether your state has in effect a statewide plan for assessing pupil achievement in subject areas.

25. Choose a field of your interest or expertness in which assessments have been made by the National Assessment of Educational Progress and report findings and implications of the results.

26. Write a brief position paper on whether you believe the National Assessment of Educational Progress should reveal norms against which individual schools and individual students could be compared.

27. Interview at least six teachers to see if they have participated in any type of evaluative study of the curriculum in the last five years. If they have, report the type of study and find out whether the study was required or not (as, for example, a study in connection with state or regional accreditation).

28. Talk with the principal of a school and ascertain his or her views on the necessity of curriculum evaluation and what he or she believes is going on in the school in the way of curriculum evaluation. Raise the same question with (1) the assistant principal for curriculum, if there is one, (2) a generalist supervisor, and (3) a specialist supervisor (the specialist could be a grade coordinator, team leader, or department head) at the same school.

29. Conduct a brief study employing the Delphi Technique.

30. Write a paper describing the roles of each of the following in curriculum evaluation:
    a. the principal
    b. the supervisor
    c. the teacher
    d. students
    e. the public

31. Identify in your school system a curriculum innovation which in its initial proposal contained a plan for evaluating its success. List criteria on which to analyze the evaluation plan and make a critique of the plan on the basis of these criteria.

32. *Those who are teaching* will design and carry out a piece of action research and report either progress or final results. *Those who are not teaching* will interview a teacher who is conducting a piece of action research and report on its design, procedures, and results.

NOTES

1. Michael Scriven, "The Methodology of Evaluation," *Perspectives of Curriculum Evaluation, AERA Monograph Series on Evaluation*, no. 1, Chicago, Rand McNally, 1967, 53.
2. Ibid.
3. Dominick Graziano, "The Curriculum Director as an Evaluator," Carbondale, Ill., Southern Illinois University, 1971. Unpublished doctoral dissertation.
4. Ibid., 175.
5. Ibid., 176.
6. Ibid., 177.
7. Ibid.

8. Ibid., 179.
9. Ibid., 180.
10. Florida Atlantic University, *Middle School Needs Assessment Performance Objectives*, Boca Raton, Fla., Division of Continuing Education, School Service Center, 1972, Section 5.
11. John W. Best, *Research in Education*, 2d ed., Englewood Cliffs, N.J., Prentice-Hall, 1970, 14.
12. Daniel L. Stufflebeam et al., *Educational Evaluation and Decision Making*, Itasca, Ill., F. E. Peacock, 1971.
13. The Center for the Study of Evaluation, *Evaluation Workshop I: An Orientation*, Del Monte Research Park, Monterey, Calif.: CTB/McGraw-Hill, 1971. See also Stephen Klein, Gary Fenstermacher, and Marvin C. Alkin, "The Center's Changing Evaluation Model," *Evaluation Comment* 4, no. 2 (1971): 9–12.
14. For other models of curriculum evaluation see J. Galen Saylor, William M. Alexander, and Arthur J. Lewis, *Curriculum Planning for Better Teaching and Learning*, 4th ed., New York, Holt, Rinehart and Winston, 1981, ch. 7.
15. The Joint Committee on Standards for Educational Evaluation, *Standards for Evaluation of Educational Programs, Projects, and Materials*, New York, McGraw-Hill, 1981.
16. Fenwick W. English and Roger A. Kaufman, *Needs Assessment: A Focus for Curriculum Development*, Alexandria, Va., Association for Supervision and Curriculum Development, 1975, 3–4.
17. See, for example, Theodore J. Czajkowski and Jerry L. Patterson, *School District Needs Assessment: Practical Models for Increasing Involvement in Curriculum Decisions*, Madison, Wisc., Madison Public Schools, 1976.
18. Willard Crouthamel and Stephen M. Preston, *Needs Assessment: User's Manual*; *Needs Assessment: Resource Guide*; *Needs Assessment: Checklist of Steps*, Atlanta, Ga., Research and Development Utilization Project, Georgia Department of Education, 1979.
19. Savannah-Chatham County Public Schools, *System-Wide Needs for a Comprehensive Educational Plan*, adopted by the Board of Public Instruction for the City of Savannah and the County of Chatham (Georgia), May 6, 1981.
20. See Olaf Helmer, "Analysis of the Future: The Delphi Method," in James R. Bright, ed., *Technological Forecasting for Industry and Government Methods and Applications*, Englewood Cliffs, N.J., Prentice-Hall, 1968, 116–122; Olaf Helmer, "The Delphi Method—An Illustration," ibid., 123–133; T. J. Gordon, "New Approaches to Delphi," ibid., 134–143. See also W. Timothy Weaver, "The Delphi Forecasting Method," *Phi Delta Kappan* 52, no. 5 (January 1971): 267–271, bibliography on the Delphi Technique, ibid., 271; Frederick R. Cyphert and Walter L. Gant, "The Delphi Technique: A Case Study," ibid., 272–273.
21. National Study of School Evaluation, *Evaluative Criteria*, 5th ed., 1978 (secondary); *Middle School/Junior High School Evaluative Criteria*, rev. ed., 1979; *Elementary School Evaluative Criteria*, 2d ed., 1981, Falls Church, Va., National Study of School Evaluation.
22. Vynce A. Hines and William M. Alexander, *High School Self-Evaluation and Curriculum Change*, Final Report, Project 3120, Contract No. OE 6–10–154, Bureau of Research, Office of Education, Washington, D.C., U.S. Department of Health, Education, and Welfare, August 1967, 64–65.
23. Fenwick W. English, "Curriculum Mapping," *The Professional Educator* 3, no. 1 (Spring 1980): 11–12.
24. Ibid., 11.
25. Fenwick W. English, "Curriculum Mapping," *Educational Leadership* 37, no. 7 (April 1980): 558.
26. Ibid., 559.
27. T. Husén, ed., *International Study of Achievement in Mathematics*, 2 vols., New York, John Wiley, 1967.

BIBLIOGRAPHY

American Educational Research Association. *American Educational Research Journal.* Washington, D.C.: American Educational Research Association, quarterly.

———. *Educational Researcher.* Washington, D.C.: American Educational Research Association, monthly.

———. *Monograph Series on Evaluation: Perspectives of Curriculum Evaluation 1–6.* Ann Arbor, Mich.: Xerox University Microfilms.

———. *Review of Educational Research.* Washington, D.C.: American Educational Research Association, quarterly.

———. *Review of Research in Education.* Itasca, Ill.: F. E. Peacock, annually.

Apple, Michael W., Michael J. Subkoviak, and Henry S. Luffler, Jr., eds. *Educational Evaluation: Analysis and Responsibility.* Berkeley, Calif.: McCutchan, 1974.

Beggs, Donald, and Ernest Lewis, *Measurement and Evaluation in the Schools.* Boston: Houghton Mifflin, 1975.

Best, John W. *Research in Education*, 2nd ed. Englewood Cliffs, N.J.: Prentice-Hall, 1970.

Borg, Walter R. *Applying Educational Research: A Practical Guide for Teachers.* New York: Longman, 1981.

Bright, James R., ed. *Technological Forecasting for Industry and Government Methods and Applications.* Englewood Cliffs, N.J.: Prentice-Hall, 1968.

California Evaluation Improvement Project. *Program Evaluator's Guide*, 2nd ed. Princeton, N.J.: Evaluation Improvement Program, Educational Testing Service, 1979.

The Center for the Study of Evaluation. *Evaluation Workshop I: An Orientation.* Monterey, Calif.: CTB/McGraw-Hill, 1971. Participant's Notebook and Leadership Manual.

Corey, Stephen M. *Action Research to Improve School Practices.* New York: Teachers College, Columbia University, 1953.

Crouthamel, Willard, and Stephen M. Preston. *Needs Assessment: Checklist of Steps*; *Needs Assessment: Resource Guide*; *Needs Assessment: User's Manual.* Atlanta: Research and Development Utilization Project, Georgia Department of Education, 1979.

"Curriculum Evaluation: Uses, Misuses, and Nonuses." *Educational Leadership* 35, no. 4 (January 1978): 243–297.

De Cecco, John P., and William R. Crawford. *The Psychology of Learning and Instruction*, 2nd ed. Englewood Cliffs, N.J.: Prentice-Hall, 1974.

Dissertation Abstracts. Ann Arbor, Mich.: University Microfilms.

Ebel, Robert, ed. *The Encyclopedia of Educational Research.* New York: Macmillan, 1979.

Education Index. New York: H. W. Wilson Company.

Eisner, Elliot W. *The Educational Imagination: On the Design and Evaluation of School Programs.* New York: Macmillan, 1979.

———. "Educational Connoisseurship and Criticism: Their Form and Functions in Educational Evaluation." *The Journal of Aesthetic Education* 10, nos. 3–4 (July–October 1976): 135–150.

English, Fenwick W. "Curriculum Mapping." *Educational Leadership* 37, no. 7 (April 1980): 558–559.

———. "Curriculum Mapping." *The Professional Educator* 3, no. 1 (Spring 1980): 8–12.

——— and Roger A. Kaufman. *Needs Assessment: A Focus for Curriculum Development.* Alexandria, Va.: Association for Supervision and Curriculum Development, 1975.

Gay, L. R. *Educational Evaluation and Measurement: Competencies for Analysis and Application.* Columbus, Ohio: Charles E. Merrill, 1980.

———. *Educational Research: Competencies for Analysis and Application*, 2nd ed. Columbus, Ohio: Charles E. Merrill 1976.

Gronlund, Norman E. *Measurement and Evaluation in Teaching*, 2nd ed. New York: Macmillan, 1971.

Husén, Torsten, ed. *International Study of Achievement in Mathematics.* New York: Wiley, 1967. 2 vols.

Johnson, Mauritz, Jr. *Intentionality in Education: A Conceptual Model of Curricular and Instructional Planning and Evaluation*. New York: Center for Curriculum Research and Services, 1977.
Joint Committee on Standards for Educational Evaluation. *Standards for Evaluation of Educational Programs, Projects, and Materials*. New York: McGraw-Hill, 1981.
Kaufman, Roger A. *Educational System Planning*. Englewood Cliffs, N.J.: Prentice-Hall, 1972.
Lewy, Arieh, ed. *Handbook of Curriculum Evaluation*. New York: Longman, 1977.
Lindvall, C. M., and Richard C. Cox with John O. Bolvin. "Evaluation as a Tool in Curriculum Development: The IPI Evaluation Program." *AERA Monograph Series on Curriculum Evaluation*, no. 5. Chicago: Rand McNally, 1970.
National Study of School Evaluation. *Elementary School Evaluative Criteria*, 2nd ed. Falls Church, Va.: National Study of School Evaluation, 1981.
———. *Evaluative Criteria*, 5th ed. Falls Church, Va.: National Study of School Evaluation, 1978.
———. *Middle School/Junior High School Evaluative Criteria*, rev. ed. Falls Church, Va.: National Study of School Evaluation,1979.
Payne, David A., ed. *Curriculum Evaluation*. Lexington, Mass.: D. C. Heath, 1974.
Phi Delta Kappa. *Research Studies in Education*. Itasca, Ill.: F. E. Peacock.
Plakos, Marie, John Plakos, and Robert Babcock. *Workbook on Program Evaluation*, 2nd ed. Princeton, N.J.: Educational Testing Service, 1978.
Popham, W. James. *Educational Evaluation*. Englewood Cliffs, N.J.: Prentice-Hall, 1975.
Provus, Malcolm. *Discrepancy Evaluation for Educational Program Improvement and Assessment*. Berkeley, Calif.: McCutchan, 1971.
Reader's Guide to Periodical Literature. New York: H. W. Wilson Company.
Saylor, J. Galen, William M. Alexander, and Arthur J. Lewis. *Curriculum Planning for Better Teaching and Learning*, 4th ed. New York: Holt, Rinehart and Winston, 1981.
Scriven, Michael. "The Methodology of Evaluation." *Perspectives of Curriculum Evaluation, AERA Monograph Series on Curriculum Evaluation*, no. 1. Chicago: Rand McNally, 1967.
Stake, Robert E. "Language, Rationality, and Assessment." In *Improving Educational Assessment and an Inventory of Measures of Affective Behavior*, Walcott H. Beatty, ed. Alexandria, Va.: Commission on Assessment of Educational Outcomes, Association for Supervision and Curriculum Development, 1969.
Stufflebeam, Daniel L. et al. *Educational Evaluation and Decision Making*. Itasca, Ill.: F. E. Peacock, 1971.
Tuckman, Bruce W. *Conducting Educational Research*. New York: Harcourt, Brace Jovanovich, 1972.
Tyler, Ralph W. *Basic Principles of Curriculum and Instruction*. Chicago: University of Chicago Press, 1949.
———, ed. *Educational Evaluation: New Roles, New Means*, 68th Yearbook of the National Society for the Study of Education. Chicago: University of Chicago Press, 1969.
———, Robert M. Gagné, and Michael Scriven. "Perspectives of Curriculum Evaluation." *AERA Monograph Series on Curriculum Evaluation*. no. 1, Chicago: Rand McNally, 1967.
Wiles, David K. *Changing Perspectives in Educational Research*. Worthington, Ohio: Charles A. Jones, 1972.
Worthen, Blaine R., and James R. Sanders. *Educational Evaluation: Theory and Practice*. Worthington, Ohio: Charles A. Jones, 1973.

Multi-Media

Filmstrip-tape programs. Vimcet Associates, Post Office Box 24714, Los Angeles, California 90024.
   #18 *Experimental Designs for School Research*
   #23 *Current Conceptions of Educational Evaluation*

#25 *Deciding on Defensible Goals Via Educational Needs Assessment*
#26 *Alternative Measurement Tactics for Educational Evaluation*
Kit. Morris, Lyon Lyons. *Program Evaluation Kit.* Beverly Hills, Calif.: Sage Publications,
   1978. The kit consists of the following volumes:
   Evaluator's Handbook
   How to Deal with Goals and Objectives
   How to Design a Program Evaluation
   How to Measure Program Implementation
   How to Measure Attitudes
   How to Measure Achievement
   How to Calculate Statistics
   How to Present an Evaluation Report

Information Services

School Research Information Service, Phi Delta Kappa, 8th Street and Union Avenue,
   Bloomington, Ind. 47401.
Smithsonian Science Information Exchange Inc., Room 300, 1730 M Street, N.W.,
   Washington, D.C. 20036.

Reports of the NAEP

Reports of the National Assessment of Educational Progress are available from the Educational
   Testing Service, Princeton, New Jersey 08541.

Videotapes

Curriculum Mapping. Fenwick English explains techniques of improving the curriculum by
   determining what is actually being taught. Association for Supervision and Curriculum
   Development, 225 N. Washington Street, Alexandria, Virginia 22314, 1981. 20 minutes.
Planning Curriculum with a Futures Perspective. Willis Harman, Arthur Lewis, Don Glines,
   Robert Bundy, and Sherry Schiller analyze trends and ways schools can help students
   prepare for the future. Association for Supervision and Curriculum Development, 225 N.
   Washington Street, Alexandria, Virginia 22314, 1982. 21 minutes.

ERIC Materials

Current Index to Journals in Education, Oryx Press, 2214 North Central at Encanto, Phoenix,
   Arizona 85004, monthly.
Resources in Education, Washington, D.C., Superintendent of Documents, U.S. Government
   Printing Office, Washington, D.C. 20402, monthly. Semiannual indexes available from
   the U.S. Government Printing Office. Annual cumulations: abstracts (2 volumes) and in-
   dex (1 volume) available from Oryx Press. *Resources in Education* replaced *Research in
   Education* in January 1975.
Thesaurus of ERIC Descriptors, 9th ed., Oryx Press, 1982.

PART **IV**

LEADERSHIP IN
STAFF DEVELOPMENT

9

Helping Teachers through In-service Programs

OBJECTIVES

After studying Chapter 9 you should be able to accomplish the following objectives:

1. Define staff development and in-service education.
2. State characteristics of an effective in-service program.
3. Describe your preferred model of in-service education.
4. Conduct an in-service needs assessment.
5. Describe features of a school district master plan for staff development.
6. Describe features of an individual school plan for staff development.
7. Propose an outline for writing in-service training components.
8. Suggest several types of in-service activities.
9. Suggest defensible incentives for teacher participation in in-service activities.
10. Explain if and when outside consultants should be used.
11. Conduct an evaluation of an in-service activity.
12. Propose criteria for evaluating a master plan for staff development.
13. Explain the purposes of a teacher education center and take a position on the teacher education center's role in staff development.

SUPERVISION AND STAFF DEVELOPMENT

Our peregrination into the world of supervision brings us now to the domain of staff development. It would be a rare specialist in supervision who would advise us not to enter and travail in this domain. Where specialists differ, as we have seen in Chapter 2, is on the following questions:

Is supervision only staff development?
Is staff development the same as in-service education?
Do we provide in-service education for groups or individuals or both?

Let's recall the model of supervision presented in Chapter 1, which appeared as in Figure 9.1.

This model depicts three domains, side by side, with no barriers to block off interaction between them. If we perceived supervision as limited to staff development, we might vary the model in several ways. We might, for example, visualize one domain with supervisory responsibilities limited to the improvement of instruction, as in Figure 9.2.

Or, if we concluded that supervisors should lead teachers only in programmatic development, we might chart a model like Figure 9.3.

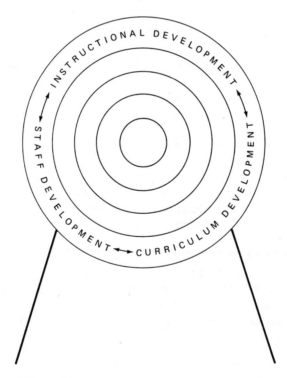

Figure 9.1 Model of Supervision

Figure 9.2   Staff Development Model 1

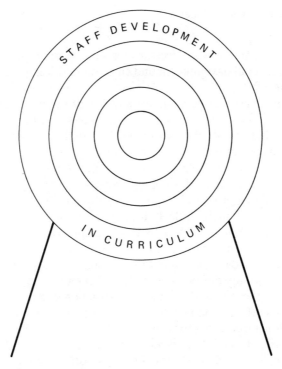

Figure 9.3   Staff Development Model 2

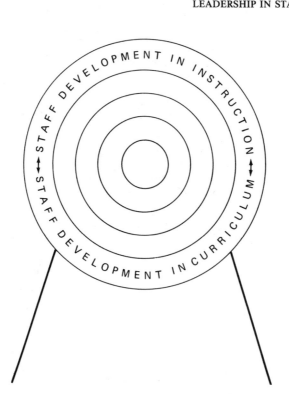

Figure 9.4 Staff Development Model 3

Were we to aver that it was necessary for supervisors to help teachers develop skills in both instructional development and curriculum development we might create the model in Figure 9.4.

Yet, although a case can be made for any one of these three staff development models, something is lacking when we examine what it is that supervisors do and what it is that teachers need. We can identify needed areas of professional development which do not fit into the rubrics of instructional development or curriculum development. Where do we place, for example, developmental activities like displaying a sense of humor, developing self-confidence, perfecting one's own language and mathematical skills, and developing a desire for continuous professional growth? I find it difficult to classify in staff development models 1 through 3 professional development activities like approved travel, delivery of talks at professional meetings, and work in the area of public relations. We could, therefore, draw a model to show three dimensions of staff development, as in Figure 9.5.

In the model of supervision presented in Chapter 1 (see Figure 9.1) I have chosen to diagram the three domains of instructional development, curriculum development, and staff development with overlap and interaction among all three. I prefer to establish three categories instead of subsuming all activities under staff development in order to make the essence of each domain stand out.

Staff development model 4 comes close to substituting for the model of supervision proposed in this text. Model 4 differs from the model of supervision in that it

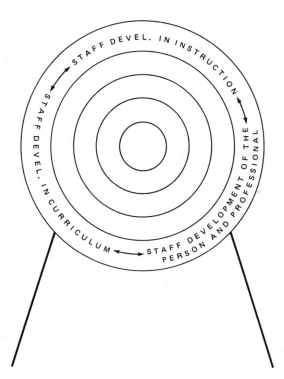

Figure 9.5 Staff Development Model 4

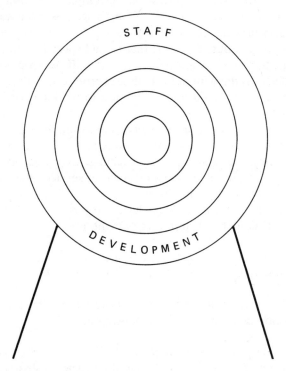

Figure 9.6 Staff Development Model 5

plays up the *staff* dimension and plays down the *instructional* and *curricular* dimensions. Were we to do that we might as well follow a model of supervision which equates supervision to staff development, as in Figure 9.6.

Staff development models 1 through 3 are too limited in their concept. Models 4, 5, and 6 would appeal to some specialists in supervision, since they would limit the focus of supervision to improvement of the *staff member*. Sometimes, however, we need to focus on improvement of *instruction* and the *curriculum* with staff development coming in as a secondary purpose. Not every activity carried out with teachers must have as its purpose the *training* of personnel. Some activities utilize the services of teachers to solve instructional and curricular problems and to create materials. There comes a time when professional teachers would reject the notion that every activity is a training experience for them.

Purposes of Staff Development

Before considering the purposes of staff development let's recap and expand upon the definitions of staff development which we introduced in Chapter 2. Most specialists in supervision agree that staff development is a function of supervision. Most specialists agree that in-service education is a function of supervision. There is considerable disagreement, however, as to whether staff development is the same as in-service education. I have used the terms staff development and in-service education synonymously in this text, as did Lloyd W. Dull,[1] since this is the way these terms are often used in present practice.

It should be pointed out, however, that not all specialists in supervision would agree with that usage. Some would maintain that staff development is the broader term which includes working with individuals and groups in both formal and informal situations whereas in-service education is limited to working with groups in formal training programs.

Ben M. Harris conceptualized in-service education as a part of staff development.[2] He divided staff development into two categories: (1) staffing and (2) training. Included in the concept of staffing were selecting, assigning, evaluating, retiring, and dismissing staff. The training aspect included in-service education and advanced preparation, which were defined in Chapter 2.

E. Lawrence Dale held in-service education to be one of several functions of staff development. Dale defined staff development as:

the totality of educational and personal experiences that contribute toward an individual's being more competent and satisfied in an assigned professional role.[3]

Thomas J. Sergiovanni and Robert J. Starratt drew the following distinctions between staff development and in-service education:

Conceptually, staff development is not something the school does to the teacher but something the teacher does for himself or herself. While staff development is basically growth-oriented, in-service education typically assumes a deficiency in the teacher and presupposes a set of appropriate ideas, skills, and methods which need developing. By focusing on these ideas, skills, and methods, in-service education works to reduce the teacher's range of alternatives—indeed, to bring about conformity. Staff development does not assume a deficiency in the teacher, but rather assumes a need for people at work to grow and develop on the job. Rather than reduce the range of alternatives, staff development works to increase this range.[4]

For our purposes staff development is an organized program for training personnel, in this case teachers, both in groups and individually to do a better job at what they are doing. Staff development is in-service education, or put another way, the staff is developed through in-service education. In-service education may be either remedial or developmental, corrective or enriching.

Why should staff development be necessary? Let's examine what happens in our profession. Every June on the campuses of hundreds of colleges and universities several thousand young people receive the long-awaited degree which certifies that they have completed their teacher-training program. With degree and state credentials in hand they join the competition for teaching jobs. In four years of training—the most common period throughout the country—they have accumulated perhaps 180 quarter-hours' credit or have completed perhaps 40 to 50 courses in a wide range of fields, or may have achieved a minimal level in a certain number of professional competencies.

Since approximately one-half of a college program consists of general education—a necessary and desirable feature—only about half of a college education for teachers consists of work in the teaching field and pedagogy. The preservice trainees' program usually culminates in a brief student-teaching experience of between 8 to 12 weeks and the amount of actual "hands on" experience during that time differs from school to school and from supervising teacher to supervising teacher. Given all the knowledge and skills necessary for successful teaching, the college training program is only a beginning. Hence the need for a continuing in-service program.

Programs for teachers in service provide the instructional staff with opportunities to expand knowledge and improve skills which have been developed in a rudimentary fashion in the college training program and to achieve new knowledge and develop new skills called for in their teaching assignments. In-service education combats complacency and satisfaction with the status quo which set in as new teachers adjust to the routines of their positions.

The Supervisor's Role in In-service Education

The supervisor as in-service leader attempts to jar teachers' complacency and create dissatisfactions with the status quo. It is the supervisor's job to stimulate teachers to want to find new and better ways of accomplishing their instructional duties and improving the curriculum. The supervisor has the responsibility for identifying teachers' in-service needs through surveys, requests from teachers, and observation. The supervisor plans, sets into operation, and evaluates in-service programs. The supervisor develops the master plan for staff development, makes its components known, and facilitates its use. The supervisor records the teachers' participation and success in in-service activities.

The supervisor's role is made more difficult by lack of agreement and uncertainties about the scope and nature of in-service education. Swirling around in-service education are the following issues some of which we touched on in Chapter 2.

1. There is no agreement that in-service education is really necessary. There is a school of thought to the effect that teachers are trained, professional people; that once they are employed there is little need for continuing education which is planned for the teacher. This school of thought holds that teachers will learn as they teach and that they can take care of what little updating they need by self-study.

2. There is no agreement on whether in-service education is effective. Summarizing several research studies, John T. Lovell commented:

It was . . . found that teachers do not perceive that they are getting the services they need and often perceive supervisors as spending much of their time in the central offices working on administrative tasks not directly related to the needs of teachers. There was also evidence that the direct services that teachers were receiving were ineffective according to certain criteria of effectiveness.[5]

Don Davies' testimony before the United States Senate's Subcommittee on Education in 1967, cited by Ben M. Harris, was one of the sharpest criticisms of in-service education. Said Davies:

In service teacher education is the slum of American education . . . disadvantaged, poverty stricken, neglected, psychologically isolated, whittled with exploitation and broken promises.[6]

Fred H. Wood and Steven R. Thompson agreed that "most staff development programs are irrelevant and ineffective, a waste of time and money."[7]

It is extremely difficult to pinpoint the effectiveness of in-service education, especially in terms of its ultimate purpose: the improvement of student achievement. Much of the research focuses on teachers' perceptions of the effectiveness or ineffectiveness of in-service programs. Harris mentioned several studies, some of which supported and some of which were critical of in-service education. Following are several examples.

Gordon Lawrence et al. reported on more than 90 in-service programs which had been well evaluated between 1968 and 1973. Of the Lawrence study Harris wrote:

Much that has long been advocated was reaffirmed: teacher positive attitudes, active participation, self-instruction, differentiated experiences, personalized or clinical approaches, continuous programmatic efforts, and freedom of choice are all consistently associated with effective in-service education. More exciting is Lawrence's conclusion that the studies show a remarkable success rate, with 80 percent of the studies showing *significant* changes in teacher behavior.[8]

In a study in Texas in 1977 Don Proctor McLendon surveyed the opinions of administrators, supervisors, and teachers about a number of principles of in-service education. Concerning this study Harris noted:

It appears from this limited evidence that teachers are highly accepting of in-service programs when they reflect some of the best-known and widely advocated principles of good practice.[9]

Francis J. Reardon found positive reactions toward in-service education in a 1975 survey of some 500 teachers in 280 school districts of Pennsylvania. Harris observed that even though the teachers responding to Reardon were on their own time in some 360 in-service programs:

Instructors were rated "excellent" by 90 percent of the teachers. Approximately 90 percent rated the activities "overall" highly positively. Similarly high positive ratings were reported for "achievement" of competencies and relevance of activities. This study reports a high level of acceptance, even enthusiasm, for a broad array of in-service offerings.[10]

Less positive attitudes of teachers toward in-service education were uncovered by Jack L. Brimm and Daniel J. Tollett in a 1974 study of 646 teachers in every school district of Tennessee. Harris summarized this study in the following way:

In responding to items about current realities, teachers reported that most in-service activities "do not appear relevant" (73 percent), "do not like to attend" (63 percent), "are not well planned" (44 percent), and "are virtually useless" (31 percent). . . . They further criticized the activities in terms of lack of specificity of objectives, inadequate follow-up, and lack of planning.[11]

David W. Champagne attributed students' improvement in basic skills, increases in SAT scores, improved student attitudes toward school, improved school attendance, and decreases in vandalism and teacher absenteeism (in a Pennsylvania study in the mid-1970s) to a staff development program which instructed teachers on how to offer high-interest projects in their classes.[12] Champagne pointed to the success of the Newington (Connecticut) Public Schools in turning around teacher attitudes toward supervision from highly negative to highly positive through a well-planned staff development program.[13] He called attention to improvement David N. Aspy achieved in interpersonal skills through a teacher-training program in which he used procedures of Robert R. Carkhuff.[14] Concluded Champagne:

These pieces of evidence taken together add up to a persuasive argument for continuing staff development, supervision, and evaluation. Successful programs will have visible, tangible results at all levels and justify the energy used to create them and the money used to sustain them.[15]

3. There is disagreement on what kinds of in-service education are best. As we have seen in the discussion of issues in Chapter 2, some specialists advocate group study; others propose clinical approaches; some want peer supervision; still others

recommend self-study by the teacher. These differing opinions make it difficult for practitioners to decide where to focus their efforts.

4. There is uncertainty of the thrust of in-service education. Should we, for example, spend our time correcting deficiencies or in providing enriching, developmental activities? Should in-service education be reactive to such forces as increased knowledge in all fields, increased use of technology, changes in students served, and changed attitudes of the public on the emphases they wish the schools to take? Or, should we be proactive and develop in-service programs which anticipate changes and take teachers to the forefront of new developments? Should supervisors wait and watch or should they move out and expand?

5. There is disagreement on the role of theory in in-service education. In simplistic terms, supervisors feel that theory is essential; teachers reject that notion. Teachers tend toward wanting practical helps with the day-to-day problems of instruction. They see little value in theory, which they believe, often erroneously, does not aid them in the classroom. Lovell confirmed the fact that most research studies "indicated that teachers and supervisors desired service directly related to the improvement of classroom instruction."[16]

Teachers, by and large, express the same negative attitudes toward theory as they do toward theory's companion, philosophy. They do not agree with John Dewey that:

Theory is in the end, as has been well said, the most practical of all things, because this widening of the range of attention beyond nearby purpose and desire eventually results in the creation of wider and farther-reaching purposes and enables us to use a much wider and deeper range of conditions and means than were expressed in the observation of primitive practical purposes.[17]

Daniel Tanner and Laurel N. Tanner stated the case for theory in the following manner:

Teachers are so caught up with the need to develop effective classroom practices that they understandably look upon educational theory as a field of esoteric specialization removed from the practical concerns of the school. Although theory will not provide simplistic answers to such questions as "What do I do on Monday?" it does provide a basis for ascertaining the implications of alternative educational pathways and destinies.[18]

6. There are uncertainties as to which teachers in-service education should assist. Should supervisors provide programs for beginning teachers or experienced or both? Should they serve effective teachers or ineffective or both? Are the beginning teachers the most ineffective, the most in need of help? There are those who believe that supervisors should not waste their time on the poorest teachers, as they cannot be salvaged anyway. On the other hand, both moral and legal considerations prevent ignoring teachers who need help. In those school systems which are bound by a union contract administrators have no choice but to exhaust every remedial measure before taking any action against an incompetent teacher.

7. There is uncertainty as to the proper focus of in-service education. Should in-service education seek to develop teachers as:

- Instructors? If so, in-service programs must concentrate on methodology.
- Curriculum developers? If so, teachers must be trained to plan, implement, and evaluate programs.
- People? If so, this focus calls for training in human relations skills.
- Subject matter specialists? If so, content of the discipline is the name of the game.
- Educated citizens? If so, supervisors would plan programs in liberal studies which enhance the teachers' general knowledge. Rarely do we find in-service education programs of this nature. Except for training programs in such areas as group dynamics and interpersonal skills, in-service education concentrates on professional development of the teacher rather than personal development.

8. There is uncertainty as to whether it is best to respond to teachers' needs through a comprehensive, long-range plan or through separate, discrete plans which are designed to satisfy particular needs. Programs more often respond to specific needs and are thus reactive in nature rather than anticipate needs and thus become proactive. Single training sessions commonly require no follow-up sessions during which teachers may demonstrate mastery of the skills and knowledge presented in the sessions. Roy A. Edelfelt commented:

In most cases needs have been translated into programs piecemeal. Programs are often one-shot sessions on a single topic (e.g., discipline techniques, management of stress and conflict, economic education) or courses that address a particular need (e.g., personal writing, conversational French, or learning activities for the gifted and talented).[19]

9. There is uncertainty how to entice teachers to participate in in-service education. It would be the best of all possible worlds if teachers were intrinsically motivated to demand in-service training for self-improvement. To a certain extent teachers will seek training to resolve immediate needs. Beyond that purpose in-service education has an uphill fight for teacher acceptance.

We can conclude without a doubt that *after school, required* in-service programs are both deadening and certain to arouse teacher hostility. We must admit that teaching is exhausting work. We need to remember that teachers are leaving the profession at alarming rates. We must recognize the phenomenon of teacher burn-out. This recognition often takes the form of in-service seminars on the maladies of stress and burn-out. Yet, these seminars usually focus on what the *teacher* can do to minimize stress and avoid burn-out. Additionally, we need more in-service programs for administrators and supervisors on what *they* may do to reduce or eliminate stress and burn-out. If in-service education is to be successful, we must look to extrinsic motivation and provide incentives. We will examine some of these incentives later in this chapter.

10. There is disagreement on who should control in-service education. Should the chief administrator or his or her director of staff development make the decisions on what will be offered through in-service education and how? Should the teachers themselves control their in-service education either through their associations and unions or through teacher education centers? Teachers are increasingly insisting on being involved in the planning of in-service education. Ninety-three percent of 646 teachers, for example, in a Tennessee survey of attitudes toward in-service education responded positively to the notion of teacher involvement in planning.[20]

Toni Sharma, a fourth-grade teacher, in an amusing but pointed article, satirized in-service education by likening it to the plight of Flossie, the cow, which Grandpop penned in a stanchion and Zeke, the inseminator, artificially inseminated. Wrote Sharma:

Too often, those in charge of inservice training make decisions for teachers just like the ones Zeke and Grandpop made for Flossie. They decide when to bring us together. They assume that injections of information they select will be helpful to all teachers, regardless of their individual needs. They assume that teachers have too narrow a perspective and that teachers' opinions are not valid. And finally, they assume that a direct and measurable outcome must result from inservice training.

Unfortunately, it's all too easy to subscribe to those assumptions. . . . I have allowed my head to be penned in the stanchion.

Now I want to take charge. . . . I want to determine my own needs, set my own goals, decide when and how and with whom I'll work toward those goals. I am going to control my own learning.[21]

ASSUMPTIONS ABOUT IN-SERVICE EDUCATION

Whatever model of in-service education a school or school system follows, it is based on certain assumptions. Fred H. Wood, Steven R. Thompson, and Sister Frances Russell outlined a model of in-service education based on a set of assumptions which I believe hold true for any model. These assumptions are:

1. *All personnel in schools, to stay current and effective, need and should be involved in inservice throughout their careers* . . .
2. *Significant improvement in educational practice takes considerable time and is the result of systematic, long-range staff development* . . .
3. *Inservice education should have an impact on the quality of the school program and focus on helping staff improve their abilities to perform their professional responsibilities* . . .
4. *Adult learners are motivated to risk learning new behaviors when they believe they have control over the learning situation and are free from threat of failure* . . .
5. *Educators vary widely in their professional competencies. readiness, and approaches to learning* . . .
6. *Professional growth requires personal and group commitment to new performance norms* . . .
7. *Organizational health including factors such as social climate, trust, open communication, and peer support for change in practice influences the success of professional development programs* . . .

8. *The school is the primary unit of change; not the district or the individual* . . .

9. *School districts have the primary responsibility for providing the resources and training necessary for a school staff to implement new programs and improve instruction* . . .

10. *The school principal is the gatekeeper for adoption and continued use of new practices and programs in a school* . . .

11. *Effective in-service programs must be based upon research, theory, and the best education practice.*[22]

Three themes come through repeatedly loud and clear in discussions of in-service education: in-service programs should be a continuing operation; they should be comprehensive in nature; and they should be cooperatively planned.

CHARACTERISTICS OF EFFECTIVE IN-SERVICE PROGRAMS

School systems vary widely in respect to both the quantity and quality of their in-service programs. Some in-service programs operate on a casual, informal, trouble-shooting basis while others offer highly structured, planned programs in addition to the informal unstructured type. Factors that appear to make the difference in respect to quantity and quality of in-service opportunities are (1) motivational level of the teachers, (2) leadership from administrators and supervisors, and (3) financial resources.

Where teachers accept the need and desirability of continuing their professional education, in-service programs thrive. Where administrators and supervisors take an active role in promoting and planning in-service opportunities, and where funds are available, teacher participation in in-service training is higher.

Citing studies made by Patricia Kells and Patricia J. Jamison, Leonard C. Burrello and Tim Orbaugh listed the following six major observations as to what constitutes effective in-service education.[23]

1. *In-service education should be designed so that programs are integrated into and supported by the organization within which they function.* A comprehensive plan for in-service education in the school and/or district should be drawn up and funding should be made available.

2. *In-service education programs should be designed to result in collaborative programs.* The plan should include ways to involve all the constituencies of the school: teachers, administrators, supervisors, nonteaching staff, students, and laypersons.

3. *In-service education programs should be grounded in the needs of the participants.* The plan should be developed from an assessment of the needs and interests of the persons to be served.

4. *In-service education programs should be responsive to changing needs.* The plan should allow for changes as conditions change and as research brings forth new knowledge.

5. *In-service education programs should be accessible.* The location, the physical facilities, and the timing are all important factors to be considered in an in-service education plan.

6. *In-service education activities should be evaluated over time and be compatible with the underlying philosophy and approach of the district.* Evaluative data are needed in order to carry out future planning and implementation.

The supervisor of staff development should lead both school and nonschool personnel in examining the assumptions and principles on which in-service education will be designed.

A MODEL FOR IN-SERVICE EDUCATION

What steps should the supervisor take in establishing an in-service education program? Let's turn to our general utility model, which you have already seen twice before, once as a simple model of instruction and once as a basic model of curriculum development. We will add two components and convert the general model into a sequence of steps for managing an in-service education program. The model for in-service education appears in Figure 9.7.

TRAINING   POST-TRAINING

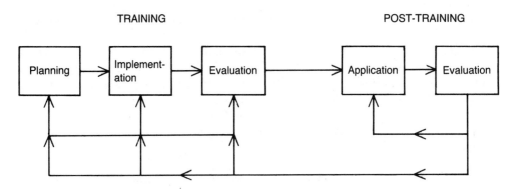

Figure 9.7 A Model for In-service Education

The foregoing diagram shows us that the training phases of in-service education consist of planning the training, carrying it out, and evaluating it. Since the purpose of training is to bring about changes in the classroom and/or in the person, we must look beyond the training programs themselves. We could actually repeat the general model and indicate that we plan for the after-training period, get the training program into operation in the classroom (or in our personal behavior), and evaluate our success in the classroom or in our personal lives. To avoid redundancy and not make the reader think that he or she has double vision, I have labeled the phases of the post-training period Application and Evaluation. Thus, we have created a model with two submodels. The feedback lines cycle within the training model, within the post-training model, and between the two submodels. Let's examine each of the five phases of the model.[24]

Planning

Most of the literature on in-service education recommends a survey of the in-service needs of the clientele to be served as a first step in the process which is called a *needs assessment*. Peter A. Williamson and Julia A. Elfman stated the steps of the in-service needs assessment succinctly as follows:

The first step is the creation of a staff development committee for the building . . .
> Next, the committee should identify the needs of the school . . .
> Third, rank the needs . . .
> Then, design a plan of action.[25]

The professional staff should have the opportunity to identify training needs. Those needs deemed to be the most critical and most pervasive should be placed at the top of the list for in-service training. It is not uncommon for teachers to be in disagreement with administrators and supervisors over which needs are most pressing in a school system. Nor is it unknown for administrators and supervisors to develop a pet idea or program which they wish to put into effect in the schools. Unless a program is mandated by the state or by the local school board administrators or supervisors would be well advised to defer to the judgment of the teachers in the case of differing opinions over training programs for teachers. Unless teachers see the value of a training program no lasting results may be expected from it.

State Assessments

One approach to determining needs of teachers is the statewide survey. Jay Lutz and Garrett Foster reported on a statewide study, for example, which asked Florida teachers, principals, superintendents, in-service directors, school board members, and university faculty to rate areas in which they believed beginning and experienced teachers were most and least proficient.[26] The survey, conducted under the auspices of the State Council for Teacher Education Centers, revealed general agreement among the groups responding that beginning teachers were least proficient in:

- familiarity with the kinds of special services provided by school systems, for example, psychological services, guidance counselors
- understanding when and how to discipline students
- ability to diagnose and prescribe for individual student differences
- ability to relate educational theory to practice

This same survey found that experienced teachers were rated least proficient in:

- ability to work with different subcultures and minority groups
- skill in helping each student develop a positive self-concept
- ability to assess oneself and to evaluate one's performance
- ability to stimulate self-direction in students

It is of interest to note differences between perceived needs of beginning teachers and those of experienced teachers. A survey of this nature yields a type of information that provides clues to areas which are worth exploring as potential areas for in-service training.

District Assessments

Two surveys conducted in Florida school systems furnish illustrations of district needs assessments. The Southwest Florida Teacher Education Center, which served six county school systems, polled teachers and administrators on possible in-service topics. The center established the following needs for in-service education in the order or priority assigned them by the groups surveyed:

1. Diagnosing and evaluating social-emotional characteristics.
2. Utilizing the community as an integral part of instruction.
3. Identifying behavior problems and possible solutions to those problems.
4. Individualizing instruction and maintaining records of performance.
5. Developing student self-concepts, attitudes, and values.
6. Using standardized tests and interpreting test data.
7. Identifying needs and planning for individual differences among students.
8. Utilizing the school campus as an instructional resource.
9. Techniques of planning and utilizing educational media.
10. Selecting, adapting, and developing materials and objectives.
11. Motivating and reinforcing students.
12. Selecting and writing goals or objectives.
13. Communicating and interacting with parents and community.
14. Conducting classroom discussion and using questioning techniques.
15. Developing and using teacher-made tests.
16. Organizing physical setting of classroom (furniture, bulletin boards, etc.).
17. Communicating and interacting with other faculty members and students.[27]

By means of an Inservice Program Survey Response Form the Dade-Monroe Teacher Education Center determined the in-service course preferences of more than 2200 teachers in 120 elementary and 53 secondary schools of the Dade County (Florida) Public Schools.[28] From a list of 43 courses on the survey response form teachers identified their choices for study. Interestingly enough, 10 of the top 11 courses chosen by both elementary and secondary school teachers were the same. Significantly, Computer Education topped the lists of both groups of teachers. Below are the top 11 choices of each of the two groups.

RANKING BY ELEMENTARY TEACHERS	COURSE TITLE	RANKING BY SECONDARY TEACHERS
1	Computer Education	1
2	Motivating the Reluctant Learner	5

RANKING BY ELEMENTARY TEACHERS	COURSE TITLE	RANKING BY SECONDARY TEACHERS
3	Discipline	3
4	Cardio-Pulmonary Resuscitation	4
5	Reading for the Young Child	—
6, 7	Motivating the Reluctant Reader	10
6, 7	Time/Stress Management	2
8	Classroom Management	7
9	Improving Student Test Performance (Test Besting)	6
10	Newspaper in the Classroom	9
11	School Law	11
—	Subject Area Methods	8

Local School Assessments

More and more educators are coming to believe that the most effective instructional, curricular, and staff development plans are those based at the individual school. The concept of school-based management generally construed as applying to budgeting is being extended to all areas of leadership, not just the managerial aspects of school operation. John I. Goodlad spoke to this point when he said, *"the optimal unit for educational change is the single school with its pupils, teachers, principal—those who live there every day—as primary participants."*[29]

The principal should exercise leadership in assessing in-service needs of teachers in his or her school, analyzing data which may reflect in-service needs, and preparing a staff development plan for that school. Among staff development activities for the 1981–1982 school year at J. H. C. Butler Elementary School (Savannah, Georgia), for example, were the following:

Orientation to Right to Learn program.
Orientation of staff to new curriculum guides in social studies, science, career education, and physical education.
Orientation to new textbooks in language arts.
Planning a file of correlated math manipulatives—coded to match checklists.[30]

Of needs assessments in general Linda L. Jones and Andrew E. Hayes cautioned:

The literature on inservice education almost always recommends a thorough assessment of teacher needs before staff development efforts. The need for doing this has been well established, but planners of staff development programs and persons conducting research on staff development may wrongly assume that statements of needs made by teachers *are* their needs rather than symptoms of needs that must be diagnosed more completely.[31]

These authors are pointing to the problem inherent in any survey of felt or perceived needs. The respondents need to know what they know and what they do not know. They may perceive themselves to have knowledge which they do not actually possess or may even ask for repetition of topics of which they can already demonstrate mastery. Jones and Hayes commented, "needs perceptions are an inadequate indicator of staff development needs."[32]

Yet, we would not want to eliminate surveys of perceived needs. Teachers want, yea demand, involvement in planning and opportunities to select the programs in which they will participate. Like curriculum needs assessments, in-service needs assessments should be verified by additional means such as data on student achievement, parental feedback, and supervisors' observations of classroom performance. In the event of discrepancy between perceived needs and actual needs, unless teachers can be persuaded otherwise, I believe we must take the path counseled by the perceptual psychologists and deal with *perceptions* before we can deal with *reality*.

By whatever means, supervisors and those who work with them must obtain from the prospective participants their preferences for in-service activities. Once the teachers' choices are made known these must be ranked in order of preferred priorities. From that point a plan must be drawn up that will indicate which of the top needs will be addressed, how, and at what cost.

Master Plans

Supervisors of staff development typically draw up master plans for their school districts. These plans are based on feedback obtained from surveys of in-service needs. Some school systems prepare new plans annually. Some develop plans to cover a longer period, sometimes up to five years, with updating annually. Master plans describe each course, workshop, and other activity, which are referred to as *components* and often read like a college catalog.

Master plans for staff development in the public school systems of Florida must cover a five-year period, be updated annually, and be approved by the state department of education. These plans provide for three types of in-service activities: basic, to develop basic teaching skills; updating, to update knowledge and skills in a subject or area; and exploratory.

A recent plan for the Dade County (Florida) Public Schools cataloged several hundred components, an example of which is the following:

1-01-50-2-2 POSITIVE ATTITUDES TOWARD LEARNING (PATL)

INDIVIDUALIZED INSTRUCTION

(Up to 2 PIP & 40 MPP Infield)*

A course designed to help teachers acquire skills in implementing individualizing instruction through the use of behavioral objectives and through the use of various media for instruction.[33]

Components are written and delivered by teachers, supervisors, and college instructors.

* For explanation of this line see discussion of incentives later in this chapter.

Each component is available at the teachers' request. Some components are delivered in the form of group study; some may be completed either in a group or independently; others are individualized components by their very nature, e.g., educational travel and supervision of student teachers.

Richmond County (Georgia) offers a wide range of staff development courses[34] and workshops,[35] as, for example:

TITLE:	COMPUTERS IN INSTRUCTION
INSTRUCTOR:	Jacquie Allison, Classroom Teacher, Westside
DESCRIPTION:	Course participants will have the opportunity to obtain:

1. knowledge and understanding of the hardware and software available in Richmond County.
2. fundamental programming skills in the BASIC language.
3. an understanding of the use of microcomputers as an instructional aid.
4. a small library of programs appropriate for use in their classroom.

CREDIT: 5 SDUs and 3 years tenure   *COST*: $25

OPEN TO: All employees *DAY OF WEEK*: Tuesday *TIME*: 4:30–9:00

BEGINNING DATE: September 21 *ENDING DATE*: December 7

LOCATION: Westside High School, Room 114

#62

OPEN TO:	All Certified Employees	**SUBJECT AREA TEACHERS: YOU CAN IMPROVE READING SKILLS!**
DATE:	February 15	
TIME:	4:30 p.m.–7:30 p.m.	This workshop will provide a look at the indicator clusters for reading and will present ways to improve student's reading skills within each subject area.
LOCATION:	Tubman, Room 315	
PRESENTER:	Linda Bledsoe	

School systems usually keep meticulous records of approvals of courses for participants, completion of courses by individuals, types of offerings, complete statistics, and evaluations of programs and instructors.

Individual School Plans

Staff development plans of the individual school and the district supplement each other. The district's master plan reaches beyond the needs of the teachers of the individual school. Studies of in-service needs of teachers in the individual school must be followed up with some kind of plan. The Savannah-Chatham County Public Schools (Georgia) provide an outline to principals for reporting staff development plans. On this outline principals must show data that were analyzed to determine needs, goals, and proposed staff development activities. Following is a sample plan from the Sol C. Johnson High School (Savannah).[36]

School/Department Improvement Plan: 1981-82

School/Department: Sol C. Johnson High School   Principal/Director: Gwendolyn P. Goodman

I. Identification of School/Department Improvement Goals:
    A. Data Based Workshop
        1. Date(s): September 1, 1981   Time: From 8:30 a.m.   To 2:15 p.m.
                      September 8, 1981 - School closing (June 1982) Meetings to be held monthly on the
                      first Tuesday

        2. Data that were analyzed:
            (a) Test Scores - Analyzed by Dr. Christine Worthington and Mrs. Mary Shank
            (b) SACS Report (Interim Evaluation to take place in March 1982)
            (c) Advisement Program - Improving school climate
            (d) Remediation Offerings - Development of modules to be used in all academic areas

    B. The school/department improvement goals and rationales were presented to the entire staff on September 4, 1981.
                                                                                                              (Date)

II. Will the improvement plan require staff development?   Yes X   No ____

III. If credit (Local and/or State SDU) is to be an option with staff development, indicate the amount below:
     Credit will not be an option   ____ 10 Contact hours (1 SDU)   ____ 20 Contact hours (2 SDU's)
     ____ 30 Contact hours (3 SDU's)   ____ 40 Contact hours (4 SDU's)   X 50 Contact hours (5 SDU's)

IV. What is the role of the Coordinating Council in the improvement plan?   Not yet clearly defined

V. School/Department Goals and Rationales

        Goals   Rationales

    (a) To improve test scores   To improve testing skills in our attempt to reach the
                                                  state and national average.

    (b) To complete interim SACS Accreditation   To maintain SACS Accreditation. We are to be evaluated
                                                  in March by SACS.

    (c) Strengthen Advisement Program   To improve school climate and assist students academically.
                                                  Mandate under CBE to assure that students meet minimal
                                                  competencies.

    (d) Offer Remediation in all academic areas To provide varied opportunities for strengthening areas
                                                  of academic weaknesses with the aid of teacher-made
                                                  materials.

364

VI. Proposed Staff Development Activities (that address improvement goals)

Topic	Objective(s)	Proposed Starting Date	Materials	Needs Consultants
How to develop a remediation program	To reduce failure	October 22, 1981	duplicating paper, stencils, construction paper, folders, labels, transparencies	Kathy O'Neill Bernard Hirshberg Mary Roberts Mary Shank Benny White
How to improve test scores	To assist students in the critical area of improving test skills	September 1, 1981	transparencies	Tina Worthington

VII. If you plan to conduct staff development for credit, which organizational format will you follow?

A. A School-based Plan: __X__
   This will require a written plan which must be approved by the Certification Renewal Committee.

B. System-wide Comprehensive Plan: _____
   This will require participation in a plan developed by appropriate staff from the Central Office in coordination with school staff.

C. Individual Teacher Plan or Group Plan: __X__
   This will require a written plan by the teacher or group which must be approved by the Certification Renewal Committee.

365

Writing Components

At some point supervisors, teachers, or outside consultants face the task of writing training programs. Though formats may differ an outline which has proved satisfactory for writing in-service components is the following:

- title page
- general description
- objectives
- pretest
- training activities
- training materials
- posttest

When teachers are asked to take on the writing of components for a master plan or individual school plan, provision should be made for released time and/or extra pay for this additional service which is over and above normal assigned teaching duties. Further, a cost accounting must be made for each in-service activity to make sure that the school and district stay within their staff development budgets.

Implementation

The in-service activities should be varied both in respect to type of activity and time devoted to each. The newer and more complex the activity, the more likely longer periods of time will need to be set aside for their study and practice. A number of possibilities for providing a varied in-service program are open to the supervisor, including:

1. *Formal college or university courses.* Perhaps the most common of all in-service activities and sometime the only organized activity is the college or university course which may be taught on the campus of a nearby college or university or off-campus in the local schools. Thousands of teachers are studying at night, on weekends, and during the summers to obtain advanced degrees and new areas of certification. Teacher education institutions have traditionally responded to in-service needs of teachers by offering courses on campus in the evening, on weekends, in intensive periods of time, and by taking the courses to teachers in the field.

One of the supervisors of a school system should be charged with the task of summarizing needs of teachers and requests for courses and transmitting that information to the teacher education institutions which serve the area. By the same token, the teacher-training institutions should be continuously seeking feedback from the public school systems they serve as to what the needs of the teachers are and in what ways their needs may best be served.

2. *Locally developed or sponsored staff development courses or modules.* Many school systems have set supervisors and teachers to work, with or without the aid of outside consultants, at writing in-service programs which are made available to other

teachers wishing to improve their knowledge and skills in certain areas. Teachers and supervisors are in the process of energetically developing components (often called "teacher-training modules") such as

- selecting standardized tests
- writing behavioral objectives
- lesson planning
- nonverbal behavior
- conducting a class discussion
- classroom management
- cooperating with parents
- questioning techniques
- behavior modification
- writing classroom tests
- assessing affective objectives

The development of teacher-training components is valuable not only in terms of product—the completed module which may be utilized in in-service education—but also in terms of process—the professional growth of the teachers who do the writing. Many of the modules which have been developed in various parts of the country by local school systems and by state and federally funded projects are now available for purchase by school systems which wish to make use of them.

3. *Workshops and institutes*. Though it is often difficult or impossible to distinguish a workshop from an institute, generally speaking, workshops provide participants with opportunities to work together to find solutions to problems which they themselves have identified, while institutes bring information and suggested solutions to problems to participants and may or may not offer opportunities for the participants to work together. Workshops and institutes typically run from one to three days, though like more formal "courses," they may last a couple of weeks or longer.

Workshops and institutes may be staffed by local personnel or by outside consultants and may or may not be tied in with a college or university for awarding academic credit for participation. In organizing workshops or institutes the supervisor has the responsibility for making sure that the participants understand the objectives, for working out logistical arrangements, and for conducting an evaluation which will provide feedback for subsequent workshops and institutes. Unless a workshop or institute offers the participants academic credit there are customarily no examinations required.

4. *Conferences.** The conference is a technique for imparting information and ideas to a large group of people in the shortest possible time. The supervisor may find it expedient to call a conference of teachers to hear a specialist on a particular topic or to clarify certain issues or problems. Whenever possible, conference pres-

---

* I.e., a group meeting in which a variety of developmental activities, such as lectures, panels, symposia, etc. takes place. In supervisory parlance *conducting a conference* can be either a phase of clinical supervision, a one-to-one talk or a meeting/convention.

entations should be followed with small-group discussions. Since the majority of participants at most conferences play a passive role, the potential of the conference as an in-service device is more limited than that of workshops, institutes, or courses.

Locally sponsored conferences take precedence over distant conferences as a typical in-service activity. Attendance of teachers at state, regional, and national conferences and conventions of the professional associations is a worthy activity but most school systems find it prohibitive in cost to send many teachers to out-of-town conferences, pay their expenses, and provide substitutes for their classes during the time they are gone. As a result, attendance at distant meetings, if permitted at all, is ordinarily limited to the few teachers who serve as officers of the associations whose expenses are often paid by the associations, who have some important role on the program of the association's convention, or who are willing to foot their own bills.

Very few schools have fully tapped the potential of state, regional, and national conferences and conventions as an in-service technique, for rarely does a participant come back and share the knowledge gained with his or her colleagues. School systems could further the use of conferences as an in-service technique by encouraging the use of professional leave days for attendance at conferences and by requiring those whose expenses are paid by the school system to prepare written (or oral) reports of what they learned from the conference and to share the reports with their peers.

5. *Supervision of student teachers.* The direction of a student teacher can be a valuable learning experience for both the student teacher and the supervisor. Unfortunately, many teachers see the supervision of a student teacher as a chore to be tolerated rather than as an in-service educational experience for them. Student teachers, if properly used, can be a tremendous help to a teacher, for they bring with them some of the latest ideas and techniques from which the observant supervising teacher can profit.

The supervisor should try to make the task of supervising a student teacher appear to be a privilege and a help rather than a burden. In cooperation with the teacher education institution from which the student teacher comes the supervisor should identify those teachers who will make effective student teacher supervisors. As word gets out that student teachers are being placed with the "better" teachers, more teachers will want to earn that label, will request student teachers, and will try to provide a worthwhile experience for these teachers-to-be.

While student teaching is ordinarily the culmination of the preservice training program for the student teacher, it should be considered a two-way street. Not only may the supervising teacher learn from the student teacher but the acts of explaining, interpreting, and providing counsel to the student teacher serve to improve the supervising teacher's effectiveness.

6. *Visiting days.* An in-service technique utilized by some school systems is the release of a teacher for a day to go to another class or school to observe fellow teachers and to discuss mutual teaching problems with them. By visiting other teachers the individual is able to broaden his or her horizon and perhaps find solutions to troubling problems. By observing other instructors visiting teachers may learn new approaches and techniques and may become acquainted with materials which are unfamiliar and which may prove helpful in their classes. At the very least

they may take comfort from discovering that others experience difficulties similar to those they encounter.

7. *Approved travel.* Some school systems permit teachers to engage in educational travel which can be directly helpful in their classrooms. In order to gain supervisory approval for travel as an in-service activity teachers frequently must submit a plan with a rationale and must report on their travel after they return.

The foregoing techniques represent seven of the most common forms of organized in-service education programs. Dynamic school systems do not limit themselves to one or two types of programs but engage in many. Supervisors of in-service education would do well to keep in mind guidelines for effective staff development programs such as the following, proposed by Wood and Thompson:

1. Include more participant control over the 'what' and 'how' of learning;
2. Focus on job related tasks that the participants consider real and important;
3. Provide choices and alternatives that accommodate the differences among participants;
4. Include opportunities for participants in inservice training to practice what they are to learn in simulated and real work settings as part of their training;
5. Encourage the learners to work in small groups and to learn from each other; and
6. Reduce the use and threat of external judgments from one's superior by allowing peer-participants to give each other feedback concerning performance and areas of needed improvement.[37]

Incentives for Participation

It is essential that the school system provide incentives for teachers to participate in organized in-service activities. Personal satisfaction and professional improvement are not sufficient incentives by themselves for teachers to participate in in-service programs. Today's school systems are encountering increasing resistance from organized teachers to demands on their time without compensation. In-service programs are going to cost a school system some money and funds for training programs must be incorporated into the total budget. Among the types of incentives school systems offer to teachers to secure their participation in in-service programs are the following:

1. *Released time.* Typically, teachers may be expected to remain after school for short periods of time and to attend faculty meetings. Contractual arrangements between a school board and an organized group of teachers often specify the exact number of hours and number of meetings which are considered a part of the teachers' obligations. Though the periods of time may often be used for in-service training, they are often too short and too few for any sustained group study. Beyond the stipulated obligations of teachers, released time during the school day (and/or other incentives acceptable to the teachers) must be provided if any meaningful in-service programs are to be operated. Some school systems use the mechanism of "teacher days," certain days during the year when teachers are on duty but children are not in attendance. Some systems allot a concentrated period of days at the end of the school year or before school opens in the late summer or fall during which teachers are paid and in-service activities may take place. Other systems release teachers for

in-service projects and hire substitutes to take their places while they are participating. Unless other incentives are operant which will induce teachers to study on
their own time, a fundamental principle for in-service activities sponsored by the local
school system is the provision of time for the teachers at the expense of the school
system.

2. *In-service credits for salary increments.* Some school systems with well-
organized in-service programs allot credit for participation in each activity. Credits are
known variously as staff development units (SDUs), master plan points (MPPs), and
professional incentive points (PIPs). In cases where the district's plan for staff development is approved by the state Department of Education, staff development units
and master plan points may be applied, like college credits, to extending or renewing
a certificate, which is an attractive inducement to many teachers. Some school
systems, e.g., Richmond County (Georgia), on their own require teachers to undertake some in-service work in order to renew their tenure for a period of three years.

Teachers earn credits on a formula basis. Five SDUs, as in the public school
systems of Georgia, require 50 hours of class time (or equivalent in self-study), which
make them roughly comparable to five quarter hours of college academic credit.
Florida master plans award credit on the basis of one master plan point for each 20
hours of class work or equivalent time in independent study.

Dade County (Florida) Public Schools have incorporated a professional incentive program through which teachers may earn professional incentive points simultaneously with master plan points. On completion of a fixed number of PIP points
teachers receive a salary increment.

With these incentives teachers may be expected to participate on their own time.

3. *Reimbursement for college tuition.* In order to encourage teachers to take
courses at nearby colleges and universities some school systems pay teachers for a
given number of college credits earned during the year. Ordinarily, college courses
for which tuition is reimbursed by the school system must be directly related to the
teacher's field of specialization.

Reimbursement for tuition makes formal study appealing to many teachers.
Since school systems pay higher salaries for teachers with master's degrees, academic
credit from a college or university, culminating in an advanced degree, is often a
sufficient incentive in itself. However, after the teacher has achieved that degree (or
a given number of college credits beyond the bachelor's degree) some device such as
reimbursement for tuition is desirable in order to encourage the teacher to continue
self-improvement.

The supervisor should work with colleges and universities in the area to secure,
if possible, favorable tuition rates for school personnel. They might also negotiate
with colleges and universities for tuition certificates for teachers who serve the higher
education institutions as supervisors of student teachers.

The supervisor should actively promote whatever means are possible to motivate
teachers to participate in in-service training. It must be reiterated that successful in-
service education cannot be provided without the investment of time and money by
the school system.

Use of Consultants

Staff development plans call heavily on administrators, supervisors, and teachers in the system to serve as instructors. On the other hand, the services of consultants from outside the school system are often called on for workshops, institutes, and conferences. The use of outside consultants is a stock response to the provision of in-service training and though the employment of outside consultants is often necessary and results in changes in teacher behavior through exposure to the consultant's views, care must be exercised in the employment of consultants and the uses which are made of their services.

It is of interest to note from the study of *High School Self-Evaluation and Curriculum Change* by Vynce A. Hines and William M. Alexander that the use of consultants from outside the school system is judged by teachers as one of the least important factors in curriculum change.[38] According to this study, teachers rate as more influential factors in curriculum change the administrative staff of one's own school, the administrative staff of the school system, the regional accrediting association, the faculty of the school, and the state Department of Education.

When planning for the use of outside consultants, the supervisor may gain the maximum productivity from their visits by following a few simple rules:

1. The supervisor should seek faculty input into the selection of consultants. This participation will make the faculty more receptive to the message the consultants may bring to them.
2. The consultants chosen should be qualified beyond question for the roles asked of them. The supervisor should do some advance checking, preferably with school systems which have called on the consultants' services in the past, to be sure that the consultants chosen are the best-qualified persons to be obtained.
3. The consultants should be oriented well in advance to the task expected of them. Far too much valuable consultant time is often lost while a consultant orients himself or herself to the task after arriving on the scene.
4. The consultants should be available for questions and discussion following their presentations. The consultant who hurries in, makes a presentation, and exits often leaves a group at the very point where some return could be obtained from interaction with him or her. It is true that some consultants have important things to say. Some share research they have conducted or new techniques they have found helpful. Others give a good pep talk and some are effective at entertaining teacher groups. Keynote speakers at conferences often fill this latter bill very well. Some of the more charismatic keynote speakers have the ability to maintain the rapt attention of audiences of a thousand or more.

For workshops and institutes, however, where teachers settle down to find specific answers to immediate problems or to learn new techniques for accomplishing their instructional duties the purely informational or the inspirational types of consultants will usually not suffice. Teachers need the services of experts who will lead them through the study they are undertaking and remain with them long enough (*at the very least* for an extended and unhurried question-and-answer session) to permit them to begin discovering answers to their many questions and problems.

Evaluation

In order to assess the effectiveness of in-service education and to strengthen subsequent programs continuing evaluation is essential. It is important to evaluate (1) the achievement of participants, (2) each in-service activity, and (3) school and master plans for staff development.

The evaluation of participants' achievement in in-service programs conducted by the school systems tends to be less formal than assessment in college courses. Teachers are unwilling to sit still for formal examinations at workshops, institutes, and conferences. More often than not the nature of an in-service activity does not lend itself to terminal examinations. Evaluation is necessary, of course. But evaluation of in-service programs can consist of the supervisor's observation of the participant's performance during the activity and after, of oral and written reports during the in-service program, and of short quizzes, e.g., pretests and posttests.

Each in-service activity must be evaluated in terms of the efficacy of the content, the delivery system, and the instructor (or consultant). It has become standard operating procedure for the staff development coordinator or the in-service activity instructor to distribute an end-of-activity evaluation form which participants fill out anonymously. Two illustrations will give us an idea of the types of information gathered from in-service education participants.

The Association for Supervision and Curriculum Development employs an evaluation card which is administered at the conclusion of every session at its annual conferences. This brief evaluation form is seen in Figure 9.8.

Consultants of the Division of Curriculum Services of the Georgia Department of Education request participants to complete the form shown in Figure 9.9.

Both master plans and individual school plans for staff development require evaluation. The Florida State Department of Education, for example, periodically evaluates master plans for staff development in each school district. Every three to five years the state Department of Education designates a visiting committee to conduct an on-site review. Criteria which guide the committee's assessment appear in the check-list in Figure 9.10.

The ultimate test of an in-service activity is translation of the knowledge and skills learned into the participant's personal and/or professional behavior. The success or failure of in-service programs rests heavily on the shoulders of those supervisors who are charged by the administrators with the direction of staff development activities. Planning, implementing, and evaluating in-service activities require a high degree of organizational skill on the part of the supervisor. Success of staff development programs correlates directly with the leadership skills of the supervisor.

ASCD ANNUAL CONFERENCE   SESSION EVALUATION FORM

I. Indicate the type of session you are evaluating by placing the appropriate number from the list below after the word Type on the evaluation card.

    1. General Session   4. Action Lab
    2. Master Lecture   5. Special Session
    3. Assembly   6. Other--Please specify, e.g., Fish Bowl
                                       Interface, Doctoral Seminar

II. Indicate the number of the activity as listed in the official program, e.g., General Session 3 or Action Lab 44 after the words number of session on the evaluation card.

III. Indicate your position from the following list by placing the appropriate number from the list below after the words your position on the evaluation card.
    1. Teacher   4. Superintendent
    2. Principal or assistant principal   5. State Department staff member
    3. School System staff member   6. College or University staff member
              7. Other--Please explain in the comments section

Please complete evaluation statements 1 and 2 and the comments section for all of the sessions you attend. Complete statements 3, 4, and 5, for the Action Labs and Special Sessions. The evaluations are to be completed by marking the appropriate number after each appropriate statement keeping the following scale in mind:
    5 = Excellent   4 = Good   3 = Acceptable   2 = Poor   1 = Very Poor

----

EVALUATION CARD

1. Type of Session___	2. Number of Session___ ___	3. Your Position___	RATING SCALE Circle the appropriate number			
			Excellent	Good	Acceptable	Poor	Very Poor
Title of Session_____			5	4	3	2	1
For All Sessions (including action labs and special sessions)							
1. Overall Quality of Session			5	4	3	2	1
2. Effectiveness of Presentation(s)			5	4	3	2	1
Complete the items below for Action Labs and Special Sessions ONLY							
3. Opportunity for Discussion/Interaction			5	4	3	2	1
4. Availability of Materials (Visuals/Handouts, etc.			5	4	3	2	1
5. Applicability of Skills/Information to your Work			5	4	3	2	1

COMMENTS

(Continue Comments on Back)

Figure 9.8   ASCD Session Evaluation Form

SOURCE: Association for Supervision and Curriculum Development, *Session Evaluation Form*, Alexandria, Va., Association for Supervision and Curriculum Development. Reprinted with permission.

CONTROL OF IN-SERVICE EDUCATION

The locus of control of in-service education is a subject of controversy. Disagreements center on questions like: Who shall make the policies pertaining to in-service education? How shall decisions be made about in-service offerings? How shall in-service budgets be expended? The school board, the superintendent, and the director of staff development are too simplistic as answers to the first question. True, the school board sets all school policies, the top executive administers them, and the administrator's aides carry out responsibilities delegated to them. But within the larger context of school management are varying opinions and practices related to the provision of in-service education.

GEORGIA DEPARTMENT OF EDUCATION
Division of Curriculum Services

WORKSHOP/PRESENTATION EVALUATION

The Division of Curriculum Services seeks constantly to improve the quality of services to the public schools of Georgia. Please assist in this effort by evaluating the workshop or presentation in which you have just participated.

Please circle the rating which most nearly agrees with your impressions about the several aspects of the presentation.

E = Excellent   G = Good   F = Fair   U = Unsatisfactory   N/A = Not applicable or Not evaluated

1. Clarity of workshop objectives	E	G	F	U	N/A
2. Appropriateness of workshop objectives	E	G	F	U	N/A
3. Appropriateness of Activities/Strategies to stated objectives	E	G	F	U	N/A
4. Quality of delivery	E	G	F	U	N/A
5. Usefulness of Activities/Strategies	E	G	F	U	N/A
6. Usefulness of Materials	E	G	F	U	N/A
7. Opportunities for participant-presenter interaction	E	G	F	U	N/A
8. Overall evaluation of the workshop or presentation	E	G	F	U	N/A

If any response is U, please explain _____

_____

_____

Use this space to write suggestions and comments which you feel may be important for planning and presenting similar services in the future.

_____

_____

_____

_____

Date: _____   Consultant's Name: _____

Topic: _____   Your job responsibility: _____

Figure 9.9 Workshop/Presentation Evaluation

SOURCE: Georgia Department of Education, Division of Curriculum Services, *Workshop/Presentation Evaluation*, Atlanta, Ga., Department of Education. Reprinted with permission.

CHECKLIST FOR ON-SITE REVIEW OF MASTER PLANS

1. AWARENESS

   a. Personnel are aware of the Master Plan for Inservice Education.

   b. New teachers have received orientation to the Master Plan activities.

2. ASSESSMENT OF NEEDS

   a. Personnel have an opportunity to identify and report inservice needs.

   b. Administrative and curriculum personnel identify and report staff development needs as it relates to programs.

   c. The assessment procedures are practical and utilized.

   d. Needs are identified and prioritized by the district Self-Study Committee.

3. INPUT

   a. Channels for providing input are known by all personnel.

   b. Representation of all appropriate personnel exists on the Self-Study Committee.

4. COMPONENTS

   a. Quality of the inservice components is highly regarded.

   b. The consultants understand their role prior to delivery date of the inservice activity.

   c. The consultants fulfill their responsibility.

   d. Evaluation is conducted for each specific objective of the component.

5. OWNERSHIP

   a. Personnel feel that it is "our" plan and not "their" plan.

   b. Support by administrative and instructional personnel exists for the Master Inservice Plan.

6. CERTIFICATE EXTENSION

   a. Some personnel are using inservice points to extend teaching certificates.

   b. Records are kept of inservice points.

   c. Component files are on record.

Figure 9.10 Checklist for On-site Review of Master Plans

SOURCE: Florida Department of Education, Bureau of Management Systems and Services, Division of Public Schools, *Checklist for On-site Review of Master Plans*, Tallahassee, Fla., State Department of Education. Reprinted with permission.

The loci for the administration of in-service education in the public schools are four in number: (1) the principal of the individual school, (2) the central office director of staff development, (3) the intermediate unit, and (4) the teacher education center. The first two loci come within the jurisdiction of the local school superintendent. The third location falls beyond the purview of the local superintendent. The fourth center may or may not lie within the complete authority of the superintendent.

Historically, in-service education has been the responsibility of the normal schools and colleges of education. From the mid-twentieth century school districts have assumed a large role in establishing and operating in-service programs. Increasingly, school district administrators are delegating responsibilities for staff development programs to the principals of the individual schools within the system. Of this trend Dull said:

During the past decade the focus of control over staff development has moved rapidly from institutions of higher education to local school districts, and even from the school district to the local school where principals are providing more and more leadership in staff development.[39]

We noted in Chapter 2 that some states have established intermediate units known as cooperative educational service agencies. These agencies, headed by a superintendent or director, serve a number of school districts. In some areas of the country, particularly the sparsely settled rural regions, the cooperative educational service agencies offer the lion's share of staff development activities. Some of the urban areas have chosen to participate in the support of the cooperative educational service agencies and utilize the services of the supervisors on the agencies' staffs. Other urban districts have remained aloof from the cooperative educational service agencies and manage their own staff development programs. Still others call on the cooperative educational service agencies as needed while at the same time conducting their own staff development programs.

Teacher Education Centers

The rise of teacher education centers has had a significant impact on the administration and operation of staff development programs. The teacher education center in America can be traced to the teacher centers which started to spring up in Great Britain in the mid-1960s. We should, however, at the onset, distinguish between the *teacher center* and the *teacher education center*. Although both types of centers have a bearing on staff development, they are not at all identical.

Teacher centers are physical plants which house all kinds of instructional, curricular, and professional materials for teachers' use. They serve as meeting places for workshops, conferences, and the like. They are sites where teachers can come together and rub elbows professionally and socially. In some respects they are glorified, staffed curriculum laboratories or curriculum materials centers. Illustrative of this type of center are not only the British teacher centers but also the Centres

Régionaux de Documentation Pédagogique which have been in existence in France for more than a quarter of a century. Some school districts in the United States are establishing British/French types of teacher centers. These centers belong to the school district and are entirely under the authority of the superintendent and school board.

The teacher education center is, if we may use slang, "a horse of a different color." Or, perhaps we should say "a concept of a different genre." Patterns of organization of teacher education centers throughout the country differ considerably. Teacher education centers may possess a single building, several buildings, or no building at all. They may or may not provide the helpful facilities and resources to be found in a teacher center. In other words, the teacher education center may or may not incorporate a teacher center within its plan.

The teacher education center is a concept based on certain assumptions, among which are the following:

- greater control over staff development programs should be placed in the hands of those most directly affected—the teachers
- to an ever-increasing extent in-service programs offered by the schools of education should be taken off the campus and placed in the real world of the teacher
- teachers, administrators, and college professors, sometimes in collaboration with students and laypersons, should cooperatively plan and carry out in-service activities

Since 10 teacher education centers were first created through state funding under the Teacher Education Center Act of 1973, the state of Florida has been a leader in the teacher education center (TEC) movement. Today all 67 of the county districts are affiliated, as a result of state mandate, with some teacher education center. Florida defined a teacher education center as follows:

an organized arrangement to promote collaboration in teacher education, both preservice and in-service. It involves teachers, school districts, and teacher education institutions. A teacher education center draws resources from existing teacher education programs. It does not replace these institutions. It is especially concerned with those aspects of teacher education requiring mutual involvement of concerned institutions.[40]

A common pattern of organization of TECs places administrative control of the center under a local school board and its superintendent. Some centers serve a single school system; others serve a number of school systems. A center director, commonly a person experienced in staff development, administers the operation of the center. The director is advised by a council composed of teachers (who constitute the majority of the council), representatives of teacher education institutions in the area, representatives of the nonteaching staff, and representatives of the community. The council sets policies and oversees the operation of the center in keeping with local and state regulations and laws. Sometimes the teacher education center director also occupies the position of director of staff development of his or her school system. Teacher education centers are operated with local and/or state funds and, in some cases, with the help of federal funding.

The program of a teacher education center includes among other activities those which are designed:

To assess in-service training needs as perceived by classroom teachers, school district personnel, college or university personnel, and other concerned agencies.

To provide adequate joint planning by school districts and colleges or universities, public or private, and to develop programs, including long-term training activities based on those identified in-service needs.

To provide human and material resources for in-service training by whichever agents are best prepared to deliver them.

To assess needs and provide the resources and experiences for clinical preservice teacher training, thus relating theoretical and practical study.

To facilitate the entry or reentry of educational personnel into the teaching profession.

To facilitate training processes which are based on assessment of needs, the development of experiences to meet those needs, and evaluation of the extent to which the needs were met.

To facilitate internal and external evaluation which would include, but not be limited to, data gathering, process evaluation, product evaluation, and validation of teaching competency.[41]

Philosophically and operationally teacher education centers are committed to:

Career-long teacher education to help teachers keep pace with the changing and diversified systems of instruction (continuity between preservice and inservice).

Cooperation and collaboration among teachers, school districts, and colleges or universities which allow for the emergence of new training strategies and procedures.

Commitment to shared power among involved agencies to encourage new kinds of collaborative models.

Pooling of resources in an organized effort to promote widespread use of new educational material and equipment for greater benefits for each agency in the teacher education center.

Field-based preservice teacher education to provide greater involvement in actual on-going classroom experiences.

Broader focus on inservice training to maintain skills for present roles and prepare for new roles and responsibilities.[42]

With the development of teacher education centers more of both the preservice and in-service education heretofore conducted on the campuses of the teacher education institutions will move off the campuses and into the regions served by the teacher education centers. The centers will provide experiences in real schools with real children and youth. If the teacher education centers throughout the country live up to their expectations, a new wave of realism will be injected into the preparation of prospective teachers and into in-service training programs.

Where teacher education centers exist, administrators and supervisors will be required to share prerogatives with the teachers, a not altogether undesirable state of affairs.

SUMMARY

Staff development and in-service education are used interchangeably in this chapter and text. Supervisors spend considerable time in planning, implementing, and evaluating staff development programs. In fact, no task looms larger on the supervisor's agenda than staff development.

In-service education programs should be planned and carried out in cooperation with those for whom the programs are designed. Several issues and assumptions were examined and a model of in-service education presented, consisting of three training components and two post-training components.

Planning for in-service education begins with an assessment of needs as perceived by the teachers. After needs are surveyed, they are ranked and top needs filled.

Active school systems make available to teachers a wide variety of opportunities for improving themselves both personally and professionally. The goal of in-service education is the continuous professional development of the teachers, which in turn will enhance the achievement of the learners. Among the types of organized in-service programs are college and university courses, workshops and institutes, conferences, supervision of student teachers, visiting days, and approved travel.

Directors of staff development of the school districts are charged with the task of preparing a comprehensive master plan. Principals are frequently assigned the job of creating a staff development plan for their schools.

In order to gain teachers' participation in organized in-service training some incentives are essential. Among the incentives found successful in school systems are released time, salary increments based on the accumulation of in-service credits, reimbursement for college and university tuition, reduced tuition rates for teachers attending colleges and universities, certificates for supervisors of student teachers entitling them to register for college or university courses, and pay differentials for advanced degrees or accumulated college and university credits.

Supervisors should plan for the evaluation of in-service activities. Participants should evaluate the contributions of the staff, the instruction, the facilities, and their own accomplishments. They should be accorded the opportunity to express their satisfaction or dissatisfaction with the activities, materials, procedures, and personnel. An evaluation form tailored to the particular in-service activity should be developed by the supervisor and staff of the in-service activity and distributed to the participants to fill out at the end of the program.

Control of in-service education is an issue. Staff development activities are sponsored by individual schools, the central office, intermediate units, schools and departments of education, and teacher education centers.

Some school districts have established teacher centers which house resources for teachers and serve as meeting places. Teacher education centers have assumed a major role in planning and administering in-service education.

ACTIVITIES FOR FURTHER STUDY

1. Poll a group of teachers and summarize their views on the following:
   a. What types of in-service activities do they prefer?
   b. Do they feel they have input into the organization of in-service training programs?
   c. What incentives do they believe are needed to secure teacher participation in in-service programs?
   d. Are they aware of in-service opportunities in their school system?
   e. Do they feel satisfied with the range and type of in-service opportunities?
2. Distinguish between a *workshop, institute, seminar*, and *course* as applied to in-service education.
3. Consult with administrators and supervisors in a school system and/or search the literature for types of organized in-service education opportunities not mentioned in this chapter.
4. Find out and report the annual cost of in-service activities of a school system you know well. Tell what percentage of funding comes from state sources, what percentage from local sources, and what percentage, if any, from federal sources. Calculate what the cost of in-service education is per pupil. Decide whether the total expenditure for in-service education is too much, too little, or about right.
5. Develop an instrument for evaluating a specific workshop, institute, conference, or other in-service activity; attend that activity; apply the instrument you have developed; summarize the data; and draw conclusions.
6. Develop a set of guidelines to help teachers achieve the maximum benefits from supervising student teachers.
7. Gather and report data from several school systems elsewhere in the state or nation on prevailing practices as to incentives provided for teachers to secure their participation in in-service training.
8. If there is a teacher education center in the area, obtain information by interview with center officials or by examining literature of the center about its in-service programs. Prepare a report that summarizes the in-service programs, shows the roles of the center and the teacher education institutions with which the center works, and contrasts in-service programs as conducted by the center with in-service programs as they exist without a center. Determine whether there is any change in the role of supervisors of a school system when a teacher education center exists in the system.
9. Analyze a master plan for staff development and using a set of criteria which you have located or developed point out its adequacies and weaknesses.
10. Analyze a staff development plan for an individual school and using a set of criteria which you have located or developed point out its adequacies and weaknesses.
11. Conduct an in-service needs assessment in your school. Verify teachers' perceived needs against empirical data.
12. Survey the attitudes of teachers in a school about in-service education. If

you discover negative attitudes, account for the negativism and suggest ways to overcome it.

13. Draw a model of in-service education.
14. Take a position pro or con on the following statements:
    a. Supervision is staff development.
    b. Staff development is in-service education.
15. Take a position on the question: Teachers should constitute the majority on the advisory council of a teacher education center.
16. Find out if an intermediate unit (cooperative educational service agency) serves your school district. If so, find out what services it provides and how many consultants it has and in what areas.
17. Draft a plan for a workshop or institute on a topic which you believe is needed by a school system you know well. Include in your plan objectives, activities, materials, personnel, and means of evaluation.
18. Draft a plan for a conference on a topic which you believe is needed by a school system you know well. Include in your plan objectives, activities, materials, personnel, and means of evaluation.
19. Write a report on the development of teacher education centers in the United States.
20. List characteristics of an effective in-service activity.

NOTES

1. Lloyd W. Dull, *Supervision: School Leadership Handbook*, Columbus, Ohio, Charles E. Merrill, 1981, 110.
2. Ben M. Harris, *Improving Staff Performance through In-Service Education*, Boston, Allyn and Bacon, 1980, 24–25.
3. E. Lawrence Dale, "What Is Staff Development?" *Educational Leadership* 40, no. 1 (October 1982): 31.
4. Thomas J. Sergiovanni and Robert J. Starratt, *Supervision: Human Perspectives*, 2d ed., New York, McGraw-Hill, 1979, 290–291.
5. John T. Lovell, "Instructional Supervision: Emerging Perspective," in A. W. Sturges, chairman, *The Role and Responsibilities of Instructional Supervisors*, Report of the ASCD Working Group on the Roles and Responsibilities of Supervisors, Alexandria, Va., Association for Supervision and Curriculum Development, October 1, 1978, 43.
6. Harris, *Improving Staff Performance through In-Service Education*, 30. See also Wagstoff and McCullough, "Inservice Educators: Education's Disaster Area," in *Administrators' Handbook*, Chicago, Midwest Administration Center, University of Chicago, May 1973.
7. Fred H. Wood and Steven R. Thompson, "Guidelines for Better Staff Development," *Educational Leadership* 37, no. 5 (February 1980): 374.
8. Harris, *Improving Staff Performance through In-Service Education*, 33. See Gordon Lawrence, Dennis Baker, Patricia Elzie, and Barbara Hansen, *Patterns of Effective In-Service Education*, Gainesville, Fla., College of Education, University of Florida, 1974.
9. Harris, *Improving Staff Performance through In-Service Education*, 36. See Don Proctor McLendon, "A Delphi Study of Agreement and Consensus among Selected Educator Groups in Texas Regarding Principles Underlying Effective Inservice Education," doctoral dissertation, Austin, Tex., University of Texas, 1977.
10. Harris, *Improving Staff Performance through In-Service Education*, 36. See Francis J.

Reardon, "Participant Survey of Pennsylvania In-service," *NCSIE Inservice*, Syracuse, N.Y., College of Education, Syracuse University, November 1977, 9–10.

11. Harris, *Improving Staff Performance through In-Service Education*, 36–37. See Jack L. Brimm and Daniel J. Tollett, "How Do Teachers Feel about In-service Education?" *Educational Leadership* 31, no. 6 (March 1974): 521–524.

12. David W. Champagne, "Does Staff Development Do Any Good?" *Educational Leadership* 37, no. 5 (February 1980): 401–402. See "An Exercise in Freedom: A Place Where Test Scores Appear to Be Rising," in *The Test Score Decline*, L. Lipsitz, ed., Englewood Cliffs, N.J., Educational Technology Publications, 1977.

13. Champagne, 402–403. See ERIC report by William P. Ward, ERIC ED 119387 + EA 008045.

14. Champagne, 403. See David N. Aspy and Flora N. Roebuck, "From Humane Ideas to Human Technology and Back Again Many Times," *Education* 95, no. 2 (Winter 1974): 163–171.

15. Champagne, 403.

16. Lovell, 35.

17. John Dewey, *The Sources of a Science of Education*, New York, Liveright, 1929, 17.

18. Daniel Tanner and Laurel N. Tanner, *Curriculum Development: Theory into Practice*, 2nd ed., New York, Macmillan, 1980, 103.

19. Roy A. Edelfelt, "Critical Issues in Developing Teacher Centers," *Phi Delta Kappan* 63, no. 6 (February 1982): 403.

20. Harris, *Improving Staff Performance through In-Service Education*, 37.

21. Toni Sharma, "Inservicing the Teachers," *Phi Delta Kappan* 63, no. 6 (February 1982): 403.

22. Fred H. Wood, Steven R. Thompson, and Sister Frances Russell, "Designing Effective Staff Development Programs," in *Staff Development/Organization Development*, 1981 Yearbook, Alexandria, Va., Association for Supervision and Curriculum Development, 1981, 61–63. See also slightly revised version in Fred H. Wood, Frank O. McQuarrie, Jr., and Steven R. Thompson, "Practitioners and Professors Agree on Effective Staff Development Practices," *Educational Leadership* 40, no. 1 (October 1982): 28–29.

23. Leonard C. Burrello and Tim Orbaugh, "Reducing the Discrepancy between the Known and the Unknown in Inservice Education," *Phi Delta Kappan* 63, no. 6 (February 1982): 385–386. See Patricia P. Kells et al., *Quality Practice Task Force Final Report*, Bloomington, Ind., National Inservice Network, 1980, and Patricia J. Jamison, *The Development and Validation of a Conceptual Model and Quality Practices Designed to Guide the Planning, Implementation, and Evaluation of Inservice Education Programs*, doctoral dissertation, College Park, Md., University of Maryland, 1981.

24. For other models of staff development, see Wood, Thompson, and Russell, 64–87; also in Wood, McQuarrie, and Thompson, 28–31. See also James C. King, "Improving Staff Development: Using a Model," *Ohio Association for Supervision and Curriculum Development Newsletter* 1 (Winter 1978): 18–21.

25. Peter A. Williamson and Julia A. Elfman, "A Commonsense Approach to Teacher Inservice Training," *Phi Delta Kappan* 63, no. 6 (February 1982): 401.

26. Jay Lutz and Garrett Foster, "Greater Involvement Urged," *Florida Schools* 37, no. 3 (February 1975): 20–21.

27. *Inservice Training Needs Assessment*, Fort Myers, Fla., Southwest Florida Teacher Education Center, 1975.

28. Dade/Monroe Teacher Education Center, *Inservice Program Survey*, Miami, Fla., Dade/Monroe Teacher Education Center, June, 1982.

29. John I. Goodlad, *The Dynamics of Educational Change: Toward Responsive Schools*, New York, McGraw-Hill, 1975, 175.

30. J. H. C. Butler Elementary School, *School/Department Improvement Plan*, 1981–82, Savannah, Ga., Savannah-Chatham County Public Schools, 1981, Section VI.

31. Linda L. Jones and Andrew E. Hayes, "How Valid Are Surveys of Teacher Needs?" *Educational Leadership* 37, no. 5 (February 1980): 390.

32. Ibid., 391.
33. Dade County Public Schools, *Master Plan for Staff Development 1979–1984*, Miami, Fla., 1979, 26.
34. Richmond County Public Schools, *Staff Development 1982–83*, Augusta, Ga., 1982, 11.
35. Ibid., 38.
36. Sol C. Johnson High School, *Staff/Department Improvement Plan: 1981–82*, Savannah, Ga., Savannah-Chatham County Public Schools, 1981.
37. Fred H. Wood and Steven R. Thompson, "Guidelines for Better Staff Development," *Educational Leadership* 37, no. 5 (February 1980): 377.
38. Vynce A. Hines and William M. Alexander, *High School Self-Evaluation and Curriculum Change*, Final Report, Project 3120, Contract no. OE 6–10–154, Bureau of Research, Office of Education, Washington, D.C., U.S. Department of Health, Education, and Welfare, August 1967, 64.
39. Dull, 111
40. Florida Department of Education, *State Council for Teacher Education Centers Annual Report*, Tallahassee, Fla., 1975, 2.
41. State Legislature of Florida, *Florida Statutes*, 1974 Supplement, Section 231.603, "Establishing Teacher Education Centers," Subsections 2(a) through (g), as amended by the 1975 session of the legislature. From *State Council for Teacher Education Centers Annual Report*, 1975, 27.
42. Florida Department of Education, *State Council for Teacher Education Centers Annual Report*, 2.

BIBLIOGRAPHY

Beegle, Charles W., and Roy A. Edelfelt, eds. *Staff Development: Staff Liberation*. Alexandria, Va.: Association for Supervision and Curriculum Development, 1977.

Bishop, Leslee J. *Staff Development and Instructional Improvement: Plans and Procedures*. Boston: Allyn and Bacon, 1976.

Burrello, Leonard C., and Tim Orbaugh. "Reducing the Discrepancy between the Known and the Unknown in Inservice Education." *Phi Delta Kappan* 63, no. 6 (February 1982): 385–388.

Champagne, David W. "Does Staff Development Do Any Good?" *Educational Leadership* 37, no. 5 (February 1980): 400–403.

Dillon-Peterson, Betty, ed. *Staff Development/Organization Development*, 1981 Yearbook. Alexandria, Va.: Association for Supervision and Curriculum Development, 1981.

Dull, Lloyd W. *Supervision: School Leadership Handbook*. Columbus, Ohio: Charles E. Merrill, 1981.

Edelfelt, Roy A. "Critical Issues in Developing Teacher Centers." *Phi Delta Kappan* 63, no. 6 (February 1982): 390–393.

Firth, Gerald R. "Ten Issues on Staff Development." *Educational Leadership* 35 (December 1977): 215–220.

Florida Department of Education. *Guidelines for Developing a Competency-Based Inservice Program*. Chipley: Panhandle Area Educational Cooperative, 1974.

Harris, Ben M. *Improving Staff Performance through In-Service Education*. Boston: Allyn and Bacon, 1980.

———. *Supervisory Behavior in Education*, 2nd ed. Englewood Cliffs, N.J.: Prentice-Hall, 1975.

Harrison, Raymond H. *Supervisory Leadership in Education*. New York: Van Nostrand Reinhold, 1968.

Huge, James. *The Role of the Building Principal as a Staff Development Leader*. Alexandria, Va.: Association for Supervision and Curriculum Development, 1977.

"Inservice Education in Practice." *Phi Delta Kappan* 63 (February 1982): 385–403.

Jones, Linda L., and Andrew E. Hayes. "How Valid Are Surveys of Teacher Needs?" *Educational Leadership* 37, no. 5 (February 1980): 390–392.

Lewis, Arthur J., and Alice Miel. *Supervision for Improved Instruction: New Challenges and New Responses.* Belmont, Calif.: Wadsworth, 1972.

Mann, Dale. "The Politics of Inservice." *Theory into Practice* 17 (June 1978): 212–217.

Rubin, Louis J., ed. *Improving In-service Education: Proposals and Procedures for Change.* Boston: Allyn and Bacon, 1971.

————. *The In-service Education of Teachers.* Boston: Allyn and Bacon, 1978.

Sergiovanni, Thomas J., ed. *Professional Supervision for Professional Teachers.* Alexandria, Va.: Association for Supervision and Curriculum Development, 1975.

Sharma, Toni. "Inservicing the Teachers." *Phi Delta Kappan* 63, no. 6 (February 1982): 403.

Sparks, Dennis C. "A Comprehensive Teacher Education Program." *Phi Delta Kappan* 63 (February 1982): 395–397.

"Staff Development." *Educational Leadership* 40 (October 1982): 4–59.

"Staff Development/New Directions." *Theory into Practice* 17 (June 1978).

Steig, Lester R., and E. Kemp Frederick. *School Personnel and In-service Training Practices.* West Nyack, N.Y.: Parker, 1969.

"Supervision as Staff Development." *Educational Leadership* 37 (February 1980): 374–423.

Unruh, Adolph, and Harold E. Turner. *Supervision for Change and Innovation.* Boston: Houghton Mifflin, 1970.

Wiles, Jon, and Joseph Bondi. *Supervision: A Guide to Practice.* Columbus, Ohio: Charles E. Merrill, 1980.

Wilhelms, Fred T. *Supervision in a New Key.* Alexandria, Va.: Association for Supervision and Curriculum Development, 1973.

Williamson, Peter A., and Julia A. Elfman. "A Commonsense Approach to Teacher Inservice Training." *Phi Delta Kappan* 63, no. 6 (February 1982): 401.

Wood, Fred H., Frank O. McQuarrie, and Steven R. Thompson. "Practitioners and Professors Agree on Effective Staff Development Practices." *Educational Leadership* 40, no. 1 (October 1982): 28–31.

Wood, Fred H., and Steven R. Thompson. "Guidelines for Better Staff Development." *Educational Leadership* 37, no. 5 (February 1980): 374–378.

Multi-Media

Florida Department of Education. The following catalogs of teacher training modules are available from Panhandle Area Educational Cooperative, P.O. Drawer 190, Chipley, Florida 32428:

Florida Catalog of Competency-Based Teacher Training Materials. Lists over 400 modules on generic teaching skills and special areas developed in Florida and elsewhere.

Florida Catalog of Competency-Based Teacher Training Materials, Addendum. Lists over 200 modules developed in projects supported by state funding.

Florida Competency-Based Modules. Lists approximately 200 "B-2" modules which were developed in federally-funded projects.

Northwest Regional Educational Laboratory, 710 S.W. Second Ave., Portland, Oregon 97204. Instructional system in *Research Utilizing Problem Solving.* Classroom Version. Participant materials, audiotape, text (*Diagnosing Classroom Learning Environments* by Fox, Luszki, and Schmuck), and leader's guide. 30 hours of instruction on (1) identifying the problem, (2) diagnosing the problem situation, (3) considering alternative actions, (4) trying out a plan of action, and (5) adapting the plan. Available from Commercial-Educational Distributing Services, P.O. Box 3711, Portland, Oregon 97208.

Weber State College. *Individualized Learning Kits.* Ogden, Utah. Eighty-five WILKITS for the preparation of elementary and secondary school teachers.

Audiotapes

Allen, Dwight. *Inservice Teacher Education*. Instructional Dynamics Incorporated, 166 E. Superior Street, Chicago, Illinois 60611, 1970.

Joyce, Bruce R. *What Research Says About In-service Education*. Association for Supervision and Curriculum Development, 225 North Washington Street, Alexandria, Virginia 22314, 1977. 45 min.

Ryan, Kevin, et al. *The Stages of Teaching: New Perspectives on Staff Development for Teachers Needs*. Association for Supervision and Curriculum Development, 225 North Washington Street, Alexandria, Virginia 22314, 1979. 90 min.

Journals and Other Periodicals

The Journal of Staff Development (twice a year) and *The Developer* (monthly). National Staff Development Council, 5198 Westgate Drive, Oxford, Ohio 45056.

Newsletters

NCSIE Inservice Newsletter. National Council of States on Inservice Education, Syracuse University, 123 Huntington Hall, Syracuse, New York 13210.

Questionnaire

Teacher Skill/Interest Questionnaire: A District Needs Assessment. Instrument for assessing in-service needs of teachers. Evaluative Research Associates, 8444 Florissant Road, Suite 207, St. Louis, Missouri 63121. Developed for use as a district needs assessment by Ferguson-Florissant Reorganized School District.

10

Helping Teachers
to Work Together

After studying Chapter 10 you should be able to accomplish the following objectives:

1. Describe leadership skills needed by the supervisor.
2. Describe types of leadership styles and decide which style you prefer and follow.
3. Explain the supervisor's role as change agent.
4. Explain key concepts in organizational development and tell how they apply to the role of the supervisor.
5. Identify problems and suggest improvements in the use of oral, written, and nonverbal language.
6. Demonstrate skills as a group leader.
7. Describe impediments to successful group work and the supervisor's role in reducing them.
8. Design a training program in group interaction.

LIVING IN GROUPS

Unless one lives in the middle of the Gobi Desert, much of one's life from the cradle to the grave will be spent in groups of some kind or other. One is a member of one's primary group, the family; one goes to school in groups, plays in groups. As giant urban concentrations or megalopolises continue to sprawl up, down, and across

America, and as the beehive high-rise condominium becomes commonplace, individuals will be thrown closer and closer together and into groups. The era of the "rugged individualist" will disappear, indeed, if it has not disappeared already, and group living will become not only a way of life but a way of survival. Even in the Gobi Desert patterns of group behavior arise when the camel trains must put in at the caravansary, and when two or more camelherders meet a group is born. If the citizens of the Gobi do not discover each other, sooner or later a group of touring American educators will discover them, and by their example of group organization reveal to them the group process in action.

Most of the world's work is conducted through group interaction. No less is true of the school; most of the work of the school is carried on through the interaction of the personnel of the school. Though the teacher in the self-contained elementary, middle school, or high school classroom may face students alone (and with them form a separate teacher-student grouping), much planning, policymaking, curriculum development, and decision making which affect the individual teacher take place in group situations.

A teacher today can no longer work completely independent of other teachers as he or she may have done in the days of the little red school house. Every decision a teacher makes has the potential of affecting other teachers. If a teacher independently, for example, decides to toss out a set of adopted textbooks and put in those more compatible with his or her objectives, the articulation of a sequence may be destroyed. If a teacher decides to make the standards of his or her grade or course so high that all pupils fail, repercussions may fall not only on him or her but on other teachers and administrators in the school. A faculty must function as a group and the success of a school is to a large measure determined by the success with which teachers are able to work together. A corollary to this statement is the proposition that the success of a supervisor is to a large measure determined by his or her success in helping teachers work together.

To some teachers it seems as if their lives are one grouping and regrouping after another, each of which requires a new set of relationships. Teachers may be members of a host of school committees and groups—the faculty as a whole, ad hoc committees, standing committees, departments, teaching teams, in-service study groups, parent-teacher associations, teacher-student organizations, school district committees, professional organizations, associations of special fields, state committees, and national groups.

Presumably, all the groups to which a teacher belongs have certain objectives. Whether a group's objectives are realized depends on a number of variables: the quality of leadership in the group, the quality of followership in the group, and the skills of interaction among all members of the group. Groups fail to achieve their objectives when any one of these variables is deficient.

Suppose an anthropologist were to study a group of teachers at their national convention. He spends the three days of the conference dropping in on various meetings and group sessions and takes copious notes. After observing the work sessions—and incidentally participating in the social agenda—he studies his notations, among which are the following:

General assembly—keynote address on "Teaching: Its Joys and Tribulations"
—the first persons to arrive fill up the last two rows in the auditorium. They are
asked to move forward.

Panel discussion on individualizing instruction—last half hour is dialogue between two of the panelists.

Seminar on computer-assisted instruction—"resource person" doesn't show—
wires regrets.

Seminar on alternative schools—guest speaker—continuous coming and going
of the audience.

Discussion group on independent study—discussion digresses to disciplinary
problems in the schools.

Seminar on reading problems—one participant cuts off others in the group,
dominates the discussion.

Seminar on open-space education—chairperson begins the session with the
question, "What would you like to discuss?"

Seminar on competency-based education—group becomes polarized, half pro,
half con.

Panel discussion on career education—two hours allotted, half-an-hour for each
of four discussants; first speaker talks 50 minutes; last speaker winds up with 10
minutes.

Round-table on developments in the language arts—everyone attempts to talk
at the same time.

Our anthropologist wonders what the participants in these groups brought away
with them from the conference. Admittedly, these were pro tempore groups
composed of persons who were relative strangers. But he wonders nevertheless if the
groups should not have been more productive. As he compares them with some of
the groups which gave evidence of productivity, he tries to sort out some of the
threads. He detects in the groups which experienced problems a lack of interest
among the participants, a lack of commitment to the group's activity, a lack of organization and planning, a lack of sensitivity among the group participants for the
concerns of others, a lack of ability or willingness to listen to each other, a lack of
communication skills, a lack of a feeling of achievement as a result of group deliberation, and often, perhaps most serious of all, a lack of purpose.

It might be conjectured that groups at a conference do not give a true picture
of groups in action. Teachers are away from home; the groups are transient and
temporary; most of the participants have little control over the organization, content,
and conduct of the deliberations of these groups. Our anthropologist would like to
test the premise that when teachers know each other intimately and work side-by-
side daily their group sessions are more productive. He learns of a junior high school
which has just begun a self-study in preparation for a year-end visit by a committee
from the regional accrediting association. He is given carte blanche to attend any of
the sessions of faculty and committees he wishes, which he takes full advantage of.
He is not surprised when he finds the following situations.

The committee on philosophy goals, aims, and objectives is about evenly divided among those who might be labeled "child-centered" and those who might be called "subject-centered." They seem unable to resolve their differences. One of the child-centered faction by default writes the committee's "report" which they will submit to the total faculty.

The committee on school and community has a difficult time apportioning the work. Much data have to be collected and put into tabular and graphic form. Several teachers protest a lack of time to do this job. Since few volunteer for specific tasks, the chairperson has to arbitrarily assign responsibilities.

When the committee on philosophy goals, aims, and objectives reports to the total faculty, several teachers sit in the back of the room talking, another is reading a newspaper, several arrive late, and two have scheduled other appointments. Time runs out before the faculty can reach consensus.

The language arts group spends an entire session hung up on pupils' deficiencies in reading and writing.

The mathematics group whips through its set of *Evaluative Criteria* without thought or discussion in 45 minutes.

The foreign language teachers engage in a prolonged, heated discussion of who should take foreign languages—require of everybody or restrict to the gifted?

The guidance committee wandered into the subject of the administrator's failings.

Are these groups productive? Some would say yes, others would say no, depending on their orientation to the group process itself. It would appear that each of these groups evidences problems.

Supervisors will spend a great part of their professional lives meeting with groups of teachers—total faculties, departments, teams, task forces, study groups, and committees. They will work with groups of teachers from single schools and with groups representative of many or all schools of a district. They will experience many meetings of groups which are unproductive. On the other hand, there will be times when the supervisors will feel that a group's effort couldn't have been more productive, and they will feel gratified at having participated in situations like the following.

1. An early childhood teaching team becomes aware of problems in handling children of minorities in its classes, proposes analysis of the problem, studies the problem thoroughly, works diligently to formulate proposals for better meeting the needs of these children, and energetically attempts to implement its proposals.

2. A committee of middle school teachers becomes concerned with the school's grading system, looks at alternate ways of grading, and drafts a proposal to take to the faculty for its consideration.

3. A junior high school faculty which feels its preadolescents as a group are lacking in motivation and are disinterested in school engages in a free-wheeling discussion of why the pupils act as they do and ends its discussion with a motion to analyze the relevance of the curriculum. A task force is created under the leadership

of the supervisor to examine the curriculum and to report back to the faculty with recommendations for making the curriculum more relevant.

4. The department of English in a high school undertakes an analysis of the reading achievement level of the students in its school. Finding many students with reading deficiencies, the teachers agree on a proposal, which, instead of blaming the elementary school, middle school, and junior high school faculties for the students' deficiencies, outlines ways for the total faculty to implement constructive remedial and developmental programs and to institute techniques of teaching reading in the content areas.

In each of the four situations above, all of the teachers have felt an obligation and responsibility to participate fully and to give of their energies and ideas. Not only has each teacher felt a responsibility for participating but everyone has also felt that his or her ideas were valued by both the group leader and other group members and that each person has had the opportunity to express himself or herself. The members of these groups felt that their missions were worthwhile.

THE SUPERVISOR AS GROUP LEADER

The successful supervisor must demonstrate the capacity to lead others. The effective instructional supervisor must not only possess leadership skills but must also be able to nurture leadership in others.

Definition of Leadership

Many studies have sought to discover the nature of leaders and leadership.[1] Unfortunately, since leadership is a human quality, like most human qualities it defies precise description, quantification, generalization, and predictability. We can find almost as many definitions of leadership as there are of supervision. Among the definitions of *leader* and *leadership* are:

> The leader is the individual in the group given the task of directing and coordinating task-relevant group activities (Fred E. Fiedler).[2]
> Leadership may be considered as the process (act) of influencing the activities of an organized group in its efforts toward goal setting and goal achievement (Ralph M. Stogdill).[3]
> . . . we define leadership as that behavior of an individual which initiates a new structure in interaction within a social system; it initiates change in the goals, objectives, configurations, procedures, inputs, processes, and ultimately the outputs of social systems (James M. Lipham and James A. Hoeh, Jr.).[4]

Although most administrators feel they are leaders and bristle when it is suggested otherwise, Lipham distinguished between an administrator and a leader:

the leader is concerned with initiating changes in established structures, procedures, or goals; he is disruptive of the existing state of affairs.

The administrator . . . may be identified as the individual who utilizes existing structures or procedures to achieve an organizational goal or objectives . . . the administrator is concerned primarily with maintaining, rather than changing established structures, procedures, or goals. Thus, the administrator may be viewed as a stabilizing force.[5]

It is unfortunately true that some school systems do not want their administrators and supervisors to be leaders. The school boards and the communities in these cases are happy with things just as they are. They want administrators and supervisors who will conserve, not disrupt, maintain rather than change. They lack dynamism and are satisfied with the status quo. What is unfortunate is that those administrators and supervisors who enter systems of this kind imbued with a zeal to exert leadership and effect change soon discover that if they wish to remain in the system they must conform and thus they become "society's children," to extrapolate on the phrase used by Carl Nordstrom, Edgar Z. Friedenberg, and Hilary A. Gold.[6]

W. H. Cowley (1928) and Robert L. De Bruyn (1976) defined *leader* and *leadership* in simple terms. Cowley saw a leader as "an individual who is moving in a particular direction and inducing others to follow after him."[7] De Bruyn's definition of leadership was "causing others to want what you are doing to accomplish the work of the school."[8] Leadership can be conceptualized as the ability to cause people to make improvements in the institution.

Traits of Leaders

It would be a boon to society and all its institutions if someone could draw up a foolproof list of traits which leaders should possess. On everyone's list would probably be:

- initiative
- forcefulness
- decisiveness
- expertise
- enthusiasm

Yet, studies of leadership have shown no consistent pattern of traits which all leaders possess.[9] The studies have revealed that in respect to their followers leaders generally are:

- more self-confident
- slightly more intelligent
- more motivated to succeed
- more mature emotionally
- more gregarious
- more goal-oriented.
- taller

Some would add that leaders are more disposed to take risks and to accept the consequences of their actions. Others would say that a leader must be assertive or aggressive. If we may assume that there are more leaders among administrators than among other school personnel, then it also pays to be male, white, Anglo-Saxon, Protestant (WASP), for more administrators in the United States possess these characteristics than do not. With the exception of sex we might write off these characteristics as the effect of sheer numbers. Since there are more WASPs, it appears logical that a higher percentage of administrators would fall into that category. The phenomenon of male dominance of school leadership positions may be explained by cultural conditioning and plain old chauvinism. But how do we explain the fact that a majority of superintendents and principals of secondary schools are social studies and physical education majors? Art, foreign language, and music majors in top positions of leadership are few and far between. Is it a matter of numbers again, for social studies and physical education are popular fields and in some parts of the country overcrowded? Then why is the English major not at the top in leadership positions, for English is also a heavily subscribed field? Do those that have it (leadership, that is) gravitate instinctively to social studies and physical education? Is this because these disciplines are people-oriented, as they are, whereas other fields are more subject-oriented? Or do the disciplines make the leader?

Stogdill conducted an extensive review of leadership studies and concluded on the basis of 10 to 15 of these studies that:

The average person who occupies a position of leadership exceeds the average member of his group in the following respects: (1) intelligence, (2) scholarship, (3) dependability in exercising responsibilities, (4) activity and social participation, and (5) socioeconomic status.

The qualities, characteristics, and skills required in a leader are determined to a large extent by the demands of the situation in which he is to function as a leader.

The average person who occupies a position of leadership exceeds the average member of his group to some degree in the following respects: (1) sociability, (2) initiative, (3) persistence, (4) knowing how to get things done, (5) self-confidence, (6) alertness to, and insight into, situations, (7) cooperativeness, (8) popularity, (9) adaptability, and (10) verbal facility. . . .

The items with the highest overall correlation with leadership are originality, popularity, sociability, judgment, aggressiveness, desire to excel, humor, cooperativeness, liveliness, and athletic ability, in approximate order of magnitude of average correlation coefficient.

In spite of considerable negative evidence, the general trend of results suggests a low positive correlation between leadership and such variables as chronological age, height, weight, physique, energy, appearance, dominance, and mood control. The evidence is about evenly divided concerning the relationship of such traits as introversion-extroversion, self-sufficiency, and emotional control.[10]

If a supervisor possessed every desirable trait on everyone's shopping list, it would not be certain that the supervisor once in the position would evidence successful leadership skills. It has become clear that successful leadership is as much a matter of the situation as of the personal skills and characteristics of the person designated to lead. Persons who may fail in one setting may very well succeed in another setting.

One trait which has not shown up as common to all leaders but which is worthy of further research is the elusive characteristic of charisma, the personal magnetism of a leader. What is surprising is how little attention has been given by the experts in administration to the phenomenon of charisma. Should we therefore deduce that charisma is unimportant to the success of leaders?

Certainly we can recall charismatic leaders out of the past. Moses and Christ must have possessed charisma. John F. Kennedy is almost always mentioned as a president who had charisma. George S. Patton and Douglas MacArthur of World War II fame were charismatic generals; most professional entertainers demonstrate charisma. It is of interest to speculate whether Adolf Hitler would have risen to a position of power if he had not been so charismatic.

Charisma is a power which enables leaders to attract persons to follow them sometimes, as it is said, to the ends of the earth. Some indefinable something in the individual's personality, whether product of the genes or the environment or both, enables the charismatic individual to assemble a following. What little literature there is on this subject seems to say that those leaders who possess charisma are fortunate; this trait adds a dimension to their leadership which is not possessed by noncharismatic individuals. On the other hand, charisma is not an essential characteristic of leadership, which is fortunate as charismatic leaders are in short supply.

Most of the literature on supervision treats leadership behavior as if it were generic, applicable to both administration and supervision. The literature assumes that the principles of leadership and leadership skills are common to both administrators and supervisors. This can only hold true if we agree that the administrator is a supervisor *and vice versa*. Since some specialists in the field believe, as I do, that the supervisor need not necessarily be an administrator, we should make a distinction between leadership skills needed by an administrator and those required of a supervisor.

Further, most administrative supervisors occupy middle-management positions. The skills necessary for success in middle management are not always identical to those needed in top management. Middle management has within it its own problems, as, for example, the need for skill in serving the demands of both administrators and teachers, which are not always in harmony.

Research which would distinguish leadership skills required of administrators from those needed by supervisors is lacking. Thus, I have done as many have and selected those skills of leadership which logically and empirically appear to apply to both supervisors, who are leaders in staff positions, and to administrators, who are leaders in line positions.

Styles of Leadership

What seems a more profitable avenue of study than traits of leaders is examination of styles or approaches to leadership. Two basic styles or approaches—three, if we include the more common mix of the basic two—have been described. Table 10.1 shows the terminology which four often cited sources have applied to the two approaches.[11]

Table 10.1   Two Basic Styles of Leadership

	Lewin, Lippitt, and White	McGregor	Fiedler	Morphet, Johns, and Reller
Style 1	Authoritarian	Theory X	Task-oriented	Traditional, monocratic, bureaucratic
Style 2	Democratic	Theory Y	Relations-oriented	Emerging, pluralistic, collegial

Though the terminologies differ, style 1 incorporates principles of directive behavior, focus on the needs of the institution, and concern for status. Style 2 emphasizes nondirective behavior, focus on the person, and openness of the system. The supervisor who embraces approach 1 is directive (ordering, prescribing, telling) in behavior, task- rather than people-oriented, and concerned about administrative efficiency. The supervisor who employs approach 2 is nondirective (helping, facilitating, counseling), conscious of interpersonal relations, and concerned about the human dimension of supervision. In practice, supervisors must learn to adapt the two styles to their situations. As there is a time to rend and a time to sew, there is a time to exhibit authoritarian behavior and a time to stress human relations skills.

The instructional supervisor who occupies a staff or advisory rather than a line or power position should be an exemplar of approach 2, using approach 1 only in rare, unavoidable instances when teacher behavior runs counter to the best interests of the students and the institution. In truth, staff personnel cannot follow approach 1 in their own right for they are not armed with line authority and must either be recipients of authority delegated by the administrator or they must refer troublesome problems to the administrator. Human relations must be the strong suit of the supervisory leader.

Human relations-oriented supervisors work in a cooperative mode with the teacher. They offer assistance; they serve as resource persons and advisers. They are concerned with building rapport and mutual trust. They evoke a nonthreatening climate where teachers' weaknesses can be revealed without punishment and where remediation can be undertaken without embarrassment. They are colleagues and friends whose purpose is helping the teachers to improve instruction so that together they may enhance student learning.

Thomas J. Sergiovanni and Robert J. Starratt would have supervisors move beyond a human relations approach to what they called human resource development. They contrasted the two in the following way:

The distinction between human relations supervision and human resources supervision is critical. Whereas human relations and human resources supervision are, for example, both concerned with teacher satisfaction, human relations views satisfaction as a means to a smoother and more effective school. . . . The human relations supervisor adopts shared decision-making to increase teacher satisfaction which in turn increases school effectiveness. . . .

The human resources supervisor, by contrast, views satisfaction as a desirable end toward which teachers will work. Satisfaction, according to this view, results from the successful accomplishment of important and meaningful work, and this sort of accomplishment is the key component of school effectiveness. . . . The human resources supervisor adopts shared decision-making practices to increase school effectiveness which in turn increases teacher satisfaction.[12]

It could be said that the human relations supervisor like the task-oriented supervisor has an increase in school effectiveness as the goal with teacher satisfaction as a means to the goal. The human resources supervisor has teacher satisfaction as the goal with increased school effectiveness as the means to that goal. Perhaps, we could say that the human resources supervisor is the *true* human relations supervisor.

At the present moment it appears to me that the term and concept of human resources supervision are encountered less frequently than human relations supervision. Human resources may well be the emerging concept as human resource development comes into its own. We now find some college departments and schools of education, for example, with their names modified to include Human Resource Development. Perhaps in years to come we will see less stress on organizational development and more on human resource development.

Though consensus is lacking on which skills are essential to the group leader, authorities on leadership appear to be in general agreement that in addition to the human orientation, supervisors should be skilled in (1) decision making, (2) effecting change, (3) organizational development, (4) communicating, and (5) group process. Let's look briefly at some of the salient points of each of these interrelated skills as they impact on the role of the supervisor.

Decision Making

President Harry S Truman summed up the heart of the administrative process in the famous slogan he kept on his desk in the Oval Office: "The buck stops here." Ultimately, the administrator must make and be responsible for decisions. Though school administrators and supervisors will not be called upon to make earth-shattering decisions like Truman's decision to drop the atomic bomb on Japan, nevertheless the ability to make decisions is the most important single ingredient of administrative and supervisory behavior. Numerous authorities have emphasized the importance of decision-making skills for the successful administrator or manager.[13]

Some would certainly add decisiveness to a list of traits which administrators and supervisors should possess. Unfortunately, teachers and others often interpret decisiveness as the ability to make snap, on-the-spot judgments. Administrators and supervisors must be able to sense when they can fulfill the desires of their followers for immediate decisions and when they should suspend judgment until more facts are available. Discretion is not only the better part of valor, it is also the better part of decision making. Administrators and supervisors who render snap judgments and call them correctly will certainly gain status. On the other hand, once they start to call the decisions wrong and suffer unpleasant consequences as a result, they can plummet in the eyes of their followers. Administrators and supervisors need to develop a companion skill known as tolerance for ambiguity. Not all decisions can, must, or should be made on the spot. Sometimes no decision is the wiser decision. The astute administrator or supervisor recognizes when it is essential to make a snap judgment, when to delay for further facts and then render a decision, and when to make no decision, allowing time for the situation to correct itself.

Administrators and supervisors are called on daily to render small or large decisions. They must make decisions about planning, implementing, evaluating, and recycling. Supervisors' decisions fall within the three domains discussed in Chapter 1: instructional, curricular, and staff development.

In Chapter 8, on curriculum evaluation, you became familiar with the CIPP model, which is a systematic process for making educational decisions. The model shows clearly the pervasiveness of the task of decision making. It shows kinds of changes which may take place, kinds of evaluation which are carried out, and types of decisions which must be made. This model features planning, structuring, implementing, and recycling decisions as tasks of educational evaluation. Though focusing on educational evaluation, the model serves as an overview of decision making generally. Evaluation is the rendering of judgments and in that respect evaluation is decision making. Every time an administrator or supervisor makes a decision he or she evaluates the situation prior to rendering a judgment, then the judgment itself must be evaluated and sometimes revised.

Decision making is so habitual to competent administrators and supervisors that they do not perceive themselves as going through a process in coming to a decision. Yet, each time we make a decision we do go through a series of steps or stages. In many instances the human brain runs through the stages so rapidly that we are not really aware that we are making any analysis of the problem before making a decision. What we are doing is actually problem solving.

We can find in the literature a number of models of the decision-making process which consist of steps to be taken by the administrator or supervisor.[14] For guidance in decision making we might fall back on the old reliable generic model for problem solving, referred to as the scientific method. In conducting research we follow certain steps of an orderly process. These steps are:

- identify the problem
- formulate a hypothesis
- collect data
- analyze data
- draw conclusions
- verify or reject the hypothesis

In one sense decision making is research. To reach some decisions we must conduct thorough research. Everyday routine decisions do not require a great deal in the way of bona fide research but the elements of collection of data, analysis, etc. are there, perhaps, only in embryo form. We can adapt the research model and make it more operational in nature as follows:

- identify the problem
- select solution from alternatives
- put solution into operation
- evaluate solution
- recycle decision, if needed

We should not confuse immediate decisions with off-the-top-of-the-head decisions. Administrators and supervisors do many times render immediate decisions. Even then, however, they should be based on the best data, which in many cases administrators and supervisors have at their fingertips. Spontaneous decisions are intuitive, hasty, ill-considered decisions which ignore data. In choosing a solution to a problem it is essential to utilize all available data, to avoid off-the-top-of-the-head judgments. Only in crises or emergencies when there is no time to gather data—the data must come out of the administrator's or supervisor's experience—can spontaneous decisions be justified.

Robert J. Alfonso, Gerald R. Firth, and Richard F. Neville have drawn 23 implications for decision theory for instructional supervisory behavior.[15] Among these are the following four propositions:

Proposition 1: Conscious decision making provides the opportunity for organizational growth and refinement.

Proposition 13: Decision making can be made more responsive and effective when it is recognized that decisions are seldom optimal, but are typically the selection of the best choice among those available.

Proposition 14: Decision making is swayed by the dynamic interaction between internal and external environments, and by the psychological makeup of the decision maker.

Proposition 16: Although executive decisions are important in establishing goals, decisions made at the operational level are still more important, since they directly affect personal commitment and, thereby, production and effectiveness.[16]

Supervisors make decisions both unilaterally and in cooperation with others in the course of their daily work. The supervisor may have to decide by himself or herself, for example, which of competing demands to meet and needs to fill. To which school and classroom will I go today? is a supervisory decision. Of course, the decision should not be purely arbitrary but should be based on the best available data.

Supervisors should, however, seek to expand the scope of cooperative decision making. The supervisor should not, for example, decide by himself or herself to initiate a curricular innovation or to select a certain series of textbooks, or to devise a system of classroom observation. These are matters for cooperative decision making.

Supervisors should be concerned not only with their own decision making but they should also seek to help teachers make decisions. Teachers want assistance with such problems as: What is the best way to handle certain types of pupils? Did I handle a particular pupil correctly? Should I introduce more inquiry learning?

Supervisors' success is gauged at least in part on how successfully they make decisions and how effective they are at helping others to reach decisions.

Effecting Change

In the span of years since the end of World War II our schools have flirted with team teaching, nongraded schools, programmed instruction, middle schools, instructional television, open-space education, computer-assisted instruction, and a host of other innovations. Change has been the order of the day.

The behavioral scientists tell us that institutions must change if they are to grow and develop. Can you imagine the Latin Grammar School as the principal secondary institution of the latter half of the twentieth century with its heavy emphasis on Latin and Greek and its absence of modern foreign languages, industrial arts, business education, interscholastic athletics, a marching band, and guidance? Can you imagine public schools which would restrict education to males as did the Latin Grammar School and early academies?

Change has been exceedingly rapid in contemporary society, toppling old mores and values as Alvin Toffler described so vividly in *Future Shock* and *The Third Wave*.[17] Whereas changes used to come slowly, modern technology, communication, and transportation catapult us into making changes often before we are emotionally ready to change.

What school systems need is planned change—not haphazard, not impulsive change. Nor can a school system afford to stand pat, wait, and maintain the status quo, no matter where the system is located. The students who are the outputs of the system suffer as much from no change as from unplanned change. Were students to spend their whole lives in a single community and in one career, the school would have a ready excuse for maintaining the status quo. Perhaps what was good enough for our grandparents would, under those conditions, be good enough for our grandchildren. But our country is large; our people are mobile; our industries are far flung. Technology has the bad habit of making careers obsolete so that more training and retraining become necessary throughout life.

The school system "on the cutting edge" will not only plan and effect change but will anticipate change. It will use such procedures as the Delphi Technique, which was mentioned in Chapter 8, consulting the experts who are willing to gaze into their crystal balls and predict where schools are going 5, 10, 15, 25 years hence. The march of the computer, the diminishing of fossil fuels, the high cost of housing, the decrease in farming population, the growth of megalopolises all have their impact on changes which will come about in our society.

The instructional supervisor is in the forefront of the change process in school systems. The supervisor is in a strategic position to influence the largest professional group, the teachers, to make changes in the system. In this process the supervisor is often referred to as a change agent. In the language of the behavioral scientist a change agent helps a client-system to bring about change. The change agent works with individuals and groups to effect improvements. In the case of the instructional

Table 10.2 Educational Innovations Probability Chart

Higher Risk ←——————————→ Lower Risk

Source of Innovation	Superimposed from outside	Outside agent brought in	Developed internally with aid	External idea modified	Locally conceived, developed, implemented
Impact of Innovation	Challenges sacrosanct beliefs	Calls for major value shifts	Requires substantial change	Modifies existing values or programs	Does not substantially alter existing values, beliefs or programs
Official Support	Official leaders active opposition	Officials on record as opposing	Officials uncommitted	Officials voice support of change	Enthusiastically supported by the official leaders
Planning of Innovation	Completely external	Most planning external	Planning processes balanced	Most of planning done locally	All planning for change done on local site
Means of Adoption	By superiors	By local leaders	By Reps	By most of the clients	By group consensus
History of Change	History of failures	No accurate records	Some success with innovation	A history of successful innovations	Known as school where things regularly succeed
Possibility of Revision	No turning back	Final evaluation before committee	Periodic evaluations	Possible to abandon at conclusion	Possible to abort the effort at any time
Role of Teachers	Largely bypassed	Minor role	Regular role in implementing	Heavy role in implementation	Primary actor in the classroom effort
Teacher Expectation	Fatalistic	Feel little chance	Willing to give a try	Confident of success	Wildly enthusiastic about chance of success
Work Load Measure	Substantially increased	Heavier but rewarding	Slightly increased	Unchanged	Work load lessened by the innovation
Threat Measure	Definitely threatens some clients	Probably threatening to some	Mild threat resulting from the change	Very remote threat to some	Does not threaten the security or autonomy
Community Factor	Hostile to innovations	Suspicious and uninformed	Indifferent	Ready for a change	Wholeheartedly supports the school

Shade the response in each category which most accurately reflects the condition surrounding the implementation of the middle school. If the "profile" of your school is predominately in the high risk side of the matrix, substantial work must be done to prepare your school for change.

SOURCE: Adapted from Jon Wiles, *Planning Guidelines for Middle Education*, Dubuque, Iowa: Kendall/Hunt Publishing Co., 1976, 30. In Jon Wiles and Joseph Bondi, *Curriculum Development: A Guide to Practice*, Columbus, Ohio: Charles E. Merrill, 1979, pp. 115–116. Reprinted with permission of Kendall/Hunt Publishing Co. and Charles E. Merrill Publishing Company.

supervisor changes are sought in instruction, in the curriculum, and in the s change agent is concerned with changes in the behavior of the people who be the organization, the goals of the organization, the structure of the organizatioı and the technical processes the organization employs.

The change agent recognizes that if an institution is to maintain a vita must grow and develop just as individuals grow and develop. The change agent to plan for change, to control and eliminate unplanned change. The change would be the first to reject the notion of change for the sake of change. Change be purposeful. It must come about because the change produces results whic better than that which preceded it.

We encounter disagreement over the question of whether a change agent s come from inside or from outside the system. Although there are cogent arguı for the employment of change agents from the outside, there are practical arguı for choosing change agents from within the system. School systems may not be to afford the services of people from the outside. They already have employe supervisory roles who can serve as agents of change. Capable supervisors have alr established a sense of trust with other school personnel; trust is an ingredient esse to the change process.

How do change agents work to effect improvements in the system? Lipham Hoeh summarized four conceptualizations of the process: "(1) a problem-sol model; (2) a research, development, and diffusion (RD&D) model; (3) an orgar tional development (OD) model; and (4) a linkage process model that includes ments of the other three."[18]

The problem-solving model is the scientific method; the RD&D model identi four phases in making changes: research, development, diffusion, and adoption; OD model emphasizes social interaction; and the linkage process model is a com nation of all three.

The behavioral scientists call the procedures they use to effect change intervؤ tion techniques or strategies. Change-agent supervisors work with teachers to impro their teaching skills by providing in-service education opportunities. They se solutions to system problems through the group process, which necessitates t formation of committees, task forces, and councils. A change to competency-basؤ education, for example, will require study and commitment of those who will ؤ expected to plan, execute, and evaluate it.

Change agents work with teachers to change the curriculum. Cooperativelؤ teachers and supervisors conduct needs assessments and decide on ways to close gaؤ in the curriculum. A change to a comprehensive high school, for example, will requir deliberation and approval of all the constituencies of the school.

Change agents work with teachers and administrators to revise school policieؤ and procedures which have become outmoded and nonfunctional. They help teacherؤ to perfect interpersonal skills through self-instruction and training sessions.

Some changes are minor, others major. Some changes affect only a single teacher, others, all school personnel and the community as well. The goal of many changes is adoption throughout the system. In fact, farsighted change agents hope that an innovation tested and found successful in their schools will be diffused and

adopted by school systems throughout the country. The behavioral objectives movement, for example, which began to develop in the late 1950s with the work of such
educators as Ralph W. Tyler at the University of Chicago, has been widely accepted
across the nation. This change was not perceived as a modification of instructional
practice for a particular school but rather a change which had a universality to it.

Change process is essentially an exercise in human relations skills. It is axiomatic
that a curriculum change, for example, can only result when people are changed. An
administrator can command change, can even bring about surface conformity. What
an administrator cannot command is a commitment to a mandated change. People
accept change when they feel they have a personal stake in it and when they believe
change will improve the lives of those affected by it.

Supervisors must be open individuals who are receptive to change themselves.
Since the impetus for change must often come from the leader, a closed personality
who sees little value in change ("if it works, don't fix it") can block a school's
progress. Schools need self-starting, energetic, future-looking persons in supervisory
positions.

Alfonso, Firth, and Neville set forth 37 propositions about change theory which
are of importance to instructional supervisors.[19] From this list we might note the
following which seem of particular significance:

Proposition 1: Planning and initiating change will be more effective when the objectives and
policies of the organization are clear, realistic, and understood.
Proposition 11: The effectiveness of a change effort will be increased when one sees the
nature of the change as enhancing one's own personal relationships and status in the
organization.
Proposition 19: Change will be more effective if it does not appear to disturb the existing
organizational structure of status, relationship, and recognition.
Proposition 29: Change agents will be more effective when the change agent, as perceived
by other group members, has prestige and acceptance within the group.[20]

Jon Wiles developed the chart shown in Table 10.2 for assessing the readiness
of a school to make changes.[21] The chart provides change agents with a means of
judging the degree to which an innovation is likely to be successful in a school on the
basis of 12 variables. Change agents hope that their schools will show up on the low
risk side of the chart.

The supervisor is a key change agent. Effecting change is what the supervisor's
job is all about. Whether as group leader or as individual counselor the supervisor
helps the people in the system and the system itself to be better than they would have
been without his or her intervention.

Organizational Development

Leaders help not only people but also their organizations to grow and develop. In
one sense organizational development is a type of change process. Richard Beckhard
defined organizational development as:

an effort (1) planned, (2) organization-wide, and (3) managed from the top, to (4) increase organization effectiveness and health through (5) planned interventions in the organization's "process," using behavioral science knowledge.[22]

Key terms in organizational development are:

- interaction of groups
- team building
- conflict resolution
- in-service education
- systems planning
- communication
- collaboration
- change agents
- role clarification
- leadership behavior

Wendell L. French and Cecil H. Bell, Jr. wove together some of the basic concepts of organizational development in the following definition:

a long-range effort to improve an organization's problem-solving and renewal processes, particularly through a more effective and collaborative management of organization culture—with special emphasis on the culture of formal work teams—with the assistance of a change agent, or catalyst, and the use of the theory and technology of applied behavioral science, including action research.[23]

Stephen J. Knezevich described the purposes of organizational development as follows:

Organizations, like individuals, are dynamic. They are born, experience frustrations, mature, and may even pass from the scene. Concern for an organization's life history, sensitivity to the conflicts within that could influence achievement of goals, and restructuring it if need be to enhance its productivity is what OD is all about.[24]

He observed that some people see organizational development as a substitute for sensitivity training.[25] This is not surprising given the heavy emphasis on team building, frequently with the assistance of an outside change agent.

The administrator or supervisor who seeks to develop the organization would help a group to gather data about its current situation, to analyze the data, to detect places where improvements in its functioning could be made, and to recommend ways to improve. Central to the process are the group's endeavors to understand itself, to become more cohesive, and to find cooperatively solutions to its problems.

Group difficulties may stem from (1) poor interpersonal relationships among groups and individuals and (2) poor management (leadership). Interpersonal relationships may be improved through group deliberation/group process and through group encounter techniques like sensitivity training (T-groups). Particularly important in the development of healthy interpersonal relationships is the reduction or elimination of conflicts.

Fred Luthans identified four types of conflict which develop in organizations. These are:

(1) hierarchical conflict (between the various organizational levels . . .); (2) functional conflict (between functional units of the organization . . .); (3) line-staff conflict (between line personnel and staff personnel . . .); and (4) formal-informal conflict (between the formal organization and the informal groupings . . .).[26]

A widely cited model of educational administration developed by Jacob W. Getzels and Egon Guba depicted the interrelationships of institutional roles and individual needs in creating the particular behavior of the social institution. Their model, which appears in Figure 10.1, posited a nomothetic (institutional, sociological) dimension and an idiographic (personal, psychological) dimension.

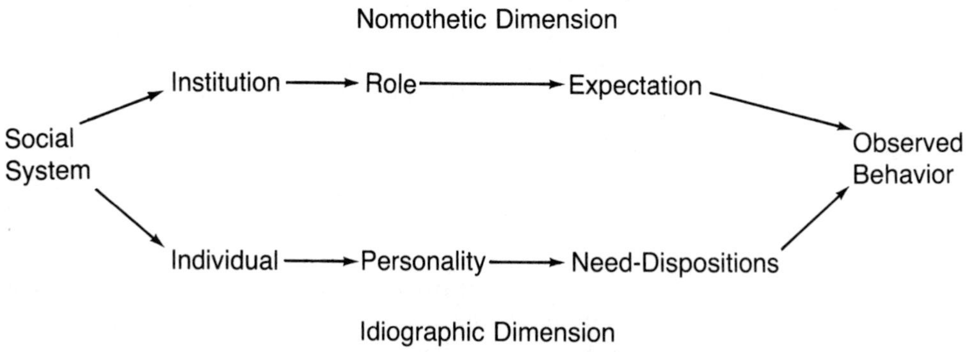

Nomothetic Dimension

Social System → Institution → Role → Expectation → Observed Behavior

Individual → Personality → Need-Dispositions → Observed Behavior

Idiographic Dimension

Figure 10.1 Getzels-Guba Model of Educational Administration as a Social Process

SOURCE: Jacob W. Getzels, "Administration as a Social Process," in Andrew W. Halpin, ed., *Administration Theory in Education*, New York, Macmillan, 1958, 152–153. Reprinted with permission.

Getzels and Herbert A. Thelen developed an even more complex model by adding anthropological (cultural), group, and biological dimensions, which further affect the observed behavior of the institution.[27]

From the Getzels-Guba model we can deduce that:

1. The school is a social system.

2. Social systems evidence two classes of phenomena (dimensions): the nomothetic by which an institution prescribes certain roles for its employees with certain expectations for each role and the idiographic by which individuals with their own peculiar personalities try to satisfy their own needs-dispositions.

3. The behavior of people within the system and the uniqueness of the system are functions of the interaction of both dimensions.

4. Leaders of a social system may be any one of three types: they may lean to the nomothetic or normative dimension emphasizing the goals of the institution; they may lean to the idiographic or human dimension emphasizing the goals of the indi-

viduals who make up the system; or they may shift from one dimension to the other as required by the needs of the institution and the persons employed by the institution. In the latter case such leadership has been referred to as transactional.

5. Three types of conflicts may arise in a social system: intrarole, intrapersonality, and role-personality. Intrarole conflicts occur when: (1) The person who holds a particular role is subjected to disagreement among groups about the expectations of the role. Teachers, for example, may view the principal's role somewhat differently from the way students or parents view the role. (2) The person who holds the role is subjected to disagreement from within a given group about the expectations of the role. Some teachers, for example, may hold a view of the principal's role which is different from that of other teachers. (3) The person who holds a role is called upon the fill more than one role at the same time. Administrators, for example, may have to perform at the same time as instructional supervisors.

Intrapersonality conflicts come about as a result of conflicting personality needs of the holder of a role. A principal, for example, may be torn between his or her desire to please teachers and his or her desire to please the superintendent.

Role-personality conflicts result from differing expectations written into the role and the needs-dispositions of the holder of the role. A principal may be expected by terms of the job description to be a strong disciplinarian but at the same time does not believe in corporal punishment.

Conflicts are resolved in a variety of ways. Some of the means for resolving and managing conflict are more effective and longer lasting than others. Some of the ways of settling conflicts are:

> *Administrative order.* This is a far from satisfactory solution. It may result in temporary conformity but leaves the conflict to fester and erupt again.
>
> *Compromise.* Some people feel that compromise is unsatisfactory since each side has to give up something. On the other hand, compromise takes place every day in our society and is especially apparent in the governmental structures of our republic.
>
> *Changing the structure of the organization to eliminate sources of conflict.* Persons can be moved around, down, up, or even out. Procedures can be changed so that the organization may function more smoothly.
>
> *Policy formulation.* Conflicts arise in the absence of policies to guide action. They can be reduced by the group's creation of policies to which all can subscribe.
>
> *New solutions.* Creative solutions may be found which are a departure from the existing practices which have provoked conflict.

Harmony and team spirit are paramount goals in organizational development.

The organization may be developed through improved management techniques. Management training, therefore, is an important feature of organizational development. Key concerns of managers interested in developing the organization are (1) planning, (2) time, and (3) stress.

Planning

A planning technique which has grown in popularity is known as MBO/R, management by objectives/results. Concerning MBO/R Knezevich wrote:

Some writers view MBO/R as a key mechanism in OD [organizational development]. Through generation of objectives and then management for results there may be revealed a need to restructure the organization. The organization's growth patterns may be directed by operating in the MBO/R mode.[28]

Those who manage or supervise by objectives follow an orderly process which is comprised of the following steps:

1. Specify the goals of the institution.
2. Specify the objectives of the institution and standards of performance of the target group(s).
3. Select strategies to accomplish the objectives.
4. Identify resources needed: human and material.
5. Establish timelines for achieving objectives.
6. Implement the strategies.
7. Evaluate success in accomplishing objectives.
8. Recycle.

Some supervisors project objectives and timelines over a five-year period, for example, and then prepare full and detailed plans annually. Management or supervision by objectives for results is a logical and systematic way of planning, implementing, and evaluating the work of the organization.

Time and Stress

If organizations are to thrive, the human beings who make the systems go must remain physically and emotionally healthy. If the human beings are to maintain vitality, they must learn to manage the bothersome and companion elements of time and stress.

To many administrators and supervisors there is never enough time to "get it all done." Work, as we know, is infinitely expandable. Compulsive, perfectionist individuals find themselves running hard just to keep up. The relentless computers and their human programmers keep grinding out paper work so that the harder we run the further behind we seem to get. At some point someone—a thoughtful administrator, a perceptive supervisor, or a facilitator from the outside—needs to blow the whistle and ask individuals to analyze what they are doing, how they are doing it, what is really necessary, how time is being utilized, and what factors are provoking stress.

Time can be managed from two perspectives. First, we can all examine whether the organizational tasks which we now feel necessary are really essential. Do we need all the committee meetings, for example? Are we, perhaps, closet meeting-lovers which is almost as bad as being overt meeting-haters? Does every administrator have to grind out requests for reports from subordinates to satisfy his or her own administrative needs and, as is sometimes said laconically, to justify his or her own position? Why, for example, must different "shops" within the *same* system demand the same factual data from subordinates, each in a slightly different format?

We need "human engineers" in our social systems who are empowered to confront each generator of paper work and require that person to justify the existence of each item. We will without doubt discover that half of the organization's paper work could be eliminated without causing the organization any harm. Imagine the savings in time and money from such a reduction in paper work!

Second, employees must make decisions on how to set priorities for demands on their time. All of us are prone sometimes to spend time on trivial matters and neglect the significant. All of us are prone sometimes to let others control our time instead of seizing the moment ourselves. The National Association of Secondary School Principals suggested 16 guidelines for managing time wisely, as follows:

1. Analyze how time is used and misused.
2. Establish priorities.
3. Budget time by appointing a time.
4. Delegate with discretion.
5. Set a deadline.
6. Develop enthusiasm.
7. Concentrate totally.
8. Be courteous.
9. Control "other imposed" time.
10. Recognize and respond to fatigue.
11. Save time in meetings.
12. Read with discrimination.
13. Help your memory.
14. Use clerical services judiciously.
15. Plan work to save time.
16. Use time to improve skills.[29]

Stress arises from a number of pressures some of which are self-imposed and some of which come from the outside. We may not be able to prevent pressures from without but we can learn to respond to them. We can certainly, at least to some degree, control self-imposed stress. If we manage our time wisely, for example, we can cut down on occasions for stress. If we take ourselves a bit less seriously, we can reduce stress. If we try to get our priorities straight, we can decrease stress. If we learn to say no on occasion, we can both reduce stress and save time. If we are a stressful type to begin with, we should not gravitate to stressful positions. It is amazing how many teachers who have difficulty managing stress in the classroom aspire to positions as administrators and supervisors. Each prospective administrator and supervisor must ask himself or herself the questions: Do I have the personality to assume a leadership position? Do I work well under pressure? Do I have a tolerance for ambiguity?

The National Association of Secondary School Principals offered several suggestions for managing stress.[30] It suggested that executives develop an awareness of their own reaction to stressful conditions, a tolerance level, and techniques for reducing stress. Executives should determine whether they are "Type A" individuals who are prone to stress and even heart attack. The National Association of Secondary School Principals provided a checklist (see Table 10.3) for executives to determine whether they are Type A personalities.

Table 10.3 Type "A" Behaving: Awareness Exercise

Are you a Type A? Do you characteristically exhibit Type A behavior? Quickly fill out the following questionnaire to see.

Yes	No	Don't Know	
___	___	___	1. I'm frequently in a hurry.
___	___	___	2. I'm typically doing several projects at the same time.
___	___	___	3. I'm always pushed by deadlines.
___	___	___	4. I usually take on as many (or a few more) projects as I can handle.
___	___	___	5. I really seek recognition from my boss and/or peers.
___	___	___	6. I believe it's important for a person to push herself or himself for success, and I seek out opportunities for promotions and advancements.
___	___	___	7. I enjoy competition in all areas.
___	___	___	8. I really enjoy winning, and hate to lose.
___	___	___	9. My job is the most important thing in my life.
___	___	___	10. I sometimes feel I neglect my family by putting my job first.
___	___	___	11. I'm usually too busy with my job to have time for many hobbies or outside activities.
___	___	___	12. When I'm given a job I really feel personally responsible for its success—i.e., even though others may be involved, I feel that it just won't come out as well unless I'm personally involved from start to finish.
___	___	___	13. I have trouble trusting people easily.
___	___	___	14. I tend to talk fast.
___	___	___	15. When speaking I believe in giving special emphasis to my meaning with strong vocal inflection and gestures.
___	___	___	16. I feel some impatience in most meetings and conversations—I just wish they would speed up and get on with it.
___	___	___	17. I tend to get irritable and lose my cool easily when obviously simple things don't go right.
___	___	___	18. I make a list of things I must get done each day.
___	___	___	19. I generally have strong opinions on most things.
___	___	___	20. I don't seem to get much time to keep up with my reading.

If you answered yes to 15 of these questions, you may be falling into the "Type A" behavior pattern.

SOURCE: Michael C. Giammatteo and Dolores M. Giammatteo, *Executive Well Being: Stress and Administrators*, Reston, Va.: National Association of Secondary School Principals, 1980, 20–21. Reprinted with permission.

Those whose answers are predominantly yes are Type A personalities, hard-driving, pushing shakers and movers; those whose answers are predominantly no are Type B personalities, relaxed, easy-going, laid-back, and less subject to stress. Obviously what is needed is an administrator or supervisor who is a combination of the two types, an A/B Type, who knows when to work hard and when to relax.

Executives should develop an ability to anticipate and avoid stressful conditions. They need to ignore minor stressful events and they need to be more trusting that their subordinates will do their jobs. Executives should learn to allocate time for personal and family interests, delegate responsibilities, and even on occasion reduce standards or expectations. We all need to remind ourselves now and then that the world can run very well without us.

Stress is a major, perhaps *the*, factor in teacher, administrator, and supervisor burn-out. The supervisor as change agent needs to help both teachers and himself or herself to use time wisely and to reduce stress.

Communication

The supervisor must be able to communicate effectively with both groups and individuals. The ability to project and understand messages is a fundamental skill of administrators and supervisors. Supervisors must give attention to (1) oral language, (2) written language, (3) nonverbal language, and (4) the silent language.

Oral Language

To some people, professionals and laypersons alike, effectiveness in communication is equated with the ability to articulate, to express oneself orally, to deliver ripostes on the spot, and to answer questions if not with lucidity, at least with verbal dexterity. Articulateness is a skill much prized by the public, who often settle for glibness over substance, for style over content.

President Jimmy Carter put his finger on this problem when he commented on his own difficulty in communicating:

I am not a great speaker and am sometimes not at ease with large groups. I acknowledge those characteristics freely. They have been pointed out to me often enough' to convince me. I can think on my feet. A poll of oldtime White House correspondents ranked me first in handling press conferences. It is hard to express effectively all sides of a complicated issue, and I tend to do that. It is much easier to take one simplistic side of an issue and express it clearly.[31]

Whether the politician says anything of substance or not, the public is impressed by the William Jennings Bryans who bestir them not to crucify mankind on a cross of gold. Like charisma, articulateness is a trait much to be desired. It puts its possessor one rung up on the status ladder. The ability to speak and respond clearly is essential.

That ability, however, should be accompanied by forthrightness, candor, and substance.

Supervisors must know how to communicate with people at various levels. They do not address adults as they do children. They do not fire a rapid barrage of idiomatic English at members of minorities who barely speak the language. They do not use the "refined" language of "high society" with the less educated. They do not use "ten-dollar" words where "half-dollar" words are needed to cement communication. They don't use football language in addressing the ladies' sewing circle, ERA notwithstanding. They do not use barroom language at a church wedding. They do not use pedagese in talking to the parents' advisory committee. They do not talk to teachers as if they were untrustworthy, lazy, disloyal, or uncooperative. They do not name-drop, throw in obtuse and incomplete references, and relate in-house jokes if they hope to communicate.

Supervisors who are aware of the power of language not only choose their words carefully, but they also watch their tone. The tone often speaks louder than the words, revealing meaning just the opposite of the words. While the lyrics may say one thing, the melody may put forth a different motif.

In our society, quite contrary to some societies, speakers are expected to be animated and cheerful. They are expected to maintain eye contact with the recipient of their messages. Americans tend to go to the heart of the problem while other cultures are less direct, indulging in small talk and social pleasantries like having tea or coffee before getting down to serious communication. It must have been an American who invented the business lunch, a custom designed to make use of every working moment and to relegate the joys of eating to a secondary role.

Sometime in their preparation supervisors should take linguistics and speech courses and, if necessary, speech therapy. They should also study basic principles of communication. Alfonso, Firth, and Neville have listed 28 propositions pertaining to communication skills.[32] Among these are the following:

> Proposition 10: Communication will be more effective when the views of the sender and the receiver(s) are in harmony.
> Proposition 14: Communication will be more effective in influencing group behavior and attitudes when it utilizes discussion and decision making.
> Proposition 15: Communication will be more effective when the sender and receiver are dealing with situations in which both have obtained previous experience.
> Proposition 18: Communication will be more effective if the style and techniques selected by the sender are consistent with the expectations of the receivers.
> Proposition 19: Communication will be more effective if senders take into account social and educational similarities and differences between themselves and receivers, as well as those *among* receivers.
> Proposition 20: Communication will be more effective if senders take into account their own personality characteristics and those of receivers.[33]

The ability to communicate orally with one's clientele is not only the stock of the salesperson, it is the primary tool of the supervisor.

Written Communication

Only slightly behind oral communication in importance is the ability of supervisors to express themselves in written form. In their daily work they write letters, memos, curriculum guides, evaluations of materials and teachers, newsletters, research reports, and other documents.

Recipients of written materials make judgments about the source and the materials on the basis of their style, accuracy, clarity, necessity, and proper use of English. As in the case of oral communication, tone is also important. We have all been recipients of imperious memoranda and you know how we reacted.

Administrators and supervisors get themselves in trouble with correspondence in which a careless phrase or word creates animosity on the part of the receiver. Senders should not write messages when they are angry or at a low ebb. Messages should always be reread for accuracy, tone, and language usage.

The sender should consider the purpose of each message. If the sender must write a negative communication, it is wise to hold the message for a day or two while he or she reconsiders the problem. It is possible that writing is the wrong way of delivering negative messages, especially if we are talking about messages destined for people in the system; oral communication may be much fairer, more effective, and even courageous. Too many people in status positions hide behind memos, fearing to confront a person in a face-to-face situation in which the recipient can respond.

Many times it is effective practice to accompany oral communication with written; the two reinforce each other. They attend to the difference in people's learning styles. Some people learn more effectively through the ears; others through the eyes. As Alfonso, Firth, and Neville posited:

Proposition 5: Communication will be more effective in promoting change if the sender utilizes many communication channels rather than a few.[34]

One final caution is in order: the supervisor should decide whether a written message, especially a memorandum, is absolutely necessary. He or she has to take the time to write it; paper is consumed; someone has to deliver it; the receiver has to read it; the receiver may be required or desire to respond, and the cycle starts all over. Supervisors who often complain about being swamped with paper work must ask themselves whether they are contributors to the paper trail.

Nonverbal Language

More attention should be given to the study of nonverbal language. Teachers are expected to be animated and convey enthusiasm. This is done as much through gestures, eye movements, interjections, smiles, frowns, posture, meaningful sounds, and laughter as through words. In fact, nonverbal language can say more than words convey. A guilty look on a person's face can betray the fact that he or she is lying. We know it and understand that the person is lying in spite of any verbal protestations to the contrary.

The supervisor needs to study the meaning of gestures in our society and in other cultures. America is, after all, a multicultural nation. Pan American World Airways in its advertising at one time touched on this theme by averring that every American has two homes—America and the nation of his or her forebears. We have only to walk down the streets of San Francisco's Chinatown, New York's Little Italy, or Miami's Little Havana to become aware of subcultures on the American scene. The adults of the subculture (and the children to a lesser extent) perpetuate the traditions, rituals, and customs of the old country.

Different cultures communicate using different gestures. In some cultures you can point a finger at a person, in others you cannot. In some cultures you can touch a person when you speak, in other you must not. Some cultures believe in eye contact, others believe that behavior to be rude. Some say no by raising their chins and giving a little click of the tongue, others shake the head from side to side. An acceptable gesture in one culture can be an obscenity in another.

Supervisors need to develop a sensitivity to nonverbal language of the persons with whom they work. They should help teachers read the nonverbal language of pupils. Regarding nonverbal communication Alfonso, Firth, and Neville advised:

Proposition 21: Communication will be more effective if verbal messages and nonverbal cues from the sender reinforce each other.[35]

Supervisors should be skillful in using and reading nonverbal language.

The Silent Language

Edward T. Hall authored a well-known little book called *The Silent Language* in which he explained pitfalls people of one culture stumble into when they find themselves in another culture without an understanding of existing but silent cultural characteristics.[36]

Although Hall included elements of nonverbal language, his concept of the silent language goes beyond nonverbal language. Hall listed 10 kinds of human activities which vary from culture to culture and which he called the Primary Message Systems, as follows:

1. *Interaction*: ways we interact with our environment, as through speech and writing. This is the only Primary Message System which involves language.
2. *Association*: ways in which human beings associate with each other, including rank and status.
3. *Subsistence*: ways in which cultures feed themselves and go about earning subsistence; attitudes toward manual labor; characteristic economy.
4. *Bisexuality*: behavior of the sexes toward each other and toward the opposite sex; behavior expected or permitted of each sex by the culture.
5. *Territoriality*: ways human beings defend their turf.
6. *Temporality*: differing conceptions of time, including punctuality or the lack of it.

7. *Learning*: differences in ways of learning to learn.
8. *Play*: recreation and leisure.
9. *Defense*: ways in which cultures protect themselves from enemies, potential and real, and from adversities of nature.
10. *Exploitation* (*use of materials*): ways of exploiting the environment, as through technology, for example.[37]

Hall's target audience was Americans going abroad. He believed that by understanding the Primary Message Systems of the other cultures, Americans could avoid cultural dissonance and conflict. His concept of a silent language, however, is useful to those supervisors who are in school systems with a multicultural population. The Primary Message Systems, though perhaps muted by the (North) American culture, can still be operant, more pronounced in some school personnel and students than in others.

I would single out bisexuality (attitudes about feminine and masculine behavior), territoriality (protecting one's vested interests), temporality (attitudes toward time and the use of it), and learning (attitudes toward curricula and methods) as having special significance to the supervisor in our pluralistic, salad-bowl society.[38]

If a supervisor is to be an effective group leader, he or she must evidence skills in communication. He or she must be both a practitioner and student of language.

Group Process

For purposes of this analysis let's zero in on the process which supervisors follow when they accept the role of group leader. Of course, the supervisor will not always serve as leader of a group and teachers may and should fill leadership positions as the situations demand. In fact, leadership from the group should be encouraged by the supervisor and opportunities for developing leadership continuously provided. It is unfortunate, perhaps, that discussing group process involves the terms leaders and followers, for the term follower implies an unthinking docility which is undesirable here. The leader-follower terminology also plants the idea that the leader is never a follower and that followers are never leaders. In professional groups such as teacher committees, teams, and faculties that is not the case at all, for leadership and followership are roles which are constantly rotated as the occasion demands and as certain kinds of expertness are called for. Some teachers who consistently play the role of follower and never seek to exert leadership do so because they have been conditioned by status leaders to believe that followership is their only role and, therefore, they have never tested their own leadership skills. The development of leadership skills from within the group should be a goal the supervisor places high on the agenda. The term follower, as used here, connotes no demeaning status but simply means a person who is not serving as a leader at that time. Let's take a look at how the supervisor's skills in group process can help teachers work together. The following guidelines are applicable to the deliberations of a task-oriented work group.

1. *A good deal of what is called processing can take place at the initial meeting of a faculty group.* It is at that time that introductions of members of the group are made and housekeeping chores dispensed with. The coffee-and-donuts routine is a commendable one for loosening up a group and setting a pleasant working atmosphere. In the introductory remarks the supervisor will attempt to make the group feel that the task they are about to undertake is an important one and that the members of the group are the ideal ones to carry out that task. Relevance of the group's task is just as important to a group as relevance of content is to a learner. If the task is trivial and unimportant the time of professional people should not be wasted.

2. *The goals and objectives of the group's work should be set at the initial or next meeting.* Commonly, the goal has already been determined prior to the group's formation. Indeed, the goal is the reason for the establishment of the group. The goal may come in the form of a mandate from the administrator or from the faculty. It is the group's task to refine the goal and from it derive the specific objectives of its work. Not only does the group need to decide upon its objectives but it must also decide on how to pursue the objectives, who will do what, on what kind of time schedule it will operate, and how it will evaluate its work. The time schedule is an important feature some groups overlook and as a result they put off a significant portion of their work until the last minute. A task force would do well to specify the completion of segments of its work by certain dates. This procedure will not only assure the work's being done on schedule but will also reassure the group periodically that it is making progress. Feedback to the group to the effect that it is making continuous progress is a strong motivator to keep the group working on the task.

3. *The supervisor has the responsibility for keeping the group on task, which is often no easy job.* The word taskmaster is too strong since it implies a despotism which is not, of course, advocated. But it is the supervisor's duty to try to prevent groups from digressing and to remind them of the topic at hand when they do go off at tangents.

Some supervisors make the mistake of interpreting their leadership role as a nondirective, laissez-faire approach. This approach permits groups to flounder, procrastinate, and fail to achieve their objectives. Someone must serve as the "gate-keeper," the work conscience of the group, and the supervisor is in a strategic position to fulfill that role.

The role of group leader requires more than mere presiding at group meetings; it necessitates planning and continuous facilitation. The leader must make sure ahead of time that those who are scheduled to present input for the group's deliberation will be ready and present. The leader must be certain that all resources needed by the group will be available at the time the group needs access to them. Equipment, materials, and resource people must be arranged for well in advance of a meeting and ready for use if the group is to be kept on task. Once the group is in session the leader continues to serve as a facilitator who attempts to secure maximum participation on the part of all members of the group.

4. *The supervisor must possess skills in the group process.* It is up to the supervisor to recognize types of behavior of members of the group which impede the group's progress and to know when individuals are performing what some call "self-

serving functions." He or she should be able to detect, for example, individuals who exhibit aggressive behavior, attempt to dominate the discussion and cut off their colleagues, make a play for attention, seek to thwart the efforts of the group, and have their own special axes to grind. At the same time the supervisor should be perceptive enough to realize that some members have withdrawn from participation, some appear disinterested, and some are fearful of expressing themselves.

As a responsible chairperson the supervisor can reduce some of the problems arising from members who are not themselves skilled in the group process. While parliamentary procedure with all its refinements is neither necessary nor desirable in most work groups, reliance on some of its more overt manifestations may prove helpful to the group leader. As a parliamentary leader the supervisor can insist that people speak one at a time. He or she can fail to recognize the attention-getter and the individual who wishes to monopolize discussion.

Ideally, the supervisor should try to bring about the participation of every member of the group. Every member should be made to feel that his or her contributions are significant enough to be considered and discussed. In almost every group, however, we find people who are "quick starters," those who are more verbal and more vocal than others and always ready to voice their opinions. The quick starter can be a boon to the group leader by helping to get discussion under way with minimal prodding from the leader. On the other hand, the quick starters should not be permitted to run away with the group discussion. It is a common malady of groups to find a subset of a few vocal participants carrying on a discussion as if they were the only persons present. This malady falls squarely in the lap of the group leader, who can neither permit nor afford to permit a few verbal individuals to usurp the discussion. The leader must seek out input from the slow starters, ask for their opinions, turn to them for reactions, and pose questions to them. For both the quick starters and slow starters the development of discussion skills may be a by-product of a task-oriented group process.

The supervisor involves group members not only in the discussion phases of the group's work but also in carrying out specific responsibilities designed to accomplish their mission. When the task is a complex one, subtasks must be assigned and distributed as broadly as possible so that as many members of the group as possible will feel a close identity with the group's work. The easiest solution to the division of labor is to leave it to volunteers but that is not always the best solution in terms of growth of both the individuals and the group. Not only does it happen that a volunteer may not be the most qualified person in the group to perform a particular task, but besides, those who participate, perhaps not vocally but silently, should be drawn into the task. The supervisor resolves this problem by requesting those who are most qualified to accept specific subtasks regardless of their verbal skills and by encouraging distribution of assignments as broadly as possible among the members of the group.

5. *At the end of each session the supervisor should summarize what the group has agreed on and decisions should be made as to what next steps will be taken.* Each person's assignments and responsibilities should be clearly understood before the group adjourns. Whenever possible the group should reach closure on issues under discussion and not leave them hanging. The supervisor has to take care not to force closure prematurely nor prevent closure by dragging out a discussion.

6. *Periodically, the group should take stock of its progress, evaluate its accomplishments, and determine if it is on schedule.* Every member of the group should know exactly where the group is at any time. If there are subgroups working, they should keep the parent group continuously advised of their progress. The supervisor helps to pace the group's progress by calling to its attention when it has completed phases of the task, what remains to be done, and when the objectives have been realized.

7. *The group must be made to feel that its efforts have been worthwhile.* When a group is working on a particular problem for which it offers a solution, the ultimate hope is that the group's recommendation will be put into practice. Nothing is more motivating to a group than to see its recommendations carried out. Teachers will realize that not every recommendation of every group can be put into operation. Barring actual adoption of a group's recommendations, however, its proposals should be granted a full hearing and if the recommendations cannot be accepted the group should be told why. Far too many times has service on a committee left teachers with the hopeless feeling that nothing will come of all the time and effort they put into the committee's work. It is small wonder that teachers are often reluctant to spend the time necessitated by some committee projects when their past experience tells them that the effort will have no pay-off.

The group leader is a key factor in the success or failure of groups to achieve their purposes. The leader sets the stage for the group's deliberations, and oversees the operation. But the success of a group is not dependent upon the leader's skills alone. Each member of the group must possess sufficient skills in interaction to further the interests of the group. When a group is involved in a task-oriented situation, it may possibly learn interaction skills incidentally as by-products of the group's work. In an ongoing task-oriented situation the supervisor should be aware that the members of the group are functioning at two levels. They are or should be working to accomplish the objectives of the group and they are or should be working on the development of their own interaction skills. While training in group interaction skills is tangential to the endeavor of a task-oriented group, special training in the functioning of groups and in group interaction is a viable in-service project.

Task versus Process

It is often said that groups are made up of two kinds of participants: those who are task oriented and those who are process oriented. Task-oriented people want to have the objectives clearly defined. They want to proceed with the job, get it done, and feel a sense of achievement. They are conscious of the time press and impatient with digressions which prevent the group from realizing its goals.

Process-oriented individuals believe that the goals of the group are of secondary importance. In their minds it is the interaction among people which really counts. As a result of interaction the goals themselves may change. It is the interaction which is the true goal and not the task imposed by a superior or by the group itself. Process-oriented people believe that everyone should have the opportunity to express himself or herself to the fullest not only about cognitive matters but also how he or she feels about the topic under discussion.

It is a rare faculty group that is not composed of persons of both persuasions. Surely a task orientation without process, can lead to sterile and perfunctory decisions while process without task orientation can lead to frustration and stagnation of a group. As a group leader, the supervisor must achieve a healthy balance between the two orientations, enough so that the task oriented will feel that the job is being accomplished and at the same time enough so the process oriented will feel that they have had sufficient opportunity to express their views.

As attendance at sessions of groups will bear out, when group deliberations fail, they do so more often because of a lack of task orientation than because of a lack of process orientation. An overemphasis on processing has caused many groups to give up on their tasks. Given the work loads of teachers and the many demands on their time and energies, teachers simply cannot tolerate unlimited processing. That teachers as a group are predisposed to a task-oriented approach is attested by Ben M. Harris and William R. Hartgraves, who made the following observations:

Are supervisors accepted by teachers as valuable members of the instructional staff?
    Yes, supervisors are highly valued, when teachers have close contact with them in project or other task-oriented situations . . .
    Are supervisors effective in improving instruction when they serve in a counseling or consultative capacity to individual teachers?
    Yes, if these consultations are task-oriented and are part of a larger program of activities for change.[39]

A certain amount of processing prior to getting down to the task must take place in any group endeavor but the leader must help the group to complete its processing so it may move ahead toward achievement of its goals.

GROUP PROCESS VERSUS GROUP COUNSELING

There is a world of difference between the type of group processing—verbal inter-action—which is related to a group's pursuit of a goal and the type of group processing that is a goal in itself. The profession has the saying that change results from a change in people. While this position is praiseworthy, issue can be taken with some of the efforts made to implement the saying. Some supervisors foster a type of group process which is designed not to accomplish a specific task but to help teachers to solve their personal problems, in effect, group counseling. When helping teachers with personal problems is the focus of group activity, the group process is the task itself rather than a forerunner of the task. Tanner and Tanner took issue with the group-counseling approach:

Although teachers demand resources for helping slow learners and behavioral problem children, while they demand the establishment of curriculum committees so that they can be involved in curriculum decisions, they do not demand help with their personal problems, nor do they seek help on matters of group process, group therapy, or ego counseling.
    Strangely enough, supervision continues to put most of its theoretical eggs in the ego-counseling-group therapy basket. This approach to helping teachers when they are looking for

substantive assistance with classroom problems has supervision on the road to self-destruction. If supervision is to avoid destroying itself, if it is to provide genuine assistance to teachers in their drive for better educational programs for children and youth, it must be task focused.[40]

I do not discount the necessity for help for some teachers with personal problems. But I do not see it as a substitute for educational decision making, nor bootlegged in under the guise of decision making, nor a compulsory or near-compulsory type of activity, nor conducted by the typical supervisor. A therapy program is something else again and should be attempted with those who seek it by those who are fully qualified to provide that type of help. Far too many supervisors have dabbled in group counseling without sufficient training. Attendance as a participant or trainee at a group therapy institute or workshop does not alone qualify supervisors to engage in the practice of group counseling, which is an effort at helping teachers to solve their personal problems. Perhaps here is an example of the "physician-heal-thyself" syndrome, in which some supervisors attempt to solve their own personal problems through attempting to help others solve theirs.

Group process as interaction among members of a group in quest of a particular task should be distinguished from group process which has as its goal the solution of personal problems of the members of a group. Ideally, the supervisor, in the role of group leader, guides a group toward accomplishment of its task but also helps the group to develop its interaction skills. In-service training in how groups operate, problems in group deliberation, and roles of leaders and followers are decidedly in order. As a matter of fact, personality modification—the goal of group counseling—may come about through training in group interaction skills. For example, it is recognized that hostility in a member of a group can impede the work of a group. To advance the work of the group, the hostility roadblock must be overcome. To do so, the group may first attempt to examine the process of group deliberation. By referring to some of the many studies of human groups, the members of the group learn about barriers to group endeavors, including the phenomenon of hostility. This is an intellectualized, conceptual approach. The aim is not to identify the hostility with a particular member of the group but the hope is that he or she will internalize the problem and change behavior. The supervisor as leader is not concerned with the roots of the member's hostility—whether the member hates his or her father or mother or this school, or whether he or she feels unfulfilled, or is in the throes of a divorce, or is short of money, or the countless sources of this type of behavior. The reasons for a person's hostility are between that person and the counselor he or she chooses, if any.

While a member's hostility is of serious import to the individual, the endeavors of the group supersede that individual's personal problems. If the supervisor is not to lose the other members of the group who are experiencing frustration as a result of interaction with the hostile member, the supervisor must, as leader of the group, move the work of the group forward. In a group-counseling situation members of the group would have every opportunity to release their aggressions, frustrations, and hostilities but it has been postulated that the typical faculty work group is not a counseling situation; it is a task-oriented work force with limits of time and energy. Since the supervisor works with faculty groups on problems of curriculum and instruction, their time and energy must be dedicated to the solution of those problems. If the supervisor attempts to keep a group on target, the hostile member may be able to intellectualize a problem to the point of being able to shelve hostility—put it on the back burner, so to speak—and permit the group to achieve its mission. This does not mean that all hostility disappears nor that the member is even a step closer to solving a personal problem. It does mean that the individual has learned to sublimate a problem at least long enough for the group to complete its task.

Nothing in these comments should be interpreted to imply that counseling of whatever persuasion—individual or group—is not important. Indeed, it is. A teacher's personality has a tremendous impact on the learners. An enlightened school system will provide opportunities for teachers to obtain individual or group counseling if they wish to so avail themselves. But group counseling in whatever form—T-groups, encounter groups, therapy groups, sensitivity groups—should not be mixed with a task-oriented group process nor should it be a required part of an in-service training program, a point elaborated toward the end of this chapter.

In this light, the supervisor who is concerned about helping teachers to work together should consider a tripartite plan consisting of the following elements:

1. The supervisor's development of his or her own leadership skills in conducting task-oriented group sessions.
2. Provision of an in-service program on the development of group interaction, human relations, and communications skills. This would be a voluntary, elective program, preferably with tangible incentives for participation.
3. Provision of group-therapy-type sessions on a completely voluntary basis and under the direction of trained psychologists.

TRAINING IN GROUP INTERACTION

When the supervisor discovers that groups he or she is working with are experiencing difficulty and members of the groups are unable to communicate with each other, it may be expeditious to set up a program designed to help teachers develop interaction skills. Training in interaction skills has application not only for teachers' relationships with each other but also for teachers' relationships with students, other school personnel, and parents. Since training in interpersonal and human relations skills skirts the fringes of awareness and sensitivity training, this type of training ought to be elective with the teacher. In fact, participation in any type of training which is primarily for personal development should be voluntary. To make participation appealing to teachers, however, some sort of incentive system should be in operation, as has been noted in the preceding chapter.

Unless the supervisor has had the necessary training, and very commonly he or she has not, it will be necessary to make arrangements for specialists in communication skills or human relations skills to conduct the training. Consultant moneys are often available for staff development programs and the supervisor might well consider bringing in consultants for this purpose to be worth the investment.

In-service education for the development of interaction skills may take a variety of forms. Two promising routes, which may be viewed as companion techniques rather than separate procedures, are (1) formal study and discussion of some the literature on the sociology and social psychology of human groups, and (2) practice in demonstrating interpersonal skills in a group setting. Although either of these techniques can be implemented without the other, the training program is much stronger if it includes both components. Consultants for the formal study may be drawn from the ranks of university specialists in sociology, psychology, education, or management. Consultants for the practice or laboratory training may come from universities' and other agencies' specialists in human relations skills, social psychology, and communications.

In the first phase of an in-service program on group interaction the consultant may take the group through the study of some of the classic literature on group formation and functioning. The participants might read and discuss, for example, such a work as George C. Homans' *The Human Group*, which provides an excellent introduction to this topic.[41] The consultant might have the participants read and discuss some of the literature on the famed Western Electric researches which provided evidence that when workers are involved in planning, research, and profit-sharing their productivity rises.[42] These researches speak also to the well-known Hawthorne Effect, a rise in productivity as a result of workers' feelings of involvement rather than from a change of technique.

A work worthy of teachers' attention is Alvin Toffler's *Future Shock*, which vividly demonstrates the necessity for human beings to work together to solve social problems which become more acute with each passing year.[43] Teachers might be made familiar with material such as Stuart Chase's popular book, *Roads to Agreement*, which interpreted the purpose and functioning of groups in layman's language and suggested ways to resolve group conflicts.[44] Chase, for example, suggested five principles for reducing conflict within groups:[45]

- *The principle of participation.* (Active participation of members of a group is essential in any type of group endeavor.)
- *The principle of group energy.* (Ways must be found to creatively channel the energies of groups.)
- *The principle of clearing communication lines.* (Leaders and followers, in-groups and out-groups must be able to communicate with each other.)
- *The principle of facts first.* (Agreement among members of a group is facilitated when the facts are known. Actions should not be taken until the facts are known.)
- *The principle that agreement is much easier when people feel secure.* (Interpersonal conflict is reduced when each person feels secure.)

Chase's five principles carry messages to both supervisor and teacher.

No study of group behavior can omit the research of Kurt Lewin, Ronald Lippitt, and Ralph K. White on experimentally created social climates.[46] In studying the effects of three types of adult leadership, authoritarian, democratic, and laissez-faire, on four groups of 11-year-old children Lewin, Lippitt, and White found:

Under the authoritarian leadership, the children were more dependent upon the leader, more discontent, made more demands for attention, were less friendly, produced less work-minded conversation than under the democratic leadership. There was no group initiative in the authoritarian group climate.

    The laissez-faire atmosphere produced more dependence on the leader, more discontent, less friendliness, fewer group-minded suggestions, less work-minded conversation than under the democratic climate. In the absence of the laissez-faire leader, work was unproductive. The laissez-faire group was extremely dependent upon the leader for information.

    . . . relationships among the individuals in the democratic leadership atmosphere were friendlier. Those under the democratic leadership sought more attention and approval from fellow club members. They depended upon each other for recognition as opposed to recognition by the leader under the authoritarian and laissez-faire systems . . . in the absence of the leader the democratic groups proceeded at their work in productive fashion.[47]

The Lewin, Lippitt, and White studies have implications for the types of group climate which leaders foster and suggest that leaders should examine the social climate of the groups they work with.

    Consultants frequently engage trainees in a study of roles played by individuals in group settings, such as "information giver," "harmonizer," "gate keeper," and "blocker," terms of great currency in studies of the inner workings of a group. Kenneth D. Benne and Paul Sheats have used these terms and others for their classification of roles played by members of a group.[48] By studying a set of descriptive terms such as the Benne-Sheats classification scheme, teachers who are investigating the functioning of groups may begin to become aware of some of the maintenance tasks required of groups and some of the positive and negative roles played by group members. In the case of negative roles a teacher may begin to realize some of the impediments to the group process, may attempt to see if any of the negative descriptors could apply to him or her, and may change behavior if it appears that a negative descriptor does, indeed, fit.

PRACTICE IN INTERACTION SKILLS

Following the more formal study of group behavior and the functioning of individuals in group settings, laboratory experiences can be created which provide participants with opportunities to demonstrate interaction skills. Training in interaction, communication, and human relations skills can supplement training in generic instructional skills and study of subject matter. Since training in interaction or interpersonal skills runs the risk of some psychological discomfort for some participants, only those trained in the use of group interaction laboratory techniques should attempt to conduct this type of training.

    Although training in group interaction comes close to group counseling and awareness training, it should be noted that it stops short of in-depth counseling on personal problems. Its aim is to improve the dynamics of the group and not to provide therapy for individuals' personal problems. Although leaders of training programs in interaction skills must possess special training, they need not necessarily be trained psychologists. Supervisors may wish to consider two approaches for offering training in interaction skills.

	Members								
	A	B	C	D	E	F	G	H	I
Task roles									
Initiator–contributor									
Information seeker									
Opinion seeker									
Information giver									
Opinion giver									
Elaborator									
Coordinator									
Orienter									
Evaluator–critic									
Energizer									
Procedural technician									
Recorder									
Building/maintenance roles									
Encourager									
Harmonizer									
Compromiser									
Gate keeper									
Standard setter									
Group–observer									
Follower									
Individual roles									
Aggressor									
Blocker									
Recognition–seeker									
Self-confessor									
Playboy									
Dominator									
Help–seeker									
Special interest pleader									

Figure 10.2 Record of Behavior of Individuals in Groups

SOURCE: Kenneth D. Benne and Paul Sheats, "Functional Roles of Group Members," *Journal of Social Issues* 4, no. 2 (Spring 1948): 43–46, as adapted by Peter F. Oliva, *Developing the Curriculum*, Boston, Little, Brown, 1982, p. 132. Reprinted with permission of Society for the Psychological Study of Social Issues and Kenneth D. Benne.

Record of Behavior of Individuals in Groups

One approach is an adaptation and application of the Benne-Sheats classification system just mentioned. An instrument can be created such as the record of behavior of individuals in groups (Figure 10.2), which can be used to analyze roles played by members of a group as they work together. The roles played by individuals in groups are shown in Table 10.4. The record of behavior converts the Benne-Sheats classification into an instrument by which an observer can record the number of times each individual plays a particular role.[49]

The record of behavior lists at the left the task, maintenance, and individual roles played by members of a group. Spaces are provided so an impartial observer can tally instances of specific role performances by individual members of the group. The purpose of such a procedure is to make members of a group more aware of the roles they play.

Using the record of behavior of individuals in groups faculty groups can devise procedures for studying their own behavior and by digesting the feedback which comes out of each study can improve the group's functioning.

Table 10.4   Roles of Individuals in Groups

GROUP TASK ROLES
a. Initiator-contributor. Suggest ideas, ways of solving problems, or procedures.
b. Information seeker. Seeks facts.
c. Opinion seeker. Asks for opinions about the values of suggestions made by members of the group.
d. Information giver. Supplies facts or facts as he/she sees them.
e. Opinion giver. Presents his/her own opinions about the subject under discussion.
f. Elaborator. States implications of suggestions and describes how suggestions might work out if adopted.
g. Coordinator. Tries to synthesize suggestions.
h. Orienter. Lets group know when it is off task.
i. Evaluator-critic. Evaluates suggestions made by group members as to criteria which he/she feels imporant.
j. Energizer. Spurs the group to acitivity.
k. Procedural technician. Performs the routine tasks which have to be done such as distributing materials.
l. Recorder. Keeps the group's record.

GROUP BUILDING AND MAINTENANCE ROLES
a. Encourager. Praises people for their suggestions.
b. Harmonizer. Settles disagreements among members.
c. Compromiser. Modifies his/her position in the interests of group progress.
d. Gatekeeper. Tries to assure that everybody has a chance to contribute to the discussion.
e. Standard setter or ego ideal. Urges the group to live up to high standards.
f. Group-observer and commentator. Records and reports on the functioning of the group.
g. Follower. Accepts suggestions of others.

INDIVIDUAL ROLES
a. Aggressor. Attacks others or their ideas.
b. Blocker. Opposes suggestions and group decisions.

Table 10.4 (*continued*)

INDIVIDUAL ROLES

c. Recognition-seeker. Seeks personal attention.
d. Self-confessor. Expresses personal feelings not applicable to the group's efforts.
e. Playboy. Refrains from getting involved in the group's work with sometimes disturbing behavior.
f. Denominator. Interrupts others and tries to assert own superiority.
g. Help-seeker. Tries to elicit sympathy for himself/herself.
h. Special interest pleader. Reinforces his/her position by claiming to speak for others not represented in the group.

SOURCE: From Kenneth D. Benne and Paul Sheats, "Functional Roles of Group Members," *The Journal of Social Issues* 4, no. 2 (Spring 1948): 43–46, as reproduced in Peter F. Oliva, *Developing the Curriculum*, Boston, Little, Brown, 1982, 130. Reprinted with permission of Society for the Psychological Study of Social Issues and Kenneth D. Benne.

Interaction Laboratory

A fully developed program for training in basic communication skills, group interaction, interpersonal skills, and professional problem solving is the Thiokol Chemical Corporation's *Interaction Laboratory for Teacher Development* created under the leadership of John J. Kampsnider.[50]

The *Interaction Laboratory* consists of 27 exercises to acquaint the participant with the need for human relations skills in teaching and to expose the trainees to "the kinds of interpersonal problems that arise with pupils, parents, and fellow teachers. Through observation, analysis, and experiencing a variety of situational problems teacher trainees will gain added insight into their own individual needs in the area of human relations."[51]

The *Interaction Laboratory* makes as its basic premise the statement: "Teachers are primarily people interacting with other people in a specialized way."[52] The *Interaction Laboratory* affords the trainee an opportunity to practice a variety of role patterns. These particular materials were developed so that they could be used by regular faculty members of a teacher education institution who have been trained in their use. They do not depend for their use on the services of specialists in psychology or group counseling and for that reason can be utilized by supervisors who gain the requisite training.

The *Interaction Laboratory* uses a group setting

to allow all individuals to examine their style of interacting with others. Such techniques as role playing, simulation exercises, and problem solving allow students to receive feedback about their effectiveness with other people. Analysis of behavior in a group setting provides the students with valuable information about their actions in a group. It also promotes understanding of future leadership roles in the classroom.[53]

Clear limitations are set for this program:

Group interaction during this training program will be limited to discussion of pertinent behavior that is transferable to the teacher's role in the school setting. Analysis of behavior beyond this limitation is to be discouraged by the trainer and is beyond the scope of this training laboratory.[54]

Requiring some 40 hours of training in groups of 15 to 20 participants, the laboratory makes use of a variety of media to help in the four areas of the program. *Communications exercises* "enable students to gain a better grasp of the complexities of the communication process." *Group discussions* "facilitate feedback from student peers and promote understanding of the group process as it might occur in school." *Interpersonal skills activities* "expand role flexibility and offer an opportunity to test and practice new behavior essential in successful teaching." *Professional problem solving* introduces the trainee "to the kinds of realistic demands placed on teachers in their professional roles."[55]

The supervisor may wish to consider either or both of the foregoing approaches when searching for ways to help teachers to work together.

PROVISION OF GROUP THERAPY-TYPE SESSIONS

It does not take an observer of the schools much time to come to the conclusion that some teachers "need help," as the euphemism goes. The critics of education have pointed out enough horrifying examples to underscore the need of some teachers for help with their personal problems. The fact, however, that some teachers "need help" does not mean ipso facto that all teachers "need help," nor does the fact that some teachers "need help" mean that they will profit from the "help" that may be given them.

Undoubtedly, as a part of a school system's program for the personal and professional development of teachers, opportunities should be made available for therapy, awareness, or sensitivity training in one or more of its many varieties. Under no circumstances, however, should this type of training be required of any or all teachers.

While school systems may provide incentives for participation in group counseling sessions, teachers should clearly understand the nature of the training program they are getting into and should have the right to refuse to participate. Sometimes sensitivity training is brought surreptitiously into task-oriented groups without the advance knowledge and consent of the participants. Other techniques for garnering attendance at awareness sessions, short of requiring participation, are the use of peer pressure to gain participation and, worst of all, administrative fiat.

Sensitivity sessions can be recommended for those participants who volunteer for the program and who recognize a need for the training. Without the individual's willing participation, results will be minimal or even harmful. If teachers are coerced or pressured to participate in awareness sessions, they start the program with a level of hostility, can actively sabotage the sessions, or can shrewdly play games with the trainer and other members of the group.

The supervisor's role in sensitivity training is to help facilitate voluntary sessions preferably systemwide (or on a broader scale yet) rather than limited to the faculty of one school who must face each other day in, day out. The supervisor should help make arrangements for the sessions, help secure thoroughly trained staff, notify faculty of the sessions, and *then step out of the trainer's way*. The supervisor should not serve either as a member of the trainer's staff or a participant in the program. The presence of a person who in any way is viewed by the trainees as a superior and in a position to penalize them for "opening up" will only impede the group and may, in fact, destroy its effectiveness.

These recommendations on sensitivity training are meant to be a middle ground between extravagant claims by some advocates of sensitivity training and unreasonable objections of some opponents of all forms of awareness training. The extreme advocates see sensitivity training as the greatest tonic since syrup of ipecac and the extreme nay-sayers view awareness training as witch's brew. Sensitivity training is one way by which some teachers can learn to work together.

SUMMARY

Supervisors spend a considerable portion of their time with teachers in groups of varying sizes and composition. In order to accomplish much of the school's work teachers must learn to work together in groups and one of the goals of supervision is the enhancement of teachers' skills in working cooperatively. Groups are composed of both task-oriented and process-oriented people. The task oriented seek to get the job done and the process oriented are concerned with individual expression and self-fulfillment. Although a certain amount of processing is necessary in any group endeavor, most faculty groups should be task oriented.

Supervisors must possess leadership skills. They should generally follow a democratic, human relations-oriented approach but must know when to use an authoritarian, task-oriented approach. To be effective leaders supervisors must be skilled in decision making, effecting change, organizational development, communication, and group process.

Decision making is at the heart of administrative and supervisory behavior. The supervisor can expect to be called on to serve as a change agent, contributing to the development of both staff members and the organization.

Organizations possess both an institutional and a personal dimension. The behavior of the members of the institution and the uniqueness of the institution itself result from the interaction of the two dimensions.

Supervisors must be able to manage their own time, stress, and conflicts while at the same time help staff members to do likewise. Supervisors must be skillful in the use of oral, written, and nonverbal language. They should help staff members develop awareness of the importance of their own oral, written, and nonverbal communication skills. Supervisors must also help teachers to understand the cultural phenomenon of the silent language.

A supervisor should exert democratic group leadership and should help teachers to develop skills in the group process. Goals and objectives should be set up at the beginning of the group's work and after the group has initiated its work it should try to keep on task. Groups should evaluate their progress and should be assured that their efforts will be recognized. The most effective type of recognition is full consideration or adoption of group decisions.

The supervisor works to develop skills in group interaction in two ways, (1) by example and direction in the performance of a task, and (2) by instituting special voluntary training in group interaction skills. Training in interaction skills should include study of group behavior and functioning and provision of opportunities for individuals to demonstrate interaction skills.

Sensitivity training should be made available to teachers on a voluntary basis and should be under the direction of specialists trained in group therapy.

ACTIVITIES FOR FURTHER STUDY

1. Distinguish between leader, administrator, and manager.
2. Identify three styles of leadership and tell which style you prefer and why.
3. Explain the difference between human relations and human resource development.
4. Make a list of your own propositions regarding (a) decision making, (b) change theory, and (c) communication skills. Also, consult Robert J. Alfonso, Gerald R. Firth, and Richard F. Neville (see bibliography) for additional propositions.
5. Tell how the supervisor works in the capacity of change agent.
6. Apply Jon Wiles' Educational Innovations Probability Chart mentioned in this chapter to a school system you know well.
7. Define the term *organizational development* and explain how this term differs from *staff development*.
8. List several sources of conflict in an organization and tell what the supervisor can do to reduce each.
9. Explain the terms *nomothetic* and *idiographic* and what their significance is.
10. Suggest ways to improve the management of your time.
11. Identify several sources of stress and tell how you would manage these.
12. Study the literature on management by objectives/results and write a critique of the process.
13. Suggest several ways of improving communications between (a) supervisor and administrator, (b) supervisor and teachers, (c) among teachers.
14. Explain and give examples of (a) nonverbal language, (b) body language, and (c) the silent language.
15. Write a report on Edward T. Hall's *The Silent Language* and draw implications for the supervisor.
16. Describe skills needed to lead (a) a faculty meeting, (b) a faculty study committee, and (c) an encounter group.
17. Distinguish between task-oriented and process-oriented groups. Draw implications for the instructional supervisor.

18. Explain the place of group therapy or sensitivity sessions in in-service education.
19. Describe the Getzels-Guba model of educational administration as a social process and draw implications for the supervisor.
20. Describe the Getzels-Thelen model of the classroom group as a social system and draw implications for the supervisor.
21. Plan a series of study sessions on group behavior to include types of consultants needed, resources to be used, and media to be employed.
22. Plan an in-service program for training in interpersonal skills.
23. Serve as a member of a task-oriented faculty group and write a report diagnosing problems in the group process. (Individuals should not be named in the report.)
24. Serve as a leader of a task-oriented faculty group and write a self-evaluation of your performance as the group's leader.
25. Write a position paper on (a) supervision must be primarily task oriented or (b) supervision must be primarily process oriented. Support your position with quotations from at least two references not mentioned in this chapter.
26. Report the specified goals and objectives of any faculty work group of which you are now a member or of which you have recently been a member. Comment on the adequacy of the statement of goals and objectives of this group.
27. Observe (with permission) a faculty group in action and apply an instrument such as one based on the Benne-Sheats classification of roles and provide the group with feedback from your observation.
28. Observe chairpersons of at least two faculty groups in action and classify their leadership as democratic, authoritarian, or laissez-faire.
29. Compile a bibliography of at least six references you would recommend to teachers on group behavior. (Omit references cited in this chapter.)
30. View the film *Future Shock*, if available, and write a critique of its implications for your school.
31. Examine the curriculum development program of a school you know well and list opportunities teachers have had to work together on that program in the last five months. (Do not list routine administrative faculty meetings.)
32. Poll at least 10 teachers and ask the following questions: In your experience are most faculty committees productive or not productive? If you believe they are not productive, what are the reasons for their lack of productivity? Summarize the teachers' comments in a short paper.
33. Discover and report to class what opportunities for group leadership have been made available to teachers of a school you know well in the last six months.
34. Determine and report to class the attitudes of at least three teachers toward a program of sensitivity training for teachers.
35. Ask at least four teachers to suggest ways by which a supervisor can help teachers to work together. Summarize the teachers' suggestions and report them to your class.

36. List a set of interaction, human relations, and communications skills which you believe are essential to the teacher in the role of group leader of your classes.

37. Write a paper using selected references on the topic, "Techniques for Developing Human Relations Skills of Teachers."

NOTES

1. See John K. Hemphill and Alvin E. Coons, *Leader Behavior Description*, Columbus, Ohio, Personnel Research Board, Ohio State University, 1950. See Ralph M. Stogdill, *Handbook of Leadership: A Survey of Theory and Research*, New York, Free Press, 1974. See Rensis Likert, *The Human Organization: Its Management*, New York, McGraw-Hill, 1967.

2. Fred E. Fiedler, *A Theory of Leadership Effectiveness*, New York, McGraw-Hill, 1967, 8 .

3. Ralph M. Stogdill, "Leadership, Membership, and Organization," *Psychological Bulletin* 47, (1950): 4. See also Stogdill, *Handbook of Leadership*, 10.

4. James M. Lipham and James A. Hoeh, Jr., *The Principalship: Foundations and Functions*, New York, Harper & Row, 1974, 182.

5. James M. Lipham, "Leadership and Administration," *Behavioral Science and Educational Administration*, 63d Yearbook, Part II, edited by Daniel E. Griffiths, Chicago, National Society for the Study of Education, 1964, 122.

6. Carl Nordstrom, Edgar Z. Friedenberg, and Hilary A. Gold, *Society's Children: A Study of Ressentiment in the Secondary School*, New York, Random House, 1967.

7. W. H. Cowley, "Three Distinctions in the Study of Leaders," *Journal of Abnormal and Social Psychology* 23, no. 2 (July-September 1928): 145.

8. Robert L. De Bruyn, *Causing Others to Want Your Leadership*, Manhattan, Kans., R. L. DeBruyn & Associates, 1976, 14.

9. See Ralph M. Stogdill, "Personal Factors Associated with Leadership: A Study of the Literature," *Journal of Psychology* 25, First Half (January 1948): 35–71. Reprinted in Stogdill, *Handbook of Leadership*, ch. 5.

10. Stogdill, *Handbook of Leadership*, 62–63.

11. Kurt Lewin, Ronald Lippitt, and Ralph K. White, "Patterns of Aggressive Behavior in Experimentally Created 'Social Climates,'" *Journal of Social Psychology* 10, no. 2 (May 1939): 271–299; Douglas M. McGregor, *The Human Side of Enterprise*, New York, McGraw-Hill, 1960; Fred E. Fiedler, *A Theory of Leadership Effectiveness*, New York, McGraw-Hill, 1967; Edgar L. Morphet, Roe L. Johns, and Theodore L. Reller, *Educational Organization and Administration: Concepts, Practices, and Issues*, 4th ed., Englewood Cliffs, N.J., Prentice-Hall, 1982.

12. Thomas J. Sergiovanni and Robert J. Starratt, *Supervision: Human Perspectives*, 2d ed., New York, McGraw-Hill, 1979, 5–6. See also Raymond Miles, "Human Relations or Human Resources?" *Harvard Business Review* 43, no. 4 (July-August 1965): 148–163; Mason Haire, Edwin Ghiselli, and Lyman Porter, *Management Thinking: An International Study*, New York, John Wiley, 1966.

13. See Chester I. Barnard, *The Functions of the Executive*, Cambridge, Mass., Harvard University Press, 1938; Daniel E. Griffiths, *Administrative Theory*, New York, Appleton-Century-Crofts, 1959; Herbert A. Simon, *The New Science of Management Decision*, New York, Harper & Row, 1960.

14. See Griffiths, 92–113. See also Alvar Elbing, *Behavior Decisions in Organizations*, 2d ed., Glenview, Ill., Scott, Foresman, 1978; Roger A. Kaufman, "Systems Approaches to Education: Discussion and Attempted Integration," in Philip K. Piele, Terry L. Eidell, and Stuart C. Smith, eds., *Social and Technological Change: Implications for Education*, Eugene, Ore., Center for the Advanced Study of Educational Administration, University of Oregon, 1970, 160.

15. Robert J. Alfonso, Gerald R. Firth, and Richard F. Neville, *Instructional Supervision: A Behavior System*, 2d ed., Boston, Allyn and Bacon, 1981, ch. 7.
16. Ibid., 228, 233, 234, 235.
17. Alvin Toffler, *Future Shock*, New York, Random House, 1970; *The Third Wave*, William Morrow, 1980.
18. Lipham and Hoeh, 108.
19. Alfonso, Firth, and Neville, ch. 8.
20. Ibid., 273, 276, 278, 282.
21. Jon Wiles, *Planning Guidelines for Middle Education*, Dubuque, Iowa, Kendall/Hunt, 1976, 30. See also Jon Wiles and Joseph Bondi, *Curriculum Development: A Guide to Practice*, Columbus, Ohio: Charles E. Merrill, 1979, 115–116.
22. Richard Beckhard, *Organization Development: Strategies and Models*, Reading, Mass., Addison-Wesley, 1969, 9.
23. Wendell L. French and Cecil H. Bell, Jr., *Organization Development*, Englewood Cliffs, N.J., Prentice-Hall, 1973, 15.
24. Stephen J. Knezevich, *Administration of Public Education*, 3d ed., New York, Harper & Row, 1975, 198.
25. Ibid., 196, 198.
26. Fred Luthans, *Organizational Behavior*, New York, McGraw-Hill, 1973, 472.
27. See Jacob W. Getzels and Herbert A. Thelen, "The Classroom Group as a Unique Social System," in Nelson B. Henry, ed., *The Dynamics of Instructional Groups: Sociological Aspects of Teaching and Learning*, 59th Yearbook, Part II, Chicago, Ill., National Society for the Study of Education, 1960, 80.
28. Knezevich, 198.
29. Gilbert R. Weldy, *Time: A Resource for the School Administrator*, Reston, Va., National Association of Secondary School Principals, 1974.
30. Michael C. Giammatteo and Dolores M. Giammatteo, *Executive Well Being: Stress and Administrators*, Reston, Va., National Association of Secondary School Principals, 1980.
31. "The Man from Plains Sums It Up," *Time* 120, no. 5 (October 11, 1982): 63.
32. Alfonso, Firth, and Neville, 174–186.
33. Ibid., 178, 179, 180, 181, 182.
34. Ibid., 176.
35. Ibid., 182.
36. Edward T. Hall, *The Silent Language*, New York, Doubleday, 1959.
37. Ibid., 45–46.
38. See Theodore Ryland Sizer, "Education and Assimilation: A Fresh Plea for Pluralism," *Phi Delta Kappan* 58, no. 1 (September 1976): 31–35.
39. Ben M. Harris and William R. Hartgraves, "Supervisor Effectiveness: A Research Résumé," *Educational Leadership* 30, no. 1 (October 1972): 78.
40. Daniel Tanner and Laurel N. Tanner, *Curriculum Development: Theory into Practice*, New York, Macmillan, 1975, 631–632.
41. George C. Homans, *The Human Group*, New York, Harcourt Brace Jovanovich, 1950.
42. F. J. Roethlisberger and William J. Dickson, *Management and the Worker*, Cambridge, Mass., Harvard University Press, 1939.
43. Toffler, *Future Shock*.
44. Stuart Chase, *Roads to Agreement*, New York, Harper & Row, 1951.
45. Ibid., 235–238.
46. Lewin, Lippitt, and White, "Patterns of Aggressive Behavior in Experimentally Created 'Social Climates.'"
47. Lewin, Lippitt, and White research as summarized by Peter F. Oliva in "High School Discipline in American Society," *The National Association of Secondary School Principals Bulletin* 40, no. 216 (January 1956): 7–8.
48. Kenneth D. Benne and Paul Sheats, "Functional Roles of Group Members," *Journal of Social Issues* 4, no. 2 (Spring 1948): 43–46. A discussion of roles as developed by the First National Training Laboratory in Group Development, 1947.

49. See also Thomas J. Sergiovanni and Robert J. Starratt, *Emerging Patterns of Supervision: Human Perspectives*, New York, McGraw-Hill, 1971, 194–199.
50. Thiokol Chemical Corporation, *Interaction Laboratory for Teacher Development*, Trainer's Manual, Trainer Aids, Student Handouts, Student Journal, and Trainer Preparation Materials, Roy, Utah, Interaction Associates 1971.
51. Ibid., *Trainer's Manual*, 2.
52. Ibid., *Trainer's Manual*, 1.
53. Ibid., *Trainer's Manual*, 1–2.
54. Ibid., *Trainer's Manual*, 2.
55. Ibid., *Trainer's Manual*, 3.

BIBLIOGRAPHY

Alfonso, Robert J., Gerald R. Firth, and Richard F. Neville. *Instructional Supervision: A Behavior System*. Boston: Allyn and Bacon, 1981.

Beckhard, Richard. *Organizational Development: Strategies and Models*. Reading, Mass.: Addison-Wesley, 1969.

Benne, Kenneth D., and Paul Sheats. "Functional Roles of Group Members." *Journal of Social Issues* 4 (Spring 1948): 41–49.

Bennis, Warren G., Kenneth D. Benne, Robert Chin, and Kenneth E. Corey, eds. *The Planning of Change*, 3rd ed. New York: Holt, Rinehart and Winston, 1976.

Bradford, Leland P., and John R. P. French, eds. "The Dynamics of the Discussion Group." *Journal of Social Issues* 4 (Spring 1948): entire issue.

Carkhuff, Robert R., David H. Berenson, and Richard M. Pierce. *The Skills of Teaching: Interpersonal Skills*. Amherst, Mass.: Human Resource Development Press, 1977.

Chase, Stuart. *Roads to Agreement*. New York: Harper & Row, 1951.

De Bruyn, Robert L. *Causing Others to Want Your Leadership*. Manhattan, Kan.: R. L. De Bruyn & Associates, 1976.

Drucker, Peter F. *Management: Tasks, Responsibilities, Practices*. New York: Harper & Row, 1974.

Fast, Julius. *Body Language*. New York: M. Evans, 1970.

Fiedler, Fred E. *A Theory of Leadership Effectiveness*. New York: McGraw-Hill, 1967.

French, Wendell L., and Cecil H. Bell, Jr. *Organization Development*. Englewood Cliffs, N. J.: Prentice-Hall, 1973.

Galloway, Charles. "The Nonverbal Realities of Classroom Life." In *Observational Methods in the Classroom*, Charles Beegle and Richard H. Brandt, eds. Alexandria, Va.: Association for Supervision and Curriculum Development, 1973.

Getzels, Jacob W. "Administration as a Social Process." In *Administrative Theory in Education*, Andrew W. Halpin, ed. New York: Macmillan, 1958.

——— and Herbert A. Thelen. "The Classroom Group as a Unique Social System." In *The Dynamics of Instructional Groups: Sociological Aspects of Teaching and Learning*, 59th Yearbook, Part II, Nelson B. Henry, ed. Chicago, Ill.: National Society for the Study of Education, 1960.

Giammatteo, Michael C., and Dolores M. Giammatteo. *Executive Well Being: Stress and Administrators*. Reston, Va.: National Association of Secondary School Principals, 1980.

Hall, Edward T. *The Silent Language*. New York: Doubleday, 1959.

Harris, Ben M., and William R. Hartgraves. "Supervisor Effectiveness: A Research Résumé." *Educational Leadership* 30, no. 1 (October 1972): 73–79.

Hemphill, John K., and Alvin E. Coons. *Leader Behavior Description*, Columbus: Ohio State University, 1950.

Homans, George C. *The Human Group*. New York: Harcourt Brace Jovanovich, 1950.

Kaufman, Roger A. *Educational System Planning*. Englewood Cliffs, J.J.: Prentice-Hall, 1972.

Kimbrough, Ralph B., and Michael Y. Nunnery. *Educational Administration: An Introduction.* New York: Macmillan, 1976.

Knezevich, Stephen J. *Administration of Public Education*, 3rd ed. New York: Harper & Row, 1975.

Landsberger, Henry A. *Hawthorne Revisited: Management and the Worker: Its Critics and Developments in Human Relations in Industry.* Ithaca, N.Y.: Cornell University, 1958.

Lewin, Kurt, Ronald Lippitt, and Ralph K. White. "Patterns of Aggressive Behavior in Experimentally Created 'Social Climates.'" *Journal of Social Psychology* 10, no. 2 (May 1939): 271–299.

Likert, Rensis. *The Human Organization: Its Management.* New York: McGraw-Hill, 1967.

Lipham, James M., and James A. Hoeh, Jr. *The Principalship: Foundations and Functions.* New York: Harper & Row, 1974.

Luthans, Fred. *Organizational Behavior.* New York: McGraw-Hill, 1973.

McGregor, Douglas M. *The Human Side of Enterprise.* New York: McGraw-Hill, 1960.

Morphet, Edgar L., Roe L. Johns, and Theodore L. Reller. *Educational Organization and Administration: Concepts, Practices, and Issues*, 4th ed. Englewood Cliffs, N.J.: Prentice-Hall, 1982.

Owens, Robert G. *Organizational Behavior in Schools.* Englewood Cliffs, N.J.: Prentice-Hall, 1970.

Rice, Berkeley. "The Hawthorne Defect: Persistence of a Flawed Theory." *Psychology Today* 16 (February 1982): 70–74.

Roethlisberger, F. J., and William J. Dickson. *Management and the Worker.* Cambridge, Mass.: Harvard University Press, 1939.

Sergiovanni, Thomas J., ed. *Professional Supervision for Professional Teachers.* Alexandria, Va.: Association for Supervision and Curriculum Development, 1975.

———, and Robert J. Starratt. *Emerging Patterns of Supervision: Human Perspectives.* New York: McGraw-Hill, 1971. See also 2d ed., *Supervision: Human Perspectives*, 1979.

Stogdill, Ralph M. *Handbook of Leadership: A Survey of Theory and Research.* New York: The Free Press, 1974.

———. "Leadership, Membership, and Organization," *Psychological Bulletin* 47 (1950): 1–14.

Tanner, Daniel, and Laurel N. Tanner. *Curriculum Development: Theory into Practice.* New York: Macmillan, 1975. 2nd ed., 1980.

Toffler, Alvin. *Future Shock.* New York: Random House, 1970.

———. *The Third Wave.* New York: William Morrow, 1980.

Weldy, Gilbert R. *Time: A Resource for the School Administrator.* Reston, Va.: National Association of Secondary School Principals, 1974.

Wiles, Jon. *Planning Guidelines for Middle Schools.* Dubuque, Iowa: Kendall/Hunt, 1976.

——— and Joseph Bondi. *Curriculum Development: A Guide to Practice.* Columbus, Ohio: Charles E. Merrill, 1979.

Films

Future Shock. Metromedia Producers Corporation. 42 min. 16 mm. Sound, color. Released by McGraw-Hill.

Sharing the Leadership. 30 min. 16 mm. Sound, black and white. Boston: WGBH-TV. Released by National Educational Television Film Service.

Multi-Media

Florida Department of Education. *Human Relations for Administrators and Supervisors.* Chipley: Panhandle Area Educational Cooperative. Sixteen training modules.

Northwest Regional Educational Laboratory, 710 S.W. Second Avenue, Portland, Oregon 97204:

Instructional system in *Interpersonal Communication*. Participant materials, nine 16 mm sound films, one audiotape, leader's manual. 30 hours.

Instructional system in *Interpersonal Influence*. Participant materials, four 16 mm sound films, two audiotapes, leader's manual. Thirty-three hours of instruction on introduction of basic concepts and tools for understanding interpersonal influence, characteristic individual patterns of response to influence situations, and analysis and interpretation of interpersonal influence in small group settings.

Instructional system in *Research Utilizing Problem Solving*, Administrators' Version. Participant materials, audiotape, text (*Diagnosing Professional Climates of Schools* by Fox, Jung, Schmuck et al.), and leader's guide. Thirty hours of instruction on (1) identifying the problem, (2) diagnosing the problem situation, (3) considering alternative actions, (4) trying out a plan of action, and (5) adapting the plan.

Teacher Education Resources. *Interdisciplinary Team Organization.* Two sound filmstrips, two cassette interviews, script books, leader's guide, and handouts. Teacher Education Resources, P.O. Box 206, Gainesville, Florida 32602.

Thiokol Chemical Corporation. *Interaction Laboratory for Teacher Development.* Ogden, Utah: Thiokol Chemical Corporation, 1971. Trainer's Manual, Trainer Aids, Student Handouts, Student Journal, and Trainer Preparation Materials.

Videotape

Cawelti, Gordon. *Selecting Appropriate Leadership Styles for Instructional Improvement.* 33 min. Association for Supervision and Curriculum Development, 225 N. Washington Street, Alexandria, Virginia 22314, 1978.

11

Helping Teachers
to Evaluate Themselves

OBJECTIVES

After studying Chapter 11, you should be able to accomplish the following objectives:

1. Identify and describe three components of teacher evaluation systems.
2. Develop and use a teacher self-appraisal instrument.
3. Explain the meaning of external and internal analysis as applied to teacher performance.
4. Describe several models of teaching.
5. Analyze your own model of teaching.
6. Produce and classify protocol materials.
7. Utilize teacher-training modules in assisting teachers to improve instruction.
8. Develop and use an instrument for student evaluation of teacher performance.
9. Develop and use an instrument for parent evaluation of teacher performance.

THREE FACES OF EVALUATION OF TEACHER PERFORMANCE

Teachers sometimes feel that they are the most scrutinized professionals in the world. They live in the public eye. They are subject to more restrictions on their behavior than most professionals, excluding the clergy. Their performance in class and their behavior out of class are evaluated by students, other teachers, administrators, and the public.

Preservice teachers should be advised to expect continuous evaluation of their performance as a way of life. The profession has come to admit that there are wide variations in knowledge, energy, dedication, and skill among the more than 2,000,000 teachers throughout this land. The profession has taken cognizance too that developments in all subject fields and in pedagogy have been rapid, necessitating continual assessment and in-service study on the part of school personnel.

At the same time there is the awareness among teachers, administrators, and supervisors that the evaluation of human performance in any field is a difficult, sensitive matter subject to gross mistakes and misjudgments. No aspect of teaching can be more threatening to teachers than evaluation of their performance. No aspect of administration can be more agonizing for a conscientious administrator that evaluation of teachers. The administrator who asserts that the evaluation of teacher performance is easy, nonthreatening, and routine seriously underestimates the complexities and effects of teacher assessment. The administrator who evidences this attitude is probably one who has forgotten his or her reactions to evaluation as a teacher and who is not subjected to systematic, formal evaluation as an administrator.

While teachers need to develop an attitude receptive to evaluation as a means of improving themselves and the profession, school systems need to devise ways to evaluate teachers which are feasible, fair, humane, and as objective as possible. What exists now are some 16,000 systems of teacher evaluation, one for each of the 16,000 school districts which make up the enterprise of American public education. Of course, I exaggerate a bit. Some states require a specific, uniform assessment program for certain purposes, e.g., state certification. Even in those cases, however, school districts within the state may follow their own systems of evaluation for their own purposes in addition to the state required program.

In the next three chapters we will examine the complex problem of evaluation of teacher performance. As we discuss teacher evaluation, we will talk about both evaluation of instruction (and to some extent, of the course or subject) and evaluation of the instructor. These two aspects are, of course, interrelated. By evaluation of instruction I mean appraisal of the effectiveness of the instructional skills and strategies chosen by the teacher. By evaluation of the instructor I mean assessment of the teacher's classroom performance (behavior), his or her effectiveness in employing the skills and strategies selected, and certain personal and professional attributes. In these three chapters I will use the words evaluation, assessment, and appraisal interchangeably.

A fully developed program of teacher appraisal consists of three components: *self-evaluation, formative evaluation,* and *summative evaluation.*

The last term, summative evaluation, is the annual assessment done by the administrator not only for purposes of improvement of instruction but also and primarily for making decisions on tenure, advancement to leadership positions, and, in those situations which have it, merit pay. Summative evaluation is discussed in Chapter 13.

The second term, formative evaluation, is ongoing assessment of teacher performance. Administrators and supervisors visit teachers periodically, observe their classes, and confer with the teachers for purposes of helping them to improve their instruction. Clinical supervision is a manifestation of formative evaluation. We will look at this component in Chapter 12.

The foci of this chapter are ways in which teachers may appraise their own performance and means by which supervisors can help them to do so. All school systems have instituted some sort of summative evaluation of teacher performance. Most school systems have implemented a formative evaluation system of one type or another. Few school systems have developed a systematic process for teacher self-appraisal. I believe that a systematic, structured way of encouraging teachers to evaluate themselves is essential and should be an integral part of the evaluation process.

A refrain from Robert Burns may run through the mind of the supervisor pondering the task of helping teachers to evaluate themselves:

> Oh wad some power the giftie gie us
> To see oursels as ithers see us
> It was frae monie a blunder free us
> And foolish notion.

The thoughtful supervisor knows that in order to make a contribution to improvement in the curriculum and in instruction he or she must possess the power to help teachers to see themselves "as ithers see" us. Perhaps power is too strong a word in reference to the supervisor's role—ability might be better. The supervisor must possess the ability or skills necessary to encourage teachers to look at their own behavior with a view to improving themselves. More, it is necessary for the supervisor to be able to look at his or her own supervisory behavior, a topic discussed in Chapter 14.

The skill of introspection is difficult to develop. When seeking ways to help teachers to evaluate themselves the supervisor is up against some formidable antagonistic attitudes. Among the notions teachers hold about evaluation of their behaviors are the attitudes that:

- It is the student alone who should be evaluated; the teacher occupies a position beyond evaluation.
- Apart from the teacher, no one is capable of making an evaluation of that teacher's behavior.
- Every teacher has reached such a high state of professional competence that evaluation of the teacher is not necessary.
- Teachers already know how to teach twice as well as they have the time or energy to teach or are permitted to teach.
- No other profession makes the assumption that a professional person must be regularly evaluated.
- Teaching is such a highly personalized and individualized art that any efforts to evaluate teacher behaviors are unproductive.

When contemplating the problem of helping teachers to evaluate themselves, the supervisor also runs into some real and often unexpressed fears of teachers, who worry that:

- They will be exposed and their shortcomings made known to the world.
- They will be subjected to ridicule if they make mistakes.
- Anything less than perfection will penalize them in terms of salary, tenure, or promotion.

Consequently, the teaching profession has built into itself some potent avoidance behaviors. The profession has resisted merit increment plans by raising questions such as: Who will do the evaluating? How do you allow for individuality? How can you identify merit in teaching? Some teachers view their own classrooms as their own territorial domains, into which the entrance of administrators, supervisors, and the public is considered an unwarranted intrusion. The flag of academic freedom is frequently hoisted to justify any type of teacher behavior. Some teachers hold to the viewpoint that if they pass the initial test of an interview, have the appropriate teaching credential, and are hired by the administrator, they have demonstrated all the competence they need to demonstrate. If it turns out that their professional skills are less than might be desired, they view that situation as the administrator's problem, not theirs.

Because of the antagonistic attitudes and fears of teachers toward evaluation, the supervisor's primary role in the evaluation of teacher competence should be one of helping teachers to evaluate themselves rather than one of evaluating teachers. This subtle distinction is crucial to the problem of evaluation. The role of the supervisor as teacher evaluator can set up barriers between the teacher and the supervisor and perpetuate the fears of teachers. In this evaluative role the supervisor can be seen as a threat to the teacher rather than a help, and rapport between the supervisor and the teacher may be most difficult to achieve.

The supervisor's role in evaluating teachers reveals the school system's concept of supervision; that is, whether supervision is conceived as a function of administration or as a service support to teachers. It has been a central theme of this text that supervision for today's schools is first of all a service function and only secondarily an administrative function.

Many school systems require supervisors to evaluate teachers, rate them on certain competencies, and fill out annual reports of performance which are submitted to the administrator. It would be preferable, however, for the administrator to assume the role of teacher-rater, removing it from the shoulders of the supervisor, and allowing the supervisor to concentrate on the role that should be fulfilled—helping teachers improve their teaching skills. If a supervisor must rate a teacher and report the rating to the administrator—and this must be done in many school systems—then the ratings themselves should be played down, teachers themselves should enter fully into the process of rating, ratings should be liberally interpreted, and emphasis throughout the process should be on helping teachers to evaluate their own performances and not to earn "brownie points" from the supervisor. Further, the confidentiality of such evaluations must be preserved and restricted to only those who have the right to see them.

Supervisors who must rate teachers are walking a tightrope. They must have built a solid base of trust and confidence and a reputation for fairness if their relationship with teachers is to withstand the trauma of teacher rating. It would be preferable if the service-oriented supervisor never had to rate a teacher but such an expectation would be unrealistic in the light of many administrators' expectations of supervisors. The challenge to the supervisor, therefore, is to make the system work to achieve the major goal being sought—improved achievement of learners through improved teacher competence.

Of course, ratings of personnel should be made, for there are teachers in the profession who should not be teaching at all. It would seem, however, that the administrator, not the supervisor, should bear the primary responsibility for making judgments about the competence or incompetence of teachers. It appears appropriate and timely for the profession as well to set up some mechanism for monitoring itself. Other professions, notably medicine and law, have devised ways to warn or remove members of the profession whom they deem unsuitable. It is often rebutted that teaching is not a profession, teachers' salaries are not comparable to those of the medical and legal professions, and therefore such monitoring would be out of line. Perhaps one of the reasons why teaching is not regarded by some of the public as a profession is the inability or unwillingness of the profession itself to spell out and monitor standards of teaching performance. The lack of a monitoring system should not thrust the burden onto the shoulders of the helpless supervisor.

In the light of these difficulties the supervisor should utilize every technique that can be mustered to help teachers evaluate their own competencies with as little stress on rating as possible. If it is the supervisor's duty to make an annual report on a teacher, the supervisor should make that evaluation an exercise in teacher self-evaluation under his or her guidance. The evaluation should be a process of discussion between the teacher and supervisor and a means for the teacher to set his or her own goals for the future. During the rating process the supervisor must present a demeanor of helping and not convey the impression that the teacher is being graded.

COMPETENCIES TO BE EVALUATED

Before considering techniques which the supervisor can employ to help teachers evaluate themselves, let us for a moment take a look at some of the competencies which school systems feel important enough to be evaluated. If teachers are to be evaluated, they should know well in advance what the criteria are on which assessments will be made.

School systems vary on the teacher behaviors they consider to be important. Among categories of behavior which appear on instruments which assess teacher performance are (1) instructional skills, (2) personal traits, and (3) professional attributes. The Appraisal of Teacher Competency of the Vidalia City Schools (Georgia) in Figure 11.1 furnishes an illustration of categories of performance which are

BOARD OF EDUCATION

Vidalia City Schools
Vidalia, Georgia

Tom P. Hutcheson
Superintendent

APPRAISAL OF TEACHER COMPETENCY

NAME (Appraisee): _____ SCHOOL: _____

CERTIFICATE TYPE AND LEVEL: _____ SOCIAL SECURITY #: _____

Present assignment and areas of responsibility: _____

_____

Number of years in present assignment: _____ Number of years in school system: _____

This appraisal is for the school year:_____

Instructions

In completing this appraisal record:

1.   Each indicator is to be rated on a five point scale. Descriptors for
     each of the five ratings for each indicator are given in the Teacher
     Performance Assessment Instruments: Competencies, Indicators, and
     Descriptors.

2.   The principal is to use his/her knowledge of the teacher's usual level
     of performance in evaluating the teacher's plans and materials, class-
     room performance, interpersonal skills, and professional standards.
     The principal is to use the daily and weekly planning skills of the
     teacher as the basis for the ratings on the Teaching Plans and Materials
     section.

3.   The signatures given do not necessarily imply agreement. They confirm
     the fact that the principal and teacher have discussed the ratings and
     the teacher has read all comments.

Figure 11.1 Appraisal of Teacher Competency

SOURCE: Vidalia City Schools, *Appraisal of Teacher Competency*, Vidalia, Ga., no date. Reprinted with permission.

TEACHING PLANS AND MATERIALS

COMPETENCY 1

PLANS INSTRUCTION TO ACHIEVE
SELECTED OBJECTIVES.

		Teacher	Teacher & Principal
1. Specifies or selects learner objectives for lessons.	1.		
2. Specifies or selects teaching procedures for lessons.	2.		
3. Specifies or selects content, materials, and media for lessons.	3.		
4. Specifies or selects materials and procedures for assessing learner progress on the objectives.	4.		
5. Plans instruction at a variety of levels.	5.		

COMPETENCY 2

ORGANIZES INSTRUCTION TO TAKE INTO
ACCOUNT INDIVIDUAL DIFFERENCES
AMONG LEARNERS.

6. Organizes instruction to take into account differences among learners in their capabilities.	6.		
7. Organizes instruction to take into account differences among learners in their learning styles.	7.		
8. Organizes instruction to take into account differences among learners in their rates of learning.	8.		

COMPETENCY 3

OBTAINS AND USES INFORMATION ABOUT
THE NEEDS AND PROGRESS OF INDIVIDUAL
LEARNERS.

		Teacher	Teacher & Principal
9. Uses teacher-made or teacher-selected evaluation materials or procedures to obtain information about learner progress.	9.		
10. Communicates with individual learners about their needs and progress.	10.		

COMPETENCY 4

REFERS LEARNERS WITH SPECIAL
PROBLEMS TO SPECIALISTS.

11. Obtains and uses information about learners from cumulative records.	11.		
12. Identifies learners who require the assistance of specialists.	12.		
13. Obtains and uses information from co-workers and parents to assist with specific learner problems.	13.		

COMPETENCY 5

OBTAINS AND USES INFORMATION ABOUT
THE EFFECTIVENESS OF INSTRUCTION
TO REVISE IT WHEN NECESSARY.

14. Obtains information on the effectiveness of instruction.	14.		
15. Revises instruction as needed using evaluation results and observation data.	15.		

CLASSROOM PROCEDURES

COMPETENCY 6

USES INSTRUCTIONAL TECHNIQUES,
METHODS, AND MEDIA RELATED TO
THE OBJECTIVES.

1. Uses teaching methods appropriate for objectives, learners
   and environment.   1.

2. Uses instructional equipment and other instructional
   aids.   2.

3. Uses instructional materials
   that provide learners with
   appropriate practice on
   objectives.   3.

COMPETENCY 7

COMMUNICATES WITH LEARNERS.

4. Gives directions and explanations related to lesson
   content.   4.

5. Clarifies directions and
   explanations when learners mis-
   understand lesson content.   5.

6. Uses responses and questions
   from learners in teaching.   6.

7. Provides feedback to learners
   throughout the lesson.   7.

8. Uses acceptable written and
   oral expression with learners. 8.

COMPETENCY 8

DEMONSTRATES A REPERTOIRE OF
TEACHING METHODS.

9. Implements learning activities
   in a logical sequence.   9.

10. Demonstrates ability to con-
    duct lessons using a variety
    of teaching methods.   10.

11. Demonstrates ability to work
    with individuals, small
    groups, and large groups.   11.

COMPETENCY 9

REINFORCES AND ENCOURAGES LEARNER
INVOLVEMENT IN INSTRUCTION.

12. Uses procedures which get
    learners initially involved
    in lessons.   12.

13. Provides learners with oppor-
    tunities for participating.   13.

14. Maintains learner involve-
    ment in lessons.   14.

15. Reinforces and encourages
    the efforts of learners to
    maintain involvement.   15.

COMPETENCY 10

DEMONSTRATES AN UNDERSTANDING OF THE
SCHOOL SUBJECT BEING TAUGHT.

16. Helps learners recognize the
    purpose and importance of
    topics or activities.   16.

17. Demonstrates knowledge in the
    subject area.   17.

COMPETENCY 11

ORGANIZES TIME, SPACE, MATERIALS, AND
EQUIPMENT FOR INSTRUCTION.

18. Attends to routine tasks.   18.

19. Uses instructional time
    effectively.   19.

20. Provides a learning environ-
    ment that is attractive and
    orderly.   20.

COMPETENCY 12

DEMONSTRATES ENTHUSIASM FOR TEACHING AND LEARNING AND THE SUBJECT BEING TAUGHT.

1. Communicates personal enthusiasm. 1. ☐☐

2. Stimulates learner interest. 2. ☐☐

3. Conveys the impression of knowing what to do and how to do it. 3. ☐☐

COMPETENCY 13

HELPS LEARNERS DEVELOP POSITIVE SELF-CONCEPTS.

4. Demonstrates warmth and friendliness. 4. ☐☐

5. Demonstrates sensitivity to the needs and feelings of learners. 5. ☐☐

6. Demonstrates patience, empathy, and understanding. 6. ☐☐

COMPETENCY 14

MANAGES CLASSROOM INTERACTIONS.

7. Provides feedback to learners about their behavior. 7. ☐☐

8. Promotes comfortable interpersonal relationships. 8. ☐☐

9. Maintains appropriate classroom behavior. 9. ☐☐

10. Manages disruptive behavior among learners. 10. ☐☐

COMPETENCY 15

MEETS PROFESSIONAL RESPONSIBILITIES.

1. Works cooperatively with colleagues, administrators, and community members. 1. ☐☐

2. Follows the policies and procedures of the school district. 2. ☐☐

3. Demonstrates ethical behavior. 3. ☐☐

4. Carries out instructional duties. 4. ☐☐

5. Carries out additional duties. 5. ☐☐

COMPETENCY 16

ENGAGES IN PROFESSIONAL SELF IMPROVEMENT.

6. Obtains and evaluates data on professional skills. 6. ☐☐

7. Obtains information to aid teaching. 7. ☐☐

8. Participates in professional growth activities. 8. ☐☐

9. Shares professional materials and ideas. 9. ☐☐

Teacher's Comments: _____
_____
_____

Principal's Comments: _____
_____
_____

Teacher's Signature: _____ Date: _____

Principal's Signature: _____ Date: _____

assessed. This instrument follows the items of the *Teacher Performance Assessment Instruments* used by the state of Georgia to assess beginning teachers for the purpose of certification.[1]

It should be pointed out that the instrument of the Vidalia City Schools is used for *summative* evaluation. The summative criteria provide a basis for teacher self-appraisal and for formative evaluation by teacher and supervisor. This particular instrument assesses teaching plans and materials, classroom procedures, interpersonal skills, and, to a very limited extent, professional standards.

When administrators and supervisors initiate the process of identification of teacher competencies and attributes and the means of evaluating these competencies and attributes, it is essential that teachers be brought into the developmental process. Participation in the development of evaluation plans from the beginning is the best means of securing commitment of teachers to the evaluation process.

In the multiplicity of evaluation systems, two general categories of teacher behavior predominate: instructional skills, which lie more in the cognitive and performance areas, and personal-professional attributes, which lie more in the affective area. It will be assumed that these two major categories of teacher behavior are worthy of appraisal and ways will be suggested by which the supervisor can help teachers to evaluate themselves in respect to these broad areas.

Evaluation of Instructional Skills

Previous chapters of this text have sought to describe instructional skills which appear desirable for teachers to master while training the evaluative spotlight on learners and their performance. Now the spotlight is focused on the teachers' performance. The supervisor mulls the question: How can I best go about helping teachers to see and analyze their own performance? Several avenues suggest themselves, one or more of which may run into a dead end:

> The supervisor may enter the teacher's classroom unannounced and unexpected, sit down at the back of the room, observe the teacher's performance, take notes while the teacher is teaching, write up a summary, and hand it to the teacher.
>
> The supervisor may appear periodically, evaluate the teacher's performances using a rating instrument, and deliver the instrument to the administrator.
>
> The supervisor may drop in informally several times to get acquainted and to see if the teacher needs help of any kind before turning to procedures for a more structured type of evaluation.
>
> The supervisor may set up some in-service training programs designed to help teachers evaluate their own performance before entering into a more structured type of evaluation.

It is imperative for the supervisor to gain the teacher's confidence before the two of them can together talk about evaluating the teacher's performance. Of the four avenues described above the last two are acceptable. The first two avenues are not acceptable, for they are grading approaches which place the teacher under threat. Provision must be made for discussion and analysis in a threat-free environment as nearly as can be accomplished.

In order to institute teachers' examination of their own competence the supervisor may follow an approach which consists of the following three stages:

1. Examination of teacher performance in general terms; that is, analysis of the teaching act in a theoretical context. This is accomplished by study of the literature and selected other media on teaching.
2. Examination of the performance of other teachers both inside and outside the school system. This is accomplished by the use of audio and visual media and by teachers' visiting each other's classrooms.
3. Examination of the teacher's own performance. This is accomplished through the use of both written materials and other selected media.

We will elaborate on these three stages in a moment. I have chosen to call the first two stages *external analysis*. At these points teachers look at teaching in general and at the performance of other teachers. They are looking beyond themselves. As they make external analyses of teaching, they begin to internalize, drawing implications for their own teaching. They begin to develop certain understandings about teaching and start to see how they can improve themselves.

The third stage is *internal analysis*, at which time the teacher focuses on his or her own behaviors. At this point the teacher comes to center stage and, instead of concentrating on the teaching act impersonally, in a general way, or on the performance of other teachers in other schools or school systems, is brought around to evaluating his or her own performance.

The purpose of this three-stage sequence from external to internal analysis is to allow time for the supervisor to help teachers build a positive mind-set toward evaluation, equip them with skills for evaluating themselves, and develop a feeling of self-confidence in their own abilities.

The literature on teacher behavior is vast and still growing. Many studies of teacher performance have been conducted and numerous training programs have been developed which permit teachers to look at teaching and at their own performance. The next section offers the prospective supervisor several strategies for developing skills of self-evaluation, briefly describes the nature of these strategies, and directs the supervisor to a number of sources and programs.

Models of Teaching

Although there is no single best point of departure for the evaluation of teacher competence, one which can be a productive route, a form of external analysis (a look at the teaching act) is the study and recognition of models of teaching. An examination of various models of teaching provides the teacher with an opportunity to identify the model or models which he or she either makes use of or can make use of. Bruce Joyce and Marsha Weil defined a model of teaching as follows:

A model for teaching is a plan or pattern that can be used to shape curriculums (long-term courses of studies), to design instructional materials, and to guide instruction in the classroom and other settings.[2]

The Joyce and Weil book described 24 models of teaching grouped into four categories: social models, information-processing models, personal models, and behavioral models. Some models of teaching are more evident than others. The following models can be identified among many that are followed by teachers:

1. *The teacher as lecturer.* This historic model conceives of the teacher as a conveyor of information from his or her mind to the minds of the learners through the medium of oral language.

2. *The teacher as expert resource person.* The teacher who follows this model is available to share information as to content and sources whenever learners have need for help.

3. *The teacher as facilitator.* Following this model the teacher does everything possible to provide resources and direction to the learners so they may go about their studies and continously guides their learning in the process of study.

4. *The teacher as counselor.* The teacher who adopts this model sees the personal development of the learner as more important than the content, advises students, encourages them, and, more importantly, listens to the learners' problems.

5. *The teacher as a leader of group meetings.* This teacher is the master of ceremonies, the group's chairperson, who promotes the work of the group, directs its activities, and encourages participation from all the group's members.

6. *The teacher as tutor.* The teacher following this model engages in instruction on a one-to-one basis, and in so doing may employ a variety of techniques, including contractual-type arrangements which provide for independent study.

7. *The teacher as manager of mediated instruction.* Various media play a primary role in the presentation of instruction via this model. The teacher selects the necessary media, arranges for their use and follows up the mediated presentations with discussion and evaluation.

8. *The teacher as laboratory supervisor.* This model requires the establishing of a laboratory approach to instruction—experimenting, constructing, researching activities which the learners carry out under the supervision of the teacher.

9. *The teacher as programmer.* From the fields of programmed instruction and computer-assisted instruction this model directs the teacher to write specific programs which the learners then work through either individually or in groups.

10. *The teacher as manipulator of the learning environment.* This behavioristic model calls for the teacher to manipulate the stimuli in the classroom environment. The teacher gives and withholds reinforcement for specific kinds of learnings which the students are attempting.

In their examination of models of teaching Joyce and Weil challenge the idea that there is any such thing as a perfect model and reject the notion that teachers should limit their personal search for a model of teaching to any single model. They believe it is a fallacy to search for the one right way to teach.

The study of models of teaching serves the worthwhile function of causing supervisors and teachers to realize that a number of models of teacher behavior are possible—how many can only be conjectured. In some respects a model of teaching resembles a style of teaching. Style injects a very personal, individualized dimension, for the concept of style of teaching includes elements of the teacher's personality— facial expressions, gesturing, kinesthetic movements, choice of vocabulary, dramatic flare, wit—the total personal delivery system.

As research into learning and teacher behavior continues, new models and adaptations of old models may be expected. A productive in-service program would lie in the identification and analysis of various models of teaching. The purpose of such an in-service program would not be to cause teachers to select from one of the models and to adopt it for exclusive use but to give them some basis for identifying their own pattern or patterns. Teachers may wish to try alternative models or develop their own eclectic models. The choice of a model or models which a teacher will follow is a function of the nature of the grade level, discipline, instructional objectives, and the teacher's own personality. Some of the models have general applicability at all grade levels and in all disciplines while others are more suited to particular grade levels and disciplines. After a study of models of teaching, the supervisor may turn the external analysis of models into an internal analysis by asking teachers to describe and classify their own models of teaching.

Critical Moments in Teaching *Films*

As an aid to examining the act of teaching, films such as the series of sound films in color developed under the leadership of Don G. Williams and David Gliessman have proved a useful tool in provoking discussion of teacher behavior. This series, known as *Critical Moments in Teaching*, presents in short (10–12 minute) films dramatizations of problems frequently encountered by elementary and secondary school teachers.[3] From initial planning in the late 1960s by a group known as the Inter-University Film Project, 16 films have appeared depicting a variety of situations which might be expected in the classroom. The films are carefully scripted and staged to bring out certain prespecified principles of teaching and learning. Each situation is intentionally left open-ended so the films can be followed with discussion and analysis. Types of classroom problems which these films show are cheating, lack of motivation of pupils, poor classroom management, lack of relevance of content, and teaching the handicapped child.

As a form of external analysis the films provide numerous insights into the teaching act. Since the situations in the films are controlled, the supervisor and teachers can zero in on specific competencies. The films have been widely used in both preservice and in-service training programs. The supervisor who wishes to use these films may select those appropriate to the particular level—elementary or secondary—and schedule them over a period of time. Since each film treats a discrete topic, each is suitable for an in-service session in itself. An instructor's manual assists the supervisor with discussion sessions which are essential as follow-up. Since discussion of the principles portrayed in the films is an integral part of the utilization of the series, it is recommended that the films be scheduled for separate meetings of faculties and not programmed in concentrated form à la film festival style, even though the films are technically and dramatically of interest. Although a bit dated now, these films are still useful in studying the teaching act.

Since the *Critical Moments in Teaching* films are intentionally structured for specific instructional purposes, they do not have the spontaneity of actual classroom situations. For spontaneous and unstructured situations the supervisor may locate or produce protocol materials.

Protocol Materials

Protocol materials are brief taped or filmed incidents of actual classroom situations. They have been described as:

vignettes of behavior which illustrate key concepts that enable the teacher to better interpret behavior in the classroom and the school. The main purpose of Protocol Materials is to develop conceptual knowledge through concept analysis and to link specific behavior to a conceptual basis.[4]

By capturing classroom behavior on tape or film teachers can study and restudy the behavior. Protocol materials differ from ordinary taping and filming of classroom situations in that the producers of protocol materials zero in on the concepts they wish to illustrate. They may be looking for examples of focusing, probing questions, verbal interaction, behavior modification, teacher enthusiasm, or other teaching skills. They capture the performance of a particular skill on tape or film so it can be studied at a future time.

Supervisors may seek protocol materials from other school systems or from commercial sources.[5] However, with today's portable videotaping equipment the supervisor can, with the help of media support personnel, produce a library of local protocol materials—taped situations in the local schools. Locally produced protocol materials will have heightened meaning for teachers in the system who make use of the materials. Needless to say, the full cooperation of classroom teachers would have to be assured in advance in order for taping to take place in their classrooms. It is most probable that only the most confident teachers would be willing—at least at first—for themselves and their classes to be taped and for the protocols to be studied by other teachers in the system.

B. Othanel Smith, Saul B. Cohen, and Arthur Pearl spoke to the purpose of protocol materials which they called "samples of behavior to be studied:"

The study of protocol materials will not only result in the prospective teacher's ability to understand and to interpret situations he will face in the classroom, school, and community; it will also increase the teacher's interest in theory, for he will see clearly for the first time that it is useful.[6]

It might be added to this quotation that it is not only the prospective teacher who can profit from the use of protocol materials but the in-service teacher as well. Smith, Cohen, and Pearl give examples of types of situations that protocols can point up: interference of concepts, conflict situations, self-image, self-fulfillment, differential reinforcement, and vicarious reinforcement.

Smith, Cohen and Pearl advised the use of protocol materials for the purpose of expanding the teacher's theoretical knowledge. They said:

Apart from situational instruction, theoretical knowledge is apt to remain pedagogically useless. Protocol materials should not be used merely to illustrate points in education courses. The whole procedure should be turned about so that the principles of the psychological, sociological, and philosophical studies, as well as those of pedagogy, are brought to the analysis of protocol materials, not the other way around. These materials suggest the knowledge that is relevant to the teacher's work.[7]

In order to make effective use of protocol materials a school system which contemplates the purchase or production of protocols will need to develop a system for classifying and cataloging behaviors. Smith et al. suggested a simple classification system:

1. Classroom situations
   a. Instructional situations
   b. Situations of classroom management and control
2. Extraclassroom situations
   a. Situations that arise in planning school programs, working with peers and the administration
   b. Situations that occur in working with parents and other members of the community
   c. Situations that occur in working in professional organizations[8]

It will be noted that protocol materials do not have to be confined exclusively to classroom behaviors. Since we are concerned at this time with the evaluation of instructional skills, we are interested primarily in classroom situations.

Two detailed systems for categorizing teacher competencies have been developed by the Florida State Department of Education.[9] The first system (Figure 11.2) classifies teacher competencies with a single topical index. The second system (Figure 11.3) employs a multiple, seven-point index system, classifying teacher competencies by teacher behavior, content area, pupil level, scope, outcome, object of change, and implied teacher performance assessment.

Though the *Florida Catalog of Teacher Competencies* was prepared to classify teacher-training modules, discussed next, a similar classification system can be applied to the development of a retrieval system for protocol materials. The supervisor must have easy access to specific protocols needed for use at specific times with teachers individually or in groups. To aid in the establishment of a bank of protocol materials the supervisor might well appoint a protocols development committee composed of teachers and other specialists in the school system.

SYSTEM I

SINGLE INDEX SYSTEM FOR
CLASSIFYING TEACHER COMPETENCIES

This system allows for competency statements to be retrieved on the basis on general headings related to teaching, such as discipline, materials, and evaluation. These general headings are designated as "Topics." This independently functioning system allows the user of the Catalog to retrieve competency statements by identifying a single topic area in which he is interested.

In some instances, competency statements may relate to more than one topic. In such cases the statements are coded for and may be retrieved under each relevant topic heading.

TOPICS (TP)

01 – Assessment Procedures	21 – Materials, activities, lessons
02 – Attitude Formation	22 – Motivation
03 – Audio-Visual aids	23 – Organization
04 – Classroom environment	24 – Parent-teacher relations
05 – Classroom management	25 – Planning
06 – Concept development	26 – Procedures/routines
07 – Community resources	27 – Professionalism
08 – Diagnosis	28 – Programmed instruction/ computer-assisted instruction
09 – Directions	29 – Pupil-teacher relations
10 – Discipline	30 – Pupil-pupil relations
11 – Discussions	31 – Questioning/responding
12 – Evaluation	32 – Records/reports/conferences
13 – Reinforcement	33 – Review/summary
14 – Goals, aims, objectives	34 – Self-concept
15 – Human relations	35 – Small group
16 – Individualized instruction	36 – Teacher self improvement
17 – Inductive teaching/ Problem solving	37 – Teacher-teacher relations
18 – Large group	38 – Test construction
19 – Learning Centers	39 – Valuing
20 – Lecture/Presentation of Information	

Figure 11.2 Classification of Teacher Competencies Using Single Topical Index

SOURCE: Florida Department of Education, *The Florida Catalog of Teacher Competencies*, Tallahassee, Fla., January 1, 1973, p. 10. Reprinted with permission.

SYSTEM II

MULTIPLE INDEX SYSTEM FOR CLASSIFYING TEACHER COMPETENCIES

(Directions for use of each Index are on subsequent pages)

TEACHER BEHAVIOR (TB)	CONTENT AREA (CA)
10. Assessing and Evaluating Student Behavior 11 – Selecting assessment instruments	01 – Agriculture 02 – Art

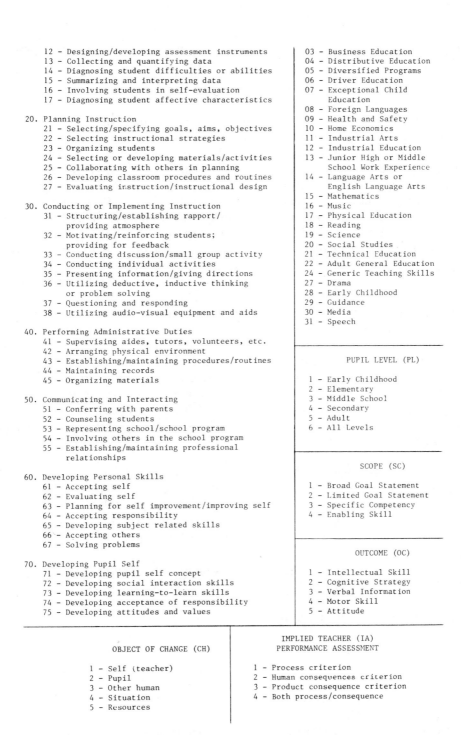

```
12 - Designing/developing assessment instruments      03 - Business Education
13 - Collecting and quantifying data                  04 - Distributive Education
14 - Diagnosing student difficulties or abilities     05 - Diversified Programs
15 - Summarizing and interpreting data                06 - Driver Education
16 - Involving students in self-evaluation            07 - Exceptional Child
17 - Diagnosing student affective characteristics           Education
                                                      08 - Foreign Languages
20. Planning Instruction                              09 - Health and Safety
    21 - Selecting/specifying goals, aims, objectives 10 - Home Economics
    22 - Selecting instructional strategies           11 - Industrial Arts
    23 - Organizing students                          12 - Industrial Education
    24 - Selecting or developing materials/activities 13 - Junior High or Middle
    25 - Collaborating with others in planning              School Work Experience
    26 - Developing classroom procedures and routines 14 - Language Arts or
    27 - Evaluating instruction/instructional design        English Language Arts
                                                      15 - Mathematics
30. Conducting or Implementing Instruction            16 - Music
    31 - Structuring/establishing rapport/            17 - Physical Education
         providing atmosphere                         18 - Reading
    32 - Motivating/reinforcing students;             19 - Science
         providing for feedback                       20 - Social Studies
    33 - Conducting discussion/small group activity   21 - Technical Education
    34 - Conducting individual activities             22 - Adult General Education
    35 - Presenting information/giving directions     24 - Generic Teaching Skills
    36 - Utilizing deductive, inductive thinking      27 - Drama
         or problem solving                           28 - Early Childhood
    37 - Questioning and responding                   29 - Guidance
    38 - Utilizing audio-visual equipment and aids    30 - Media
                                                      31 - Speech
40. Performing Administrative Duties
    41 - Supervising aides, tutors, volunteers, etc.
    42 - Arranging physical environment
    43 - Establishing/maintaining procedures/routines          PUPIL LEVEL (PL)
    44 - Maintaining records
    45 - Organizing materials                         1 - Early Childhood
                                                      2 - Elementary
50. Communicating and Interacting                     3 - Middle School
    51 - Conferring with parents                      4 - Secondary
    52 - Counseling students                          5 - Adult
    53 - Representing school/school program           6 - All Levels
    54 - Involving others in the school program
    55 - Establishing/maintaining professional
         relationships
                                                            SCOPE (SC)
60. Developing Personal Skills
    61 - Accepting self                               1 - Broad Goal Statement
    62 - Evaluating self                              2 - Limited Goal Statement
    63 - Planning for self improvement/improving self 3 - Specific Competency
    64 - Accepting responsibility                     4 - Enabling Skill
    65 - Developing subject related skills
    66 - Accepting others
    67 - Solving problems
                                                           OUTCOME (OC)
70. Developing Pupil Self
    71 - Developing pupil self concept                1 - Intellectual Skill
    72 - Developing social interaction skills         2 - Cognitive Strategy
    73 - Developing learning-to-learn skills          3 - Verbal Information
    74 - Developing acceptance of responsibility      4 - Motor Skill
    75 - Developing attitudes and values              5 - Attitude
```

```
                                          IMPLIED TEACHER (IA)
         OBJECT OF CHANGE (CH)            PERFORMANCE ASSESSMENT

         1 - Self (teacher)               1 - Process criterion
         2 - Pupil                        2 - Human consequences criterion
         3 - Other human                  3 - Product consequence criterion
         4 - Situation                    4 - Both process/consequence
         5 - Resources
```

Figure 11.3 Classification of Teacher Competencies Using Multiple Index

SOURCE: Florida Department of Education, *The Florida Catalog of Teacher Competencies*, Tallahassee, Fla., January 1, 1973, p. 11. Reprinted with permission.

Teacher-Training Modules

In the last few years, teacher-training institutions, state departments of education, and other educational agencies have been producing materials which are known to the profession as teacher-training modules. A large number of these modules is now available for use in preservice and in-service teacher training. Each module focuses on the development of a particular competency. In format a module consists of printed materials often accompanied by other media. The modular approach is an individualized process of training and though modules may be utilized in a group setting, each individual teacher must work through his or her own module.

The Florida Catalog of Teacher Competencies is one of the most comprehensive references to modules currently available. The catalog draws from many sources around the country, including Brigham Young University, Dade County (Florida) Public Schools, *Florida B-2 Modules* project, Florida Department of Education, Florida Middle School Module Project, The Florida State University, the University of Georgia, Northwest Regional Laboratory, Southwest Minnesota State College, State University College at Buffalo, Thiokol Chemical Corporation, University of Toledo, University of Houston, Weber State College, and Western Washington State College. To illustrate the utility of this reference to the supervisor let us employ the aforementioned classification systems and cite one example. Suppose a group of teachers is interested in a teacher's behavior as an empathetic listener. Competency #258 indexes training modules for the development of this particular behavior.[10]

TP 29	258— serve as an empathetic listener for students.
TB 52	*Source: The Role of the Teacher in Individually Prescribed*
CH 1	*Instruction*/C. M. Lindvall and John O. Bolvin.
IA 1,2	*Material*: (1) Weber State *WILKIT* #57,
CA 24	*Tutorial Techniques and School Records.*
PL 6	
SC 2	(2) Fla. B-2 Module. I-1, *Building*
OC 5	*One-to-One Relationships, Human Relations Cluster.*

The symbols to the left refer to the two indexing systems:

TP 29 — Topic 29, Pupil-teacher relations
TB 52 — Teacher Behavior 52, Counseling students
CH 1 — Object of Change 1, Self (teacher)
IA 1,2 — Implied Teacher Performance Assessment 1, Process criterion and 2, Human consequence criterion
CA 24 — Content Area 24, Generic Teaching Skills
PL 6 — Pupil Level 6, All Levels
SC 2 — Scope 2, Limited Goal Statement
OC 5 — Outcome 5, Attitude

Each competency is accompanied by a reference to a source of the particular behavior. Many of the modules have been designed for use in preservice teacher training programs but they are equally valuable in in-service training programs. Not only do the modules provide training in the development of particular skills and competencies but they also serve as standards against which the teacher can evaluate self-performance. The evaluative dimension enters the picture as teachers work through the modules, consider their own performance in relation to the recommendations of the modules, and convince themselves that there are improvements they can make in their performance.

The development of teacher-training modules is a reflection of the interest of institutions and states in the competency-based approach to teacher education.

Two of the better-known sets of teacher-training modules are the *WILKITS* and *B-2 Modules*. The *WILKITS* (Weber State College, Utah *Individualized Learning Kits*) have been produced for Weber State College's preservice training program.[11] Weber State College, one of the early developers of competency-based teacher education programs, has eschewed the traditional approach to teacher education and confronts the students with a series of 85 modules, each of which trains them in some phase of professional education. To give the supervisor an idea of the content of the *WILKITS* a few titles may be cited:

#4 Classroom Management and Discipline
#12 Self-concept
#13 Motivation and Learning
#17 Professional Relationships
#22 Purposes and Methods of Classroom Evaluation
#26 Reading Study Techniques
#81 Classroom Strategies Inquiry

Another source of training materials is the *Florida B-2 Modules* which were developed through a grant from the U.S. Office of Education to the Florida State Department of Education under Part B, Subpart 2, of the Education Professions Development Act.[12] Modules have been prepared and grouped into 10 clusters: I-Teacher Aide Training, II-Planning Skills for Teachers, III-Presentation Skills for Teachers, IV-Classroom Procedures, V-Questioning Skills, VI-Assessment, VII-Special Skills, VIII-Assessing Educational Personnel, IX-School Volunteer Training, and X-Occupational Specialist Program. A variety of films, filmstrips, and audiotapes accompany the printed materials.

The development of modules for teacher training has proceeded at a rapid rate. Schools of education and teacher education centers are sources which the supervisor should check for materials of this type.

Laboratory Approaches

Several approaches to the evaluation of teacher behavior now followed to a large extent in preservice programs are equally suitable to in-service training programs, although in the latter case they pose special operational and motivational problems. Referred to as laboratory or clinical approaches, they include peer teaching and microteaching, both with and without videotaping.

Central to the laboratory approach is microteaching in which a teacher or prospective teacher demonstrates in a clinical setting a particular teaching skill before a small group of students (preferably not his or her own) or peers. The purpose of microteaching is to enable the teachers to gain feedback about their teaching so that they may make improvements. When the microteaching session is conducted with colleagues serving as students, it is called peer teaching. Although microteaching and peer teaching can be carried out in a clinic which is not equipped with videotaping facilities, they gain added impact when videotaped. Taping permits the teacher to view his or her own performance and allows repeated analysis.

Dwight Allen and Kevin Ryan identified 14 general teaching skills which might be developed through microteaching:[13]

- stimulus variation
- set induction
- closure
- silence and nonverbal cues
- reinforcement of student participation
- fluency in asking questions
- probing questions
- higher-order questions
- divergent questions
- recognizing attending behavior
- illustrating and use of examples
- lecturing
- planned repetition
- completeness of communication

The process of microteaching calls for a presentation of a very short (mini) lesson, after which the teacher's performance is critiqued on the basis of an instrument or prespecified set of criteria. After the critique the teacher repeats the lesson and it is again analyzed. When the subjects are students, it is preferable for the lesson repetition to be conducted with a different group of students. The critique of the lesson may be directed by the supervisor or other consultant, a peer, or by the teacher if the lesson is videotaped.

The supervisor should take the initiative to establish a microteaching laboratory in the school or school system. Space and equipment needed are minimal. The laboratory, a small room which is reasonably free from external noise, is usually equipped with a desk, blackboard, video camera, recording and playback unit, and television monitor.

The laboratory approach establishes an artificial, simulated, controlled situation but it provides an opportunity for development or refinement of a particular technique or skill prior to its introduction in a real classroom. A motivational problem exists in stimulating the willingness of the teacher to be placed in a learner-type situation, to appear before colleagues and/or students, and to face criticism, albeit constructive, of his or her performance. An operational problem arises in finding suitable space, providing necessary equipment, and finding a convenient time for all personnel involved—teachers, students, peers, observers, and media maintenance personnel. None of these sets of problems is insurmountable if the laboratory is an accepted and voluntary part of a total in-service program. It is likely that beginning teachers who have not yet begun to develop all the defense mechanisms of experienced teachers will make the most use of the laboratories or clinics. A special incentive such as released time, additional pay, or university credit will make the use of a laboratory approach more palatable to teachers.

Observation Systems

The intensive research into teaching performance has brought into being a number of systems for studying, analyzing, and recording teacher behavior in the classroom. These systems provide a means by which trained observers may record the actual performance of a teacher and by which teachers may evaluate their own performance through the use of videotaped recordings. The ultimate purpose of an observation system is the provision of an opportunity for teachers to systematically analyze their own teaching in order to make improvements. An observation system structures the teacher's evaluation by enabling him or her to look for prespecified aspects of teaching.

Although a few systems of observation analysis are very well known to the profession, many exist which are not as well known. Anita Simon and E. Gil Boyer compiled in 1974 an anthology of 99 observation instruments.[14] It is probable that the present number of observation instruments exceeds twice that figure.

The aspects of teacher performance that the numerous instruments choose for observation vary somewhat from system to system. Some focus on the teacher, some on the pupil, and other on teacher-pupil interaction. Some stress cognitive learning whole others watch for affective behavior. Some emphasize verbal behavior, others, nonverbal behavior. Some instruments are refinements of previously created instruments, capitalizing on the research that has taken place.

"The question naturally arises," said Smith, Cohen, and Pearl, "as to which of the many observation systems should be used for the training of teachers. But a review of the literature indicates that the analyses differ more in the labels used than in the substance of the categories themselves. In other words, there is not as much variation among the analyses as the terminology seems to indicate."[15] A viable procedure for selecting an observation instrument, assuming the decision has been cooperatively reached to engage in analysis of classroom behavior, is the supervisor's appointment of a committee of teachers to study various systems and choose an instrument which they would be willing to use. If they were a particularly creative group, they might even wish to develop their own instrument, an activity which the supervisor might well encourage. The process of selecting or developing an instrument would be valuable in-service training for those participating on the committee.

Teacher Talk	Response	1. *Accepts feeling.* Accepts and clarifies an attitude or the feeling tone of a student in a nonthreatening manner. Feelings may be positive or negative. Predicting and recalling feelings are included. 2. *Praises or encourages.* Praises or encourages students; says "um hum" or "go on"; makes jokes that release tension, but not at the expense of a student. 3. *Accepts or uses ideas of students.* Acknowledges student talk. Clarifies, builds on, or asks questions based on student ideas.
		4. *Asks questions.* Asks questions about content or procedure, based on teacher ideas, with the intent that a student will answer.
	Initiation	5. *Lectures.* Offers facts or opinions about content or procedures; expresses his own ideas, gives his own explanation, or cites an authority other than a student. 6. *Gives directions.* Gives directions, commands, or orders with which a student is expected to comply. 7. *Criticizes student or justifies authority.* Makes statements intended to change student behavior from nonacceptable to acceptable patterns; arbitrarily corrects student answers; bawls someone out. Or states why the teacher is doing what he is doing; uses extreme self-reference.
Student Talk	Response	8. *Student talk—response.* Student talk in response to a teacher contact that structures or limits the situation. Freedom to express own ideas is limited.
	Initiation	9. *Student talk—initiation.* Student initiates or expresses his own ideas, either spontaneously or in response to the teacher's solicitation. Freedom to develop opinions and a line of thought; going beyond existing structure.
Silence		10. *Silence or confusion.* Pauses, short periods of silence, and periods of confusion in which communication cannot be understood by the observer.

Based on Ned A. Flanders, *Analyzing Teaching Behavior*, 1970. No scale is implied by these numbers. Each number is classificatory; it designates a particular kind of communication event. To write these numbers down during observation is to enumerate, not to judge a position on a scale.

Figure 11.4 Flanders Interaction Analysis Categories (FIAC)

SOURCE: Ned A. Flanders et al., *Interaction Analysis: Teacher Handbook*, San Francisco, Calif., Far West Laboratory for Educational Research and Development, 1972, p. 5.

It would be impossible and superfluous for this text to examine all of the observation instruments now available. The Simon and Boyer reference analyzed 99 of these instruments as to focus of the system, coding units used, uses to which the system can be put, and setting in which the systems have been used. The supervisor and the committee might begin their work by sending for copies of the instruments and accompanying explanatory literature of systems in which they may have a particular interest.

To give an idea of what kinds of behavior the developers of observation instruments consider important enough to be observed and analyzed—and as a consequence, to be improved—we will examine the categories of two instruments: Ned A.

Flanders' Flanders Interaction Analysis Categories (FIAC) (Figure 11.4) and Bruce W. Tuckman's *Tuckman Teacher Feedback Form* (Figure 11.5).

Observation analysis has been introduced in this chapter with the Flanders and Tuckman instruments in order to point out that teachers can utilize a systematic form of observation in analyzing their own performance. Classroom observation by the supervisor will be discussed at greater length with additional examples of observation instruments in the chapter on clinical supervision which follows.

Flanders' system concentrates on verbal interaction while Tuckman's instrument assesses classroom climate. Flanders' system prescribes a tally every three seconds while Tuckman's system uses a simple checklist. Both instruments may be used for either self-appraisal or appraisal to judge teachers' performance on items assessed by these instruments. When teachers apply the Flanders' instrument to assess their own performance, they may do so by reviewing a transcript, audiotape, or videotape of the lessons. The Tuckman instrument may be converted from an appraisal form to a teacher preference or self-appraisal form by changing the data at the top of the in-

Person Observed_____   Observer_____
Date: _____

1.	ORIGINAL	—:—:—:—:—:—	CONVENTIONAL
2.	PATIENT	—:—:—:—:—:—	IMPATIENT
3.	COLD	—:—:—:—:—:—	WARM
4.	HOSTILE	—:—:—:—:—:—	AMIABLE
5.	CREATIVE	—:—:—:—:—:—	ROUTINIZED
6.	INHIBITED	—:—:—:—:—:—	UNINHIBITED
7.	ICONOCLASTIC	—:—:—:—:—:—	RITUALISTIC
8.	GENTLE	—:—:—:—:—:—	HARSH
9.	UNFAIR	—:—:—:—:—:—	FAIR
10.	CAPRICIOUS	—:—:—:—:—:—	PURPOSEFUL
11.	CAUTIOUS	—:—:—:—:—:—	EXPERIMENTING
12.	DISORGANIZED	—:—:—:—:—:—	ORGANIZED
13.	UNFRIENDLY	—:—:—:—:—:—	SOCIABLE
14.	RESOURCEFUL	—:—:—:—:—:—	UNCERTAIN
15.	RESERVED	—:—:—:—:—:—	OUTSPOKEN
16.	IMAGINATIVE	—:—:—:—:—:—	EXACTING
17.	ERRATIC	—:—:—:—:—:—	SYSTEMATIC
18.	AGGRESSIVE	—:—:—:—:—:—	PASSIVE
19.	ACCEPTING (people)	—:—:—:—:—:—	CRITICAL
20.	QUIET	—:—:—:—:—:—	BUBBLY
21.	OUTGOING	—:—:—:—:—:—	WITHDRAWN
22.	IN CONTROL	—:—:—:—:—:—	ON THE RUN
23.	FLIGHTY	—:—:—:—:—:—	CONSCIENTIOUS
24.	DOMINANT	—:—:—:—:—:—	SUBMISSIVE
25.	OBSERVANT	—:—:—:—:—:—	PREOCCUPIED
26.	INTROVERTED	—:—:—:—:—:—	EXTRAVERTED
27.	ASSERTIVE	—:—:—:—:—:—	SOFT-SPOKEN
28.	TIMID	—:—:—:—:—:—	ADVENTUROUS

Figure 11.5 Tuckman Teacher Feedback Form (Short Form)

SOURCE: Bruce Wayne Tuckman, "New Instrument: The Tuckman Teacher Feedback Form (TTFF), *Journal of Educational Measurement* 13, no. 3 (Fall 1976), p. 234. Reprinted with permission.

strument shown in Figure 11.5 from "Person Observed," "Observer," and "Data" to "Name," "Date," and "My Preference for."

Observation analysis can be implemented in a number of ways. Proceeding from an external approach to an internal approach, the means of utilizing observation instruments are prescribed below.

The teacher may view videotapes of classroom sessions or protocol materials showing other teachers in action and apply an instrument to these recordings of teacher performance. The teacher may analyze that performance and make recommendations *for that teacher*. By indirection the teacher may also be making self-recommendations.

The teacher may permit an observation of his or her teaching to be made live in the classroom—without taping—by an outside, trained observer, by a colleague, or by the supervisor who will employ an observation instrument and review the observation with the teacher. This approach is, perhaps, the most threatening of all approaches and one which many teachers cannot constitutionally take. It requires extremely broad shoulders for a teacher to ask for and receive what amounts to a criticism, even in the most positive terms, of his or her teaching, especially in the kind of face-to-face arrangement of this approach.

The teacher may allow himself or herself to be taped and may ask a trained observer, colleague, or supervisor to apply an observation instrument to the taped session and then review the analysis with the teacher. The element of threat is still present but it is softened by the relative remoteness of the videotape. It is less threatening because the teacher is not undergoing analytical observation while teaching but afterward when the observer views the tape.

The teacher may arrange for himself or herself to be taped and then personally use an observation instrument to critique the performance. Except in the case of research studies when observations must be carried out by trained members of a research staff, this approach holds the most promise for lasting change and continuous improvement in teaching performance. This threat-free approach encourages teachers to look at their own teaching, knowing that no one is present to criticize them for poor performance.

In order to achieve reliable observation, the observer (who may actually be the teacher) must be thoroughly familiar with the categories of behavior to be observed and the procedures for recording and interpreting the data. The observer should undergo a training period and a number of practice sessions, perhaps with video-tapes or protocols, to gain skill in using the instrument. Since the supervisor will wish each teacher to develop the proficiency of analyzing his or her own behavior, in-service training in the observation system must precede actual utilization of the system.

Access to portable videotaping equipment is a must if teachers are ever going to see themselves in action and be able to study their own performance. No matter how helpful an observer may be to a teacher there is nothing which can replace a teacher's viewing his or her own performance.

Flanders' observation instrument and one designed by E. Wayne Roberson,[16] were utilized in a research project which permitted teachers of the Tucson Public

Schools to study their own behavior from videotape recordings made in their own classrooms.[17] This research study, known as the Teacher Self-Appraisal Program, stated its purpose as follows:

The basic purpose of the program is to help teachers to be aware of their attitudes and classroom behavior in light of their behavioral objectives. Then, if they see that their classroom behavior is not in accord with their attitudes and behavioral objectives, they can initiate a change in their behavior.[18]

The study hypothesized that "if teachers could see themselves interacting with their students in the classroom, in the light of their behavioral objectives, they would be better able to appraise and analyze their behavior."[19] To test the hypothesis the project used the following procedures:[20]

1. Instruction in writing behavioral objectives.
2. Group situations so teachers could communicate their attitudes and ideas to each other.
3. Videotapes of their classroom behavior.
4. Instruction in analytically viewing their classroom behavior through the use of Flanders' and Roberson's codes.

The Tucson study concluded that teachers who participated in the program were:

• spending significantly less time giving information
• spending significantly more time calling for responses from students
• spending significantly less time on Demonstration
• using significantly more Receptive Verbal and Non-Verbal expressions
• using significantly less Routine Verbal and Non-Verbal expressions[21]

The study found no significant overall change in cognitive objectives or methods used by the teachers but it did find overall significant changes in the affective objectives and verbal and nonverbal behavior.

Faculties considering the use of observation instruments might wish to create and try out a simplified, even rough or crude, instrument to become familiar with the concept of observation analysis. Their initial efforts at creating an instrument might result in a simple instrument such as the one shown below on which an observer would make tallies of each evidence of the specified behaviors of the teacher and students.

Teacher Behavior		*Student Behavior*	
	TALLY		TALLY
Lecturing _____		Responding to teacher's questions _____	
Leading discussion _____		Asking questions of the teacher _____	
Questioning orally _____		Participation in class discussion _____	

Teacher Behavior		*Student Behavior*	
	TALLY		TALLY
Reinforcing pupil responses _____		Participating in work activities _____	
Directing class activities _____		Performing leadership role _____	
Moving about the class _____		Misbehaving _____	

When utilizing an instrument of this nature the observer—who could be the teacher with the use of videotapes of his or her own classes—makes a tally mark every time the teacher evidences any of the specified teacher behaviors and every time any pupil shows any of the behaviors in the student behavior column. Such a simplified instrument may be used as an introduction to more sophisticated and validated instruments. Observation analysis through the use of coding instruments offers a productive route for helping teachers to evaluate themselves.

Through the study of models of teaching, the use of selected media and training modules, the use of laboratories, and the application of observation systems, teacher performance can be evaluated. With the utilization of videotaping equipment in the classroom and clinic teachers can be helped to appraise and improve their own teaching.

Evaluation of Personal-Professional Attributes

Moving from the evaluation of cognitive and instructional skills to the areas of personal and professional attributes presents new problems. Not only is it difficult to define the personal and professional attributes which teachers ought to possess and on which there is universal agreement but it is also difficult to measure these and, if they are found to be lacking, to effect a change in the teacher.

How does one judge relationships with administrators, for example? Should subservience be rewarded over outspokenness? How do you rate appearance? Should a teacher be penalized for obesity, for example? Does an attractive, handsome teacher rate higher in appearance than a plain, unattractive person? Are the teacher's memberships and participation in professional organizations of concern to administrators? If so, should the teacher be evaluated by number of memberships or by degree of participation? In the eyes of the administrator is membership in a professional organization today a plus or a minus?

If teachers are to be evaluated by someone else—or by themselves—on personal-professional attributes, these traits must be clearly spelled out and instances of behavior wherein the attributes can be demonstrated must be described. The democratic approach to supervision would dictate the principle that teachers be involved in deciding what personal-professional attributes will be evaluated and what evidences of these traits will be recorded. Beyond insubordination and criminal and moral offenses, personal and professional attributes are most difficult to nail down.

Certain personality characteristics and certain human relations skills are essential to successful teacher performance, such as:

- sense of humor
- ability to relate to other teachers, students, administrators, and the public
- adequate self-concept
- open personality
- respect for the individual
- absence of prejudice
- respect for excellence
- respect for the confidentiality of school matters
- cooperative attitude
- industriousness

These are but a few of the general personality traits which are necessary for success in any field or in life as a whole.

The problem for the supervisor when trying to help teachers evaluate their personal and professional attributes is to find ways by which they may reflect on their own traits, agree that there is need for improvement, and make changes accordingly. Personality traits are especially difficult to change, engrained as they are in the individual's history, life style, and philosophy of life.

Are there any techniques which may help teachers evaluate themselves on personal and professional attributes? There are, but as every clergyman realizes, no amount of sermonizing will succeed in moving a person to change behavior if the person does not wish to change.

The supervisor may once again begin with an external approach—an intellectualizing of traits which individuals feel teachers should possess. The process of identifying these traits and agreeing on ways they can be observed are the first hurdles to be cleared. The supervisor might direct teachers to some of the literature on the development of the self-concept and the meaning of the self-actualizing personality, such as found in the writings of Arthur W. Combs,[22] Earl C. Kelley,[23] and Abraham H. Maslow.[24] The popular 1962 Yearbook of the Association for Supervision and Curriculum Development is another helpful source of writings on these topics.[25]

It is in this area that consultants may be helpful to groups of teachers, if only for the purpose of bringing them inspirational messages. The use of certain personality inventories and attitude instruments such as William C. Schutz' *FIRO-B*, a series of 54 statements designed to explore ways in which individuals interact with other people, may lead teachers into greater awareness of certain personal traits.[26]

There is a school of thought which warmly endorses encounter groups or sensitivity training—"touchy-feely," in the vernacular—as the answer to the search for ways for individuals to change their behavior. Yet, some reservations have been expressed about possible negative effects of sensitivity training on some participants and caution is required that such training be on a voluntary basis, free of pressure to participate, and stringently controlled.[27]

The issue of evaluating personal and professional attributes leads to two conclusions: (1) If a supervisor is called on to evaluate a teacher in respect to these traits, the attributes to be evaluated should cover a very limited, specifically defined, and observable set of characteristics agreed on in advance by teachers. (2) Lasting change can only come about as teachers evaluate their own behavior and internalize the necessity for change.

Using Evaluation Instruments

If the supervisor is required to evaluate teachers annually or periodically for reporting purposes, a task discussed more fully in Chapter 13, teachers should enter fully into the evaluation process. What William Goldstein called "goal-oriented supervision"[28] is a desirable approach. With this approach the teacher and supervisor agree on what areas of performance the teacher will work on during the year. When it comes time for an evaluation at the end of the year, the supervisor and teacher meet and evaluate whether or not and to what degree the teacher has improved in the performance areas.

Thomas J. Watman reported on the goal-oriented evaluation process carried out in Keene, New Hampshire.[29] Watman outlined the steps followed in the process.

1. Each teacher evaluates himself or herself on 26 performance standards grouped under five categories of growth: professional preparation, instructional skills, management abilities, personal characteristics, and performance level of students.
2. The supervisor evaluates the teacher on the same 26 performance standards.
3. The supervisor and teacher discuss the evaluations and agree on three to five standards which the teacher will work on during the year.
4. The supervisor and teacher jointly monitor the performance of the teacher on the agreed-on standards during the year.
5. At the end of the year both the supervisor and teacher evaluate the teacher's performance on the agreed-on standards and further agree on the job targets for the next year.

This approach to evaluation fulfills the principle of bringing the teacher into the evaluation process. Further, it delimits the job targets and the teacher is not required to demonstrate improvement across the board, which is a much more realistic approach than expecting improvement in many or all performance areas.[30]

The Cincinnati Public Schools have developed an in-depth teacher appraisal system which consists of evaluation by principals[31] and teacher self-evaluation.[32] The process of evaluation of the teacher (appraisee) by the administrator (appraiser) consists of the following steps:

I. Review appraisees' responsibilities as specified in the following documents:
   A. *Board Policies—Cincinnati Board of Education*

    B. The *Collective Bargaining Contract*

    C. Individual employee's contract

    D. Local school handbook/faculty manual

    E. Instructional guides provided by the school system and/or local school.

  II. Conduct orientation sessions and respond to inquiries related to the appraisal process.

 III. Conduct observations, on at least a monthly basis from the beginning of the school year, which should be followed by conferences when feasible during which appraisees are informed of their performance levels. Complete "Observation Report Forms" and distribute copies within one week of observations.

 IV. Hold appraisal conference during which job targets will be finalized and the five major roles discussed in detail. Job targets should be demonstrable, observable, and measurable. They should relate to the teaching assignment. The *Manual for Self-Appraisal* contains performance standards which should be helpful in formulating job targets. In the event it is necessary for job targets to be specified by appraisers, this fact shall be indicated on the "Job Development Form."

  V. Complete "Job Target Progress Report" and "Performance Evaluation Summary" and hold final appraisal conference.

 VI. Submit copies of completed forms to participants and Certificated Personnel Branch in compliance with designated dates.[33]

JOB TARGET DEVELOPMENT FORM

This form is to be used by the appraisee and appraisers to develop tentative job targets and also to list the negotiated job targets established during the initial appraisal conference.

Appraisee_____School_____Grade/Subject_____

Appraisers_____Date_____

STATEMENT OF JOB TARGETS MUTUALLY AGREED UPON BY APPRAISEE AND APPRAISERS IN ORDER OF PRIORITY:

_____

STATEMENT OF SPECIFIC MEANS TO BE EMPHASIZED IN THE ATTAINMENT OF EACH JOB TARGET.

_____   _____
   Appraisee's Signature   Appraisers' Signature(s)

Distribution: Copy 1 - Principal; Copy 2 - Instructional Consultant;
               Copy 3 - Appraisee

Figure 11.6 Job Target Development Form

SOURCE: Cincinnati Public Schools, *Teacher Appraisal Manual*, Cincinnati, Ohio, Certificated Personnel Branch, July 1978, p. 17. Reprinted with permission.

The supervisor may participate as an appraiser if requested to do so by the principal or the teacher. Whether serving as an appraiser or not, the supervisor (called "instructional consultant") is kept informed of the teacher's performance and progress and receives copies of the completed evaluation forms.

To gather, report, and record the data required by the evaluation process the Cincinnati Public Schools have created five instruments or forms as follows:

1. *Job Target Development Form.* On this form (Figure 11.6), which the principal fills out, the teacher and principal state agreed on job targets for the year and means of achieving these targets. The role of the supervisor at this stage of the evaluation process is described in the following terms, "It is recommended that all supervisors be involved in the establishment of job targets even though they may not be identified as appraisers."[34]

2. *Observation Report Form.* The appraiser using this form (Figure 11.7) reports observations of teacher classroom performance relative to the job targets and five major roles mentioned above.

3. *Job Targets Progress Report.* The teacher and principal fill out a copy of this form (Figure 11.8) prior to the final appraisal conference between the teacher and principal. On this form the teacher and principal report in the respective comment sections how well they perceive the teacher to have done in relation to job targets. If the teacher or principal feels that certain job targets have not been reached, an explanation is provided. Copies of a completed form are attached to the summary of the final appraisal.

CINCINNATI PUBLIC SCHOOLS
Certificated Personnel Branch

OBSERVATION REPORT FORM

Appraisee_____School_____Grade/Subject_____

Appraiser_____Date_____

Time of Arrival_____Time of Departure_____

Type of Activity Observed_____

(Note: Not Carbonized - Use carbon paper)

Distribution: Copy 1 - Personnel (to be submitted with final appraisal reports)
               Copy 2 - Observer; Copy 3 - Other Appraiser; Copy 4 - Appraisee

Figure 11.7 Observation Report Form

SOURCE: Cincinnati Public Schools, *Teacher Appraisal Manual*, Cincinnati, Ohio, Certificated Personnel Branch, July 1978, p. 18. Reprinted with permission.

```
                          JOB TARGETS PROGRESS REPORT


This form is to be completed during the final appraisal conference between the
appraisee and appraisers.

Appraisee_____School_____Grade/Subject_____

Appraisers_____Date_____

                         Appraisee's Comments          Appraisers' Comments
 Job Target(s)              on Progress                   on Progress
```

```
_____          _____
    Appraisee's Signature               Appraisers' Signature(s)
```

```
Distribution:  Copy 1 - Personnel; Copy 2 - Instructional consultant;
               Copy 3 - Principal; Copy 4 - Appraisee
```

Figure 11.8 Job Targets Progress Report

SOURCE: Cincinnati Public Schools, *Teacher Appraisal Manual*, Cincinnati, Ohio, Certificated Personnel Branch, July 1978, p. 19. Reprinted with permission.

4. *Performance Evaluation Summary for Teachers.* The principal completes the form (Figure 11.9) prior to the final appraisal conference with the teacher, evaluating the teacher's progress in respect to the five major roles. While both the principal and teacher sign the completed summary form, the teacher's signature does not necessarily imply agreement with the principal's evaluation.

5. *Self-Appraisal Instrument.* The self-appraisal instrument, *Principles of the Self-Appraisal* (Figure 11.10), is an extensive personal inventory designed to permit the teacher to make a self-appraisal on the five major roles considered important by the school system. This is a personal exercise in which the teacher may decide to participate or not. The *Teacher Appraisal Manual* observes, "Appraisees are encouraged to administer the self-appraisal process which is voluntary."[35]

PERFORMANCE EVALUATION SUMMARY FOR TEACHERS

Appraisee_____ School_____ Grade/Subject_____

Appraiser(s)_____ Date_____

U - Unsatisfactory   S - Satisfactory   O - Outstanding
M - Marginal   VG - Very Good

			U	M	S	VG	O

I. Instructional Leader
    Knowledge of and preparation for field of
    specialization; use of appropriate methods,
    techniques and resources.
    COMMENTS:

II. Social Interaction Leader
    Teacher-pupil rapport; classroom interpersonal
    relationships; provision for appropriate success
    experiences for each student.
    COMMENTS:

III. Promoter of Healthful Emotional Growth
     Use of appropriate techniques and school-community
     resources in resolving adjustment problems;
     maintains a positive learning environment.
     COMMENTS:

IV. Communications Facilitator among school personnel,
    parents and community participants
    Presents positive image as an employee of Board of
    Education; provides adequate, accurate information
    about educational programs.
    COMMENTS:

V. Professional Educator
    Behavioral characteristics and professional
    relationships related to successful job performance.
    COMMENTS:

OVERALL PERFORMANCE EVALUATION
COMMENTS:

_____   _____
    Appraisee's Signature   Appraisers' Signature(s)

The appraisee's signature does not necessarily signify agreement with the evaluation.
Distribution: Copy 1 - Staff Personnel; Copy 2 - Principal;
               Copy 3 - Instructional Consultant; Copy 4 - Appraisee

Figure 11.9 Performance Evaluation Summary for Teachers

SOURCE: Cincinnati Public Schools, *Teacher Appraisal Manual*, Cincinnati, Ohio, Certificated Personnel Branch, July 1978, p. 20. Reprinted with permission.

ROLE I—INSTRUCTIONAL LEADER

CATEGORY A

The teacher understands and applies psychological readiness principles. Readiness for new learning is a state of mastery of simpler skills that permits a pupil to master more advanced skills. Readiness is a complex product of the interactions of physiological maturation, psychological abilities, prerequisite learning, and motivation. New experience presented too early or too late may be less effective and even damaging to pupil development.

CODE: FP—Frequently Practiced IP—Infrequently Practiced
NA—Non Applicable

		FP	IP	NA
A-1	The teacher ascertains each student's mastery of simpler tasks prerequisite to the task at hand.	☐	☐	☐
A-2	The teacher recognizes that there are often wide variations in psychological-readiness levels within each pupil, and adjusts instructional techniques accordingly or provides experiences designed to raise low levels of readiness.	☐	☐	☐
A-3	The teacher persists in his efforts to raise skill level in cases of individuals who have apparently reached plateaus, since some may be "late bloomers" capable of surpassing formerly superior students.	☐	☐	☐
A-4	The teacher gives the child enough experiences with several materials that incorporate the same concept, words, or skill before he shifts to another concept, word, or skill.	☐	☐	☐
A-5	The teacher obtains knowledge of the child's past achievement, his intellectual ability, and utilizes this knowledge in preparing for the classwork and assignments.	☐	☐	☐
A-6	The teacher gives the child time to assimilate learning experiences before the presentation of new learning experiences.	☐	☐	☐
A-7	The teacher uses a variety of objective evaluation techniques to assess student readiness.	☐	☐	☐

NUMBER OF PRINCIPLES IN THE CATEGORY LESS THOSE WHICH DO NOT APPLY	NUMBER OF PRINCIPLES IN THE CATEGORY PRACTICED FREQUENTLY	PERFORMANCE INDEX FOR CATEGORY I-A

CATEGORY B

The teacher provides a success-oriented learning environment for each student. Tasks that establish such an environment for a pupil tend to facilitate motivation, feelings of competence, adjustment, and achievement.

		FP	IP	NA
B-1	The teacher provides classroom challenges within the range of ability of the pupils in the class.	☐	☐	☐
B-2	The teacher demonstrates awareness that classroom challenges may make demands on social and motor-coordination skills as well as on academic skills.	☐	☐	☐

(9 principles)

Figure 11.10 Principles of the Self-appraisal

The teacher plans skillfully for an effective teaching-learning situation.

	FP	IP	NA
C-1 The teacher endeavors to make the physical setting conducive to learning.	☐	☐	☐
C-2 The teacher, whenever possible or appropriate, involves his students in formulating educational objectives and in planning instructional activities.	☐	☐	☐

(6 principles)

CATEGORY D

The teacher individualizes instruction where appropriate. Pupils may vary in readiness for new learning due to a number of factors. A good teacher makes routine provision for readiness through effective assessment and through adjustment in the "range of challenge" presented to individual students.

	FP	IP	NA
D-1 The teacher uses recent "IQ" scores available, achievement test results, pupil-interest levels, etc., as possible predictors of readiness to learn.	☐	☐	☐
D-2 The teacher reclassifies, when possible, advanced or retarded pupils as recent evidence indicates that variation in the rate of intellectual growth has occurred.	☐	☐	☐

(8 principles)

CATEGORY E

The teacher facilitates student motivation toward academic and social achievement. Teachers who motivate pupils to learn contribute to pupil growth in cognitive abilities and academic and social-skill mastery.

	FP	IP	NA
E-1 The teacher helps pupils believe that achievement at a higher level is possible.	☐	☐	☐
E-2 The teacher helps pupils believe that they should try harder to achieve.	☐	☐	☐

(9 principles)

CATEGORY F

The teacher facilitates intellectual development. Pupils' cognitive abilities increase when there is deliberate attempt to (a) help the pupil perceive differences and arrive at generalizations, and (b) increase the pupil's ability to use words and deal with abstractions.

	FP	IP	NA
F-1 The teacher encourages logical reasoning.	☐	☐	☐
F-2 The teacher points out relevancy and provides organizational guidelines for pupils prior to learning new material.	☐	☐	☐

(11 principles)

Figure 11.10 (continued)

The teacher facilitates motor-skill development. Speaking, singing, playing games, and physical activities are skill areas that may be facilitated by the teacher.

	FP	IP	NA
G-1 The teacher helps pupils grow in articulation abilities.	☐	☐	☐
G-2 The teacher helps pupils grow in the ability to walk, run, skip, dance, climb, throw, catch, etc.	☐	☐	☐

(8 principles)

CATEGORY H

The teacher uses effective reinforcement techniques. Learning is more rapid and less apt to be lost if performance is accompanied or followed by reinforcement in general accordance with principles of effective reinforcement.

	FP	IP	NA
H-1 The teacher provides opportunities for pupils to experience intrinsic satisfaction from successful performance whenever possible.	☐	☐	☐
H-2 The teacher selects extrinsic satisfactions according to the unique needs of each individual pupil.	☐	☐	☐

(14 principles)

CATEGORY I

The teacher accurately interprets evaluation results and uses the information to improve the conditions of learning.

	FP	IP	NA
I-1 The teacher takes into account general characteristics affecting the testing situation, such as reading speed, vocabulary, comprehension, "clerical" test-taking skills, the chance factor, and test anxiety.	☐	☐	☐
I-2 The teacher takes into account temporary characteristics affecting the testing situation, such as: health, motivation and set, environmental testing conditions, fatigue, and memory lapse.	☐	☐	☐

(11 principles)

CATEGORY J

The teacher understands and applies sound principles of learning.

	FP	IP	NA
J-1 The teacher understands that transfer of learning occurs whenever previous learning is related to later learning.	☐	☐	☐
J-2 The teacher teaches for the application of the principles underlying the content of his subject.	☐	☐	☐

(17 principles)

Figure 11.10 (*continued*)

ROLE II—SOCIAL INTERACTION LEADER

The teacher establishes a democratic classroom atmosphere. The democratic classroom atmosphere as referred to here is defined as one containing elements of warmth *and effective limit-keeping*. Such an atmosphere has been shown to promote higher levels of creativity, peer interaction, motivation, sex-role identification, and acceptable public behavior.

	FP	IP	NA
A-1 The teacher provides a level of acceptance in the classroom that allows pupils to feel socially worthy.	☐	☐	☐
A-2 The teacher reacts sympathetically to pupil problems.	☐	☐	☐

(7 principles)

CATEGORY B

The teacher guides peer interactions effectively. Teachers who are knowledgeable about the principles of group dynamics can increase peer acceptance of isolates, guide peer groups into socially acceptable paths, encourage individual development of social skills.

	FP	IP	NA
B-1 The teacher serves as a constructive influence on the nature and direction of peer relationships by establishing rapport with students.	☐	☐	☐
B-2 The teacher attempts to determine the reasons a social isolate is not participating in peer activities.	☐	☐	☐

(13 principles)

CATEGORY C

The teacher adjusts social interaction activities to group norms. Since social readiness is determined by physiological maturation and various kinds of social experiences, the teacher must be aware of the general level of motivation and skill in peer interaction of the pupils in his classroom and be able to promote those activities within the "range of challenge" of the group.

	FP	IP	NA
C-1 The teacher takes into account that the student's ability to perceive intentions and motivations of others, to perform social roles, and to control aggressive impulses develops gradually throughout the school years.	☐	☐	☐
C-2 The teacher takes into account that adolescents must show more initiative in order to achieve peer acceptance than they did as children.	☐	☐	☐

(3 principles)

Figure 11.10 (*continued*)

The teacher adapts classroom activities to the pupil who is atypical in terms of social skills. A good teacher makes routine provision for immature and advanced pupils by adjusting social demands toward their "range of challenge."

	FP	IP	NA
D-1 The teacher gives support to pupils experiencing social stress due to late or early physical maturation.	☐	☐	☐
D-2 The teacher makes a special effort to discover isolates and to increase their social acceptability with classmates.	☐	☐	☐

(7 principles)

CATEGORY E

The teacher facilitates development of moral character and moral behavior. Teachers who help pupils develop favorable attitudes toward moral and social values, who encourage growth in the understanding of values, and who provide practice in moral behavior, contribute to the ability of the pupil to guide his own behavior in a mature manner.

	FP	IP	NA
E-1 The teacher takes into account that moral character and moral behavior are learned in part by the student's identification with an imitation of admired, respected models.	☐	☐	☐
E-2 The teacher takes into account that moral character and moral behavior are learned in part by experiencing repeated satisfaction from the possession of the expression of moral values.	☐	☐	☐

(5 principles)

ROLE III—PROMOTER OF HEALTHFUL EMOTIONAL DEVELOPMENT

CATEGORY A

The teacher recognizes symptoms of poor adjustment. Depending upon the adaptive habits of individual pupils, the teacher should be able to recognize the subtle symptoms of high emotional tension as well as the withdrawal and aggressive responses pupils resort to in an effort to reduce uncomfortable levels of emotional tension.

	FP	IP	NA
A-1 The teacher takes into account that thumb sucking, fingernail biting, tics, hyperactivity, overreacting, etc., function as tension-reduction behaviors, and may be symptomatic of high anxiety.	☐	☐	☐
A-2 The teacher takes into account that low self-esteem and inappropriate levels of aspiration are symptomatic of high anxiety.	☐	☐	☐

(6 principles)

Figure 11.10 (*continued*)

The teacher reduces disabling levels of anxiety. Teachers should be aware of techniques useful in reducing anxiety and be able to skillfully apply the most appropriate techniques in the classroom situation.

		FP	IP	NA
B-1	The teacher absolutely avoids the use of psychotherapy techniques requiring a great deal of sophisticated training for safe, effective practice.	□	□	□
B-2	The teacher gives extra emotional support to those pupils who are experiencing high-stress feelings.	□	□	□

(11 principles)

CATEGORY C

The teacher strengthens weak skill areas as an aid to adjustment. Pupils often exhibit high anxiety because of a lack of ability to adapt to the demands of their situation. Teachers should attempt to engage in academic and social skill remediation with these pupils.

		FP	IP	NA
C-1	The teacher takes into account that pupils are often anxious because of a chronic lack of ability to adapt and because of a lack of ability to achieve normal satisfactions through their own efforts.	□	□	□
C-2	The teacher encourages independent pupil behavior, provides acceptance for the pupil in spite of mistakes and failures, and gives guidance appropriate to meeting the demands of the task.	□	□	□

(8 principles)

CATEGORY D

The teacher uses effective case-study methods and employs necessary referral techniques. In order to provide the most supportive situation for an anxious pupil, the teacher must be able to gather and analyze background information bearing on the emotional disorder, and develop tentative plans for the amelioration of the problem.

		FP	IP	NA
D-1	The teacher takes into account the need for careful analysis of a pupil's situation when the usual trial-and-error approaches to reducing pupil anxiety have not been effective.	□	□	□
D-2	The teacher asks for the help of and works with parents and school specialists when conducting an analysis of a pupil's situation.	□	□	□

(7 principles)

ROLE IV—COMMUNICATOR WITH PARENTS AND COLLEAGUES

CATEGORY A

The teacher communicates information and suggestions to parents and colleagues about the intellectual, social, and emotional development of his students. Teachers should be aware of the effect of parental behavior and attitudes on children and should be able to interpret

Figure 11.10 (*continued*)

progress of students to parents or colleagues in a positive fashion and make suggestions for enhancing or remediating intellectual, social and emotional development.

	FP	IP	NA
A-1 The teacher takes into account that parents are given the prime responsibility for educating their child and that the teacher is acting as agent for the parents.	☐	☐	☐
A-2 The teacher takes into account that parental patterns of supervision lead to different patterns of performance in children.	☐	☐	☐

(10 principles)

ROLE V—PROFESSONAL EDUCATOR

CATEGORY A

All staff members in the Cincinnati Public Schools are expected to contribute to the overall functioning of the school system by assuming responsibilities other than classroom teaching, conducting themselves appropriately and developing positive professional relationships.

	FP	IP	NA
A-1 The staff member's attire and grooming is appropriate for the instructional setting in which he performs.	☐	☐	☐
A-2 The staff member completes all required records promptly, legibly and accurately.	☐	☐	☐

(6 principles)

Figure 11.10 (*continued*)

SOURCE: Cincinnati Public Schools, *Teacher Self-Appraisal Manual*, Cincinnati, Ohio, Certificated Personnel Branch, August 1974, p. 8–27.

The self-appraisal instrument is divided into five sections, each section corresponding to one of the five major roles previously mentioned. A description of one or more categories within each of the major roles is given and each description is followed by a number of teaching principles to which the teacher responds "frequently practiced," "infreqently practiced," and "non-applicable."

The teacher can compute a performance index for each category of the instrument by (1) counting the number of principles in each category less those which do not apply, (2) counting the number of principles in each category to which he or she has responded "frequently practiced," and (3) consulting a Performance Index Calculation Chart to determine the performance index for each category. After calculating the performance index on each category, the teacher can plot the indices on a Profile Blank which shows graphically the teacher's perceived strengths and weaknesses in relation to the five major roles.

To show how the self-appraisal instrument is constructed Role I-Instructional Leader-Category A is reproduced in its entirety (seven principles) while portions of the remaining roles and categories are also reproduced. Space precludes reproduction of the entire instrument since the complete instrument contains 183 principles divided into 21 categories.

The Teacher Facilitates Motor-Skill Development...

		FP	IP	NA
G-1	The teacher helps pupils grow in articulation abilities.	☑	☐	☐
G-2	The teacher helps pupils grow in the ability to walk, run, skip, dance, climb, throw, catch, etc.	☐	☐	☑
G-3	The teacher helps pupils grow in the ability to manipulate objects and instruments with their hands and fingers.	☑	☐	☐
G-4	The teacher gives training and provides opportunity for well-motivated practice.	☐	☑	☐
G-5	The teacher relates achievement standards for motor-skill development to student maturation.	☑	☐	☐
G-6	The teacher groups pupils for motor-skill practice to avoid loss of social acceptability that usually accompanies demonstrated motor-skill inadequacy.	☐	☑	☐
G-7	The teacher refrains from making predictions about pupil abilities in various motor-skills on the basis of demonstrated ability in one or two skills.	☐	☑	☐
G-8	The teacher refers motor-skill deficiencies to appropriate diagnostic and treatment specialists such as school psychologist, speech therapist, school nurse, etc. when deviations from normal standards occur.	☑	☐	☐

Now here is what the particular category you have been working with will look like. There are eight teaching principles determining that one (1) was not applicable, four (4) were frequently practiced, and three (3) were infrequently practiced. You have subtracted the one (NA) from the total of eight and entered the total number of principles that you work with in some form, which is seven (7), in the proper blank at the bottom. You have also entered the number of principles frequently practiced, four (4), in the proper blank at the bottom of the category. YOU ARE NOW READY TO COMPUTE YOUR PERFORMANCE INDEX FOR THIS CATEGORY!

7	4	↘
Number of Principles in the Category Less Those Which Do Not Apply	Number of Principles in the Category Frequently Practiced	Performance Index

Figure 11.11 Calculation of a Performance Index

SOURCE: Cincinnati Public Schools, *Teacher Self-Appraisal Manual*, Cincinnati, Ohio, Certificated Personnel Branch, August 1974, p. 5. Reprinted with permission.

When the teacher has completed the self-appraisal inventory, the next steps are the calculation of performance indices for each category and the construction of a profile. The *Teacher Self-Appraisal Manual* provides an illustration of the calculation of a performance index (Figure 11.11).

As the instructions for calculating the performance will show, a teacher who responds to the eight principles of Category G, Role I, deciding that one principle is not applicable and that he or she frequently practices four of the seven applicable principles, writes the numbers seven and four at the bottom of the section of the instrument on the appropriate blanks. To determine quickly the performance index for a particular category the teacher turns to the Performance Index Calculation Chart (shown in Figure 11.12), which is in reality a chart of quotients in which the numbers

The Number of Principles In The Category Frequently Practiced

The Number Of Principles In The Category Less Those Which Do Not Apply	1	2	3	4	5	6	7	8	9	10	11	12	13	14	15	16	17
1	1.00																
2	.50	1.00															
3	.33	.67	1.00														
4	.25	.50	.75	1.00													
5	.20	.40	.60	.80	1.00												
6	.17	.33	.50	.67	.83	1.00											
7	.14	.29	.43	.57	.71	.86	1.00										
8	.13	.25	.38	.50	.63	.75	.88	1.00									
9	.11	.22	.33	.44	.56	.67	.78	.89	1.00								
10	.10	.20	.30	.40	.50	.60	.70	.80	.90	1.00							
11	.09	.18	.27	.36	.45	.55	.64	.73	.82	.91	1.00						
12	.08	.17	.25	.33	.42	.50	.58	.67	.75	.83	.92	1.00					
13	.08	.15	.23	.31	.38	.46	.54	.62	.69	.77	.85	.92	1.00				
14	.07	.14	.21	.29	.36	.43	.50	.57	.64	.71	.79	.86	.93	1.00			
15	.07	.13	.20	.27	.33	.40	.47	.53	.60	.67	.73	.80	.87	.93	1.00		
16	.06	.13	.19	.25	.31	.38	.44	.50	.56	.63	.69	.75	.81	.88	.94	1.00	
17	.06	.12	.18	.24	.29	.35	.41	.47	.53	.59	.65	.71	.76	.82	.88	.94	1.00

A given performance index is determined by locating the intersection of a line and column representing the appropriate number of principles.

Figure 11.12 Performance Index Calculation Chart

SOURCE: Cincinnati Public Schools, *Teacher Self-Appraisal Manual*, Cincinnati, Ohio, Certificated Personnel Branch, August 1974, p. 28. Reprinted with permission.

across the top of the chart are divided by the numbers in the left-hand column. To find the performance index for the results on Role I-Category G the teacher reads down to 7 in the left-hand (vertical) column and across to 4 in the horizontal row across the top. He or she reads across the 7 line and down the 4 column to find the block where the two figures intersect. The 7–4 block contains the number 57 (4.00 ÷ 7), which is the performance index for that category.

The teacher can then plot .57 on the Profile Blank under Role I, Category G. Taking some purely arbitrary figures, a profile of performance indices for a hypothetical teacher might look as shown in Figure 11.13.

The Profile Blank readily shows areas of teacher performance to which the teacher may wish to give consideration with a view to improving. The Cincinnati appraisal program, which was developed by a committee of teachers, administrators, and supervisors, utilizes not only appraisal of teachers by administrators and, in some cases, by supervisors but also teacher self-appraisal.

STUDENT EVALUATIONS

More frequently than in days gone by the recipients of instruction—the learners—are being asked to give their reactions to the teacher's performance. The learners can provide insights into the instruction which cannot be gained otherwise.

Conscientious teachers seek the counsel of their students about the effectiveness of their instruction. They want to know whether students perceive that they have learned. Student evaluations of the instructor and the instruction provide one more source of data about the effectiveness of teaching.

Teachers at all levels should be encouraged by their supervisors to solicit student reactions to their performance. Student evaluations should be gathered anonymously (or as anonymously as possible given the teacher's intimate knowledge of the students' handwriting).

Supervisors should help teachers to fashion student evaluation instruments if the teachers feel the need for such help. Instruments may be simple checklists or rating scales. A place for comments can allow for observations which students may wish to make. It is in the comments section, however, that the learners are most likely to reveal their identity by the distinctiveness of their handwriting. The teacher must be professional enough not to retaliate for negative comments they are able to ascribe to a particular student. In order to reduce the potential threat implicit in student evaluations the results should be available only to the teacher for his or her own guidance and should be shared only if the teacher decides to do so.

The results should be given close attention but at the same time teachers should realize that student evaluations represent the learners' perceptions of instruction and not their actual achievement. Perceptions, however, are extremely important and must be dealt with. Thus, if the majority of learners feel, for example, that the teacher's grading system is unfair, the teacher needs to decide whether there is merit to the criticisms. If the teacher agrees that the students have justification for their beliefs, he or she can modify the system. If the teacher finds that the criticisms are not accurate, he or she should spend some time explaining the rationale for the grading procedures.

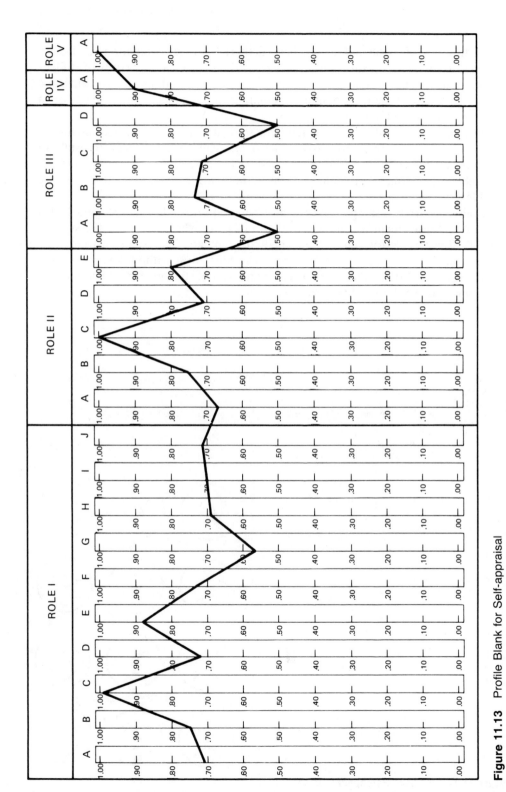

Figure 11.13 Profile Blank for Self-appraisal

SOURCE: Cincinnati Public Schools, *Teacher Self-Appraisal Manual*, Cincinnati, Ohio, Certificated Personnel Branch, August 1974, p. 29. Reprinted with permission.

Institutions of higher education have gathered student evaluations of faculty performance for years. In the case of colleges and universities the results of student evaluation are regularly shared with the faculty member's administrative superiors and become a part of the documentation required for decisions on merit increases in salary, promotion, and tenure.

In recent years with the movements for student rights, teacher accountability, and student participation in governance the public schools have begun to establish procedures for the collection of student reactions to instruction. Student input about the teacher's performance is being sought at both the elementary and secondary school levels.

Following are two samples of student evaluation forms. The first (Figure 11.14) is an optional instrument for grades three through five which is part of the state of Georgia's Teacher Performance Assessment Instruments. This same instrument is used in grades six through adult level in a checklist form without the faces. The second (Figure 11.15) is a checklist for senior high school students from Miami Southridge Senior High School, Miami, Florida.

SCHOOL____________________

DATE____________________

TEACHER____________________

Check the face that is most like your teacher.

Never Sometimes Often

1. My teacher enjoys teaching.

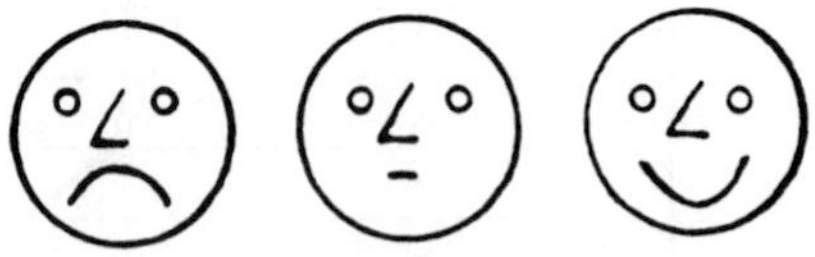

2. My teacher keeps me interested in my school work.

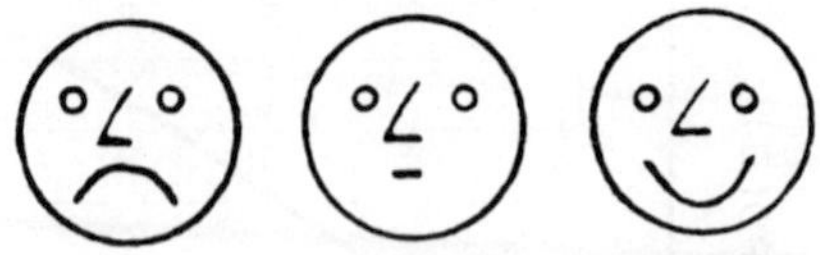

3. My teacher knows what to do and how we are going to do it.

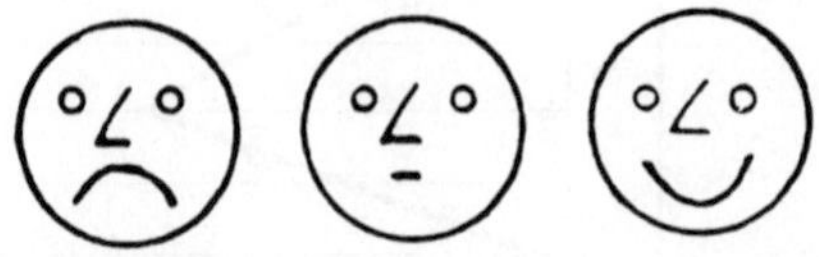

4. My teacher is friendly.

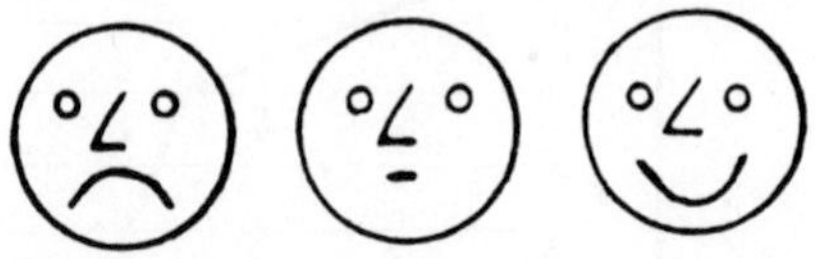

Figure 11.14 Student Perceptions (grades 3–5)

	Never	Sometimes	Often

5. My teacher cares about my
    feelings.

6. My teacher is patient and
    understands me.

7. My teacher lets me know if I am
    behaving right or wrong.

8. My teacher is polite and nice.

9. My teacher does things that keep
    children well-behaved.

10. My teacher is fair when
    children misbehave.

11. My teacher teaches in ways that
    help me learn.

12. My teacher uses things like charts,
    movies, filmstrips, and records.

13. My teacher chooses books, workbooks,
    worksheets, and other things that
    help me learn.

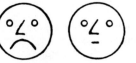

	Never	Sometimes	Often

14. My teacher gives clear explanations
and directions about my class work.

15. My teacher explains things again if
I don't understand.

16. My teacher listens to me and uses
my ideas.

17. My teacher tells me when my
answers are right or wrong.

18. My teacher talks and writes so that
I can understand.

19. My teacher teaches things in an
order that makes sense.

20. My teacher uses more than one way
to teach.

21. My teacher works with large groups,
small groups, and individual children.

22. My teacher gets me interested in new
lessons.

	Never	Sometimes	Often

23. My teacher gives me a chance to do things in this class.

24. I work or pay attention during a whole lesson.

25. My teacher does things to keep me working or paying attention during a lesson.

26. My teacher tells me why the things we learn in school are important.

27. My teacher knows a lot about what is taught in school.

28. My teacher does things like checking the roll and handing out papers quickly.

29. My teacher is ready to begin a new activity as soon as we finish one.

30. My teacher makes my classroom look like a nice place to be.

SOURCE: Georgia State Department of Education, *Teacher Performance Assessment Instruments: A Handbook for Interpretation*, Atlanta, Ga., Division of Staff Development, revised 1980, pp. 139–142. Reprinted with permission.

MIAMI SOUTHRIDGE SENIOR HIGH SCHOOL

Student Evaluation of Classroom Instruction

PURPOSE: To provide your teachers with information that will be useful in improving classroom instruction.

Directions: Check the space that you feel best describes the classroom atmosphere. Be fair and honest. You do not have to sign your name. (This is a voluntary exercise.)

		Always	Often	Seldom	Never
1.	The classroom atmosphere is free from bias and prejudice.	___	___	___	___
2.	The lessons are clear and well organized.	___	___	___	___
3.	The lessons and assignments have meaning and are purposeful.	___	___	___	___
4.	Student participation in class discussions is encouraged.	___	___	___	___
5.	Individual help is available when needed.	___	___	___	___
6.	The students have the right to express their own opinions on controversial issues without jeopardizing relations with the teacher.	___	___	___	___
7.	My personal rights as a student are respected.	___	___	___	___
8.	All tests are graded and reviewed. Questions regarding the test are answered.	___	___	___	___
9.	The classroom discipline is fair, consistent and encourages learning.	___	___	___	___
10.	The test schedule is announced and adhered to.	___	___	___	___
11.	A variety of teaching methods is used in classroom instruction.	___	___	___	___

12. The attendance procedures and classroom policies are clearly explained at the beginning of the semester. Yes ___   No ___

13. The grading policy is explained at the beginning of each semester. Yes ___   No ___

14. The students are notified of unsatisfactory progress with sufficient time for corrective action. Yes ___   No ___

COMMENTS: _____

_____

THANK YOU!

Figure 11.15 Student Evaluation of Classroom Instruction

SOURCE: Dade County Public Schools, *Student Evaluation of Classroom Instruction*, Miami, Fla., Miami Southridge Senior High School. Reprinted with permission.

Students can provide valuable insights about the course, the instruction, and the instructor. Though somewhat threatening to teachers at first, student evaluations come to be a valuable tool in the improvement of instruction.

PARENT EVALUATIONS

Schools by and large, although they involve parents in a variety of ways, such as serving on advisory committees and PTAs, working as volunteer aides, and expressing their views on curricular needs, rarely seek out in any systematized fashion parental feedback about the teacher's performance. Schools poll parents on many things except what they think about the teacher's instructional skills. Questionnaires to parents could be easily modeled on student questionnaires with such items as:

> My child's teacher enjoys teaching.
> My child's teacher is patient and understanding.
> My child's teacher is fair when students misbehave.
> My child's teacher gives clear directions and explanations.
> My child's teacher seeks my advice concerning my child.

This dimension of evaluation is lacking in most school systems. The solicitation of anonymous parent evaluations about the teacher's performance is a path yet to be trod in the evaluation of instruction. Both student and parent evaluations can help teachers to evaluate themselves.

SUMMARY

Supervisors effect changes in instruction as they help teachers to evaluate themselves. The supervisor must master a variety of techniques for getting teachers to look at their own behavior. An external approach is recommended as a step to be taken prior to an internal approach—the provision of opportunities for the teachers to analyze their own performances. Teacher evaluation systems should include three components: self-appraisal, formative evaluation during the year, and summative or annual evaluation.

Competencies that school systems consider important enough to be evaluated tend to fall within two major categories: instructional skills and personal-professional attributes. Techniques for evaluating instructional skills include an examination of models of teaching, the use of selected training films, the utilization of protocol materials, the study of teacher-training modules, and the application of observation analysis systems.

Teacher self-appraisal should be the goal of efforts to evaluate teaching competency. Self-appraisal can be realized through the use of videotaping in the classroom or clinic. Clinical approaches—peer teaching and microteaching—offer the opportunity to try out new techniques and skills in a controlled learning situation.

Personal and professional attributes are difficult to identify and evaluate. Agreement of the faculty on those personal and professional traits that should be evaluated is essential. Self-evaluation of personal and professional characteristics may be initiated by a review of the literature on personality development and by the use of selected personal attitude inventories.

In addition to the teachers' appraisal of their own performance student and parental evaluations of instruction can aid teachers in analyzing their own behavior and making needed improvements.

Many school systems require supervisors to evaluate teachers periodically. The supervisor is advised to institute a goal-oriented evaluative process, whereby the supervisor and teacher agree on the teacher's job targets for the year, jointly monitor, and jointly evaluate. Though the supervisor may evaluate *teachers*, his or her primary role should be helping teachers to evaluate *themselves*. Changes in behavior, whether in instructional skills or in personal-professional attributes, can only come about if the teacher sees the need for change and agrees to try to improve.

ACTIVITIES FOR FURTHER STUDY

1. Choose one of the models of teaching found in Bruce Joyce and Marsha Weil, *Models of Teaching*, 2d ed., and describe its characteristics and uses.
2. Write a paper analyzing your own model of teaching.
3. Create a classification system for retrieval of protocol materials.
4. Employ videotaping equipment and create a protocol, identifying the behavior shown in the protocol.
5. Preview a protocol material and write a brief evaluation of it as to its effectiveness in bringing out the particular point it aims to portray.
6. Develop a plan for a clinical laboratory, with complete specifications of equipment, including costs.
7. Prepare a five-minute lesson to demonstrate one generic teaching skill, have it videotaped, watch the tape of your performance, select and apply an observation instrument, and present a critique of your own performance.
8. Select an observation instrument and train a teacher to use it to analyze (1) a film or videotape of another teacher teaching and (2) a videotape of the teacher himself or herself teaching.
9. Prepare a presentation using appropriate visual materials on Ned A. Flanders' Flanders Interaction Analysis Categories.
10. Draft a proposal describing personal-professional attributes which you feel should be evaluated and how they would be assessed.
11. Administer to yourself the *FIRO-B* instrument mentioned in this chapter. Make a self-diagnosis of your responses.
12. Obtain samples of teacher training modules and analyze their suitability as materials for studying the teaching act.

13. Create and, if you are teaching, use an instrument for student evaluation of your teaching performance.
14. Create and, if you are teaching, use an instrument for parent evaluation of your teaching performance.

NOTES

1. Georgia State Department of Education, *Teacher Performance Assessment Instruments: A Handbook for Interpretation*, Atlanta, Ga., State Department of Education, Division of Staff Development, revised 1980.
2. Bruce Joyce and Marsha Weil, *Models of Teaching*, 2d ed., Englewood Cliffs, N.J., Prentice-Hall, 1980, 1.
3. See bibliography heading *Films, Critical Moments in Teaching*, New York, Holt, Rinehart and Winston.
4. National Resource and Dissemination Center, *Protocol Materials for Use in Preservice and Inservice Teacher Education*, Tampa, Fla., n.d., unnumbered page 1. Center is no longer operating.
5. See bibliography heading *Protocol Materials*.
6. B. Othanel Smith, Saul B. Cohen, and Arthur Pearl, *Teachers for the Real World*, Washington, D.C., American Association of Colleges for Teacher Education, 1969, 63.
7. Ibid., 63.
8. Ibid., 51–52.
9. Florida Department of Education, *The Florida Catalog of Teacher Competencies*, Tallahassee, Fla., January 1, 1973.
10. Ibid., 72.
11. Weber State College, *Wilkits*, Ogden, Utah: Weber State College.
12. Florida Department of Education, *B-2 Teacher Education Modules*, Chipley, Fla., Panhandle Area Educational Cooperative.
13. Dwight Allen and Kevin Ryan, *Microteaching*, Reading, Mass., Addison-Wesley, 1969, 15.
14. Anita Simon and E. Gil Boyer, *Mirrors for Behavior III: An Anthology of Observation Instruments*, Philadelphia, Pa., Research for Better Schools, 1974.
15. Smith, Cohen, and Pearl, 55.
16. See E. Wayne Roberson, "The Preparation of an Instrument for the Analysis of Classroom Behavior," Tucson, Ariz., University of Arizona, 1967. Unpublished doctoral dissertation.
17. Russell N. Jensen, Darleen Videen, and Charles F. Grubbs, *Teacher Self-Appraisal Program*, 1967–68, Tucson, Ariz., Research and Development, Tucson Public Schools, July 1968.
18. Ibid., 3.
19. Ibid., 1.
20. Ibid., 4.
21. Ibid., 17.
22. Arthur W. Combs, *Individual Behavior: A Perceptual Approach*, rev. ed., Harper & Row, 1959.
23. Earl C. Kelley, *Education for What Is Real*, New York, Harper and Row, 1947.
24. Abraham H. Maslow, *Motivation and Personality*, 2d ed., New York, Harper & Row, 1970.
25. Arthur W. Combs, ed., *Perceiving, Behaving, Becoming*, 1962 Yearbook, Alexandria, Va., Association for Supervision and Curriculum Development, 1962.

26. William C. Schutz, *FIRO-B*, Palo Alto, Calif., Consulting Psychologists Press, 1957. See also William C. Schutz, *FIRO: A Three Dimensional Theory of Interpersonal Behavior*, New York, Holt, Rinehart and Winston, 1958.
27. See Max Birnbaum, "Sense and Nonsense about Sensitivity Training," *Saturday Review* (November 15, 1969): 82–83; and Ted J. Rakstis, "Sensitivity Training: Fad, Fraud or New Frontier?" *Today's Health* (January 1970): 20–25ff.
28. William Goldstein, "An Enlightened Approach to Supervising Teachers," *The Clearing House* 46, no. 7 (March 1972): 391–394.
29. Thomas J. Watman, "Instructional Media: Supervision for Growth," *The Clearing House* 46, no. 9 (May 1972): 567–568.
30. For specification of the objectives of the individual within the framework of the objectives of the institution see some of the literature on management by objectives such as John William Humble, ed., *Management by Objectives in Action*, New York, McGraw-Hill, 1970; George S. Odiorne, *Management by Objectives: A System of Managerial Leadership*, New York, Pitman, 1965; and Robert O. Riggs, "Management by Objectives: Its Utilization in the Management of Administrative Performance," *Contemporary Education* 63, 3 (January 1972): 129–133. See also reference, Robert E. Boston and David A. Spencer, *Management by Objectives*, bibliography heading *Multi-Media*.
31. Cincinnati Public Schools, *Teacher Appraisal Manual*, Cincinnati, Ohio, Certificated Personnel Branch, July 1978.
32. Cincinnati Public Schools, *Teacher Self-Appraisal Manual*, Cincinnati, Ohio, Certificated Personnel Branch, August 1974.
33. Cincinnati Public Schools, *Teacher Appraisal Manual*, 7–8.
34. Ibid., 14.
35. Ibid., 5.

BIBLIOGRAPHY

Allen, Dwight, and Kevin Ryan. *Microteaching*. Reading, Mass.: Addison-Wesley, 1969.

Allen, Paul M., William D. Barnes, Jerald L. Reece, and E. Wayne Roberson. *Teacher Self-Appraisal: A Way of Looking over Your Own Shoulder*, Worthington, Ohio: Charles A. Jones, 1970.

Amidon, Edmund J., and Ned A. Flanders. *The Role of the Teacher in the Classroom: A Manual for Understanding and Improving Classroom Behavior*, rev. ed. Minneapolis: Association for Productive Teaching, 1971.

——— and John B. Hough, eds. *Interaction Analysis Theory, Research, and Application*. Reading, Mass.: Addison-Wesley, 1967.

——— and Elizabeth Hunter. *Improved Teaching: The Analysis of Classroom Verbal Interaction*. New York: Holt, Rinehart and Winston, 1966.

Bellack, Arno A., H. M. Kliebard, R. T. Hyman, and F. L. Smith, Jr. *The Language of the Classroom*. New York: Teachers College Press, 1966.

Borg, Walter R., et al. *The Minicourse: A Microteaching Approach to Teacher Education*. Beverly Hills, Calif.: Macmillan, 1970.

Briggs, Leslie J. *The Use and Evaluation of "Protocol" Materials in Teacher Education Program*. Tallahassee, Fla.: State Department of Education, 1971.

Brighton, Stayner F. *Increasing Your Accuracy in Teacher Evaluation*. Englewood Cliffs, N. J.: Prentice-Hall, 1965.

Brophy, Jere E., and Thomas L. Good. *Teacher-Child Dyadic Interaction: A Manual for Coding Classroom Behavior*, Austin: University of Texas at Austin, 1969.

Brown, Bob Burton, Richard L. Ober, Robert S. Soar, and Jeannine N. Webb. *The Florida Taxonomy of Cognitive Behavior*. Gainesville, Fla.: Institute for Development of Human Resources, 1968. Manual and instrument.

Brown, George. *Microteaching: A Programme of Teaching Skills*. London: Methuen, 1975.

Burke, Caseel. *The Individualized, Competency-Based System of Teacher Education at Weber State College*. Washington, D. C.: American Association of Colleges for Teacher Education, 1972.

Cincinnati Public Schools. *Teacher Appraisal Manual*. Cincinnati: Certificated Personnel Branch, Cincinnati Public Schools, 1978.

———. *Teacher Self-Appraisal Manual*. Cincinnati: Certificated Personnel Branch, Cincinnati Public Schools, 1974.

Combs, Arthur W. *Individual Behavior: A Perceptual Approach*, rev. ed. New York: Harper & Row, 1959.

———, ed. *Perceiving, Behaving, Becoming*, 1962 Yearbook. Alexandria, Va.: Association for Supervision and Curriculum Development, 1962.

———. *The Professional Preparation of Teachers: A Perceptual View of Teacher Preparation*. Boston: Allyn and Bacon, 1965.

Flanders, Ned A. *Analyzing Teacher Behavior*. Reading, Mass.: Addison-Wesley, 1970.

———. *Interaction Analysis: Teacher Handbook*. San Francisco: Far West Laboratory for Educational Research and Development, 1972.

——— et al. *Interaction Analysis: A Minicourse from the Far West Laboratory: Handbook*. St. Paul, Minn.: Paul S. Amidon and Associates, 1974.

Florida Department of Education. *The Florida Catalog of Teacher Competencies*, 1st ed. Tallahassee: Florida Department of Education, 1973.

Florida Project for Changing Teacher Education through the Use of Protocol Materials. *Protocol Materials Catalog*. Tallahassee: Protocol Materials Project, Florida Department of Education, 1975.

Goldstein, William. "An Enlightened Approach to Supervising Teachers." *The Clearing House* 46, no. 7 (March 1972): 391–394.

Hamachek, Don E. *Encounters with the Self*, 2nd ed. New York: Holt, Rinehart and Winston, 1978.

Houston, W. Robert, et al. *Resources for Performance-Based Education*. Albany: Division of Teacher Education and Certification, New York State Education Department, 1973.

———, Karen S. Nelson, and Elizabeth C. Houston. *Resources for Performance-Based Education, Supplement A*. Albany: Division of Teacher Education and Certification, New York State Education Department, 1973.

Hudgins, Bruce B., and associates. *A Catalogue of Concepts in the Pedagogical Domain of Teacher Education*. St. Louis: Graduate Institute of Education, Washington University, 1974. Available from the Multi-State Consortium on Performance-Based Teacher Education, New York State Education Department, Albany, New York.

Humble, John William, ed. *Management by Objectives in Action*. New York: McGraw-Hill, 1970.

Hunter, Madeline. "Teacher Competency: Problem, Theory, and Practice." *Theory into Practice* 15, (April 1976): 162–171.

Hutchins, C. L., Barbara Dunning, Marilyn Madsen, and Sylvia I. Rainey. *Minicourses Work*. San Francisco: Far West Laboratory for Educational Research and Development, 1971. Available from the U.S. Government Printing Office, Washington, D. C.

Hyman, Ronald T. *School Administrator's Handbook of Teacher Supervision and Evaluation Methods*. Englewood Cliffs, N. J.: Prentice-Hall, 1975.

Institute for Development of Human Resources. *Teacher Practices Observation Record*. Gainesville, Fla.: Institute for Development of Human Resources. Handbook and instrument.

Jensen, Richard N. *Microteaching: Planning and Implementing a Competency-Based Training Program*. Springfield, Ill.: Charles C. Thomas, 1974.

Jourard, Sidney M. *The Transparent Self*. New York: Van Nostrand Reinhold, 1971.

Joyce, Bruce, and Marsha Weil. *Models of Teaching*, 2nd ed. Englewood Cliffs, N. J.: Prentice-Hall, 1980.

Kelley, Earl C. *Education for What Is Real*. New York: Harper & Row, 1947.

McNergney, Robert F., and Carol A. Carrier. *Teacher Development*, New York: Macmillan, 1981.

Maslow, Abraham H. *Motivation and Personality*, 2nd ed. New York: Harper & Row, 1970.

———. *Toward a Psychology of Being*, 2nd ed. Princeton, N. J.: D. Van Nostrand, 1968.

Nuthall, Graham, and Ivan Snook. "Contemporary Models of Teaching." In *Second Handbook of Research on Teaching*, Robert M. W. Travers, ed. Chicago: Rand McNally, 1973.

Ober, Richard L. "Theory and Practice through Systematic Observation." *Research Bulletin of the Florida Educational Research and Development Council* 4 (Spring 1968).

Odiorne, George S. *Management by Objectives: A System of Managerial Leadership*. New York: Pitman, 1965.

Roberson, E. Wayne. *A Manual for Utilizing the Teacher Self-Appraisal Observation System*. Tucson: Educational Innovators Press, 1973.

———. "The Preparation of an Instrument for the Analysis of Teacher Classroom Behavior." Tucson: University of Arizona, 1967. Unpublished doctoral dissertation.

Rogers, Carl R. *Being, Becoming, and Behavior*. Boston: Houghton Mifflin, 1961.

Simon, Anita, and E. Gil Boyer. *Mirrors for Behavior III: An Anthology of Observation Instruments*. Philadelphia: Research for Better Schools, 1974.

Smith, B. Othanel, Saul B. Cohen, and Arthur Pearl. *Teachers for the Real World*. Washington, D.C.: American Association of Colleges for Teacher Education, 1969.

Travers, Robert M. W., ed. *Second Handbook of Research on Teaching*. Washington, D.C.: American Educational Research Association, 1973.

Tucson Public Schools. *The Teacher Self-Appraisal Program: An Inservice Program for Classroom Accountability: A Five-Year Overview*. Tucson: Research Department, Tucson Public Schools, 1971.

Turner, Robert L., ed. *A General Catalog of Teaching Skills*, Bloomington: Indiana University, 1973. Ten chapters paged separately. Available from Multi-State Consortium on Performance-Based Teacher Education, New York State Education Department, Albany, New York.

Watman, Thomas J. "Instructional Media: Supervision for Growth." *The Clearing House* 46, no. 91 (May 1972): 567–568

Films

Critical Moments in Teaching. New York: Holt, Rinehart and Winston. Series of 16 mm films, sound color. Available from BFA Educational Media, 468 Park Avenue South, New York, New York 10016. Titles as follows:

Title	Time	Topic	Level
A Child Who Cheats	10 min.	Cheating	elementary
The Day The Insects Took Over	10 min.	Class discussion	secondary
The First and Fundamental R	12 min.	Teaching reading	elementary
Give Me Instead a Catastrophe	11 min.	Child's anxiety over testing	elementary
Image in a Mirror	9 min.	Pupil's lack of self-confidence	elementary
I Walk Away in the Rain	11 min.	Motivating a bright underachiever	secondary
Julia	10 min.	Handicapped child	elementary
Just a Simple Misunderstanding	11 min.	Use of controversial material	secondary
Less Far Than the Arrow	8 min.	Motivating a class in poetry	secondary
The Poetry in Paul	9½ min.	Plagiarism	secondary
Report Card	12 min.	Grading practices	secondary (JHS)

Title	Time	Topic	Level
Some Courses Don't Count	$9\frac{1}{4}$ min.	Selecting courses	secondary
Tense: Imperfect	12 min.	Teaching lower socio-economic students	secondary
Walls	$10\frac{1}{2}$ min.	Motivating an unresponsive group	secondary
Welcome to the Third Grade	12 min.	Retention and promotion	elementary
What Do I Know About Benny?	10 min.	Scholastic aptitude	elementary

Inventory

William C. Schutz, *FIRO-B*, Consulting Psychologists Press, Inc., 557 College Avenue, Palo Alto, California, 1957. Survey of Interpersonal Skills.

Multi-Media

Boston, Robert E., and David A. Spencer. *Management by Objectives*. How-To booklet on implementation of Management by Objectives in the local school district. Five filmstrips with cassette tapes. Available from Paul S. Amidon and Associates, Inc., 1966 Benson Avenue, St. Paul, Minnesota 55116.

Flanders, Ned A., Edwenna Werner, Rachel Ann Elder, Jacomina Newman, and Morris K. Lai. *Interaction Analysis: A Minicourse from the Far West Laboratory*. Minneapolis: Paul S. Amidon and Associates, Inc., 1966 Benson Avenue, St. Paul, Minnesota 55116, 1974. Workbook, Coordinator's Manual, and two cassette tapes.

Florida Department of Education. *B-2 Teacher Education Modules*. Chipley: Panhandle Area Educational Cooperative.

Weber State College. *Individualized Learning Kits*. Ogden, Utah: Weber State College. Eighty-five *WILKITS* for the preparation of elementary and secondary school teachers.

Protocol Materials

Bucknell University, Lewisburg, Pennsylvania. *Developmental Reading*. Ten 16 mm films, black and white.

California State University, Northridge. *Responding to Literature*. Ten 16 mm films, color.

Far West Laboratory for Educational Research and Development, San Francisco. *Classroom Interaction*. Five 16 mm films, black and white. *Group Process*. Four 16 mm films, black and white.

Indiana University, Bloomington. *Concepts and Patterns in Teacher/Pupil Interaction*. Nine 16 mm films, color.

Michigan State University, East Lansing. *Tasks of Teaching*. Two 16 mm films, color.

Southern Illinois University at Edwardsville. *Black Dialect*. Twelve cassette tapes.

University of Colorado, Boulder. *Instructional Concepts*. Five 16 mm films, color. Two filmstrips, color. *Role Concepts*. Four filmstrips, color with cassettes.

University of Southern California, Los Angeles. *Interaction in Multicultural Classrooms*. Seven 16 mm films, color.

Utah State University, Logan. *Classroom Management*. Four 16 mm films, color. *Teacher Language*. Six 16 mm films, black and white.

12

Helping Teachers
on a One-to-One Basis

OBJECTIVES

After studying Chapter 12 you should be able to accomplish the following objectives:

1. Define formative evaluation as applied to teacher performance.
2. Distinguish between clinical supervision and general supervision.
3. Describe one or more models of clinical supervision.
4. Describe skills needed by the supervisor for clinical supervision.
5. Select or create and apply appropriate classroom observation instruments.
6. Demonstrate selected techniques of classroom observation.
7. Assess your own readiness to render clinical supervision.
8. Plan for the use of teacher peers in supervision.

FORMATIVE EVALUATION

Let's recall for a moment two of the three components of a teacher evaluation system: formative evaluation and summative evaluation. Formative evaluation is assessment of teacher performance by an instructional supervisor during the year for the purpose of improving instruction. Summative evaluation is assessment of teacher performance by an administrator for the purpose of making decisions about tenure, retention, and the like.

If the school system is large enough, an instructional supervisor will serve as the formative evaluator and the administrator will be the summative evaluator. However, the summative evaluator may also be the formative evaluator, as in the case of a principal in a small school which has no other supervisory personnel. The principal's summative evaluations will be based on formative evaluation. The formative evaluations in this case fulfill a double purpose: improvement of instruction and personnel decisions.

If a school system is large enough, it should provide for two sets of formative evaluation: one set by the instructional supervisor with no summative evaluation and one set by the administrator culminating in a summative evaluation.

When two sets of formative evaluation are possible, those of the instructional supervisor should not be reported to the administrator unless the teacher requests it or agrees to it. In this chapter we are concerned with formative evaluation as carried out by the instructional supervisor. We will examine in particular that structured approach to formative evaluation which is known as clinical supervision.

CLINICAL SUPERVISION

In Chapter 2 we raised the issue of whether supervisors should work primarily with groups or with individuals. A growing number of specialists in supervision believe that supervisors should concentrate their energies on working with individual teachers in their classrooms. These specialists believe that supervisors should take what has come to be called a clinical approach.

The term *clinical supervision* came into vogue in 1961 when Morris Cogan used it in a proposal he made at Harvard University entitled *Case Studies and Research in Clinical Supervision*. As Cogan himself pointed out, the term met with a great deal of resistance.[1] The word invokes images of doctors and laboratory technicians analyzing and diagnosing a patient's ailments. No one looks forward with delight to a trip to the clinic.

Yet, the concepts of analysis, diagnosis, and remediation can apply as well in professional education as in medicine or dentistry or athletics. When Cogan spoke of supervision, he meant clinical supervision unless he specified otherwise. Cogan defined clinical supervision in the following way:

Clinical supervision may therefore be defined as the rationale and practice designed to improve the teacher's classroom performance. It takes its principal data from the events of the classroom. The analysis of these data and the relationship between teacher and supervisor form the basis of the program, procedures, and strategies designed to improve the students' learning by improving the teacher's classroom behavior.[2]

Cogan offered a simple test for distinguishing between what he referred to as *general supervision* from clinical. He described general supervision as follows:

general supervision subsumes supervisory operations that take place principally outside the classroom. . . . *General supervision*, therefore, denotes activities like the writing and revision of curriculums, the preparation of units and materials of instruction, the development of processes and instruments for reporting to parents, and such broad concerns as the evaluation of the total educational program.[3]

It is clear that Cogan felt that clinical supervision should be stressed over general supervision. Although clinical supervision as a concept appears to be a rather recent development in supervision, in some respects, without the newer label, we can find in the early history of this field a type—albeit quite different—of clinical supervision.

The earliest supervisors served as inspectors. They visited classrooms, observed the teacher's performance, and checked on the condition of the classroom. They did analyze; they did diagnose; and, if they proposed remediation, it was more in line with the concept of a medical prescription. Supervision in the individual teacher's classroom preceded organized in-service education of groups of teachers. The supervising principal, headmaster, or superintendent felt it his or her obligation to discover what was happening in the various classrooms. The intent was more to see if the teacher was carrying out approved policies, procedures, and programs than to provide assistance to the teacher for the improvement of instruction. Under an aura of investigation early "snoopervisors" were decidedly clinical in the purest sense of the word: detached, aloof, critical, and judgmental. They felt it incumbent upon themselves to find out if rooms were kept clean, bulletin boards neat, property protected, shades properly drawn, children well disciplined, and lessons heard and repeated by the learners.

Of course, the purposes and practices of clinical supervision today differ radically from historic approaches to supervision of individual teachers. One factor, however, remains constant. Clinical supervision takes place in the classroom. Thus, it is an individualized approach to supervision.

Robert H. Anderson and Robert J. Krajewski in revising the work of Robert Goldhammer attributed nine characteristics to clinical supervision. They wrote that it:

1. is a technology for improving instruction.
2. is a deliberate intervention into the instructional process.
3. is goal-oriented, combining school and personal growth needs.
4. assumes a working relationship between teacher(s) and supervisor.
5. requires mutual trust, as reflected in understanding, support, and commitment for growth.
6. is systematic, yet requires a flexible and continuously changing methodology.
7. creates productive tension for bridging the real-ideal gap.
8. assumes the supervisor knows more about instruction and learning than the teacher(s).
9. requires training for the supervisor.[4]

Clinical supervision should be perceived as a concept, not a single, fixed set of procedures. Practices may vary—though as we shall see when we examine models of clinical supervision below, they do not vary as widely as might be supposed—but fundamental to clinical supervision is, as Goldhammer said, "a face-to-face relationship between supervisors and teachers."[5] In this chapter we will be concerned with the basic model of clinical supervision—the one-to-one relationship between supervisor and teacher. Goldhammer took note of "variations of the basic model that include group supervision, that is, supervision of individual teachers by groups of supervisors, groups of teachers by groups of supervisors, and groups of teachers by an individual supervisor."[6]

Though group supervision may be possible, I feel the group variations of the model to be limited in both feasibility and practicality. Whereas a one-to-one basis appears to me the most effective approach to clinical supervision, one possible application of the principle of groups' supervising individual teachers may occur in the case of well-knit teaching teams in which peers collaborate to provide guidance to their own members.

Clinical supervision is one of the more apparent trends in the field of instructional supervision. Barbara Nelson Pavan noted:

With the advent of the 1980's, clinical supervision has almost become an educational fad, at least in word, if not in practice. For the first time since the seeds were sown, cultivated, and fertilized by groups of faculty members, students, and classroom teachers interacting in various training projects at Harvard beginning in the 1960's, mentioning clinical supervision to a group of educators does not result in blank stares . . . clinical supervision has come of age.[7]

THE SUPERVISOR'S ROLE IN CLINICAL SUPERVISION

Goldhammer, Anderson, and Krajewski conceptualized supervision and, ipso facto, clinical supervision, as teaching.[8] They took the position that "a supervisor in order to be helpful must have a larger and deeper understanding of teaching than the persons he or she seeks to help . . ."[9] and charted the supervisor's role as shown in Figure 12.1.

Keith A. Acheson and Meredith Damien Gall pictured the supervisor as primarily a facilitator.[10] They took note, however, of the continuing dilemma supervisors face when they must fulfill the dual roles of facilitator and evaluator. Concerning this conflict they commented in their book:

This book is strongly oriented toward the role of clinical supervisor as facilitator, yet we acknowledge that most supervisors must also evaluate teachers. . . .

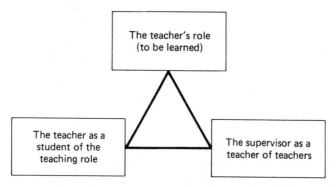

Figure 12.1 The Supervisor's Role (revised illustration)

SOURCE: Robert Goldhammer, Robert H. Anderson, and Robert J. Krajewski, *Clinical Supervision: Special Methods for the Supervision of Teachers*, 2nd ed., New York, Holt, Rinehart and Winston, 1980, p. 29. Reprinted with permission.

The conflict between facilitation and evaluation is not unique to teacher supervision; supervisors in all occupations and professions face the same problem. Even teachers must play the dual role of evaluator and facilitator.[11]

When the same person is charged with the responsibility for both formative and summative evaluation, the dilemma may be minimized by a high degree of competence and interpersonal skills on the part of the supervisors. Teachers will accept evaluation of the rating type (summative) and evaluation of the helping variety (formative) from the same person if they have confidence in that person. The dilemma, of course, is eliminated when formative evaluation is carried out by a staff supervisor and summative by a line administrator-supervisor.

The role of the supervisor as facilitator is compatible with the role of the supervisor as teacher. In fact, facilitating behavior is both a generic skill in one sense and a model of teacher behavior in another sense.

Like this textbook, most of the literature on clinical supervision emphasizes the analysis of teaching for the purpose of improving instruction. Acheson and Gall viewed clinical supervision as "supervision to help a teacher improve his/her instructional performance."[12] In that sense they agreed with Goldhammer, Anderson, and Krajewski, who saw clinical supervision as a "technology for improving instruction."[13]

Ralph L. Mosher and David E. Purpel called for clinical supervisors skilled not only in analyzing teaching but also in curriculum development. They explained:

Clinical supervision has, since its inception, been based on specialized, expert knowledge of the content of instruction. A current and related development, largely attributable to Purpel, is emphasis on supervision as instruction in curriculum. Specialized knowledge of curriculum theory and development is therefore a prerequisite to a comprehensive analysis of teaching.[14]

They went on to state:

Clinical supervision is one means by which teachers can confront and modify both the content and the practice of teaching. Indeed, it is virtually inseparable from curriculum development activity, both in its theoretical principles and as a strategy for involving teachers in analysis of their instruction. The most productive way to get teachers to analyze and change *how* they teach, in the writer's experience, is to involve them in analysis of *what* they teach.[15]

Noreen Garman saw the role of the supervisor in clinical supervision as friend, confidante, and respected colleague.[16] Garman described clinical supervision as embracing four concepts:

- Collegiality: an internal state embodying a spirit of "connectedness," i.e., identification with another person for whom you hold respect and affection.
- Collaboration: teacher and supervisor sharing a common language so that they may share each other's perceptions.
- Skilled service: the supervisor's special competence based on training and experience from which teachers can benefit.
- Ethical conduct: exercising judgment and maintaining trust.[17] Said Garman, "In clinical supervision one doesn't have ethics, one does ethics."[18]

Replying to the question, "When are we really clinical supervisors?" Garman painted the following word-picture:

A person becomes a clinical supervisor when he/she begins to think and act as if the "cycle of supervision" were a metaphor as well as a method; when observation and analysis are not only procedural phases for actions in classrooms, but also represent the empirical approach inherent in a skilled service; when the notion of conference not only means two people meeting before and after classroom visits, but also suggests dynamic forms of collaboration in educational alliances; when the image of "cycle" not only guarantees repeated performance, but also refers to high levels of involvement and commitment that press participants toward the "connectedness" of collegiality; when the teacher-supervisor relationship stands for ethical conduct as it is lived out in important choices.[19]

There is considerable disagreement among specialists in a supervision over the question of whether the supervisor-teacher relationship should be a superior-subordinate relationship or a relationship between equals. Some experts feel that the superior-subordinate relationship is necessary to nudge teachers to make changes. These people believe that since the superior-subordinate relationship does exist, we should make the best of it. Others feel that although the superior-subordinate relationship exists, the inequality of the partners should be deemphasized or ignored. Still others feel that a superior-subordinate relationship has no place in the modern-day supervision of professionals and can be dispensed with, at least in the case of staff supervisors who do not possess line authority.

Robert J. Alfonso and Lee Goldsberry made clear the existence of the supervisor's authority status when they said:

Supervision is a formal organizational act; moreover, supervision always implies a superordinate-subordinate relationship. The terms "peer supervision" and "colleague supervision" may be contradictions, for one cannot be both a peer/colleague and a supervisor at the same time. Clearly, teachers can and should help each other in a variety of ways, but a supervisor is vested with organizational authority for decision making about others.[20]

In another context Alfonso with coauthors Firth and Neville examined the dimensions of leadership and included among a number of propositions the following: "The probability of successful leadership will be increased if the leader maintains some degree of psychological distance from subordinates."[21] They developed this point in the following passage:

Supervisors are likely to be more effective if they do not become an integral part of the teacher group. While obviously joined to them and responsible for them, a sense of psychological distance is necessary. This is not to suggest that supervisors need to be aloof, undemocratic, or "company people," but rather that their relationships to teachers must permit psychological freedom and objectivity. While writing in supervision has often suggested a close relationship, research indicates that maintaining some degree of psychological distance enhances a supervisor's ability to make discriminations between teachers and to assess their ability and effectiveness more clearly and objectively. Supervisors need to maintain the delicate balance that enables one to operate freely as a member of a group while still retaining a recognized degree of psychological detachment.[22]

In a different vein Garman advocated a close relationship when she said: "A heightened sense of collegiality is possible when I can imagine myself as a member of an organic unit, when the distinction between supervisor and teacher is less discernible and I can transcend my conventional role status."[23]

Differing interpretations of the supervisor's role highlight once again the problem of the dual roles of many supervisors: helper and evaluator. The helper has little or no need of psychological distance whereas the evaluator finds maintaining distance useful and, perhaps, necessary. The clinical supervisor who works in a helping, face-to-face relationship with teachers has less need to maintain a superior-subordinate relationship than the administrative supervisor who must make the hard decisions about retention and dismissal.

The supervisor enters the process of clinical supervision as a knowledgeable helper. He or she brings to the process skills in pedagogy and personal relations. He or she knows how to analyze teaching, diagnose difficulties, confer with teachers, and make recommendations to the teacher for improvement. The supervisor knows sources of information and materials, is able to help with assessment of student performance, and can assist in interpreting applicable research. In addition, the supervisor possesses skills to help teachers with curriculum development.

MODELS OF CLINICAL SUPERVISION

The literature offers us a number of models of clinical supervision which recommend certain steps or stages to be followed. As early as 1930 George C. Kyte proposed such a model. Though he did not use the label "clinical," he suggested a pattern which anticipated the clinical approach 30 years later. Referring to supervisory observation—the heart of clinical supervision—Kyte outlined a three-phase process which included:

1. planning for the observation of teaching.
2. getting the most out of the observation period.
3. analyzing the teaching observed.[24]

Kyte's discussion of the first phase placed emphasis on plans the supervisor would make for the forthcoming observation as well as on preobservation conferencing, a key feature of clinical supervision models. He made note of the desirability of conferences with the teacher both before and after observing. Kyte described the two kinds of conferences as follows:

Two kinds of individual conferences are conducted in supervision. The less common one in practice, though markedly important, is that which is preparatory to work projected. The series of first conferences with a new teacher, the consultations planned in response to a teacher's request for help on a new undertaking, and the interviews for the purpose of planning classroom experimentation frequently are of this nature. The more common type of conference, however, is that which occurs after a supervisory visit has been made to the classroom, or the products of pupils' efforts have been submitted to a supervisory officer.[25]

Thus, by putting these elements together, we could create, in effect, the following four-stage model:

1. Preobservation conference and planning for the observation
2. Observation
3. Analysis of the data
4. Postobservation conference

Some of Kyte's recommendations are remarkably contemporary. He proposed, for example:

a. Regarding planning and preparation for observation:
Purposeful planning includes (a) the selection of sound objectives, (b) the analysis of teacher personnel, (c) the survey of learning conditions, (d) the diagnosis of teaching difficulties, (e) the determining of teacher needs, and (f) the choice of supervisory aid. . . .[26]

When the supervisor has made adequate preparation for the visit to a classroom, he will enter the room with a clear understanding of what he expects to stress in his observation, why he should so place his emphasis, and how he will make use of the results to aid the teacher.[27]

Table 12.1 Distribution of Items Regarding the Technique of Teaching Listed Frequently in Twenty-Five Teacher-Rating Devices

Nature of Items Listed	Rating Devices	
	Number	Percent
Making the assignment	19	76
Discipline of the pupils	19	76
Training pupils to study	17	68
Attention to individual needs	17	68
Participation of pupils	16	64
Skill in questioning	16	64
Care of hygienic conditions	16	64
Skill in stimulating thought	15	60
Selection of subject matter	15	60
Organization of subject matter	15	60
Definiteness of instructions	14	56
Skill in motivating work	13	52
Skill in habit formation	13	52
Securing and holding interest	12	48
Definite and clear aims	12	48
Careful preparation of teacher	12	48
Care of routine	12	48
Economic use of school time	11	44
Use of instructional materials	10	40
Neatness of room	10	40
Orderliness of room	10	40
Evidence of growth of pupils	10	40

SOURCE: George C. Kyte, *How to Supervise*, Boston, Houghton Mifflin, 1930, 151.

496   LEADERSHIP IN STAFF DEVELOPMENT

b. Regarding observation:

[The author] has observed teaching, taking personal notes, and using a trained secretary to obtain stenographic notes. . . . The reaction of the teachers to their first experience of this nature was somewhat unfavorable. . . . When copies of the notes were given to them and they were told that the stenographic records would be used as the basis of the conference, they frankly admitted that the notes proved helpful to them before they came to the conference, and very helpful as a basis for getting help through the conference. . . . After the third experience, they were unanimous in their recommendation that detailed records be made during the supervisory observation, because of the greater aid resulting. . . .[28]

Frequently the supervisors utilize published forms, or ones that they have improvised for their own use in recording their observations. . . .[29]

Kyte found 25 "teacher-rating devices," which we would now call observation instruments, published between 1920 and 1930. He summarized the items assessed by these devices as shown in Table 12.1. You will note that many of the items are skills which present-day observation systems seek to assess.

Kyte suggested ways of recording classroom observations in the following passage:

In addition to long-hand and stenographic accounts of observations, other means of attempting to gather objective data are used. Many printed forms exist which suggest various ways of collecting the desired information. Check-lists, word- or phrase-responses, and complete sentences are typical methods of recording the supervisor's reactions. Still another and a more recent type is exemplified by the chart of the classroom used, with a legend for recording child-participation.[30]

Kyte made reference to a recording system suggested by Roswell C. Puckett in 1928. The seating chart and detailed legend, shown in Figure 12.2, are similar in nature to some of the observational techniques in use today.

c. Regarding analysis of the observation data:

Just as soon after the observation as possible, the supervisor should set aside time to go over his notes in order to add items which may recur to him while the observed lesson is still freshly impressed upon him. He should give careful thought to the lesson as a whole, and to the points which he noted with a view to preparing for the conference . . . A careful analysis of the lesson should be made by the supervisor before conferring with the teacher. If the supervisor is to be a super-teacher, he must make the same sort of preparation for his "recitation" with the teacher, the conference, as the teacher is expected to make for his classroom recitation.[31]

Kyte dealt with the continuing questions of whether to make announced or unannounced visits (both have their place)[32] and how long a visit to make (elementary: 30 minutes; secondary: one period).[33] Kyte's work was very much in line with the present movement toward clinical supervision.

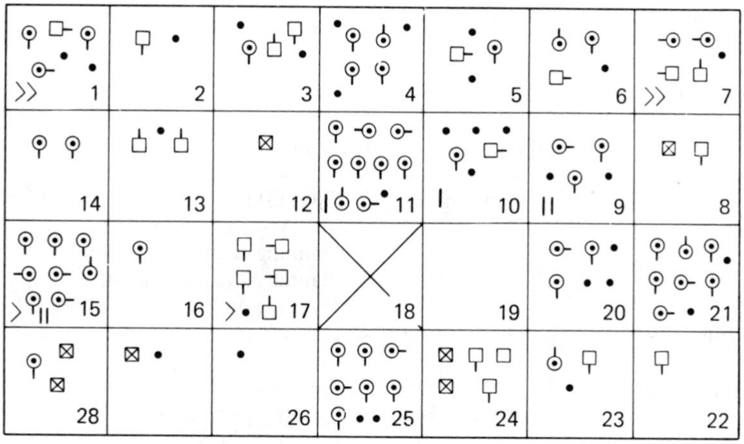

Pupil responses in a IX B civics class

- Pupil raised hand.
- ⊙ Pupil raised hand and was called on by teacher.
- ⊚ Pupil raised hand, was called on by teacher, and made a single-word response.
- ⊙- Pupil raised hand, was called on by teacher, and made a fair response.
- ⊙ Pupil raised hand, was called on by teacher, and made a good response.
- -⊙ Pupil raised hand, was called on by teacher, and made a very good response.
- □ Pupil called on when he did not have hand raised.
- ⊔ Pupil called on when he did not have hand raised; made a single-word response.
- □- Pupil called on when he did not have hand raised; made a fair response.
- ⊔ Pupil called on when he did not have hand raised; made a good response.
- -□ Pupil called on when he did not have hand raised; made a very good response.
- ⊠ Pupil called on when he did not have hand raised; made no response.
- > Pupil asked a question.
- | Pupil spoke without being addressed by teacher.

Figure 12.2 Record of Pupil Participation in a Recitation

SOURCE: Roswell C. Puckett, "Making Supervision Objective," *School Review*, 36, no. 3 (March 1928) 210–211. Reprinted with permission of The University of Chicago, Chicago, Illinois, publisher.

Four Models

It will be helpful in understanding the concept of clinical supervision if we perceive it, as did Cogan, in terms of a cycle consisting of a number of recurring stages or phases.[34] Several authorities have suggested models to guide the practice of teachers and supervisors as they engage in the cycle of supervision. Table 12.2 shows the stages or phases recommended by the models of Goldhammer,[35] Mosher and Purpel,[36] Cogan,[37] and Acheson and Gall.[38]

Table 12.2 Four Models of Clinical Supervision*

Goldhammer (1969) Goldhammer, Anderson and Krajewski (1980) Five stages	Mosher and Purpel (1972) Three stages	Cogan (1973) Eight phases	Acheson and Gall (1980) Three phases
1. Preobservation conference	1. Planning	1. Establishing the teacher-supervisor relationship 2. Planning with the teacher 3. Planning the strategy of observation	1. Planning conference
2. Observation	2. Observation	4. Observing instruction	2. Classroom observation
3. Analysis and strategy	3. Evaluation or analysis	5. Analyzing the teaching-learning processes 6. Planning the strategy of the conference	
4. Supervision conference		7. The conference	3. Feedback conference
5. Postconference analysis		8. Renewed planning	

*Modification of *Table 1: The Process of Clinical Supervision*, in Barbara Nelson Pavan, "Clinical Supervision: Some Signs of Progress," *Texas Tech Journal of Education*, 7, no. 3 (Fall 1980), 248. Reprinted with permission.

Although models differ in number of stages or phases, they all possess three essential ingredients: (a) there is some kind of contact or communication with the teacher prior to an observation; (b) there is some type of classroom observation; and (c) there is some kind of follow-up of the observation. For some of the proponents of clinical supervision the process involves two—and only two—players: one supervisor and one teacher. To others a teacher-peer may substitute for the supervisor. In still more complex versions of the process a number of peers, as, for example, in the case of teaching teams, may substitute for the supervisor.

The practice of peer supervision is growing even though some feel that the concept itself is an anomaly since the very word supervision implies a superordinate-subordinate relationship. Where mutual respect and trust exist, peer or collegial supervision can be an effective process.[39] Alfonso and Goldsberry took note of studies that showed that "teachers report other colleagues to be their first source of professional help, even when supervisory assistance is available."[40] Goldhammer, Anderson, and Krajewski saw value in peer supervision, commenting, "In the case of peer supervision (for example, within a teaching team) we are confident that teachers at whatever respective levels of skill can be extremely helpful to each other."[41]

Extensions of the more common supervisory-teacher model of clinical supervision may very well result in drastic changes in the role of the supervisor. For example, Garman discussed the formation of an "organic team" of six teaching colleagues who directed their own activities.[42] A supervisor who works with a group of this nature would serve as a facilitator and resource person.

Colleagueship in supervision can supplement or conceivably even replace more customary modes of instructional supervision. Recognizing the need for instructional supervision and the shortage of instructional supervisors, Alfonso and Goldsberry suggested:

a new role for supervisors. They might become "orchestrators" of instructional supervision, persons who serve a broker role in the school system, identifying needs and then selecting and recruiting from throughout the school or school system those persons who can contribute to specific tasks of instructional improvement.[43]

These authors recommended that instructional supervisors take on the responsibility for developing colleagueship in supervision.

Whether the helper's role in clinical supervision is performed by a supervisor from the central office or from the individual school or by a teacher's peer(s), three phases appear to be essential to the process: (a) preobservation conference, (b) observation, and (c) postobservation conference.

Preobservation Conference

The word *conference* as used in the cycle of clinical supervision is, I believe, almost too formal a term. It implies an atmosphere, structure, and length which can almost turn a teacher off. Add the term *clinical* and we have a potentiality for setting up an avoidance behavior on the part of the teacher. Teachers might be more accepting and solicitous of help if in their presence we used words like *chat, talk*, or *dialogue* instead of *conference* and *individualized, tailor-made*, or *classroom* instead of *clinical*. Among supervisors, however, we could continue to use the technical language which has already been invented.

A preobservation conference is a face-to-face talk between teacher and supervisor prior to the supervisor's visit to the teacher's classroom. It is the purpose of the preobservation conference to settle on necessary preliminaries. It is already agreed or assumed by the two participants to the conference that the supervisor will visit the teacher and observe the teacher's performance. It is hoped that the teacher is as desirous of having the supervisor visit as the supervisor is of making the visit. Whether the teacher looks forward to help of this nature from the supervisor will depend on whether a feeling of mutual respect has been developed between the two. Conceivably, clinical supervision can be carried on without the existence of mutual respect but in that event the cycle is perfunctory, resented by the teacher, and doomed to failure. Though I would limit the concept of peer supervision to assistance given by one teacher to another, the clinical supervisor should be a peer in the best sense of the term.

It sometimes seems as if clinical supervision, or, for that matter, any type of supervision, is the supervisor's show. In all stages of the cycle of clinical supervision the teacher and supervisor should perceive each other as working together for the ultimate benefit of the learners.

At the preobservation conference the teacher and supervisor together should decide what class the supervisor will visit and when. Thus, the supervisor's schedule is set in advance. Whereas the evaluator of teacher performance may feel the need for unannounced visits, the clinical supervisor has no need of these. The clinical supervisor is not seeking to check on teachers, to keep them "on the ball," or to assess their competence or professionalism for administrative purposes. The clinical supervisor is coming to visit and observe as a trained, skilled aide.

Once the teacher and supervisor have pinpointed the specific class, the teacher will provide background to help the supervisor understand the composition of the group. The teacher will inform the supervisor about the background of the learners and will describe the group. The teacher will discuss special problems he or she is encountering with the group.

In the preobservation conference the teacher will identify special teaching problems he or she is encountering and with which he or she would like some help. Thus, the two participants focus on specific teacher and student behaviors which the supervisor will observe. The teacher may feel the need for someone to observe and provide feedback about such specific behaviors as:

- verbal interaction between students and teacher
- the teacher's use of oral questioning
- the teacher's methods of subgrouping
- students' interaction with each other
- the teacher's presentation of a particular item of content
- the teacher's use of simple control techniques
- the teacher's nonverbal behavior
- classroom management techniques
- provision of individualized help to learners
- the teacher's awareness of what's happening in the classroom
- the teacher's use of media in presenting a lesson
- the clarity with which the teacher gives directions

The teacher will acquaint the supervisor with the unit and lesson plans which will be taught when the supervisor visits. The teacher will explain the objectives of the lesson, the methods of presentation, and techniques of evaluating student performance. The teacher and supervisor will agree on the supervisor's role during the visit. Although some experts allow for the possibility of the supervisor's playing an active role during the visit, e.g., talking with students, the more common and most appropriate role of the supervisor is unobtrusive observer. Also, if the supervisor is to make an accurate record of what is taking place during an observation, he or she cannot be distracted from this task nor should he or she distract the teacher with interjections into the proceedings. I am in complete agreement with Goldhammer, who said:

As a rule, Supervisor should not intervene in the teaching in any manner during Observation. . . . Supervisor should only intervene by explicit prior agreement with Teacher, and in a manner seeming mutually agreeable and appropriate to both except, of course, in physical emergencies.[44]

The supervisor and teacher should agree on procedures the supervisor will follow to record data. Thus, the teacher will not be upset when the supervisor makes marks on an observation instrument or sits busily writing a verbatim account of the events.

The teacher and supervisor should decide whether the use of audio- or video-taping is desirable and, if so, must work out details of their usage. The participants need to agree on how long the supervisor will remain in the classroom and where the supervisor will be seated.

Regarding the time needed Acheson and Gall advised:

Planning conferences need not be long. As a supervisor, you might allow twenty to thirty minutes for the first planning conference unless the teacher has a particularly difficult problem to discuss. Later planning conferences might require only five to ten minutes.[45]

The supervisor should seek to calm the anxieties the teacher may have about the visit. Assuring the teacher of the confidentiality of the data will help. Specialists suggest that conferences be conducted either in the teacher's classroom or office or at another mutually agreed upon location, not in the supervisor's office. Conferencing in the supervisor's office perpetuates the notion of a superordinate-subordinate relationship which the supervisor should attempt to deemphasize.

The supervisor should let the teacher know when he or she will be able to provide feedback about the observation. The supervisor will explain to the teacher that he or she will need some time after the conference to analyze the data and prepare for a postobservation conference. In the preobservation conference the groundwork is laid for the observation.

Observation

If we were to draw up a list of supervisor's tasks which require specialized skills, classroom observation would head the list. On the surface observation would seem a simple task. The supervisor enters the classroom, sits down at the back of the room, watches for a half-hour to an hour, gets up, and leaves. Yet, classroom observation demands a high level of technical and analytical skills. The supervisor must know what to look for, how to look, how to record what is seen, and, later, how to analyze the data and provide the teacher with feedback.

Every observation is a new situation; classroom transactions are never the same. The supervisor must draw on all his or her training and experience to turn in a creditable performance at observing the teacher and students in action.

What to Observe

Two basic approaches to observation are possible, the choice of which is dependent upon the purpose of the supervisor's visit. For want of better terms, we'll call the two approaches *specific* and *global*.

Specific Approach.   If we follow through with the cycle of clinical supervision, the teacher and supervisor in the preobservation conference have decided on the specific behaviors of teachers and students which the supervisor will observe. The supervisor concentrates on the evidence of the presence or absence of the specific behaviors. Thus, if the teacher and supervisor have agreed, for example, that the supervisor will diagnose the teacher's skill in providing reinforcement to the learner, he or she does not attempt to analyze the extent of student participation or testing techniques.

Karolyn J. Snyder has developed on observation training program centering around four variables identified by Benjamin S. Bloom: cues and directives, reinforcement, participation, and corrections and feedback.[46] Mosher and Purpel listed the following factors in teaching:

> The teacher's ability to communicate.
> The logic of the teaching strategy or method employed.
> The teacher's performance of "instrumental tasks."
> The motivational effect of the teaching.
> The quality of the personal relationship established between the teacher and his pupils.
> Content.[47]

A number of specific, observable behaviors are subsumed under each factor.

At each preobservation conference the teacher and supervisor specify the particular behaviors to be observed at the next observation. It is the analysis of these behaviors which the teacher and supervisor discuss in the postobservation conference.

Global Approach.   It is probable that the global approach to teacher evaluation is the more common approach followed by both staff and line supervisors. The global approach is a generalized assessment of teacher performance on a wide variety of teaching skills, usually generic in nature. The supervisor often uses an instrument of some type to guide the assessment of teacher performance, although he or she may record the classroom events without resorting to an instrument. Whatever instrument or system is to be used, the teacher must be made familiar with it.

A global approach is a useful technique for the staff supervisor when the teacher and supervisor wish to make a general appraisal of the teacher's performance. Since the global approach is essentially an assessment of the teacher's total performance, it is particularly suitable for the use of line supervisors, i.e., administrator-supervisors, as a basis for summative evaluation. The administrator-supervisor by observing a teacher several times and assessing the teacher's overall performance can compile sufficient data to make an annual, summative appraisal of performance.

As we have noted in the previous chapter, efforts have been made in recent years to identify the generic skills or competencies which make up the teaching act. The profession has moved closer to the concept of teaching as a science. Thus, supervisors have adopted what we might call a scientific approach, diagnosing teacher performance in respect to specific, identifiable behaviors.

Some of the experts would have us look more closely at teaching as an art rather than a science and, thus, supervision as an art rather than a science. Elliot W. Eisner listed several of the fallacies he saw in scientific supervision as follows:

the *fallacy of additivity* which is committed by attempting to study or supervise teaching using a procedure that implies or assumes that the incidence of particular teaching behaviors—structuring, giving examples, positive and negative reinforcement, and so forth—all have equal pedagogical weight and can be added together to secure an index of the quality of teaching . . .

the *fallacy of composition*, that the whole is equal to the sum of its parts. This is committed when the quality of teaching is determined by counting the incidence of teacher behaviors in a variable or category and then adding to this sum the scores produced in other variables . . .

the *fallacy of the act* . . . the tendency to neglect the process of educational life as it the exclusive referent for observation is the manifest behavior of the student. . . . When we observe pupils or teachers we do not merely look at the behavior they display, but also at its meaning and the quality of their experience . . .

the *fallacy of the act*, . . . the tendency to neglect the process of educational life as it unfolds in classrooms and schools . . .

the *fallacy of method*: neglecting those aspects of teaching that are immune to the criteria and instruments that the researcher employs. . . .[48]

Eisner advocated an artistic approach to supervision. By an artistic approach to supervision Eisner meant:

an approach to supervision that relies on the sensitivity, perceptivity, and knowledge of the supervisor as a way of appreciating the significant subtleties occurring in the classroom, and that exploits the expressive, poetic, and often metaphorical potential of language to convey to teachers or to others whose decisions affect what goes on in schools, what has been observed.[49]

Instead of focusing on just the readily observable specific teaching skills, Eisner would have the supervisor attempt "to improve the quality of educational life in the school."[50]

Eisner believed that the supervisor must "hear the music" as well as observe the action; he/she must judge the character and quality of the teacher's performance, not just the quantitative aspects. Eisner commented:

teachers, too, are differentiated by their style and by their particular strengths. Artistically oriented supervision would recognize this style and try to help the teacher exploit it by strengthening the positive directions already taken.... The connoisseur of teaching, like the connoisseur of the violin or cello, would appreciate these characteristic traits of the performer in addition to the general overall quality of the performance. In other words, both the general level of teaching competence and the unique characteristics of the performance would be perceived and appraised.[51]

Eisner did not believe that artistic supervision could be accomplished using rating instruments. The artistic supervisor, according to Eisner, must possess the ability to appreciate what is happening in the classroom, which he labeled "educational connoisseurship" and to interpret the quality of performance to the teacher, which he called "educational criticism."[52]

The thrust of instructional supervision at the present time is clearly in the direction of a scientific approach with its emphasis on diagnosis of specific, observable teaching behaviors and on the collection of objective data which can be discussed with the teacher.

Artistic supervision would require, I believe, a virtuoso performance beyond the range of many persons who hold supervisory positions. The preparation of specialists who can tune into the many nuances of teaching poses a problem. Present training programs appear more nearly geared to the concept of supervision as a science than as an art.

How to Record

Depending on what the teacher and supervisor have agreed should be observed, they have the choice of recording the events of the classroom by electronic means, written means, or a combination of the two. If they elect to use the former, a decision must be made, assuming the necessary equipment is available, between audio- and video-taping. An audiotape is a helpful supplement to the supervisor's observation and provides an oral verbatim record of what has transpired. An audio record is deficient in that it does not reveal movement and nonverbal behavior of both teachers and students. For this reason the supervisor's presence is necessary even if an audiotape is made of the lesson.

Videotaping holds much promise as a supervisory tool. The videotape reveals most or sometimes, if the group is small, all of the class transaction. Conceivably, with videotaping the supervisor might not need to be present in order to analyze the classroom events. Analysis could be done from the tapes. Attempts have been made to apply this techinique to the supervision of student teachers. While videotaping in the absence of the supervisor is not to be encouraged as a standard practice, such a technique could augment the supervisor's help by providing additional data beyond the data which the supervisor has garnered from classroom visitations.

Regardless of means for recording, electronic or otherwise, the teacher and supervisor must be in agreement on their use. It is true that the presence of electronic equipment can cause teachers and students to be distracted. A practice run or two, however, will take the edge off the novelty. After a time or two the taping loses its newness and the teacher and students shed their self-consciousness at being before the camera.

In order for the supervisor to concentrate on the lesson, a technician should be available for the actual taping. This could be done by a trained cadre of older students if media technicians are not available.

Even if electronic equipment is used in observing, the supervisor must become proficient in recording classroom events by written means. Among the techniques available to the supervisor are (1) verbatim recording, (2) note taking, (3) instruments, and (4) charting.

Verbatim Recording. Goldhammer strongly recommended that the supervisor make verbatim records of the classroom events.[53] He argued logically that verbatim records provide an accurate record of what has taken place and permit the supervisor to recall with the teacher exactly what transpired. Verbatim records are the written counterpart of electronic records. The supervisor has taken down what has been said word for word.

To record a lesson verbatim the supervisor must be adept at recording either by longhand or shorthand. It has been suggested that supervisors learn shorthand or speedwriting[54] or that the ability to stenotype would help.[55] I am not an advocate of verbatim recording. I feel this technique keeps the supervisor so busy that he or she does not have time to discern the nuances of what is happening in the classroom. Unless the supervisor is isolated at the back of the room, the recording of the lesson word for word can in itself be distracting to the teacher and students.

Note Taking. The supervisor may discreetly take notes on everything and anything that he or she sees. It should be remembered that the majority of observations conducted by clinical supervisors will center on specific behaviors. Whereas a verbatim transcript of the lesson would include these behaviors, it does not seem necessary to record behaviors beyond those which the supervisor has agreed to observe. A verbatim record is not necessary at all if the lesson is taped by either audio or video means. The making of notes is less conspicuous and therefore less distracting than verbatim recording. Judicious notes made by a keen observer can provide an adequate recording of the classroom activities.

Acheson and Gall suggested the use of note taking, which they called an "anecdotal record," as a technique which could be used when the teacher and supervisor have *not* identified specific behaviors to observe.[56] The anecdotal record, composed of "short," "objective," and "nonevaluative" handwritten notes, forms the basis of a "protocol."[57] Acheson and Gall recommended that the handwritten notes be typed so they may be more easily studied by the teacher.[58]

Somewhat less than a complete verbatim transcript and somewhat more than simple notes is *selected verbatim*, which Acheson and Gall described as follows:

As the term implies, the supervisor makes a written record of exactly what is said, that is, a verbatim transcript. Not all verbal events are recorded, however. Supervisor and teacher select beforehand certain kinds of verbal events to be written down; in this sense, the verbatim record is intended to be "selective."[59]

CLASSROOM OBSERVATION FORM
Full-time Teachers
DADE COUNTY PUBLIC SCHOOLS

NAME Last	First	Middle	Date of Observation

Subject Area or Grade Observed

OVERALL SUMMARY RATING: ACCEPTABLE ( )   UNACCEPTABLE ( )

REMARKS:_____

SIGNATURE OF OBSERVER:_____ DATE:_____

                                                    Title

SIGNATURE OF TEACHER:_____ DATE:_____

Teacher's signature means the teacher has seen and received the document.

CATEGORY I - Preparation and Planning The teacher shows evidence of preparation and planning in structuring the learning experiences of students.			OVERALL CATEGORY RATING: Acceptable Unacceptable ( ) ( )
Indicators	Rating	Supporting Statement	Recommendations for improvement and support the teacher will receive to achieve recommendations
A. The classroom activities reflect evidence of effective instructional planning.	( ) A ( ) U		
B. The teacher develops lesson plans.	( ) A ( ) U		
C. The teacher plans and makes necessary arrangements for materials, equipment and supplies.	( ) A ( ) U		
CATEGORY II - Knowledge of Subject Matter The teacher shows evidence of subject area competency.			Acceptable Unacceptable ( ) ( )
CATEGORY III - Classroom Management The teacher administers classroom procedures effectively and maintains control.			Acceptable Unacceptable ( ) ( )
CATEGORY IV - Techniques of Instruction The teacher employs instructional techniques which motivate and enable students to learn.			Acceptable Unacceptable ( ) ( )
A. Adapts materials and methods to the interests, needs and abilities of the students.	( ) A ( ) U		
B. Provides opportunities for students to express their ideas.	( ) A ( ) U		
C. Uses instructional strategies for teaching the subject matter.	( ) A ( ) U		
D. Gives clear assignments and directions and allows ample time for completion of tasks.	( ) A ( ) U		

CATEGORY V – Assessment Techniques The teacher utilizes assessment techniques which motivate and enable students to learn.		Acceptable ( )	Unacceptable ( )
A. Makes assessments of each student's academic and/or vocational progress.	( ) A ( ) U		
B. Utilizes information from a variety of sources (e.g., parents, school personnel, records) in order to identify each student's learning levels, interests and needs.	( ) A ( ) U		
C. Maintains records of student acheivement.	( ) A ( ) U		
CATEGORY VI – Teacher-Student Relationships The teacher establishes relationships with students which reflect equal recognition of and respect for every individual.		Acceptable ( )	Unacceptable ( )
CATEGORY VII – Professional Responsibility The teacher assumes professional responsibility.		Acceptable ( )	Unacceptable ( )
A. Complies with established School Board Rules, administrative directives and contract provisions duly ratified by the appropriate bargaining unit and the School Board.	( ) A ( ) U		
B. Performs responsibilities and required school routines with punctuality.	( ) A ( ) U		

A = Acceptable   U = Unacceptable

Observations rated Unacceptable in any specific category are documented by incidents and/or annotations in the appropriate section.

White copy – Principal
Yellow copy – Teacher

Figure 12.3 Classroom Observation Form

SOURCE: Dade County Public Schools, *Classroom Observation Form*, Miami, Fla., July 19, 1977. Reprinted with permission.

The supervisor may elect to limit recording only to selective verbatim which focuses on specific behaviors, may jot down only brief notes, or may use a combination of verbatim recording and note taking. Recording of observation data can be a very personal undertaking and, like handwriting, may not be decipherable from one supervisor to the other.

Instruments.   Many supervisors prefer to utilize an instrument of some kind to guide their observations. Which instrument they use will depend on the decision made by the teacher and supervisor as to whether the supervisor will make a comprehensive, i.e., global analysis of the teacher's performance or whether he or she will limit the observation to specific behaviors. Let's briefly examine the nature of two types of instruments: one to make a comprehensive or global assessment and one to evaluate specific behaviors.

1. *Global.* We do not have to look far to find examples of instruments designed to survey teaching behaviors rather broadly. The movement toward the specification of generic competencies has stimulated school systems to create instruments for assessing those competencies. The checklist shown at the end of Chapter 4 is an illustration of an instrument which could be used—and subsequently has been used—to assess the generic competencies discussed in the early chapters of this book.[60]

The Dade County (Florida) Public Schools have developed a coordinated formative and summative evaluation system which encompasses the generic competencies defined by the state of Florida. Reproduced in Figure 12.3 is the formative evaluation instrument used for classroom observation in Dade County. In the next chapter you will find the companion instrument used for annual evaluation of teachers by their principals.

As an additional illustration of a formative, global instrument we can look at the Classroom Observation Form used in the Richmond County (Georgia) Public Schools (see Figure 12.4). The Richmond County Classroom Observation Form is part of a coordinated system which includes a self-appraisal instrument and a teacher appraisal instrument as well as the Classroom Observation Form. All three of the Richmond County instruments are based on the generic competencies specified by the state of Georgia. The form requires an understanding of the competencies, indicators (subdivisions of the competencies), and descriptors (statements by which the indicators are rated) built into the state's beginning teacher assessment program.[61]

```
                    RICHMOND COUNTY BOARD OF EDUCATION
                       CLASSROOM OBSERVATION FORM

  Name_____School/Dept._____

  All of this form or part of this form may be used to record teacher observation
  data.  The observer is to refer to the descriptors in the Teacher Appraisal
  Guidebook.  The descriptors that describe what the observer sees are to be
  circled.  The number of descriptors circled determines the ratings.

                        COMPETENCIES AND INDICATORS                      Rating

  PLANS INSTRUCTION                                            Descriptors

   1.  Specifies or selects learner objectives for lessons........ a  b  c  d  _____
   2.  Specifies or selects teaching methods for lessons.......... a  b  c  d  _____
   3.  Specifies or selects contents, materials, and equipment
       for lessons............................................... a  b  c  d  _____
   4.  Specifies or selects materials and procedures for assessing
       learner progress on the objectives........................ a  b  c  d  _____
   5.  Plans instruction at a variety of levels.................. a  b  c  d  _____

  Comments:_____
  _____
```

USES TECHNIQUES, METHODS, AND MEDIA RELATED TO THE OBJECTIVES

6. Uses teaching methods appropriate for objectives, learners,
    and environment.. a b c d _____
7. Uses instructional equipment and other instructional aids.. a b c d _____
8. Uses instructional materials that provide learners with
    appropriate practice on objectives........................ a b c d _____
9. Provides for individual differences among learners......... a b c d _____

Comments:_____

_____

COMMUNICATES WITH LEARNERS

10. Gives directions and explanations related to lesson
    content... a b c d _____
11. Provides feedback to learners throughout the lesson........ a b c d _____
12. Uses acceptable written and oral expression with learners.. a b c d _____

Comments:_____

_____

DEMONSTRATES A VARIETY OF TEACHING METHODS

13. Implements learning activities in a logical sequence....... a b c d _____
14. Uses a variety of teaching methods......................... a b c d _____
15. Group arrangement(s) is appropriate for teaching
    procedures.. a b c d _____

Comments:_____

_____

REINFORCES AND ENCOURAGES LEARNER INVOLVEMENT IN INSTRUCTION

16. Uses procedures which get learners involved in lessons..... a b c d _____
17. Maintains learner involvement in lessons................... a b c d _____
18. Reinforces and encourages the efforts of learners to
    maintain involvement...................................... a b c d _____

Comments:_____

_____

DEMONSTRATES AN UNDERSTANDING OF THE SUBJECT

19. Helps learners recognize the purpose/importance of
    topics or activities...................................... a b c d _____
20. Demonstrates knowledge in the subject area................. a b c d _____

Comments:_____

_____

ORGANIZES TIME, SPACE, MATERIALS, AND EUQIPMENT FOR INSTRUCTION

21. Attends to non-instructional tasks......................... a b c d _____
22. Uses instructional time efficiently....................... a b c d _____
23. Provides a learning environment that is attractive and
    orderly... a b c d _____

Comments:_____

_____

```
DEMONSTRATES ENTHUSIASM FOR TEACHING, LEARNING, AND THE SUBJECT                  Rating

                                                              Descriptors

24.  Communicates personal enthusiasm.......................... a  b  c  d  _____
25.  Stimulates learner interest.............................. a  b  c  d  _____

Comments:_____

_____


HELPS LEARNERS DEVELOP POSITIVE SELF-CONCEPTS

26.  Demonstrates warmth and friendliness...................... a  b  c  d  _____
27.  Demonstrates patience, empathy, and understanding.......... a  b  c  d  _____

Comments:_____

_____


MANAGES CLASSROOM INTERACTIONS

28.  Provides feedback to learners about their behavior......... a  b  c  d  _____
29.  Promotes comfortable interpersonal relationships........... a  b  c  d  _____
30.  Maintains appropriate classroom behavior................... a  b  c  d  _____
31.  Manages disruptive behavior among learners................. a  b  c  d  _____

Comments:_____

_____


GENERAL COMMENTS:_____

_____

_____

_____

_____


Date: _____        Observer: _____

Distribution:  Principal - White      Teacher - Canary            Page 2 of 2
```

Figure 12.4 Classroom Observation Form

SOURCE: Richmond County Public Schools, *Classroom Observation Form*, Augusta, Ga. Reprinted with permission.

Comprehensive observation instruments of the type shown by these examples are widely used by both staff supervisors and line administrators.

2. *Specific.* When it comes to the use of instruments for evaluating specific behaviors, the range of possibilities is both expanded and narrowed. It is expanded because the specific behaviors are so varied; it is narrowed because the number of instruments for evaluating particular behaviors is so small. In fact, for some specific behaviors there are no existing instruments in which case the supervisor will either have to create one or use another means for gathering the data.

The supervisor may or may not be fortunate enough to find a ready-made instrument. The Flanders Interaction Analysis Categories mentioned in the preceding chapter are one example of an instrument created to evaluate one specific set of behaviors: verbal interaction.[62] Charles M. Galloway designed a system for evaluating nonverbal behavior, primarily the teacher's.[63] Jacob S. Kounin developed a system for evaluating classroom management and discipline.[64] A search of the literature will reveal a number of instruments which may be useful to the supervisor. Among references helpful on this topic are the following:

> Ronald T. Hyman, *School Administrator's Handbook of Teacher Supervision and Evaluation Methods*, Englewood Cliffs, N.J., Prentice-Hall, 1975.

> Robert F. McNergney and Carol A. Carrier, *Teacher Development*, New York, Macmillan, 1981.

> Anita Simon and E. Gil Boyer, *Mirrors for Behavior III: An Anthology of Observation Instruments*, Philadelphia, Pa., Research for Better Schools, 1974.

If the supervisor is unable to find or create an instrument to evaluate specific behaviors agreed on by the teacher and supervisor, he or she may turn to recording classroom events verbatim or making notes. If using an instrument, recording verbatim or taking notes does not appear feasible, charting may provide an answer to the observation of certain classroom behaviors.

Charting.   We have already seen an example of charting earlier in this chapter—Puckett's system for recording pupil participation in a recitation. Starting with a class seating chart and a devised key the supervisor can record a wide variety of data. He or she can determine which pupils are on task and which off task. He or she can observe and record the flow of communication between teacher and pupils and among students. The supervisor can record the movement of the teacher and students about the room.[65]

By the careful use of symbols of his or her own choosing the supervisor can record on a class chart a great deal of information about what is taking place. Observation is the stage of the cycle of clinical supervision during which data are collected. The supervisor must master skills of observing and recording classroom events.

Postobservation Conference

Soon after the observation the teacher and supervisor meet once again at a mutually satisfactory location to carry out the phase which most specialists believe to be the most difficult and most important in the entire cycle: the postobservation or follow-up conference. The major purpose of the postobservation conference is to give feedback to the teacher about the teacher's performance. It is true that perceptive teachers can think through and make an analysis of their own performance. With a video-tape of their own performance teachers should be able to diagnose their teaching almost as well as the supervisor can. But the provision of feedback from an interested helper enables teachers to see their performance as others see it.

The discussion at the follow-up conference should center on the data collected by the supervisor, not on the supervisor's experiences, biases, and feelings. The supervisor must take every precaution to keep the conference from being a threatening situation to the teacher. Therefore, the proper subject of the conference is *the teaching* observed by the supervisor, not *the teacher.*

It is generally agreed by the experts that a short period of time should elapse before the supervisor and teacher get together to discuss the data. This allows the supervisor time to organize and analyze the data and to prepare for the ensuing conference. Thus, at the preobservation conference the supervisor will have advised the teacher that he or she will need a day or two (or more, if necessary) to take care of such tasks as transcribing notes; listening to or looking at tapes, if any; searching for evidence of the behaviors which were to be observed; organizing his or her notes in some coherent form; and deciding what approach to take in the conference. The supervisor may make some bland comments at the end of the observation assuring the teacher that he or she will be back in touch in a day or two to set a time for the conference. At this point they might even talk about tentative days and times which would be convenient to both the teacher and supervisor.

Madeline Hunter identified six types of supervisory conferences: five instructional (i.e., postobservation) and one evaluative ("the summation of what has occurred in and resulted from a series of instructional conferences").[66] Hunter set forth purposes and objectives for each of the five types of instructional conferences as follows:

1. Type A Instructional Conference—*Purpose*: To identify, label, and explain the teacher's effective instructional behaviors giving research-based reasons for their effectiveness so the teacher knows what he or she has done and why it worked, and in the future can do it on purpose. *Objective*: At the end of the conference (not in some nebulous future) the teacher will identify teaching decisions and behaviors that promoted learning and state why they were effective....

2. Type B Instructional Conference—*Purpose*: To stimulate the development of a repertoire of effective teaching responses so the teacher is not limited to those most frequently used. *Objective*: Teacher and observer will generate alternatives to behaviors which were effective in the observed lesson in case they should be less effective in a different situation....

3. Type C Instructional Conference—*Purpose*: To encourage teachers to identify those parts of a teaching episode with which they were not satisfied so that, in collaboration with the observer, strategies for reducing or eliminating future unsatisfactory outcomes will be developed. *Objective*: The teacher will identify solutions with potential for changing unsatisfying aspects of the lesson....

4. Type D Instructional Conference—*Purpose*: To identify and label those less effective aspects of teaching that were not evident to the teacher and to develop alternative procedures that have potential for effectiveness. *Objective*: The teacher will select alternative behaviors he or she might substitute for behaviors perceived by the observer (and hopefully by the teacher) as not so effective ...

5. Type E Instructional Conference—*Purpose*: To promote continuing growth of excellent teachers. *Objective*: The teacher will select next steps in expanding his or her own professional growth.[67]

The postobservation conference should not be perceived by the participants as an assessment of the teacher's performance in the same vein as the principal's summative evaluation but rather as an opportunity for the supervisor to provide valuable feedback for the teacher's consideration.

The conduct of an effective conference requires a special set of technical and personal skills on the part of the supervisor. He or she must know how to give helpful, and sometimes negative, feedback without injuring the teacher's ego or arousing defensive behaviors. Kyte long ago suggested a three-point outline for the conference which remains good procedure:

1. strong points of the lesson
2. weak points in the lesson
3. doubtful points not clearly understood[68]

Mosher and Purpel recommended that the supervisor avoid making two types of analysis with the teacher: the simple inventory of events and recounting of critical incidents which took place during the observation. Instead they advised that the supervisor help the teacher to discern *"recurring patterns* in content, teaching or student behavior and of their *possible interrelations."*[69]

The supervisor's manner and attitudes are as important as the technical analysis which he or she makes for the teacher. In Chapter 2 we contrasted directive and nondirective behavior. A nondirective posture can put the teacher at ease. For example, a few processing-type comments at the beginning of the conference can go a long way toward establishing rapport. A question to the teacher such as, "How did you feel about the lesson?" can be useful in breaking the ice. Surely, the supervisor should not come to the conference with a rigid analysis on the basis of which he or she proceeds to lecture the teacher. The supervisor needs to avoid sermonizing and conveying a loftier-than-thou superiority. The supervisor should remember that it is far easier to tell a person, especially after the fact, how to do something than to do it oneself.

The supervisor should keep in mind that teachers want specific help, specific suggestions. They want supervisors to talk to specific points which can help them to improve. The supervisor should eschew extended chattiness and effusive behavior. He or she needs to strike a friendly, professional mien.

Whereas a generally nondirective approach which probes for the teacher's feelings and an analysis of his or her own performance appears to me appropriate, directive behavior at times may be necessary. For example, the supervisor may need to focus on a point with an expression such as, "Here's the way I see it. I believe it would have been more effective if. . . ." As a matter of fact, the degree of directiveness and nondirectiveness needs to be tailored to the individual teacher and to the relationship between the teacher and the supervisor. When nondirective measures fail with an uncommunicative and inarticulate teacher, the supervisor may need to resort to more directive means.

Carl D. Glickman has introduced a collaborative orientation between directive and nondirective behavior.[70] Glickman described a supervisory behavior continuum from directive to collaborative to nondirective orientation. For each of these dominant behaviors Glickman outlined a pattern of specific behaviors, as follows:[71]

Directive Orientation	Collaborative Orientation	Nondirective Orientation
Clarifying	Listening	Listening
Presenting	Clarifying	Clarifying
Demonstrating	*Presenting	Encouraging
Directing	Problem solving	*Presenting
Standardizing	*Negotiating	*Negotiating
Reinforcing		
	*Supervisor-initiated	*Teacher-initiated

The supervisor must detect which dominant behavior will be most effective with a particular teacher and adjust his or her style accordingly. Thus, the supervisor's behavior is not a monolithic, unchanging, machine-like process with a single orientation which will be unfailingly successful in all situations, but a flexible, changing, human process.

The postobservation conference has maximum chance for success if both the teacher and supervisor manifest a sense of confidence in their own roles. A successful conference cannot occur without a feeling of rapport, which the supervisor should have established with the teacher long before initiating the cycle of clinical supervision.

PROBLEMS IN CLINICAL SUPERVISION

Clinical supervision is not without its critics, who raise the following questions:

Who will do the supervising?
Do we have the necessary resources?
For whom should clinical supervision be provided?
Are there other models for assisting teachers which are as effective or more effective than clinical supervision?

Let's briefly examine each of these issues.

Who Will Do the Supervising?

We have already explored in Chapter 2 two issues as they relate to supervision in general. First, we have the continuing question, which we have reexamined in this chapter in the context of clinical supervision: whether the administrator can be or should be the clinical supervisor. Since this issue has been dealt with in preceding pages of this book, I shall not belabor the point. However, it is worth reiterating that in some schools where the principal serves as both administrator and instructional supervisor, help in supervising is often available and unused in the form of department heads, grade coordinators, team leaders, and lead teachers.

Second, another question is raised about clinical supervision which we considered in Chapter 2 in reference to supervision in general: should the clinical supervisor be a generalist or a specialist? Both prevailing practice and present-day preservice and in-service training programs appear to be slanted toward the use of generalists who can appraise generic teaching skills. Much of the literature, including this textbook, aims at the development of skills in supervising across disciplines and levels.

Mosher and Purpel stressed the importance of the supervisor's specialization in the teaching field when they wrote:

The supervisor is, first, a content specialist, because it is not considered feasible to analyze teaching effectiveness independently of the content of what is being taught. This may appear to labor the obvious. Nonetheless, the question of whether people can supervise *across* subject-matter areas is very much an issue in supervision.[72]

Given the choice, I would incline toward utilizing the services of instructional supervisors who are trained and experienced in their fields of specialization *as well as* general methods of instruction. But, as Voltaire made us realize, the quest for the best of all possible worlds can be both ludicrous and not very productive. Wealthier school systems can probably afford to deploy a cadre of specialists who are at the same time generalists. The less-well-to-do school districts may have to work with one or more generalists who are not familiar with specialties outside of their own field(s) of specialization. In any case, whether a school system uses administrators or supervisors, generalists or specialists, effective supervision is still possible with appropriate in-service training.

Do We Have the Necessary Resources?

Time, money, and personnel—all interrelated—pose problems when a school system is deciding whether or not to launch a program of clinical supervision. We can calculate a large amount of time per teacher if we tally the hours for each phase of clinical supervision. Let's postulate a bare minimum of time to be spent for each teacher as follows:

Preobservation conference	20 minutes
Observation	30 minutes
Analysis of data	30 minutes
Postobservation conference	30 minutes
	110 minutes

Thus, the supervisor needs at the very least approximately two hours per teacher per cycle of clinical supervision; this figure is somewhat unrealistically on the low side.

You can see the enormity of the time problem if you multiply this estimate by the number of times the teacher and supervisor repeat the cycle; allow time for the supervisor to make a record of the preobservation and postobservation conferences; allocate time for typing transcripts or notes of observation; increase the time of observation from 30 minutes to 50; set aside time for what Goldhammer called a "postmortem" or "post-conference analysis."[73] The time factor is enlarged if arrangements must be made for electronic media, and observation time is doubled if the supervisor is to review an audio- or videotape of the lesson.

School system administrators will need to decide how to allocate their dollars for personnel, equipment, and materials between clinical supervision and general supervision, including curriculum and staff development.

For Whom Should Clinical Supervision Be Provided?

Ideally, clinical supervision should be available to all teachers—experienced, inexperienced, effective, ineffective, pedestrian, and talented. Given the paucity of resources and the demands of the job, it appears unlikely that an adequate program of clinical supervision can be made available to every teacher. Consequently, those teachers who are experiencing problems are more likely to need and call for assistance of this nature.

Some supervisors feel it best to ignore those teachers who are doing quality work. On the other hand, Hunter argued against neglecting excellent teachers. She commented, "We have learned to challenge gifted students to encourage continuing growth, but often our gifted teachers are left to provide their own stimulation or to become bored and atrophied."[74]

If adequate material and human resources are, indeed, available, clinical supervision should be provided for all teachers who wish to secure this type of aid. The instructional supervisor as contrasted with the administrative supervisor cannot and should not thrust himself or herself on the teacher. Thus, a number of teachers may opt out of the opportunity for receiving help from the supervisory consultant. To some degree supervisors can judge their own success by the demand of teachers for their services.

If a school system is not able to cater to the supervisory needs of all teachers, it must do what school systems have always done—set priorities and/or put out fires. Those that are most in need must be assured of help if for no other reason than the well-being of their students. A better solution, of course, would be sufficient funding for our schools so that adequate supervision can be made available to all who need and want it.

Are There Models Other Than the Clinical?

The clinical model calls for diagnosis of teaching behaviors and prescriptions to change. Theresa Reilkoff took note of problems with the clinical supervision model when she said:

principals, researchers, and theoreticians seem to view clinical supervision as it is currently conceived to be of limited practical value in the classroom because of its formalism, its time constraints, its drain on the personal and professional resources of teachers and supervisors, and its paternalism.[75]

To overcome these difficulties she advocated instead what she called "supportive supervision," which she defined as follows:

Supportive supervision is that system in which supervisor and teacher collaborate to assess and maximize student performance. Unlike clinical supervision, which focuses on teaching behavior, supportive supervision focuses on the student. Student attitudes, behaviors, and learning outcomes are analyzed for the purpose of their improvement. At no time during this action-oriented process is the teacher evaluated or negatively criticized.[76]

Yet, the clinical model has begun to take root. It is reinforced by the movement toward competency-based teacher education. It fits in well with the newer emphasis placed by teacher educators on field-based training. It offers a system which has had a lengthy period of development. There is even some degree of evidence that clinical supervision may be helpful, as Reilkoff duly noted in the following passage:

Although outcomes of clinical supervision have not as yet been subject to rigorous statistical analysis, emergent work does suggest that the practice of clinical supervision contributes to statistically significant changes in teachers' verbal interactions, teaching strategies, and teaching behavior, at least in carefully controlled laboratory conditions.[77]

Cheryl Granade Sullivan observed that the research on clinical supervision has not reached a point where we can safely make generalizations about the clinical model.[78] Mosher and Purpel took note of some of the difficulties with clinical supervision but saw value in the process:

Clinical supervision is full of gaps. It is a fact—an extremely sobering one—that we don't know, either theoretically or empirically, who the effective teacher is or what effective teaching is. It is a fact that there is evidence of very low validity and reliability in the analyses, inferences and evaluations supervisors make about teaching behavior. It is a fact that there is no conclusive empirical evidence that clinical supervision changes what teachers do. We do, however, have significant clinical opinion and experience on these questions. A decade of practice, some attempt to conceptualize clinical supervision and considerable experience suggest that this method of instructing teachers *does* make a difference.[79]

We can argue about process and procedures but logic supports a one-to-one, face-to-face relationship between a teacher and an able supervisor as an incomparable means of helping the teacher grow. In fact, it is a way of helping both the teacher and supervisor to grow. When personal and professional growth takes place, the entire school system and its clientele benefit. Clinical supervision provides a setting for such growth to occur.

SUMMARY

Clinical supervision is the provision of supervisory help to the individual teacher. It is formative in nature, designed to assist the teacher to improve instruction. The typical clinical model calls for a one-to-one, face-to-face relationship between the teacher and supervisor. Clinical supervision focuses on the events which take place in the classroom. Thus, it is both data based and field based.

Models of clinical supervision posit a cycle which consists of a number of stages or phases. Minimally, a model would encompass three stages: preobservation conference, observation, and postobservation conference.

In the preobservation conference the teacher and supervisor make plans for the supervisor's forthcoming visit to the classroom. They decide on specific behaviors to be observed. During the observation the supervisor looks for evidence of the behaviors and makes a record of what transpired. Among the means for recording classroom events are (1) electronic media, (2) verbatim and selective verbatim transcripts, (3) note taking, (4) instruments, and (5) charting.

A postobservation conference should take place after the supervisor has had time to analyze and organize the data. Both pre- and postobservation conferences should occur in a mutually acceptable location. In the cycle of clinical supervision the supervisor plays the role of knowledgeable, trained, and experienced peer of the teacher.

Clinical supervision requires the supervisor to possess skills in observing, diagnosis, prescribing, and conferencing. In addition, the supervisor must manifest attitudes of a helping relationship and interest in the teacher.

The aim of clinical supervision is improvement of instruction and thereby improvement in student achievement. It is not designed for evaluating teachers for administrative purposes.

It is possible for a teacher's peer to assume the role of clinical supervisor. The provision of adequate time, personnel, equipment, and materials poses a problem for school systems which desire to conduct a program of clinical supervision.

Alternatives to the clinical model have been suggested such as an artistic approach to supervision and supportive supervision. Although more research is needed, there is some indication that clinical supervision can be effective.

ACTIVITIES FOR FURTHER STUDY

1. Describe each of the following:
   a. Clinical supervision
   b. Peer supervision
   c. Developmental supervision
   d. Supportive supervision
2. Prepare a report on Morris Cogan's model of clinical supervision.
3. Prepare a report on Robert Goldhammer's model of clinical supervision.
4. Contrast the first edition of Robert Goldhammer's book with the second edition revised by Robert H. Anderson and Robert J. Krajewski.

5. Report on any existing programs of clinical supervision which you can locate.
6. Role-play a preobservation conference.
7. Observe a class in action and record the events verbatim for 20 minutes.
8. Observe a class in action and record the events by means of notes for 30 minutes.
9. Report on kinds of data which can be recorded by means of a class seating chart.
10. Using the book by Keith A. Acheson and Meredith Damien Gall as a guide select a seating chart exercise, try it out on a class, and report on your experience in using the technique.
11. Videotape a class and analyze the tape. If the teacher of the class wishes, conduct a second analysis with him or her.
12. Prepare a review of Elliot W. Eisner's views on artistic supervision.
13. Critique Theresa Reilkoff's proposal for supportive supervision.
14. Prepare an analytical report on Carl D. Glickman's monograph, *Developmental Supervision*.
15. Report on recommendations for observing made by writers on the subject prior to 1950.
16. Collect and analyze samples of classroom observation instruments.
17. Respond to the question: Under what conditions should clinical supervisors conduct global assessments of the teacher's performance?
18. Defend or challenge the concept of peer supervision, stating reasons.
19. Locate in the literature or in practice models of clinical supervision which are *not* on a one-teacher to one-supervisor basis. Discuss the pros and cons of group models.
20. Select one of the following specific behaviors and choose or create an instrument by which you would assess it. If you use an existing instrument, cite the specific instrument and source:
    a. verbal interaction
    b. nonverbal behavior
    c. providing feedback to the students
    d. stimulus variation
    e. individualization of instruction
21. Design, conduct, and report on a simple study to determine the following:
    a. Whether principals feel they can be effective as instructional supervisors.
    b. Whether teachers feel the principal can be effective as an instructional supervisor.
22. Design, conduct, and report on a simple study to determine the following:
    a. Whether supervisors feel they can assist teachers effectively in a field of specialization for which they have not been trained.
    b. Whether teachers feel supervisors can assist them effectively in a field of specialization for which the supervisors have not been trained.
23. Design your own classroom observation instrument for global evaluation of teacher performance.
24. Apply the observation instruments you created for activities 20 and 23 in

a live situation or with a videotape of an actual classroom situation and interpret the data.

25. Select or create and apply in a live situation an observation instrument designed to assess overall performance of a teacher on *specific* rather than *generic* teaching skills in a particular subject area, such as the evaluation of teaching third-grade reading, the teaching of sixth-grade science, the teaching of beginning algebra, and the teaching of tenth-grade physical education.

NOTES

1. Morris L. Cogan, *Clinical Supervision*, Boston, Houghton Mifflin, 1973, 8.
2. Ibid., 9.
3. Ibid.
4. Robert Goldhammer, Robert H. Anderson, and Robert J. Krajewski, *Clinical Supervision: Special Methods for the Supervision of Teachers*, 2d ed., New York, Holt, Rinehart and Winston, 1980, 26–27.
5. Goldhammer, 1st ed., 1969, 54.
6. Ibid.
7. Barbara Nelson Pavan, "Clinical Supervision: Some Signs of Progress," *Texas Tech Journal of Education* 7, no. 3 (Fall 1980): 241, 250.
8. Goldhammer, Anderson, and Krajewski, 27. See also Robert H. Anderson in William H. Lucio, ed., *Supervision: Perspectives and Propositions*, Alexandria, Va., Association for Supervision and Curriculum Development, 1967, 29–41.
9. Goldhammer, Anderson, and Krajewski, 28.
10. Keith A. Acheson and Meredith Damien Gall, *Techniques in the Clinical Supervision of Teachers: Preservice and Inservice Applications*, New York, Longman, 1980, 15–16.
11. Ibid.
12. Ibid., 8.
13. Goldhammer, Anderson, and Krajewski, 26.
14. Ralph L. Mosher and David E. Purpel, *Supervision: The Reluctant Profession*, Boston, Houghton Mifflin, 1972, 84.
15. Ibid., 110–111.
16. Noreen Garman, "The Clinical Approach to Supervision," in Thomas J. Sergiovanni, ed., *Supervision of Teaching*, 1982 Yearbook, Alexandria, Va., Association for Supervision and Curriculum Development, 1982, 35–52.
17. Ibid., 38.
18. Ibid., 52.
19. Ibid.
20. Robert J. Alfonso and Lee Goldsberry, "Colleagueship in Supervision," in Thomas J. Sergiovanni, ed., *Supervision of Teaching*, 1982 Yearbook, Alexandria, Va., Association for Supervision and Curriculum Development, 1982, 94.
21. Robert J. Alfonso, Gerald R. Firth, and Richard F. Neville, *Instructional Supervision: A Behavior System*, 2nd ed., Boston, Allyn and Bacon, 1981, 121.
22. Ibid.
23. Garman, 42.
24. George C. Kyte, *How to Supervise: A Guide to Educational Principles and Progressive Practices of Educational Supervision*, Boston, Houghton Mifflin, 1930, 138.
25. Ibid., 171.
26. Ibid., 142.
27. Ibid., 147.
28. Ibid., 149–150.

29. Ibid., 150.
30. Ibid., 156–157.
31. Ibid., 160.
32. Ibid., 139.
33. Ibid., 158.
34. Cogan, 10.
35. Goldhammer, 1st ed., 57. Goldhammer, Anderson, and Krajewski, 32.
36. Mosher and Purpel, 81.
37. Cogan, 10–13.
38. Acheson and Gall, 8–11.
39. Richard D. Hawthorne distinguished between a peer model and a collegial model. With a peer model, according to Hawthorne, one teacher evaluates another whereas with a collegial model a small group of teachers evaluates another teacher. See Richard D. Hawthorne, "Teacher Evaluation," in Lloyd W. Dull, *Supervision: School Leadership Handbook*, Columbus, Ohio, Charles E. Merrill, 1981, 270.
40. Alfonso and Goldsberry, 91.
41. Goldhammer, Anderson, and Krajewski, 28–29.
42. Garman, 48–49.
43. Alfonso and Goldsberry, 107.
44. Goldhammer, 1st ed., 89.
45. Acheson and Gall, 43.
46. Goldhammer, Anderson, and Krajewski, 74.
47. Mosher and Purpel, 92–95.
48. Elliot W. Eisner, "An Artistic Approach to Supervision," in Thomas J. Sergiovanni, ed., *Supervision of Teaching*, 1982 Yearbook, Alexandria, Va., Association for Supervision and Curriculum Development, 1982, 55–57.
49. Ibid., 59.
50. Ibid., 60.
51. Ibid., 60–61.
52. Ibid., 62.
53. Goldhammer, 1st ed., 88–89.
54. Goldhammer, Anderson, and Krajewski, 78.
55. Goldhammer, 1st ed., 87.
56. Acheson and Gall, 128.
57. Ibid.
58. Ibid., 129.
59. Ibid., 88.
60. This checklist has been used in a form slightly modified at the suggestion of Dr. Sarah W. J. Pell of Florida International University. The modified form omits the sections selection of resources and selection of strategies, provides a space for comments to the right of the *Yes* and *No* columns, and adds at the bottom places for data on duration of time in minutes, names of teacher and school, grade, and date.
61. For further explanation of competencies, indicators, and descriptors see Chapter 13.
62. Ned A. Flanders, *Analyzing Teacher Behavior*, Reading, Mass., Addison-Wesley, 1970.
63. Charles M. Galloway, *An Exploratory Study of Observational Procedures for Determining Teacher Nonverbal Communication*, doctoral dissertation, University of Florida, 1962. *Dissertation Abstracts International*, 1962, 2310.
64. Jacob S. Kounin, *Discipline and Group Management in Classrooms*, New York, Holt, Rinehart and Winston, 1970.
65. See Acheson and Gall, Chapter 7, for helpful discussion of techniques of this type.
66. Madeline Hunter, "Six Types of Supervisory Conferences," *Educational Leadership* 37, no. 5 (February 1980): 412.
67. Ibid., 409–412.
68. Kyte, 187–188.

69. Mosher and Purpel, 97–98.
70. Carl D. Glickman, *Developmental Supervision: Alternative Practices for Helping Teachers Improve Instruction*, Alexandria, Va., Association for Supervision and Curriculum Development, 1981, 17–37.
71. Ibid., 22, 29, 34.
72. Mosher and Purpel, 83.
73. Goldhammer, 1st ed., 273.
74. Hunter, 412.
75. Theresa Reilkoff, "Advantages of Supportive Supervision over Clinical Supervision of Teachers," *The National Association of Secondary School Principals Bulletin* 65, no. 448 (November 1981): 30.
76. Ibid., 31.
77. Ibid., 29.
78. Cheryl Granade Sullivan, *Clinical Supervision: A State of the Art Review*, Alexandria, Va., Association for Supervision and Curriculum Development, 1980, 22–23.
79. Mosher and Purpel, 111.

BIBLIOGRAPHY

Acheson, Keith A., and Meredith Damien Gall. *Techniques in the Clinical Supervision of Teachers: Preservice and Inservice Applications*. New York: Longman, 1980.
Alfonso, Robert J. "Will Peer Supervision Work?" *Educational Leadership* 34 (1977): 594–601.
———— and Lee Goldsberry. "Colleagueship in Supervision." In *Supervision of Teaching*, 1982 Yearbook, Thomas J. Sergiovanni, ed. Alexandria, Va.: Association for Supervision and Curriculum Development, 1982.
Beegle, Charles W., and Richard M. Brandt, eds. *Observation Methods in the Classroom*. Alexandria, Va.: Association for Supervision and Curriculum Development, 1973.
Bellon, Jerry J., Robert E. Eaker, James O. Huffman, and Richard V. Jones. *Classroom Supervision and Instructional Improvement: A Synergetic Process*. Dubuque, Iowa: Kendall/Hunt, 1978.
Berman, Louise M., and Mary Lou Usery. *Personalized Supervision: Sources and Insights*. Alexandria, Va.: Association for Supervision and Curriculum Development, 1971.
Champagne, David W. and R. Craig Hogen. *Consultant Supervision: Theory and Skill Development*. Wheaton, Ill.: CH Publications, 1981.
"Clinical Supervision." *Contemporary Education* 49 (Fall 1977).
"Clinical Supervision." *Journal of Research and Development in Education* 9 (1976).
Cogan, Morris L. *Clinical Supervision*. Boston: Houghton Mifflin, 1973.
————. "Rationale for Clinical Supervision." *Journal of Research and Development in Education* 9 (Winter 1976): 3–19.
Dull, Lloyd W. *Supervision: School Leadership Handbook*. Columbus, Ohio: Charles E. Merrill, 1981.
Eisner, Elliot W. "An Artistic Approach to Supervision." In *Supervision of Teaching*, 1982 Yearbook, Thomas J. Sergiovanni, ed. Alexandria, Va.: Association for Supervision and Curriculum Development, 1982.
Flanders, Ned A. "Interaction Analysis and Clinical Supervision." *Journal of Research and Development in Education* 9 (Winter 1976): 47–57.
Garman, Noreen B. "The Clinical Approach to Supervision." In *Supervision of Teaching*, 1982 Yearbook, Thomas J. Sergiovanni, ed. Alexandria, Va.: Association for Supervision and Curriculum Development, 1982.
Glickman, Carl D. *Developmental Supervision: Alternative Practices for Helping Teachers Improve Instruction*. Alexandria, Va.: Association for Supervision and Curriculum Development, 1981.

Goldhammer, Robert. *Clinical Supervision: Special Methods for the Supervision of Teachers.* New York: Holt, Rinehart and Winston, 1969.

————, Robert H. Anderson, and Robert J. Krajewski. *Clinical Supervision: Special Methods for the Supervision of Teachers*, 2nd ed. New York: Holt, Rinehart and Winston, 1980.

Griffith, Francis. *A Handbook for the Observation of Teaching and Learning.* Midland, Mich.: Pendell, 1973.

Harris, Ben M. "Limits and Supplements to Formal Clinical Procedures." *Journal of Research and Development in Education* 9 (Winter 1976): 3–19.

Hawthorne, Richard D. "Teacher Evaluation." In *Supervision: School Leadership Handbook*, Lloyd W. Dull, ed. Columbus, Ohio: Charles E. Merrill, 1981.

Hosford, Philip, and J. Jeuenfeldt. "Teacher Evaluation Via Videotape: Hope or Heresy?" *Educational Leadership* 36 (March 1979): 418–422.

Hunter, Madeline. "Six Types of Supervisory Conferences." *Educational Leadership* 37, no. 5 (February 1980): 408–412.

Hyman, Ronald T. *School Administrator's Handbook of Teacher Supervision and Evaluation Methods.* Englewood Cliffs, N.J.: Prentice-Hall, 1975.

Kindsvatter, Richard, and William W. Wilen. "A Systematic Approach to Improving Conference Skills." *Educational Leadership* 38 (April 1981): 525–529.

Krajewski, Robert J. "Clinical Supervision: To Facilitate Teacher Self-Improvement." *Journal of Research and Development in Education* 9 (Winter 1976): 58–66.

————. "Instructional Supervision: Dollars and Sense." *Contemporary Education* 49 (Fall 1977): 5–15.

Krey, Robert D., Lanore A. Netzer, and Glen G. Eye. "Assumptions Supporting Structure in Clinical Supervision." *Contemporary Education* 49 (Fall 1977): 16–23.

Kyte, George C. *How to Supervise: A Guide to Educational Principles and Progressive Practices of Educational Supervision.* Boston: Houghton Mifflin, 1930.

Lerch, Robert D. "The Clinical Model: The Optimum Approach to Supervision." *The Clearing House* 53 (January 1980): 238–240.

Lovell, John T., and Kimball Wiles. *Supervision for Better Schools*, 5th ed. Englewood Cliffs, N.J.: Prentice-Hall, 1983.

McLeary, Lloyd E. "Competencies in Clinical Supervision." *Journal of Research and Development in Education* 9 (Winter 1976): 30–35.

McNeil, John D. "A Scientific Approach to Supervision." In *Supervision of Teaching*, 1982 Yearbook, Thomas J. Sergiovanni, ed. Alexandria, Va.: Association for Supervision and Curriculum Development, 1982.

McNergney, Robert F., and Carol A. Carrier. *Teacher Development.* New York: Macmillan, 1981.

Marks, James R., Emery Stoops, and Joyce King-Stoops. *Handbook of Educational Supervision*, 2nd ed. Boston: Allyn and Bacon, 1978.

Mattaliano, Anthony. "Clinical Supervision: The Key Competencies Required for Effective Practice." Amherst: University of Massachusetts, 1977. Unpublished doctoral dissertation.

Mosher, Ralph L., and David E. Purpel. *Supervision: The Reluctant Profession.* Boston: Houghton Mifflin, 1972.

Pavan, Barbara Nelson. "Clinical Supervision: Some Signs of Progress." *Texas Tech Journal of Education* 7, no. 3. (Fall 1980): 241–251.

Reavis, Charles A. "Clinical Supervision: A Timely Approach." *Educational Leadership* 33 (February 1976): 360–363.

Reilkoff, Theresa. "Advantages of Supportive Supervision over Clinical Supervision of Teachers." *National Association of Secondary School Principals Bulletin* 65, no. 448 (November 1981): 28–34.

Salek, Charles Jerrold. "Helping Teachers vs. Evaluating Teachers." *National Association of Secondary School Principals Bulletin* 59, no. 392 (September 1975): 34–38.

Sergiovanni, Thomas J., ed. *Supervision of Teaching*, 1982 Yearbook. Alexandria, Va.: Association for Supervision and Curriculum Development, 1982.

————. "Toward a Theory of Clinical Supervision." *Journal of Research and Development in Education* 9 (Winter 1976): 3–19.
"Sharpening Supervision Skills." *Educational Leadership* 38, no. 7 (1981).
Synder, Karolyn J. "Clinical Supervision in the 1980's." *Educational Leadership* 38, no. 7 (April 1981): 521–524.
Stallings, Jane. *Learning to Look*. Berkeley, Calif.: Wadsworth, 1977.
Sullivan, Cheryl Granade. *Clinical Supervision: A State of the Art Review*. Alexandria, Va.: Association for Supervision and Curriculum Development, 1980.
Wingspan: The Pedamorphosis Communique. Vol. 1, No. 1, 1981. Issue on clinical supervision. Pedamorphosis, Inc., 1220 Broadway, Suite 605, Lubbock, Texas 79401.

Audiotapes

Carl D. Glickman. *Developmental Supervision: Alternative Approaches for Helping Teachers*. Alexandria, Va.: Association for Supervision and Curriculum Development, 1981. 90 min.
Madeline Hunter. *Improving the Quality of Instruction through Professional Development*. Alexandria, Va.: Association for Supervision and Curriculum Development, 1977. 50 min.
————. *Supervisory Conferences with Teachers*. Alexandria, Va.: Association for Supervision and Curriculum Development, 1980. 55 min.
Alan E. Simon. *Peer Supervision: An Alternative*. Alexandria, Va.: Association for Supervision and Curriculum Development, 1979. 40 min.

Videotape

Association for Supervision and Curriculum Development. *The Supervisory Process: Helping Teachers to Improve Instruction*. Alexandria, Va.: Association for Supervision and Curriculum Development, 1978. 30 min.

Multi-Media

Ingersoll, Gary M., and Joy Kleucker. *Analysis of Teacher-Pupil Interaction: Reacting to Pupil Responses*. Bloomington, Ind.: National Center for the Development of Teacher Training Materials, c. 1972. Manual and films: *Pattern in Teacher-Pupil Interaction: Reacting to Pupil Responses I and II.*
Northwest Regional Educational Laboratory, 710 S.W. Second Ave., Portland, Oregon 97204. Instructional system in *Systematic and Objective Analysis of Instruction*. Participant materials and training manual. 100 hours of instruction in learning skills in interpersonal relations, supervisory techniques, and teaching strategies in analysis of teachers and self-analysis for the improvement of instruction. Available from Commercial-Educational Distributing Service, P.O. Box 3711, Portland, Oregon 97208.
Okey, James, James Walden, Jerry Ciesla, Maurie Hendrickson, and Joy Kleucker. *Skills in Teacher-Pupil Interaction: Developing Comprehension through Accepting and Probing Reactions*. Bloomington, Ind.: National Center for the Development of Teacher Training Materials, 1972. Manual and films: *Patterns in Teacher-Pupil Interaction: Reacting to Pupil Responses I and II.*

13

Administrative Assessment of Teacher Performance

OBJECTIVES

After studying Chapter 13 you should be able to accomplish the following objectives:

1. Define summative evaluation as applied to teacher performance.
2. Distinguish between administrative assessment and clinical supervision.
3. Describe the principal's role in summative evaluation.
4. Describe the instructional supervisor's role, if any, in summative evaluation.
5. Describe how to collect data for purposes of summative evaluation.
6. State what teacher behaviors should be administratively assessed. Defend your choice of behaviors.
7. Describe how you would assess each behavior which you believe should be assessed.
8. Distinguish between and write competencies, indicators, and descriptors.
9. Select or create and apply, if required by the job, an instrument by which the administrator may assess teacher performance.

SUMMATIVE EVALUATION

Summative evaluation as the term is used in this chapter is the overall assessment of teacher performance made by the administrator (or the administrator and others) which culminates in a comprehensive appraisal either annually or as otherwise required by the state or locality. Included within the concept of summative evaluation are the periodic (some would say formative) evaluations made during the year for the purpose of collecting data in order to make the summative appraisal at the end of the year.

525

Tentatively, I had considered titling this chapter "Helping Teachers through Assessment of Performance." Yet, in reality, there is some question as to the degree to which teachers benefit from summative evaluations even though it is claimed that the purpose of summative assessment is the improvement of instruction. On receipt of their "report cards," a copy of the principal's written report of the periodic and summative appraisals, if they have earned "passing grades," many teachers simply file the reports away and wait for the next one.

Some educators attribute the lack of help in evaluation systems to misuse of the process. Arthur Shaw took this position when he said:

Evaluation is often dreaded by principals, feared by teachers, and seldom utilized by school districts for the purposes for which it was intended—the improvement of instruction and the subsequent facilitation of learning.[1]

Actually, the effective, conscientious, professional teachers will try out recommendations made by the administrator, if they feel the recommendations are sound. Ineffective teachers who receive low ratings are forced to attempt to make improvements in their teaching if they wish to maintain their positions. Thus, summative or administrative assessment does have as a goal the improvement of instruction. It might be said that the system succeeds in this goal to some degree in spite of itself.

The major purpose of administrative assessment of teachers, however, lies in another direction. Summative evaluation is essentially an exercise, albeit a necessary one, in personnel, not instructional management. Whereas the primary purpose of formative evaluation as carried out in clinical supervision, for example, is to improve the teacher's instructional skills, the main purpose of summative evaluation is the making of decisions about personnel. Both formative and summative evaluation have as their ultimate purpose the improvement in student learning.

On the college level annual evaluations of faculty are made for the purpose of deciding on tenure, promotion, and salary increments. On the public school level, the decisions to be made are primarily retention, including tenure or continuation of contract and dismissal or termination of contract. Occasionally, summative evaluations are used for making decisions about transfer of teachers to other schools or assignments, or to other responsibilities, e.g., team leader, grade coordinator, lead teacher, department head, teacher on special assignment, and workshop staff.

Since most school systems presently are on single-salary schedules based exclusively on number of years of experience and training, decisions on pay for meritorious service are not ordinarily made about public school teachers. The profession has flirted with merit salary systems in the past, as in New York State in the 1940s. Most teachers' groups reject the practice of awarding merit pay on the grounds of subjectivity and unreliability. The teachers argue with some reason that if we cannot agree on what good teaching is, how can we fairly evaluate finely enough to make distinctions among teachers in salary? Distrust of administration is rampant in the merit pay issue. In spite of problems involved in creating and administering a system for rewarding meritorious teachers, there is nevertheless increasing sentiment both within and outside the profession in support of merit pay systems. Discussions on this issue are going on at the local, state, and national levels. In the near future we may expect to find merit pay systems as a standard feature of school personnel practices.

Although almost any evaluation system has to some degree the improvement of instruction as its purpose, summative evaluation aims ultimately to rid the profession of incompetent teachers. As such, summative evaluation is a necessary function of administration. True, effective (however defined) teachers may take to heart suggestions made by the evaluation for improving instruction. True, ineffective (however defined) teachers may be pressured by the administrator to undergo some remedial training to remedy deficiencies. But the bottom line—which gives summative evaluation an aura of threat—is the potential for dismissal. Even the mere existence of written evaluations which are good to excellent but less than perfect is cause for concern to teachers who know that personnel files can dog them the same way cumulative records can hound students. A careless, inaccurate, or biased comment of an evaluator can be a source of both professional and psychological harm to the teacher.

You may well ask why, if summative assessment is a personnel rather than an instructional matter, a chapter on this subject is included in this textbook. I offer the following reasons:

1. In some schools, particularly small ones, the principal *is* the instructional supervisor. He or she takes on responsibilities for both formative and summative evaluation, combining the functions.

2. In some school systems the instructional (staff) supervisor is either charged with the responsibility for both formative and summative evaluation even though the administrator may actually sign the year-end assessment report or is called on to participate with the administrator and/or others in the summative evaluation process.

3. It is important that instructional supervisors and administrators be able to distinguish between the purposes and processes of formative and summative evaluation of teachers.

4. Both staff and line supervisors owe it to the profession, to teachers, to students, to the public, and to themselves to make the summative assessment of teachers as fair, meaningful, and constructive as possible.

5. The summative evaluation process should be coordinated with the processes of teacher self-appraisal and formative evaluation.

In evaluating teachers for personnel purposes school systems must provide answers to the following questions:

> Who should be evaluated?
> Who should do the evaluating?
> What should be evaluated?
> How should the evaluations be done?
> How should the data be used?

Answers to these questions appear at first deceptively simple. But simple they are not. Our decentralized system of education has produced, as is the case with many other aspects of American education, a variety of answers. In just a moment we will examine each of these questions.

It is of interest to note, as Perry A. Zirkel reported, that "fewer than half ($n = 23$) of the states have statutes or administrative regulations directly dealing with the evaluation of public school teachers."[2]

It comes as a surprise to learn that there are states which have no established regulations to control a process so fundamental to education as the evaluation of teachers. Zirkel went on to point out that even in the majority of states with teacher evaluation laws the local level is "the primary locus for establishing the policies and procedures for teacher evaluation."[3] As a result, the responsibility for establishing policies about teacher evaluation fall on the local boards of education. In some states "the input of local teachers is provided for in the form of either advice (Arizona, California), consultation (Nevada, Oklahoma), or negotiation (Connecticut)."[4] Thus, responsibility for establishing procedures for the evaluation of school personnel rests with the state and local levels, with the latter playing the dominant role.

Zirkel called attention to the fact that local regulations must conform to state minimum statutory standards and that both state and local regulations must abide by federal constitutional and statutory provisions which include the First and Fourteenth Amendments, the Civil Rights Act of 1964, Section 504 of the Rehabilitation Act of 1973, and the Age Discrimination in Employment Amendments of 1978.[5]

Who Should Be Evaluated?

Teachers, of course, should be evaluated. But the answer is not that simple. To begin with, some states require evaluation of all certificated personnel (Florida and Georgia, for example). Some states (Arizona, for example) limit evaluation to certificated *teachers*. Other states (Kansas and West Virginia, for example) require that all employees be evaluated. Some states (Florida, Louisiana, and Nevada) list the personnel to be evaluated by category, as teachers, counselors, librarians, etc. Some states (Massachusetts and Michigan, for example) call for the evaluation of nontenured teachers only, whereas others (Florida, for example) stipulate that both tenured and nontenured teachers be evaluated.[6]

A great diversity of practice in respect to the assessment of school personnel can be seen. It might be argued that after teachers have gone through their probationary period and have been accorded tenure, they are fully competent and need no further supervision or evaluating. The argument might be pushed back even further and a case made that if teachers were carefully selected, once on the job there'd be no need for continuing supervision and evaluation. Would that this were so! In that utopian world instruction would be superb and school administration would be child's play. We all know, however, that the presence of poor teachers in our midst makes that argument specious and untenable. Though much can be said in defense of tenure, and I would not advocate giving it up, on the negative side is the presence of tenured teachers who are performing poorly, lack motivation, are barely meeting minimum professional standards, or are actually incompetent. Tenure is no guarantee of the presence of able teachers. Consequently, evaluation of teacher performance is necessary. The evaluation of all teachers, tenured and nontenured, which I would advocate, appears to be prevailing practice.

Who Should Evaluate Teachers?

Unless you are of the persuasion that school administrators are ill qualified to evaluate teachers, you would probably answer the question, "Who should evaluate teachers?" with, "The principal." But this is not an answer which is universal. Zirkel observed that Florida, Hawaii, New Jersey, New Mexico, and Wyoming specify that the evaluation of teachers be performed by the principal or immediate supervisor.[7] In most of the states which have concerned themselves with teacher evaluation the choice of who will do the evaluating is left to the local board of education.[8] In some states (Connecticut and Pennsylvania, for example) the decision on who will do the evaluating is left to the superintendent.[9]

A rather unique process is followed by Massachusetts in which a committee of three people does the evaluating. One person is selected by the teacher to be evaluated, one by the local school board, and one by the two selected committee members.[10]

Generally speaking, either by state mandate, local board regulations, or just tradition—or we might add, by reasonable administrative practice—responsibility for evaluating personnel of his or her school falls to the principal. As a matter of fact, most principals regard this task as their responsibility, indeed, prerogative. Whether they carry out that responsibility themselves is another matter. In some cases where principals bear the responsibility, they delegate to their assistant principals the task of collecting data and reporting to them. The principal in these instances evaluates teachers on secondary data rather than firsthand.

Some persons hold that the principal should not perform the task of evaluating teachers. Shaw, for example, voiced the sentiment to the effect that administrators should not be evaluating teachers when he spoke about the problem of evaluating teachers:

The answer to the problem lies not so much in changing the attitudes of the administrators who now do the bulk of the evaluation, but with teachers who must somehow wrest the privilege away from administrative personnel in order to come full cycle as a viable profession and emerge as the leaders of instruction. As the Texas Federation of Teachers proposes: "Control and entry into and egress from the teaching profession should be in the hands of the practicing professionals."

As long as teachers allow themselves to be capriciously evaluated, the teaching profession will not assume its proper role in the educational world. A profession sets its own standards and requires members to adhere to these standards. Improved teacher evaluation techniques may be the key to realizing these standards.[11]

Who may do the evaluating is bound not only by state and local board regulations but also by contracts negotiated between school management and teachers' organizations. The contracts usually specify who may do the evaluating, how often, how the data will be used, and what records will be kept.

Controversy swirls around the issue of whether staff supervisors from the central office or individual school should be involved in the summative evaluation of teachers. In some school systems which have negotiated contracts department chairpersons are forbidden to do any formal evaluating of teachers, as the chairpersons are considered members of the bargaining unit, i.e., teachers, and summative evaluations (and formative evaluations as well which are for the purpose of making a summative evaluation) must be done by management, i.e., administrators.

Many of us in supervision believe, as I have noted elsewhere in this book, that instructional supervisors should be as far removed from summative evaluation as possible. They should try to avoid summative assessments which require the data to be furnished to the administrator for personnel action. They should become involved only under the following conditions:

1. If such evaluations are standard practice agreed on by the teachers when the evaluation process was set up.
2. If a teacher requests the supervisor to do so.
3. If the principal requests the supervisor to do so *and the teacher consents.*
4. If a teacher is facing dismissal for incompetence and an expert judgment is needed.
5. If so ordered by the superintendent.
6. If doing so does not violate the state law, school board policy, or terms of a negotiated contract.

Generally speaking, the principal is responsible for the summative evaluation of teachers, which, I believe, is as it should be. The principal should personally observe all teachers a sufficient number of times in their classrooms to form a judgment about their performance and to provide a basis for a written annual assessment. In this respect the principal is engaging in formative evaluation. The principal may, if he or she chooses, seek additional evaluations by his or her assistant administrators as supplementary to but not in place of the principal's own evaluating. Although the principal is charged with many duties, it appears to me that if he or she must delegate certain tasks, he or she should delegate almost any task other than teacher evaluation. It is the principal who should possess the highest degree of competence in evaluating personnel and should therefore feel it is incumbent upon him or her to put those skills to use. I believe teachers have the right to expect an evaluation of their performance, if it is done at all, from their status leader—the principal. None of the principal's activity in formative or summative evaluation obviates the formative evaluation carried on by instructional supervisors.

What Should Be Evaluated?

Would that we could give a simple answer to the question: What should be evaluated? Some would say teacher competence, which is both a simple answer and a simplistic one. The response made by some evaluators to how they know good teaching is like the response that is given to the question, "How do you know a good painting?" The answer, "I know it when I see it," does not tell us very much. Teaching is often judged in the same way. To some extent we can all identify good teachers and good teaching. The problem lies in the fact that we are often not in agreement on who the good teachers are and what good teaching is.

John D. McNeil, in referring to studies of teaching effectiveness summarized by A. S. Barr observed:

He [Barr] correctly saw that the problem that needs clarifying before all others is the criterion of teaching effectiveness. Different people employ different criteria and approaches to the evaluation of teachers. Some prefer to approach effectiveness from the point of view of personal prerequisites; some from teacher-pupil behaviors; some from basic knowledge, attitudes, and skill; and some from the point of view of results or products. These different approaches give different answers to the question, "Is this teacher an effective teacher?"[12]

Teaching effectiveness like beauty can be in the eyes of the beholder. We need to come to grips with the basic problem: What is effectiveness in teaching? We may arrive at an answer to this question in a number of ways. First, we may accept what the experts, for example, professors of education, tell us is good or effective teaching. We find, however, that, lacking hard data, the experts are in disagreement about what constitutes good teaching. Some look for a heavy affective orientation in teaching; others advocate a heavy cognitive load. Some professors have a fondness for a particular methodology and feel other methods to be inferior. For example, some champion inquiry learning and small-group instruction. Others favor didactic teaching and the use of large groups.[13]

In spite of disagreements there is, however, considerable uniformity of thought about teaching effectiveness. We know that teachers who like children are more effective instructors than those who do not. We know that student achievement is higher when teachers reinforce correct responses. We know that as a rule if students are to be motivated, the teacher must be motivated. We know that a teacher cannot teach what he or she does not know. Many educators follow what Allen R. Warner and Dora H. Scott referred to as "the contemporary conventional wisdom of teaching."[14] Both the experts and the not-so-expert rely heavily on conventional wisdom, which itself is derived from research, personal and vicarious experiences, and common sense.

Second, we can base a definition of teacher effectiveness on description of what teachers actually do. We can observe what most teachers do and try to describe the teaching act from the data gleaned from those observations. We could sharpen our observation by first identifying good teachers and poor teachers and then studying what it is that good teachers do. But that puts us in a Catch-22 situation, for the good teachers must be identified and we will certainly encounter differences among the identifiers as to what good teaching is. We might be fortunate enough, however, to achieve consensus among the indentifiers.

Third, we can gather empirical data about teaching behaviors which are related to certain learner variables, for example, student achievement. We can try to find out which behaviors have a positive effect on student achievement so that teachers may repeat those behaviors.

Donald M. Medley summarized close to 300 studies of teacher effectiveness and concluded that the following variables are related to student achievement: an orderly and supportive learning environment, time on task, instruction in large groups, and, surprisingly, the use of low-level questioning.[15] Barak V. Rosenshine discovered engaged time, content covered, and direct instruction as factors in teacher effectiveness.[16] Other researchers affirmed the importance of direct instruction and academic focus for student achievement.[17]

Fourth, we can ask a group of teachers or a mixed group of professional educators to describe effective teaching behaviors. Many professional educators have been involved in identifying generic competencies in their states. Although the lists of competencies vary from state to state, which once again reveals the uncertainty in the profession as to what good teaching is, nevertheless the competencies are uniform within those states which have undertaken the task and thus provide some direction for the evaluation of teachers.

In the absence of recommended or mandated systemwide or statewide processes which have already specified the teaching competencies to be evaluated, or even as supplementary to state and local systems of evaluation, the faculty of each school should reach consensus on what it believes is good teaching. No exercise could be a more valuable in-service activity than the production of a description of what is effective teaching as perceived by the local school teachers and administrators.

Since the principal, who is a generalist, will ordinarily be the person doing the evaluating, he or she will evaluate teacher performance in relation to specified generic competencies. Since the principal's major purpose in observing and evaluating is to gather reliable data for annual assessment and making personnel decisions, his or her observations will usually be of the global variety. The principal will evaluate teachers each time he or she observes them on all of the specified competencies.

Ben M. Harris, Kenneth E. McIntyre, Vance C. Littleton, Jr., and Daniel F. Long suggested that competencies possess the following characteristics:

1. There should be relatively few *important* competencies that are demonstrably related to effective teaching and learning.
2. The competencies should be sufficiently specific so that they are clearly definable.
3. The competencies should be amenable to reliable measurement.
4. For formative evaluation purposes, the performance manifestation of the competencies should be subject to change through school-sponsored, in-service programs and instructional supervision.[18]

I would add to the fourth characteristic "for summative evaluation purposes also."

Any study of personnel evaluation as carried out in the schools reveals the fact that administrators seek to evaluate more than teaching competencies. The process extends beyond the classroom into personal and professional attributes of teachers. Harris et al. wrote of three approaches to personnel evaluation:

Basically, there are three approaches to the evaluation of personnel: (1) the characteristics of the individual, sometimes called "presage criteria," (2) the products attributed to the individual, and (3) the processes used by the individual.[19]

Let's take a quick look at these three approaches.

Characteristics of the Teacher

It is obvious that the personal characteristics of the teacher do make a difference to the learners, to the school, and to the community. It was not uncommon in days gone by for administrators and school boards to prescribe in detail how a teacher would dress. Male teachers have been required to wear suits; female teachers have been prohibited from wearing cosmetics; both male and female teachers have been required to teach Sunday school. And, of course, neither could touch alcoholic beverages or smoke.

The number of restrictions on personal behavior has diminished in recent years. We now find general statements in school board policies about clean and appropriate dress and grooming and general decorum in behavior. This is not to say that personal and professional characteristics are not important; they are; nor that they should not be evaluated; they should be. John C. Reynolds commented:

Four factors generally differentiate effective teachers from ineffective teachers—superior personality organization, good judgment/reasoning, capacity to relate to others, and a knowledge of basic content and instructional methods.[20]

The first three factors are largely personal in nature. Faculties can and should draw up their own list—if it is not already a part of the evaluation system—of personal and professional characteristics which they deem essential to the teacher, as, warmth, enthusiasm, communication skills, etc.

Products

Current practice in teacher evaluation seeks to assess teacher performance in terms of the school's products, i.e., the performance of students. The accountability movement aims to discover what success teachers have had in promoting student achievement. National, state, and local assessments of student achievement have evolved in order to determine whether students have mastered the content with which they have been confronted. Test data reveal one dimension of product evaluation. They do not disclose, however, less observable behaviors, particularly those in the affective domain. An assessment of the products of teaching should be built into the teacher evaluation system. As Shaw said in responding to the question, What is to be evaluated? "at least some of the evaluation should center on whether the teacher has changed any student behavior; has the teacher taught the student anything?"[21]

Processes

Evaluation systems usually stress this approach. The majority of items on evaluation instruments center on process or methods used by the teacher. In some respects the processes are easier to observe and evaluate than personal and professional characteristics or products of teaching.

Personal and professional characteristics, products, and processes are all applicable elements to be evaluated. Whether an element is to be evaluated, however, should be agreed on by both the evaluators and the evaluatees. Together the representatives of the administrators and teachers should create a system which meets with general consensus, which does not conflict with state or federal laws and constitutional provisions, and which, of course, the local school board endorses.

How Should the Evaluations Be Done?

Sampling of Behavior

The evaluator should make enough visits to a teacher's classroom and observe long enough each time to obtain a generous sampling of the teacher's performance. The principal or other evaluator must decide how many times he or she will visit, observe, and evaluate each teacher on his or her staff. Practice varies widely; the states offer no uniform answer to this problem. Concerning the question, How frequently should evaluations be made? Zirkel wrote:

A few states (*n* = 3) answer this question with a weasel word—"continuously" in Connecticut, "on a regular basis" in West Virginia, and "periodically" in Wyoming. What such continual evaluation means is left immediately to professional discretion and ultimately to judicial determination.[22]

Some states (Alaska, Florida, Michigan, Oregon, and Washington, for example) specify that evaluations be conducted yearly. Some states require more frequent evaluations for nontenured teachers than for tenured teachers. California and Louisiana, for example, require an annual evaluation for nontenured teachers but every two years for tenured teachers. In Oklahoma and South Dakota nontenured teachers are evaluated twice a year; tenured teachers every three years. Nontenured teachers in New Jersey are evaluated three times a year; tenured teachers once.[23]

Hawaii takes into consideration the number of years of experience of a teacher, requiring evaluations four times the first year, twice the second year, and annually each year thereafter. Kansas follows a different pattern, requiring evaluations twice during the first and second years, annually during the third and fourth years, and once every three years thereafter.[24]

Which pattern is best? Who can say? It can be argued that the more frequently an administrator observes a teacher, the better he or she is able to judge that teacher's performance and the fairer will be any personnel decisions made as a result.

We have, perhaps, neglected to mention one of the purposes of administrative evaluation besides evaluation of the teacher—that is, to keep the administrator apprised of what is going on in the school. The principal who sits in his or her office behind the desk cannot know what is happening. He or she has no idea of what is being taught, what delivery methods are being used, whether lesson plans are being followed, whether students and teachers are using their time wisely.

The number of visits to observe the teacher must be tempered to the size of the staff and the number of evaluators. I know administrators who visit each teacher once a month. I know others who visit all teachers five times a year; still others who visit teachers on annual contract (nontenured) four times a year and tenured teachers twice a year. There is no magic number. However, when the principal sums up his or her observations in an end-of-year report for each teacher, he or she should have observed each teacher a sufficient number of times to complete the report accurately and fairly. Further, if the principal begins to detect evidence of incompetence on the part of a teacher, he or she should very well visit that teacher often enough so that if the time comes to build a case for dismissal, he or she will have the necessary documentation.

As far as length of each visit is concerned, the principal or other evaluator should remain in the classroom long enough to obtain a fair appraisal of the teacher's performance. Unfortunately, that is rather vague advice. Like graduate students who invariably want to know how long a term paper should be, evaluators want more than the answer "long enough to do the job." Thus, I would fall back on the rule of thumb for formative clinical observations: at least 30 minutes at the elementary school level, one period for the secondary school level.

Announced versus Unannounced Visits

Whereas I believe the clinical supervisor should always schedule visits in advance at a time agreeable to the teacher, the summative evaluator may find it desirable to make a combination of announced and unannounced visits. Since entrapment is not the name of the game, a sufficient number of prearranged visits should be made. The teacher should be seen at his or her best. On the other hand, unannounced visits can confirm whether the observations made at announced times revealed the teacher's typical performance. They can introduce an element of simple control, tacitly advising the teacher that he or she is expected to be prepared every day. They can let the teacher know that the principal is on the job and is interested in what is happening in the school.

Collecting and Recording the Data

If an evaluation system is not already in place, the faculty and administrators will need to decide what data they want collected and how the data will be gathered. They will need to select or create instruments for recording both the periodic observations and the final appraisal.

For the periodic observations in the teacher's classroom a global instrument such as the ones described in the preceding chapter is desirable. These instruments known generally as classroom observation forms are designed to help the evaluator assess what is transpiring in the classroom. Occasionally, these forms include items for which evidence must be found by means other than classroom observation.

The summative evaluation instrument, called by some the teacher appraisal form, must bear some relationship to both the classroom observation form and any teacher self-appraisal form in use. In some cases the teacher appraisal form is identical to the classroom observation form. It would be my preference to limit the classroom observation form to *only* those items which can be observed in the classroom. The teacher appraisal form then could include all the items on the classroom observation form plus items for which data must be obtained in other ways, e.g., certain personal and professional characteristics, products, and processes in extra-class activities.

Some of the data to be collected will come from classroom observations. Other data will result from examination of the teacher's lesson and unit plans. Some data will be derived from conferences with the teacher. Student test data will furnish clues to teacher performance. Comments from students, parents, teachers, and even other administrators about a given teacher should be, as the cliché goes, treated with a grain of salt until firsthand evidence confirms or refutes the statements made either on behalf of or in criticism of the teacher.

NAME OF TEACHER BEING EVALUATED   SCHOOL   DATE

CLASS IDENTIFICATION (LEVEL, ETC.)

EVALUATIVE LEVEL CODE:
5—Superior
4—Above Average
3—Average
2—Below Average
1—Poor

A. TEACHING EFFECTIVENESS

	1 2	3	4 5
1. Competence in teaching field	*Knowledge of subject needs improving*	*Average knowledge of subject*	*Has strong mastery of subject*
2. Organization of course content	*Lacks direction; planning seems vague*	*Organized as per course objectives*	*Very well organized; shows thorough planning*
3. Preparation for each class	*Not enough preplanning; too much wasted time*	*Activities well planned*	*Definite evidence of excellent planning*

Figure 13.1 Teacher Evaluation Criteria

	1 2	3	4 5
4. Teaching skill	*Classes are not stimulating, student interest appears low*	*Teaching procedure seldom changes; interest average*	*Produces steady interest; creates desire to learn*
5. Individualized instruction	*Same content and activities planned for all students*	*Some evidence of planning for various levels*	*Students working at their own pace, with supervision. Enrichment work and pursuance of advanced topics in evidence*
6. Student-teacher interaction	*Discussions ramble and sometimes without purpose; little pupil participation; student-teacher rapport poor*	*Questions rather routine. Average pupil participation student-teacher rapport good*	*Questions challenging: discussions interesting, high degree of pupil participation, student-teacher rapport excellent*
7. Discipline (learning environment)	*Students constantly talking; confusion in classroom hampers instruction. Poor learning environment*	*Students generally follow instructions. Distractions seldom interfere with instructional environment*	*Students always working; or attentive. Good learning atmosphere and environment*
8. Instructional objectives	*Given too hurriedly; vague and sometimes unreasonable or indefinite*	*Usually adequate and understood*	*Students clearly understand objectives and know what is desired*
9. Originality of approach	*Instructional pattern seldom changes; new ideas seldom tried*	*Some evidence of new approaches*	*Demonstrates unusual creative ability and awareness of new subject field developments*
10. Closure	*Class ends abruptly with the bell, no plans for continuity*	*Some carry over from one day to the next*	*Students clearly understand what is expected and have a goal for future classes*
11. Classroom management	*Student care of school property poor, classroom untidy and unorganized*	*School property and classroom appearance average*	*School property respected by student; room neat or used purposefully*
12. Evaluation	*Evaluation results not always used purposefully; too few evaluations*	*Average evaluation and use of results*	*Tests and other criteria used very effectively; results used in planning*
13. Attendance register	*Register returned for corrections: 6–10 times, 4–5 times*	*3 times*	*2 times, 0–1 times*

Figure 13.1 (*continued*)

B. PERSONAL QUALIFICATIONS

	1 2	3	4 5
1. Emotional stability	*Is upset easily; has problems with unusual classroom situations*	*Generally even-tempered; can cope with most unusual classroom events*	*Unusually calm and collected; takes most unusual class situation in stride*
2. Judgment	*Sometimes makes very poor decisions; some problems intensified by poor handling*	*Generally uses good common sense in making decisions and handling problems*	*Decisions and action are exceptionally appropriate*
3. Initiative	*Avoids extra duties; minimum planning and classroom effort*	*Handles average share of extra duties; exhibits some extra planning and interest in students*	*Seeks extra duties; puts extra effort in planning and classroom work. Eager to help individual students*
4. Accuracy	*Records, reports, grades, plans are often inaccurate*	*Occasional mistakes on records, reports, grades, plans*	*Seldom makes errors in grading, records, reports, and plans*
5. Punctuality	*Often late to school and classroom; seldom meets schedules or deadlines for grades, reports, etc.*	*Occasionally late to school and classroom; usually meets schedules or deadlines for grades, reports, etc.*	*On time to school and classroom; always meets schedules or deadlines for grades, reports, etc.*
6. Personal grooming	*Attire not always appropriate for classroom; good grooming practices not always followed*	*Attire and grooming habits are acceptable*	*Personal attire and grooming sets good example for students*
7. Communicative skills	*Occasionally uses poor grammar; voice is weak or monotonous; students bored*	*Grammar usually good; voice level adequate and pleasant*	*Sets good example with speech habits; voice adequate, pleasant, and used effectively to arouse interest*
8. Poise	*Teacher appears ill at ease, lets irritations and temper influence behavior*	*Teacher seldom becomes upset over minor incidents*	*Teacher appears relaxed; maintains composure under stress*
9. Attendance	*Days absent: 11 or more, 9–10*	*5–8*	*3–1, 1–2*
10. Dependability	*Duties and details of teaching sometimes not done; constant supervision necessary*	*Performs duties and assignments reliably*	*Performs duties and handles assignments unusually well*

Figure 13.1 (*continued*)

C. PROFESSIONAL ATTITUDES (USE SCALE 1-5: LOW 1, HIGH 5)

1. Understands and adheres to school board policies, administrative policies, and school policies   ————
2. Respects the confidential nature of matters relating to pupils, parents, and school personnel.   ————
3. Refrains from derogatory remarks and uses discretion in remarks about students, teachers, or school matters.   ————
4. Participates willingly in in-service activities designed to stimulate professional growth; exhibits an interest in continuing professional growth.   ————
5. Joins professional organizations and actively participates.   ————
6. Maintains appropriate pupil-teacher relationship.   ————

D. PERSONAL-PROFESSIONAL RELATIONSHIPS

1. Maintains professional relations with fellow teachers.   ————
2. Cooperates with the school administration.   ————
3. Is respected by pupils and parents.   ————
4. Provides opportunities for parent-teacher conference.   ————
5. Responds well to constructive criticism and shows evidence of professional growth.   ————

How long has the evaluator known the teacher being evaluated in a teaching capacity?

_____

| _____ | _____ | _____ |
| SIGNATURE (EVALUATOR) | POSITION | DATE OF EVALUATION CONFERENCE |

SOURCE: Monroe County Public Schools, *Teacher Evaluation Criteria*, Key West, Fla. Reprinted with permission.

Figure 13.1 (*continued*)

Personnel evaluation calls for the rating of teachers. Harris et al. underscored the care that must be taken in rating personnel when they said, "It is *crucial* that the decisions concerning ratings be based on relevant, descriptive, and verifiable data."[25] The evaluator must have firm evidence for each behavior rated or else he/she should not rate that behavior.

After each evaluation, periodic and final, the evaluator should confer with the teacher. The administrator does hope that the periodic evaluations will result in improvement in instruction during the year and that the summative appraisal will work the same way for instruction during the ensuing year. It is customary for both the administrator and the teacher to sign the summative evaluation report. The teacher's signature does not necessarily signify agreement with the administrator's rating but that the tacher has seen the evaluation, acknowledges it, and has received a copy.

It is of interest to note the evolution of some evaluation systems. Monroe County (Florida) quite some time ago used a comprehensive teacher appraisal form

(Figure 13.1) which is typical of many earlier forms. You will note that the form attempted to evaluate teaching effectiveness, personal qualifications, professional attitudes, and personal-professional relationships. Several years ago Monroe Country dropped this extensive rating scale and substituted in its place a more open-ended type of summative appraisal (Figure 13.2).

Both the rating scale and the open-ended instrument have their advantages and disadvantages. A rating scale is easier to fill out: it focuses on specific behaviors; the data can be treated quantitatively, if you prefer to do so. The open-ended instrument permits greater flexibility for the evaluator: it is a more personal, individualized approach which avoids quantification of the data.

Several years ago Dade County (Florida) Public Schools used a teacher evaluation form (Figure 13.3) which required quantification of the data. Using a rating scale with a low of 1 and a high of 5, principals rated nine competencies and averaged them. If the teacher's average score fell below 3.5, he or she was considered to be performing unsatisfactorily and might expect to suffer whatever the consequences were which accrued to unsatisfactory work.

With an evaluation system of this type principals encounter the same type of difficulty as teachers who must decide whether a student has earned a 78 or an 82, a C+ or a B–. When a cutoff score signals the boundary between satisfactory and unsatisfactory performance, the sagacious principal, aware of his or her own fallibility in judgment, tends to inflate the "grades." The open-ended system eliminates this problem but introduces other problems of its own.

A binary rating system reduces the necessity for making fine numerical distinctions, but since behavior is reported with but two symbols, as, for example, S (satisfactory) and U (unsatisfactory), a wide range of behavior is encompassed within each of the two symbols. A few years ago Dade County teachers and administrative personnel jointly developed and instituted an annual evaluation form (Figure 13.4) which required principals to rate teacher competencies as acceptable or unacceptable. Although many teachers prefer the broader symbols, some teachers feel that the term acceptable does not do justice to those teachers who are performing at a high level. In this respect teachers who reject the binary approach emulate those students who object to satisfactory-unsatisfactory, pass-fail, credit-no credit systems and demand A through F letter grades which recognize superior achievement. You will note that this newer annual evaluation form correlates with the classroom observation form shown in the preceding chapter.

You will recall that in Chapter 12 we looked at the Classroom Observation Form used by the Richmond County (Georgia) Public Schools. Figure 13.5 reproduces the Teacher Appraisal Record, the summative evaluation form, used by this Georgia county. Paralleling the Classroom Observation Form the Teacher Appraisal Record is constructed in such a way that principals make a numerical rating for each indicator of each competency. This appraisal form groups the numerical ratings into two categories: improvement needed and satisfactory. Unlike the Classroom Observation Form the Teacher Appraisal Record does not include descriptors. Both the Classroom Observation Form and the Teacher Appraisal Record are based on the state's Teacher Performance Assessment Instruments.

MONROE COUNTY SCHOOL DISTRICT

Teacher's Annual Evaluation

NAME _____ DATE _____

SCHOOL _____

POSITION_____ CLASS & LEVEL _____

I. Performance of Teaching Duties

    A. Strengths _____

    _____

    _____

    B. Needed Improvement _____

    _____

II. Relationships with Students, Staff, Parents

    A. Strengths _____

    _____

    B. Needed Improvement _____

    _____

III. Involvement in Total Educational Program

    A. Strengths _____

    _____

    B. Needed Improvement _____

    _____

IV. Personal Qualities

    A. Strengths _____

    _____

    _____

    B. Needed Improvement _____

    _____

V. Summary

    A. Recommendations made during year _____

    _____

    B. Steps taken for improvement _____

    _____

    C. Comments _____

    _____

Date _____   Signature of Principal _____

VI. I have read the above evaluation.

    Comments _____

    _____

    _____

Date _____   Signature of Teacher _____

Figure 13.2 Teacher's Annual Evaluation

SOURCE: Monroe County Public Schools, *Teacher's Annual Evaluation*, Key West, Fla. Reprinted with permission.

DADE COUNTY EVALUATION FORM
(Instructional)

SOCIAL SECURITY #
_____

LAST NAME   FIRST   MIDDLE   ( ) TEACHER   ( ) LIBRARIAN
                                ( ) COUNSELOR ( ) OTHER

             ANNUAL   CONTINUING   EMPLOYEE NUMBER
             _____   _____

                                 ASSIGNMENT THIS YEAR
_____   _____   _____
AVERAGE SCORE   CONTRACT STATUS
                                 NAME OF SCHOOL WHERE EMPLOYED

Mark each item according to the code below. The original of this evaluation is due in the Personnel Office no later than June 1. For persons on A-3 and above contracts, this form must accompany reappointment recommendations.

CODE: LOW - 1.0; 1.5; 2.0; 2.5; 3.0; 3.5; 4.0; 4.5; 5.0 - HIGH
(Leave no item blank; use N for any item which does NOT apply.)

APPRAISAL ITEMS:

1. *Maintains good discipline.*   1._____
   (Establishes and maintains reasonable and fair boundaries,
   understood by pupils, that will promote self-discipline and
   allow both pupils and teacher to operate effectively.)
2. *Is alert to and provides for individual pupil needs.*   2._____
   (Uses cumulative folders and test data, confers with staff
   members and parents, and makes every effort through personal
   observation to identify and provide for individual differences.)
3. *Uses evaluative criteria effectively.*   3._____
   (Maintains classroom folders which reflect effective use of
   evaluative material that shows pupil progress.) (Test, assigned
   papers and other samples of pupil work.)
4. *Makes definite plans for class activities and procedures.*   4._____
   (Prepares and uses a plan book which is meaningful to the
   teacher.)
5. *Stimulates pupil interest and eagerness to learn.*   5._____
6. *Shows knowledge of educational developments and shows sound*   6._____
   judgment in the use of techniques and materials.
7. *Works well with others.*   7._____
   (Cooperates with teachers, the principal, other administrators,
   and the entire school staff; has good rapport with pupils,
   parents and community.)
8. *Understands and supports school policies and demonstrates a*   8._____
   professional attitude in implementing them.
   (Is punctual and accurate in maintaining required records and
   reports; i.e., grade books, cumulative folders, attendance
   reports, etc.; follows directives and communicates suggested
   changes in a professional manner.)
9. *Contributes to the total school program.*   9._____
   (Recognizes own subject field in relation to the educational
   program; willingly accepts and performs responsibilities
   beyond the classroom; contributes to the esprit de corps of
   the staff.)

CLASSROOM VISITATION DATES: ____ ____ ____ ____ ____ ____ ____ ____
(If on leave for year, name type.)

Signature of Evaluator: _____

This evaluation has been
reviewed with the evaluator. _____ _____
                             Signature of employee evaluated   Date

AN AVERAGE RATING OF BELOW 3.5 INDICATES UNSATISFACTORY WORK IN THE DADE COUNTY SCHOOLS.

Figure 13.3 Dade County Evaluation Form (Instructional)

SOURCE: Dade County Public Schools, *Dade County Evaluation Form (Instructional)*, Miami, Fla. Reprinted with permission.

```
                    ANNUAL EVALUATION
                    Full Time Teachers
                 DADE COUNTRY PUBLIC SCHOOLS

NAME_____          19      -19_____
      Last       First       Middle                     School Year

CONTRACT STATUS (Circle one):  A-1  A-2  A-3  CC  _____
                                                  Dates of employment (if less than 1 year)

_____         _____   _____
Other Contract Status (Please Specify)            Employee No.    Soc. Sec. No.

SCHOOL_____        _____
                                                  Teaching Assignment this Year

SUBJECT AREAS OF CERTIFICATION (if teaching out of field):_____
```

PRINCIPAL'S RECOMMENDATION (Check only one):
1. Recommended for Employment   ( )   3. Recommended for Annual Contract A-4 ( )
                                                    (Documentation Attached)
2. Not Recommended for Employment   ( )   4. Other (Specify)_____   ( )
    (Documentation Attached)   (Documentation Attached)

CATEGORIES:	ACCEPTABLE	UNACCEPTABLE
A. OBSERVABLE CHARACTERISTICS:		
1. PREPARATION AND PLANNING The teacher shows evidence of preparation and planning in structuring the learning experiences of students.	( )	( )
2. KNOWLEDGE OF SUBJECT MATTER The teacher shows evidence of subject area competency.	( )	( )
3. CLASSROOM MANAGEMENT The teacher administers classroom procedures effectively and maintains control.	( )	( )
4. TECHNIQUES OF INSTRUCTION The teacher employs instructional techniques which motivate and enable students to learn.	( )	( )
5. ASSESSMENT TECHNIQUES The teacher utilizes assessment techniques which motivate and enable students to learn.	( )	( )
6. TEACHER-STUDENT RELATIONSHIP The teacher establishes relationships with students which reflect equal recognition of and respect for every individual.	( )	( )
7. PROFESSIONAL RESPONSIBILITY The teacher assumes professional responsibility.	( )	( )
B. SUPPORTIVE CHARACTERISTICS:		
The teacher contributes to the total school program.	( )	( )

```
OBSERVATION DATE(S):_____

REMARKS:_____
            _____


SIGNATURE OF PRINCIPAL:_____  DATE:_____

*SIGNATURE OF TEACHER:_____  DATE:_____
*Teacher's signature means the teacher has seen and received this document.

White Copy - Personnel Office; Yellow Copy - Teacher; Pink Copy - Principal
```

Figure 13.4 Annual Evaluation

SOURCE: Dade County Public Schools, *Annual Evaluation*, Miami, Fla. Reprinted with permission.

RICHMOND COUNTY BOARD OF EDUCATION
Teacher Appraisal Record

TEACHER'S NAME_____ SSN_____

SCHOOL_____

GRADE/SUBJECT_____

The circled ratings on this record reflect a summative evaluation
of the teacher's teaching performance for the school year(s)_____

COMPETENCIES AND INDICATORS	Improvement Needed	Satisfactory
PLANS INSTRUCTION		
1. Specifies or selects learner objectives for lessons.	1 2	3 4 5
2. Specifies or selects teaching methods for lessons.	1 2	3 4 5
3. Specifies or selects contents, materials, and equipment for lessons. .	1 2	3 4 5
4. Specifies or selects materials and procedures for assessing learner progress on the objectives	1 2 3	4 5
5. Plans instruction at a variety of levels	1 2 3	4 5
USES TECHNIQUES, METHODS, AND MEDIA RELATED TO THE OBJECTIVES		
6. Uses teaching methods appropriate for objectives, learners, and environment.	1 2 3	4 5
7. Uses instructional equipment and other instructional aids.	1 2	3 4 5
8. Uses instructional materials that provide learners with appropriate practice on objectives	1 2 3	4 5
9. Provides for individual differences among learners	1 2	3 4 5
COMMUNICATES WITH LEARNERS		
10. Gives directions and explanations related to lesson content.	1 2 3	4 5
11. Provides feedback to learners throughout the lesson.	1 2 3	4 5
12. Uses acceptable written and oral expression with learners.	1 2 3 4	5
DEMONSTRATES A VARIETY OF TEACHING METHODS		
13. Implements learning activities in a logical sequence	1 2	3 4 5
14. Uses a variety of teaching methods	1 2	3 4 5
15. Group arrangement(s) is appropriate for teaching procedures.	1 2 3	4 5
REINFORCES AND ENCOURAGES LEARNER INVOLVEMENT IN INSTRUCTION		
16. Uses procedures which get learners involved in lessons	1 2	3 4 5
17. Maintains learner involvement in lessons	1 2	3 4 5
18. Reinforces and encourages the efforts of learners to maintain involvement.	1 2 3	4 5
DEMONSTRATES AN UNDERSTANDING OF THE SUBJECT		
19. Helps learners recognize the purpose/importance of topics or activities	1 2	3 4 5
20. Demonstrates knowledge in the subject area	1 2 3	4 5
ORGANIZES TIME, SPACE, MATERIALS, AND EQUIPMENT FOR INSTRUCTION		
21. Attends to non-instructional tasks	1 2	3 4 5
22. Uses instructional time efficiently.	1 2 3	4 5
23. Provides a learning environment that is attractive and orderly	1 2 3	4 5
DEMONSTRATES ENTHUSIASM FOR TEACHING, LEARNING, AND THE SUBJECT		
24. Communicates personal enthusiasm	1 2 3	4 5
25. Stimulates learner interest.	1 2 3	4 5
HELPS LEARNERS DEVELOP POSITIVE SELF-CONCEPTS		
26. Demonstrates warmth and friendliness	1 2 3	4 5
27. Demonstrates patience, empathy, and understanding.	1 2 3	4 5
MANAGES CLASSROOM INTERACTIONS		
28. Provides feedback to learners about their behavior	1 2 3	4 5
29. Promotes comfortable interpersonal relationships	1 2 3	4 5
30. Maintains appropriate classroom behavior	1 2 3	4 5
31. Manages disruptive behavior among learners	1 2 3	4 5

Principal Comments:_____
_____

Date:_____   Signature of Principal:_____

Teacher Comments:_____
_____

I have read and am aware of the contents of this form which are based on observations by my
principal and his/her designee during this school year.

Date:_____   Signature of Teacher:_____

    Distribution: Personnel - White   Principal - Canary   Teacher - Pink

Figure 13.5 Teacher Appraisal Record

SOURCE: Richmond County Public Schools. *Teacher Appraisal Record*, Augusta. Ga. Reprinted with
permission.

544

Competencies, Indicators, and Descriptors

If you incline to the use of instruments which detail specific competencies, as I do, you should collect data utilizing instruments which break the competencies into more specific indicators and, if so desired, into descriptors of the indicators.

We may define a competency as a particular teaching behavior or skill. The Georgia State Department of Education defined a competency as follows: "A generic *teacher competency* is a conceptualization of a responsible and purposeful performance essential to the effective professional conduct of all teachers."[26]

The Georgia State Department of Education notes, however, that "This definition results in statements which are too broad for assessment purposes."[27]

Planning for instruction, using student responses, and managing the classroom are examples of generic competencies. We make a mistake if we try to evaluate these competencies without detailing what they mean. We need some guidelines to help us gather evidence that the teacher possesses the competency. Indicators serve as those guideposts. The Georgia State Department of Education explained indicators in the following way:

competency *indicators* . . . define behaviors representative of the competency. The more indicators a person demonstrates proficiently, the more likely it is that that person is demonstrating the target competency.[28]

If you will refer to the Dade County Public Schools Classroom Observation Form in Chapter 12 (Figure 12. 4) for a moment, you will see seven generic competencies, six of which may be observed in the classroom. Each competency bears a descriptive statement and is then described by a number of indicators. Take the first category, preparation and planning, for example. The descriptive statement reads, "The teacher shows evidence of preparation and planning in structuring the learning experiences of students." This statement is followed by three indicators:

A. The classroom activities reflect evidence of effective instructional planning.
B. The teacher develops lesson plans.
C. The teacher plans and makes necessary arrangements for materials, equipment, and supplies.[29]

Those are the items on which the teacher should be evaluated in respect to the first competency, no more, no less. Look now at the Annual Evaluation form for this same school shown in Figure 13.4. You will see recurring the descriptive statement which is all that is necessary for the summative form, for this report is based on the periodic classroom observations and is not an observation form. Indicators should appear, however, on summative instruments which are also used as formative instruments.

Most of the evaluation instruments which I have seen divide the competencies no further than the indicator level. The Georgia Teacher Assessment program breaks the indicators into descriptors. The Georgia Department of Education defined descriptors as follows:

They are more specific than either competencies or indicators, and are used to describe the quality of a teacher's performance relevant to a competency indicator. Descriptors are usually expressed in sentence-length statements and are scored on a scale from 1 to 5.[30]

To use the Richmond County Public Schools' Classroom Observation Form (see Figure 12.5) requires familiarity with the descriptors and ratings, which are explained in an accompanying manual. Let's take the first competency on the Richmond County Classroom Observation Form: plans instruction. This competency is divided into five indicators, as follows:

1. Specifies or selects learner objectives for lessons.
2. Specifies or selects teaching methods for lessons.
3. Specifies or selects contents, materials, and equipment for lessons.
4. Specifies or selects materials and procedures for assessing learner progress on the objectives.
5. Plans instruction at a variety of levels.[31]

For each indicator, by referring to the guidebook, the evaluator selects what he or she judges are the appropriate descriptors and rating. Let's illustrate this point by showing the descriptors and ratings possible for the first indicator of the first competency:

1. Specifies or selects learner objectives for lessons.

Ratings	Descriptors
1. None of the descriptors is evident.	a. The lesson plan includes objectives for learners.
2. Descriptor (a) is evident.	b. Objectives are appropriate to the unit and curriculum guide.
3. Descriptors (a) and (b) are evident.	c. Objectives are appropriate to the learners.
4. Descriptors (a) and (b) and either (c) or (d) are present.	d. The objectives in the lesson plan have been chronologically or conceptually sequenced,
5. All descriptors are present.	or sequencing is not appropriate.[32]

Instead of descriptive statements which are rated acceptable or unacceptable as on Dade County's summative form, Richmond County chose to repeat the competencies and indicators. The numerical ratings on the Richmond County summative form would be based on the periodic visits made by the principal or his or her designee and recorded on the Classroom Observation Form.

Indicators and descriptors are helpful in refining a competency. They serve as guides for the evaluator's observations and provide a basis for assessment. When a teacher asks, "What do you mean by this competency?" the evaluator can easily reply, "It means these indicators," or "It means these indicators and descriptors."

How Should the Data Be Used?

The data collected about a teacher's performance are used by the administrator for (1) conferences with the teacher and (2) decisions about retention or dismissal.

Conferences should be held with the teacher after each observation and for the summative evaluation. Since the administrator will be doing global assessments on each visit, preobservation conferences are less important and may be transacted in a few short minutes to schedule a visit or to obtain any special information the administrator would need to know about the class.

Conferences

Conferences between the teacher and administrator serve two purposes. First, they offer an opportunity for the administrator to gather data not witnessed during a classroom visits; they provide the teacher an opportunity to describe some of the events which the administrator viewed. Second, they are the setting for an evaluation. It should be pointed out that although the administrator's periodic observations are or can be formative in nature, they are also evaluations. Each conference, then, with the administrator is evaluative in nature. As the leopard cannot shed his or her spots, the administrator cannot wash away his or her line authority. The administrator is simply not the same person, nor should he or she be, as the staff instructional supervisor. Consequently, the administrator cannot and should not avoid the evaluative dimension of observations and conferences.

The rules of the game are different for the line administrator and the staff supervisor. The staff supervisor divulges to persons other than the teacher only what is necessary or required about a teacher's performance. The line administrator tells everything, in writing, and forwards it to the superintendent's office. In the case of teachers charged with incompetence the data go beyond the superintendent's office. The staff supervisor does not have to make the hard personnel decisions; the line administrator does. The staff supervisor relies on the authority of persuasion and expertise, the line administrator on the authority of the office.

Administrators or supervisors who must be both evaluator and instructional supervisor at the same time have a difficult role. Their observations and conferences must be both formative and evaluative. While they diagnose and prescribe, they must also rate. While they may try to minimize the element of threat, a certain amount of teacher anxiety remains.

Administrators cannot, and should not if they could, obliterate all traces of status. Though I believe protocol is overdone in many cases, a modicum of protocol is essential to the efficient operation of the program. As a matter of fact, teachers want and expect their administrators to maintain some semblance of status. Thus, whereas I would argue that the clinical supervisor should confer with a teacher in the teacher's classroom or on neutral territory, I would take the position that it is proper for evaluative conferences to be held in the administrator's office or in the administrator's conference room. The administrator can ease the tension by coming out from behind the desk and conferring with the teacher at a table or in comfortable chairs.

Madeline Hunter referred to the summative conference as the *evaluative conference* and made it clear that the evaluative conference should be based on previous conferences during the year which she called instructional conferences. She described an evaluative conference as follows:

The objective of an *evaluative conference* is that a teacher's placement on a continuum from "unsatisfactory" to "outstanding" will be established and the teacher will have the opportunity to examine the evidence used. . . . An evaluative conference should be the summation of what has occurred in and resulted from a series of instructional conferences. Information given and conclusions reached in an evaluative conference should come as no surprise to the teacher because the supporting evidence has been discussed in previous instructional conferences. As a result, the evaluative conference has high probability for being perceived as fair, just, and supportable by objective evidence rather than based on subjective opinion. This conference is the culmination of a year's diagnostic, prescriptive, collaborative work with a teacher and supervisor who shared responsibility for the teacher's continuous professional growth.[33]

During each of the series of conferences it is incumbent upon the administrator to make suggestions for improvement if he or she feels the teacher needs to improve certain behaviors. It is generally perceived that it is the administrator's responsibility, not the teacher's, to recommend remedial measures for a teacher who evidences deficiencies. If the principal seeks to dismiss a teacher for incompetence, the first question which will be asked is, "What did you do to help the teacher overcome the deficiencies?" Thus, rating a teacher is not enough. The principal must propose actions which the teacher can take if deficiencies are noted. Further, the principal has the obligation to monitor the teacher's progress in overcoming the deficiencies.

Retention and Dismissal

The decision to retain a teacher is much easier to make than a decision for dismissal. The dismissal of a teacher is a heavy, stressful burden both for the administrator and, of course, for the teacher to be dismissed. It is particularly stressful if the administrator was the person who hired the teacher in the first place. The necessity for dismissing a teacher whom the administrator has hired reflects on that administrator's judgment in selecting people to begin with.

Retention becomes acute at the point where a teacher is being considered for a continuing contract or tenure, usually at the end of three years of teaching in a school system. The administrator knows that a decision to retain will mean that the teacher will be with the school a long time, possibly a lifetime. The administrator knows also that it is far easier to dismiss a nontenured teacher than a tenured one. Although there may be moral and ethical reasons for informing a nontenured teacher of causes for nonretention, there are not usually legal reasons compelling an administrator to do so. The teacher on annual contract may simply be notified that the contract will not be renewed the following year.

Dismissal of a teacher after the teacher has earned tenure status is much more difficult. Teachers may be discharged if their positions are abolished. The major grounds for dismissal, however, are what I call the three I's: insubordination, immorality, and incompetence. Proving insubordinate and immoral behavior is relatively easy, although immorality is becoming an increasingly difficult question since standards of behavior differ greatly from community to community. Incompetence is the bear for administrators. We all know that there are incompetent people in teaching positions. We know that there are teachers who are deficient in knowledge of subject matter, in use of English, in teaching skills, and in interpersonal skills. Yet, it is difficult to prove incompetence. How incompetent does one have to be declared incompetent enough for removal from the teaching profession? Neither the teacher's organizations nor the profession in general has fully come to grips with this question. The major burden for removing an incompetent teacher is placed on the shoulders of the principal. Some teachers' groups take the position that since the principal hires teachers, it is the principal's responsibility to fire an incompetent teacher.

Dismissal for incompetence requires a great deal, some principals would say an excessive amount, of documentation. The principal must build a case carefully, citing chapter and verse, to remove a teacher who is tenured. State laws and local policies have set certain specific procedures concerning notices to be given to the teacher, hearings provided for, and appeals that may be taken before a teacher can be discharged. Many educators believe that if a state has a strong due process law, tenure is not an essential provision. Teachers, however, somewhat distrustful of administration in general, still incline to preservation of the principle of tenure.

Harris and others noted the importance of selection, formative evaluation, and summative evaluation in the making of personnel decisions:

If formative evaluation is well done, most summative evaluation decisions should be routine (e.g., continuation on the job for the majority of the teachers) or nonthreatening (e.g., transfer, change of function, or placement in a tenure status). Recommendations for termination of contract or other unpleasant eventualities are and should be relatively rare. They should be extremely rare if initial selection of personnel is carefully done and if formative evaluation and follow-up growth activities are carried out.[34]

The profession regulates to some degree standards of professional competence through professional practices commissions established in some states. The Professional Practices Commission of Georgia, for example, "was established for the purpose of setting and enforcing standards of competent professional performance and ethical conduct for educators in Georgia."[35] The commission, composed of 17 practicing members of the education profession, advises in matters of school law, counsels members of the profession, investigates complaints brought against educators, holds hearings to adjudicate matters brought before a local board of education, conducts professional, on-site reviews of the services of an educator whose performance has been questioned, and makes recommendations to the state Board of Education or the Department of Education in matters concerning denial, suspension or revocation of teaching certificates.[36] A state professional practice commission can be of help to teachers, administrators, and the profession by setting standards of competence and assisting schools in maintaining those standards.

When recommendations have been made and the conference terminated, copies of the completed instruments, duly signed by both the administrator and principal, should be placed on file. Normally, the teacher would receive a copy, the principal would retain one, and a copy would be sent to the appropriate official at the central office.

PROBLEMS IN SUMMATIVE EVALUATION

I am sure that you can name teachers who, having received their summative appraisal reports, declare, "How can the principal know how well I am doing? He (she) has never been into my classroom." Even when they receive glowing reports from the administrators, the teachers resent this type of administrative behavior. A variation on this theme is the comment voiced by numerous teachers, "But he (she) has been to visit me only once this year and then he (she) stayed only 10 minutes." One of the scandals of summative evaluation practices is the failure of the administrator to obtain an adequate sampling of a teacher's performance. The teacher should be visited, observed, and evaluated several times during the year. It is not uncommon for some administrators to limit their visits to a few minutes once or twice during the year. It is not unheard of for administrators to render summative judgments without a single visit to the teacher's classroom!

Many principals delegate teacher evaluation to their assistant principals. In fact, this is accepted practice in some school systems. There is nothing inherently wrong with such a process but if I, as principal, am required to sign my name to evaluation reports, if I am the person who must make personnel decisions or recommendations to the superintendent about personnel, and if I am the one who must document teaching performance, I would want more than secondhand information. Otherwise, the process should be turned over completely to the assistant principals, who would not only do the observing, the conferencing, and the evaluating, but would also sign the appraisal reports and defend them if challenged.

Principals err in evaluating personnel when they skew their ratings to the high side of the scale. The easy rater may be compensating for failure to gather enough data to make accurate evaluations, may feel that the whole process is burdensome and unnecessary, may be striving to maintain rapport with teachers or may simply feel that teachers need positive reinforcement for their efforts. Overrating of teacher performance is, therefore, a much more common error than is underrating. Permit me to generalize: if we were to analyze the administrative evaluations of both public school and college faculties, we would conclude that almost all of our teachers have reached a state of perfection which calls for very little improvement. Giving high ratings is an easy way out for the administrator who wishes to avoid the stress which comes from conflicts with teachers over low ratings.

Ratings should be as objective as possible. Since we all have room for growth, suggestions should be made which will lead to improvement. Teachers have reason to be concerned about the lack of reliability between evaluators. Teachers are confused and resentful when one evaluator rates a teacher's performance high while another rates the same teacher's performance low. Evaluators must take care not to let their own biases about teaching and about individual teachers affect their ratings.

Still another problem sometimes encountered is the lack of feedback to the teacher. If teachers are to profit from an assessment, they must know what it is they need to do to be more effective. Personal conferences between the teacher and evaluator are essential to the process. Sufficient time must be allocated for each conference so that the teachers feel they have had adequate opportunities to express themselves and to understand what it is the administrator wishes.

Most of the problems associated with summative evaluation can be alleviated through appropriate in-service training of the evaluators. Administrators are in as great a need of in-service education as are the teachers they supervise.

SUMMARY

Summative evaluation of teacher performance is the assessment administrators make toward the end of the year for purposes of arriving at personnel decisions. The summative appraisal is based on periodic or formative evaluations conducted during the year. All teachers should be evaluated periodically. The frequency and length of visits to the classroom vary greatly from school system to school system. In practice, nontenured teachers are evaluated more frequently than are tenured teachers. The frequency of summative appraisals varies from state to state.

Principals should evaluate the teachers of their schools. They may call on help from assistants as needed. Administrators and teachers should be in agreement as to what should be evaluated. Generally speaking, administrators collect data concerning personal and professional characteristics of teachers, products of teaching, and processes.

Administrators normally use a classroom observation instrument for making the periodic or formative evaluations during the year. This type of instrument permits a comprehensive assessment of specific teacher competencies. Competencies are best evaluated if defined with indicators and, if desired, descriptors of the indicators. The year-end summative appraisal is based on the periodic evaluations made during the year and any additional data required by the instrument in use. The summative instrument is usually correlated with the classroom observation form and with any teacher self-appraisal instrument.

If teachers are expected to make improvements in their teaching, the administrator must give them feedback. This means at the very least a conference following each formative evaluation and at the summative appraisal.

Copies of the written evaluations should be given the teacher and placed on file in the principal's office and in the appropriate office of the central administration. Evaluative data are used for administrative decisions on retention and dismissal. In presenting a case for dismissal of a teacher the administrator must adhere to due process. Administrators must make their ratings of teachers as fair and objective as possible. If a teacher is found to be deficient in some way, it is the administrator's responsibility to recommend and monitor measures which may assist the teacher in overcoming the deficiencies.

ACTIVITIES FOR FURTHER STUDY

1. Define: (a) administrative assessment, (b) summative evaluation of teacher performance, and (c) formative evaluation of teacher performance.
2. Create a set of correlated instruments for (a) teacher self-appraisal, (b) classroom observation, and (c) summative evaluation of teachers.

3. Interview and report on views of at least three teachers regarding administrative ratings of teacher competence as to categories rated and procedures.
4. Locate samples of summative evaluation instruments used by school systems to evaluate teacher competencies (other than those mentioned in this chapter) and compare them as to similarities and differences. Choose the one you would prefer.
5. Report (if the data can be obtained) on the performance of a faculty as a group (not as individuals) on annual ratings of competence in one school by percentages of faculty on each category rated.
6. Report (if data are available) on the number of dismissals or terminations of contract in a particular school system for the past five years. Classify the data as to reasons for dismissal and whether each teacher was tenured or nontenured.
7. Interview several teachers and determine (a) whether recommendations for improving instruction are regularly made by evaluators, (b) whether the teachers try to follow the recommendations, and (c) whether the evaluator monitors their progress in implementing the recommendations.
8. Report on a principal's perceptions of teacher evaluation, treating processes, difficulties, and suggestions for prospective evaluators.
9. Write several indicators for each of the following competencies:
    a. The teacher demonstrates the ability to communicate clearly to learners.
    b. The teacher demonstrates the ability to motivate the learners.
    c. The teacher demonstrates skill in classroom management.
    d. The teacher demonstrates professional behavior.
    e. The teacher demonstrates enthusiasm.
10a. For each of the following indicators suggest a competency of which it might be indicative:
    1. The teacher uses strategies which are appropriate to the learners.
    2. The teacher uses evaluation techniques which relate to the objectives.
    3. The teacher varies the stimuli.
    4. The teacher uses English correctly.
    5. The teacher shows personal interest in the learners.
10b. For each indicator write several descriptors.
11. Of the following types of summative instruments tell which you prefer and why:
    a. rating scale with numbers, as 1 to 5
    b. rating scale with two categories, as satisfactory and unsatisfactory
    c. open-ended, narrative
    d. other (specify).
12. Show your position on the following:
    a. How often should a principal visit and observe each teacher?
    b. How long should a principal remain in the classroom when observing?
    c. Should the principal's visits be (1) all announced, (2) all unannounced, or (3) a combination of announced and unannounced?

13. Reply to the following questions:
    a. Is annual evaluation of each teacher necessary?
    b. If you believe an annual evaluation of each teacher is not necessary, how often should a summative appraisal be made for each teacher?
    c. Should the frequency of summative evaluation be varied on the basis of tenured and nontenured status of the teachers?
14. Prepare a position statement on the question: Should the principal delegate responsibility for teacher evaluation to an assistant principal?
15. Show your position on the question: Can the principal serve as a clinical supervisor?
16. Describe some observable symptoms of teacher incompetence.
17. Report on the work of the professional practices commission or similar body, if there is one in your state.
18. Prepare a statement on what you believe the profession should do to weed out incompetent teachers. Be specific as to persons or groups within the profession who you believe should take responsibility for this task.
19. Suggest procedures for selection of teachers which would help to assure the employment of competent teachers. Specify the school personnel who you feel should be involved in the selection of teachers.
20. Debate the question: Teacher salary schedules should make provision for salary increments based on merit. If you take the affirmative side of this issue, suggest how merit will be defined and determined.

NOTES

1. Arthur Shaw, "Improving Instruction Through Evaluation: One Teacher's View," *Action in Teacher Education* 2, no. 1 (Winter 1979–80): 1.
2. Perry A. Zirkel, "Teacher Evaluation: An Overview," *Action in Teacher Education* 2, no. 1 (Winter 1979–80): 19.
3. Ibid.
4. Ibid.
5. Ibid., 17, 19.
6. Some of the data from Zirkel, 19.
7. Ibid.
8. Ibid.
9. Ibid.
10. Ibid.
11. Shaw, 4.
12. John D. McNeil, "A Scientific Approach to Supervision," in Thomas J. Sergiovanni, ed., *Supervision of Teaching*, 1982 Yearbook, Alexandria, Va., Association for Supervision and Curriculum Development, 1982, 23.
13. See Peter F. Oliva and Kenneth T. Henson, "The Expert Syndrome," *Contemporary Education* 53, no. 2 (Winter 1982): 61–64.
14. Allen R. Warner and Dora H. Scott, "Evaluating Teacher Effectiveness: Professional Dimensions," *Action in Teacher Education* 2, no. 1 (Winter 1979–80): 30.
15. See Donald M. Medley, "The Effectiveness of Teachers," in Penelope L. Peterson and Herbert J. Wahlberg, eds., *Research on Teaching: Concepts, Findings, and Implications*,

Berkeley, Calif., McCutchan, 1979, 11–27. See also Donald M. Medley, "Research in Teacher Effectiveness—Where It Is and How It Got Here," *Journal of Classroom Interaction* 13, no. 2 (Summer 1978): 20.

16. See Chapter 4 of this textbook for references to Barak V. Rosenshine, "Academic Engaged Time, Content Covered, and Direct Instruction," *Journal of Education* 160, no. 3 (August 1978): 38–66; and Barak V. Rosenshine, "Content, Time, and Direct Instruction," in Penelope L. Peterson and Herbert J. Wahlberg, eds., *Research on Teaching: Concepts, Findings, and Implications*, Berkeley, Calif., McCutchan, 1979, 52.

17. See N. L. Gage, *The Scientific Basis of the Art of Teaching*, New York, Teachers College Press, 1978; David C. Berliner et al., *Phase III of the Beginning Teacher Effectiveness Study*, San Francisco, Calif., Far West Laboratory for Educational Research and Development, 1976; Jere E. Brophy and C. M. Evertson, *Process-Product Correlation in the Texas Teacher Effectiveness Study*, Austin, Texas, University of Texas, 1974.

18. Ben M. Harris, Kenneth E. McIntyre, Vance C. Littleton, Jr., and Daniel F. Long, *Personnel Administration in Education: Leadership for Instructional Improvement*, Boston, Allyn and Bacon, 1979, 290–291.

19. Ibid., 298.

20. John C. Reynolds, "In Search of Mr. (Ms.) Goodteacher," *Action in Teacher Education* 2, no. 1 (Winter 1979–80): 37.

21. Shaw, 4.

22. Zirkel, 19–20.

23. Ibid., 20.

24. Ibid.

25. Harris et al., 304.

26. Georgia Department of Education, *Teacher Performance Assessment Instruments: A Handbook for Interpretation*, Atlanta, Ga., rev. 1980, 3.

27. Ibid.

28. Ibid.

29. Dade County Public Schools, *Classroom Observation Form*.

30. Georgia Department of Education, 4.

31. Richmond County Public Schools, *Classroom Observation Form*.

32. Richmond County Public Schools, *Teacher Appraisal Guidebook*, rev., Augusta, Ga., 1982.

33. Madeline Hunter, "Six Types of Supervisory Conferences," *Educational Leadership*, 37, no. 5 (February 1980): 408, 412.

34. Harris et al., 304.

35. Professional Practices Commission, *Professional Practices Commission: Serving Education in Georgia*, brochure, Atlanta, Ga. For an illustration of the rules of a Professional Practices Council see State of Florida Statutes: Chapter 6B-1, *The Code of Ethics of the Education Profession in Florida* and Chapter 6B-5, *Standards of Competent Professional Performance*.

36. Professional Practices Commission, brochure.

BIBLIOGRAPHY

Allred, Malcolm, et al. *Teaching Skills: A Dimension of Professional Competence*. Salt Lake City: Utah State Board of Education, 1978.

Association of Teacher Educators. "Evaluating Teacher Effectiveness." *Action in Teacher Education* 2 (Winter 1979–80): 1–66.

Berliner, David D., et al. *Phase III of the Beginning Teacher Effectiveness Study*. San Francisco: Far West Laboratory for Educational Research and Development, 1976.

Borich, G. D., and S. K. Madden. *Evaluating Classroom Instruction: A Sourcebook of Instruments*. Reading, Mass.: Addison-Wesley, 1977.

Brophy, Jere E., and C. M. Evertson. *Process-Product Correlation in the Texas Teacher Effectiveness Study*. Austin: University of Texas, 1974.

"Evaluating School Personnel." *National Elementary Principal* 52 (February 1973).

Evertson, Carolyn, and Freda M. Holley. "Classroom Observation." In *Handbook of Teacher Evaluation*, Jason Millman, ed. Beverly Hills, Calif.: Sage, 1981.

Flanders, Ned A. *Analyzing Teacher Behavior*. Reading, Mass.: Addison-Wesley, 1970.

Gage, N. L., ed. *Handbook of Research on Teaching*. Chicago: Rand McNally, 1963.

———. *The Scientific Basis of the Art of Teaching*. New York: Teachers College Press, 1978.

———. *Teacher Effectiveness and Teacher Education: The Search for a Scientific Basis*. Palo Alto, Calif.: Pacific Books, 1972.

Georgia Department of Education. *Teacher Performance Assessment Instruments: A Handbook for Interpretation*. Atlanta: Georgia State Department of Education, 1980.

Glass, Gene. "Teacher Effectiveness." In *Evaluating Educational Performance*, Herbert J. Wahlberg, ed. Berkeley, Calif.: McCutchan, 1974.

Haefele, Donald L. "How to Evaluate Thee, Teacher—Let Me Count the Ways." *Phi Delta Kappan* 61 (January 1980): 349–352.

Harris, Ben M., Kenneth E. McIntyre, Vance C. Littleton, Jr., and Daniel F. Long. *Personnel Administration in Education: Leadership for Instructional Improvement*. Boston: Allyn and Bacon, 1979.

Hawley, Robert C. *Assessing Teacher Performance: Task and Analysis*. Amherst, Mass.: Education Resources Associates, 1982.

Hunter, Madeline. "Appraising Teaching Performance: One Approach." *The National Elementary Principal* 52 (February 1973): 62–63.

———. "Six Types of Supervisory Conferences." *Educational Leadership* 37, no. 5 (February 1980): 408–412.

Hyman, Ronald T. *School Administrator's Handbook of Teacher Supervision and Evaluation Methods*. Englewood Cliffs, N.J.: Prentice-Hall, 1975.

Kowalski, J. D. S. *Evaluating Teachers' Performance*. Arlington, Va.: Educational Research Services, 1978.

Levin, Benjy. "Teacher Evaluation—A Review of Research." *Educational Leadership* 37 (December 1979): 240–245. See bibliography at end of this article.

McNeil, John D. "A Scientific Approach to Supervision." In *Supervision of Teaching*, 1982 Yearbook, Thomas J. Sergiovanni, ed. Alexandria, Va.: Association for Supervision and Curriculum Development, 1982.

——— and W. James Popham. "The Assessment of Teacher Competence." In *Second Handbook of Research on Teaching*, Robert M. W. Travers, ed. Chicago: Rand McNally, 1973.

Marks, James R., Emery Stoops, and Joyce King-Stoops. *Handbook of Educational Supervision: A Guide for the Practitioner*, 2nd ed. Boston: Allyn and Bacon, 1978.

Medley, Donald M. "The Effectiveness of Teachers." In *Research on Teaching: Concepts, Findings, and Implications*, Penelope L. Peterson and Herbert J. Wahlberg, eds. Berkeley, Calif.: McCutchan, 1979.

Millman, Jason, ed. *Handbook of Teacher Evaluation*. Beverly Hills, Calif.: Sage, 1981.

———. "Student Achievement as a Measure of Teacher Competence." In *Handbook of Teacher Evaluation*, Jason Millman, ed. Beverly Hills, Calif.: Sage, 1981.

Oliva, Peter F., and Kenneth T. Henson. "The Expert Syndrome." *Contemporary Education* 53, no. 2 (Winter 1982): 61–64.

———. "What Are the Essential Generic Teaching Competencies?" *Theory into Practice* (Spring 1980): 117–121.

Reynolds, John C. "In Search of Mr. (Ms.) Goodteacher." *Action in Teacher Education* 2, no. (Winter 1979–80): 35–38.

Rosenshine, Barak V. "Academic Engaged Time, Content Covered, and Direct Instruction." *Journal of Education* 160, no. 3 (August 1978): 38–66.

———. "Classroom Instruction." In *The Psychology of Teaching Methods*, N. L. Gage, ed. Chicago: National Society for the Study of Education, 1976.

————. "Content, Time, and Direct Instruction." In *Research on Teaching: Concepts, Findings, and Implications*, Penelope L. Peterson and Herbert J. Wahlberg, eds. Berkeley, Calif.: McCutchan, 1979.

———— and Norma Furst. "The Use of Direct Observation to Study Teaching." In *Second Handbook of Research on Teaching*, Robert M. W. Travers, ed. Chicago: Rand McNally, 1973.

Shavelson, Richard, and Nancy Dempsey-Atwood. "Generalizability of Measures of Teaching Behavior." *Review of Educational Research* 46, no. 4 (Fall 1976): 553–611.

Shaw, Arthur. "Improving Instruction through Evaluation: One Teacher's View." *Action in Teacher Education* 2, no. 1 (Winter 1979–80): 1–4.

Simon, Anita, and E. Gil Boyer. *Mirrors for Behavior III: An Anthology of Observation Instruments*. Philadelphia: Research for Better Schools, 1974.

Stallings, Jane. *Learning to Look*. Belmont, Calif.: Wadsworth, 1977.

Strike, Kenneth A., and Barry Bull. "Fairness and the Legal Context of Teacher Evaluation." In *Handbook of Teacher Evaluation*, Jason Millman, ed. Beverly Hills, Calif.: Sage, 1981.

Travers, Robert M. W., ed. *Second Handbook of Research on Teaching*. Chicago: Rand McNally, 1973.

University of Florida. *Teacher Competence Research Project*. Gainesville: University of Florida.

Wahlberg, Herbert J., ed. *Evaluating Educational Performance*. Berkeley, Calif.: McCutchan, 1974.

Warner, Allen R., and Dora H. Scott. "Evaluating Teacher Effectiveness: Professional Dimensions." *Action in Teacher Education* 2, no. 1 (Winter 1979–80): 27–34.

Zirkel, Perry A. "Teacher Evaluation: A Legal Overview." *Action in Teacher Education* 2, no. 1 (Winter 1979–80): 17–25.

Audiotapes

Elliot W. Eisner. *Educational Connoisseurship and Educational Criticism: A New Evaluation Approach*. Association for Supervision and Curriculum Development, Alexandria, Virginia 22314, 1978. 55 min.

Don Holste and Richard J. Bodine. *Stimulating Professional Growth through Systematic Personnel Appraisal*. Association for Supervision and Curriculum Development, Alexandria, Virginia 22314, 1979.

Thomas McGreal. *Alternative Models for Use in Designing Local Teacher Evaluation Systems*. Association for Supervision and Curriculum Development, Alexandria, Virginia 22314, 1980. 92 min.

Videotapes

Richard Manatt. *Evaluating Teacher Performance: Part I. The Process*. Association for Supervision and Curriculum Development, Alexandria, Virginia 22314, 1981. 60 min.

————. *Evaluating Teacher Performance: Part II. Teaching Episodes*. Association for Supervision and Curriculum Development, Alexandria, Virginia 22314, 1981. 60 min.

Barak V. Rosenshine, Ronald Edmonds, and Peter Mortimore. *Teacher and School Effectiveness*. Association for Supervision and Curriculum Development, Alexandria, Virginia 22314, 1981. 21 min.

Kit

Ben M. Harris and Jane Hill. *DeTek: The Developmental Teacher Evaluation Kit*. Southwest Educational Development Laboratory, 211 East Seventh Street, Austin, Texas 78701.

Multi-Media

Florida Department of Education. "Techniques for Evaluating Teacher Performance." Cluster VIII, *Assessing Educational Personnel, No. 4*, B-2 Teacher Education Module, Panhandle Area Educational Cooperative, Chipley, Florida 32428.

Multi-Media Association, Inc. Filmstrips and audio cassettes on Behavior, Evaluation, Management, and Needs Assessment. Educational Innovators Press, P.O. Box 13052, Tucson, Arizona 85732.

PART **V**

INSTRUCTIONAL SUPERVISION: EVALUATION AND CHANGE

14

Improving Instructional Supervision

OBJECTIVES

After studying Chapter 14 you should be able to accomplish the following objectives:

1. Design an instrument by which administrators can evaluate supervisors.
2. Design an instrument for self-evaluation of the supervisor.
3. Design an instrument for evaluation of the supervisor by the teachers.
4. Design a plan for evaluating the supervisory program.
5. Predict likely developments in supervision in the future.

THE ROLE OF THE SUPERVISOR: A REPRISE

Throughout this text the supervisor has been seen performing a variety of roles. He or she has been conceptualized as an individual whose primary role is the improvement of instruction and the curriculum through individual and group assistance to teachers. The instructional supervisor is a service-oriented staff person who would be more effective if freed of administrative responsibilities.

As stated in the beginning, there are many types of supervisors: generalists, specialists, supervisor-administrators, building supervisors, district supervisors, county supervisors, department heads, team leaders, and state supervisors. The role and function of each of these supervisors differ to some extent though their primary roles are similar—the improvement of programs for young people through the professional development of teachers. Consequently, the principles of supervision which have been discussed in this text have relevance for all supervisors. Modifications of specific practices and procedures, however, will need to be made to fit the various types of supervisors.

All supervisors, for example, must be concerned with helping teachers with planning, selection of strategies and resources, and evaluation. Some supervisors, for example those on the state level, may be more remote from the firing line than local supervisors but they still follow similar principles of supervision in somewhat modified ways. The supervisors at each higher level of the educational hierarchy may aid supervisors below them as well as the teachers and therefore must be thoroughly conversant with duties and responsibilities of supervisors at lower levels of the echelon.

The responsibilities of the supervisor imply a number of roles. The supervisor is:

- *An expert on instruction*, knowledgeable about the latest and best methodology.
- *A curriculum expert*, knowledgeable about the curriculum and ways to improve it.
- *A communicator*, who can relate information and ideas to teachers and is a good listener.
- *An organizer*, skillful in establishing various kinds of programs of value to teachers.
- *A master teacher*, able to demonstrate good teaching as well as talk about it.
- *A group leader* who knows how to work with groups and get the most out of them.
- *An evaluator*, who helps teachers evaluate instruction, the curriculum, and themselves.
- *A stimulator*, who suggests ideas for teachers to consider.
- *A coordinator*, who seeks to achieve articulation between programs and levels, and helps teachers to become aware of each other's problems.
- *An orienter*, who takes responsibility for helping teachers who are new to the system and community to become acquainted.
- *A consultant*, on call to individual teachers and groups who wish to take advantage of his or her expertise.
- *A public relations person*, who may be invited to interpret the school's curriculum to the public either in written communications or in talks to lay groups.
- *A researcher*, who instigates research studies, particularly action research.
- *A change agent*, a catalyst for helping teachers to change and improve.

Although the roles of a supervisor could be extended, those mentioned show to a small degree the scope of the supervisor's job in today's schools. It is obvious that a special kind of person is required to fill the shoes of the supervisor, one with extended training and experience.

Once appointed the supervisor must not assume that the training period is over. As is the case with the teachers supervised, the supervisor must keep up with developments in the field of supervision. To remain up-to-date and to maintain effectiveness the supervisor should (1) participate in in-service activities for professional development, (2) regularly and systematically evaluate himself or herself, and (3) regularly and systematically request teachers to evaluate his or her effectiveness.

Supervisors can improve themselves by participating in some of the workshops, institutes, and conferences sponsored by both teacher education institutions and professional associations. They can participate in the activities of state and national organizations of particular service to supervisors, for example, the Association for Supervision and Curriculum Development. In large school systems, supervisors can come together periodically to discuss mutual problems to which they are seeking solutions. Formal course work during the year or during the summer at a teacher education institution is another means of self-improvement. Supervisors can keep up on current developments by establishing their own professional libraries and reading regularly the professional journals which have the most significance for them and the teachers they supervise.

The supervisor may learn some of the skills of supervision by on-the-job training. For example, skill in writing curriculum guides may be gained by participating with a group of teachers in that activity. Skill in conducting a research study may be developed by participating in research under the direction of a research specialist. The supervisor may develop the skills of organizing in-service activities by drafting plans for specific activities and putting them to the test. It should be stressed that supervisors should not become complacent about their own professional development or so busy directing the professional development of teachers as to ignore their own growth. Nothing can be more incongruous in a school system than to see a faculty experiencing professional growth while the supervisory staff remains stagnant. The supervisor must continue to develop professionally if for no other reason than to set an example for teachers which communicates to them the idea that professional growth is an expected part of the life of a professional.

EVALUATION OF THE SUPERVISOR

Supervisors should continuously evaluate their effectiveness. In seeking evaluation supervisors serve as models to teachers, demonstrating a personal need for continuous evaluation of their performance. Feedback on performance is necessary for all professionals if they are to grow and develop. Supervisors can gain feedback on their performance in three ways. First, they are ordinarily evaluated by their administrators. Second, they can evaluate their own performance. Third, they can survey the perceptions of teachers about their work.

Evaluation by Superordinates

It is rather general practice for administrators and supervisors to be evaluated by their superordinates. Central office supervisors and principals are evaluated by their supervisors in the central administration. Principals assess the performance of assistant

CLARKE COUNTY SCHOOL DISTRICT-SUPERVISOR-COORDINATOR ASSESSMENT RECORD

NAME _____ SCHOOL _____

ASSESSOR _____ SUBJECT OR GRADE_____ DATE _____

THREE COPIES FOR: PART ①- PERSONNEL FILE   PART ②- STAFF MEMBER   PART ③- ASSESSOR'S FILE

PLEASE USE BLACK BALL POINT PEN FOR THIS FORM

RATING   RATING

Rating columns: Excellent | Satisfactory | Improvement Necessary | Not Observed

A. PERSONAL QUALITIES

1. Demonstrates sufficient stamina and energy to perform assignment at an effective level.

2. Demonstrates punctual and regular attendance.

3. Manifests poise and self control.

4. Dresses in a manner appropriate to the particular role.

5. Demonstrates competency in language usage .

6. Voice Quality: Speaks with clarity, appropriate tone and volume.

B. HUMAN AND INTERPERSONAL RELATIONSHIPS

1. Accepts constructive criticism positively.

2. Establishes and maintains positive relationships with teachers.

3. Establishes and maintains positive relationships with co-workers.

4. Establishes and maintains positive relationships with the community.

5. Is supportive of the school program.

C. PROFESSIONAL QUALITIES

1. Takes pride in teaching and is supportive of the profession.

2. Demonstrates cooperation in areas of assigned responsibilities within the school and/or school system.

3. Actively pursues a program of self-improvement.

4. Recognizes an obligation to understand and support administrative policies and procedures while offering dissent in a constructive manner.

D. PROFESSIONAL PERFORMANCE

1. Demonstrates adequate knowledge of area of responsibility.

2. Diagnoses strengths and weaknesses of persons/programs supervised or coordinated.

3. Provides appropriate assistance to teachers for the improvement of their performance.

4. Communicates clearly and effectively with school staff and co-workers.

5. Creates an atmosphere which stimulates interest and enthusiasm for teaching.

6. Supports the adopted policies and procedures of the school system.

7. Demonstrates ability to organize and manage area of responsibility.

E. COMMENTS (OPTIONAL)

Staff Member's Comments _____

_____

Assessor's Comments _____

_____

_____

* SIGNATURE OF STAFF MEMBER _____ DATE _____

* SIGNATURE OF ASSESSOR _____ DATE _____

* This signature does not necessarily imply agreement; it indicates that the person has seen it.

If any area is checked as "improvement necessary" the "PERFORMANCE IMPROVEMENT PLAN" must be filled out by the assessor and the person being assessed.

1   PERSONNEL FILE

SPEEDIPLY® Patent Pending. MCP® Patented 3,429,827;3,016,308; Moore Business Forms, Inc., A

Figure 14.1 Clarke County District-Supervisor-Coordinator Assessment Record

SOURCE: Clarke County Public Schools, *Clarke County District-Supervisor-Coordinator Assessment Record*, Athens, Ga. Reprinted with permission.

principals, lead teachers, department heads, grade coordinators, team leaders, and other supervisory personnel.

Administrators and supervisors who rise through the ranks often hold tenure as *teachers*. They do not, as a rule, have tenure in administrative or supervisory positions. They serve in leadership positions at the discretion of their superordinates. Even the superintendent is evaluated one way or another by his or her superordinates: the people. If the superintendent is elected to office, the people may turn him or her out at the next election. If the superintendent is appointed, he or she serves at the pleasure of the people's representatives, the local board of education. If the board is dissatisfied with the performance of the superintendent, it may refuse to renew his or her contract. If the board becomes dissatisfied enough with the superintendent during the period of the contract, it may discharge him or her and buy up the remaining time of the contract.

Thus, school personnel are evaluated by their superordinates. Administrators and supervisors are evaluated for two purposes: (1) to provide them with feedback so they can improve their performance and (2) to provide their superiors with data on which to base personnel decisions, as, whether to retain them in their administrative or supervisory positions.

Many school systems rate their administrative and supervisory personnel using instruments which detail the specific criteria considered important in those systems. Some school systems use the same instrument to rate both administrators and supervisors without distinguishing between these two types of personnel. In that respect they emulate the preservice training programs of professional education institutions which stipulate the same course requirements for both administrators and supervisors.

The evaluation instrument of the Clarke County (Georgia) Public Schools shown in Figure 14.1 provides an illustration of the kinds of criteria which supervisory personnel may be expected to demonstrate. It behooves prospective administrators and supervisors to discover the criteria on which they will be evaluated before accepting a leadership position, so they can decide whether or not they feel they would wish to or could fulfill the requirements of the position.

In selecting people for administrative or supervisory positions, especially those with no previous track record in administration or supervision, the employing officials need to gather as much evidence as they can to predict whether or not the persons to be employed will be successful on the job. They should certainly investigate whether the prospective administrators and supervisors were successful as teachers, whether they were, in fact, superior teachers. They should make it a point to learn something of their philosophy of education, their organizational and problem-solving skills, and especially important, their skills in communicating and working with people.

Self-evaluation

A conscientious supervisor will stop periodically for self-assessment. Such a supervisor will raise questions about the effectiveness of the help provided teachers, look for evidence of the kind of assistance rendered, and gauge his or her competencies

Rate yourself on each of the items below by checking the appropriate number.
1 is lowest and 5 highest. NA is not applicable.

Characteristics	1	2	3	4	5	NA
1. I provide assistance as needed.						
2. I am open to communication.						
3. I show concern for the individual teacher.						
4. I transmit pertinent information.						
5. I am receptive to others' ideas.						
6. I interact effectively with teachers.						
7. I communicate clearly.						
8. I provide leadership in curriculum development.						
9. I am up-to-date on curriculum developments.						
10. I am effective as a demonstration teacher.						
11. I am skillful in diagnosing instructional difficulties.						
12. I am skillful in prescribing measures for instructional improvement.						
13. I am effective as a group leader.						
14. I involve teachers in decision making.						
15. I am skillful in conducting conferences with teachers.						
16. I plan in-service activities in response to teachers' needs.						
17. I perceive my primary role as a helper to teachers.						

Figure 14.2 Self-assessment Instrument

against some standards of performance such as those described in the literature on supervision. Supervisors look at the objectives they have specified for the year or other period of time and determine whether the objectives have been met. Not only do they assess the effectiveness of the supervisory program per se but they also evaluate the quality of the roles they have played in that supervisory program. While encouraging teachers to evaluate themselves, supervisors can do no less than practice what they preach, evaluate their own traits and accomplishments, and make changes as a result of self-discovery. It is often helpful to make use of a check-list or inventory to direct a self-appraisal. Figure 14.2 is an example of such a checklist.

Instead of following a check-list the supervisor could keep in mind a few basic questions to which he or she could periodically and privately respond, such as:

Am I meeting my objectives?
Am I providing any real help to teachers?
Where are the gaps in my help?
Am I using my time wisely?
In what areas do I need in-service education?
Am I behaving like a supervisor or like an administrator?

Professional supervisors evaluate their own performance continuously.

Evaluation by Teachers

It is axiomatic that supervisors will be evaluated by their superiors in the educational hierarchy. What is much rarer but an obvious necessity is the provision of opportunities for teachers to evaluate administrators and supervisors. Administrative and supervisory personnel at all levels of the educational spectrum commonly omit what could be a vital source of feedback—evaluation by "the troops."

Although there exists a growing movement toward a process by which teachers evaluate the performance of those who administer and supervise their work, evaluation of superiors by subordinates in the hierarchy is a relatively recent development. The traditional point of view held by both teachers and administrators/supervisors has been that the administrators and supervisors were immune from evaluation by those lower on the table of organization. Historically, the bureaucratic approach to administration and supervision has dominated most formal organizations. Authority and communication in bureaucratic organizations proceed from the top down, not vice versa.

Only in recent times with a growing emphasis on the democratic or collegial approach to administration have superordinates begun to permit and encourage subordinates to participate in the administration of the organization. Evaluation of the leadership by the members of the organization is a part of the collegial approach to administration. In school settings the evaluation of administrators and supervisors by the subordinates, the teachers, is analogous to the evaluation of teachers by their students and by the parents of their students. Since administrators and supervisors suggest or require student evaluations and often recommend parents' evaluations of teachers, they should set an example by seeking teachers' perceptions of their performance.

The accountability movement, which has rubbed off not only on teachers but also on their administrators and supervisors, and the growing power of teachers' organizations have also contributed to the notion that administrators and supervisors are accountable to their subordinates as well as to their superiors. The new supervisor can forge a strong link in the chain of rapport with teachers by promptly and voluntarily instituting a process by which the teachers supervised can periodically—at least annually—evaluate his or her achievements. Feedback from the teachers is the best way to find out whether or not the supervisor is actually accomplishing the mission. The teachers whom the supervisor serves are in a real sense the consumers of the product brought to them, and they are in the best position to judge whether that product is effective.

The supervisor may design with the assistance of teachers an instrument which teachers can fill out toward the end of the year. To obtain valid results the instrument should be administered in a threat-free environment. The best means of accomplishing this is to have teachers fill out the instrument anonymously and turn it in to an elected committee of their colleagues, who will tabulate the data and furnish the supervisor with a summary of the data, after which the original evaluations will be destroyed by the committee.

With some minor changes the self-evaluation instrument which appeared in Figure 14.2 can be transformed into an instrument by which teachers can evaluate the performance of the supervisor (Figure 14.3). Descriptive terms are used in place of numbers. A space is provided for the response "no information" if teachers feel they have inadequate data on which to base a judgment. Appropriate directions on how to fill out the instrument and to whom it is to be given would accompany the instrument.

EVALUATION OF THE SUPERVISORY PROGRAM

In addition to looking at how well he or she fulfills his or her role the supervisor should gather data on how effective the program has been. The supervisor should make an effort to judge the results of the supervision program. We want to know not only how well the supervisor functions but also whether and what results have been achieved. Two approaches to evaluation of the supervisory program have proved helpful. For want of better terminology let's call them simply (1) evaluation by objectives and (2) evaluative questioning.

Evaluation by Objectives

In keeping with the approach to administration referred to as management by objectives, supervision by objectives requires the supervisor to establish specific objectives which are to be carried out during the year. Just as the specification of instructional (behavioral) objectives simplifies the task of evaluating student achievement, the specification of supervisory objectives makes the task of evaluating the success of the supervisory program simpler.

Please rate your supervisor on the following characteristics.

Characteristics	Outstanding	Very Good	Good	Fair	Poor	No Information
1. Provides assistance as needed.						
2. Is open to communication.						
3. Shows concern for the individual teacher.						
4. Transmits pertinent information.						
5. Is receptive to others' ideas.						
6. Interacts effectively with teachers.						
7. Communicates clearly.						
8. Provides leadership in curriculum development.						
9. Is up-to-date on curriculum developments.						
10. Is effective as a demonstration teacher.						
11. Is skillful in diagnosing instructional difficulties.						
12. Is skillful in prescribing measures for instructional improvement.						
13. Is effective as a group leader.						
14. Involves teachers in decision making.						
15. Is skillful in conducting conferences with teachers.						
16. Plans in-service activities in response to teachers' needs.						
17. Perceives his or her primary role as a helper to teachers.						

Figure 14.3 Teacher Evaluation of the Supervisor

Let's assume for the moment the role of assistant principal for curriculum and instruction in an elementary school. In this school the principal, assistant principal, grade coordinators, and central office supervisors regularly visit and observe teachers. During the summer the assistant principal drafts the following objectives which will become his or her supervisory job targets for the ensuing academic year:

By December 1 a videotaping system will have been put in place for teachers to evaluate their own performance.

By January 1 each tenured teacher will have been visited once and each nontenured teacher twice; a conference will have been held with each teacher.

By February 1 assessment tests in the basic skills of fifth graders will have been completed.

By March 1 a curriculum mapping study will have been completed at each grade level.

By April 1 curriculum guides in social studies and science will have been completed.

By May 1 the in-service needs of teachers will have been surveyed for purposes of planning next year's staff development program.

By May 31 the following workshops based on last year's survey of teachers' needs will have been offered; times and dates to be scheduled in September with the faculty.

By June 5 each teacher will have had the opportunity to visit and observe for a day another teacher in the school system.

The foregoing objectives are typical of those which might be specified by a school-based supervisor. In evaluating the supervisory program the supervisor can readily determine which objectives have been achieved. Establishing the objectives in advance is an earmark of sound planning. Specifying objectives clarifies the program directions in the supervisor's own mind, communicates the targets to others, and eases the problem of evaluation of the program.

Evaluative Questioning

The supervisor who follows this approach seeks answers to questions designed to cast light on results achieved. John T. Lovell and Kimball Wiles illustrated this approach by suggesting the following questions, which might be asked by the supervisor:

1. How many more teachers are experimenting?
2. Has there been an increase in the calls for help in thinking through problems?
3. Has there been a change in the nature of the problems presented?
4. Is there an increased demand in the staff for professional materials?
5. Is there more sharing of materials among members of the staff?
6. Is the faculty identifying the problems it has to face further ahead, so that it isn't confronted with so many emergencies?

7. Is there a greater use of evidence in deciding issues?
8. Is there within the faculty a greater acceptance of difference?
9. How many more parents are involved in the school?
10. How many rooms are attractive?
11. How many more teachers are active in professional organizations?
12. How many more teachers are seeking in-service experience?
13. How many more teachers are planning with other teachers?
14. How many more pupils are being included in planning and evaluating?
15. Is a larger percentage of the staff assuming responsibility for the improvement of the program?
16. Are staff meetings becoming more faculty directed?
17. How many more teachers are using a wider range of materials?
18. How are students scoring on achievement tests?[1]

Answers to the foregoing questions will reveal a great deal about the effectiveness of the supervisory program. If the two approaches to program evaluation are both followed, that is, if prespecified objectives are assessed and if probing, evaluative questions are answered, a thorough assessment of the program may be made. Where deficiencies are uncovered, it is the supervisor's responsibility to take the initiative for making plans to overcome the deficiencies.

FUTURE DIRECTIONS IN SUPERVISION

It is almost pro forma for the author of an education textbook to gaze into a crystal ball and prophesy what he or she sees portending for the future. We have seen the emergence of a new academic specialty called Futurism, which has its own organization composed of Futurists, whose writings appear in the organization's journal, *The Futurist*.[2] We can identify any number of books and films which predict what life will be like in the twenty-first century and beyond. The beauty of prophesying is that no one can prove the prophet wrong. Not until the future arrives can the prophecies be pronounced "right" or "wrong," or perhaps judged on the scale employed by some of those tough standardized test items "more right than wrong" or "more wrong than right."

So I cannot resist becoming a bit delphic and very briefly playing the game of Prophecy. I'd like to consider with you the question: What will supervision be like 10 years from now?

Clarification of Roles

During the next 10 years the supervisor's duties will continue to be more clearly spelled out and roles will continue to be clarified. Increasingly, job descriptions of the supervisor's duties will be written and differentiation of responsibilities among various types of supervisors will be made.

Supervision still exists as it has for many years in a kind of half-world between teaching and administration. While supervision may not in 10 years end its long-time marriage with administration, it will at least come out of the shadow of administration as a viable career in its own right. As a step toward achieving this career status, the training program of supervisors will be stiffer, more extensive, and more precise. Training programs will be tailored to the needs of those who see their careers specifically as supervisors, not as administrators-in-waiting or as teachers-once-removed. More states will emulate the programs of those states requiring a sixth year or specialist's certificate for state certification as a supervisor. In addition to the more general background needed by professional personnel, training components will call for heavier stress on such areas as curriculum development, instructional technology, microteaching, human relations, communication skills, measurement and evaluation, and classroom management.

Emphasis on Observable Teaching Competencies

In spite of some recommendations to the contrary, continuing emphasis will be placed on the identification and development of specified, measurable, and observable competencies of teachers. It will be the supervisor's task to work with teachers to identify those competencies and to devise strategies for achieving and evaluating them.

The principle of accountability will continue taking root at least to the extent of joint efforts by teachers and supervisors to ascertain whether the demonstrated instructional competencies of the teacher make a difference in respect to the product of instruction—the students. In this respect, teacher competency will be considered effective when teachers succeed in helping learners to reach instructional objectives.

The profession may even make a breakthrough in settling on an answer to the question: What is effective teaching? The advent of merit pay systems will force school systems to define what they mean by effective teaching.

Clinical Supervision

Clinical supervision will establish its place in the total supervisory program. Instructional supervisors will increase the help they render to individual teachers. Together with the teacher they will identify specific behaviors with which the teacher would like assistance. They will follow a cycle of supervision which includes observation and pre- and postobservation conferences. Clinical supervisors will focus on the improvement of instruction rather than rating teachers for personnel purposes.

Peer Supervision

We may expect to see a greater camaraderie among teachers and an increased willingness for them to help each other. Supervisors will train teachers to analyze their own performance and the performance of other teachers. Teachers, then, will alternate the roles of teacher and supervisor. Helping each other to improve instruction will be routine with teaching teams. The use of peers will help extend our supervisory resources. By giving teachers a role in supervision the "cold war" between teachers and supervisors may be defused.

School-based Supervision

More frequently individual schools will assume responsibilities for providing instructional supervision for their faculties. Schools will seek to develop teachers' supervisory skills so they may aid each other. The schools will make better use of the supervisory personnel they already have aboard: assistant principals, lead teachers, department heads, grade coordinators, team leaders, and others.

With the movement toward school-based supervision the role of the central office supervisor will change. Typically, the services of central office supervisors have been spread thin throughout the system. These personnel have tried with varying degrees of success to meet all of the supervisory needs of all the schools in their districts. As school-based personnel take over some of these supervisory responsibilities central office supervisors can give more attention to coordinating programs among the various schools and providing back-up help to school-based supervisory personnel who are experiencing difficult problems.

Use of Technology

More teachers will be willing to have their lessons videotaped so they and their supervisors may carefully analyze the teachers' performance. Media will become less of a mystery and more of an aid to both teachers and supervisors. Teachers will feel less threatened and students less distracted by the repeated appearance of video equipment in the classroom.

Enterprising school systems will create a professional library of videotaped protocol materials to be used for the analysis of teaching. We are just beginning to realize the implications of using computers in education. Supervisors will need sophistication in the application of computers not only to help them do their own job more effectively but also to help teachers utilize computers for instructional purposes.

Teacher Involvement

Either by invitation of the administrators or by pressure from the teachers' organizations teachers will have more say in the management of the schools. The collegial approach to administration which stresses participation of subordinates will continue to make inroads into the traditional bureaucratic approach. Teacher education centers provide one vehicle for teachers to become intimately involved in supervision, particularly in staff development.

Teacher education centers have affected the role of the supervisor in at least two ways. First, the decision-making process is now more widely shared with the various constituencies of the school. The teacher constituency has become the dominant force in the teacher education center, since teachers make up the majority of a center's advisory council. Supervisors who are accustomed to working closely with teachers, assessing their needs, and responding to their suggestions welcome the effect of the teacher education center. Those supervisors who are accustomed to more independent decision making feel that some of their power has slipped away and they are confronted with the need for a change in their style of leadership.

A second effect of the teacher education center may be seen in the centralized coordination responsibilities of the center through the office of its director. Since staff development programs are coordinated at least to some degree through the center, individual supervisors must work more frequently through the center's agency rather than independently, as they had been accustomed to do previously.

Some of the supervisor's present responsibilities will be assumed by the teachers' organizations. Even without the existence of a teacher education center, supervisors may expect to see increasingly the development of teacher evaluation by their peers and teacher involvement in making decisions on the competence or incompetence of particular teachers.

A more concerted effort will be made to develop supervisory leadership from within the teachers' organizations. Some of the decision-making process which the supervisor now enjoys will be shared to a greater extent with teachers and the representatives of their organizations.

Goal-oriented Supervision

Goal-oriented supervision will be a viable alternative to or a supplement to across-the-board or global evaluation of teacher competencies. Supervisors and teachers will identify specific job targets on which the teachers will focus during a particular period of time, usually a year. The supervisor will help the teacher to delimit areas in which they agree the teacher needs improvement. Teacher self-appraisal will be increasingly used as a technique for identification of areas where improvement is needed and as a means by which job targets can be selected.

Systematic Planning

The supervisor will develop more systematic approaches to planning for supervision. Systems principles will be more commonly applied. The supervisor will work with teachers to specify objectives of long-term staff development plans, to choose procedures for carrying out the objectives, and to design means of evaluating the attainment of objectives. Continuous feedback during the implementation of staff development plans will permit alteration of the objectives and procedures.

The supervisor will learn to set and schedule supervisory activities, specify goals and objectives of the supervisory program for a specific period of time, and establish priorities. He or she will develop the technique of drafting a planning calendar which will specify target objectives for the year, activities designed to reach the objectives, personnel and facilities required, time by which the objectives should be reached, and means by which the activities will be evaluated.

Increased Use of Specialists

To compensate for the heavy emphasis on generic teaching skills, increased services of subject matter specialists will be made available either at the individual school level or from the central office. As the sum of knowledge in all disciplines continues to grow and as methodology in the special areas becomes more complex the services of specialist supervisors will be more in demand. Not only will there be a place for specialists in the traditional disciplines but school districts will find the need for specialists in fields which cut across the curriculum such as instructional design, computer literacy, human relations, learner exceptionalities, media, communication skills, tests and measurement, and community involvement.

Like all branches of education supervision will undergo changes, some simple, some profound, in the years ahead.

SUMMARY

Today's supervisor plays a number of varied roles. Throughout this text his or her primary role is conceived as that of a service-oriented helper to teachers in the areas of curriculum and instruction. While giving attention to the in-service needs of teachers, supervisors must not neglect their own in-service training.

Supervisors are regularly evaluated by their supervisors. Conscientious supervisors regularly engage in self-evaluation and seek evaluation of their performance by the teachers being served. The supervisory program may be evaluated by determining whether objectives have been met and by responding to searching questions about the effects of the program.

The field of supervision is undergoing numerous changes. Among developments which might be predicted are the following:

> Supervisory roles will be clarified and differentiated.
> Emphasis will continue on observable teaching competencies.
> Clinical supervision will be practiced more widely.
> Peer supervision will be more common.
> The individual school will assume greater responsibility for supervision of its own faculty.
> Supervisors will make greater use of technological aids.
> Teachers will play a greater role in school management.

Goal-oriented supervision will be an alternative to or supplement to global assessment of teaching performance.

Supervisors will follow more systematic approaches to planning, implementing, and evaluating their work.

The services of specialist supervisors will be made more readily available to teachers.

ACTIVITIES FOR FURTHER STUDY

1. Create a self-evaluation instrument for supervisors.
2. Create an instrument by which administrators may evaluate supervisors' performance.
3. Create an instrument by which teachers may evaluate supervisors' performance.
4. Locate and report on one or more self-evaluation instruments for supervisors which are in use in school systems.
5. Locate and report on one or more instruments in use in school systems by which administrators rate their supervisors' performance.
6. Locate and report on one or more instruments in use in school systems by which teachers may evaluate supervisors' performance.
7. Obtain and analyze a set of objectives for a year which have been drawn up by one or more of the following:
   a. an assistant principal
   b. a department head
   c. a grade coordinator
   d. a lead teacher
   e. a team leader
   f. a central office supervisor (coordinator)
8. Obtain and analyze a set of objectives for a year which have been drawn up by a principal. Identify which objectives pertain to instructional supervision.
9. Make a list or probable questions which you would ask as a supervisor in order to assess the results of your supervisory program.
10. Interview a supervisor (preferably in the type of position to which you aspire) and construct a job analysis of that supervisor's duties.
11. Survey at least 10 teachers and see if they have ever had the opportunity to evaluate an administrator or supervisor.
12. Talk with a number of supervisors and report on in-service activities in which they have participated for their own professional development in the past 12 months.
13. Write a paper on the meaning and application of the systems approach to supervision.
14. Write a paper on how computers might be used in the field of supervision.

15. Draw up your own list of prophecies as to what developments are likely to take place in the field of supervision within the next 10 years.
16. Analyze the future directions in supervision discussed in this chapter and state whether you agree or disagree with each position and why you take that position.
17. Locate and report on several articles or books which make predictions for changes which may occur in respect to the areas of curriculum and instruction.
18. Identify professional organizations and their major publications which are of special significance to the development and growth of the supervisor.
19. Compile a bibliography of books on supervision copyrighted within the past five years which would be suitable as the nucleus of a professional library for supervisors.

NOTES

1. John T. Lovell and Kimball Wiles, *Supervision for Better Schools*, 5th ed., Englewood Cliffs, N.J., Prentice-Hall, 1983, 287–290.
2. See *The Futurist: A Journal of Forecasts, Trends, and Ideas about the Future*, World Future Society, P.O. Box 30369, Bethesda Branch, Washington, D.C. 20014.

BIBLIOGRAPHY

Douglas, Harl R., Rudyard K. Bent, and Charles W. Boardman. *Democratic Supervision in Secondary Schools*, 2nd ed. Cambridge, Mass.: Riverside, 1961.
Dull, Lloyd W. *Supervision: School Leadership Handbook*. Columbus, Ohio: Charles E. Merrill, 1981.
Feyereisen, Kathryn Y., A. John Fiorino, and Arlene T. Nowak, *Supervision and Curriculum Renewal: A Systems Approach*. New York: Meredith, 1970.
Franseth, Jane. *Supervision as Leadership*. Evanston, Ill.: Row, Peterson, 1961.
Gwynn, J. Minor. *Theory and Practice of Supervision*. New York: Dodd, Mead, 1961.
Harris, Ben M. *Supervisory Behavior in Education*, 2nd ed. Englewood Cliffs, N.J.: Prentice-Hall, 1975.
Lewis, Arthur J., and Alice Miel. *Supervision for Improved Instruction: New Challenges, New Responses*. Belmont, Calif.: Wadsworth, 1972.
Lovell, John T., and Kimball Wiles. *Supervision for Better Schools*, 5th ed. Englewood Cliffs, N.J.: Prentice-Hall, 1983.
Marks, James R., Emery Stoops, and Joyce King-Stoops. *Handbook of Educational Supervision: A Guide for the Practitioner*, 2nd ed. Boston: Allyn and Bacon, 1978.
Neagley, Ross L., and N. Dean Evans. *Handbook for Effective Supervision of Instruction*, 3rd ed. Englewood Cliffs, N.J.: Prentice-Hall, 1980.
Odiorne, George S. *Management Decisions by Objectives*. Englewood Cliffs, N.J.: Prentice-Hall, 1969.
Wiles, Jon, and Joseph Bondi. *Supervision: A Guide to Practice*. Columbus, Ohio: Charles E. Merrill, 1980.
Wilson, L. Craig, T. Madison Byar, Arthur S. Shapiro, and Shirley H. Schell. *Sociology of Supervision: An Approach to Comprehensive Planning in Education*. Boston: Allyn and Bacon, 1969.

Appendix A: Competencies

Below are the major competencies (objectives) of this textbook. After studying this textbook you should be able to demonstrate each of these competencies. By demonstrating these competencies you will reflect a repertoire of knowledge and skills needed to be a successful supervisor. The numbers after each competency are the chapters in which the major discussion of the competency can be found.

1. Write a working definition and draw a working model of supervision.   1
2. Describe minimal qualifications of a supervisor.   1
3. Identify several unresolved problems (issues) in supervision and show your position on each.   2
4. Describe and apply a model of instruction.   3
5. Demonstrate the ability to write instructional goals and objectives in a particular discipline.   3
6. Write behavioral objectives for each major category of the taxonomies of the three domains of learning.   3
7. Demonstrate the ability to describe learning tasks.   3
8. Demonstrate the ability to construct a unit plan.   3
9. Demonstrate the ability to construct a lesson plan.   3
10. Select instructional resources applying appropriate criteria.   4
11. Select instructional strategies applying appropriate criteria.   4
12. Demonstrate selected generic teaching skills.   4
13. Demonstrate the ability to specify entry skills for study of topics in your discipline.   5
14. Distinguish between norm-referenced and criterion-referenced measurement and state the uses of each.   5
15. Distinguish between formative and summative evaluation as the terms are used in the instructional process.   5
16. Create well-constructed essay tests.   5
17. Create well-constructed objective tests.   5

18. Describe and defend a marking system for your school. 5
19. Describe and defend a system for reporting marks assigned by teachers in your school. 5
20. Describe principal causes of student misbehavior. 6
21. Describe ways by which a teacher can promote self-discipline. 6
22. Recommend corrective measures appropriate to specific age levels. 6
23. Draw a model for curriculum development and explain each of its components. 7
24. Demonstrate the ability to write curriculum goals and objectives. 7
25. Describe and apply a rationale for selecting curricular content. 7
26. Define the concepts of scope, sequence, and balance as they relate to curriculum development. 7
27. Draw a model for curriculum evaluation and explain each of its components. 8
28. Distinguish among different types of educational research. 8
29. Apply principles of action research. 8
30. Explain selected research concepts. 8
31. Demonstrate the ability to plan a curricular needs assessment. 8
32. Describe the techniques of curriculum mapping. 8
33. Demonstrate the ability to apply the *Evaluative Criteria* for your particular level of schooling. 8
34. Identify several general references useful in conducting research on an educational topic. 8
35. Conduct an in-service needs assessment. 9
36. Plan a comprehensive in-service program for teachers of a school system. 9
37. Plan a comprehensive in-service program for teachers of a particular school. 9
38. Write in-service training components (modules). 9
39. Plan and conduct various types of in-service activities. 9
40. Identify and demonstrate skills necessary to lead task-oriented groups. 10
41. Analyze the performance of individuals in groups. 10
42. Design training programs for group interaction. 10
43. Design a comprehensive teacher evaluation system. 11
44. Demonstrate skill in training teachers to evaluate themselves. 11
45. Use media in evaluating and improving teacher performance. 11
46. Train teachers to gather student evaluations of their performance. 11
47. Train teachers to gather parent evaluations of their performance. 11
48. Describe and apply a model of clinical supervision. 12
49. Select or create and apply appropriate classroom observation instruments. 12
50. Demonstrate selected techniques of classroom observation. 12

51. Conduct pre- and post-observation conferences. 12
52. Develop a plan for utilizing teacher peers in supervision. 12
53. Distinguish between formative and summative evaluation of teacher performance and explain the instructional supervisor's role, if any, in each. 12, 13
54. Select or create and apply an instrument by which an administrator can evaluate teacher performance. 13
55. Select or create and apply an instrument by which an administrator can evaluate the supervisor's performance. 14
56. Select or create and apply an instrument by which you can evaluate your own performance as a supervisor. 14
57. Select or create and apply an instrument by which teachers can evaluate the supervisor's performance. 14
58. Describe ways to evaluate the supervisory program. 14
59. Describe trends and probable future developments in the field of supervision. 14

Appendix B:
Examples of Descriptions
of Supervisory Positions

JOB DESCRIPTION 1

TITLE: Assistant Superintendent for Instructional Services

QUALIFICATIONS: 1. B.S. Degree in Elementary Education
2. M.A. Degree in Guidance/Counseling
3. Sixth-Year Specialist Certificate, Curriculum Director
4. Sixth-Year Specialist Certificate, Administration/Supervision

REPORTS TO: Associate Superintendent of Schools

SUPERVISES: 1. Secretary for Instructional Division
2. Instructional Specialist
3. Director of Special Education
4. Coordinator of Staff Development and Career Education
5. CESA Specialists

JOB GOAL: To furnish leadership in the improvement of the curriculum and the Instructional Program

PERFORMANCE RESPONSIBILITIES:
1. Program Planning, Instruction, Resources, and Evaluation
   a. Study curriculum in continuous evaluation and development with the ultimate aim to fit the needs of all students involved;
   b. Study and evaluate the results of all testing programs, both county and state;
   c. Help identify curriculum needs which cut across subject areas;
   d. Seek for continuity in the scope and sequence of subject matter;
   e. Help create a conducive atmosphere for curriculum change and innovation and develop readiness for curriculum improvement in specific areas;
   f. Initiate and assist in curriculum improvement activities;
   g. Conduct systemwide studies for improving instruction;
   h. Coordinate curriculum and help develop curriculum guides;

    i. Help teachers and principals with teaching methods, instructional materials, and implementation of the instructional program;

    j. Coordinate textbook adoptions and library activities;

    k. Maintain book inventories;

    l. Assist in the evaluation of and selection of instructional materials;

    m. Assist in orientation of new teachers;

    n. Work with the administration to solve instructional problems of a systemwide or area-wide nature;

    o. Work closely with curriculum committee chairmen and members in planning for committee meetings, participate in the meetings, and carry out committee actions;

    p. Coordinate activities within certain curriculum committees and among other committees;

    q. Coordinate and direct activities of consultants of Cooperative Educational Service Agency (CESA);

    r. Request and coordinate activities of consultants from the State Department of Education;

    s. Request and coordinate activities of consultants from colleges and universities;

    t. Help coordinate music and band programs at the county level;

    u. Coordinate preparation of the Comprehensive Plan for Vocational Education at the county level;

    v. Coordinate preparation of the State Plan for Staff Development at the county level;

    w. Confer with publishers, representatives, salesmen, etc. in order to keep abreast of current materials;

    x. Develop criteria for purchase and utilization of instructional materials and equipment;

    y. Visit schools on a scheduled and call basis;

    z. Assist in the development of federal, state, and other approved projects;

  aa. Assist in the implementation of federal, state, and other approved projects.

2. Studies, Demonstration, and Research
    a. Assist teachers with research and experimentation;
    b. Conduct studies for improving instruction;
    c. Keep informed on research findings and make available to staff;
    d. Initiate and assist in research projects, experimental studies, and evaluation programs.

3. Human Relations in School and Community
    a. Help to build good rapport between the school and community;
    b. Work with lay and professional groups.

4. In-Service, Workshops, and Teacher Education
    a. Plan, provide, and coordinate workshops and staff development for teachers;
    b. Stay informed on current philosophy, methodology, and materials;
    c. Help teachers to keep abreast of new curriculum development and gain new insights into the teaching-learning process;
    d. Coordinate program of Coastal Area Teacher Education Service (CATES);

    e. Encourage professional growth and higher certification of teachers;
    f. Help coordinate student teaching in the schools;
    g. Serve on Teacher Education Committee at Augusta College;
    h. Serve on Coastal Area Teacher Education Service (CATES) Advisory Committee;
    i. Plan and arrange for visiting speakers and consultants.
5. Conferences, Professional Meetings, and Organizations
    a. Be a member and active participant in professional organizations;
    b. Attend conferences and professional meetings.
6. Other Duties
    a. Carry out assignments as directed by the Superintendent and the Associate Superintendent;
    b. Cooperate with everyone in the improvement of the total teaching-learning process;
    c. Participate in and help coordinate task force;
    d. Participate in and help coordinate reading evaluations;
    e. Serve on the Disciplinary Committee;
    f. Assist in the recognition of outstanding achievements in various areas of instruction;
    g. Coordinate the Governor's Honors Program at the county level;
    h. Coordinate the Teacher of the Year Program at the county level;
    i. Coordinate visits made by other counties who desire to observe certain phases of Columbia County's Instructional Program.
7. Administration and Personnel
    a. Provide direction for other personnel at central office level in the instructional department;
    b. Provide direction for principals and teachers in the instructional program;
    c. Attend superintendent's central staff meetings;
    d. Prepare the instructional part of the school budget;
    e. Keep financial records on special projects;
    f. Prepare local, state, and national reports and records dealing with instruction.
TERMS OF EMPLOYMENT: 12 months

APPROVED BY: _____ DATE: _____
REVIEWED AND AGREED BY: _____ DATE: _____

SOURCE: Columbia County Public Schools, Appling, Ga., March 1978. Reprinted with permission.

JOB DESCRIPTION 2

TITLE: Curriculum Director

QUALIFICATIONS: 1. Master's degree or equivalent in curriculum development or school administration.
                2. Three years' successful teaching experience.

3. Three years' successful administrative experience.
4. Three years' successful experience in curriculum development or related activity.
5. Such alternatives to the above qualifications as the Board may find appropriate and acceptable.

REPORTS TO: Superintendent

JOB GOAL: To provide leadership in the ongoing development and improvement of the entire instructional program of the district.

PERFORMANCE RESPONSIBILITIES:

1. Provides staff leadership to insure understanding of and promote the educational objectives of the district, and plans and administers programs of inservice educational activities for instructional personnel.
2. Coordinates all formal efforts of the professional staff in projects of curriculum improvement.
3. Works with principals and teacher committees in organizing and coordinating grade level and departmental meetings, in order to effect horizontal and vertical continuity and articulation of the instructional program throughout the district.
4. Plans and presents a series of meetings each year for the express purpose of interpreting the educational program to the Board, to parent groups, and to other interested patrons of the district.
5. Directs creation of and edits for publication all curriculum guides and materials prepared by and to be distributed among the instructional staff.
6. Secures and distributes instructional resources such as filmstrips, sample textbooks, and curriculum guides from other districts, and the like.
7. Maintains a curriculum library for staff use.
8. Coordinates the selection of textbooks for the district through use of faculty committees.
9. Keeps abreast of and interprets for the staff current research in the area of curriculum development.
10. Establishes a program for the ongoing evaluation of instruction and curriculum.
11. Assists in the development and coordination of the sections of the budget that pertain to curriculum and instruction.

TERMS OF EMPLOYMENT: Ten, eleven, or twelve month year. Salary and work year to be established by the Board.

EVALUATION: Performance of this job to be evaluated annually in accordance with provisions of the Board's policy on Evaluation of Administrative Personnel.

Approved by: _____ Date:_____
Reviewed and agreed to by: _____ Date:_____
                              (Incumbent)

SOURCE: Johnson County Public Schools. Wrightsville, Ga. Reprinted with permission.

JOB DESCRIPTION 3

Elementary Curriculum Director

1. To supervise the curriculum through the direction of the school principal of grades kindergarten through sixth grade.
2. To improve the quality of instruction through supervision, demonstration, selection of materials, and the organization of instruction.
3. Assist in the formulation of philosophy and objectives for the total curriculum in kindergarten through sixth grade and assist the principal in directing the implementation of these plans.
4. Guides development, implementation, and evaluation of inservice training for instructional personnel in kindergarten through sixth grade. This includes aides and teachers. This will be directed through the principal.
5. Assist in the selection of textbooks and instructional materials in textbook adoption. Textbook orders should go through instructional supervisor for final ordering.
6. Assist instructional personnel in compiling, interpreting, and using test data for the improvement of instruction.
7. Guides the development of a sequential program in all areas in grades K-6.
8. Be responsible for directing the following projects (includes writing projects, expenditures, etc.)
   A. Beginning Teacher Project
   B. State Testing Project
   C. Compensatory Education
   D. Preschool Incentive Project
   E. State Staff Development
   F. Policy Coordinator
9. Be responsible for working in conjunction with Secondary Curriculum Director on the following projects:
   A. Textbook Adoption
   B. Act as a consultant to the Instructional-Media Committee.
10. Evaluation and amending of Chapter I and delegated projects.
11. Evaluate requests by personnel and aid in determining the extent of the need of the request through the direction of the principal. All purchase orders must be signed by the principal and then have final approval of the superintendent.
12. Keeping an inventory of all materials and equipment purchased through your specific project funds.
13. Make sure that programs are in accordance with the regulations governing the project.
14. Visit classrooms on a regular basis. A minimum of 50% of job time should be spent in the classroom with documentation to verify instructional supervision.

15. Aid in the directing of testing of children in grades K-6. (Chapter I, Migrant, Reading, Math)
16. Assume other responsibilities as deemed necessary by the person himself, the principal or the superintendent.
17. Attend meetings as assigned by the superintendent. Principals may request your attendance to special meetings but this must be approved through the superintendent's office.
18. Work with principals and central staff as services and knowledge are needed.
19. Turn in weekly performance sheet to inform superintendent of instructional supervision and other areas of concern.

SOURCE: Jenkins County Public Schools, Millen, G., 1982–83. Reprinted with permission.

JOB DESCRIPTION 4

Job Title: *Coordinator, Secondary Curriculum*   Class Title: *Coordinator III*
Position Location: *Curriculum & Instruction*   Class Code: *1267*

General Summary Statement:
Under general direction provides leadership and direction to the secondary (7–12) curriculum support section including supervision of the Secondary Curriculum Consultants and the Secondary Teacher Resource Center.

Duties and Responsibilities

1. Establish and implement goals and objectives for the section; coordinate the determination of goals and objectives for assigned curriculum consultants.
2. Coordinate the development of basic District curriculum and the assessment of needs for secondary curriculum development.
3. Direct the consultative services provided by curriculum consultants and the Teacher Resource Center for secondary teachers and administrators.
4. Coordinate the provision of consultative services to secondary schools concerning instructional programs, teaching strategies, organizational patterns, groupings of students, classroom management, computer managed instruction, criterion-referenced tests and other areas related to District curriculum.
5. Plan, coordinate and facilitate appropriate in-service activities for secondary school staffs as determined by needs assessments and as required to meet Board goals and objectives.
6. Participate in the review and update of District policies, regulations and procedures regarding secondary curriculum.
7. Coordinate the development, editing, review, publication and dissemination of documents and bulletins concerning the District course of study.
8. Provide consultation to central administrators and building administrators regarding the course of study and instructional program.

9. Supervise the staff selections and placements; ensure performance evaluations; prepare and administer the section budget in conformance with established fiscal procedures.
10. Evaluate section activities and provide interpretations and reports for District personnel, the public and for management decision-making.
11. Perform related duties as assigned.

Indicate the minimum education experience, and/or specialized training required for this position.

Education (cite major area of study if above high school):
M. A. degree in education with an emphasis in curriculum and instruction.

Length and type of experience:
Five (5) years successful teaching and/or administrative experience at elementary level.
Two (2) years in supervision and/or development of curriculum or related activities.

Special licenses, registration, or certification:
A valid Washington State Teaching Certificate.

Skills:
Curriculum development; supervision and evaluation of personnel and programs; human relations and interpersonal communications.

Knowledge of:
Theories, techniques and methodologies related to K-12 education and curriculum development.

Ability to:
Provide leadership and direction for assigned functional areas; communicate effectively both orally and in writing with all levels of staff; relate positively and effectively with District staff, students and the public; work in a multiethnic environment.

Desired (but not required):
Approval: Approval:

(Signature of Immediate Supervisor)   (Signature of Next Highest Supervisor)
FOR CLASSIFICATION OFFICE USE ONLY

Class Title	Class Code	Class Level
Coordinator III	1267	CS-39

Job Family	Working Title
Administrative/Managerial	Coordinator, Secondary Curriculum

Work Year	Bargaining Unit
260 days	Nonrepresented

Title of Immediate Supervisor	Title of Next Highest Supervisor
Director, Curriculum Services	Assistant Superintendent, C & I

Unit/Section	Department	Division
	Curriculum Services	Curriculum & Instruction

Date: March 1983

Approved:
Asst. Superintendent
Human Resources Administration

SOURCE: Seattle Public Schools, Seattle, Wash. Reprinted with permission.

JOB DESCRIPTION 5

PRINCIPAL, ELEMENTARY OR SECONDARY

FUNCTIONS: To serve as the instructional and administrative leader of assigned school

DIRECTLY RESPONSIBLE TO: Area Assistant Superintendent

IMMEDIATE SUBORDINATES: Assistant Principals, teachers; other staff as assigned.

ASSIGNED RESPONSIBILITIES:

1. Plans, evaluates, and recommends programs, policies, goals, and objectives in area of responsibility.
2. Supervises the instructional program, and evaluates, develops, and reviews the curricular offerings and instructional program of assigned building.
3. Trains, supervises and evaluates personnel assigned to area of responsibility.
4. Interviews and makes recommendations to the Personnel Office for the selection and assignment of certificated and classified employees.
5. Works with the Area Assistant Superintendent and other authorized personnel in the development and implementation of programs, and in modification and utilization of the building, physical facilities, and school playgrounds.
6. Conducts a community relations program and coordinates it with the district program.
7. Organizes and works with a school advisory committee within policy.
8. Conducts a program of inservice education for assigned personnel.
9. Conducts meetings of the staff as are necessary to the proper functioning of the school.
10. Insures that all School Board and administration policies are effectively explained and implemented.

11. Requisitions and maintains adequate supplies and equipment.
12. Submits such reports and records as required by law, Board policies, and administrative directives.
13. Supervises building custodial care.
14. Performs related duties as required.

REQUIRED KNOWLEDGE, SKILLS AND ABILITIES:

Knowledgeable of school administration, organization, curriculum, and possesses the ability to work effectively with people.

MINIMUM TRAINING AND EXPERIENCE:

Three years experience as a successful classroom teacher.
Master's degree.
Certification to meet State and Southern Association standards.
Approved:

SOURCE: Richland County School District One, Columbia, S.C., Feb. 29, 1980. Reprinted with permission.

JOB DESCRIPTION 6

A. POSITION TITLE: Assistant Principal

B. PRIMARY FUNCTION: Assists the principal in providing effective leadership in the organization, administration, and supervision of the educational program of a school.

C. QUALIFICATIONS:

1. *Educational*   Master's degree in addition to the educational requirements prescribed by the State of Indiana.

2. *Experience*   Minimum of five years of successful classroom teaching.

3. *Certification*   Indiana certificate for principalship.

D. MAJOR RESPONSIBILITIES AND KEY DUTIES:

1. Assists in providing educational leadership which strives for an effective educational program which meets the individual needs of all students.
2. Cooperates in constant evaluation of curriculum and suggests needed improvements and measures to implement these changes.
3. Assists teachers in interpreting curriculum and adapting it to meet individual needs.
4. Assists in evaluating the needs of the professional staff and recommends in-service meetings to enhance previous educational experiences.
5. Encourages and participates in educational research.
6. Aids in developing and implementing innovative programs of instruction.
7. Aids in regular teaching assignments when necessary.

8. Assumes a leading role in developing and sustaining efficient operation of the school through effective use of human and material resources.
9. Assumes complete charge of the school in the absence of the principal.
10. Assists with the organization of classes each semester, including assignments and scheduling of teachers, placement of pupils and rooms.
11. Aids in requisitioning, assigning, distributing, and making best use of supplies, equipment, and other instructional materials.
12. Assists in maintaining accurate and up-to-date records and submits required reports promptly.
13. Takes initiative in the organization and operation of the lunchroom, and the assignment of staff to necessary duties for the supervision of children involved in the lunch program.
14. Cooperates with the principal and staff in establishing and maintaining democratic policies and procedures within the school.
15. Assists in orientation of personnel new to the school.
16. Aids in providing necessary orientation and instructions for substitute teachers.
17. Aids in achieving effective use of the school plant in implementing the school program.
18. Shares with the principal the task of supervision and formal evaluation of both new and experienced teachers.
19. Is responsible for gaining experiences and becoming familiar with all areas of instruction at all levels of the elementary school.
20. Assists teachers in effective grouping of children for optimum achievement.
21. Assists teachers in developing effective techniques for solving problems of pupil behavior.
22. Assists teacher in providing experiences that will foster self-direction or self-control in children.
23. Utilizes services of the parents, social worker, school psychologist, and other community resources in working with individual pupil problems.
24. Cooperates in establishing positive relationships between home, school, and community.
25. Aids in the organization of an effective health and safety program.
26. Assists in surveying grounds and building needs; reports needed maintenance repairs, alterations, and improvements.
27. Assists the principal by serving as liaison in establishing line of communication between teaching staff and custodial staff.
28. Helps to organize an effective program of good housekeeping.

E. ORGANIZATIONAL RELATIONSHIPS:
1. *Responsibility*   Is responsible to the principal.

SOURCE: Indianapolis Public Schools, Indianapolis, Ind. Reprinted with permission.

JOB DESCRIPTION 7

POSITION GUIDE—INSTRUCTIONAL PROGRAM FACILITATOR

Acountable to: Principal

Broad Function

    As a faculty member of the local school, the Instructional Program Facilitator will assist the school principal and the classroom teachers in effectively implementing the prescribed curriculum and instructional program as designed systemwide for the Crisp County School System. A portion of the day will be spent in classroom instructional activities which provide for direct services to students such as working with small groups of students with special needs in reading, mathematics, and other identified areas.

Professional Qualifications and Personal Characteristics

    Any person employed as an Instructional Program Facilitator must possess a T–5 certificate.

    Any person employed as an Instructional Program Facilitator should have the capacity to build and maintain effective interpersonal relationships with co-workers and central office personnel.

    Any person employed as an Instructional Program Facilitator should have the ability to work cooperatively with classroom teachers, interpret adopted curriculum to the faculty, and to train new and beginning teachers in the use of adopted materials.

    Any person employed as an Instructional Program Facilitator should exhibit the organizational skills necessary to facilitate the school's instructional program and to balance his/her time between direct teaching activities and other instruction related activities.

    The Instructional Program Facilitator should be knowledgeable of current trends and practices in the teaching of reading and/or mathematics.

Principal Responsibilities

A. *Total Reading and Mathematics Program*

1. To assist the classroom teacher with the teaching of specific reading and mathematics groups.
2. To test students for placement in the reading and mathematics program.
3. To assist the classroom teacher in charting progress in the reading and mathematics program.
4. To assist with maintenance of the student's reading and mathematics folder.
5. To design and duplicate reteaching lessons for the basal reading and mathematics program.
6. To orient new teachers to the reading and mathematics program.
7. To establish and maintain a mathematics materials resource center.
8. To inventory and order reading and mathematics materials.
9. To develop materials for an individual student in the classroom.
10. To assist with preparing materials for parents to use at home with students.
11. To develop strategies for content area teachers to improve student achievement.

APPENDIX B

12. To provide the link between teachers of special education and regular classroom teachers, to assist with referral paperwork, staffings, and IEP implementation and review.
13. To assist with the coordination of the Title I teacher and the state-paid teacher.
14. To assist classroom teachers in scheduling Title I and Special Education services.

B. *Testing Program*
1. To inventory, schedule and distribute practice CRT [Criterion-Referenced Test] materials (grades 2, 3, 4, and 6).
2. To assist teachers in determining deficient skill areas on CRT.
3. To assist teachers in designing and/or acquiring materials to work on deficient CRT objectives.
4. To inventory and distribute CRT materials to teachers.
5. To assist teachers in administering the Metropolitan Readiness Tests and the Metropolitan Achievement Tests.
6. To begin the initial screening for special education services by administering the Slosson Intelligence Test and/or other diagnostic measures.
7. To assist teachers in understanding and utilizing test results.
8. To assist in the implementation of the promotion policy.

C. *Staff Development*
1. To plan and assist with staff development in the schools.
2. To provide support to teachers in their classrooms through visitation, demonstration teaching, and problem solving.
3. To assist the principal in monitoring classroom organization (management, placement, and grouping).
4. To train and coordinate parent volunteers.
5. To assist in aide orientation and training.
6. To attend staff development sessions conducted by the central office.
7. To assist in workshops with parent groups, grade level meetings, and system-wide curriculum development activities, etc.

D. *Other Responsibilities*
1. To enhance school-community relations by assisting with a school newsletter or providing articles for the local paper.
2. To cooperate with and assist the school media specialist with media center motivational activities such as Book Week, Media Fairs, Book Fairs, etc.
3. To assist the principal and teachers with parent conferences.

SOURCE:Crisp County Public Schools, Cordele, Ga., July 1982. Reprinted with permission.

JOB DESCRIPTION 8

INSTRUCTIONAL LEAD TEACHER

MINIMUM QUALIFICATIONS:

1. Holder of a T-5 certificate in reading or elementary education and a minimum of three courses in elementary mathematics or methods of teaching elementary mathematics. AJ–5 certification will be acceptable provided the applicant also holds a minimum of T–4 certification in reading or elementary education.
2. IS-5 or AS-5 certificate
3. Five years of teaching experience in grades K–7 (or 6–8 middle school) with the final year of teaching experience within Richmond County.

SALARY:

The lead teacher's salary will be determined using the County Teacher Salary Schedule based on certification and experience plus a supplement of $1,000. Travel will be paid according to the location of assignment.

JOB DESCRIPTION:

1. The lead teacher serves under the direct supervision of the Principal and addresses instructional components of the school program within the assigned school.
2. The lead teacher, whose salary, for the major part, is paid through the State CEP [Compensatory Education Program], will work with remedial teachers and classroom teachers of grades 3–7 particularly in language arts and mathematics, and may work with small groups of students with special needs in reading, mathematics, and other identified areas. The portion of the salary paid by the local Board of Education enables the lead teacher to serve teachers in grades K–2 and in special programs.
3. The lead teacher works closely with the principal of the school to which he/she is assigned, keeping him/her informed of the progress of instructional programs. The lead teacher will serve the same hours as the teachers of the school to which he/she is assigned. The lead teacher will conform to Richmond County school policies and the policies of the individual schools. The principal is in charge of all aspects of the instructional program in the school. The lead teacher will assist the principal in coordinating the instructional program in the school.
4. Specifically, the lead teacher's responsibilities may include:
   a. Maintaining and making available for previewing by the central office staff and/or a state department auditing team a current file documenting overall school instructional needs.
   b. Serving as school testing coordinator and liaison person between the elementary testing consultant and the school staff.
   c. Assisting teachers with testing, diagnosing, and prescribing for students.
   d. Assisting all teachers with planning, implementing, and evaluating the instructional program.
   e. Demonstration teaching, when needed, by prior arrangement.
   f. Keeping records needed for planning and evaluating of staff development.

g. Scheduling of individual conferences with teachers as requested by principal, teacher, and/or parents.
h. Keeping Principal and Curriculum Director informed of all plans, developments, guides, bulletins, handouts, etc.
i. Providing Instructional Department with records as requested through the principal.
j. Providing, with principal and staff, for students' emotional, social, mental, and physical needs.
k. Visiting all classroom teachers according to plans and procedures developed with the principal.
l. Assisting teachers with learning and interest centers upon request by principal, teacher, or central office staff member.
m. Keeping a daily log of duties performed and furnishing copies to Curriculum Director and Principal for State monitoring purposes of CEP.
n. Assisting with interviewing of personnel when requested.
o. Participating on the teacher assessment team as a support member.
p. Attending school staff meetings and other related school activities.
q. Attending lead teacher staff development meetings as scheduled by the Curriculum Director.
r. Coordinating all staff development sessions within the school.
s. Attending pertinent conferences for professional growth and enrichment.
t. Assisting the Instructional Department as requested through the principal.
u. Serving as chairman of school screening committee.
v. Assisting the principal to determine that the promotion policy is being implemented.
w. Conducting substitute teacher workshops as scheduled.
x. Assisting principal in obtaining Bilingual information as students enter Richmond County Schools.

SOURCE: Richmond County Public Schools, Augusta, Ga. Reprinted with permission.

JOB DESCRIPTION 9

Descriptor Term: JOB DESCRIPTION Department Head	Descriptor Code: GBBAF-R Rescinds:	Issued Date: 9/15/79 Issued:

QUALIFICATIONS: 1. Master's Degree with a major in assigned curricular area.
2. A valid state teacher's certificate.
3. A minimum of five years of teaching experience.
4. Such alternatives as the Board may find advisable.

REPORTS TO: Principal

JOB GOAL: To provide leadership, coordination, and innovation in assigned curricular area, so that each student may derive maximum benefit from the continuing pursuit of the subject area involved.

PERFORMANCE RESPONSIBILITIES:

1. Establishes curriculum objectives for the department.
2. Develops a program for the implementation and evaluation of these objectives.
3. Conducts departmental meetings as necessary.
4. Assists department teachers in the handling of day to day problems of instruction.
5. Acts as resource person for department teachers on curriculum questions.
6. Manages the department supplies, textbooks, equipment, and supplementary materials.
7. Maintains an up-to-date inventory of department materials.
8. Serves as a member of the Instructional Media Committee.
9. Advises the principal on the Master schedule and the assignment of department teachers.
10. Makes classroom visitations of department personnel when requested and provides follow-up consultation.
11. Develops and maintains a department library.
12. Provides orientation and inservice training programs for department personnel.
13. Assists in the recruitment, screening, and hiring of department personnel.
14. Assists the principal in interpreting general grading and promotional policies.
15. Attends relevant school, district, and professional meetings.
16. Meets with other department heads to promote interdisciplinary programs.
17. Assists in identifying and utilizing community resources for the department program.
18. Keeps informed on educational innovations and trends as they relate to department concerns.
19. Assists in planning goals and objectives with feeder schools.

TERMS OF EMPLOYMENT: Ten month year. Salary based on state and local index with an additional $500 supplement.

EVALUATION: Performance of this job will be evaluated annually by the Principal.

SOURCE: Wayne County Public Schools, Jesup, Ga. Reprinted with permission.

JOB DESCRIPTION 10

GRADE LEVEL CHAIRPERSON, ELEMENTARY SCHOOL

Experience
1. At least two school years of teaching service within the past five years in the grade level(s) of the assignment.
2. At least one school year of teaching service at the assigned school.
3. Service as a training and/or demonstration teacher.
4. Leadership as a coordinator of instructional projects or inservice education, school health or safety programs, extracurricular activities, community affairs, or other related school programs and activities.
5. Membership on a school advisory board, faculty advisory committee, or school representative to the P.T.A.
6. Membership on District-wide committees for the selection and evaluation of textbooks, audio-visual aids, supplies, equipment, and other related instructional materials.

Knowledges, skills, abilities, and personal characteristics
1. Leadership ability in planning and improving the instructional program of the grade level(s) department including inservice education activities for department members.
2. Knowledge and understanding of the local school organization and programs.
3. Understanding of the instructional program of and knowledge of current trends in curriculum development for the grade level(s) of assigned responsibility.
4. Knowledge of the local school and District resources available to teachers in the grade level(s) of the department.
5. Ability to work effectively with students, parents, staff members and community representatives in providing a suitable education program.
6. Ability to properly use and to care for the textbooks, supplies, equipment, and related instructional materials of the grade level(s) of assigned responsibility.
7. Facility in oral and written expression.
8. Cleanliness and appropriate personal appearance and manner.
9. Poise, tact, good judgment and commitment to the education of students.

Statement of Duties
A. *Primary function*
In addition to service as a teacher, serves as head of a grade level(s) in an elementary school; provides educational leadership for, and coordinates the organization and implementation of, the instructional program and activities for the assigned grade level(s).
B. *Responsible to*
Principal, Elementary School or his/her designee

C. *Subordinates*

None; provides technical direction and advises the members of the grade level(s) for which responsible

D. *Responsibilities—Under the direction of the principal*

1. Provides instructional leadership for a grade level(s) including the following:
   a. Plans and organizes grade level(s) meetings, in-school workshops to improve instruction and develop teaching techniques and assists in the planning of faculty meetings
   b. Reviews and assesses grade level(s) standards with teachers of the grade level in relationship to the total school educational program
   c. Serves as a resource person regarding current trends, developments, and publications in the grade level(s) of assigned responsibility
   d. Develops resources for the improvement of instruction
   e. Encourages creative instructional practices
   f. Assists in the evaluation of the instructional work of the grade level(s) as it relates to student achievement
   g. Assists in identifying and developing leadership potential within the grade level(s).

2. Coordinates and contributes to the organization and implementation of the instructional program and activities of the grade level(s) including the following:
   a. Grade level articulation with the total school program
   b. Assists in orientation of teachers new to the grade level
   c. Assists in review and recommendation of changes in curriculum
   d. Assists in the selection of textbooks and other materials; aids in the preparation of requisitions and allocation of textbooks, supplies, equipment, and other materials
   e. Acts as liaison between grade level(s) teachers and the appropriate school administrator or his/her designee

3. Provides assistance to teachers with problems in class control and management and with curriculum and course of study content; and confers with the appropriate school administrator regarding teacher problems.

4. As directed, serves as a member of school or District committees, such as advisory, faculty, PTA, curriculum development, and textbook selection.

5. Contributes information for or maintains records of grade level(s) program or materials; gathers and compiles information as requested by the principal.

6. During periods of critical personnel shortage or other emergency situation, shall temporarily perform any duties, as directed, within the authorization of any credentials held by the incumbent which are registered with the Office of the Los Angeles County Superintendent of Schools and which are a part of the class description requirements in effect at the time such duties are performed.

7. Performs other duties as assigned.

SOURCE: Los Angeles Unified School District, Los Angeles, Calif., April 1981. Reprinted with permission.

JOB DESCRIPTION 11

TEAM LEADERS

Specific Duties of the Team Leader

1. Plans and conducts regular team meetings.
2. Cooperates with team members to ensure proper placement of students and recommends students to the guidance department where appropriate.
3. Works cooperatively with counselors in the implementation of the advisory program.
4. Gives assistance to substitute teachers within his/her team.
5. Discusses and implements administrative directives with his/her team and directs all necessary actions thereto.
6. Encourages and stimulates enrollment in professional groups and attendance at professional meetings.
7. Works with team members in developing long-range plans for the team, planning and writing units of instruction, and other methods of improving the total program of instruction.
8. Determines the need for modification and updating of the team program through constant evaluation which involves the usage of all available objective data.
9. Integrates the work of the team into the total instructional program of the school.
10. Cooperates with the subject area leaders to recommend new or additional materials of instruction and textbooks for his/her team.
11. Suggests books, magazines or pamphlets to be purchased by the school librarian.
12. Nominates and evaluates instructional materials and equipment to be purchased by the principal and/or County Media Center.
13. Aids in the preparation of in-service courses.
14. Recommends to the Assistant Principal for Instruction individual teaching assignments for the members of his/her team.
15. Attends formal meetings with building administrators and other team leaders so as to promote the integration of learning experiences of the students and the elimination of needless duplication of effort and experience.
16. Responsible for all other duties assigned by the Building Principal, Assistant Principals, or the Superintendent.

SOURCE: Richmond County Public Schools, Augusta, Ga. Reprinted with permission.

JOB DESCRIPTION 12

LANGUAGE ARTS DIVISION

Title: Language Arts Consultant
Qualifications: 1. A master's degree or higher with a major in English or reading or the equivalent

   2. A valid state certificate to teach in Georgia

   3. An Instructional Supervision Certificate (within one year) or as an AS [Administration and Supervision certificate]

   4. At least three years of successful teaching experience

   5. Ability to work with individuals and groups in a consultative capacity

Reports to: Language Arts Coordinator

Job Goal: To assist client systems program development and staff development, primarily in Language Arts.

Performance Responsibilities

  I. Program Development

    A. Needs Assessment

      1. Assist with selection and/or development of instruments for needs assessment.

      2. Assist with development of procedures and plans for carrying out needs assessment.

      3. Assist with implementation of needs assessment plan.

      4. Assist with analyzing and prioritizing needs.

      5. Assist with identifying and evaluating programs to meet needs.

      6. Assist with testing students for placement.

    B. Planning

      1. Assist with development and/or revision of curriculum materials or guides.

      2. Assist with reviewing and selecting programs and materials.

      3. Recommend implementation strategies.

      4. Assist with identifying resources for implementing programs.

      5. Assist with the development of project proposals.

    C. Comprehensive Planning

    D. Program Implementation

      1. Visit classrooms at request of local personnel.

      2. Assist with organizing materials.

      3. Assist with evaluation of program implementation.

 II. Staff Development

    A. Professional

      1. Plan staff development.

      2. Assist teachers in selecting and acquiring materials.

      3. Conduct and/or coordinate in-service workshops.

    B. Non-Professional

      1. Coordinate and/or conduct staff development programs for aides/parents/volunteers/substitutes.

III. Internal Operations

    A. Office Maintenance—Reports

      1. Assist in maintaining division and personal files, materials, and equipment.

      2. Record activities and complete activity-travel reports.

B. Professional Growth
   1. Participate in staff meetings with other CESA [Cooperative Educational Service Agency] personnel.
   2. Participate in staff development activities.
   3. Attend professional meetings and conferences.

Term of Employment: 190 work days with the dates specified to include 195 days, five of which the consultant may take as unspecified holidays based upon the approval of the division coordinator.

Evaluation: Performance of the job will be evaluated annually by the coordinator and the consultant. The results will be discussed and signed by both parties.

Approved by: _____ Date _____

Reviewed and
agreed to by: _____ Date _____

SOURCE: First District Cooperative Educational Service Agency, Statesboro, Ga. Reprinted with permission.

JOB DESCRIPTION 13

Descriptor Term:	Descriptor Code: GBBAI
INSTRUCTIONAL SPECIALIST/CONSULTANT	Issued Date:

DUTIES AND RESPONSIBILITIES:
   1. Works with individual system administrators and teachers to identify and deliver priority requested services for program and staff development.
   2. Develops teaching strategies to implement new curricula.
   3. Performs classroom visitations and demonstrations.
   4. Serves as representative to curriculum projects.
   5. Works with individuals and committees on identified needs.
   6. Informs members of the staff in the content area of major trends and developments affecting them.
   7. Writes and constructs performance criteria.
   8. Analyzes pupil progress and teaching methods in the content area.
   9. Promotes the content relevance and effectiveness in terms of established objectives.
   10. Confers with principals and others on content problems.
   11. Orients new teachers in the content area.
   12. Other appropriate duties and responsibilities assigned by the Director.

SOURCE: Okefenokee Cooperative Educational Service Agency Board of Control, Waycross, Ga., July 1, 1972. Reprinted with permission.

Index